# Lecture Notes in Computer Science

576

Edited by G. Goos and J. Hartmanis

Advisory Board: W. Brauer   D. Gries   J. Stoer

Lecture Notes in Computer Science

Edited by G. Goos and J. Hartmanis

570

J. Feigenbaum (Ed.)

# Advances in Cryptology – CRYPTO '91

Proceedings

Springer-Verlag Berlin Heidelberg GmbH

Series Editors

Gerhard Goos
Universität Karlsruhe
Postfach 69 80
Vincenz-Priessnitz-Straße 1
W-7500 Karlsruhe, FRG

Juris Hartmanis
Department of Computer Science
Cornell University
5148 Upson Hall
Ithaca, NY 14853, USA


Volume Editor

Joan Feigenbaum
AT&T Bell Laboratories, Room 2C473
600 Mountain Avenue, Murray Hill, NJ 07974-0636, USA

CR Subject Classification (1991): E. 3–4


ISBN 978-3-540-55188-1     ISBN 978-3-540-46766-3 (eBook)
DOI 10.1007/978-3-540-46766-3

This work is subject to copyright. All rights are reserved, whether the whole or part of the
material is concerned, specifically the rights of translation, reprinting, re-use of illustrations,
recitation, broadcasting, reproduction on microfilms or in any other way, and storage in data
banks. Duplication of this publication or parts thereof is permitted only under the provisions
of the German Copyright Law of September 9, 1965, in its current version, and permission
for use must always be obtained from Springer-Verlag Berlin Heidelberg GmbH. Violations
are liable for prosecution under the German Copyright Law.

© Springer-Verlag Berlin Heidelberg 1992
Originally published by Springer-Verlag Berlin Heidelberg New York in 1992

Typesetting: Camera ready by author

45/3140-543210 - Printed on acid-free paper

# Preface

The Crypto '91 conference, sponsored by the International Association for Cryptologic Research (IACR), took place at the University of California in Santa Barbara, August 11–15, 1991. The conference was very enjoyable and ran very smoothly, largely because of the efforts of General Chair Burt Kaliski and his colleagues at RSA Data Security, Inc.

There were 115 submissions, two of which were not considered because they arrived after the deadline. Three of the remaining 113 were withdrawn by their authors. Of the 110 submissions considered by the Program Committee, 36 were chosen for presentation at the conference; in two cases, the results presented were combinations of two related submissions. In addition, the Committee chose three invited speakers. All of the contributed talks and two of the invited talks resulted in papers for this volume. Please remember that these are unrefereed papers and that the authors bear full responsibility for their contents. Many of these papers represent work in progress; we expect that the authors will write final papers for refereed journals when their work is complete.

For the third year in a row, submissions were required to be anonymous. This year, we had an explicit rule that each Program Committee member could be an author or coauthor of at most one accepted paper. Program Committee members' submissions were anonymous and went through the same reviewing process as other submissions.

It is my pleasure to acknowledge the efforts of those who contributed to making the conference a success. First of all, I wish to thank the Program Committee, which consisted of Tom Berson (Anagram Laboratories), myself, Ingemar Ingemarsson (University of Linkoping), Ueli Maurer (Princeton University and ETH Zürich), Kevin McCurley (Sandia National Laboratories), Michael Merritt (AT&T Bell Laboratories), Moni Naor (IBM Almaden), Eiji Okamoto (NEC Japan), Josef Pieprzyk (University of New South Wales), Tony Rosati (Newbridge Microsystems), and Moti Yung (IBM Yorktown). Many of us relied on colleagues and friends for help in evaluating the submissions – those who helped include Martín Abadi, Josh Benaloh, Ernie Brickell, Mike Burrows, Don Coppersmith, Uriel Feige, Matt Franklin, Stuart Haber, Mike Luby, Andrew Odlyzko, Alon Orlitsky, and Jim Reeds. As usual, we all thank Whit Diffie for organizing the rump session. I thank Gilles Brassard for agreeing at the last minute to chair the first session of the conference and for providing all of the Latex macros that I used to put together the proceedings. Ruth Shell was extremely helpful in processing all of the submissions, acknowledgements, acceptances, and rejections.

Finally, I thank the authors for sending in their submissions (even the ones that were rejected), the speakers, and all of the participants in this and other IACR conferences. We have established a good tradition, and I hope it continues.

Murray Hill, NJ                                                                 Joan Feigenbaum
December, 1991

# Contents

# Session 4: Cryptanalysis
Tom Berson

# Session 5: Complexity Theory
Joan Feigenbaum

# Session 6: Cryptographic Schemes Based on Number Theory
Kevin McCurley

## Session 7: Pseudorandomness
Josef Pieprzyk

## Session 8: Applications and Implementations
Tony Rosati

## Session 9: Secure Computation Protocols
Moti Yung

# Session 10: Public-Key Cryptosystems and Signatures
Eiji Okamoto

# A Calculus for Access Control
# in Distributed Systems

M. Abadi*    M. Burrows*    B. Lampson*    G. Plotkin[†]

### Abstract

We study some of the concepts, protocols, and algorithms for access control in distributed systems, from a logical perspective. We account for how a principal may come to believe that another principal is making a request, either on his own or on someone else's behalf. We also provide a logical language for access control lists, and theories for deciding whether requests should be granted.

## 1   The Problem

At least three ingredients are essential for security in computing systems:

- A trusted computing base: the hardware and systems software should be capable of preserving the secrecy and integrity of data.

- Authentication: it should be possible to determine who made a statement; for example, a user should be able to request that his files be deleted and to prove that the command is his, and not that of an intruder.

- Authorization, or access control: access control consists in deciding whether the agent that makes a statement is trusted on this statement; for example, a user may be trusted (hence obeyed) when he says that his files should be deleted.

These ingredients are fairly well understood in centralized systems.

Distributed systems pose new problems. Scale becomes an issue, as ultimately one would want to envision a global distributed system, with a global name space and global security. In addition, there are difficulties with communication, booting, loading, authentication, and authorization.

The computing base of a distributed system need not reside in a single location, under a single management. This implies, in particular, that secure communication cannot be taken for granted. Since it is hard to provide physically secure communication lines, some form of encryption is typically required. In what follows, we assume that shared-key encryption (e.g., [7]) and public-key encryption (e.g., [8, 19]) are available where needed, but we use them frugally. In addition, there are problems of secure booting and

---

*Digital Equipment Corporation, Systems Research Center. 130 Lytton Avenue, Palo Alto, California 94301, USA.

[†]Department of Computer Science, University of Edinburgh, King's Buildings, Edinburgh EH9 3JZ, UK. Part of this work was completed while at Digital Equipment Corporation, Systems Research Center.

J. Feigenbaum (Ed.): Advances in Cryptology - CRYPTO '91, LNCS 576, pp. 1-23, 1992.
© Springer-Verlag Berlin Heidelberg 1992

secure loading of software. For instance, the operating system that a host runs may be obtained from a repository across the network; a mechanism is needed to guarantee that this software is an authentic release, free of viruses. This mechanism will inevitably rely on authentication and access control, as it is necessary to restrict who can make a release.

The nodes of a distributed system may act on their own behalf, or on behalf of users. Users and nodes trust one another to different extents. Moreover, a user may be trusted only when he is working at certain nodes; he may have more rights at his office than when working from a remote public terminal. Therefore, both users and nodes need to be authenticated, and their identities considered in access control decisions.

These issues give rise to a change in the nature of authentication and access control. The basic questions of authentication and access control are, always, "who is speaking?" and "who is trusted?" Typically the answer is the name of a simple principal (a user or a host). In a distributed environment, these questions can receive a variety of answers; the notion of principal can be extended, to include:

- Users and machines.

- Channels, such as input devices and cryptographic channels. There is no formal reason to distinguish channels from users and machines, and it is advantageous not to. Cryptographic channels are identified by keys, and so we may write that the key $K$ says $s$ when $s$ is asserted in a message decrypted with $K$.

- Conjunctions of principals, of the form $A \wedge B$. If $A$ and $B$ make the same statement $s$, then $A \wedge B$ says $s$ as well. It often happens that $A \wedge B$ is trusted on $s$, but neither $A$ nor $B$ is trusted by himself—a "joint signature" is required.

- Groups. It is often inconvenient to list explicitly all of the principals that are trusted in some respect, both because the list would be long and because it may change too often. Groups provide an indirection mechanism. The use of groups implies the need for a scheme for deciding whether a principal is a member of a group. This is not always straightforward, for example when the registrar for a group is remote; group membership certificates then become necessary.

- Principals in roles, of the form $A$ *as* $R$. The principal $A$ may adopt the role $R$ and act under the name $A$ *as* $R$ when he wants to diminish his powers, in particular as a protection against blunders. For example, a system manager may act in the role *normal-user* most of the time, and enable the *manager* role only on occasion. Similarly, a machine may adopt a weak role before beginning to run a piece of untrusted software, or before delegating authority to an untrusted machine.

- Principals on behalf of principals, of the form $B$ *for* $A$. The principal $A$ may delegate authority to $B$, and $B$ can then act on his behalf, using the identity $B$ *for* $A$. In the most common case, a user $A$ delegates to a machine $B$. It is also possible for a machine to delegate to another machine, and for delegations to be cascaded (iterated); then we encounter expressions such as $C$ *for* $(B$ *for* $A)$.

This list raises formal questions of some practical importance. First, there is a need to determine which of the operations on principals should be viewed as primitive, and which can be defined from the others. Then one may ask what laws the operations satisfy, as for example whether $B$ *for* $(A \wedge A')$ and $(B$ *for* $A) \wedge (B$ *for* $A')$ are in some sense equivalent; if two principals are equivalent then they should be granted the same requests. The resulting theory of principals should provide a reasonable degree of expressiveness, and it should be amenable to a mathematical justification. It is also essential that the theory of principals be simple, because users need to specify permissions on resources and programs need to make access control decisions.

Further, a variety of protocols and algorithms must be designed and analyzed. Mechanisms are required for secure booting and loading, for joining groups and for proving membership, for adopting roles, for delegations of authority and for certifying such delegations, and for deciding whether a request should be granted.

This paper is a study of some of the concepts, protocols, and algorithms for security in distributed systems, with a focus on access control. Our treatment is fairly formal, as it is based on logics. We account for how a principal may come to believe that another principal is making a request, either on his own or on someone else's behalf. We also provide a logical language for access control lists (ACLs), and theories for deciding whether requests should be granted. The logics enable us to explain a variety of protocols which can differ from one another in subtle ways.

On occasion, the formal analysis has suggested ideas useful to implementations, for example that some digital signatures could be saved. Moreover, logics make it possible to describe protocols and policies at a reasonable level of abstraction; we avoid the need for *ad hoc* arguments about particular implementations. This abstraction is important in the context of heterogeneous distributed environments, where several implementations of a design may coexist.

Our study is intended as a formal basis for parts of a security architecture, and for the Digital Distributed Systems Security Architecture (DSSA) in particular [10]; this architecture is currently under implementation. Other formal explanations of security are conceivable. We hope that this work clarifies some of the issues that these alternative accounts may address.

The next section is an overview. We describe the basic logical framework in section 3. Sections 4 and 5 extend the treatment with roles and delegation. Finally, in section 6, we consider delegation schemes and algorithms for making access control decisions.

This paper does not cover many issues in the area; some of these issues are briefly mentioned in passing. Since an implementation of the ideas presented is not complete, we leave most implementation considerations to a companion paper [14] and to future work. In particular, more thought needs to be given to the user interface and to the policies for the writing of ACLs.

## 2 Overview

Composite principals play a central role in informal reasoning; for example, one often talks about "$A$ and $B$" and "$B$ on behalf of $A$." Therefore, we start by introducing formal notations for composite principals.

Some classical constructors for composite principals such as conjunction and disjunction come to mind first:

- $A \wedge B$: $A$ and $B$ as co-signers. A request from $A \wedge B$ is a request that both $A$ and $B$ make. (It is not implied that $A$ and $B$ make this request in concert.)

- $A \vee B$ is the dual notation; $A \vee B$ represents the group of which $A$ and $B$ are the sole members.

Conjunction is important in our designs. Disjunction is often replaced with implication, in particular in dealing with groups. As discussed further below, "$A$ is a member of the group $G$" can be written $A \Rightarrow G$. The group $G$ can be named, as all other principals; it need not be given a definition beyond that implicit in formulas such as $A \Rightarrow G$. The ability to write out a group in full (as a disjunction) is not essential in practice.

There are also new connectives, in particular:

- $A$ *as* $R$: the principal $A$ in role $R$.

- $B|A$: the principal obtained when $B$ speaks on behalf of $A$, not necessarily with a proof that $A$ has delegated authority to $B$; by definition, $B|A$ says $s$ if $B$ says that $A$ says $s$; we pronounce $B|A$ as "$B$ quoting $A$."

- $B$ *for* $A$: the principal obtained when $B$ speaks on behalf of $A$, with appropriate delegation certificates; $B$ *for* $A$ says $s$ when $A$ has delegated to $B$ and $B$ says that $A$ says $s$, possibly after some checking that $s$ is reasonable.

Of these, only $|$ is primitive in our approach; *for* and *as* are important, but they are coded in terms of $\wedge$ and $|$. Since *for* is stronger than $|$, we tend to use $|$ only for encoding *for* and *as*.

In order to define the rights of these composite principals, we develop an algebraic calculus. In this calculus, one can express equations such as $(B \wedge C)$ *for* $A = (B$ *for* $A) \wedge (C$ *for* $A)$, and then examine their consequences. Since $\wedge$ is the standard meet in a semilattice, we are dealing with an ordered algebra, and we can use a partial order $\Rightarrow$ among principals: $A \Rightarrow B$ stands for $A = A \wedge B$, and it means that $A$ is at least as powerful as $B$; we pronounce this "$A$ implies $B$" or "$A$ speaks for $B$."

A modal logic extends the algebra of principals. In this logic, $A$ *says* $s$ represents the informal statement that the principal $A$ says $s$. Here $s$ may function as an imperative ("the file should be deleted") or not ("$C$'s public key is $K$"); imperative modalities are not explicit in the formalism.

The modal logic is a basis for various algorithms and protocols. For example, it is possible to explain logically how two principals $A$ and $B$ establish a public key $K_d$ for $B$ *for* $A$.

The logic also underlies a theory of ACLs. We write $\supset$ for the usual logical implication connective, and $A$ *controls* $s$ as an abbreviation for $(A$ *says* $s) \supset s$, which expresses trust in $A$ on the truth of $s$; in the logic, an ACL for a formula $s$ is a list of assertions of the form $A$ *controls* $s$. If $s$ represents a command to a server, then the ACL entry $A$ *controls* $s$ records the server's trust in $A$ on $s$, and hence that $A$ will be obeyed when he says $s$. When $s$ is clear from context, the ACL for $s$ may simply be presented as the list of principals trusted on $s$.

If $A \Rightarrow B$ and $B$ *controls* $s$ then $A$ *controls* $s$ as well. Therefore, ACLs may not mention all trusted principals explicitly; when $B$ is listed, access should be granted to any $A$ such that $A \Rightarrow B$. It is not always entirely trivial to decide whether a request should be granted.

Encryption is not treated formally, as its use is not essential for security—it is just present in the most reasonable implementations. The logic does not consider the problems associated with timestamps and lifetimes, either. Therefore, we do not explain how principals come to believe that messages are recent, and not replays. In this, and in the treatment of cryptographic channels as mere principals, the logic is more abstract than the logic of authentication proposed in [4]. The logic of authentication has as its goal describing and debugging fairly low-level authentication protocols; in contrast, the logic discussed here is intended as an aid in developing and applying a general design.

# 3 The Basic Logic

This section describes the basic logical framework, with syntax, axioms, and semantics. The last subsection presents some axioms that we do not adopt. The laws for *as* and *for* appear in sections 4 and 5.

## 3.1 A calculus of principals

We study a calculus of principals, in a minimal syntax. As discussed later in the paper, this syntax suffices for expressing roles and the needed delegation connectives.

Principals form a semilattice under the operation of conjunction, and obey the usual semilattice axioms:

- $\land$ is associative, commutative, and idempotent.

As usual, $A \Rightarrow B$ can be taken as an abbreviation for $A = A \land B$, or $=$ can be defined in terms of $\Rightarrow$.

Implication is often used to represent group membership. This notion of membership is slightly peculiar, and in particular it is transitive. We have found that transitivity is rather convenient for reasoning about hierarchical groups. Moreover, $\Rightarrow$ has a fairly pleasant interaction with the other connectives of our calculus.

However, our treatment of groups is incomplete. It would be desirable to provide group subtraction and intersection operations. It would also be desirable to provide naming support for usual subgroups—so that there would be a standard operation that one applies to a group name $G$ to obtain the group of principals with a certain position or job in $G$. Most probably, these operations would appear only at the lowest level of logical formulas, and would not mix with other constructs. Therefore, we do not include these additional operations here; intersection and subtraction are discussed in the full paper [2].

The principals form a semigroup under $|$:

- $|$ is associative.

The final axiom is the multiplicativity of $|$ in both of its arguments, which means:

- $|$ distributes over $\land$.

Multiplicativity implies monotonicity.

In short, the principals are organized as a multiplicative semilattice semigroup. Often, these same axioms are taken for structures with some sort of union or disjunction (instead of $\land$), and then the term additive is preferred to multiplicative.

A common example of a multiplicative semilattice semigroup is an algebra of binary relations over a set, with the operations of union and composition; a multiplicative semilattice semigroup isomorphic to an algebra of binary relations is called representable. In fact, the binary-relation example is common in a mathematical sense: every free multiplicative semilattice semigroup is representable (e.g., [3, 18]). This implies that the equational theory of multiplicative semilattice semigroups coincides with that of binary-relation algebras.

Equational theories do not suffice for reasoning about access rights, as for example group-membership assumptions are needed. Since the binary-relation model is a clear, appealing one, it is then natural to hope that every multiplicative semilattice semigroup is representable. Andréka has recently proved that this is not the case [3]. She has also studied the distributive multiplicative semilattice semigroups, which are defined by the additional distributivity axiom:

- if $B \wedge C \Rightarrow A$ then there exist $B'$ and $C'$ such that $B \Rightarrow B'$, $C \Rightarrow C'$, and $A = B' \wedge C'$.

Every distributive multiplicative semilattice semigroup is representable. The class of distributive multiplicative semilattice semigroups is a quasi-variety, but neither a variety nor finitely axiomatizable.

The algorithmic applications of the distributivity axiom are hard to see, because of its existential nature. Therefore, in the remainder of the paper, we examine both the axiomatic and the model-theoretic possibilities. We tend to work axiomatically, with the theory of multiplicative semilattice semigroups, but rely on binary relations as a way of constructing models. Moreover, section 6 describes an algorithm for the binary-relation model.

Several extensions to the signature are possible, and natural. For example, a unit 1 turns the semigroup into a monoid; 1 can be viewed as a perfectly honest principal. We describe these extensions in the full paper.

The syntax for reasoning about principals is much the obvious one. We manipulate equations between principal expressions, built from atoms $A_0$, $A_1$, $A_2$, ... with the symbols $\wedge$ and $|$. We combine equations into boolean formulas, and then adopt the usual axioms from propositional logic, and the axioms for the algebraic structures of choice (multiplicative semilattice semigroups, when not stated otherwise).

Section 6 discusses decidability issues for the calculus of principals.

## 3.2 A logic of principals and their statements

Here we develop a modal logic based on the calculus of principals.

### Syntax

The formulas are defined inductively, as follows:

- a countable supply of primitive propositions $p_0$, $p_1$, $p_2$, ... are formulas;

- if $s$ and $s'$ are formulas then so are $\neg s$ and $s \wedge s'$;

- if $A$ and $B$ are principal expressions then $A \Rightarrow B$ is a formula;

- if $A$ is a principal expression and $s$ is a formula then $A$ *says* $s$ is a formula.

We use the usual abbreviations for boolean connectives, such as $\supset$, and we also treat equality between principals ($=$) as an abbreviation. In addition, $A$ *controls* $s$ stands for $(A \; says \; s) \supset s$.

## Axioms

The basic axioms are those for normal modal logics [12]:

- if $s$ is an instance of a propositional-logic tautology then $\vdash s$;

- if $\vdash s$ and $\vdash (s \supset s')$ then $\vdash s'$;

- $\vdash A \; says \; (s \supset s') \supset (A \; says \; s \supset A \; says \; s')$;

- if $\vdash s$ then $\vdash A \; says \; s$, for every $A$.

The calculus of principals is included:

- if $s$ is a valid formula of the calculus of principals then $\vdash s$.

Other axioms connect the calculus of principals to the modal logic:

- $\vdash (A \wedge B) \; says \; s \equiv (A \; says \; s) \wedge (B \; says \; s)$;

- $\vdash (B|A) \; says \; s \equiv B \; says \; A \; says \; s$;

- $\vdash (A \Rightarrow B) \supset ((A \; says \; s) \supset (B \; says \; s))$.

The last axiom is equivalent to $(A = B) \supset ((A \; says \; s) \equiv (B \; says \; s))$, a substitutivity property.

Let us write $A \rightarrow B$ if, for every $s$, if $A$ *says* $s$ then $B$ *says* $s$. Although $\rightarrow$ is weaker than $\Rightarrow$, it suffices in many of the situations where we currently use $\Rightarrow$, and hence we have contemplated adding it to the formalism. It may also be convenient to have second-order quantification over formulas and over principals. Second-order quantification enables us to define $A \rightarrow B$ as $\forall x.((A \; says \; x) \supset (B \; says \; x))$. We do not adopt any of these additional constructs, for the sake of minimality. However, there is no difficulty in giving a semantics for them, and the proof rules needed in examples would be simple.

Another important relation between principals is defined by the formula $(A \; says \; false) \supset (B \; says \; false)$, which we abbreviate $A \mapsto B$. Intuitively, $A \mapsto B$ means that there is something that $A$ can do (say *false*) that yields an arbitrarily strong statement by $B$ (in fact, *false*). Thus, $A \mapsto B$ means that $A$ is at least as powerful as $B$ in practice. Clearly, $A \Rightarrow B$ implies $A \mapsto B$. We do not have the converse, and actually the converse does not seem attractive, as for example $B \mapsto (B|A)$ is valid but we would not want $B \Rightarrow (B|A)$. Nevertheless, the relation $\mapsto$ serves as a point of reference in axiomatizing the algebra of principals; a careful study of $\mapsto$ may be of some interest.

## 3.3   Semantics

The simplest semantics is a Kripke semantics, based on accessibility relations [12]. A structure $\mathcal{M}$ is a tuple $\langle W, w_0, I, J \rangle$, where:

- $W$ is a set (as usual, a set of possible worlds);

- $w_0$ is a distinguished element of $W$;

- $I$ is an interpretation function which maps each proposition symbol to a subset of $W$ (the set of worlds where the proposition symbol is true);

- $J$ is an interpretation function which maps each principal symbol to a binary relation over $W$ (the accessibility relation for the principal symbol).

The meaning function $\mathcal{R}$ extends $J$, mapping a principal expression to a relation:

$$\begin{aligned} \mathcal{R}(A_i) &= J(A_i) \\ \mathcal{R}(A \wedge B) &= \mathcal{R}(A) \cup \mathcal{R}(B) \\ \mathcal{R}(B|A) &= \mathcal{R}(A) \circ \mathcal{R}(B) \end{aligned}$$

There is no difficulty in giving a semantics to other operations on principals such as infinite conjunctions, disjunctions, 0, and 1.

Then the meaning function $\mathcal{E}$ maps each formula to its extension, that is, to the set of worlds where it is true:

$$\begin{aligned} \mathcal{E}(p_i) &= I(p_i) \\ \mathcal{E}(\neg s) &= W - \mathcal{E}(s) \\ \mathcal{E}(s \wedge s') &= \mathcal{E}(s) \cap \mathcal{E}(s') \\ \mathcal{E}(A \text{ says } s) &= \{w \mid \mathcal{R}(A)(w) \subseteq \mathcal{E}(s)\} \\ \mathcal{E}(A \Rightarrow B) &= W \text{ if } \mathcal{R}(B) \subseteq \mathcal{R}(A) \text{ and } \emptyset \text{ otherwise} \end{aligned}$$

where $\mathcal{R}(C)(w) = \{w' \mid w\mathcal{R}(C)w'\}$.

A formula $s$ holds in $\mathcal{M}$ at a world $w$ if $w \in \mathcal{E}(s)$, and it holds in $\mathcal{M}$ if it holds at $w_0$. In the latter case, we write $\mathcal{M} \models s$, and say that $\mathcal{M}$ satisfies $s$. Moreover, $s$ is valid if it holds in all models; we write this $\models s$. The axioms are sound, in the sense that if $\vdash s$ then $\models s$. Although useful for our application, the axioms are not complete. For example, the formula

$$(C \text{ says } (A \Rightarrow B)) \equiv ((A \Rightarrow B) \vee (C \text{ says false}))$$

is valid but not provable. A more interesting source of incompleteness is that the algebras of principals that underly the semantics are obviously representable, while some multiplicative semilattice semigroups are not. (We do obtain a completeness result for a sublanguage, in section 6.)

This simple relational model provides some justification for the axioms for principals. If $\mathcal{R}(A) = \mathcal{R}(B)$, then it is natural to have $A = B$, and this holds in the semantics. For example, $\mathcal{R}(C|(B|A)) = \mathcal{R}((C|B)|A)$ provides a justification for the associativity of $|$.

A more abstract model may be desirable in order to avoid the requirement of representability. Dynamic algebras suggest such a model (see Pratt's [18] for a recent discussion of dynamic algebras). The operator *says* is directly analogous to the usual partial correctness operator [ ] of dynamic logic. It connects the two sorts of the algebras, that of principals and that of propositions.

## 3.4  On idempotence

Idempotence postulates are attractive. For example, when $A$ is a user, there seems to be little advantage in distinguishing $A|A$ and $A$; in fact, this distinction seems quite artificial. Therefore, we may postulate that $A|A = A$, for all $A$, and hence that $A$ *says* $A$ *says* $s$ and $A$ *says* $s$ are equivalent. The idempotence of $|$ implies the idempotence of *for* (see section 5 for details). Here we discuss the idempotence of $|$ and *for*; most of the remarks below are written in terms of $|$, but exactly the same arguments apply to *for*.

The idempotence axiom is rather convenient for handling chains of principals. For instance, suppose that $G$ represents a collection of nodes, that $B$ and $C$ represent members of $G$, and that an ACL includes $G|A$. Thanks to idempotence, $C|B|A$ obtains access. This means that multiple "hops" within a collection of nodes does not reduce rights and should not reduce security. In particular, there is no need to postulate that $G|G \Rightarrow G$, or to make sure that $G|G|A$ appears in the ACL explicitly.

In addition, idempotence yields $(A \wedge B) \Rightarrow (B|A)$, since $(A \wedge B) = (A \wedge B)|(A \wedge B)$ and $|$ is monotonic, and similarly $(A \wedge B) \Rightarrow (B \text{ for } A)$. These implications are rather pleasing, but not necessarily intuitive. They complicate the problem of making access control decisions. When $(A \wedge B)$ makes a request, one must check whether either $(B|A)$ or $(A|B)$ is trusted, and grant access if either is trusted.

Finally, the semantics of subsection 3.3 does not validate idempotence. We have been unable to find a sensible condition on binary relations that would force idempotence and would be preserved by both union and composition. A related symptom is that idempotence seems less compelling for complex principals than for simple ones.

For all these reasons, we prefer to do without idempotence; in compensation, we often rely on assumptions of the form $G|G \Rightarrow G$, or write less elegant but more explicit ACLs.

We give a similar treatment to other possible axioms related to idempotence. Although in many cases it is reasonable to assume formulas of the forms $A$ *controls* $(B \Rightarrow A)$ and $A$ *controls* $(t \supset A \text{ says } s)$, this does not seem well founded in general. In particular, when $A$ is a group, if $A$ *controls* $(B \Rightarrow A)$ for all $B$ then any member of $A$ can add members to $A$. Therefore, we choose to adopt neither $A$ *controls* $(B \Rightarrow A)$ nor $A$ *controls* $(t \supset A \text{ says } s)$ as general axioms.

# 4  Roles

The formal systems we have presented so far include no exotic connective, such as *for*. Neither do they include a primitive for roles. We discuss roles in this section and delegation in the next one. We start with an informal argument on the nature of roles and then describe their logic.

## 4.1 Roles versus groups

Roles are often related to groups. For example, a member of a group $G$ can act in the role of member of $G$. It is tempting to establish a formal identification between the group $G$ and a corresponding role $G\_role$. We find that this identification is harmful.

In particular, roles make it possible to reduce privileges as a protection against accidents. The roles used for this purpose need not correspond to groups. For example, there may be a role such that adopting it makes it possible to access only a certain directory in the file system; the role corresponds naturally to a set of resources (files) rather than to any group of principals.

In what follows, then, we do not identify roles and groups. In fact, this confusion would interact somewhat strangely with our encoding of roles, given below. We do allow roles related to groups (such as $G\_role$), but this relation is not formal; a formal operator for relating groups and roles may be a useful extension of our calculus.

It is reasonable to expect that not all roles make sense for all principals, and that a principal can act only in certain roles. For example, a principal may be allowed to act as $G\_role$ only if he is a member of $G$. The simplest implementation of this idea relies on the judicious writing of ACLs. Roles can be adopted freely, and any $A$ can speak in the role $G\_role$, with the identity $A$ *as* $G\_role$. However, it may be that no ACL in the system grants access to $A$ *as* $G\_role$, and for example the ACL $G$ *as* $G\_role$ does not. It is this implementation that we choose.

## 4.2 The encoding

Given the view that roles can be freely adopted, it is quite satisfactory to define $A$ *as* $R$ to equal $A|R$.

In many cases, this encoding makes some intuitive sense. For example, let $A$ be a machine and $R$ a (possibly untrusted) piece of software that $A$ is running. The requests that $A$ makes while running this software should not emanate from $A$ with full powers; rather, they should emanate from $A$ in some restricted role. The role can be named after the piece of software, or after its class (e.g., *untrusted-software*). In any case, when $A$ makes a request $s$ in this role, $A$ says that $R$ says $s$. This is precisely $A|R$ *says* $s$. Similarly, if $A$ is a user and $R$ is one of his positions, we can think of $R$ as a program that $A$ is following, and apply the analysis above.

Furthermore, this presentation of roles offers formal advantages, thanks to the monotonicity, the multiplicativity, and the associativity of $|$.

- Since $|$ is monotonic in both arguments, if $R$ is a more trusted role than $R'$ and $A$ a more trusted principal than $A'$, then $A$ *as* $R$ is more trusted than $A'$ *as* $R'$, that is, if $R \Rightarrow R'$ and $A \Rightarrow A'$ then $(A$ *as* $R) \Rightarrow (A'$ *as* $R')$. Thus, it is possible to exploit a hierarchy of roles.

- The multiplicativity of $|$ yields that $A \wedge B$ in a role $R$ is identical to the conjunction $A$ and $B$ both in role $R$:

$$(A \wedge B) \text{ as } R = (A \text{ as } R) \wedge (B \text{ as } R)$$

Similarly, we can exploit the conjunction operation for roles:

$$A \text{ as } (R \wedge R') = (A \text{ as } R) \wedge (A \text{ as } R')$$

Both of these properties seem reasonable for roles as we conceive them informally, and they are quite handy.

- Associativity yields a satisfactory interaction between roles and delegation. In particular, the user $A$ in role $R$ on a machine $B$ is identical to the user $A$ on a machine $B$, with the compound in role $R$:

$$B|(A \text{ as } R) = (B|A) \text{ as } R$$

and then the encoding of *for*, given in the next section, yields:

$$B \text{ for } (A \text{ as } R) = (B \text{ for } A) \text{ as } R$$

Some special properties for roles can be expected:

- We sometimes rely on the postulates that all roles are idempotent ($R|R = R$) and commute with one another ($R'|R = R|R'$). This yields:

$$A \text{ as } R \text{ as } R = A \text{ as } R$$

and

$$A \text{ as } R \text{ as } R' = A \text{ as } R' \text{ as } R$$

(We make it explicit when these properties are assumed.)

- We assume $A \Rightarrow (A \text{ as } R)$ for all $A$. With a unit, this could just be written $1 \Rightarrow R$. In the binary-relation model, $1 \Rightarrow R$ means that roles are subsets of the identity relation; note that the previous idempotence and commutativity properties follow from this.

# 5 Delegation

Delegation is a fairly ill-defined term. Here we explain our approach to delegation; some example schemes for delegation illustrate the use of the logic. Then we give an encoding of delegation.

## 5.1 The forms of delegation

Delegation is a basic primitive for secure distributed computing. It is the ability of a principal $A$ to give to another principal $B$ the authority to act on $A$'s behalf. When $B$ requests a service from a third principal, $B$ might present credentials which are supposed to demonstrate that $B$ is making the request and that $A$ has delegated to $B$.

Naturally, access control decisions need to take delegations into account. A range of designs is possible.

In the simplest case, $A$ delegates all of his rights to $B$. Upon $B$'s request, a service will be granted if it would have been granted to $A$, had $A$ requested it directly.

An obvious improvement is for $A$ to delegate only some of his rights, such as the right to read certain files from a file server. Capability systems (e.g., [9, 20, 15]) embody this approach in the case where delegation certificates can be transferred; the containment of capabilities is a serious concern. If delegation certificates are not transferrable, cascaded delegations are hampered, as $A$ may have to prepare adequate certificates for any expected collaborators to $B$ in advance. In all cases, the provider of the service never checks that $B$ is a reasonable delegate for $A$.

These considerations suggest more sophisticated designs, where access control decisions may depend on the identities of both $A$ and $B$. For example, the file server may not let a known malicious workstation read a user's files, even if the user was unlucky enough to log onto the workstation. The file server may also let a trusted node read files over which the user has execute-only rights, in the belief that these files will not be shown to the user, but just executed; here the node acts as a protected subsystem, and offers guarantees that its clients cannot provide by themselves. These examples illustrate a desirable flexibility. It exists in some form in a few designs and systems [21, 13], and it is a prominent component of DSSA [11]. We believe that it should and will become widespread.

Different mechanisms embody the concept of delegation in different settings. A user might rely on a smart-card for delegating to a workstation, while delegation across the address spaces of a machine might benefit from operating system support. (The use of smart-cards is discussed in [1], with a simplistic view of delegation.) Similarly, credentials can be signed with either shared-key cryptography or with public-key cryptography, or they might not be signed at all when a secure physical channel is available. Recognizing and treating all these variants as mere instances of delegation makes possible a uniform view of access control throughout an entire distributed system.

Delegation relies on authentication, which is often achieved through authentication protocols (see for example [17, 5, 16, 13, 4]). In fact, some of the messages for delegation can be combined with those for authentication. However, in our study, it is often convenient to view delegation as independent.

## Delegation without certificates

The framework outlined so far enables us to describe and compare various schemes for delegation. In what follows, $A$ delegates to $B$, who makes requests to $C$. For instance, $A$ may be a user with a sufficiently powerful smart-card, $B$ a workstation, and $C$ a file server. For simplicity, the authority delegated from $A$ to $B$ is not limited to any particular class of requests, and $A$ does not adopt a special role before the delegation.

We assume that synchronized clocks are available, and that appropriate timestamps, lifetimes, sequence numbers, and message type fields are included and checked for all messages. We also assume that all principals can perform digital signatures, for example with the RSA algorithm [19]. We denote by $K_A$ and $K_B$ the public keys for $A$ and $B$, and by $K_A^{-1}$ and $K_B^{-1}$ the matching secret keys. The formula $K$ *says* $X$ represents the certificate $X$ encrypted under $K^{-1}$, which is commonly written $\{X\}_{K^{-1}}$.

A certification authority $S$ provides certificates for the principals' public keys as needed. The necessary certificates are $K_S$ *says* $K_A \Rightarrow A$ and $K_S$ *says* $K_B \Rightarrow B$, where $K_S$ is $S$'s public key.

We consider three instances of delegation. In each case, we are led to ask whether composite principals, such as $B|A$, appear on $C$'s ACL. The simplest instance of delegation is delegation without certificates:

1. When $B$ wishes to make a request $r$ on $A$'s behalf, $B$ sends the signed request along with $A$'s name, for example in the format $K_B$ *says* $A$ *says* $r$.

2. When $C$ receives the request $r$, he has evidence that $B$ has said that $A$ requests $r$, but not that $A$ has delegated to $B$; then $C$ consults the ACL for request $r$, and determines whether the request should be granted under these circumstances.

The logic serves in describing the reasoning of the service provider, $C$, who makes the access control decision. Some assumptions are needed. First, $C$ must believe that $K_S$ is $S$'s public key:

$$K_S \Rightarrow S$$

and $C$ obtains a certificate encrypted under the inverse of $K_S$:

$$K_S \; says \; (K_B \Rightarrow B)$$

These two formulas yield:

$$S \; says \; (K_B \Rightarrow B)$$

We should assume that $C$ trusts $S$ for such statements:

$$S \; controls \; (K_B \Rightarrow B)$$

and we immediately obtain that $C$ has $B$'s key:

$$K_B \Rightarrow B$$

In addition, $C$ sees a message under the inverse of $K_B$, requesting $r$ on behalf of $A$; in other words,

$$K_B \; says \; A \; says \; r$$

Immediately, $C$ obtains:

$$B \; says \; A \; says \; r$$

that is,

$$(B|A) \; says \; r$$

Now $C$ consults an ACL for $r$. If $B|A$ appears in this ACL, that is, if $B|A$ is trusted on $r$, then $C$ believes $r$—access is granted.

## Delegation with certificates

The protocol just described can hardly be considered satisfactory in general. It is preferable for $A$ to issue a delegation certificate that proves the delegation to $B$:

1. After mutual authentication, $A$ issues a certificate to $B$, under $A$'s key. This certificate states that $A$ has delegated some authority to $B$.

2. When $B$ wishes to request $r$ on $A$'s behalf, no further interaction with $A$ is needed: $B$ can present $A$'s certificate to $C$, along with $K_B$ *says* $A$ *says* $r$.

3. At this point $C$ has evidence that $B$ has requested $r$ on behalf of $A$; now $C$ consults the ACL for $r$, and determines whether the request should be granted.

For the time being, let us use the notation $B$ *serves* $A$ to mean that $B$ is a delegate for $A$. (But *serves* need not be primitive; see subsection 5.2.) Then the delegation certificate from $A$ for $B$ can be expressed:

$$K_A \; says \; (B \; serves \; A)$$

and the usual checking of public-key certificates from $S$ yields:

$$A \; says \; (B \; serves \; A)$$

If $C$ trusts $A$ on this statement, $C$ gets:

$$((B|A) \; says \; r) \wedge (B \; serves \; A)$$

In our theories, this implies:
$$(B \; for \; A) \; says \; r$$

Again $C$ can consult the ACL for $r$, and $r$ will be granted if the list includes $B$ *for* $A$. In particular, $r$ will be granted if the list mentions $B|A$, a weaker principal, but may be granted even otherwise.

This scheme is illustrated in more detail by an example in section 6. An important variant consists in omitting the authentication between $B$ and $C$, leaving the responsibility of authenticating $B$ solely to $A$; we study it in the full paper.

## 5.2   The encoding

The delegation of all powers can be defined convincingly: $A$ delegates to $B$ when $A$ says that $B$ speaks for $A$ (that is, when $A$ *says* $(B \Rightarrow A)$ holds). The concept of delegation that interests us here is subtler. When $A$ delegates to $B$, the powers of $B$ on behalf of $A$ depend on the contents of the ACLs in the distributed system; $A$ may be more reckless with delegations if these powers are small. In turn, the contents of the ACLs depend on how their writers understand the meaning of delegation. There is a circularity here. We conclude that the meaning of delegation is purely conventional—it is a convention between the writers of ACLs, the delegators, and the delegates.

These remarks suggest an approach where the notion of delegation is primitive; we now sketch this approach. The operator *serves* is taken as primitive, and axiomatized. Some straightforward axioms come to mind, and in particular that $B$ *serves* $A$ is anti-monotonic in $B$, and that if $B_i$ *serves* $A$ for all $i$, then $\bigvee_i B_i$ *serves* $A$. Let $E(A)$ be the weakest principal to which $A$ has delegated, and let $E_B(A)$ be the weakest principal stronger than $B$ to which $A$ has delegated. (If disjunction is available, such principals always exist.) Then $B$ *for* $A$ can be defined to be $E_B(A)|A$, and this equals $(B \wedge E(A))|A$. Axioms for delegation yield properties of *for*; for example, the axioms given yield that *for* is multiplicative in its second argument. We have not found a satisfactory way to obtain associativity.

We prefer not having delegation as a primitive; the following thought experiment inspires an alternative approach. Imagine that there is a distinguished principal $D$ in the distributed system who operates as a delegation server. The function of $D$ is to certify delegations. When $A$ wants to delegate to $B$, it suffices for $A$ to tell $D$ that if $B$ says that $A$ says $s$, then $D$ should back $B$. Thus, if $B|A$ *says* $s$ then $D|A$ *says* $s$. Intuitively, $D$ says that $A$ says $s$ when a delegate of $A$'s makes this assertion. Thus, we can take $(B \land D)|A$ as a formal encoding for $B$ *for* $A$. Notice the striking similarity between this encoding of *for* and the previous formulation.

It is not actually necessary for $D$ to be implemented, just as typical roles do not correspond to real users and machines. When $A$ wishes to delegate to $B$, $A$ says that for all $s$, if $B$ says that $A$ says $s$ then $D$ says that $A$ says $s$; formally, it suffices to have $A$ *says* $(B|A \Rightarrow D|A)$. The statement $A$ *controls* $(B|A \Rightarrow D|A)$ then represents that $A$ can delegate to $B$. These two assertions together immediately yield $(B|A \Rightarrow D|A)$, and when $(B|A)$ *says* $s$, we obtain $(D|A)$ *says* $s$, and then $((B \land D)|A)$ *says* $s$. In this formal derivation, it is irrelevant whether $D$ is a real server or not. (It is perhaps even better if $D$ is not a real server, for then it cannot be attacked.)

Thus, we can take $B$ *for* $A$ to mean $(B \land D)|A$, where $D$ is a distinguished fictional principal. Similarly, $(B|A \Rightarrow D|A)$ can represent $B$ *serves* $A$; hence, if $B$ *serves* $A$ then $(B|A \Rightarrow B$ *for* $A)$. This expresses the intuition that *for* is | "plus a delegation." The logical framework also allows the possibility of weaker delegation statements, where $A$ delegates only some of this rights; we prefer the use of roles for limiting the power of delegations.

Our encoding has sensible formal consequences:

- *for* is monotonic in both arguments.

- *for* is multiplicative in both arguments, in fact. This follows from the multiplicativity of | and the definition of *for*:

$$
\begin{aligned}
(B \land B') \ for \ (A \land A') &= (B \land B' \land D)|(A \land A') \\
&= ((B \land D) \land (B' \land D))|(A \land A') \\
&= ((B \land D)|A) \land ((B \land D)|A') \land ((B' \land D)|A) \land ((B' \land D)|A') \\
&= (B \ for \ A) \land (B \ for \ A') \land (B' \ for \ A) \land (B' \ for \ A')
\end{aligned}
$$

- $B$ *for* $A$ is always defined, even if $A$ has not delegated to $B$. In fact, we have:

$$
(B|A) \land (C \ for \ A) \Rightarrow ((B \land C) \ for \ A)
$$

and hence also

$$
(B|A) \land (C \ for \ A) \Rightarrow (B \ for \ A)
$$

This somewhat surprising theorem is the consequence of two desirable, basic properties: the monotonicity of *for*, and the antimonotonicity of delegation (which means that if $A$ delegates to $C$, then it also delegates to the stronger principal $B \land C$).

Additional properties of $D$ yield further consequences:

- If $D|D \Rightarrow D$ then *for* possesses a weak associativity property:

$$
C \ for \ (B \ for \ A) \Rightarrow (C \ for \ B) \ for \ A
$$

which follows from the associativity and the multiplicativity of |:

$$
C \ for \ (B \ for \ A) = (C \land D)|((B \land D)|A)
$$

$$= (C|B|A) \land (C|D|A) \land (D|B|A) \land (D|D|A)$$
$$\Rightarrow (C|B|A) \land (C|D|A) \land (D|B|A) \land (D|A)$$
$$\Rightarrow (C|B|A) \land (D|B|A) \land (D|A)$$
$$= ((C\ for\ B)|A) \land (D|A)$$
$$= (C\ for\ B)\ for\ A$$

The other direction of the implication is not valid. The essential reason for this is that $C\ for\ (B\ for\ A)$ implies $C|D|A$, while $(C\ for\ B)\ for\ A$ does not. Intuitively, this is because $C$'s part in $(C\ for\ B)\ for\ A$ need not involve checking evidence that $B$ is a delegate for $A$, or even that $A$ exists.

- If $A \Rightarrow D|A$ then $(A \land (B|A)) \Rightarrow (B\ for\ A)$, because | is multiplicative:

$$
\begin{aligned}
A \land (B|A) &\Rightarrow & (D|A) \land (B|A) \\
&=& ((B \land D)|A) \\
&=& B\ for\ A
\end{aligned}
$$

This property means that when $A$ makes a statement himself, there is no need to find a corresponding statement by the delegation server.

- If $A \Rightarrow D|A$ and $A = A|A$ then $A = A\ for\ A$, that is, the idempotence of | implies the idempotence of *for*:

$$
\begin{aligned}
A\ for\ A &=& ((A \land D)|A) \\
&=& (A|A) \land (D|A) \\
&=& A \land (D|A) \\
&=& A
\end{aligned}
$$

The additional properties for $D$ are reasonable, and we adopt them. These properties are reminiscent of those for roles. In the binary-relation model, for example, these properties of $D$ and those for roles all amount to saying the same thing, that the associated binary relations are subsets of the identity.

# 6  Protocols and Algorithms

In this section we consider some mechanisms for delegation and for access control decisions. The last subsection presents an example.

## 6.1  Delegation

While delegation has a single semantics, substantially different implementations are recommended for users and for nodes.

### 6.1.1 Delegation from users to nodes

The schemes for delegation discussed in section 5 do not seem adequate for users. Delegation from users to nodes poses special problems. One difficulty is that it is inconvenient for users to refresh delegation certificates. Refreshing a delegation certificate may require reintroducing a smart-card, for example. Therefore, it seems desirable that delegation certificates be relatively long-lived (valid for many hours).

Long-lived delegation certificates pose a security threat, because a delegation certificate may be valid long after the user has stopped using the node. An attacker may subvert the node over a relatively long time period, and abuse the user's delegation. To prevent this from happening, it is best to introduce an auxiliary delegation key that the node can forget deliberately when the user leaves. The delegation certificate remains valid, but becomes useless.

In more detail, the protocol goes as follows. First the user $A$ delegates to the node $B$ and to a public key $K_d$ provided by the node:

$$A \; says \; ((K_d \wedge B) \; serves \; A)$$

The node has the inverse of the public key, and it can set up a channel $Ch$ for $(K_d \wedge B)$ for $A$:

$$K_d \; says \; A \; says \; (Ch \Rightarrow (K_d \wedge B) \; for \; A)$$

and

$$B \; says \; A \; says \; (Ch \Rightarrow (K_d \wedge B) \; for \; A)$$

Hence

$$((K_d \wedge B) \; for \; A) \; says \; (Ch \Rightarrow (K_d \wedge B) \; for \; A)$$

follows logically. When this statement is believed, it yields:

$$Ch \Rightarrow (K_d \wedge B) \; for \; A$$

and then monotonicity leads to the desired result:

$$Ch \Rightarrow B \; for \; A$$

Hereafter $B$ can make requests for $A$ through the channel $Ch$. In practice, the channel may be obtained by multiplexing a longer-term secure channel from $B$; this longer-term channel may well be a DES channel.

The delegation from $K_d$ to the channel has a relatively short lifetime, and needs to be renewed frequently. When the node forgets $K_d$ deliberately, it loses the ability to refresh the certificate for the channel $Ch$.

### 6.1.2 Delegation from nodes to nodes

For nodes, the schemes of section 5 are convenient enough. The one corresponding to the *for* operator is simple, reasonably secure, and it can be made efficient enough for implementation.

The same ideas work for cascaded delegations. Suppose that user $A$ has delegated to node $B$, and $B$ can operate with the identity $B$ for $A$. If a further delegation is needed, to a node $C$, the precise delegation statement is:

$$(B|A) \; says \; (C \; serves \; (B \; for \; A))$$

Since $A$ has delegated to $B$, it follows logically that:

$$(B \text{ for } A) \text{ says } (C \text{ serves } (B \text{ for } A))$$

This statement is believed, and it yields:

$$C \text{ serves } (B \text{ for } A)$$

Now $C$ can make a request $r$ on behalf of $B$ for $A$:

$$C \text{ says } (B \text{ for } A) \text{ says } r$$

and then the delegation from $A$ yields:

$$(C \text{ for } (B \text{ for } A)) \text{ says } r$$

## 6.2 Access control decisions

Unfortunately, the set of valid formulas of the calculus of principals is not recursive for any useful definition of validity, but it is recursively enumerable. Undecidability can be proved by a reduction from the word problem for Thue systems, for example. On the other hand, the formulas that arise in access control are not arbitrary; the next two parts discuss decidable access control problems.

### 6.2.1 A general access control problem

The problem of making access control decisions is computationally complex. It is important therefore to understand the precise form of its instances. The parts of an instance are:

- An expression $P$ in the calculus of principals represents the principal that is making the request. In particular, all appropriate delegations are taken into account in constructing this expression. The various relevant certificates are presented for checking.

- A statement $s$ represents what is being requested or asserted; the statement is presented explicitly by the requestor, and the service provider does not need to derive it logically from other statements. The precise nature of $s$ is ignored—it is treated as an uninterpreted proposition symbol.

- Assumptions state implications among principals; these typically represent assumptions about group memberships. They have the form $P_i \Rightarrow G_i$, where $P_i$ is an arbitrary expression in the calculus of principals and $G_i$ an atom. Note that this syntax is liberal enough to write $G|G \Rightarrow G$ for every appropriate $G$ of interest, obtaining some of the benefit of the idempotence axiom.

- Certain atomic symbols $R_0, \ldots, R_i, \ldots$ are known to denote roles. This may be obvious from their names.

- An ACL is a list of expressions $E_0, \ldots, E_i, \ldots$ in the calculus of principals; these represent the principals that are trusted on $s$.

The problem of access control is deciding whether $\bigwedge_i (P_i \Rightarrow G_i)$ and $\bigwedge_i (E_i \; controls \; s)$ imply $P \; controls \; s$, given the special properties of roles and of the delegation server $D$.

As discussed in the full paper, this problem is intractable. (We have sketched a reduction from the acceptance problem for alternating pushdown automata [6].) Further restrictions are wanted.

### 6.2.2 A more tractable problem

A second version of the access control problem is based on some further simplifications:

- The *for* operator takes a more prominent role. Since it is expected to be common, one would want an algorithm that does not treat it by expanding it in terms of $\wedge$ and $|$, with an exponential blow-up.

- In effect, *for* is treated as an associative operator. More precisely, we assume that all ACLs have the weakest parenthesization possible. This enables us to ignore the parenthesization of the requestor.

- The $|$ operator occurs only in the encoding of *for* and *as*, and $D$ occurs only in the encoding of *for*.

- Roles are differentiated from other principals (called proper principals), and occur in special positions. The set of atomic symbols for proper principals is $\mathcal{P}$; the set of atomic symbols for roles is $\mathcal{Q}$.

- Assumptions (group memberships) are restricted to be of the form $atom \Rightarrow atom$, where both atoms are either in $\mathcal{P}$ or in $\mathcal{Q}$. In particular, this forbids the assumptions of the form $G|G \Rightarrow G$, which would give us some benefits of idempotence where appropriate.

- It is therefore necessary to include a construct for writing, in an ACL, that any positive number of iterations of a principal are allowed. We introduce a metalogical construct $(\;)^+$ for this purpose; for example $F \; for \; G^+$ is a shorthand for the list $F \; for \; G, \; (F \; for \; G) \; for \; G, \; \ldots$.

An ACL is a list of ACL entries. In turn, an ACL entry is a conjunction of ACL entries free of $\wedge$, called *for*-lists. A *for*-list is a list connected by *for*'s, that is, it has the form $P_0 \; for \; \ldots \; for \; P_m$, where each $P_i$ is a principal in roles. A principal in roles is of the form $Q \; as \; R_1 \; as \; \ldots R_n$, where $Q$ is a proper principal and each $R_j$ is a role.
' This definition is summarized by a grammar:

$$
\begin{aligned}
ACL \;\; &= \;\; list \; of \; Entry \\
Requestor \;\; &= \;\; Entry \\
Entry \;\; &= \;\; conjunction \; of \; for\text{-}list \\
for\text{-}list \;\; &= \;\; Principal\text{-}in\text{-}Roles \mid for\text{-}list \; for \; Principal\text{-}in\text{-}Roles \\
Principal\text{-}in\text{-}Roles \;\; &= \;\; Proper\text{-}Principal \mid Principal\text{-}in\text{-}Roles \; as \; Role \\
Membership \;\; &= \;\; Proper\text{-}Principal \Rightarrow Proper\text{-}Principal \mid Role \Rightarrow Role
\end{aligned}
$$

The syntactic conditions can be loosened, as this normal form for ACL entries can be obtained by two syntactic transformations justified by the laws of the logic. Conjunctions can be pushed outwards, since both *as* and *for* distribute over $\wedge$; this normalization is the only source of exponential behavior, and it can be expected to be unimportant in the common examples where conjunctions are rare. Roles can be pushed inwards, into the delegator argument of *for*'s; this step is efficient.

With these syntactic restrictions, a more efficient access control algorithm is possible:

- The request is granted if the requestor implies one of the ACL entries.

- Each ACL entry is a conjunction of *for*-lists, and so is the requestor. For the requestor to imply an ACL entry, it must be that for each conjunct of the ACL entry there exists some conjunct of the requestor that implies it.

- A *for*-list implies another if they are of the same length, and each principal in roles of the requestor implies the corresponding one of the entry.

- A principal in roles $Q$ *as* $R_1$ *as* ... *as* $R_n$ implies another $Q'$ *as* $R_1'$ *as* ... *as* $R_{n'}'$ if $Q$ implies $Q'$ and for each $R_j$ there exists $R_k'$ such that $R_j$ implies $R_k'$.

- An atomic symbol $P$ implies another atomic symbol $P'$ if there is a chain of assumptions $P = P_0 \Rightarrow \ldots \Rightarrow P_n = P'$.

It is simple to describe this algorithm to users, and it is also simple to implement it. The adequate speed of a prototype implementation suggests that the algorithm might well be practical. The metalogical construct $( )^+$ does not introduce any major algorithmic difficulty. Its treatment is well understood, as it is standard in the context of regular languages.

The algorithm is sound for the binary-relation model, where we take all roles to be subsets of the identity. The algorithm is also complete for the binary-relation model. Note in particular that the algorithm treats all roles as idempotent, and they all commute with one another.

**Theorem 1 (Soundness and Completeness)** *Let* $E_0, \ldots, E_i, \ldots$ *be an ACL, $P$ a requestor, and* $\bigwedge_i (B_i \Rightarrow B_i')$ *a conjunction of assumptions. The algorithm grants the request if and only if*

$$\bigwedge_i (B_i \Rightarrow B_i') \wedge \bigwedge_i (E_i \text{ controls } p) \supset (P \text{ controls } p)$$

*is valid for all p over binary-relation models.*

## 6.3 An example

The most typical, complete example is that of a user logging into a workstation, and the workstation making requests on a server.

- The user $A$ authenticates and delegates in some role $R_A$ to a workstation $B$ in role $R_B$. The user may rely on a smart-card, and use the scheme for user delegation outlined in subsection 6.1. The delegation certificate is:

$$K_A \text{ says } R_A \text{ says } ((K_d \wedge (B \text{ as } R_B)) \text{ serves } (A \text{ as } R_A))$$

- The workstation sets up a secure channel to a server. Logically, this requires two statements:

$$K_d \; says \; (A \; as \; R_A) \; says \; (Ch \Rightarrow ((B \; as \; R_B) \; for \; (A \; as \; R_A)))$$

under the delegation key, and

$$K_B \; says \; R_B \; says \; (A \; as \; R_A) \; says \; (Ch \Rightarrow ((B \; as \; R_B) \; for \; (A \; as \; R_A)))$$

(For simplicity, the workstation acts in the role $R_B$, but any stronger role would do just as well.)

- The server needs to check that $K_A$ is the user's key and that $K_B$ is the workstation's key, that is, $K_A \Rightarrow A$ and $K_B \Rightarrow B$. Typically this requires looking at certificates from a certification authority; it is possible that a chain of certification authorities needs to be involved, as there may be no single universally trusted certification authority.

- With these properties of the keys, it follows from the delegation certificate that:

$$(A \; as \; R_A) \; says \; ((K_d \wedge (B \; as \; R_B)) \; serves \; (A \; as \; R_A))$$

and this statement is believed. The channel set-up certificates yield:

$$((K_d \wedge (B \; as \; R_B))|(A \; as \; R_A)) \; says \; (Ch \Rightarrow ((B \; as \; R_B) \; for \; (A \; as \; R_A)))$$

and this leads to

$$((B \; as \; R_B) \; for \; (A \; as \; R_A)) \; says \; (Ch \Rightarrow ((B \; as \; R_B) \; for \; (A \; as \; R_A)))$$

and then

$$Ch \Rightarrow ((B \; as \; R_B) \; for \; (A \; as \; R_A))$$

as $(B \; as \; R_B) \; for \; (A \; as \; R_A)$ is trusted on this matter.

- The user may indicate to the workstation that he wishes to reduce his privileges, and adopt a further role $R'_A$, in order to make a request $r$; or the workstation may do this on behalf of the user, on its own initiative:

$$(Ch \; as \; R'_A) \; says \; r$$

The requestor here is $((B \; as \; R_B) \; for \; (A \; as \; R_A)) \; as \; R'_A$, which is equivalent to $(B \; as \; R_B) \; for \; (A \; as \; R_A \; as \; R'_A)$.

- The ACL at the server may contain $(G' \; as \; R_B) \; for \; (G \; as \; R''_A)$. The server may have, or the workstation may present, certificates that prove that $A \Rightarrow G$, $R_A \Rightarrow R''_A$, $R'_A \Rightarrow R''_A$, and $B \Rightarrow G'$.

- Actually, the group membership certificates come signed with someone's public key. In each case it must be possible to resolve this public key into a name, and then to discover that the name is that of someone who is trusted to certify membership in the group.

- At this point, the algorithm for access control can easily determine that access should be granted.

# 7 Conclusions

Our main goal in this paper has been to isolate some useful and mathematically tractable concepts. We have only touched on many practical and theoretical matters that deserve more detailed treatments. In addition, the basic logic could be extended in many interesting ways. The full paper describes some of these extensions.

# Acknowledgements

Morrie Gasser, Andy Goldstein, and Charlie Kaufman were at the origin of many of the ideas discussed here. Tim Mann, Garret Swart, and Ted Wobber participated in fruitful discussions about implementations and examples. Greg Nelson and Vaughan Pratt helped in understanding the algebra of principals. Roger Maddux told us about Andréka's work. Luca Cardelli and Cynthia Hibbard provided editorial suggestions.

# References

[1] M. Abadi, M. Burrows, C. Kaufman, and B. Lampson. Authentication and Delegation with Smart-Cards. Digital Equipment Corporation Systems Research Center report No. 67, October 1990.

[2] M. Abadi, M. Burrows, B. Lampson, and G. Plotkin. A Calculus for Access Control in Distributed Systems. Digital Equipment Corporation Systems Research Center report No. 70, February 1990.

[3] H. Andréka. Representations of Distributive Lattice-ordered Semigroups with Binary Relations. Manuscript, August 1989.

[4] M. Burrows, M. Abadi, and R.M. Needham. A Logic of Authentication. *Proceedings of the Royal Society of London A* Vol. 426, 1989, pp. 233–271.

[5] CCITT. CCITT Blue Book, Recommendation X.509 and ISO 9594-8: The Directory-Authentication Framework. Geneva, March 1988.

[6] A. Chandra, D. Kozen, and L. Stockmeyer. Alternation. *JACM* Vol. 28, No. 1, January 1981, pp. 114-133.

[7] National Bureau of Standards. Data Encryption Standard. Fed. Inform. Processing Standards Pub. 46. Washington DC, January 1977.

[8] W. Diffie and M. Hellman. New Directions in Cryptography. *IEEE Transactions on Information Theory* IT-22, No. 6, November, 1976, pp. 644–654.

[9] R. Fabry. Capability-based Addressing. *CACM* Vol. 17, No. 7, July 1974, pp. 403-412.

[10] M. Gasser, A. Goldstein, C. Kaufman, and B. Lampson. The Digital Distributed System Security Architecture. Proceedings of the 1989 National Computer Security Conference, October 1989, pp. 305-319.

[11] M. Gasser and E. McDermott. An Architecture for Practical Delegation in a Distributed System. Proceedings of the 1990 IEEE Symposium on Security and Privacy, May 1990, pp. 20–30.

[12] G.E. Hughes and M.J. Cresswell. An Introduction to Modal Logic. Methuen Inc., New York, 1968.

[13] J. Kohl, C. Neuman, and J. Steiner. The Kerberos Network Authentication Service (version 5, draft 3). Available by anonymous ftp from athena-dist.mit.edu as /pub/doc/kerberos/V5DRAFT3-RFC.{PS,TXT}, October 1990.

[14] B. Lampson, M. Abadi, M. Burrows, and E. Wobber. Authentication in Distributed Systems: Theory and Practice. To appear in the Proceedings of the Thirteenth Symposium on Operating System Principles, October 1991.

[15] H. Levy. Capability-based Computer Systems. Digital Press, 1983.

[16] S.P. Miller, C. Neuman, J.I. Schiller, and J.H. Saltzer. Kerberos Authentication and Authorization System. *Project Athena Technical Plan* Section E.2.1, MIT, July 1987.

[17] R.M. Needham and M.D. Schroeder. Using Encryption for Authentication in Large Networks of Computers. *CACM* Vol. 21, No. 12, December 1978, pp. 993–999.

[18] V. Pratt. Dynamic Algebras as a Well-behaved Fragment of Relation Algebras. In *Algebraic Logic and Universal Algebra in Computer Science*, Springer-Verlag LNCS 425, 1990.

[19] R.L. Rivest, A. Shamir, and L. Adleman. A Method for Obtaining Digital Signatures and Public-key Cryptosystems. *CACM* Vol. 21, No. 2, February 1978, pp. 120-126.

[20] J. Saltzer and M. Schroeder. The Protection of Information in Computer Systems. *Proceedings of the IEEE* Vol. 63, No. 9, September 1975, pp. 1278-1308.

[21] K. Sollins. Cascaded Authentication. Proceedings of the 1988 IEEE Symposium on Security and Privacy, April 1988, pp. 156-163.

# Deriving the Complete Knowledge of Participants in Cryptographic Protocols
## (Extended Abstract)

Marie-Jeanne Toussaint
Université de Liège
Institut Montefiore, B28, Sart Tilman
B 4000 Liège (Belgium)
toussain@montefiore.ulg.ac.be

**Abstract**

This paper shows how to derive a representation of the participants' knowledge in a cryptographic protocol. The modelization is based on the assumption that the underlying cryptographic system is perfect and is an extension of the "Hidden Automorphism Model" introduced by Merritt. It can be used to establish the security of the protocols.

# 1  Introduction

A fair amount of research is devoted to developing cryptographic systems that are as secure as possible. Unfortunately, this is not sufficient: if a cryptographic system is used in an incorrect protocol, security can be compromised even if the cryptographic system is perfect. In the literature, the analysis of the security of the protocols is often strongly linked to the particular structure of the used cryptosystem ([Moo88, Dam87, EGS86]).

We adopt the point of view of Merritt in [Mer83] who studied the problem of reasoning about cryptographic protocols, assuming the underlying cryptographic system to be perfect. In [Mer83] and [MW85], a cryptosystem is represented by an algebra (called the *crypto-algebra*) and its perfection is modeled by the fact that the crypto-algebra is isomorphic to the free algebra of the same type.

In [TW91], we introduced a new representation of the participants' knowledge. The messages and keys whose a participant knows the meaning are represented in his state of knowledge by constants of the free-algebra whereas the ones whose he does not know the meaning are represented by variables defined on the free-algebra. This representation enabled us to obtain a new method to prove the security of cryptographic protocols. But, as we have seen by studying some examples in [Tou91], it is not sufficient because it does not model all the inferences and computations that the participants (and opponents) are able to make from their states of knowledge.

J. Feigenbaum (Ed.): Advances in Cryptology - CRYPTO '91, LNCS 576, pp. 24-43, 1992.
© Springer-Verlag Berlin Heidelberg 1992

In this paper, we refine the representation by modeling all the knowledge that a participant is able to obtain. We assume that the set of all the messages and keys that a participant knows is closed under the enciphering and deciphering operators. However, if in the computation of this closure he finds by two distinct ways the same sequence of bits, the participant will often be able to deduce from that the meaning of some messages and keys i.e. to infer from that the values of the free-algebra variables representing these messages and keys. In fact, the two ways of computing the same sequence of bits correspond to two distinct expressions in the free-algebra; the inferences that the participant is able to draw consist in unifying these two expressions. When this unification is not possible, an inconsistency is detected and an attempt at cheating is discovered. Moreover, a participant can instantiate some variables of his state of knowledge (we talk then about a 'state of belief') and try to obtain some informations by inferences. These inferences are also modeled by unifications between expressions of the free-algebra and the probability that such unifications really bring some informations is studied. In fact, other types of inferences exist and are all modeled in this paper by unifications or contra-unifications (i.e. elimination of some values from the domain of the variables because some expressions in the free or crypto-algebra which could be unified correspond to distinct elements in the other algebra) of elements of the free-algebra or the crypto-algebra.

The main originalities of our method are its generality (we can apply this method to protocols using public or private key cryptography, preserving the secret of data, to authentication protocols, signature schemes,... (see [Tou91])), the consideration of the probabilistic knowledge of the participants and the use of a model based on the assumption of a 'perfect' cryptosystem. Other papers [BAN89, Bie89, Kem89, Mea89, Var89, MCF87] mainly prove the security of keys distribution protocols where the probabilistic choice does not occur: the properties of the cryptosystem that ensure security are there modeled by axioms and the proofs often use logics of knowledge or belief.

This paper is organized as follows. In Section 2, we present our model of the representation of knowledge of the participants in a cryptographic protocol. In Section 3 (Subsection 3.1), we introduce some examples to show that this model has to be refined. Afterwards we formalize the inferences that a user is able to draw from his state of knowledge (Subsection 3.2) and we define the notion of 'inferred state of knowledge' which contains all the informations that a user can obtain by computations and inferences (Subsection 3.3).

# 2 Modeling States of Knowledge

## 2.1 Modeling the Cryptosystem

A cryptosystem is seen as an algebraic system called the *crypto-algebra* $C$. For simplicity, we suppose that the plaintexts and ciphertexts belong to the same set $\mathcal{M}$ and the keys to a set denoted $\mathcal{K}$. The operators of the crypto-algebra $C$ are usually the enciphering function $E$ and the deciphering function $D$ which are linked by some relations.

Following [MW85], we consider an idealization of the cryptosystem. It is the quotient by the relations between $e$ and $d$ of the free algebra of the same type as the crypto-algebra. This free-algebra represents the structure of the cryptosystem and is denoted here by $\mathcal{F}$. The operators of the free-algebra are respectively denoted by $e$ and $d$ corresponding to $E$ and $D$ in the crypto-algebra. The 'perfection' of the cryptosystem is modeled by assuming that the crypto-algebra is isomorphic to the free-algebra.

## 2.2 Modeling Participants' Knowledge

As in [TW91], the state of knowledge of a participant is seen as a partial knowledge of the isomorphism (denoted here $\varphi$) between the free and crypto-algebras.

**Definition 2.1** A state of knowledge *about a cryptosystem is a subset of* $\mathcal{F} \times C$.

This definition is very general. However, we only consider states of knowledge which can be partitioned in three special finite sets $F$, $V$ and $SV$: these states of knowledge are called *representable*.

1. $F$ (for *F*ixed) is formed by pairs $(a, b)$ which define a one to one mapping from a subset of $\mathcal{F}$ to a subset of $C$. That corresponds to elements the participant has seen or that he knew at the start of the protocol and that he can label by a fixed element of the free-algebra. The set $F$ will be described by specifying the free-algebra component of the pairs.

2. $V$ (for *V*ariables) is formed by pairs $(x, y)$ where $x$ is a fixed generator of the free-algebra whereas $y$ ranges over a subset of the generators of the crypto-algebra. The pairs of this type correspond to generators of the crypto-algebra that the participant has not seen but the existence of which he is aware of; they will be represented by a variable denoted by a tilded symbol, $\tilde{x}$, ranging over the image

under the isomorphism $\varphi^{-1}$ of the domain of $y$. The variable $y$ is then called the 'dual variable' of $\tilde{x}$. In the rest of this paper, we consider $V$ as a set of variables of the free-algebra instead of a set of pairs.

3. $SV$ (for $Semi$-$Variables$) is formed by pairs $(z, a)$ where, for each pair, $a$ is a fixed element of the crypto-algebra and $z$ belongs to a finite subset of

$$Cl(F \cup V) \setminus (Cl(F) \cup V)$$

where $Cl(X)$ (for any subset $X$ of $\mathcal{F}$) denotes the closure of $X$ under the enciphering and deciphering operators. These pairs correspond to elements that the user has seen but is unable to label. A pair $(z, a)$ of $SV$ is represented by a variable (denoted $z^*$) defined on the free-algebra with an inclusion constraint on this variable in the corresponding subset of $Cl(F \cup V) \setminus (Cl(F) \cup V)$ and occasionally inequality relations between variables.

The participants make some computations on their states of knowledge. We overvalue them by assuming that each participant is able to compute the closure $Cl(F \cup SV)$: this closure is called the *seen fraction* of the participant (because it corresponds to the closure of the set of elements of the crypto-algebra that he has seen) whereas $Cl(F)$ is called his *known fraction*.

A participant can also consider some instantiations of the variables of his state of knowledge: the obtained set is then called a 'state of belief'.

**Definition 2.2** *A state of belief compatible with a knowledge state* $K = F \cup V \cup SV \subset \mathcal{F} \times C$ *is a maximal restriction of* $K$ *to a one to one mapping ('maximal' means here that there is no other restriction of* $K$ *to a one to one mapping including this state of belief).*

Even if the elements of $V$ are represented, for simplicity, as variables in the free-algebra, their free-algebra components can be fixed whereas their crypto-algebra components vary. It is thus more natural to define an instantiation of an element of $V$ as an element of the crypto-algebra. On the other hand, the elements of $SV$ (or more exactly their free-algebra components) are really variables in the free-algebra and are instantiated by elements of the free-algebra. By definition, the *free-part* of an instantiation of the variables of a knowledge state is the restriction of this instantiation to the elements of $SV$ and its *crypto-part* is its restriction to the elements of $V$.

For each state of belief $Be$ compatible with a knowledge state $K = F \cup V \cup SV$, there is one and only one instantiation $i$ of the variables of this knowledge state such that

$$Be = F \cup \{(\tilde{v}, i(\tilde{v})) : \tilde{v} \in V\} \cup \{(i(x^*), SV(x^*)) : x^* \in SV\} \tag{1}$$

where $SV$ is considered as a function which maps the variable representing an element (i.e. a pair) of $SV$ to its second component. The instantiation $i$ is called the *instantiation relative to the belief state Be*.

We can divide the set of belief states compatible with a given state of knowledge in (finite) equivalence classes for the relation: "their relative instantiations have the same crypto-part". We could obtain a similar relation for the free-part of the relative instantiations of the belief states but this relation would not be used below.

# 3 Modeling the Possible Inferences of a User from his State of Knowledge

## 3.1 Problem Statement

Each participant tries to obtain some additional informations by analyzing his state of knowledge. We have overvalued the power of computation of a participant by assuming that he is able to compute his seen fraction. But that is not sufficient: we have not modeled the different inferences the participant is able to draw by analyzing his seen fraction or a finite number of his belief states.

**Example 3.1** In [TW91], we studied the following example of coin-flip protocol which can use any secret key cryptosystem.

1. $A$ chooses randomly a key $k$ in $\mathcal{K}$ and different messages $m_1, m_2$ in $\{T, H\}$. $A$ sends $em_1 = E(k, m_1)$ (the enciphering of $m_1$ under key $k$) and $em_2 = E(k, m_2)$ to $B$.

2. $B$ picks $u$ in $\{em_1, em_2\}$ and sends $u$ to $A$.

3. $A$ sends $k$ to $B$ and they both know the answer $a$ of the coin flip by applying the deciphering transformation $D$ to $u$.

$B$'s knowledge at the end of the first step is modeled as in Subsection 2.2 by $K(B, 1) = F(B, 1) \cup V(B, 1) \cup SV(B, 1)$:

$$F(B, 1) = \{T, H\}; \quad V(B, 1) = \{\tilde{k}\}; \quad SV(B, 1) = \{em_1^*, em_2^*\}$$

where

$$\tilde{k} \in \mathcal{K}; \quad em_1^*, em_2^* \in \{e(\tilde{k}, T), e(\tilde{k}, H)\}$$
$$em_1^* \neq em_2^*.$$

The representation of $B$'s knowledge has not changed at the end of the second step and becomes at the end of the third step $K(B,3) = F(B,3) \cup V(B,3) \cup SV(B,3)$:

$$F(B,3) = \{T,H,k\}; \quad V(B,3) = \emptyset; \quad SV(B,3) = \emptyset.$$

This model is not sufficient: it only represents the knowledge that $B$ directly obtains but not the inferences that he is able to draw. Indeed, at the end of the first step, $B$ tries to obtain more informations. For this, he studies some belief states. If he considers the right instantiation of the key $k$, he will find out that it is the right value and $B$'s knowledge at the end of the first step can be represented by $K(B,3)$. We have to prove that the probability that happens is zero. Moreover, the transmission of $k$ by $A$ at the third step enables $B$ to verify that $em_1$ and $em_2$ had the right form. Otherwise, an inconsistency is detected. This is not translated in $K(B,3)$. In fact, $B$ computes his seen fraction which contains $e(k,T)$ and $e(k,H)$ at the end of the third step; then he compares their crypto-algebra components with the crypto-algebra components of $em_1^*$ and $em_2^*$ and deduces from that the values of $em_1^*$ and $em_2^*$ if there was no cheat at step 1 or detects an inconsistency if there was a cheat. We have to translate these inferences in our model. ∎

Let us now consider simple abstract examples in order to introduce our model.

### 3.1.1  Inferences Obtained by Computing the Participant's Seen Fraction

Assume that the state of knowledge $K = F \cup V \cup SV$ of a participant is the following:

$$F = \{k_1, m_1\}; V = \{\tilde{k}, \tilde{m}\}; SV = \{e(\tilde{k}, \tilde{m})\}, \quad \tilde{k} \in \mathcal{K}, \tilde{m} \in \mathcal{M}.$$

The seen fraction of this participant contains the pair formed by the element $e(k_1, m_1)$ and the corresponding element of the crypto-algebra. If the images of $e(k_1, m_1)$ and $e(\tilde{k}, \tilde{m})$ under this seen fraction coincide, the participant will directly deduce that $\tilde{k} = k_1$ and $\tilde{m} = m_1$: we will say that there has been a *unification* of the elements $e(k_1, m_1)$ and $e(\tilde{k}, \tilde{m})$ of the free-algebra and $\tilde{k} = k_1$ and $\tilde{m} = m_1$ are the *constraints required by this unification*. If the images of $e(k_1, m_1)$ and $e(\tilde{k}, \tilde{m})$ are different, the user will directly deduce that $\tilde{k} \neq k_1$ or $\tilde{m} \neq m_1$: we will then talk about a *contra-unification* because it is as the opposite of a unification and $\tilde{k} \neq k_1$ or $\tilde{m} \neq m_1$ are the *constraints required by this contra-unification*.

However, the second components of the elements in the seen fraction of a user are fixed sequences of bits. If a given element of the free-algebra has as image two different elements of the crypto-algebra, there is some inconsistency in the corresponding state of knowledge and a failure is detected: it can be a failure in the communication or a cheating of another participant or of an opponent. These cases are treated in the same way and result in the rejection by the user of the current execution of the protocol.

Moreover, if the domain of the seen fraction of a user contains some variables of $V$, he directly deduces the value of these variables: they have thus to be removed from the set $V$. In order to have a uniform model for all the inferences drawn from the computation of the seen fraction, we treat this case as a unification of elements of the crypto-algebra. Indeed, the state of knowledge $K = F \cup V \cup SV$ is represented by giving the free-algebra component of the elements of $F$, the variables of $V$ and $SV$, and the corresponding constraints defined in the free-algebra. $K$ can thus be considered as a function which associates with the free-algebra component of an element of $F$ its crypto-algebra component, to a variable of $V$ its dual variable, and to a variable of $SV$ its image under $SV$; $K$ can then be written in a way rather similar to the representation (1) of a belief state

$$K = F \cup \{(\widetilde{v}, \widetilde{v}^d) : \widetilde{v} \in V\} \cup \{(x^*, SV(x^*)) : x^* \in SV\} \tag{2}$$

where $\widetilde{v}^d$ denotes the dual variable of $v$. If the domain of $Cl(F \cup SV)$ contains some variables of $V$, each of these variables will have for image under $Cl(F \cup SV)$ a sequence of bits fixed in the crypto-algebra and under $V$ its dual variable: it is then sufficient to unify these two images i.e. to restrict the domain of the dual variable to a singleton containing the sequence of bits in order to model the additional information obtained by the user.

### 3.1.2 Inferences Obtained from the Closure of Belief States

Let us assume now that $K = F \cup V \cup SV$ is the following knowledge state

$$F = \emptyset; V = \{\widetilde{k}, \widetilde{m}\}; SV = \{e(\widetilde{k}, \widetilde{m})\}; \widetilde{k} \in \mathcal{K}, \widetilde{m} \in \mathcal{M}. \tag{3}$$

The user thus knows the element of the crypto-algebra corresponding to $e(\widetilde{k}, \widetilde{m})$ but not the ones corresponding to $\widetilde{k}$ and $\widetilde{m}$.

Let $Be$ be a belief state compatible with $K$ such that

$$Be = \{(\widetilde{k}, k^c), (\widetilde{m}, m^c)\} \cup \{e(\widetilde{k}, \widetilde{m}), SV(e(\widetilde{k}, \widetilde{m}))\}; \text{ for some } k^c \in \mathcal{K}, m^c \in \mathcal{M} \tag{4}$$

where $\mathcal{K}$ and $\mathcal{M}$ represent respectively the set of keys and the set of messages in the crypto-algebra. If, in the computation of the closure of the belief state, the encryption of $m^c$ under the key $k^c$ gives $SV(e(\widetilde{k}, \widetilde{m}))$, the user can deduce from this that the value of $\widetilde{k}$ truly is $k^c$ and that the value of $\widetilde{m}$ is $m^c$. On the other hand, if the encryption of $m^c$ under $k^c$ does not yield $SV(e(\widetilde{k}, \widetilde{m}))$, the user will reject this belief state.

However, when we want to model and systematize this reasoning, we have some difficulties in the case where the belief state associates the right values to $\widetilde{k}$ and $\widetilde{m}$ because nothing enables us to distinguish the case where the image of the free-algebra element $e(\widetilde{k}, \widetilde{m})$ is computed from the values $k^c$ and $m^c$ from the case where we simply take its image under $SV$. We have to distinguish these two ways of computing this image. Therefore, let us reason on the notion of belief state.

In a belief state, the variables of $V$ are instantiated by elements of the domain of their dual variables without considering the elements of $SV$ which are expressed as functions of those variables: because of the isomorphism between $\mathcal{F}$ and $\mathcal{C}$, the variables of $V$ appearing in the expressions representing the domain of the elements of $SV$ cannot be replaced by their instantiations except if these instantiations correspond to their real values. We thus distinguish the variables of $V$ from the free-algebra elements corresponding to their instantiations under the isomorphism $\varphi$ between $\mathcal{F}$ and $\mathcal{C}$. We will denote these elements by overindexing them by the letter '$f$' (for $f$ixed and $f$ree-algebra). In the above example, the belief state becomes

$$Be = \{(k^f, k^c), (m^f, m^c)\} \cup \{(e(\widetilde{k}, \widetilde{m}), SV(e(\widetilde{k}, \widetilde{m})))\}; k^c \in \mathcal{K}, m^c \in \mathcal{M}. \qquad (5)$$

Thus, $k^f$ (resp. $m^f$) is the free-algebra element image under $\varphi^{-1}$ of the crypto-algebra element $k^c$ (resp. $m^c$).

We proceed then exactly in the same way as for the computation of the seen fraction of a user. If the images of $e(k^f, m^f)$ and $e(\widetilde{k}, \widetilde{m})$ under the closure of $Be$ are the same, we unify these two expressions and deduce that

$$\widetilde{k} = k^f \text{ and } \widetilde{m} = m^f;$$

if these images are not identical, we deduce by what we have called a "contra-unification" that

$$\widetilde{k} \neq k^f \text{ or } \widetilde{m} \neq m^f,$$

which amounts to rejecting the belief state $Be$ under consideration.

The example that we have just examined is extremely simple. Let us complicate slightly the knowledge state $K$ which becomes for instance

$$F = \emptyset; V = \{\widetilde{k}_1, \widetilde{m}_1, \widetilde{k}_2, \widetilde{m}_2\}; SV = \{z^*\}; \qquad (6)$$

$$\widetilde{k}_1, \widetilde{k}_2 \in \mathcal{K}; \widetilde{m}_1, \widetilde{m}_2 \in \mathcal{M}; z^* \in \{e(\widetilde{k}_1, \widetilde{m}_1), e(\widetilde{k}_2, \widetilde{m}_2), d(\widetilde{k}_1, e(\widetilde{k}_2, \widetilde{m}_1))\}.$$

A belief state compatible with $K$ could then be

$$Be = \{(k_1^f, k_1^c), (m_1^f, m_1^c), (k_2^f, k_2^c), (m_2^f, m_2^c)\} \cup \{e(\widetilde{k}_1, \widetilde{m}_1), SV(z^*)\}; \qquad (7)$$

$$k_1^c, k_2^c \in \mathcal{K}; m_1^c, m_2^c \in \mathcal{M}.$$

If the encryption of $m_1^c$ under $k_1^c$ is equal to $SV(z^*)$, we can not directly deduce that $\widetilde{k}_1 = k_1'$ and $\widetilde{m}_1 = m_1'$; that would only be true if the instantiation of $z^*$ is correct (otherwise, we would have $\widetilde{k}_2 = k_1'$ and $\widetilde{m}_2 = m_1'$): note that the instantiation $i(z^*) = d(\widetilde{k}_1, e(\widetilde{k}_2, \widetilde{m}_1))$ can directly be rejected but not the instantiation $i(z^*) = e(\widetilde{k}_2, \widetilde{m}_2)$. In the same way, if this encryption is not equal to $SV(z^*)$, we can deduce that $\widetilde{k}_1 \neq k_1'$ or $m_1 \neq \widetilde{m}_1'$, only if the instantiation of $z^*$ is correct.

We see that the conclusions obtained by computing the closure of a belief state can be considered only under the auxiliary hypothesis that the instantiation of some variables relative to this belief state corresponds to the current instantiation of these variables. When can we remove this hypothesis and really obtain some information to add to the state of knowledge?

Before answering this question, let us remark that in the case of the belief state (4), we have directly been able to add the deduced information to the state of knowledge without any auxiliary hypothesis. The difference between the states of knowledge (3) and (6) is that in (3) the set $SV$ contains an element whose domain can be considered as a singleton which only varies when the variables of $V$ vary; whereas in (6) the domain of $z^*$ contains three elements and thus for the same values of the variables of $V$, $z^*$ can take three different values. The problem in (6) appears because two elements in the domain of $z^*$ have the same form i.e. are unifiable. The instantiation of the element of $SV$ in (3) i.e. the free-part of the instantiation relative to the state of belief (4) is thus always correct contrary to the one relative to the state of belief (7).

Note also that with the notation used in relations (5) and (7), the variables of $V$ appear only in the instantiated values of the elements of $SV$. The different constraints are thus necessarily the result of a unification of the instantiated values of variables of $SV$ with other computed elements and are valid only if these instantiated values correspond to the real values of the elements of $SV$. We thus see that the auxiliary hypothesis is concerned only with the elements of $SV$, i.e. with the free-part of the instantiation relative to the belief state.

A constraint will be added to the state of knowledge of a user only if it is valid for every instantiation of the elements of $SV$. For a given instantiation of the variables of $V$, we have thus to successively study the different possible instantiations of the variables of $SV$: a constraint will then only be considered if it appears for all the instantiations of the variables of $SV$. In other words, a constraint will be added to the state of knowledge of a user only if it is required by the unifications and contra-unifications made in the analysis of each of the states of belief whose the relative instantiations have the same crypto-part. At the end of Section 2, we have grouped these belief states in an equivalence class for the relation

"their relative instantiations have the same crypto-part".

Each equivalence class contains a finite number of belief states because the domain of the elements of $SV$ expressed in terms of the variables of $V$ is finite.

A constraint on the variables required by a unification or contra-unification in the computation of the closure of a belief state can be added to the state of knowledge only if it is deduced from the computation of the closure of each (nonrejected) belief state of a same class. We will then say that this constraint is *characteristic of the considered class*. A way of obtaining the constraints characteristic of a class consists in taking the disjunction of all the constraints required in the analysis of the belief states of this class.

**Remark 3.1** In the case of the above example (6), each instantiation of the variables $\widetilde{k_1}, \widetilde{k_2}, \widetilde{m_1}, \widetilde{m_2}$ leads to an equivalence class which contains three belief states corresponding to the three possible instantiations of $z^*$. If the encryption of $m_1^c$ under $k_1^c$ is equal to $SV(z^*)$, the constraint

$$(\widetilde{k_1} = k_1' \text{ and } \widetilde{m_1} = m_1') \text{ or } (\widetilde{k_2} = k_1' \text{ and } \widetilde{m_2} = m_1')$$

is characteristic of the class of the belief state $Be$ given in (7) and can be added to the state of knowledge (6), but if this encryption is not equal to $SV(z^*)$, the constraint

$$(\widetilde{k_1} \neq k_1' \text{ or } \widetilde{m_1} \neq m_1') \text{ or } (\widetilde{k_2} \neq k_1' \text{ or } \widetilde{m_2} \neq m_1') \text{ or } (z^* = d(\widetilde{k_1}, e(\widetilde{k_2}, \widetilde{m_1})))$$

is characteristic of the class of $Be$. ∎

We assume that a user is able to compute the closure of any fixed finite number of belief states. The best strategy to add as much information as possible to a state of knowledge seems to consist in analyzing all the belief states of some classes (rather than to consider some belief states of some classes): the disjunction of the obtained constraints can then directly been added to the state of knowledge without any auxiliary hypothesis. Because these classes are finite, we can assume that a user is able to compute the closure of all the belief states of a fixed finite number of classes. A user who wants to obtain a maximum of informations will thus choose a finite number of classes and analyze all the belief states of these classes: the choice of a finite number of belief states without considering their belonging to the equivalence classes would be much less useful because the constraints obtained by their analysis would only be valid under the auxiliary hypothesis that the corresponding instantiation of the variables of $SV$ is correct.

### 3.1.3 Summary of the Possible Inferences

The seen fraction of a user and the closure of each belief state of a finite number of chosen classes are successively examined. Several cases can appear.

- When two elements of the free-algebra (resp. of the crypto-algebra) have for image (resp. are image of) a same element of the crypto-algebra (resp. of the free-algebra), we have to be able to unify these two elements; if it is not possible, either a failure is detected if the seen fraction of the user is analyzed or, in the case of the computation of the closure of a belief state, this belief state is rejected. Note that the rejection of a belief state can be translated as a constraint on the variables: at least one of the variables is not instantiated as specified in this belief state. If all the belief states are rejected at the end of the analysis, a cheating has been detected.

- If two unifiable elements (i.e. such that we can reduce the domain of the variables so that they become equal) of the free-algebra have different images in the crypto-algebra, we introduce what we call a contra-unification, i.e. we exclude the values of variables which would unify these two elements.

In the case of the computation of the seen fraction, the constraints required by the unifications and contra-unifications are directly added to the state of knowledge; in the case of the closure of a belief state, they are added only if they are characteristic of the class of this belief state. Moreover, the domains of the variables satisfying all these constraints have to be not empty; otherwise an attempt to cheat is again detected and the current execution of the protocol is stopped and rejected.

Now, we are going to formalize all these different concepts.

## 3.2 Unifiable Elements

Before building the inferred state of knowledge of a user, which has to contain all the informations directly obtained or deduced by this user, we need to introduce some definitions and make some remarks.

The notion of 'domain' which is very usual in mathematics can seem a little strange here for the elements of $V$: as we have defined in Subsection 2.2, the domain of these elements is the free-algebra subset corresponding to the domain of their dual variable. Moreover, by extension, we say that the domain of a constant of the free-algebra or the crypto-algebra is the singleton including this constant.

As we have seen above, in a given state of knowledge $K = F \cup V \cup SV$, the variables introduced in the free-algebra are the variables of $V$ and $SV$, and those introduced in the crypto-algebra are the dual variables. The free and crypto-algebras components of the elements of the seen fraction and of the closure of a belief state can be expressed in terms of the corresponding variables. The problem is to unify two elements of one of the two algebras.

Let $\mathcal{A}$ be the free-algebra or the crypto-algebra; the set of variables defined in $\mathcal{A}$ given the state of knowledge $K$ of a user is denoted $V_{\mathcal{A}}$. As we have seen previously, the variables of $V_{\mathcal{A}}$ are introduced in the representation of the state of knowledge $K$ and thus depend on this state of knowledge. Let us consider the elements of $\mathcal{A}$ which can be expressed in terms of the variables of $V_{\mathcal{A}}$ and of the corresponding enciphering and deciphering operators. Unifying two elements of $\mathcal{A}$ in the state of knowledge $K$ amounts to limiting the domain of the variables of $V_{\mathcal{A}}$ so that these two elements are equal for the remaining values of the variables.

Let $K = F \cup V \cup SV$ be a (assumed to be representable) state of knowledge, the set $V_{\mathcal{A}}$ is finite and can be denoted

$$V_{\mathcal{A}} = \{v_1, \ldots, v_n\}$$

with the constraints

$$v_1 \in D_{v_1}, \ldots, v_n \in D_{v_n}$$

where $D_{v_1}, \ldots, D_{v_n}$ denote respectively the domain of $v_1, \ldots, v_n$. An element of $\mathcal{A}$ expressed in terms of $0, 1, \ldots$ or $n$ variables of $\mathcal{A}$ and of the enciphering and deciphering operators is denoted by an expression like

$$exp(v_1, \ldots, v_n);$$

its domain is

$$\{exp(v_1, \ldots, v_n) : v_1 \in D_{v_1}, \ldots, v_n \in D_{v_n}\}$$

and is denoted here briefly

$$exp(D_{v_1}, \ldots, D_{v_n}).$$

The unification of the two elements $exp_1(v_1, \ldots, v_n)$ and $exp_2(v_1, \ldots, v_n)$ amounts to replacing their domain by the set

$$\{exp_1(v_1, \ldots, v_n) : v_1 \in D_{v_1}, \ldots, v_n \in D_{v_n} \text{ such that } exp_2(v_1, \ldots, v_n) = exp_1(v_1, \ldots, v_n)\}.$$

We will call this set *the parametric intersection* of the domains of the elements

$$exp_1(v_1, \ldots, v_n) \text{ and } exp_2(v_1, \ldots, v_n)$$

because it is the union on all the variables of the intersection of the domains of these two elements i.e.

$$\bigcup_{v_1 \in D_{v_1}, \ldots, v_n \in D_{v_n} : \, exp_1(v_1, \ldots, v_n) = exp_2(v_1, \ldots, v_n)} \{exp_1(v_1, \ldots, v_n)\}.$$

We would like to reduce this intersection to the two equivalent forms

$$\{exp_1(v_1, \ldots, v_n) : v_1 \in D'_{v_1}, \ldots, v_n \in D'_{v_n}\} \text{ or } \{exp_2(v_1, \ldots, v_n) : v_1 \in D'_{v_1}, \ldots, v_n \in D'_{v_n}\}$$

where $D'_{v_1} \subseteq D_{v_1}, \ldots, D'_{v_n} \subseteq D_{v_n}$ or to a finite (disjoint) union of such sets. In our notation, the two sets above are respectively represented by

$$exp_1(D'_{v_1}, \ldots, D'_{v_n}) \text{ and } exp_2(D'_{v_1}, \ldots, D'_{v_n}).$$

When such a reduction is possible, we say that the parametric intersection of the domains of the two elements is *projectable* and we have the following definition.

**Definition 3.1** *Let $K = F \cup V \cup SV$ be a given state of knowledge; $A$ denotes the free or crypto-algebra and $V_A = \{v_1, \ldots, v_n\}$ ($v_1 \in D_{v_1}, \ldots, v_n \in D_{v_n}$) is the set of variables in $A$ where $D_{v_i}$ denotes the domain of $v_i$ ($i = 1, \ldots, n$). Let $exp_1(v_1, \ldots, v_n)$ and $exp_2(v_1, \ldots, v_n)$ be two elements of $A$ expressed in terms of the variables of $V_A$ and the operators of $A$. The parametric intersection of their domains is projectable in the state of knowledge $K$ if there is a finite partition of this intersection, denoted*

$$\{\{exp_1(v_1, \ldots, v_n), v_1 \in D_{v_1}^{(i)}, \ldots, v_n \in D_{v_n}^{(i)}\}; i = 1, \ldots, r\}$$

*such that, for every $i = 1, \ldots, r$,*

$$D_{v_1}^{(i)} \subset D_{v_1}, \ldots, D_{v_n}^{(i)} \subset D_{v_n}.$$

Intuitively, the parametric intersection of the domains of two elements of $A$ is projectable in $K$ if it can be partitioned in a finite number of sets which can be represented by any of the two expressions representing the initial domains but where the variables $V_A$ vary on more limited domains.

The unification of the two elements $exp_1(v_1, \ldots, v_n)$ and $exp_2(v_1, \ldots, v_n)$ of Definition 3.1 will consist in replacing the domains of these elements by their parametric intersection i.e. in requiring of the variables of $V_A$ the following additional constraint

$$\bigvee_{i=1}^{r} (v_1 \in D_{v_1}^{(i)} \wedge \ldots \wedge v_n \in D_{v_n}^{(i)});$$

this constraint is called the 'constraint required by the unification'.

Moreover, the contra-unification of the two elements

$$exp_1(v_1,\ldots,v_n) \text{ and } exp_2(v_1,\ldots,v_n)$$

of Definition 3.1 will consist in preventing these two elements from belonging to the parametric intersection of their domains i.e. in requiring of the variables $V_A$ the following additional constraint

$$\bigwedge_{i=1}^{r}(v_1 \notin D_{v_1}^{(i)} \vee \ldots \vee v_n \notin D_{v_n}^{(i)});$$

this constraint is called the '*constraint required* by the contra-unification'.

For simplicity, we assume that the parametric intersection of the domains of any two elements of the free or crypto-algebra is projectable in any state of knowledge of a user. Note that, in most practical cases, the partition in Definition 3.1 includes only one term.

We can now precisely define 'unification' and 'contra-unification'.

**Definition 3.2**

- *Two elements of the free-algebra or of the crypto-algebra are* unifiable *in a state of knowledge $K = F \cup V \cup SV$ if the parametric intersection of their domains is not empty.*

- *Let $E_1$ and $E_2$ be two unifiable elements of the free (resp. crypto)-algebra in a state of knowledge $K = F \cup V \cup SV$.*

  *The unification of $E_1$ and $E_2$ consists in limiting the domains of the variables of $V$ and $SV$ (resp. of the dual variables) by some constraints such that $E_1$ and $E_2$ become equal and vary in the parametric intersection of their initial domains. The constraints on the variables are called the* constraints required *by the unification.*

  *The contra-unification of $E_1$ and $E_2$ consists in limiting the domains of the variables of $V$ and $SV$ (resp. of the dual variables) by some constraints such that $E_1$ and $E_2$ can not become equal and thus can not belong to the parametric intersection of their initial domains. The constraints on the variables are called the* constraints required *by the contra-unification.*

## 3.3    Inferred States of Knowledge and "Known Fractions" of the Participants

When can we conclude that a state of knowledge is consistent or, on the contrary, that an attempt of cheating has occurred? As we have already mentioned previously, we analyze the seen fraction of a user, then successively the closure of belief states belonging to a finite number of equivalence classes as defined in Subsections 2.2 and 3.1.2. All the free-algebra elements (resp. crypto-algebra) which have the same image in the crypto-algebra (resp. which are the image of an identical element of the free-algebra) must be unified: if they are not unifiable, the state of knowledge is said to be *inconsistent* in the case of the seen fraction of the user or the belief state is rejected in the case of the closure of a belief state. The unifiable elements remaining in the free-algebra are then contra-unified. All the required constraints have to be '*compatible*' i.e. there must be at least one value in the domain of the variables which satisfies all these constraints. More generally, we have the following definition

**Definition 3.3**

- *A relation included in $\mathcal{F} \times C$ is* consistent *if*
    - *all the elements*
        * *of the domain which have the same image on one hand or*
        * *of the codomain which are image of an identical element of the domain on the other hand*
    
    *are unifiable and*
    - *all the constraints required*
        * *by these unifications and*
        * *by the contra-unifications of the unifiable elements of the domain which have not the same image*
    
    *are compatible.*
- *The* unified function *of a consistent relation f included in $\mathcal{F} \times C$ is the one to one function obtained by*
    - *unification of the elements of the domain (resp. codomain) which have the same image in the codomain (resp. are image of an identical element of the domain) and*
    - *contra-unification of the other unifiable elements of the domain.*
    
    *The procedure to obtain the unified function from a consistent relation is called* the unification *of this relation.*

The unified function of a relation can be seen as this relation to which the constraints required by the possible unifications and contra-unifications are imposed.

We want to apply these definitions to the state of knowledge of a participant in an execution of a protocol in order to determine if he will accept or reject this execution. A state of knowledge is said 'consistent' if the probability that the different inferences drawn by the corresponding participant (for any adopted strategy) do not introduce any inconsistency is 1, i.e. if the probability that this participant chooses to analyze a finite number of classes of belief states such that all the deduced informations are compatible is 1. (Remark that, if the number of classes is infinite, that does not necessarily mean that all these informations have to be compatible for every choice of a finite number of classes).

In the following definition, we explicitly consider a state of knowledge and the corresponding sets $F, V, SV$ as sets of pairs belonging to $\mathcal{F} \times \mathcal{C}$.

**Definition 3.4** *A state of knowledge* $K = F \cup V \cup SV$ *is consistent if*

1. $Cl(F \cup SV) \cup V$ *is consistent and*

2. *the probability to choose a fixed finite number (which depends on the computational power of the corresponding user) of classes of belief states compatible with* $K$ *such that all the following constraints are compatible is 1 (for any adopted strategy to choose the belief states). These constraints are*

   - *the constraints required by the unification of* $Cl(F \cup SV) \cup V$,
   - *the constraints representing the rejection of the belief states belonging to one of these classes and whose closure is not consistent,*
   - *the constraints required by the unification of the closure of the consistent belief states of these classes and characteristic of at least one of these.*

An 'inferred state of knowledge' is a state of knowledge increased by all the informations that the corresponding participant can deduce by inferences as specified in the following definition.

**Definition 3.5** *Given a consistent state of knowledge* $K = F \cup V \cup SV$ *and a finite number of classes of belief states compatible with* $K$, *the inferred state of knowledge is the state of knowledge* $K_i = F_i \cup V_i \cup SV_i$ *obtained from* $K$ *by the addition of all the constraints*

   - *required by the unification of* $Cl(F \cup SV) \cup V$,

- *representing the rejection of the belief states belonging to one of the considered classes and which closure is not consistent,*

- *required by the unification of the closure of the consistent belief states of these classes and characteristic of at least one of these.*

Note that the inferred state of knowledge defined in Definition 3.5 depends on the choice of the classes of belief states: when we do not specify the chosen classes, we talk about '*an*' inferred state of knowledge.

The purpose of a malicious participant is to detect the belief states whose closure is consistent. If the number of classes of belief states is finite, the participant can analyze the consistency of the closure of each state of belief: in that case, we assume that $n$ (the number of classes whose all the states of belief can be examined) is larger than the total number of classes of belief states. If the number of classes of belief states is infinite, an exhaustive analysis is impossible; the participant can test the consistency of the closure of belief states of only a finite number of classes that he chooses.

Remark that if its set $SV$ is empty (it is for example the case in a simple state of knowledge), the state of knowledge $K$ is always consistent and can not be increased: the inferred state of knowledge is identical to the initial state of knowledge $K$.

An inferred state of knowledge is thus a representation of all the information that the user is able to obtain. We can extend the definition of the 'known fraction of a user' from that.

**Definition 3.6** *Given a state of knowledge $K$ and an inferred state of knowledge $K_i = F_i \cup V_i \cup SV_i$, the inferred known fraction of the corresponding user is the closure of $F_i$ under the operations of the free and crypto-algebras whereas the inferred seen fraction of this user is the closure of $(F_i \cup SV_i)$ under the same operations.*

Note that these inferred known and seen fractions are not unique but depend on the choice of the classes of belief states (because the given inferred state of knowledge $K_i$ depends on that choice): when we do not specify the chosen classes, we talk about '*an*' inferred known fraction and '*an*' inferred seen fraction.

**Example 3.2** The knowledge states of user $A$ at the different steps of Example 3.1 are always simple: they are thus consistent. Whereas, at the end of the first step, $B$ has an infinite number of belief states which correspond to the different possible instantiations of the variables $\tilde{k}, em_1^*$ and $em_2^*$: these belief states are divided in an infinite number of equivalence classes depending on the instantiation of $\tilde{k}$. When user $B$ chooses a finite set of classes of his belief states, i.e. in fact a finite set of instantiations of the variable $\tilde{k}$, two cases are possible:

- if the real instantiation of $\tilde{k}$ is chosen, $B$ will find out, by unifications, that it is the right value; $B$'s inferred state of knowledge is then

$$F(B,1) = \{T,H,k\}; V(B,1) = \emptyset; SV(B,1) = \emptyset;$$

- if the real instantiation of $\tilde{k}$ is not chosen, all the belief states of the chosen classes are rejected and the chosen values of $\tilde{k}$ are removed from its domain; $B$'s inferred state of knowledge is his initial state of knowledge where a finite number of values are removed from the domain of $\tilde{k}$.

Note that, in any case, there still are values of the variables which satisfy all the required constraints: the states of knowledge are thus consistent.

The security of our coin-flip example is preserved only if $B$ is not able to find the value of the variable $\tilde{k}$. Intuitively, choosing the real value of $\tilde{k}$ has a probability equal to zero and in the other case, rejecting a finite number of belief states does not matter. In the full paper, we will prove this formally by applying the probabilistic measure introduced in [Tou91]. Moreover, when $B$ analyzes his seen fraction at the end of the third step, this fraction contains $e(k,T)$, $e(k,H)$, $em_1^*$, $em_2^*$. If the crypto-algebra components of $em_1^*$ and $e(k,T)$ or $e(k,H)$ are identical, $B$ deduces the values of $em_1^*$ and $em_2^*$. Otherwise, an inconsistency is detected. ∎

# 4 Conclusions

We have proposed a model of all the knowledge that a participant in a cryptographic protocol can obtain by inferences and computations. Among other things, our model enables us to represent the probabilistic knowledge of the participants in a cryptographic protocol and to prove some probabilistic properties of these protocols. This representation is necessary to enable us to find out by the method described in [TW91] and [Tou91] all the possible attacks of the participants and of the intruders against cryptographic protocols.

# Acknowledgements

A large part of this work was developed in collaboration with Prof. P.Wolper; I would like to thank him very much. I wish to thank also Dr. M.Merritt and Prof. J.-J.Quisquater for several helpful discussions about this work. I thank also Philippe Lejoly for useful commentaries.

# References

[BAN89] M. Burrows, M. Abadi, and R. Needham. A Logic of Authentication. Technical Report 39, Digital — Systems Research Center (SRC), 1989.

[Bie89] P. Bieber. *Aspects Epistémiques des Protocoles Cryptographiques.* PhD thesis, Université Paul-Sabatier de Toulouse (Sciences), October 1989.

[BM84] M. Blum and S. Micali. How to Generate Cryptographically Strong Sequences of Pseudo-Random Bits. *SIAM Journal on Computing,* 13(4):850–864, 1984.

[Dam87] I. B. Damgard. *The Application of Claw Free Functions in Cryptography; Unconditional Protection in Cryptographic Protocols.* PhD thesis, Mathematical Institute, Aarhus University (Denmark), 1987.

[EGS86] S. Even, O. Goldreich, and A. Shamir. On the Security of Ping-Pong Protocols using the RSA. In H. C. Williams, editor, *Lecture Notes in Computer Science. Advances in Cryptology — CRYPTO'85, #218,* pages 58–72. Springer-Verlag, 1986.

[GMR89] S. Goldwasser, S. Micali, and C. Rackoff. The Knowledge Complexity of Interactive Proof-Systems. *SIAM Journal on Computing,* 18(1):186–208, 1989.

[GNY90] L. Gong, R. Needham, and R. Yahalom. Reasoning about Belief in Cryptographic Protocols. In *Proceedings of the 1990 IEEE Computer Society Symposium on Research in Security and Privacy,* pages 234–248. IEEE Computer Society Press, 1990.

[Kem89] R. A. Kemmerer. Analyzing Encryption Protocols Using Formal Verification Techniques. *IEEE Journal on Selected Areas in Communications,* 7(4):448–457, 1989.

[MCF87] J. K. Millen, S. C. Clark, and S. B. Freedman. The Interrogator: Protocol Security Analysis. *IEEE Transactions on Software Engineering,* 13(2):274–288, 1987.

[Mea89]   C. Meadows.  Using Narrowing in the Analysis of Key Management Proto-
          cols. In *Proceedings of the 1989 IEEE Symposium on Research in Security and
          Privacy*, pages 138–147. IEEE Computer Society Press, 1989.

[Mea90]   C. Meadows. Representing Partial Knowledge in an Algebraic Security Model.
          In *Proceedings of the Computer Security Foundations Workshop III*, pages 23–
          31. IEEE Computer Society Press, 1990.

[Mer83]   M. J. Merritt. *Cryptographic Protocols*. PhD thesis, Georgia Institute of Tech-
          nology, 1983.

[Moo88]   J. H. Moore. Protocol Failures in Cryptosystems. *Proceedings of the IEEE*,
          76(5):594–602, May 1988.

[MW85]    M. Merritt and P. Wolper. States of Knowledge in Cryptographic Protocols
          (extended abstract). Unpublished Manuscript, 1985.

[Syv91]   P. Syverson. The Use of Logic in the Analysis of Cryptographic Protocols. In
          *Proceedings of the 1991 IEEE Symposium on Research in Security and Privacy*,
          pages 156–170. IEEE Computer Society Press, 1991.

[Tou91a]  M-J. Toussaint. Formal Verification of Probabilistic Properties in Crypto-
          graphic Protocols (Extended Abstract). to appear in the proceedings of ASI-
          ACRYPT'91, 1991.

[Tou91b]  M.-J. Toussaint. *Verification of Cryptographic Protocols*. PhD thesis, Univer-
          sité de Liège (Belgium), 1991.

[TW91]    M-J. Toussaint and P. Wolper. Reasoning about Cryptographic Protocols
          (Extended Abstract). In Joan Feigenbaum and Michael Merritt, editors, *Dis-
          tributed Computing and Cryptography (October 1989)*, pages 245–262. DI-
          MACS - Series in Discrete Mathematics and Theoretical Computer Science
          (AMS - ACM), 1991. Volume 2.

[Var89]   V. Varadharajan. Verification of Network Security Protocols. *Computers &
          Security*, 8(8):693–708, 1989.

# Systematic Design of Two-Party Authentication Protocols[*]

Ray Bird        Inder Gopal        Amir Herzberg        Phil Janson
Shay Kutten        Refik Molva        Moti Yung

## Abstract

We investigate protocols for *authenticated exchange* of messages between two parties in a communication network. Secure authenticated exchange is essential for network security. It is not difficult to design simple and seemingly correct solutions for it, however, many such 'solutions' can be broken. We give some examples of such protocols and we show a useful methodology which can be used to break many protocols. In particular, we break a protocol that is being standardized by the ISO.

We present a new authenticated exchange protocol which is both *provably secure* and *highly efficient and practical*. The security of the protocol is proven, based on an assumption about the the cryptosystem employed (namely, that it is secure when used in CBC mode on a certain message space). We think that this assumption is quite reasonable for many cryptosystems, and furthermore it is often assumed in practical use of the DES cryptosystem. Our protocol cannot be broken using the methodology we present (which was strong enough to catch all protocol flaws we found). The reduction to the security of the encryption mode, indeed captures the non-existence of the exposures that the methodology catches (specialized to the actual use of encryption in our protocol). Furthermore, the protocol prevents chosen plaintext or ciphertext attacks on the cryptosystem.

The proposed protocol is efficient and practical in several aspects. First, it uses only conventional cryptography (like the DES, or any privately-shared one-way function) and no public-key. Second, the protocol does not require synchronized clocks or counter management. Third, only a small number of encryption operations is needed (we use no decryption), all with a single shared key. In addition, only three messages are exchanged during the protocol, and the size of these messages is minimal. These properties are similar to existing and proposed actual protocols. This is *essential* for integration of the proposed protocol into existing systems and embedding it in existing communication protocols.

# 1   Introduction

The extensive use of open networks and distributed systems poses increasing threats to the security of communications and operations involving end-users and network com-

[*]R. Bird is with IBM Networking Systems, I. Gopal, A. Herzberg, S. Kutten and M. Yung are with IBM T. J. Watson Research Center, P. Janson and R. Molva are with IBM Zurich Research Laboratory.

J. Feigenbaum (Ed.): Advances in Cryptology - CRYPTO '91, LNCS 576, pp. 44-61, 1992.
© Springer-Verlag Berlin Heidelberg 1992

ponents [29]. One essential function for achieving security in a network is a mechanism to reliably authenticate the exchange of messages between two communicating parties. Such an authenticated exchange allows the establishment of the fact that the exchange of messages have passed via the other (legal) party, which provides to each party some weak proof of the identity of the other party (in some sense). This operation further enables various applications on top of it, e.g., verifying that a fresh session key agreement is taken place between the legal parties.

The basic idea of cryptographic authentication is to authenticate a message from $A$ to $B$ we use a *challenge* which $B$ previously sent to $A$. Usually, $A$ cryptographically combines the challenge with the authenticated message, and $B$ verifies this combination. These cryptographic operations are done usually, and in our protocol, using conventional cryptosystem such as DES, with a key known to both parties. (Alternately, the cryptographic operations may use public key cryptosystems [19], Digital signatures [22], or Zero-Knowledge based methods [10, 11], but these alternatives require much more processing.)

Since the key changes quite rarely, the challenge should ideally be different in every authentication instance (and from security standpoint it better be "random"). There are three alternative techniques to guarantee that the challenge is different. First, the challenge may be derived from a real-time clock reading; this is called *time-stamp* challenge. Second, the challenge may be a counter that is incremented after each operation. Third, the challenge may be selected randomly from a huge space; this is called a *nonce* challenge. We concentrate on nonce-based methods which does not require clock synchronization or consistent counter maintenance, both of which are difficult to maintain especially when dealing with parallel sessions. (Note that, if desired, a nonce can be replaced by a counter value or the time-stamp, we assume a good random source is generating the nonces in use).

## 1.1  Scenario and attacks

We consider two parties $A$ and $B$ which share a key to a 'secure' cryptosystem $E$. The parties execute possibly many instances of the protocol, where each instance is an authenticated exchange independent of the other instances (exchanges can be executed in parallel and in an interleaving fashion, representing multiple connections between "parties" in an open network environment). Whenever a party completes an instance, it marks the instance as either *accept* (for successful authentication) or otherwise *reject*. The goal is that instances marked as accept were really an exchange of messages with a specific instance of the protocol at the other party. An *error-free history*, is one in which if one takes the history of all instances in both parties except rejected instances, the remaining accepted instances *match exactly*, except, maybe, for some last messages being still in transit. Note that this captures that indeed accepted instances indeed "passed" via the other party.

An attacker on such a protocol can be intuitively described as a third party who has no access to the key. However, the attacker has access to past legal communication. In addition, the attacker is able to start or interfere in the middle of such protocol instances many times. The attacker tries that a party will mark an instance as "accept" incorrectly. Namely, without the other legal party recording this instance (so that the exchange is not recorded correctly). This captures the fact that the adversary is able to fool one side into accepting an exchange without the other party being actually involved.

Note that the attacker may adaptively send any message to both parties, initiate new instances of the protocol, and intercept messages sent by the parties. We do not impose response-time constraints on these actions. As noted above, in real networks, two parties that share a key may often initiate many instances simultaneously.

Our definition of correctness does not prevent the attacker from acting as a 'relay' between the two parties (by being in the middle). This is equivalent to cutting the communication lines *after* or just before the last message of the instance (and then taking the role of the legal party). However, this does not contradict the authentication of the exchange of the messages. Note that the requirement is that the *exchange* be authenticated, and not the parties themselves. Also, an attacker that removes messages on links between the parties only creates a long delay in the execution of the instance, and the correctness (and authentication) is preserved, thus, we do not consider such attacks.

We investigate both one-way and two-way authenticated exchange protocols. The difference is in the requirements in executions where messages are exchanged correctly between the two parties. In one-way protocols, it is sufficient that one party marks accept; in two-way protocols we require both parties to mark accept. In most one-way protocols, only the initiator of the protocol accepts, and therefore these protocols are not applicable to most tasks. We discuss one-way protocols mainly in order to simplify the discussion of two-way protocols.

## 1.2   Related Works

Many works dealing with authentication in networks combine the issues of key distribution with the issues of authentication. These works avoid our assumption that the two parties share a secret key. They use an entity, trusted by all network processors, called usually a *key distribution center* (KDC). The KDC initially shares a secret key with each of the two parties. These protocols are called *three party protocols*, and have been studied extensively, e.g. in [23, 2, 9, 24, 5, 28, 17, 3, 18]. Also, most of these protocols, e.g. [17, 23, 28], use long messages which makes them unsuitable for low network layers (where the field size devoted to security overhead should be small). Some require synchronized clocks, e.g. [23, 28], or counters, e.g. [17]. While some others require heavy computations such as public key cryptography [18].

Two-party protocols received less attention in the literature, despite their application in many networks. Some works achieve this by using public-key cryptography, e.g. [19, 21]. With a public-key cryptosystem, each party only has to know or verify the public key of the other party, and there is no need to share secret keys. However, for reasons such as efficiency we want to use only private key cryptosystems (specifically, we believe that the block size of public-key and the computation involved with it are too large an overhead for frequent authentication of entities). The basic published proposal using private key that we have found is the ISO proposed standard [16], which we break in this paper.

Many practical authentication protocols were proposed without a convincing proof of (or argument for) security. We prove the security of our protocol by showing how one can successfully forge CBC-mode encryption using the cryptosystem, given an attacker that breaks the protocol using this cryptosystem. Since cryptosystems, e.g. DES, are usually considered to be provide secure CBC-mode, it is reasonable to consider the protocol quite secure. This is basically an application of the basic method of proof used in many of the recent works in cryptography, originating e.g. in [25, 26].

A different method of analyzing the security of protocols was presented in [5, 1] and used in other works (e.g., [6, 15]). This method applies formal logic to state assumptions and analyze the properties of protocols. This innovative approach enables better comparison of protocols, often revealing critical weaknesses or possible improvements, as was successfully done for several protocols in [5] and in subsequent works. However, the proofs of security obtained using this logic depends on assumptions which concern the protocol itself, not only the specific cryptosystem. Furthermore, the assumptions and the analysis view the cryptographic primitive (cryptosystem) as secure in a very idealized sense which is obviously much stronger than that of any candidate cryptosystem, our approach is to try to quantify the relationship between the cryptosystem and the protocol in a complexity-theoretic sense. Also, the axiomatic system may assume certain mode of use of the system and certain basic believes which may or may not exist in real environments (thus, again, assumptions may be too strong).

For example, one common assumption in logic-of-authentication is that if $A$ and $B$ share a secret key and $A$ receives a message encrypted using that key with source field $B$, then $A$ believes that $B$ sent that message. This basically means that it is impossible to find an encrypted strings with a specific source field, without knowing the key. However, if the space of messages is small (say we encrypt one bit using half of the ciphertexts as zero and half as one as in "probabilistic encryption" [14]), by guessing enough strings, the attacker can find such an encryption. Also note that the assumption makes use of a property of the protocol, i.e. the use of a source field in the message. Hence, the logic cannot be used for protocols which do not follow several implicit requirements (but it may be extendable?). In particular, the protocols we investigate *cannot be analyzed* using this logic, since they combine the identity of the sender within the message, rather than having a separate field. This was required in order to use short messages, which in turn is essential for integration into existing systems. It seems that the combination of the logic approach with approaches like we take here (computational-complexity and reducing the properties of protocols to basic properties of cryptographic tool) is a useful research direction.

The present work addresses only the exchange of a single message in each instance. Obviously, in many applications we need to exchange reliably many messages, preserving the order between them. A solution to this problem was presented in [12], however it uses longer messages since it concatenates random fields into them. It seems possible to combine our results and [12] and provide a solution which does not increase the amount of bits communicated.

## 1.3 Objectives and Results

The goal of this work is to design two-way authentication protocols that are provably secure yet remain realistic, efficient and simple. We require that security be proven (assuming that the cryptosystem used in the protocol is secure in some reasonable sense). Indeed, the protocol we present is secure if the cryptosystem may be used to generate secure CBC-encryption (on some message space). While we define this concept and assumption in this paper, it nevertheless appears to be an assumption made, implicitly, in many systems which employ cryptosystems such as DES in CBC mode to encrypt or to generate hash or 'fingerprint' also called MAC (Message Authentication Code).

Another security requirement is to prevent the attacker from using strong cryptanalysis techniques. In particular, we prevent chosen ciphertext attacks, which enable powerful methods such as the differential cryptanalysis [4].

The non-security requirements are all motivated by the need to present alternative to existing and proposed insecure protocols such as [16]. Such insecure protocols are already designed into systems (using existing flows of messages). It is very difficult to replace them by secure protocols which have significantly higher requirements, are substantially less efficient or behave very differently. This motivated the following requirements, all of which we meet:

- Nonce-based protocol, not requiring either synchronized clocks or stable counters. (The use on nonce implies the possibility of using time or counter value, but vice versa is not true).

- The protocol uses short messages, to be usable in low layers of the network where messages often have fixed sizes.

- Only one key is shared between the two parties, and only this key is used with the cryptosystem. This is both for compatibility with existing systems and to save loading time and secure storage requirements.

- Any secure cryptosystem may be used (in fact, we do not require decryption, so a secure one-way (or random) function suffices).

- Only three flows are used in the protocol.

- A small number of encryption operations (3) is made by each party.

- No context information is used, but the simple fact that "different parties have different names". (No use is made of assumptions like: order of names, number of key owners, temporal constraints, sequential mode of operation, and so on).

Note that by avoiding decryption, it may become easier to obtain governments approval for the (international) use and the export of the protocol. A well-defined interface to an encryption-only device/system suffices.

For simplicity, we only include the cryptographic data fields in the protocols.

# 2 One Way Authentication

## 2.1 A trivial, but insecure, one way protocol

One-way authentication is simply "authenticated acknowledgment", namely a protocol to let the sender of a message know that it was received. Figure 1 shows a trivial one way authentication protocol. This protocol may be used to authenticate $B$ to $A$ (right hand side) or to authenticate $A$ to $B$ (left hand side). Here, $N_1$ is a nonce generated by $B$ (or $A$) and $E(N_1)$ is the value of $N_1$ enciphered by $E$. The idea is that since only $A$ and $B$ can decipher, then when $B$ sends $E(N_1)$ and gets it deciphered, it believes that $A$ was the one who deciphered.

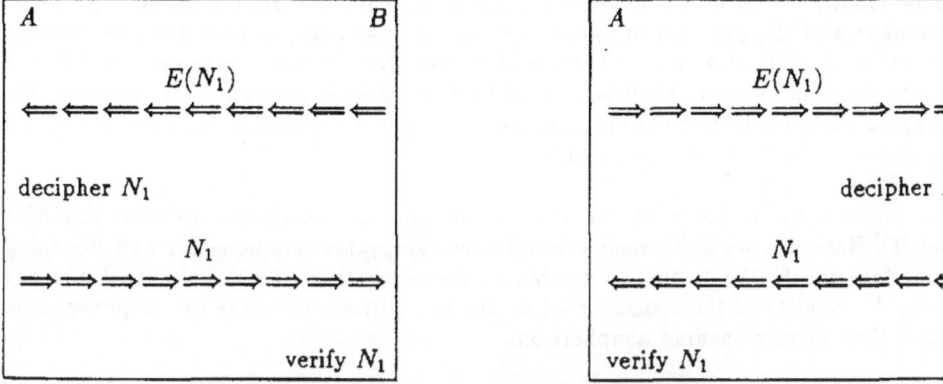

Figure 1: Trivial and insecure one way protocol

We now demonstrate an attack on this protocol. Party $A$ tries to authenticate a message to $B$. An attacker $X$ intercepts the first flow (i.e. $E(N_1)$) sent by $A$ to $B$. The attacker wishes to pretend to be $B$, although it cannot decipher $E(N_1)$ directly. However, the attacker uses $A$ itself to perform this decryption. For this purpose, the attacker starts a second instance with $A$, pretending to be $B$ starting the protocol. (In figure 2 we use a different kind of arrows to distinguish between instances.) We named this kind of attack a *parallel session attack*, and we say that $A$ served as an *oracle* to the attacker. In addition, notice that the protocol exposes the key to chosen-ciphertext attacks. Using it with e.g. Rabin cipher system [25] is insecure.

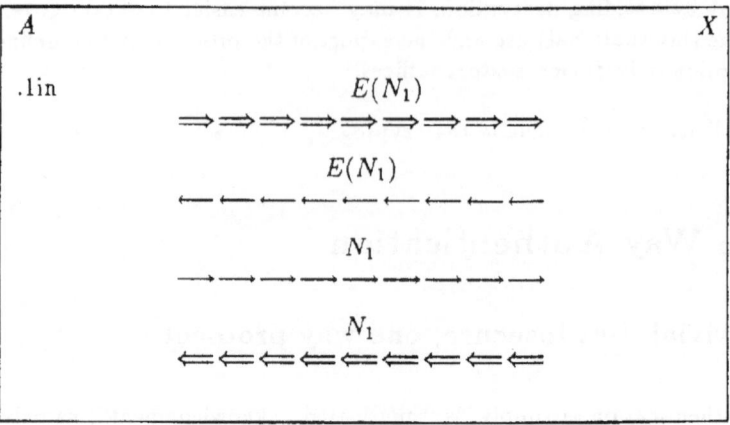

Figure 2: Parallel session attack on the simple one-way protocol

## 2.2 A Secure One-Way Authentication Protocol

We now modify the protocol of figure 1 slightly, to make it a secure one-way protocol. The weakness of the protocol of figure 1 is that the same key is used for two different purposes: verification of $A$ and verification of $B$. One trivial solution is to use two different keys, one for each purpose. However, recall that we allow just one key. In addition, the challenging party controlled the entire ciphertext to be decrypted in the protocol, which made chosen-ciphertext attacks possible.

The solution to the first problem is to use the same key, but in two different ways (for $A$ and $B$). Basically, we implement two different encryption functions $E_A$ and $E_B$ using just one function $E$. We do this by combining the encryption $E(m)$ of plaintext message $m$, with the identity of the processor ($A$ or $B$). In addition, we make the response more complex than merely opening a ciphertext.

The security of this scheme relies on what we may call the 'pseudo-independence' of $E_A(m)$ $E_B(m)$, and $E(m)$ (to be explained in the definition below). As an example for operations that are *not* 'pseudo-independent' the reader is encouraged to break the protocol with $E_A(m) = E(A + m)$ and $E_B(m) = E(B + m)$, where $+$ stands for the bit-wise exclusive or operation over the strings. Intuitively these operations are 'dependent' since given $m$, it is easy to find $m'$ so that $A + m$ is identical to $B + m'$. We need a more secure way of combining the identity and and $m$.

Such 'secure combination' of values is assumed to hold for the fingerprint produced by the CBC mode of DES or any good block cipher (also when produces only last block called MAC, given $S = a, b, c$ then $MAC(S) = E(c + (b + E(a)))$, in the context of a fixed length messages and when the first field is chosen at random and the rest is fixed or a fixed function of dependent on this initial choice. The exact context is important for our assumption to be reasonable. MAC is considered secure in many cases, and furthermore, in our context, the two common attacks on MAC calculations do not apply. The first attack is the *birthday attack* [7] when the message space is cut into two parts and using the known birthday paradox, a new message is found with some much larger probability (rather than being order of $1/n$ for $n = 2^l$, it becomes $1/\sqrt{n}$). The second attack is a *splay attack*, where given two strings $S_1 = b_1, b_2, ..., b_n$ and $S_2 = c_1, c_2, ..., c_m$, and their MAC's: $MAC(S_1) = E(b_n + (E(b_{n-1} + ...(E(b_1))..)))$, and similarly $MAC(S_2)$, one can manipulate and get the following string

$$S' = b_1, b_2, ..., b_n, \{MAC(S_1) + c_1\}, c_2, ..., c_m$$

and notice that $MAC(S_2) = MAC(S')$ so we have a new string and its MAC.

We now present a formal notion of the security usually attributed to the CBC mode fingerprint [13]. This notion is sufficient to show the security of the selection of $E_A$, $E_B$ below. We present it in the context of a general size block-cipher (size $l$) as is customary in complexity theory. It is assumed (for practice) that length of 64 bits DES (or 128) already provides strong enough security.

**Definition 2.1** *A cryptosystem* $E : \{0,1\}^l \rightarrow \{0,1\}^l$ *is* **depth-2 CBC secure** *if the following holds. Select arbitrary:*

- *two different identities* $A, B \in \{0,1\}^l$.

- *a small set of chosen messages* $CHOSEN \subset \{0,1\}^l$ *(size poly(l)).*

- *An efficient algorithm ATTACKER.*

*Randomly select a key for* $E$ *for blocks of size* $l$, *and two strings* $w, x \in \{0,1\}^l$.

*Run ATTACKER on inputs* $x$, $E(B + E(x))$, $E(A + E(w))$, $E(B + E(w))$ *and let attacker choose* $CHOSEN$, *as long as* $x \notin CHOSEN$ *(note that* $E(B+E(x))$ *was given to the attacker). Get* $E(A + E(z))$, $E(B + E(z))$ *for every* $z \in CHOSEN$. *The probability that ATTACKER produces either* $w$ *or* $E(A + E(x))$ *is negligible (smaller than inverse polynomial in* $l$).

**Lemma 1** *If* $E$ *is a depth-2 CBC secure cryptosystem then the selection* $E_A(m) = E(A + E(m))$ *and* $E_B(m) = E(B + E(m))$ *gives a secure one-way authentication protocol.*

The proof reduces all on-line (and replay and off-line) attacks to the adversary attacking the CBC mode as above. It captures any cryptographic attempt to produce the answer to the challenge in some feasible way with some non-negligible probability (as long as the assumption is correct and the query power of the attacker in its definition does not enable the attack). Note that the definition above captures both, the security of the exact challenge in a protocol where the challenge is decryption as in the protocol above, as well as an attack on a dual protocol where the challenge involves encryption (in the CBC mode) of a challenge (which is just a plaintext $w$).

If the assumption would have been that the message space encrypted under CBC is not $(m, A)(m, B)$ given all random $m$'s, but actually $(m, A+m)(m, B+m)$, then a similar assumption about CBC on this message space could be postulated. This message space increases the variability of the second block of the strings (and we call it the *variability heuristics*, which combines ciphertext chaining with plaintext chaining mode).

## 2.3 Two-way authentication is not simply twice one-way!

A natural proposition for a two-way authentication protocol is to combine two applications of a secure one-way authentication protocol, i.e. to use the one-way protocol to authenticate each party to the other. We show this simple two-way protocol in figure 3. The second flow in figure 3 simply sends in parallel both the second flow of the first application and the first flow of the second application.

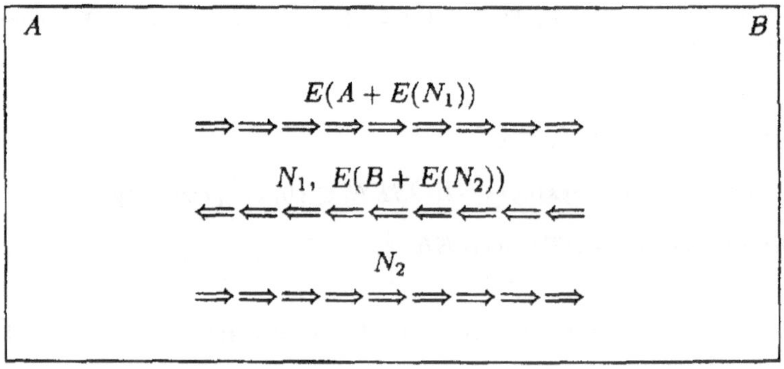

$A$                                                  $B$

$$E(A + E(N_1))$$
$$\Rightarrow \Rightarrow \Rightarrow \Rightarrow \Rightarrow \Rightarrow \Rightarrow \Rightarrow \Rightarrow$$

$$N_1, \ E(B + E(N_2))$$
$$\Leftarrow \Leftarrow \Leftarrow \Leftarrow \Leftarrow \Leftarrow \Leftarrow \Leftarrow \Leftarrow$$

$$N_2$$
$$\Rightarrow \Rightarrow \Rightarrow \Rightarrow \Rightarrow \Rightarrow \Rightarrow \Rightarrow \Rightarrow$$

Figure 3: Combination of two runs of one-way authentication

We now show why this protocol is not a secure two way authentication protocol. Basically the same kind of message is used in the first flow and in the second flow. Therefore, an attacker can initiate a few sessions and as a result can successfully impersonate one of the parties by supplying the third flow: It gets the value of the third flow from a legal party in the second flow. This attack is demonstrated in figure 4.

## 3  A Technique for Breaking Protocols

We have broken many protocols suggested during this investigation. In most cases it was done as follows: we searched for the values the attacker had to send, then we search for

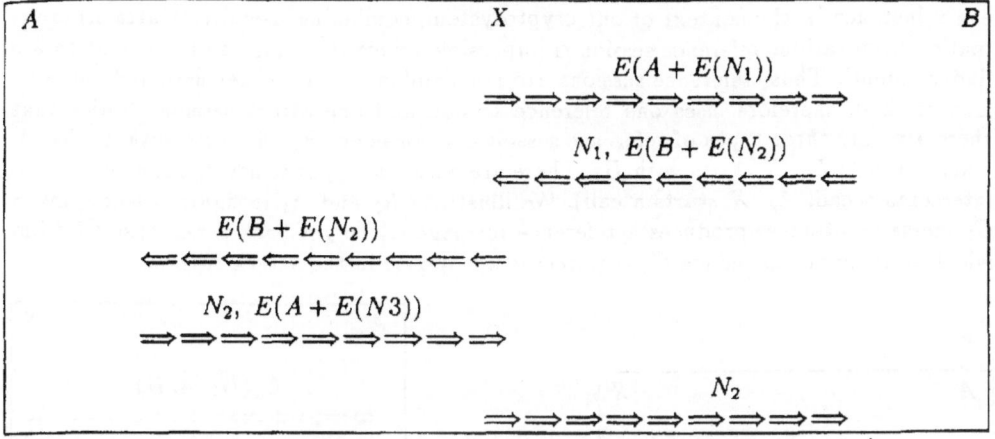

Figure 4: An attack on two-way authentication by twice one-way

a session in which a honest party could send this value (or a response from which the value can be derived by an easy computation).

The list can, of course, be used in order to check a candidate protocol. Of course, a protocol not broken by this method may still be breakable by some other method. However, *all the attacks we found* on protocols can be found using this list. Section 4 presents such an attack. Postulating an exact assumption about the underlying cryptosystem which captures the fact that using various activations of the protocol in any context and attacking the protocol directly using cryptanalysis, is the core of our security proof.

**Example 3.1** *Consider the attack of figure 4. In order to attack the session with B, called the* attack *session, the attacker X started another session with A, called a* reference *session. In the reference session X sent to A exactly the same challenge, $E(B + E(N_2))$, as X got in the attack session.*

In general, the attacker can send something that depends on the attack session in a more subtle way. For example, change the protocol in such a way that the challenge in the first flow is XORed with the name of the sending party. That is: $A + E(A + E(N_1))$, while the rest of the protocol remains without change. To break this protocol $X$ would need to send in the reference session the message $A + E(B + E(N_2))$, although in the attack session it receives $E(B + E(N_2))$.

The method is, therefore, to try to compute any of the response to challenge flows required to in an attack session, using the flows available in reference sessions (computing in any feasible way in polynomial time is allowed). Since we are going to assume that the responses to challenges include an encryption of a truly random field in each and every instance in the context of our cryptosystem, combining useful (for attack) information from various reference session is impossible (since these pieces of information are 'independent'. Thus, reference sessions are not combined, but rather used individually. The method, therefore, uses one reference session and one attack session. Notice that there are only three types of reference sessions to consider ($R_1$: $A$ starts with $B$; $R_2$: $X$ starts with $A$; $R_3$: $X$ starts with $B$). There are only two types of attack sessions ($A_1$: $X$ intercepts a call; $A_2$: $X$ starts a call). We illustrate $R_3$ and $A_1$ in figure 5 where given $C_1$ message, attacker produces a reference message $C_1'$ to get back a response $C_2'$ from which it attempts to deduce $C_2$ required as a response in the attack session.

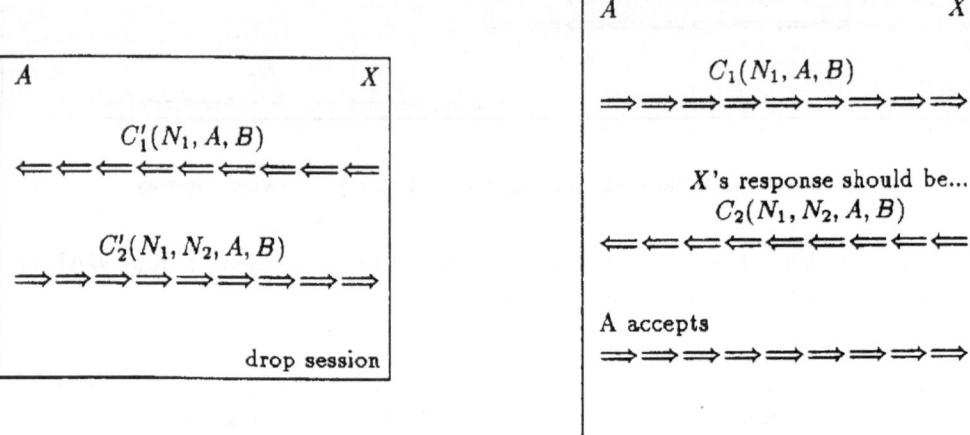

Figure 5: Reference session $R_3$ (left) and attack session $A_1$ (right).

# 4 Attack on ISO Protocol

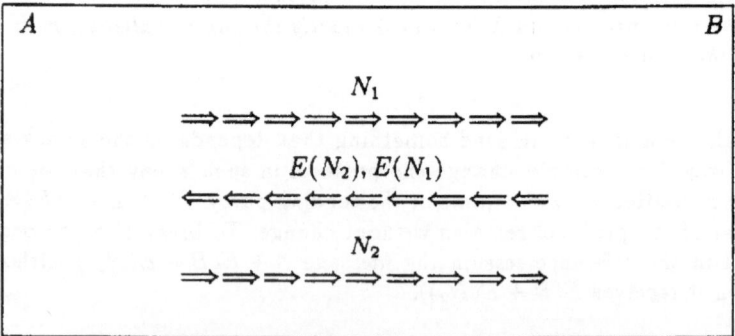

Figure 6: ISO standard proposed protocol

Due to lack of space, this version contains only one example of an attack. In Figure 6 we show a protocol proposed as a standard for "Entity Authentication Using Symmetric Techniques" by the ISO [16]. It seems that the designer of this protocol have realized the problem of using the same flow in both directions, and thus the challenges in the different directions are different.

The reader may exercise now by breaking this protocol, directly by experimentation or by applying the approach presented in the previous section. The attack we found is shown in figure 7. Notice that $B$ is impersonated while not even being present in the communication.

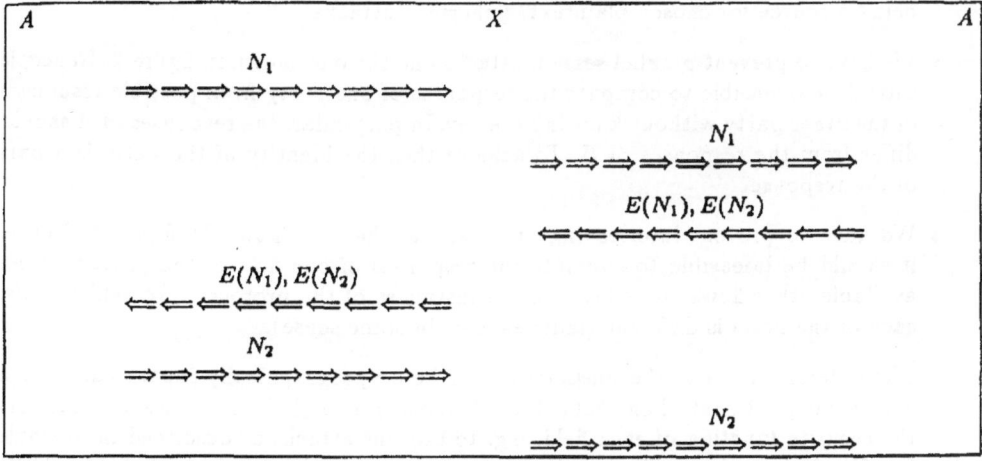

Figure 7: An attack on the ISO protocol

This attack is generated by the technique presented in section 3, as follows. We use attack session $A_1$ and reference session $R_3$. The attacker uses the second flow of $R_3$ to be the second flow of $A_1$.

# 5 A Secure Two-Way Authentication Protocol

## 5.1 Avoiding Security Weaknesses

We have tried to identify and avoid the security weaknesses of other protocols. The attacker cannot directly perform the cryptographic operations required to generate the response to a given challenge, since the key is secret and we made the protocol strong in the sense that it is defined over random instances and does not expose data for attacks (such as chosen message, say). However, the attacker may attempt to generate the response by using the the services of a legal party by applying an instance of the protocol itself. This implies several requirements from the protocol:

- The attacker should not be able to use either party as an 'oracle'. In particular, the protocol should never perform a cryptographic operation on inputs which may be completely selected by the attacker. Instead, in every cryptographic operation, there should be at least one field which is selected randomly by a honest party. We achieve this by having a random field selected by the party performing the cryptographic operation. This ensures "pseudo-independence" of responses in various sessions (and combination of many reference sessions). This also prevents the protocol from being a source for chosen plaintext/ciphertext attacks.

- We have to prevent parallel session attacks like the one shown in figure 2. Hence, it should be infeasible to compute the responses of one party from possible responses of the other party without knowing the key. In particular, the responses of $A$ should differ from the responses of $B$. To achieve this, the identity of the party is a part of the response.

- We have to prevent interleaving attacks, like the one shown in figure 4. Hence, it should be infeasible to compute the responses of one flow of the protocol from available other flows (possibly of other instances of the protocol). To achieve this, each of the flows is different (independent, in some sense).

- The different fields in the message should be cryptographically separated, i.e. the attacker cannot control one field through another field. This is necessary to support the security function of each field, e.g. to prevent attacks as described in example 3.1. We achieve this, while keeping the message short, by sending a MAC (or CBC encryption) of the concatenation of all the fields.

## 5.2 A secure protocol

In figure 8 we present a secure two-way authentication protocol, following the design considerations presented above. In order to find a secure protocol, we follow the security considerations above. Then, we tried to break the protocol using the methodology presented in section 3.

During this evolutionary development, we realized that it is very helpful for the protocol to use the well established CBC mode of the DES [13], Namely, it seems good to use expressions of the form $E(a + E(b + E(c)))$, where some of $c, b$ and $a$ are random values and others are constants or constants exclusive-ored with random values. The protocol in figure 8 follows from this form for the expressions combined with the security considerations presented above.

The proof of the security of this protocol relies heavily on an assumption about the security of the CBC mode. This assumption is an extension of the depth-2 CBC assumption presented in section 2.2. The assumption first asserts that producing something like

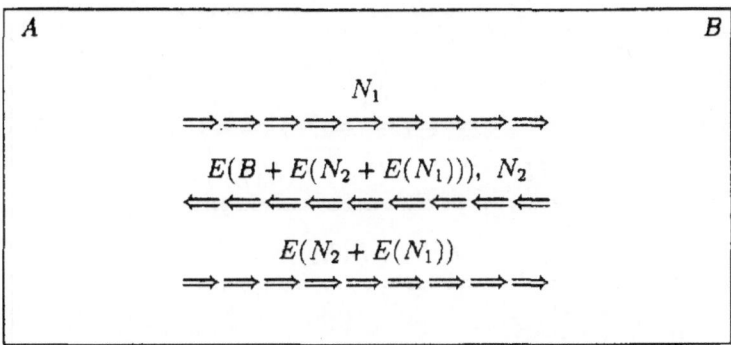

Figure 8: A secure two party authentication protocol

a response on the second message given $N_1$ is impossible given many choices of other challenges. Then, the assumption also takes care of the independence of the two encryptions used in the second and third flow of the protocol (as explained in the next paragraph). The proof actually reduces the general attack on a session to a direct violating of the CBC-encryption mode on the message space, thus capturing directly the hardness of attacks along the lines of the search methodology above on the protocol above. Both the proof and the exact assumption are omitted from this abstract. We just outline the properties achieved.

Notice that the response on the second flow includes a random data field $N_2$, so these responses in different instances are 'pseudo-independent', and there is no exposure to chosen plaintext attack. The response in the second flow is independent from the response on the third flow. We, indeed, assume that given $E(B + E(w))$, for a constant $B$, it is hard to produce $E(w)$ (which is an assumption equivalent to assuming one can get $m$ from $E(m)$. If this is possible with non-negligible probability, then the depth-2 CBC assumption does not hold. Note further that our $m$ in turn is of the form $E(N_2 + E(N_1))$ for known $N_1, N_2$ and getting it is, in turn, also equivalent to a violation of the depth-2 CBC. Thus, we actually build on a previous assumption in this extension. Therefore, we can justifyingly assume that encryptions done by $A$ at the third-flow response are independent from those done by $B$ on the second response (and vice versa).

Note that this protocol is optimal in all of the efficiency criteria, except for requiring three encryptions. The third encryption assures further strength of the method against possible statistical attacks (like birthday attacks— it isolates every block of plaintext of a given fixed format).

Also note that the use of CBC encryption is extendible in case more fields are needed to be hashed in the messages, e.g. information to be exchanged and authenticated or longer names (as long as the format is determined once and for all.

As a further improvement we suggest the protocol of figure 9. This is the previously

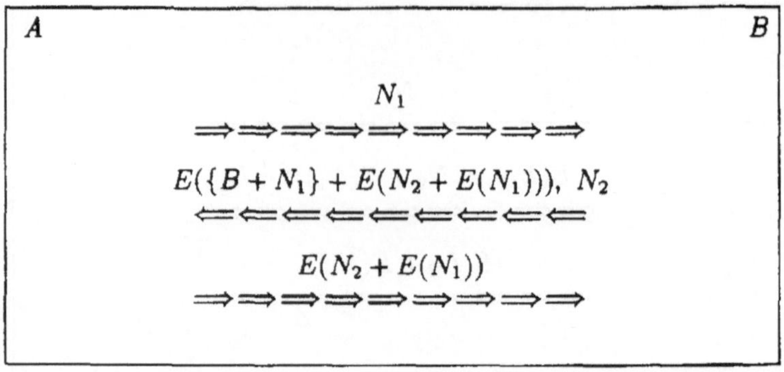

$$A \qquad\qquad\qquad\qquad\qquad\qquad\qquad\qquad\qquad\qquad B$$

$$N_1$$
$$\Rightarrow \Rightarrow \Rightarrow \Rightarrow \Rightarrow \Rightarrow \Rightarrow \Rightarrow \Rightarrow$$

$$E(\{B + N_1\} + E(N_2 + E(N_1))), \ N_2$$
$$\Leftarrow \Leftarrow \Leftarrow \Leftarrow \Leftarrow \Leftarrow \Leftarrow \Leftarrow$$

$$E(N_2 + E(N_1))$$
$$\Rightarrow \Rightarrow \Rightarrow \Rightarrow \Rightarrow \Rightarrow \Rightarrow \Rightarrow \Rightarrow$$

Figure 9: Heuristically improved protocol

mentioned variability heuristics. Heuristically, we change the third block in the plaintext of the response of the second flow from $B$ to $B + N_1$ to increase the variability of this block. The security of this protocol seems to be stronger since the attacker cannot collect many pairs of the form $E(B + m)$, $m$ for a fixed $B$.

Similar improvement is achieved if the name of $B$ is long (say, mandatorily contains two blocks $B_1$ and $B_2$ and the second flow computes $E(B_1 + E(B_2 + E(N_2 + E(N_1))))$; however this introduces an additional encryption. This does not give the attacker any direct pair $m, E(m)$. But this alternative still gives the attacker a collection of pairs forming a deterministic relation $E(B_1 + E(B_2 + m))$ and $m$, for fixed $B_1, B_2$. We can combine the last two suggestions and add the variability heuristics here and get

$$E(\{B_1 + N_1\} + E(\{B_2 + N_1\} + E(N_2 + E(N_1))))$$

which seems to be the strongest combination.

# 6 Open Questions

The work presented a protocol which is shown to be as secure as its underlying block-cipher system in a CBC-mode. That is, this protocol encrypts only in the CBC mode over a plaintext space which includes a random block of a fixed size and fixed format. The CBC-encryptions and CBC-fingerprints, also called Message Authentication Code (MAC) (which was shown strong in our message space), are widely used in practice. Hence, this security assumption is accepted in practice, although we are not aware of it being formally defined so far. The obvious question is whether this assumption can be reduced to the security of a cryptosystem itself (or some weaker assumption). Say, can the security of the protocol be proven based solely on the assumption that we use a block-cipher which is (ideally) a random permutation.

Another question concerns the methodology which we used while developing this protocol. We used this methodology to check the protocol against a family of 'interleaving' attacks. An obvious challenge is to identify exactly the full generality of this family of attacks, and to prove that the methodology, or some modification of it, ensures security against the general set of attacks, based on any reasonable underlying encryption method (not necessarily our encryptions).

## Acknowledgments

The authors are grateful to Reid Sayre for suggesting the problem and useful discussions. It is also a pleasure to thank Martin Abadi, Sekar Chandersekaran, Don Coppersmith, Mark Davis, Bob Elander, Virgil Gligor, Don Johnson, Mike Matyas, and Jim Randall for useful discussions and comments.

# References

[1] M. Abadi and M. Tuttle, *A semantics for a logic of authentication*, PODC 1991, pp. 201–216

[2] R. K. Bauer, T. A. Berson and R. J. Freiertag, *A key distribution protocol using event markers*. ACM TOCS 1 3 (1983) pp. 249-255.

[3] S. M. Bellovin and M. Merritt, Limitations of the Kerberos Authentication System. ACM Computer Communication Review 30,5 (1990) 119-132.

[4] E. Biham and A. Shamir, *Differential cryptanalysis of des-like cryptosystems*. Crypto-90.

[5] M. Burrows, M. Abadi and R. M. Needham, *A logic of authentication*. Proc. 12th ACM SOSP, ACM OSR 23 5 (Dec.89) 1 13. (Also in ACM TOCS).

[6] P-C Cheng and V. Gligor, *On the formal specification and verification of a multiparty session protocol*. IEEE Sym. on Research in Security and Privacy (1990), pp. 216–233.

[7] D. Coppersmith, *Another birthday attack*. Crypto-85, pp. 14-17.

[8] D. E. R. Denning, *Cryptography and Data Security*. Addison-Wesley, Reading, MA, 1982.

[9] D. E. Denning and G. M. Sacco, *Timestamps in key distribution systems*. CACM 24 8 (Aug.81) 533-536.

[10] A. Fiat and A. Shamir, *How to Prove Yourself: practical solutions to identification and signature problems*. Proc. of Crypto-86, Springer-Verlag LNCS 263, (1987) pp. 186-194.

[11] Z. Galil, S. Haber, and M. Yung, *Symmetric Public-Key Cryptography*. Crypto 85, pp. 128–137.

[12] O. Goldreich, A. Herzberg and Y. Mansour, *Source to Destination Communication in the Presence of Faults*. PODC 1989, pp. 85–102.

[13] *Data Encryption Standard, FIPS 46, NBS (Jan.77)*..

[14] S. Goldwasser and S. Micali, *Probabilistic encryption*. J. Comp. Systems Sci. 28 (1984), pp. 270-299.

[15] L. Gong, R. Needham and R. Yahalom, *Reasoning about belief in cryptographic protocols*. IEEE Sym. on Research in Security and Privacy (1990), pp. 234-248.

[16] *Working Draft: Entity Authentication Using Symmetric Techniques.* ISO Project JTC1.27.02.2(20.03.1.2) 06/21/1990.

[17] *Banking - Key management (wholesale). ISO 8732, Geneva (1988).*

[18] *OSI Directory - Part 8: Authentication Framework.* ISO 9594-8, Geneva (1988).

[19] J. J. Jueneman, S. M. Matyas, and C. H. Meyer, *Message Authentication. IEEE Communication Magazine*, pp. 29–40, 1985.

[20] M. J. Merritt, *Cryptographic protocols. Ph.D. dissertation GIT-ICS-83/06, The Georgia Institute of Technology, Atlanta, Ga., 1983*

[21] C. H. Meyer and S. M. Matyas, *Cryptography: a new dimension in computer data security.* Willey, New York, 1982

[22] M. Naor and M. Yung, *Universal one-way hash functions and their cryptographic applications.* ACM annual Symp. on Theory of Computing, 1989.

[23] R. M. Needham, M. D. Schroeder, *Using encryption for authentication in large networks of computers.* CACM 21 12 (1978) 993-998.

[24] D. Otway, O. Rees, *Efficient and timely mutual authentication.* ACM OSR 21 1 (Jan.87) 8-10.

[25] M. O. Rabin, *Digital signature and public-key functions as intractable as factoring.* MIT Tech. reprt TM-212 Lab. for Comp. Sci. (1979).

[26] R. L. Rivest, A. Shamir, and L. Adleman, *A method for obtaining digital signatures and public-key crypto-systems.* CACM 21 2 (1978) 120-126 (and CACM 26 1 (1983) 96-99).

[27] D.D. Sidhu, Authentication Protocols for Computer Networks:I. *Computer Networks and ISDN Systems*, 11, pages 297–310, 1986.

[28] J. G. Steiner, et al., *Kerberos: an authentication server for open network systems.* Proc. Usenix Conf. (Winter 88).

[29] V.L. Voydoc and S.T. Kent, *Security Mechanisms in High Level Network Protocols.* Computing Surveys. 15 (1983).

# Appendix: an Exhaustive Search of Sessions' Interleaving

Let $Ai.j$ {$Ri.j$} be the $i$th flow of attack session $Aj$ {Reference session $Rj$} in Figure 5. Assume further that the message in the first flow contains the challenge in the first message $C_1$ which is a function of $N_1$, and possibly $A$ and $B$. The message in the second flow containing the challenge $C_2$: a function of $N_2$ and $A$ and $B$ and $C_1$ (and $N_1$), etc. We deal with the attack session and at least one other session. Thus let $C_1'$, $C_2'$ $N_1'$ and $N_2'$ be the values used in the other session, to distinguish between them and the value used in the attack session in question.

The attacker can break the protocol if it can solve one of the equations below. (We have written just $N_1$, $N_2$, but in fact the attacker may control only $C_1$ and $C_2$, since it may not know $N_1$ and $N_2$.)

**Example 6.1** *Example- in Figure 4 Equation 7 is solved trivially by the attacker. In Example 3.1 the attackers does a minor computation on $C_2$ to obtain $C_1$.*

# The Equations

- (1) $A_1.2 = R_1.3$, where $N_2$ is free and $N_1 \neq N_1'$
- (2) $A_1.2 = R_1.2$, where $N_2$ is free and $N_1 \neq N_1'$
- (3) $A_1.2 = R_2.2$, where $N_1'$ and $N_2$ are free but $N_1'$ cannot depend on $N_2'$ and $N_1' \neq N_2'$ as this would be a trivial relay (observe and cut) attack where $X$ is just a passive observer between $A$ and $B$, who have actually authenticated one another in real-time
- (4) $A_1.2 = R_3.2$, where $N_1'$ and $N_2'$ are free but $N_1'$ cannot depend on $N_2'$
- (5) $A_2.3 = R_1.3$, where $N_1$ is free but cannot depend on $N_2$
- (6) $A_2.3 = R_1.2$, where $N_1$ is free but cannot depend on $N_2$
- (7) $A_2.3 = R2.2$, where $N_1$ is free but cannot depend on $N_2$ and $N_1'$ is free but cannot depend on $N_2'$
- (8) $A_2.3 = R_3.2$, where $N_1$ is free but cannot depend on $N_2$ and $N_1'$ is free but cannot depend on $N_2'$
- (9) $A_2.3 = A2.2$, where $N_1$ is free but cannot depend on $N_2$

The following example shows a case of a breakable protocol that cannot be broken by the method as described so far. This is since the attacker does not send in the attack session the *very same* value it received in the reference session. Instead it receives a value, does some trivial operation and sends the result. The method can be generalized further to cope with this additional operation. However, in order to be sure that the protocol is indeed secure one should actually have a formal proof of security stating exactly the attacker's poser and reducing it to some statement about the underlying cryptosystem, (also presented in this paper) rather than to be sure that one has coped with every possible attack. Still, we present the method as a very useful checking tool. An extension of the method should take into account derivation of responses based on easy calculations from reference sessions. Here is the example:

**Example 6.2** *Let us change the protocol of Figure 4 slightly. Instead of sending $N_1$ in the second flow, the party (say B) sends $N_1$ XORed with the party name $(B + N_1)$ in the example of Figure 4). The rest of the algorithm remains the same. In particular, in the third flow $N_2$ is sent, rather than $(A + N_2)$.*

*In order to break the protocol we need now to change the attack in Figure 4 slightly. The attacker who receives $A + N_2$ from A in the second flow of the reference session needs to perform an easy computation of XORing this with A to obtain the value $N_2$ it needs to send B.*

# Combinatorial characterizations of authentication codes

D. R. Stinson
Computer Science and Engineering
University of Nebraska
Lincoln, NE 68588-0115
stinson@bibd.unl.edu

**Abstract**

In this paper, we prove two new combinatorial characterizations of authentication codes. Authentication codes without secrecy are characterized in terms of orthogonal arrays; and general authentication codes are characterized in terms of balanced incomplete block designs.

# 1 Introduction

In this paper, we prove some new characterizations of authentication codes. By a characterization theorem, we mean a theorem of the form "an authentication code with certain properties exists if and only if a certain combinatorial structure exists". Typically, the properties of the authentication code that are considered are natural, desirable properties such as having the minimum possible deception probabilities and the minimum number of encoding rules.

In the past, bounds have been proved on these quantities, and constructions have been given for classes of authentication codes that meet such bounds with equality. Many of these constructions have used combinatorial designs. The characterizations in this paper show that, in certain cases, the known constructions are essentially the "only way" to obtain codes with the specified properties. Of course, a characterization of this type has intrinsic interest. However, a characterization also proves that it is impossible to find "different" constructions from those already known.

In this paper, we prove two new characterizations of this type. The first result (Theorem 3.1) concerns authentication codes without secrecy, i.e. codes where an observed message can correspond to only one possible source state. Such a code is equivalent to one where a message consists of a source state concatenated with an authenticator. A code where the deception probabilities and the number of encoding rules meet the lower bounds with equality is equivalent to a combinatorial design called an orthogonal array. This characterization has been previously proved in the case where the number of possible

J. Feigenbaum (Ed.): Advances in Cryptology - CRYPTO '91, LNCS 576, pp. 62-73, 1992.
© Springer-Verlag Berlin Heidelberg 1992

source states is at most 1 + the number of possible of authenticators. Here, we extend the characterization so that this assumption is no longer needed. The proof uses an elegant linear-algebraic technique which has not previously been used in authentication theory.

Our second characterization concerns "general" authentication codes. Again, we consider those codes where the deception probabilities and the number of encoding rules are the minimum possible. It has been previously shown that such a code can exist only if a certain balanced incomplete block design (BIBD) exists. Conversely, it has been previously shown that one can use the BIBD to construct the desired code *if the source states are known to be equiprobable*. In this paper, we complete the characterization by showing that the assumption of equiprobable sources is necessary. Our result is stated as Theorem 4.1.

Finally, the second characterization can be extended to include codes that, in addition, provide perfect secrecy. An extra numerical condition is necessary and sufficient to provide secrecy (see Theorem 4.2).

The paper is organized as follows. Section 2 gives necessary background from the theory of authentication codes. In Section 3, we prove our characterization for authentication codes without secrecy. In Section 4, we prove the characterization of general authentication codes.

# 2    Basic results on authentication codes

The general theory of of unconditional authentication has been developed by Simmons (see e.g. [Si1] and [Si2]), and has been extensively studied in recent years. In this section, we will give a brief review of some relevant known results concerning authentication without secrecy.

In the usual model for authentication, there are three participants: a *transmitter*, a *receiver*, and an *opponent*. The transmitter wants to communicate some information to the receiver using a public commmunications channel. The *source state* (or plaintext) is encrypted to obtain the *message* (ciphertext), which is sent through the channel. An *encoding rule* (or key) $e$ defines the message $e(s)$ to be sent to communicate any source state $s$. Each encoding rule will be a one-to-one function from the source space to the message space. We assume the transmitter has a key source from which he obtains a key. Prior to any messages being sent, this key is communicated to the receiver by means of a secure channel.

We will use the following notation. Let $S$ be a set of $k$ source states; let $M$ be a set of $v$ messages; and let $\mathcal{E}$ be a set of $b$ encoding rules. Since each encoding rule is a one-to-one function from $S$ to $M$, we can represent a code by a $b \times k$ matrix, where the rows are indexed by encoding rules, the columns are indexed by source states, and the entry in row $e$ and column $s$ is $e(s)$. We call this matrix the *encoding matrix*. For any encoding rule $e \in \mathcal{E}$, define $M(e) = \{e(s) : s \in S\}$, i.e. the set of valid messages under encoding rule $e$. For an encoding rule $e$, and a message $m \in M(e)$, define $e^{-1}(m) = s$ if $e(s) = m$.

Suppose the opponent has the ability to introduce messages into the channel and/or to modify existing messages. When the opponent places a (new) message $m'$ into the channel, this is called *impersonation*. When the opponent sees a message $m$ and changes it to a message $m' \neq m$, this is called *substitution*. In either case, his goal is to have $m'$ accepted as authentic by the receiver. That is, if $e$ is the encoding rule being used (which is *not* known to the opponent), then the opponent is hoping that $m' = e(s)$ for some source state $s$.

We assume that there is some probability distribution on $S$, which is known to all the participants. Given the probability distribution on the source states, the receiver and transmitter will choose a probability distribution for $\mathcal{E}$, called an *encoding strategy*. Once the transmitter/receiver have chosen the encoding strategy, it is possible to determine, for $i = 0, 1$, a probability denoted $P_{d_i}$, which is the probability that the opponent can deceive the transmitter/receiver by impersonation and substitution, respectively.

$P_{d_0}$ is calculated as follows. The opponent can compute, for each message $m$, a quantity $payoff(m)$ which denotes the probability that $m$ will be accepted as authentic by the transmitter/reciever. It is easy to see that

$$payoff(m) = \sum_{\{e \in \mathcal{E} : m \in M(e)\}} p(E = e).$$

Then it follows that

$$\sum_{\{m \in M\}} payoff(m) = k.$$

Hence, there exists a particular message $m_0 \in M$ such that $payoff(m_0) \geq k/v$. Further, $P_{d_0} = k/v$ if and only if $payoff(m) = k/v$ for every message $m$. We summarize this as follows.

**Theorem 2.1** *[Si1]* $P_{d_0} \geq k/v$. *Further,* $P_{d_0} = k/v$ *if and only if*

$$\sum_{\{e \in \mathcal{E} : m \in M(e)\}} p(E = e) = \frac{k}{v}$$

*for every message* $m$.

Now, let's turn our attention to the computation of $P_{d_1}$. The situation is quite different depending on whether we have an authentication code without secrecy as opposed to a general authentication code. Let's first consider authentication codes without secrecy. This means that $e(s) = e'(s')$ only if $s = s'$; i.e. the message uniquely determines the source state, irrespective of the encoding rule being used. Hence, we can partition the set of messages $\mathcal{M}$ into $k$ subsets $\mathcal{M}_s$, $s \in S$, such that $\mathcal{M}_s = \{e(s) : e \in \mathcal{E}\}$.

Suppose $P_{d_0} = k/v$. For codes providing authentication without secrecy, this can happen only if $|\mathcal{M}_s| = v/k$ for every source state $s$. In this situation, we can define a set $\mathcal{A}$ of $\ell = v/k$ authenticators and a mapping $\phi : \mathcal{M} \to \mathcal{A}$ such that, for every $s \in S$, $\{\phi(m) : m \in \mathcal{M}_s\} = \mathcal{A}$. We can then obtain an isomorphic code by defining for every encoding rule $e$ an *authentication rule* $e^\phi$ defined by $e^\phi(s) = \phi(e(s))$ for every source state $s$. In this new code, every message consists of a source state concatenated with an authenticator from $\mathcal{A}$, i.e. source state $s$ is mapped to $(s, e^\phi(s))$, where $e^\phi$ is an authentication rule. In terms of $\ell = |\mathcal{A}|$, we have $P_{d_0} = 1/\ell$.

We will henceforth assume that every message consists of a source state with a concatenated authenticator, since there is no loss of generality in doing so. Also, we will think of $\mathcal{E}$ as being a collection of authentication rules, and we will speak of an *authentication matrix* rather than an encoding matrix.

Suppose the opponent sees the message $m = (s, a)$ in the channel. He can substitute this message with any message $m' = (s', a')$, where $s' \neq s$. Denote by $payoff(m, m')$ the probability that the message $m'$ will be accepted as authentic, given that $m$ is observed in the channel. Denote by $e_0$ the authentication rule being used by the transmitter/receiver (again, we emphasize that $e_0$ is unknown to the opponent). Then we have the following:

$$payoff(m, m') = \frac{\sum_{\{e:e(s)=a, e(s')=a'\}} p(E = e)}{\sum_{\{e:e(s)=a\}} p(E = e)}.$$

Now, it follows that

$$\sum_{a' \in A} payoff(m, (s', a')) = 1$$

for any $s' \neq s$. Hence, for every $s'$, there exists an authenticator $a' = f(m, s')$ such that $payoff(m, m') \geq 1/\ell$, and it follows that $P_{d_1} \geq 1/\ell$.

Suppose that $P_{d_0} = 1/\ell$. Then, from Theorem 2.1, we have

$$\sum_{\{e:e(s)=a, e(s')=a'\}} p(E = e) = \frac{1}{\ell}.$$

Hence, we obtain the following theorem.

**Theorem 2.2** *[St2] Suppose we have an authentication code without secrecy in which* $P_{d_0} = k/v = 1/\ell$. *Then* $P_{d_1} \geq 1/\ell$. *Further,* $P_{d_1} = 1/\ell$ *if and only if*

$$\sum_{\{e : e(s) = a, e(s') = a'\}} p(E = e) = \frac{1}{\ell^2}$$

*for every* $s, s', a, a', s \neq s'$.

The above considerations also lead to a lower bound on the number of authentication rules and a characterization as to when equality can occur. We give this characterization in terms of orthogonal arrays, which we now define. An *orthogonal array* $OA(n, k, \lambda)$ is a $\lambda n^2 \times k$ array of $n$ symbols, such that in any two columns of the array every one of the possible $n^2$ pairs of symbols occurs in exactly $\lambda$ rows. If $\lambda = 1$, then we write $OA(n, k)$. Orthogonal arrays are well-studied structures in combinatorial design theory, and are equivalent to other structures such as transversal designs, mutually orthogonal Latin squares and nets.

**Theorem 2.3** *[St2] Suppose we have an authentication code without secrecy in which* $P_{d_0} = P_{d_1} = k/v = 1/\ell$. *Then* $b \geq \ell^2$, *and equality occurs if and only if the authentication matrix is an orthogonal array* $OA(\ell, k)$ *and the authentication rules are used with equal probability.*

**Proof:** Suppose $P_{d_0} = P_{d_1} = k/v = 1/\ell$. Let $s \neq s'$. Then, for every $a, a'$, $|\{e : e(s) = a, e(s') = a'\}| \geq 1$. Hence, $b \geq \ell^2$.

In order that $b = \ell^2$, it must be the case that $|\{e : e(s) = a, e(s') = a'\}| = 1$ for every $s, s', a, a'$, where $s \neq s'$; and $p(E = e) = 1/\ell^2$ for every $e \in \mathcal{E}$. The authentication matrix is clearly an orthogonal array $OA(\ell, k)$.

Conversely, suppose we start with an orthogonal array $OA(\ell, k)$. Use each row as an authentication rule with equal probability $1/\ell^2$. Then we obtain a code with the stated properties. □

The above theorem provides a nice characterization, as far as it goes. However, existence of an $OA(\ell, k)$ requires that $k \leq \ell + 1$. The two parameters $k$ and $\ell$ are independent parameters, so it is also of interest to characterize authentication codes in the situation $k > \ell + 1$; i.e. when $v < k^2 - k$. We shall do this in Section 3. The characterization involves orthogonal arrays with $\lambda > 1$.

Let's turn to general authentication codes. Now, the set $\mathcal{E}$ is a set of encoding rules. As before, we compute a quantity $payoff(m, m')$ which is the property that the receiver will be deceived by a substitution of $m$ by $m'$. We have

$$payoff(m, m') = \frac{\sum\limits_{\{e:m,m' \in M(e)\}} p(E = e)p(S = e^{-1}(m))}{\sum\limits_{\{e:m \in M(e)\}} p(E = e)p(S = e^{-1}(m))}.$$

Fix a message $m$. Then we can compute $\sum_{m' \neq m} payoff(m, m') = k - 1$. Hence, there exists a message $m' = f(m)$ such that

$$payoff(m, m') \geq \frac{k-1}{v-1},$$

and it follows that $P_{d_1} \geq (k-1)/(v-1)$.

**Theorem 2.4** *[Ma], [St1] In any authentication code, $P_{d_1} \geq (k-1)/(v-1)$. Further, $P_{d_1} = (k-1)/(v-1)$ if and only if*

$$\frac{\sum_{\{e:m,m' \in M(e)\}} p(E = e)p(S = e^{-1}(m))}{\sum_{\{e:m \in M(e)\}} p(E = e)p(S = e^{-1}(m))} = \frac{k-1}{v-1}$$

*for all $m, m', m \neq m'$.*

If we have a code in which $P_{d_0} = k/v$ and $P_{d_1} = (k-1)/(v-1)$, then we can obtain an immediate lower bound on the number of encoding rules and a partial characterization. We need the concept of a *balanced incomplete block design*, or BIBD. A $(v, k, \lambda)$–BIBD is a pair $(X, \mathcal{A})$, where $|X| = v$ is a set of elements called *points* and $\mathcal{A}$ is a family of $k$–subsets of $X$ (called *blocks*) such that every pair of points occurs in exactly $\lambda$ blocks. It is not difficult to see that every point occurs in precisely $r = \lambda(v-1)/(k-1)$ blocks and that the total number of blocks is $b = \lambda v(v-1)/(k(k-1))$.

**Theorem 2.5** *[Ma], [St2] Suppose we have an authentication code in which $P_{d_0} = k/v$ and $P_{d_1} = (k-1)/(v-1)$. Then $b \geq (v^2 - v)/(k^2 - k)$, and equality can occur only if the rows of the encoding matrix, taken as unordered sets, form a $(v, k, 1)$–BIBD.*

**Proof:** For every two distinct messages, $m, m'$, $|\{e : m, m' \in M(e)\}| \geq 1$. Hence, $b \geq (v^2 - v)/(k^2 - k)$. If $b = (v^2 - v)/(k^2 - k)$, then $|\{e : m, m' \in M(e)\}| = 1$ for every $m, m'$. $\square$

The following partial converse was shown in [St2].

**Theorem 2.6** *[St1] Suppose there is a $(v, k, 1)-BIBD$. Then there exists an authentication code for $k$ equiprobable sources in which $P_{d_0} = k/v$, $P_{d_1} = (k-1)/(v-1)$ and $b = (v^2 - v)/(k^2 - k)$.*

**Proof:** For every block $A \in \mathcal{A}$, arbitrarily define an encoding rule $e_A$ such that $\{e_A(s) : s \in \mathcal{S}\} = A$. Use every encoding rule with equal probability $1/b$. $\square$

In Section 4, we complete the characterization by showing that existence of an authentication code with $P_{d_0} = k/v$, $P_{d_1} = (k-1)/(v-1)$ and $b = (v^2 - v)/(k^2 - k)$ *requires* that the source states and encoding rules be equiprobable.

# 3   Authentication without secrecy

Suppose there is an authentication code (without secrecy) for $k$ source states, having $b$ authentication rules and $\ell$ authenticators, such that $P_{d_0} = P_{d_1} = 1/\ell$. Denote $\mathcal{M} = \mathcal{S} \times \mathcal{A}$; $\mathcal{M}$ is the set of messages. For an authentication rule $e \in \mathcal{E}$, $M(e) = \{(s, e(s)) : s \in \mathcal{S}\}$ is the set of messages arising from authentication rule $e$.

Define a $k\ell$-dimensional real vector space $V$ having as its basis $\mathbf{B} = \{\overline{m} : m \in \mathcal{M}\}$. For every authentication rule $e \in \mathcal{E}$, define a vector $\overline{e} = \sum_{s \in \mathcal{S}} \overline{(s, e(s))}$. For every $s \in \mathcal{S}$, define $\overline{v_s} = \sum_{a \in \mathcal{A}} \overline{(s, a)}$. Next, define $\overline{X} = \sum_{m \in \mathcal{M}} \overline{m} = \sum_{s \in \mathcal{S}} \overline{v_s}$. Finally, for every $m = (s, a) \in \mathcal{M}$, define $\overline{v_m} = \ell \sum_{e \in \mathcal{E}, e(s) = a} p(E = e)\overline{e}$.

Using Theorems 2.1 and 2.2, it is not difficult to see that

$$\overline{v_m} = \overline{m} + \frac{1}{\ell}(\overline{X} - \overline{v_s}). \tag{1}$$

Now fix a source state $s_j \in \mathcal{S}$. Define $V' = \langle \mathbf{B}' \rangle$, where

$$\mathbf{B}' = \{\overline{v_s} : s \in \mathcal{S}, s \neq s_j\} \bigcup \{\overline{e} : e \in \mathcal{E}\}.$$

Note that the dimension of $V'$ is at most $b + k - 1$. We shall prove that $V' = V$.

First, from Theorem 2.1, we observe that

$$\ell \sum_{e \in \mathcal{E}} p(E = e)\overline{e} = \overline{X}, \tag{2}$$

so $\overline{X} \in V'$. Next, we have

$$\overline{v_{s_j}} = \overline{X} - \sum_{s \in S, s \neq s_j} \overline{v_s},$$

so $\overline{v_{s_j}} \in V'$. At this point, we have $\{\overline{v_s} : s \in S\} \subseteq V'$. Then it follows from Equation (1) that

$$\overline{v_m} - \frac{1}{\ell}(\overline{X} - \overline{v_s}) = \overline{m} \in V'$$

for any $m \in \mathcal{M}$. Hence, $V' = V$.

Since $V$ has dimension $k\ell$ and it is generated by $\mathbf{B}'$, a set of $b + k - 1$ vectors, we have that $b \geq k(\ell - 1) + 1$.

Now, let's consider the case of equality, i.e. $b = k(\ell - 1) + 1$. In this case, $\mathbf{B}'$ is a basis for $V$. We shall show that every authentication rule is used with equal probability $1/b$, and that the matrix of authentication rules is an orthogonal array $OA(\ell, k, \lambda)$, where $\lambda = b/\ell^2$.

Fix an authentication rule $e_i \in \mathcal{E}$. Using Equations (1) and (2), we compute

$$\sum_{m \in M(e_i)} \overline{v_m} = \overline{e_i} + \frac{k-1}{\ell}\overline{X}$$

$$= \overline{e_i} + (k-1)\sum_{e \in \mathcal{E}} p(E = e)\overline{e}$$

But we also have that $\overline{v_m} = \ell \sum_{e \in \mathcal{E}, e(s) = a} p(E = e)\overline{e}$, where $m = (s, a)$, by definition. Hence, we have

$$\sum_{m \in M(e_i)} \overline{v_m} = \ell \sum_{m \in M(e_i)} \sum_{\{e : m \in M(e)\}} p(E = e)\overline{e}.$$

Since $\mathbf{B}'$ is a basis for $V$, we can extract the coefficient of $\overline{e_i}$ and we obtain $\ell k p(E = e_i) = 1 + (k - 1)p(E = e_i)$. Hence, $p(E = e_i) = 1/(k(\ell - 1) + 1) = 1/b$. Since $e_i$ was an arbitrary authentication rule, it follows that all authentication rules are used with equal probability $1/b$.

Now, define the $b \times k$ authentication matrix $M = (a_{ij})$ where $a_{ij} = e_i(s_j)$, $1 \leq i \leq b$, $1 \leq j \leq k$.

Consider any message $m = (s, a)$; since $p(E = e) = 1/b$ for any $e$, we have the equation

$$\overline{v_m} = \frac{\ell}{b} \sum_{e \in \mathcal{E}, e(s)=a} \overline{e} = \frac{1}{\ell}(\overline{X} - \overline{v_s}) + \overline{m}.$$

We write this equation with respect to the basis $\mathbf{B}$. Define $r_m = |\{e \in \mathcal{E}, e(s) = a\}|$, and for any $m' = (s', a')$, $s' \neq s$, define $\lambda_{mm'} = |\{e \in \mathcal{E}, e(s) = a, e(s') = a'\}|$. Then we obtain the following relation:

$$\frac{\ell}{b}(r_m \overline{m} + \sum_{m'=(s',a'),s'\neq s} \lambda_{mm'} \overline{m'}) = \overline{m} + \frac{1}{\ell} \sum_{m'=(s',a'),s'\neq s} \overline{m'}.$$

Extracting the coefficient of $\overline{m}$, we see that $r_m = b/\ell$. Then extracting the coefficient of any $\overline{m'}$ ($m' = (s', a')$, $s' \neq s$), we see that $\lambda_{mm'} = b/\ell^2$. Since $m$ is an arbitrary message, it follows that the authentication matrix $M$ is an $OA(\ell, k, \lambda)$.

Conversely, suppose we start with an orthogonal array $OA(\ell, k, \lambda)$. Use each row as an authentication rule with equal probability $1/(\lambda \ell^2)$. Then we obtain a code with $P_{d_0} = P_{d_1} = 1/\ell$.

We summarize the above discussion in the following theorem, which complements Theorem 2.3.

**Theorem 3.1** *Suppose we have an authentication code without secrecy in which $P_{d_0} = P_{d_1} = k/v = 1/\ell$. Then $b \geq k(\ell - 1) + 1$, and equality occurs if and only if the authentication matrix is an orthogonal array $OA(\ell, k, \lambda)$ where $\lambda = (k(\ell - 1) + 1)/\ell^2$ and the authentication rules are used with equal probability.*

# 4    General authentication codes

Suppose there is an authentication code for $k$ source states, having $b$ encoding rules and $v$ messages, such that $P_{d_0} = k/v$ and $P_{d_1} = (k - 1)/(v - 1)$. Recalling Theorem 2.5, we know that $b \geq v(v - 1)/(k(k - 1))$ and equality can occur only if the encoding matrix is a $(v, k, 1)-$BIBD. Here, we consider the case of equality, i.e. $b = v(v - 1)/(k(k - 1))$.

From Theorem 2.4, it must be the case that

$$\sum_{\{e:m,m' \in M(e)\}} p(E = e)p(S = e^{-1}(m)) = \sum_{\{e:m,m^* \in M(e)\}} p(E = e)p(S = e^{-1}(m))$$

for all $m \neq m', m \neq m^*$. As noted earlier, since $b = v(v-1)/(k(k-1))$, it follows that $|\{e : m, m' \in M(e)\}| = 1$ for all $m \neq m'$. Hence, it follows that

$$p(E = e)p(S = s) = p(E = e')p(S = s')$$

if $e(s) = e'(s')$.

For any $m \in \mathcal{M}$, let

$$x_m = \sum_{\{e:m \in M(e)\}} p(E = e)p(S = e^{-1}(m)).$$

Then,

$$p(S = s)p(E = e) = \frac{x_m}{r}$$

for all $e, s$ such that $e(s) = m$ (recall that $r = (v-1)/(k-1)$ is the number of encoding rules in which any message $m$ occurs). Also, note that $\sum_{m \in \mathcal{M}} x_m = 1$.

Now, for any $e \in \mathcal{E}$, we have

$$p(E = e) = \sum_{s \in S} p(E = e)p(S = s) = \sum_{m \in M(e)} \frac{x_m}{r}. \tag{3}$$

Fix a message $m_0$. Now, applying Theorem 2.1 and Equation (3), we get the following:

$$\frac{k}{v} = \sum_{\{e:m_0 \in M(e)\}} p(E = e)$$

$$= \sum_{\{e:m_0 \in M(e)\}} \sum_{m \in M(e)} \frac{x_m}{r}$$

$$= x_{m_0} + \frac{1}{r} \sum_{m \in \mathcal{M}, m \neq m_0} x_m$$

$$= (1 - \frac{1}{r})x_{m_0} + \frac{1}{r}$$

since $\sum_{m \in \mathcal{M}} x_m = 1$. Solving for $x_{m_0}$, we get

$$x_{m_0} = (\frac{k}{v} - \frac{1}{r})\frac{r}{r-1} = \frac{r}{bk}.$$

This quantity is independent of $m_0$, so we have

$$p(E = e)p(S = s) = \frac{1}{bk}$$

for all $s \in S, e \in \mathcal{E}$. Fixing $e$ and summing over $s$, we get $p(E = e) = 1/b$ for every $e \in \mathcal{E}$. Similarly, fixing $s$ and summing over $e$, we get $p(S = s) = 1/k$ for every $s \in S$. Hence both the set of source states and the set of encoding rules must be equiprobable in order to obtain the desired deception probabilities.

Summarizing this discussion, we have our main theorem.

**Theorem 4.1** *Suppose we have an authentication code in which* $P_{d_0} = k/v$ *and* $P_{d_1} = (k-1)/(v-1)$. *Then* $b \geq (v^2 - v)/(k^2 - k)$, *and equality occurs if and only if the rows of the encoding matrix (taken as unordered sets) form a* $(v, k, 1)-BIBD$, *and both the source states and encoding rules are equiprobable.*

We can extend this result to include codes that provide perfect secrecy. The following theorem follows immediately from Theorem 2.5 and [St2, Theorem 6.4].

**Theorem 4.2** *Suppose we have an authentication code which provides perfect secrecy and in which* $P_{d_0} = k/v$ *and* $P_{d_1} = (k-1)/(v-1)$. *Then* $b \geq (v^2 - v)/(k^2 - k)$, *and equality occurs if and only if* $v - 1 \equiv 0 \bmod k(k-1)$, *there exists a* $(v, k, 1)-BIBD$, *and both the source states and encoding rules are equiprobable.*

# Acknowledgements

This research was supported by NSERC grant A9287 and by the Center for Communication and Information Science at the University of Nebraska.

This paper is a preliminary version. A final version has been submitted for publication in Designs, Codes and Cryptography.

# References

[Ma] J. L. Massey. *Cryptography – a selective survey*, in *Digital Communications*, North-Holland (pub.) (1986), 3–21.

[Si1] G. J. Simmons. *Message authentication: a game on hypergraphs*, Congr. Numer. **45** (1984), 161–192.

[Si2] G. J. Simmons. *Authentication theory / coding theory*, Lecture Notes in Comput. Sci. **196** (1985), 411–432 (proceedings of CRYPTO 84).

[St1] D. R. Stinson. *Some constructions and bounds for authentication codes*, J. Cryptology **1** (1988), 37–51.

[St2] D. R. Stinson. *The combinatorics of authentication and secrecy codes*, J. Cryptology **2** (1990), 23–49.

# Universal hashing and authentication codes

D. R. Stinson
Computer Science and Engineering
University of Nebraska
Lincoln, NE 68588-0115
stinson@bibd.unl.edu

### Abstract

In this paper, we study the application of universal hashing to the construction of unconditionally secure authentication codes without secrecy. This idea is most useful when the number of authenticators is exponentially small compared to the number of possible source states (plaintext messages). We formally define some new classes of hash functions and then prove some new bounds and give some general constructions for these classes of hash functions. Then we discuss the implications to authentication codes.

# 1   Introduction

In this paper, we study the application of universal hashing to the construction of unconditionally secure authentication codes without secrecy. This idea is due to Wegman and Carter [We], who gave a construction which is useful when the number of authenticators is exponentially small compared to the number of possible source states (plaintext messages). We generalize the Wegman and Carter construction by formally defining some new classes of hash functions. We prove some new bounds and give some general constructions for these classes of hash functions. Then we discuss the implications to authentication codes. We are able to decrease the key *length* by a factor of four compared to the Wegman and Carter construction, while maintaining the same security.

The paper is organized as follows. In this introduction we give an informal discussion of the motivation for this paper. Section 2 is a brief review of the necessary background of authentication codes. Section 3 gives relevant definitions from universal hashing. Section 4 presents proofs of new lower bounds on the number of hash functions in certain types of universal classes and gives the basic construction for authentication codes from universal classes of hash functions. Section 5 gives a variety of new constructions for universal classes of hash functions. In Section 6, we bring all the theory together and discuss its implications to the construction of authentication codes. Section 7 makes further comments and discusses open questions.

J. Feigenbaum (Ed.): Advances in Cryptology - CRYPTO '91, LNCS 576, pp. 74-85, 1992.
© Springer-Verlag Berlin Heidelberg 1992

Here are couple of hypothetical examples to motivate the problems we study. Suppose we have an authentication code with $k$ possible source states and $\ell$ possible authenticators. That is, we wish to authenticate a $\log k$-bit message with a $\log \ell$-bit authenticator. An opponent who plays either impersonation or substitution can deceive the transmitter with a probability of at least $1/\ell$ (in either case).

One important point is that $k$ and $\ell$ are independent parameters. $k$ is the number of possible source states; $\ell$ is a security parameter. For purposes of discussion, we identify two "reasonable" situations:

case 1 $k = 2^{20}$, $\ell = 2^{20}$

case 2 $k = 2^{2560}$, $\ell = 2^{20}$

Researchers have generally concentrated on the construction of codes which ensure that the opponent's deception probabilities are limited to these lower bounds. The main tool for constructing such codes has been a structure from combinatorial design theory called an orthogonal array (or equivalent structures, such as mutually orthogonal Latin squares, transversal designs or nets). Codes constructed by this method contain the minimum possible number of encoding rules, which is an important consideration since the encoding rule is secret information that must be exchanged over a secure channel before the transmission of a message.

In this paper, we shall use the language of orthogonal arrays. An $OA(n, k, \lambda)$ is a $\lambda n^2 \times k$ array of $n$ symbols, such that in any two columns of the array every one of the possible $n^2$ pairs of symbols occurs in exactly $\lambda$ rows. It is shown in [St1] that an $OA(n, k, \lambda)$ gives rise to an authentication code for $k$ source states, with $n$ authenticators and $\lambda n^2 \times k$ encoding rules (each row of the array gives rise in an obvious way to an encoding rule which assigns an authenticator to every possible source state, and the encoding rules are each used with equal probability). It has been known since 1945 (see [Pl]) that if an $OA(n, k, \lambda)$ exists, then

$$\lambda \geq \frac{k(n-1)+1}{n^2}.$$

It follows that $\lambda n^2 \geq n^2$ if $k \leq n+1$ and $\lambda n^2 \geq k(n-1)+1$ if $k \geq n+1$ ($\lambda n^2$ is the number of encoding rules in the resulting code).

In case 1, we can obtain a code with $2^{40}$ encoding rules; i.e. 40 bits of key are required. In case 2, the minimum number of encoding rules using this method is $2^{2560}(2^{20}-1)+1$, or about 2580 bits of key.

The observation of Wegman and Carter [We] is that by *not* requiring the deception probabilities to be the theoretical minimum (i.e. $1/\ell$), one can sometimes reduce the number of encoding rules significantly, at least in the case where $k \gg \ell$.

# 2 Authentication codes

The general theory of of unconditional authentication has been developed by Simmons (see e.g. [Si1] and [Si2]), and has been extensively studied in recent years. In this section, we will give a brief review of some relevant known results concerning authentication without secrecy.

In the usual model for authentication, there are three participants: a *transmitter*, a *receiver*, and an *opponent*. The transmitter wants to communicate some information to the receiver using a public communications channel. The *source state* (or plaintext) is encrypted to obtain the *message* (ciphertext), which is sent through the channel. An *encoding rule* (or key) $e$ defines the message $e(s)$ to be sent to communicate any source state $s$. Each encoding rule will be a one-to-one function from the source space to the message space. We assume the transmitter has a key source from which he obtains a key. Prior to any messages being sent, this key is communicated to the receiver by means of a secure channel.

We will use the following notation. Let $S$ be a set of $k$ source states; let $\mathcal{M}$ be a set of $v$ messages; and let $\mathcal{E}$ be a set of encoding rules. Since each encoding rule is a one-to-one function from $S$ to $\mathcal{M}$, we can represent a code by an $|\mathcal{E}| \times k$ matrix, where the rows are indexed by encoding rules, the columns are indexed by source states, and the entry in row $e$ and column $s$ is $e(s)$. We call this matrix the *encoding matrix*. For any encoding rule $e \in \mathcal{E}$, define $M(e) = \{e(s) : s \in S\}$, i.e. the set of valid messages under encoding rule $e$. For an encoding rule $e$, and a message $m \in M(e)$, define $e^{-1}(m) = s$ if $e(s) = m$.

In this paper, we are studying authentication codes without secrecy. This means that $e(s) = e'(s')$ only if $s = s'$; i.e. the message uniquely determines the source state, irrespective of the encoding rule being used. Hence, we can partition the set of messages $\mathcal{M}$ into $k$ subsets $\mathcal{M}_s$, $s \in S$, such that $\mathcal{M}_s = \{e(s) : e \in \mathcal{E}\}$.

Suppose the opponent has the ability to introduce messages into the channel and/or to modify existing messages. When the opponent places a (new) message $m'$ into the channel, this is called *impersonation*. When the opponent sees a message $m$ and changes it to a message $m' \neq m$, this is called *substitution*. In either case, his goal is to have $m'$ accepted as authentic by the receiver. That is, if $e$ is the encoding rule being used (which is *not* known to the opponent), then the opponent is hoping that $m' = e(s)$ for some source state $s$.

We assume that there is some probability distribution on the source states, which is known to all the participants. Given the probability distributions on the source states, the receiver and transmitter will choose a probability distribution for $\mathcal{E}$, called an *encoding strategy*. Once the transmitter/receiver have chosen the encoding strategy, it is possible to determine, for $i = 0, 1$ a probability denoted $P_{d_i}$, which is the probability that the opponent can deceive the transmitter/receiver by impersonation and substitution, respectively.

It is not difficult to show that $P_{d_0} \geq k/v$ and that $P_{d_0} = k/v$ only if $|\mathcal{M}_s| = v/k$ for every source state $s$ [Si1]. In this paper, we will confine our attention to codes in which $P_{d_0} = k/v$. In this situation, we can define a set $\mathcal{A}$ of $\ell = v/k$ *authenticators* and a mapping $\phi : \mathcal{M} \to \mathcal{A}$ such that, for every $s \in \mathcal{S}$, $\{\phi(m) : m \in \mathcal{M}_s\} = \mathcal{A}$. We can then obtain an isomorphic code by defining for every encoding rule $e$ an *authentication rule* $e^\phi$ defined by $e^\phi(s) = \phi(e(s))$ for every source state $s$. In this new code, every message consists of a source state concatenated with an authenticator from $\mathcal{A}$; i.e. $m = (s, e^\phi(s))$. In terms of $\ell = |\mathcal{A}|$, we have $P_{d_0} \geq 1/\ell$. It then follows that $P_{d_1} \geq 1/\ell$, as well [St2].

Codes with $P_{d_0} = P_{d_1} = 1/\ell$ are in fact equivalent to orthogonal arrays, as follows.

**Theorem 2.1** *[St4] Suppose we have an authentication code without secrecy in which $P_{d_0} = P_{d_1} = k/v = 1/\ell$. Then $b \geq k(\ell - 1) + 1$, and equality occurs if and only if the authentication matrix is an orthogonal array $OA(\ell, k, \lambda)$ where $\lambda = (k(\ell - 1) + 1)/\ell^2$ and the authentication rules are used with equal probability.*

# 3  Universal hashing

Universal classes of hash functions were introduced by Carter and Wegman [Ca], and were studied further by Sarwate [Sa], Wegman and Carter [We] and Stinson [St3]. In this paper, we are interested in the application of universal hashing to authentication codes. First, let us review the relevant definitions.

Let $A$ and $B$ be finite sets, and denote $a = |A|$ and $b = |B|$, where $a \geq b$. A function $h : A \to B$ will be termed a *hash function*. For a hash function $h$, and for $x, y \in A$, $x \neq y$, define $\delta_h(x, y) = 1$ if $h(x) = h(y)$, and $\delta_h(x, y) = 0$ otherwise. That is, $\delta_h(x, y) = 1$ if and only if the hashed values of $x$ and $y$ collide. For a finite set $H$ of hash functions, define $\delta_H(x,y) = \sum_{h \in H} \delta_h(x,y)$. Hence, $\delta_H(x,y)$ counts the number of hash functions in $H$ under which $x$ and $y$ collide.

The idea of a universal class of hash functions is to define a collection $H$ of hash functions in such a way that a random choice of a function $h \in H$ yields a low probability that any two distinct inputs $x$ and $y$ will collide when their hashed values are computed using the function $h$. Note that this probability can be computed to be $\delta_H(x,y)/|H|$. By choosing $H$ suitably, it is possible to make this probability small for *all* choices of $x$ and $y$.

However, for the purpose of practical applications, it is important not only to have $\delta_H(x,y)/|H|$ small for every $x$ and $y$, but $|H|$ should be small as well.

First, let's consider $\delta_H(x,y)$. We state without proof a bound that was noted in [Sa, p. 42].

**Theorem 3.1** *For any class $H$ of hash functions from $A$ to $B$, there exist distinct elements $x,y \in A$ such that $\delta_H(x,y) \geq |H|(a - b)/(b(a - 1))$, where $a = |A|$ and $b = |B|$.*

Here now are two definitions of classes of hash functions.

1. Let $\epsilon$ be a positive real number. $H$ is $\epsilon-almost$ $universal_2$ (or $\epsilon - AU_2$) if $\delta_H(x,y) \leq \epsilon|H|$ for all $x,y \in A$, $x \neq y$.

2. Let $\epsilon$ be a positive real number. $H$ is $\epsilon-almost$ $strongly$-$universal_2$ (or $\epsilon - ASU_2$) if the following two conditions are satisfied:

   (a) for every $x_1 \in A$ and for every $y_1 \in B$, $|\{h \in H : h(x_1) = y_1\}| = |H|/|B|$

   (b) for every $x_1, x_2 \in A$ ($x_1 \neq x_2$) and for every $y_1, y_2 \in B$,

   $$|\{h \in H : h(x_1) = y_1, h(x_2) = y_2\}| \leq \epsilon|H|/|B|.$$

The first definition is saying that the probability of collision is at most $\epsilon$ for any two inputs $x$ and $y$. The second definition says that any input $x_1$ is mapped to any hashed value $y_1$ with probability $1/b$; and given that $x_1$ is mapped to $y_1$, the conditional probability that $x_2$ is mapped to $y_2$ is at most $\epsilon$, for any $x_2, y_2, x_2 \neq x_1$.

Special cases of these definitions have been previously studied in the literature. For example, $(a - b)/(ab - b) - AU_2$ has been called *optimally universal* [Sa], $(1/b) - AU_2$

has been called *universal* [Ca], and $(1/b) - ASU_2$ has been called *strongly universal* [We]. Note that in an $\epsilon - ASU_2$ class, it must be the case that $\epsilon \geq 1/b$.

$\epsilon - ASU_2$ classes of hash functions can be used for authentication. If we have such a class $H$ of hash functions from $A$ to $B$, then we can think of the elements of $A$ as source states and the elements of $B$ as authenticators. Each hash function gives rise to an encoding rule, and the encoding rules are used with equal probability. The following result is immediate.

**Theorem 3.2** *If there exists an $\epsilon - ASU_2$ class $H$ of hash functions from $A$ to $B$, then there exists an authentication code for $|A|$ source states, having $|B|$ authenticators and $|H|$ encoding rules, such that $P_{d_0} = 1/|B|$ and $P_{d_1} \leq \epsilon$.*

# 4 Lower bounds on the size of classes of hash functions

In view of the fact that classes of hash functions give rise to authentication codes, it is of interest to compute lower bounds on the number of hash functions required. We present two lower bounds in this section, which generalize some previously known bounds. The proofs use a nice variance technique, but are omitted from this extended abstract due to space limitations.

**Theorem 4.1** *If there exists an $\epsilon - AU_2$ class $H$ of hash functions from $A$ to $B$, where $a = |A|$ and $b = |B|$, then*

$$|H| \geq \frac{a(b-1)}{a(\epsilon b - 1) + b^2(1 - \epsilon)}.$$

By substituting $\epsilon = 1/b$ and $\epsilon = (a - b)/(ab - b)$ into the above bound, respectively, we obtain the following corollary.

**Corollary 4.1** *[St3] Suppose $H$ is a class of hash functions from $A$ to $B$, where $a = |A|$ and $b = |B|$. If $H$ is $U_2$, then $|H| \geq a/b$. If $H$ is $OU_2$, then $|H| \geq (a - 1)/(b - 1)$.*

We next present a lower bound on the number of hash functions in a $\epsilon - ASU_2$ class.

**Theorem 4.2** *If there exists an $\epsilon - ASU_2$ class $H$ of hash functions from $A$ to $B$, where $a = |A|$ and $b = |B|$, then*

$$|H| \geq 1 + \frac{a(b-1)^2}{b\epsilon(a-1) + b - a}.$$

In the case $\epsilon = 1/b$, we get the following corollary.

**Corollary 4.2** *[St3] If there exists an $SU_2$ class $H$ of hash functions from $A$ to $B$, where $a = |A|$ and $b = |B|$, then $|H| \geq 1 + a(b-1)$. Further, $|H| = 1 + a(b-1)$ if and only if there is an $OA(b, a, \lambda)$, where $\lambda = (a(b-1) + 1)/a^2$.*

# 5 Constructions

In this section, we give some direct and recursive constructions for universal classes of hash functions. First, we recall some direct constructions that are special cases of constructions from [St3] and [Ca].

**Theorem 5.1** *Let $q$ be a prime power. Then there exists a $U_2$ class $H$ of hash functions from $A$ to $B$, where $|A| = q^2$, $|B| = q$ and $|H| = q$ (hence $\epsilon = 1/q$).*

**Proof:** Let $A = GF(q) \times GF(q)$, let $B = GF(q)$ and let $H = \{h_x : x \in GF(q)\}$, where $h_x(a, b) = b - ax$. □

**Theorem 5.2** *Let $q$ be a prime power. Then there exists an $SU_2$ class $H$ of hash functions from $A$ to $B$, where $|A| = q^2$, $|B| = q$ and $|H| = q^3$ (hence $\epsilon = 1/q$).*

**Proof:** Let $A = GF(q) \times GF(q)$, let $B = GF(q)$ and let $H = \{h_{xyz} : x, y, z \in GF(q)\}$, where $h_{xyz}(a, b) = x + ay + bz$. □

**Theorem 5.3** *Let $q$ be a prime power. Then there exists an $SU_2$ class $H$ of hash functions from $A$ to $B$, where $|A| = q$, $|B| = q$ and $|H| = q^2$ (hence $\epsilon = 1/q$).*

**Proof:** Let $A = B = GF(q)$ and let $H = \{h_{xy} : x, y \in GF(q)\}$, where $h_{xy}(a) = x + ay$. $\square$

Now we present some methods of combining classes of hash functions which generalize similar constructions from [We] and [Sa].

**Theorem 5.4 (Cartesian Product)** *If there exists an* $\epsilon - AU_2$ *class* $H$ *of hash functions from* $A$ *to* $B$, *then, for any integer* $i \geq 1$, *there exists an* $\epsilon - AU_2$ *class* $H^i$ *of hash functions from* $A^i$ *to* $B^i$ *with* $|H| = |H^i|$.

**Proof:** For every $h \in H$, define a hash function $h^i : A^i \to B^i$ by the rule $h^i(a_1, \ldots, a_i) = (h(a_1), \ldots, h(a_i))$. Define $H^i = \{h^i : h \in H\}$. $\square$

**Theorem 5.5 (Composition 1)** *For* $i = 1, 2$, *suppose there exists an* $\epsilon_i - AU_2$ *class* $H_i$ *of hash functions from* $A_i$ *to* $B_i$, *where* $A_2 = B_1$. *Then there exists an* $\epsilon - AU_2$ *class* $H$ *of hash functions from* $A_1$ *to* $B_2$, *where* $\epsilon = \epsilon_1 + \epsilon_2$ *and* $|H| = |H_1| \times |H_2|$.

**Proof:** For every $h_i \in H_i$, $i = 1, 2$, we define a hash function $h : A_1 \to B_2$ by the rule $h(a) = h_2(h_1(a))$. Let $H$ be the set of all such hash functions. For any two inputs, the probability of collision is at most $\epsilon_1 + (1 - \epsilon_1)\epsilon_2 < \epsilon_1 + \epsilon_2$. $\square$

**Theorem 5.6 (Composition 2)** *Suppose* $H_1$ *is an* $\epsilon_1 - AU_2$ *class of hash functions from* $A_1$ *to* $B_1$, *and suppose* $H_2$ *is an* $\epsilon_2 - ASU_2$ *class of hash functions from* $B_1$ *to* $B_2$. *Then there exists an* $\epsilon - ASU_2$ *class* $H$ *of hash functions from* $A_1$ *to* $B_2$, *where* $\epsilon = \epsilon_1 + \epsilon_2$ *and* $|H| = |H_1| \times |H_2|$.

**Proof:** For every $h_i \in H_i$, $i = 1, 2$, define a hash function $h : A_1 \to B_2$ by the rule $h(a) = h_2(h_1(a))$. Let $H$ be the set of all such hash functions. Let $x_1, x_2 \in A_1$ ($x_1 \neq x_2$) and let $y_1, y_2 \in B_2$. How many functions in $H$ map $x_1$ to $y_1$ and $x_2$ to $y_2$? Suppose first that $y_1 = y_2$. Let $p$ denote that probability that $x_1$ and $x_2$ collide under a hash function from $H_1$. Then the maximum number is at most

$$p|H_1| \times \frac{|H_2|}{b} + (1 - p)|H_1| \times \frac{\epsilon_2|H_2|}{b} \leq (\epsilon_1 + \epsilon_2)|H_1| \times \frac{|H_2|}{b}.$$

If $y_1 \neq y_2$ then the number is less. Since $p \leq \epsilon_1$, it follows that we have an $\epsilon - ASU_2$ class with $\epsilon = \epsilon_1 + \epsilon_2$. $\square$

# 6 The application of universal hashing to authentication

We now combine the constructions of the previous section to obtain authentication codes.

**Theorem 6.1** *Let $q$ be a prime power and let $i \geq 1$ be an integer. Then there exists an $(i/q) - AU_2$ class of $q^i$ hash functions from $A$ to $B$, where $|A| = q^{2^i}$ and $|B| = q$.*

**Proof:** Apply Theorems 5.1, 5.4 and 5.5. $\square$

**Theorem 6.2** *Let $q$ be a prime power and let $i \geq 1$ be an integer. Then there exists an $((i+1)/q) - ASU_2$ class of $q^{i+2}$ hash functions from $A$ to $B$, where $|A| = q^{2^i}$ and $|B| = q$.*

**Proof:** Apply Theorems 6.1, 5.3 and 5.6. $\square$

**Theorem 6.3** *Let $q$ be a prime power and let $i \geq 1$ be an integer. Then there exists an $(i/q^2 + 1/q) - ASU_2$ class of $q^{2i+3}$ hash functions from $A$ to $B$, where $|A| = q^{2^i}$ and $|B| = q$.*

**Proof:** Apply Theorems 6.1 (replacing $q$ by $q^2$), 5.2 and 5.6. $\square$

Let's look at the codes we can obtain via Theorem 3.2 for case 2 of the Introduction using the above results. If we apply Theorem 6.2 with $q = 2^{20}$ and $i = 7$, we get an authentication code with $2^{180}$ encoding rules in which $P_{d_0} = 2^{-20}$ and $P_{d_1} = 2^{-17}$. On the other hand, if we apply Theorem 6.3, we get an authentication code with $2^{340}$ encoding rules in which $P_{d_0} = 2^{-20}$ and $P_{d_1} < 2^{-19}$. On the other hand, if we require $P_{d_0} = P_{d_1} = 2^{-20}$ then Theorem 2.1 tells us that the number of encoding rules is at least $2^{2560}(2^{20} - 1) + 1 \approx 2^{2580}$. Hence, we obtain an enormous reduction in the size of the key space by increasing $P_{d_1}$ only slightly.

Taking logarithms, we can rephrase the above discussion by saying that authentication of a 2560-bit source with a 20-bit authenticator requires 180, 340 and 2580 bits of key, respectively.

The following bound, obtained from Theorem 6.2, is similar to that given in [We].

**Theorem 6.4** *There exists an authentication code for an $a'$-bit source with a $b'$-bit authenticator, obtaining deception probabilities $P_{d_0} = 2^{-b'}$ and $P_{d_1} = (\log a' - \log b' + 1)2^{-b'}$, with a key of length $(\log a' - \log b' + 2)b'$.*

**Proof:** Write $b = 2^{b'} = q$ and $a = 2^{a'} = b^{2^i}$. Then $i = \log a' - \log b'$. Apply Theorem 6.2. □

In Section 3 of [We], a similar construction for a $2/b - ASU_2$ class of hash functions is presented, in which $\log |H|$ is $4(b' + \log \log a') \log a'$. However, it appears to me that the analysis of $\epsilon$ too low by a factor of $\log a'$, and that the class is in fact an $\epsilon - ASU_2$ class where $\epsilon = (2 \log a')2^{-b'}$. With respect to our example of case 2, the key length would be about 1056. In general, our bound on the key length (Theorem 6.4) is lower by a factor of four.

# 7 Further comments and open questions

We have been emphasizing the application of hash functions to the construction of authentication codes with $k \gg \ell$. This is because previously known techniques are already quite good when $k$ and $\ell$ are even polynomially related. For, suppose we have an $\epsilon - ASU_2$ class $H$ of hash functions from $A$ to $B$ where $|A| = a(= k)$ and $|B| = b(= \ell)$. Consider the effect of increasing $\epsilon$ from $1/b$ to $2/b$ in the bound of Theorem 4.2. The ratio of the two bounds is about $(a + b)/b$. Hence, the potential for decreasing $|H|$ significantly is much greater when $a \gg b$.

The constructions for $\epsilon - ASU_2$ classes of hash functions given in Theorems 6.1 and 6.2 have $|H|$ considerably larger than the lower bound given in Theorem 4.2. There are relatively few situations where the bound of Theorem 4.2 is known to be met with equality. The only cases known to us are as follows. First, if $\epsilon = 1/b$, then the class is an $SU_2$ class and is equivlent to an orthogonal array $OA(b, a, \lambda)$, where $\lambda = (a(b-1)+1)/a^2$. (Corollary 4.2). Some infinite classes of these are known to exist; see [St3].

The only examples with $\epsilon > 1/b$ known to us are given below as Theorem 7.1. The construction uses a *balanced incomplete block design*, or BIBD. A $(v, k, \lambda)-$BIBD is a pair $(X, \mathcal{A})$, where $|X| = v$ is a set of elements called *points* and $\mathcal{A}$ is a family of $k-$subsets of $X$ (called *blocks*) such that every pair of points occurs in exactly $\lambda$ blocks. It is not difficult to see that every point occurs in precisely $r = \lambda(v - 1)/(k - 1)$ blocks and that the total number of blocks is $b = \lambda v(v - 1)/(k(k - 1))$. A $(v, k, \lambda)-$BIBD is *resolvable* if the blocks can be partitioned into $r$ parallel classes, each of which consists of $v/k$ blocks that partition the set of points.

**Theorem 7.1** *Suppose there exists a resolvable $(v, k, 1)-BIBD$. Then there exists an $\epsilon - ASU_2$ class $H$ of hash functions from $A$ to $B$, where $|A| = (v-1)/(k-1)$, $|B| = v/k$, $\epsilon = 1/k$ and $|H| = v$.*

**Remark:** In terms of $a = |A|$ and $b = |B|$, $|H| = b(a-1)/(a-b)$.

**Proof:** Let $(X, \mathcal{A})$ be the hypothesized $(v, k, 1)-BIBD$, and let $\mathcal{P}_1, \ldots, \mathcal{P}_r$ be the $r$ parallel classes. Name the blocks in each $\mathcal{P}_i$ as $P_{ij}$, $1 \leq j \leq v/k$. Let $A = \{1, \ldots, r\}$ and $B = \{1, \ldots, v/k\}$. For each point $x \in X$, we define a hash function $h_x$ by the rule $h_x(i) = j$ if and only if $x \in P_{ij}$. □

The following example illustrates the construction of Theorem 7.1 with $v = 8$, $k = 2$.

**Example 7.1** *A $1/2-ASU_2$ class of 8 hash functions from $\{1, 2, 3, 4, 5, 6, 7\}$ to $\{1, 2, 3, 4\}$:*

|       | 1 | 2 | 3 | 4 | 5 | 6 | 7 |
|-------|---|---|---|---|---|---|---|
| $h_1$ | 1 | 1 | 1 | 1 | 1 | 1 | 1 |
| $h_2$ | 1 | 2 | 3 | 2 | 4 | 4 | 3 |
| $h_3$ | 3 | 1 | 2 | 3 | 2 | 4 | 4 |
| $h_4$ | 4 | 3 | 1 | 2 | 3 | 2 | 4 |
| $h_5$ | 4 | 4 | 3 | 1 | 2 | 3 | 2 |
| $h_6$ | 2 | 4 | 4 | 3 | 1 | 2 | 3 |
| $h_7$ | 3 | 2 | 4 | 4 | 3 | 1 | 2 |
| $h_8$ | 2 | 3 | 2 | 4 | 4 | 3 | 1 |

For applications to authentication codes, the construction of Theorem 7.1 is not of much use, since $a \approx b$ and many other constuctions are known in this case.

A very interesting open problem would be to find examples of $\epsilon - ASU_2$ classes of hash functions $H$ with $\epsilon > 1/b$ and $a \gg b$, such that $|H|$ meets the lower bound of Theorem 4.2 with equality.

# Acknowledgements

This research was supported by NSERC grant A9287 and by the Center for Communication and Information Science at the University of Nebraska.

This paper is a preliminary version. A final version has been submitted for publication in the IEEE Transactions on Information Theory.

# References

[Ca] J. L Carter and M. N. Wegman. *Universal classes of hash functions*, J. Comput. System Sci. **18** (1979), 143–154.

[Pl] R. L. Plackett and J. P. Burman. *The design of optimum multi-factorial experiments*, Biometrika **33** (1945), 305–325.

[Sa] D. V. Sarwate. *A note on universal classes of hash functions*, Inform. Proc. Letters **10** (1980), 41–45.

[Si1] G. J. Simmons. *Message authentication: a game on hypergraphs*, Congr. Numer. **45** (1984), 161–192.

[Si2] G. J. Simmons. *A survey of information authentication*, Proc. of the IEEE **76** (1988), 603–620.

[St1] D. R. Stinson. *Some constructions and bounds for authentication codes*, J. Cryptology **1** (1988), 37–51.

[St2] D. R. Stinson. *The combinatorics of authentication and secrecy codes*, J. Cryptology **2** (1990), 23–49.

[St3] D. R. Stinson. *Combinatorial techniques for universal hashing*, submitted to J. Comput. System Sci.

[St4] D. R. Stinson. *Combinatorial characterizations of authentication codes*, submitted to Designs, Codes and Cryptography (a preliminary version appears elsewhere in these proceedings).

[We] M. N. Wegman and J. L. Carter. *New hash functions and their use in authentication and set equality*, J. Comput. System Sci. **22** (1981), 265–279.

# On Correlation-immune functions [1]

## P. Camion, C. Carlet, P. Charpin & N. Sendrier

INRIA, Domaine de Voluceau, Rocquencourt,
BP 105, 78153 Le Chesnay Cedex, FRANCE
camion@hades.inria.fr

### Abstract

We establish the link between *correlation-immune* functions and *orthogonal arrays*. We give a recursive definition of any correlation-immune function of maximal degree. We describe the set of quadratic balanced correlation-immune functions of maximal order. Some constructions are then deduced.

# 1 Introduction

In a general type of running-key generator, the output sequences of $m$ Linear Feedback Shift Registers are taken as arguments of a single non linear combining function $f$. If the function $f$ is not properly chosen, it can happen that the generator structure is not resistant to a *correlation attack*: there is a statistical dependence between any small subset of the $m$ subgenerator sequences and the keystream sequence (cf. an example in [8], p. 116).

A function $f$ which provides an immunity to a correlation attack is called *a correlation-immune function*. The $k$th-order correlation-immune functions (denoted $k$-CI functions) were introduced by T. SIEGENTHALER in [11]. X. GUO-ZHEN and J.L. MASSEY later gave an equivalent definition of the $k$-CI functions, using the WALSH transform of the boolean functions. It is their definition, recalled in Section 2, which is used in the present paper.

We wish to show that Algebraic Coding Theory provides an alternative point of view for the concept of correlation-immunity. We present two new definitions of the $k$-CI functions, related to coding theory, and deduce some constructions.

In Section 3 we point out that a $k$-CI function is an *orthogonal array of strength $k$*. We later give a recursive definition of any $k$-CI function of maximal degree. Using algebraic properties - which are in fact properties of REED and MULLER codes (RM-codes) and subcodes of RM-codes - we show that the recursive definition permits to obtain explicitly some $k$-CI functions.

In Section 4 we present some constructions. Using the recursive definition, we describe

---

[1] Research supported by CNET-FRANCE, n.885B016 007909245/PAA

J. Feigenbaum (Ed.): Advances in Cryptology - CRYPTO '91, LNCS 576, pp. 86-100, 1992.
© Springer-Verlag Berlin Heidelberg 1992

a large class of 1-CI functions of maximal degree. We after give a full description of the set of the quadratric balanced correlation-immune function of maximal order. In the last paragraph we propose, in fact, an algorithm producing some balanced correlation-immune functions of maximal order.

The present paper is a shortened version of the scientific report [3]; the reader can find in [3] more explanations and examples.

# 2 Correlation-immune functions

Let $\mathbf{F} = GF(2)$ and $\mathbf{G} = \mathbf{F}^m$. An element $x$ of $\mathbf{G}$ is an $m$-tuple $(x_1, \ldots, x_m)$ over $\mathbf{F}$. Let $x \in \mathbf{G}$ and $\lambda \in \mathbf{G}$, and define their dot product as: $x \cdot \lambda = x_1\lambda_1 + \ldots + x_m\lambda_m \in \mathbf{F}$.

Let $f$ be a boolean function of $m$ binary variables. The *Walsh transform* of $f(x)$ is the real-valued function over $\mathbf{G}$:

$$F(\lambda) = \sum_{x \in \mathbf{G}} f(x)\,(-1)^{x \cdot \lambda} \ . \tag{1}$$

The set of the elements $x \in \mathbf{G}$ such that $f(x) = 1$ is a binary array $M \times m$, where $M$ is the weight of the value of $f$. This array is the *truth-table* of $f$.

In this paper, the weight of a binary vector $u$ is always *the Hamming weight*, ie the number of nonzero components in $u$, and is denoted by $W(u)$.

**Definition 2.1** [7] *Let $k \in [1, m-1]$. The function $f$ is $k$th-order correlation immune (ie is a $k$-CI function) if and only if its Walsh transform satisfies:*

$$F(\lambda) = 0, \quad for \ \ 1 \le W(\lambda) \le k \ , \tag{2}$$

*where $W(\lambda)$ denotes the Hamming weight of the binary $m$-tuple $\lambda$.*

In the following, we denote by $v(f)$ the binary vector $\{f(x) \mid x \in \mathbf{G}\}$ and we say that $v(f)$ is *the value of $f$*. In general we shall suppose that the value of a $k$-CI function $f$ is balanced, ie that $F(0) = 2^{m-1}$ ; we shall say that *the function $f$ is balanced*.

**Proposition 2.1** [11] *Let $f$ be a $k$-CI function. Let $d(f)$ be the degree of $f$. Then $d(f) \le m - k$. Moreover if $f$ is balanced then $d(f) < m - k$ unless $k = m - 1$ .*

Hence if $f$ is a $(m-2)$-CI function and is balanced , $f$ is an affine function. The only possible $(m-1)$-CI functions are [11]: $f(x) = x_1 + \ldots + x_m + c$ , $c \in \mathbf{F}$. In [11], T. SIEGENTHALER showed how to construct by iteration a limited family of $k$-CI functions : a $k$-CI function is obtained from two linear functions of $m - (k+1)$ variables.

# 3 Others definitions

## 3.1 Orthogonal arrays

The characterization given by X. GUO-ZEN and J.L. MASSEY [7] for correlation-immune functions, concept introduced by T. SIEGENTHALER [11] was taken as Definition 2.1. That characterization corresponds precisely to the one by P. DELSARTE of orthogonal arrays, concept introduced by C.R. RAO [10] - as we point out in Theorem 3.1 -.

**Definition 3.1** [6, Ch. 11] *An* $M \times m$ *matrix* $V$ *with entries from a set of* $q$ *elements is called an orthogonal array of size* $M$, $m$ *constraints,* $q$ *levels, strength* $k$, *and index* $\mu$ *if any set of* $k$ *columns of* $V$ *contains all* $q^k$ *possible row vectors exactly* $\mu$ *times. Such an array is denoted by* $(M, m, q, k)$ . *Clearly* $M = \mu q^k$ .

**Theorem 3.1** *A boolean function* $f$ *on* $G$ *is correlation immune of order* $k$ *if and only if its truth table is an orthogonal array* $(M, m, 2, k)$ .

*Proof:* Let $f$ be a boolean function of $m$ variables. Let $M$ be the weight of $v(f)$; let $T$ be the truth-table of $f$.

1. Suppose that $T$ is an orthogonal array $(M, m, 2, k)$; let $\mu = 2^{-k}M$. Let $\lambda \in G$ such that $W(\lambda) = k$. Then we have:

$$
\begin{aligned}
F(\lambda) &= \sum_{x \in G} f(x)\,(-1)^{x.\lambda} = \mu \sum_{y \in \mathbf{F}^k} (-1)^{W(y)} \\
&= \mu\,(\,|\,\{\, y \in \mathbf{F}^k \,;\, W(y)\ \text{is even}\,\}\,| - |\,\{\, y \in \mathbf{F}^k \,;\, W(y)\ \text{is odd}\,\}\,|\,) = 0 \ .
\end{aligned}
$$

It is clear that an orthogonal array $(M, m, 2, k)$ is also an orthogonal array $(M, m, 2, i)$ for $i \in [1, k]$. Hence $F(\lambda) = 0$ for all $\lambda$ such that $W(\lambda) \in [1, k]$. So $f$ satisfies (2).

2. Suppose that $f$ is a $k$-CI function. Let $\lambda \in G$ such that $W(\lambda) = k$. Define the projection $\pi : G \longmapsto \mathbf{F}^k$ as

$$\pi(x) = (x_i)_{i \in I} \quad , \quad I = \{\, i \in [1, m] \mid \lambda_i = 1 \,\} \ ,$$

and $\eta : \mathbf{F}^k \longmapsto \mathbf{Z}$ as

$$\eta(g) = |\,T_g\,| \quad , \quad T_g = \{\, x \in G \mid f(x) = 1, \pi(x) = g \,\} \ .$$

We define the *support* $s(x)$ of any element $x \in \mathbf{F}^m$ by: $s(x) = \{\, i \mid x_i \neq 0 \,\}$ . We now use the fact that $T$ is an orthogonal array $(M, m, 2, k)$ if and only if for any $\lambda \in G$ such that $W(\lambda) = k$ , then the value $\eta(g)$ defined above is $\eta(g) = 2^{-k}M$, for all $g \in \mathbf{F}^k$. For any $\lambda' \in \mathbf{G}$ with $s(\lambda') \subset s(\lambda)$ , we have:

$$F(\lambda') = \sum_{x \in T}(-1)^{\lambda'.x} = \sum_{g \in \mathbf{F}^k}\sum_{x \in T_g}(-1)^{\lambda'.x} = \sum_{g \in \mathbf{F}^k}\eta(g)\,(-1)^{\pi(\lambda').g} \quad .$$

On the other hand, denote by $H$ the abelian group $(\mathbf{F}^k, +)$ and consider the abelian group algebra $\mathbf{C}H$. An element $z \in \mathbf{C}H$ is denoted by $\sum_{g \in H}z_g X^g$ . The *Walsh-Fourier transform* $\hat{z}$ of $z$ is given by

$$\hat{z}_h = \sum_{g \in H}z_g(-1)^{h.g}, \quad \text{for all } h \in H \ .$$

Thus for $z = \sum_{g \in H}\eta(g)X^g$ , we observe that for every $\lambda'$ such that $s(\lambda') \subset s(\lambda)$ , then if $\pi(\lambda') = h$ , we have that $F(\lambda') = \hat{z}_h$ and therefore $\hat{z}_h = 0$ for every nonzero $h$. Hence inversing the Fourier transform $z \rightarrow \hat{z}$ , we obtain:

$$\eta(g) = 2^{-k}\sum_{g \in H}\hat{z}_h(-1)^{h.g} = 2^{-k}\hat{z}_0 = 2^{-k}\,M \quad . \quad \square$$

**Example 3.1** $m = 4$ , $M = 2^{m-1} = 8$ , $f(x) = x_1 + x_3 + x_4$ . *Let $V$ be the truth table of $f$; we study the transposed array :*

$$\tilde{V} = \begin{bmatrix} 1 & 1 & 0 & 0 & 0 & 0 & 1 & 1 \\ 0 & 1 & 0 & 1 & 0 & 1 & 0 & 1 \\ 0 & 0 & 1 & 1 & 0 & 0 & 1 & 1 \\ 0 & 0 & 0 & 0 & 1 & 1 & 1 & 1 \end{bmatrix} \begin{matrix} x_1 \\ x_2 \\ x_3 \\ x_4 \end{matrix}$$

*Each line of $\tilde{V}$ contains 4 times "0" and 4 times "1". Thus $f$ is an 1-CI function. Moreover any set of two lines of $\tilde{V}$ contains all 2-dimensional vectors exactly twice. So $f$ is an 2-CI function.*

## 3.2  A recursive definition

The correlation-immune functions of maximal degree (for a fixed order), the value of which is **balanced**, are more interesting in applications; for this reason, we have chosen to present our results with these hypotheses. From now on we only consider balanced correlation-immune functions.

**Definition 3.2** *A balanced $k$-CI function of $m$ variables is said to be a $ci(k, m)$ function; such a function is said to have the maximal degree if and only if $d(f) = m - (k+1)$. By convention a $ci(0, m)$ function is a balanced function the degree of which equals $m - 1$.*

For any $m$, we denote by $\mathcal{F}^m$ the set of boolean functions of $m$ variables $x_1, \ldots, x_m$. Let $f \in \mathcal{F}^m$ with degree $\leq m - 1$. Using the polynomial form of $f$, it is easy to prove that, after possibly permuting the indices, then $f$ can always be written as follows:

$$f = (x_m + 1)\, f_1 + x_m\, f_2 \qquad \begin{cases} f_1 \text{ and } f_2 \in \mathcal{F}^{m-1} \\ d(f_1) = d(f_2) = d(f) \\ d(f_1 + f_2) < d(f) \end{cases} \qquad (3)$$

**Theorem 3.2** *Let $f_1$ and $f_2$ be functions derived from $f$ by (3). Let $F_1$ and $F_2$ be respectively the Walsh transforms of $f_1$ and $f_2$. Then $f$ is a $ci(k, m)$ function if and only if:*

(i) *$f_1$ and $f_2$ are $ci(k - 1, m - 1)$ functions*

(ii) *For all $\lambda' \in \mathbf{F}'^{n-1}$ with $W(\lambda') = k$ we have:*

$$F_1(\lambda') + F_2(\lambda') = 0 \quad . \qquad (4)$$

*Moreover $f$ has maximal degree if and only if $f_1$ and $f_2$ have maximal degree.*

*Proof:* Let $\lambda \in \mathbf{F}^m$, $\lambda = (\lambda', \epsilon)$ with $\epsilon \in \mathbf{F}$ and $\lambda' \in \mathbf{F}^{m-1}$. Let $x' = (x_1, \ldots, x_{m-1})$. Then

$$F(\lambda) = \sum_{x \in G} f(x)(-1)^{x'.\lambda' + x_m.\epsilon} = \sum_{x_m = 0} f_1(x')(-1)^{x'.\lambda'} + \sum_{x_m = 1} f_2(x')(-1)^{x'.\lambda' + \epsilon};$$

$$F(\lambda) = F_1(\lambda') + (-1)^\epsilon F_2(\lambda') \quad . \qquad (5)$$

1. Suppose that $f$ satisfies (i) and (ii). In accordance with (5), we have:

$$F(0) = F_1(0) + F_2(0) = 2^{m-1} \quad ;$$

if $\lambda$ is such that $0 < W(\lambda') < k$ then $F(\lambda) = 0$, from (i); if $\lambda$ is such that $W(\lambda') = k$ and $\epsilon = 0$ then $F(\lambda) = 0$, from (ii). So $f$ is a $ci(m, k)$ function.

2. Suppose now that $f$ is a $ci(k, m)$ function. Then for all $\lambda = (\lambda', \epsilon)$ such that $W(\lambda) \in [1, k]$, formula (5) yields:

$$0 = F_1(\lambda') + (-1)^\epsilon F_2(\lambda') \quad . \qquad (6)$$

For $\lambda = (0, 1)$, we obtain $F_1(0) = F_2(0)$. Then $f_1$ and $f_2$ are balanced. If $0 < W(\lambda') < k$, we obtain: $F_1(\lambda') = F_2(\lambda')$ for $\epsilon = 1$ and $F_1(\lambda') = -F_2(\lambda')$ for $\epsilon = 0$. Then $F_1(\lambda') = F_2(\lambda') = 0$ - ie (i) is satisfied. If $W(\lambda') = k$ and $\epsilon = 0$, we obtain (ii) immediately from (6).

3. A $ci(k, m)$ function has maximal degree $m - (k + 1)$. A $ci(k - 1, m - 1)$ function has

maximal degree $(m-1)-k$. Since by definition $d(f)$ equals $d(f_1)$ and $d(f_2)$, then $f$ has maximal degree if and only if $f_1$ and $f_2$ have maximal degree. $\square$

REMARK : Theorem 3.2 means that a $ci(k,m)$ function, has its truth-table $T$ in the following form ($\tilde{T}$ is the transposed T):

$$
\tilde{T} \;=\;
\begin{array}{|c|c|}
\hline
\tilde{T}_1 & \tilde{T}_2 \\
\hline
0\;0\;\ldots\;0\;0 & 1\;1\;\ldots\;1\;1 \\
\hline
\end{array}
\qquad \text{where}
$$

- $T_1$ and $T_2$ are orthogonal arrays $(2^{m-2}, m-1, 2, k-1)$,
- let $\mu = 2^{m-k-1}$; let $u \in \mathbf{F}^k$ and a set of $k$ rows containing $a$ times $u$ in $\tilde{T}_1$ and $b$ times $u$ in $\tilde{T}_2$; then $a+b = \mu$.

## 3.3   Correlation-immune functions and Reed-Muller codes

Recall that $\mathbf{G} = \mathbf{F}^m$. The Reed-Muller code of length $2^m$ and order $r$, denoted by $R(r,m)$, can be identified with the set of the boolean functions of $m$ variables and of degree $\leq r$. The codewords are the values of the functions. Let $f \in \mathcal{F}^m$; the order of the correlation-immunity of $f$ is obtained in studying the weights of the coset $f + R(1,m)$: for each $\lambda \in \mathbf{G}$, the function $h_\lambda : x \in \mathbf{G} \longmapsto x.\lambda$ is an element of $R(1,m)$; then

$$
F(\lambda) = 0 \quad \Longleftrightarrow \quad W(\,v(f) + v(h_\lambda)\,) = 2^{m-1} \quad . \tag{7}
$$

Thus $f$ is $ci(k,m)$ if and only if for all $\lambda$, with $W(\lambda) < k$, then $f + h_\lambda$ has weight $2^{m-1}$. The writing of $f$ as in (3) means that $f_1$ and $f_2$ are in $R(d(f), m-1)$ and in a same coset of the code $R(d(f)-1, m-1)$. It appears in Theorem 3.2 that it will be interesting to know the codewords $g$ of weight $2^{m-2}$ of a coset $f_1 + R(d(f)-1, m-1)$ and, for such $g$'s the weights of the codewords of the coset $g + R(1,m)$. So it seems difficult to obtain the overall description of the set of the $ci(k,m)$ functions, because this problem is related with open problems on Reed-Muller codes. However some well-known properties may be used:

1. In Corollaries 4.1 and 4.2 we use some transformations which preserve a given coset and carry a balanced word in another balanced word.

2. We are able to easily construct $ci(1,m)$ functions, because the set of the $ci(0,m')$ functions is well-known for any $m'$. So we can prove in the following Section that Theorem 3.2 expresses a constructive definition of $k$-CI functions with maximal degree.

A $ci(0,m')$ function is a function of degree $m'-1$ and of $m'$ variables, the value of which has weight $2^{m'-1}$. The class of the functions $ci(0,m')$ was studied in [2] and [5];

it is very simple to construct such a function : let $V(g)$ be the truth-table of a function $g$ of $m'$ variables and of weight $2^{m'-1}$ . Then the degree of $g$ is $m' - 1$ if and only if there exists an hyperplane $H$ of $\mathbf{F}^{m'}$ such that the size of the set $V(g) \cap H$ is odd (see the construction of $f_1$ in Example 4.1). The number $N$ of such functions $g$ can be calculated with formulae given in [2]; for small values of $m'$, we obtain:

$m' = 3 \Rightarrow N = 56$ ; $m' = 4 \Rightarrow N = 12000$ ;

$m' = 5 \Rightarrow N = 582\ 284\ 160$ ;

$m' = 6\ , \Rightarrow N = 1.803.989.388.148.674.048$ .

# 4  Construction of correlation-immune functions

## 4.1  Extending an orthogonal array to a stronger one

In accordance with Theorem 3.1 and 3.2, we shall construct a $k$-CI function by extending the truth-table of a $(k-1)$-CI function to an orthogonal array of strength $k$. So we define two simple applications on $\mathcal{F}^m$ which preserves the zeros of the Walsh transform.

**Proposition 4.1** *Let $f \in \mathcal{F}^m$ and denote by $\nu$ the weight of the value of $f$; let us define the applications from $\mathcal{F}^m$ onto itself:*

$$\Lambda \ : \ f \ \longmapsto \ 1 + f \ ; \tag{8}$$

*for $a \in G$ and $\tau_a \ : \ x \in G \ \to \ x + a$,*

$$\Omega_a \ : \ f \ \longmapsto \ f \circ \tau_a \ . \tag{9}$$

*Let $F$, $F'$ and $F''$ be the Walsh transforms of $f$, $\Lambda(f)$ and $\Omega_a(f)$ respectively. Then for all $\lambda$ in $G$, $\lambda \neq 0$, we have:*

**(i)** $F'(\lambda) = -F(\lambda)$     **(ii)** $F''(\lambda) = (-1)^{\lambda \cdot a}\ F(\lambda)$ .

*Moreover $F'(0) = 2^m - \nu$ and $F''(0) = F(0) = \nu$ .*

*Proof:* By definition we have $F'(\lambda) + F(\lambda) = \sum_{x \in G / f(x) = 0} (-1)^{x \cdot \lambda} + \sum_{x \in G / f(x) = 1} (-1)^{x \cdot \lambda}$ ; this sum equals 0 if $\lambda \neq 0$ and equals $2^m$ otherwise. Formula (ii) and the value of $F''(0)$ become from:

$$F''(\lambda) = \sum_{x \in G} f(x + a)\ (-1)^{(x+a) \cdot \lambda + a \cdot \lambda} = (-1)^{\lambda \cdot a}\ F(\lambda) . \ \square$$

Then from (i) of Proposition 4.1 and from Theorem 3.2 we immediatly have:

**Corollary 4.1** *Let $f_1 \in \mathcal{F}^{m-1}$. Then the function of $m$ variables $(x_1, \ldots, x_m)$*

$$f = (x_m + 1) \, f_1 \; + \; x_m \, \Lambda(f_1) = f_1 \; + \; x_m \tag{10}$$

*is a $ci(k, m)$ function if and only if $f_1$ is a $ci(k-1, m-1)$ function; moreover $f$ has maximal degree if and only if $f_1$ has maximal degree.*

**Corollary 4.2** *Let $k$ be an odd integer. Let $a \in \mathbf{F}^{m-1}$, $a = (1, 1, \ldots, 1)$; $\tau_a$ and $\Omega_a$ are denoted by $\tau_1$ and $\Omega_1$. Let $f_1 \in \mathcal{F}^{m-1}$. Then the function of $m$ variables $(x_1, \ldots, x_m)$*

$$f = (x_m + 1) \, f_1 \; + \; x_m \, \Omega_1(f_1) = f_1 \; + \; x_m \, (f_1 + f_1 \circ \tau_1) \tag{11}$$

*is a $ci(k, m)$ function if and only if $f_1$ is a $ci(k-1, m-1)$ function; moreover $f$ has maximal degree if and only if $f_1$ has maximal degree.*

*Proof:* Since $a = (1, 1, \ldots, 1)$, formula (ii) of Proposition 4.1 becomes $F''(\lambda) = (-1)^{W(\lambda)} F(\lambda)$. When $k$ is odd we can apply Theorem 3.2 with $f_2 = \Omega_1(f_1)$. $\square$

REMARK : If $k$ is even we can also apply Theorem 3.2 with $f_2 = \Lambda(\Omega_1(f_1))$; indeed calculating the Walsh transform of $f_2$ with $F''$ given above, we then see by (i) of Proposition 4.1, that formula (ii) of Theorem 3.2 is satisfied.

REMARK : Starting from functions given by (10) and (11), the construction of SIEGEN-THALER permits to obtain other correlation-immune functions. Indeed his algorithm is based on this result: *let $f$ be a boolean function defined by (3); if $f_1$ and $f_2$ are $ci(k, m-1)$ functions, then $f$ is a $ci(k, m)$ function.* Note that the order is not increased in that construction.

REMARK : In fact, Corollary 4.1 is obvious. It consists in the addition of a variable; that is an addition of a binary symmetric channel having capacity zero [11].

**Example 4.1 A construction of a $ci(k, m)$ functions using Corollaries 4.1 and 4.2.** *We explained in Section 3.3 how we can construct a $ci(0, m-1)$ function; from Corollaries 4.1 and 4.2 that yields the construction of at least one $ci(1, m)$ function. First assume that $m = 5$ and $f_1 \in \mathcal{F}^4$. Let $H$ be the hyperplane generated by the basis $\{x_1, x_2, x_3\}$. The following array shows the values of $f_1$, $\Lambda(f_1)$ and $\Omega_1(f_1)$. The value of $f_1$ has weight 8. The transposed truth-table $\tilde{V}$ of $f_1$ is such that the set $\tilde{V} \cap H$ has 5* *elements. Then $f_1$ is a $ci(0,4)$ function - ie a balanced function of degree 3 -.*

$$
\begin{array}{c}
x_1 \\
x_2 \\
x_3 \\
x_4 \\
f_1 \\
\Lambda(f_1) \\
\Omega_1(f_1)
\end{array}
\left[
\begin{array}{cccccccccccccccc}
0 & 1 & 0 & 1 & 0 & 1 & 0 & 1 & 0 & 1 & 0 & 1 & 0 & 1 & 0 & 1 \\
0 & 0 & 1 & 1 & 0 & 0 & 1 & 1 & 0 & 0 & 1 & 1 & 0 & 0 & 1 & 1 \\
0 & 0 & 0 & 0 & 1 & 1 & 1 & 1 & 0 & 0 & 0 & 0 & 1 & 1 & 1 & 1 \\
0 & 0 & 0 & 0 & 0 & 0 & 0 & 0 & 1 & 1 & 1 & 1 & 1 & 1 & 1 & 1 \\
0 & 1 & 1 & 1 & 1 & 0 & 0 & 1 & 0 & 0 & 0 & 0 & 0 & 1 & 1 & 1 \\
1 & 0 & 0 & 0 & 0 & 1 & 1 & 0 & 1 & 1 & 1 & 1 & 1 & 0 & 0 & 0 \\
1 & 1 & 1 & 0 & 0 & 0 & 0 & 0 & 1 & 0 & 0 & 1 & 1 & 1 & 1 & 0
\end{array}
\right]
$$

*According to Corollary 4.2, the function* $f' = f_1 + x_5(f_1 + \Omega_1(f_1))$ *is a $ci(1,5)$ function with degree 3. The polynomial forms of $f_1$ and $f'$ are*

$$
\begin{aligned}
f_1(x_1,\ldots,x_4) &= x_1 + x_2 + x_3 + x_1x_2 + x_1x_4 + x_2x_4 + x_3x_4 \\
&\quad + x_1x_2x_3 + x_1x_2x_4 + x_1x_3x_4 + x_2x_3x_4 \ .
\end{aligned}
$$

$$
\begin{aligned}
f'(x_1,\ldots,x_5) &= f_1(x_1,\ldots,x_4) + x_5(f_1(x_1,\ldots,x_4) + f_1(x_1+1,\ldots,x_4+1)) \\
&= x_1 + x_2 + x_3 + x_5 + x_1x_2 + x_1x_4 + x_1x_5 + x_2x_4 + x_2x_5 \\
&\quad + x_3x_4 + x_1x_2x_3 + x_1x_2x_4 + x_1x_3x_4 + x_2x_3x_4 \ .
\end{aligned}
$$

*The truth-table $T$ of $f'$ is an orthogonal array $(16,5,2,1)$:*

$$
\tilde{T} =
\begin{array}{c}
x_1 \\
x_2 \\
x_3 \\
x_4 \\
x_5
\end{array}
\left[
\begin{array}{cccccccccccccccc}
1 & 0 & 1 & 0 & 1 & 1 & 0 & 1 & 0 & 1 & 0 & 0 & 1 & 0 & 1 & 0 \\
0 & 1 & 1 & 0 & 1 & 0 & 1 & 1 & 0 & 0 & 1 & 0 & 1 & 0 & 0 & 1 \\
0 & 0 & 0 & 1 & 1 & 1 & 1 & 1 & 0 & 0 & 0 & 0 & 0 & 1 & 1 & 1 \\
0 & 0 & 0 & 0 & 0 & 1 & 1 & 1 & 0 & 0 & 0 & 1 & 1 & 1 & 1 & 1 \\
0 & 0 & 0 & 0 & 0 & 0 & 0 & 0 & 1 & 1 & 1 & 1 & 1 & 1 & 1 & 1
\end{array}
\right]
$$

## 4.2 Quadratic balanced correlation-immune functions of maximal order

Let $f$ be a boolean function on $G$, and define $\forall \lambda \in G : f_\lambda(x) = f(x) + x.\lambda$ . According to Definition 3.2, the function $f$ is a $ci(k,m)$ function, $k > 0$, if and only if for any $\lambda$ such that $0 < W(\lambda) \le k$ the function $f_\lambda$ is balanced. Indeed, for any $\lambda \ne 0$, we have:

$$
\sum_{x \in G}(-1)^{f(x)+x.\lambda} = \sum_{x \in G}(-1)^{x.\lambda} - 2\sum_{x \in G} f(x)(-1)^{x.\lambda} = -2F(\lambda) \ ,
$$

where $\sum_{x \in G}(-1)^{f_\lambda(x)}$ equals zero if and only if $f_\lambda$ is balanced. We say that $f$ is *quadratic if and only if its degree equals exactly 2* (i.e. $f \in R(2,m)\backslash R(1,m)$). If $f$ is quadratic, then $f_\lambda$ is also quadratic. Then we can determine whether $f_\lambda$ is balanced or not (for instance see [4]):

**Lemma 4.1** *Let $g$ be a quadratic boolean function. Let the symplectic form associated with $g$:*

$$\phi_g \ : \ (x,y) \ \longmapsto \ g(0) + g(x) + g(y) + g(x+y) \ ,$$

*Recall that the kernel of $\phi_g$ is the subspace of $G$: $E_g = \{ \ x \in G \mid \forall y \in G, \ \phi_g(x,y) = 0 \ \}$ (of even codimension). Then $g$ is balanced if and only if its restriction to $E_g$ is not constant.*

**Theorem 4.1** *A $ci(m-3,m)$ quadratic function takes one of the polynomial forms given in (12), (13), (14) or (15).*
*Moreover, we can obtain all the $ci(m-3,m)$ quadratic functions by applying several times Corollaries 4.1 and 4.2 to $ci(0,3)$ quadratic functions.*

*Proof:* For any function $f$ of degree 2 on $G$, define: $A_f = \{ \ \lambda \in G \mid f_\lambda$ is not balanced $\}$ . By definition, the immunity order of $f$ is equal to the smallest weight of the elements of $A_f$ minus 1. In accordance with Lemma 4.1, $A_f$ is the set of all $\lambda \in G$ such that $f_\lambda$ is constant on $E_f$, or, equivalently:

$$A_f = \{ \ \lambda \in G \mid \forall x, \ x \in E_f \ : \ f(x) + f(0) = \lambda . x \ \} \ .$$

The function $f + f(0)$ is linear on $E_f$, and is therefore the restriction to $E_f$ of at least one linear form on $G$. As the linear forms on $G$ all are of the type $x \longrightarrow \lambda . x$ , $A_f$ has at least one element. Let $\lambda_0 \in A_f$; then we have: $A_f = \{ \ \lambda \in G \mid \forall x \in E_f, \ \lambda . x = \lambda_0 . x \ \}$ . We denote by $E_f^\perp$ the linear space: $E_f^\perp = \{ \ \lambda \in G \mid \forall x \in E_f, \ \lambda . x = 0 \ \}$ . Then $\lambda$ is in $A_f$ if and only if $\lambda + \lambda_0$ is in $E_f^\perp$; $A_f$ is an affine subspace of $G$, of direction $E_f^\perp$, and therefore of even dimension. We will now determine such subspaces, and deduce the corresponding functions $f$.

Let $A$ be an affine subspace of $G$, of even dimension, and whose elements have weights at least equal to $m-2$. Let $\{e_1, \ldots, e_m\}$ be the natural basis of $G$, and the space $A' = A + e_0$, where $e_0 = e_1 + \ldots + e_m$ . So $A'$ is an affine-subspace, of even dimension, whose elements have weights at most equal to 2; it is clear that we can determine equivalently $A$ or $A'$. If $A'$ contains 0, then it is the linear space equal to:

$$A^{(1)} = \{0, e_i, e_j, e_i + e_j\} \quad \text{or} \quad A^{(2)} = \{0, e_i + e_j, e_i + e_k, e_j + e_k\} \ ,$$

where $i$, $j$ and $k$ are distincts elements of $[1, m]$.
If $A'$ contains at last one element of weight 1, then it is equal to:

$$A^{(3)} = \{e_i, e_j, e_i + e_k, e_j + e_k\} \ .$$

If $A'$ contains only elements of weight 2, then it is equal to:

$$A^{(4)} = \{e_i + e_j, e_i + e_k, e_l + e_j, e_l + e_k\} \ ,$$

where $i$, $j$, $k$ and $l$ are distincts elements of $[1, m]$.

Now we are able to examine the four possible definitions of $A_f$:

$$\text{(i)} \quad A_f = A^{(1)} + e_0 \qquad \text{(ii)} \quad A_f = A^{(2)} + e_0$$
$$\text{(iii)} \quad A_f = A^{(3)} + e_0 \qquad \text{(iv)} \quad A_f = A^{(4)} + e_0 \ .$$

(i) $A_f = \{e_0, e_0 + e_i, e_0 + e_j, e_0 + e_i + e_j\}$ . Since $A_f$ is a coset of $E_f^\perp$, we have:

$$E_f^\perp = \{0, e_i, e_j, e_i + e_j\} \quad \text{and then} \quad E_f = \{x \in G \mid x_i = x_j = 0\}.$$

Let the function $g \ : \ x \in G \ \longrightarrow \ x_i x_j$ . Clearly $E_g = E_f$. There exists only one symplectic form admitting $E_f$ as kernel, since $E_f$ has codimension 2 and since there exists only one non-zero symplectic form on a linear space of dimension 2. So $f$ belongs to the same coset of the code $R(1, m)$ as $g$. Hence there exists $\lambda \in G$ and $\epsilon \in F$ such that: $f(x) = g(x) + \lambda.x + \epsilon$. Since $g$ is not balanced, then $\lambda$ must be in $A_f$. So we obtain the algebraic normal form of $f$:

$$f = x_i x_j + \sum_{t \in [1,m]-\{i,j\}} x_t + \epsilon_i x_i + \epsilon_j x_j + \epsilon \ , \quad \epsilon_i \in F, \ \epsilon_j \in F, \ \epsilon \in F \ . \tag{12}$$

For m=3 the following functions are clearly balanced:

$$x_1 x_2 + x_1 + x_2 + x_3 \ , \quad x_1 x_2 + x_1 + x_3 \ , \quad x_1 x_2 + x_2 + x_3 \ , \quad x_1 x_2 + x_3 \ .$$

Indeed their expressions all contain a linear function which is linearly independant from $x_1$ and $x_2$ and so they are $ci(0, 3)$ functions. By using Corollary 4.1, $m - 3$ times, we obtain the following $ci(m - 3, m)$ functions:

$$x_1 x_2 + x_1 + x_2 + x_3 + \ldots + x_m \qquad x_1 x_2 + x_1 + x_3 + \ldots + x_m$$
$$x_1 x_2 + x_2 + x_3 + \ldots + x_m \qquad x_1 x_2 + x_3 + \ldots + x_m \ .$$

By permuting the variables we can check that all $ci(m - 3, m)$ functions described by (12) are then obtained.

(ii) $A_f = \{e_0, e_0 + e_i + e_j, e_0 + e_i + e_k, e_0 + e_j + e_k\}$ . Then

$$E_f^\perp = \{0, e_i + e_j, e_i + e_k, e_j + e_k\} \quad , \quad E_f = \{x \in G \mid x_i + x_j = x_i + x_k = 0\},$$

and $\quad f(x) = (x_i + x_j)(x_i + x_k) + \lambda.x + \epsilon \quad$ with $\quad \lambda \in A_f$ , where

$$\lambda.x = \sum_{t=1}^{m} x_t \ \text{or} \sum_{t \in [1,m]-\{i,j\}} x_t \ \text{or} \sum_{t \in [1,m]-\{i,k\}} x_t \ \text{or} \sum_{t \in [1,m]-\{j,k\}} x_t. \tag{13}$$

Now the following functions are balanced, since their expressions all contain a linear function which is linearly independant from $x_1 + x_2$ and $x_1 + x_3$; so they are $ci(0,3)$ functions:

$$(x_1 + x_2)(x_1 + x_3) + x_1 + x_2 + x_3 \quad , \quad (x_1 + x_2)(x_1 + x_3) + x_2 + x_3 ,$$
$$(x_1 + x_2)(x_1 + x_3) + x_1 + x_3 \quad , \quad (x_1 + x_2)(x_1 + x_3) + x_1 + x_2 .$$

We then obtain all the functions described by (13), for the same reasons as in (i).

(iii) $A_f = \{e_0 + e_i, e_0 + e_j, e_0 + e_i + e_k, e_0 + e_j + e_k\}$ . Then

$$E_f^{\perp} = \{0, e_i + e_j, e_k, e_i + e_j + e_k\} \quad , \quad E_f = \{x \in G \mid x_i + x_j = x_k = 0\},$$

and $\quad f(x) = (x_i + x_j)x_k + \lambda.x + \epsilon \quad$ with $\quad \lambda \in A_f$ , where

$$\lambda.x = \sum_{t \in [1,m]-\{i\}} x_t \quad \text{or} \quad \sum_{t \in [1,m]-\{j\}} x_t \quad \text{or} \quad \sum_{t \in [1,m]-\{i,k\}} x_t \quad \text{or} \quad \sum_{t \in [1,m]-\{j,k\}} x_t. \quad (14)$$

Now the following functions are balanced, since their expressions all contain a linear function which is linearly independant from $x_1 + x_2$ and $x_3$; so they are $ci(0,3)$ functions:

$$(x_1 + x_2)(x_1 + x_3) + x_1 + x_2 + x_3 \quad , \quad (x_1 + x_2)(x_1 + x_3) + x_2 + x_3 ,$$
$$(x_1 + x_2)(x_1 + x_3) + x_1 + x_3 \quad , \quad (x_1 + x_2)(x_1 + x_3) + x_1 + x_2 .$$

We then obtain all the functions described by (14), for the same reasons as in (i).

(iv) $A_f = \{e_0 + e_i + e_j, e_0 + e_i + e_k, e_0 + e_l + e_j, e_0 + e_l + e_k\}$ . Then

$$E_f^{\perp} = \{0, e_j + e_k, e_i + e_l, e_i + e_j + e_k + e_l\} \quad , \quad E_f = \{x \in G \mid x_j + x_k = x_i + x_l = 0\},$$

and $\quad f(x) = (x_j + x_k)(x_i + x_l) + \lambda.x + \epsilon \quad$ with $\quad \lambda \in A_f$ , where

$$\lambda.x = \sum_{t \in [1,m]-\{i,j\}} x_t \quad \text{or} \quad \sum_{t \in [1,m]-\{i,k\}} x_t \quad \text{or} \quad \sum_{t \in [1,m]-\{l,j\}} x_t \quad \text{or} \quad \sum_{t \in [1,m]-\{l,k\}} x_t. \quad (15)$$

Let us consider once again the $ci(0,3)$ functions using in (iii). Using Corollary 4.2 with $m = 4$, we obtain the $ci(1,4)$ functions:

$$(x_1 + x_2)(x_3 + x_4) + x_2 + x_3 \quad , \quad (x_1 + x_2)(x_3 + x_4) + x_1 + x_3 ,$$
$$(x_1 + x_2)(x_3 + x_4) + x_2 \quad , \quad (x_1 + x_2)(x_3 + x_4) + x_1 .$$

So we can use Corollary 4.1 and obtain all the functions described by (15). □

REMARK : It is easy to check that all the $ci(0,3)$ functions we use in the proof, are equivalent; that is natural since their symplectic forms have the same rank and since they all are balanced.

In accordance with (12), (13), (14) and (15), we can state the number of the $ci(m-3, m)$ quadratic functions:

**Corollary 4.3** *Let $Q_m$ be the number of $ci(m-3,m)$ quadratic functions. Then:*

$$Q_m = \frac{1}{3}m(m-1)(3m-2)(m+1) . \tag{16}$$

*Proof:* Counting the functions described by (12), (13), (14) and (15), we obtain respectively:

$$8\binom{m}{2} \quad , \quad 8\binom{m}{3} \quad , \quad 8\binom{m}{2}(m-2) \quad \text{and} \quad 4\binom{m}{2}\binom{m-2}{2} \quad . \quad \Box$$

**Corollary 4.4** *If an orthogonal array $(2^{m-1}, m, 2, m-3)$ (with index 4) is the truth table of a quadratic boolean function, that function is given by (12), (13), (14) or (15). The number of such orthogonal arrays is given by (16).*

There are $NQ_m = (2^u - 1)2^{m+1}$ , $u = \binom{m}{2}$, quadratic functions. One can see, with the following array, that few of them are $ci(m-3,m)$ quadratic functions. We denote by $BQ_m$ the number of balanced quadratic functions.

| $m$ | $NQ_m$ | $BQ_m$ | $Q_m$ |
|---|---|---|---|
| 3 | 112 | 56 | 56 |
| 4 | 2016 | 840 | 200 |
| 5 | 65472 | 36456 | 520 |
| 6 | 4194176 | 1828008 | 1120 |
| 7 | 536870656 | 300503336 | 2128 |
| 8 | 137438952960 | 60273666600 | 3696 |

## 4.3 More balanced correlation-immune functions of maximal orders

**Proposition 4.2** *Let $r \in [1, m[$ , $g$ a boolean function on $\mathbf{F}^{m-r}$, and $\phi$ a mapping from $\mathbf{F}^{m-r}$ to $\mathbf{F}^r$. Let $f$ be the boolean function $f$ such defined:*

$$\mathbf{D} = \mathbf{F}^r \times \mathbf{F}^{m-r} , \quad \forall\, (x,y) \in \mathbf{D} \; : \; f(x,y) = <x, \phi(y)>_r + g(y) , \tag{17}$$

*where $<,>_r$ denotes the usual dots product on $\mathbf{F}^r$. Then $f$ is a $ci(k,m)$ function, with*

$$k \geq \inf\{ W(\phi(y)) \mid y \in \mathbf{F}^{m-r} \} - 1 .$$

*Proof:* Let $a \in \mathbf{F}^r$ and $b \in \mathbf{F}^{m-r}$. We have

$$L = \sum_{(x,y)\in \mathbf{D}} (-1)^{f(x,y)+<a,x>_r+<b,y>_{m-r}} = \sum_{y\in \mathbf{F}^{m-r}} (-1)^{g(y)+<b,y>_{m-r}} \sum_{x\in \mathbf{F}^r} (-1)^{<a+\phi(y),x>_r} .$$

The function $x \rightarrow <a + \phi(y), x >_r$ is a linear form on $\mathbf{F^r}$, and therefore is either null or balanced. Then

$$L = 2^r \sum_{y \in \phi^{-1}(a)} (-1)^{g(y) + <b, y>_{m-r}} \quad.$$

Hence: $a \notin \phi(\mathbf{F}^{m-r}) \;\Rightarrow\; L = 0$. Let $\mu = inf \{ W(\phi(y)) \mid y \in \mathbf{F}^{m-r} \} - 1$. If $W(a) + W(b) \leq \mu$ then $a$ does not belong to $\phi(\mathbf{F}^{m-r})$ and $L = 0$. That means : for all $\lambda = (a, b)$, $\lambda \in D$, such that $W(\lambda) \leq \mu$, the function $f_\lambda$ is balanced. Then $f$ is $ci(k, m)$, with $k \geq \mu$. □

**Corollary 4.5** *There exist functions of type (17), which have degree $m - r + 1$ and are $ci(r - 2, m)$ - i.e. they have a maximum immunity order for their degree.*

*Proof:* Let $r > 2$; then $m - r \leq m - 2$. We get $\phi(y) = (\phi_1(y) + 1, \ldots, \phi_r(y) + 1)$ :

$$\phi_i : \mathbf{F}^{m-r} \rightarrow \mathbf{F}, \quad V(\phi_i) \cap V(\phi_j) = \emptyset, \quad \exists i : |V(\phi_i)| \text{ is odd} \tag{18}$$

($V(\phi_i)$ is the truth-table of $\phi_i$). Then , for any $y \in \mathbf{F}^{m-r}$, the weight of $\phi(y)$ is at least equal to $r - 1$. Therefore $f$ is a $ci(r - 2, m)$ function; moreover $f$ has degree $m - r + 1$, since one of the function $\phi_i$ has degree $m - r$. □

**Example 4.2** **A construction of a $ci(2, 7)$ function using corollary 4.5.** *We get $m = 7$ and $r = 4$. Using Corollary 4.5, we are able to construct a $ci(2, 7)$ function $f$ of maximal degree $d(f) = 4$. We choose the $\phi_i$'s, satisfying (18):*

$$\begin{matrix}
x_5 \\ x_6 \\ x_7 \\ \phi_1 \\ \phi_2 \\ \phi_3 \\ \phi_4
\end{matrix}
\begin{bmatrix}
0 & 1 & 0 & 1 & 0 & 1 & 0 & 1 \\
0 & 0 & 1 & 1 & 0 & 0 & 1 & 1 \\
0 & 0 & 0 & 0 & 1 & 1 & 1 & 1 \\
0 & 0 & 1 & 0 & 1 & 0 & 0 & 1 \\
1 & 0 & 0 & 0 & 0 & 0 & 1 & 0 \\
0 & 1 & 0 & 1 & 0 & 0 & 0 & 0 \\
0 & 0 & 0 & 0 & 0 & 1 & 0 & 0
\end{bmatrix}$$

*The polynomial form of the $\phi_i$'s:*

$$\begin{aligned}
\phi_1(x') &= x_5 x_6 + x_6 + x_5 x_7 + x_7 + x_6 x_5 x_7 & \phi_2(x') &= x_5 x_6 + x_5 x_7 + x_5 + x_6 + x_7 + \\
\phi_3(x') &= x_5 x_7 + x_5 & \phi_4(x') &= x_6 x_5 x_7 + x_5 x_7
\end{aligned}$$

*where $x' = (x_5, x_6, x_7)$. Then the function:*

$$f(x) = x_1(\phi_1(x') + 1) + x_2(\phi_2(x') + 1) + x_3(\phi_3(x') + 1) + x_4(\phi_4(x') + 1),$$

*where $x = (x_1, x_2, x_3, x_4, x_5, x_6, x_7)$, is a $ci(2, 7)$ function. Its polynomial form is :*

$$\begin{aligned}
f(x) = \; & x_1 x_5 x_6 x_7 + x_5 x_6 x_7 x_4 + x_1 x_5 x_6 + x_1 x_5 x_7 + x_5 x_6 x_2 + x_5 x_7 x_2 + x_5 x_7 x_3 \\
& + x_5 x_7 x_4 + x_1 x_6 + x_1 x_7 + x_5 x_2 + x_5 x_3 + x_6 x_2 + x_7 x_2 + x_1 + x_3 + x_4
\end{aligned}$$

In accordance with Theorem 3.2, we can construct two  $ci(1,6)$  functions:

$$f(x) = (x_1 + 1)\, f_1(x_2,\ldots,x_7) \;+\; x_1\, f_2(x_2,\ldots,x_7) \quad \text{with}$$

$$f_1 = x_5x_6x_7x_4 + x_5x_6x_2 + x_5x_7x_2 + x_5x_7x_3 + x_5x_7x_4 + x_5x_2 + x_5x_3 + x_6x_2 + x_7x_2 + x_3 + x_4$$

$$f_2 = x_5x_6x_7x_4 + x_5x_6x_7 + x_5x_6x_2 + x_5x_7x_2 + x_5x_7x_3 + x_5x_7x_4 + x_5x_6$$
$$+ x_5x_7 + x_5x_2 + x_5x_3 + x_6x_2 + x_7x_2 + x_6 + x_7 + x_3 + x_4 + 1.$$

From Theorem 3.2,  $f_1$  and  $f_2$  are  $ci(1,6)$  functions with maximal degree.

# References

[1]  R.C. BOSE & K.A. BUSH *Orthogonal arrays of strength two and three*, Am. Math. Stat., 23(1952) 508-524.

[2]  P. CAMION *Etude de codes binaires abéliens modulaires autoduaux de petites longueurs*, Revue du CETHEDEC, NS 79-2 (1979) 3-24.

[3]  P. CAMION, C. CARLET, P. CHARPIN & N. SENDRIER *Definition and construction of correlation-immune functions*, to appear as INRIA report.

[4]  C. CARLET *Codes de Reed et Muller, codes de Kerdock et de Preparata*, Thèse de l'Université PARIS 6, LITP 90-59.

[5]  P. CHARPIN *Etude sur la valuation des H-codes binaires*, Cahiers du B.U.R.O. , n. 41, Univ. P. et M. Curie , Paris 1983.

[6]  P. DELSARTE *An algebraic approach to the association schemes of coding theory*, Thesis, Université Catholique de Louvain, June 1973.

[7]  X. GUO-ZHEN & J.L. MASSEY *A spectral characterisation of Correlation-immune Combining functions*, IEEE, vol. 34, n.3, May 88.

[8]  R.A. RUEPPEL *Analysis and Design of stream ciphers*, Communications and Control Engineering Series, Springer-Verlag Berlin Heidelberg 1986.

[9]  F.J. MACWILLIAMS & N.J.A. SLOANE *The theory of Error Correcting Codes*, North-Holland 1986.

[10]  C.R. RAO *Factorial experiments derivable from combinatorial arrangements of arrays*, J. Roy. statist. Soc. 9, 128-139.

[11]  T. SIEGENTHALER *Correlation-Immunity of nonlinear combining fonctions for Cryptographics Applications*, IEEE on Inf. Theory, vol IT-30, n.5, Sept. 84.

# On the Size of Shares
# for Secret Sharing Schemes[*]

R. M. Capocelli[1], A. De Santis[2], L. Gargano[2], U. Vaccaro[2]

[1] Dipartimento di Matematica, Università di Roma, 00185 Roma, Italy
[2] Dipartimento di Informatica, Università di Salerno, 84081 Baronissi (SA), Italy

### Abstract

A secret sharing scheme permits a secret to be shared among participants in such a way that only qualified subsets of partecipants can recover the secret, but any non-qualified subset has absolutely no information on the secret. The set of all qualified subsets defines the access structure to the secret. Sharing schemes are useful in the management of cryptographic keys and in multy-party secure protocols.

We analyze the relationships among the entropies of the sample spaces from which the shares and the secret are chosen. We show that there are access structures with 4 participants for which any secret sharing scheme must give to a participant a share at least 50% greater than the secret size. This is the first proof that there exist access structures for which the best achievable information rate (i.e., the ratio between the size of the secret and that of the largest share) is bounded away from 1. The bound is the best possible, as we construct a secret sharing scheme for the above access structures which meets the bound with equality.

## 1 Introduction

Secret Sharing is an important tool in Security and Cryptography. In many cases there is a single master key that provides the access to important secret information. Therefore, it would be desirable to keep the master key in a safe place to avoid accidental and malicious exposure. This scheme is unreliable: if the master key is lost or destroyed, then all information accessed by the master key is no more available. A possible solution would be that of storing copies of the key in different safe places or giving copies to trusted people. In such a case the system becomes more vulnerable to security breaches

---

[*]This work was partially supported by the Italian Ministry of the University and Scientific Research, within the framework of the Project: Progetto ed Analisi di Algoritmi and by the National Council of Research, Progetto Finalizzato Sistemi Informatici e Calcolo Parallelo.

J. Feigenbaum (Ed.): Advances in Cryptology - CRYPTO '91, LNCS 576, pp. 101-113, 1992.
© Springer-Verlag Berlin Heidelberg 1992

or betrayal [Sham], [De]. A better solution would be breaking the master key into pieces in such a way that only the concurrence of certain predefined trusted people can recover it. This has proven to be an important tool in the management of cryptographic keys and in multy-party secure protocols (see for example [GoMiWi]).

As a solution to this problem, Blakley [Bl] and Shamir [Sham] introduced $(k, n)$ threshold schemes. A $(k, n)$ threshold scheme allows a secret to be shared among $n$ participants in such a way that any $k$ of them can recover the secret, but any $k - 1$, or fewer, have absolutely no information on the secret (see [Simm] for a comprehensive bibliography on $(k, n)$ threshold schemes).

Ito, Saito, and Nishizeki [ItSaNi] described a more general method of secret sharing. An access structure is a specification of all the subsets of participants who can recover the secret and it is said monotone if any set which contains a subset that can recover the secret, can itself recover the secret. Ito, Saito, and Nishizeki gave a methodology to realize secret sharing schemes for arbitrary monotone access structures. Subsequently, Benaloh and Leichter [BeLe] gave a simpler and more efficient way to realize secret sharing schemes for any given monotone access structure.

An important issue in the implementation of secret sharing schemes is the size of shares, since the security of a system degrades as the amount of the information that must be kept secret increases. Unfortunately, in all secret sharing schemes the size of the shares cannot be less than the size of the secret[1]. Moreover, there are access structures for which any corresponding secret sharing scheme must give to at least a participant a share of size strictly bigger than the secret size. Indeed, [BeLe] proved that there exists an access structure for which any secret sharing scheme must give to some participant a share which is from a domain larger than that of the secret. Recently, Brickell and Stinson [BrSt] improved on [BeLe] by showing that for the same access structure, the number of elements in the domain of the shares must be at least $2|S| - 1$ if the cardinality of the domain of the secret is $|S|$. Ideal Secret Sharing schemes, that is sharing schemes where the shares are taken from the same domain than that of the secret were characterized by Brickell and Davenport [BrDa] in terms of matroids.

All above results regarding the size of the domain of the shares and that of the secret, can be interpreted as relations between the entropies of the corresponding sample spaces

---

[1] This property holds since non-qualified subset of participants have *absolutely* no information on the secret. If we relax this requirement (as is done in ramp schemes) the size of the shares might be less than the size of the secret.

when only uniform probability distributions are involved. A more general approach has been considered by Karnin, Greene, and Hellman [KaGrHe] who initiated the analysis (limited to threshold schemes) of secret sharing schemes when arbitrary probability distributions are involved.

We extend the approach of [KaGrHe] to general access structures deriving several relations among the entropies of the secret and those of the shares even when partial informations are taken into account. When we restrict probability distributions to be uniform, our results implies an improvement over the above mentioned results on the size of shares.

In this paper we prove that for any secret sharing scheme, for any set $A$ of participants which are not qualified to recover the secret, the average uncertainty on each share of participants in another set $B$ given that the shares of $A$ are known ($A$ and $B$ are sets of participants such that they can recover the secret by pooling together their shares) must be at least as great as the *a priori* uncertainty on the secret. This is a generalization and also a sharpening of a result in [KaGrHe]. We also analyze the relationships between the size of the shares and that of the secret. We improve on the result of [BrSt] proving that there are access structures with 4 participants for which any secret sharing scheme must give to some participant shares which are from a domain of size at least $|S|^{1.5}$, $|S|$ being the secret domain size. In other words, we show that the number of bits needed for a single share is 50% bigger than those needed for the secret. This is the first proof that there exist access structures for which the best achievable information rate (i.e., the ratio between the size of the secret and that of the largest share) is bounded away from 1. We construct a secret sharing scheme for the above access structures which meets the bound with equality. Finally, the bound is generalized to access structures with any number of participants.

# 2 Preliminaries

In this section we shall review the information theoretic concepts we are going to use. For a complete treatment of the subject the reader is advised to consult [CsKo], [Ga], [Shan].

Given a probability distribution $\{p(x)\}_{x \in X}$ on a finite set $X$, define the *entropy* of $X$,

$H(X)$, as

$$H(X) = -\sum_{x \in X} p(x) \log p(x)^2.$$

The entropy $H(X)$ is a measure of the average information content of the elements in $X$ or, equivalently, a measure of the average uncertainty one has about which element of the set $X$ has been chosen when the choices of the elements from $X$ are made according to the probability distribution $\{p(x)\}_{x \in X}$. It is well known that $H(X)$ is a good approximation to the average number of bits needed to faithfully represent the elements of $X$. The following useful property of $H(X)$ will be used in the following:

$$0 \le H(X) \le \log |X|, \tag{1}$$

where $H(X) = 0$ if and only if there exists $x_0 \in X$ such that $p(x_0) = 1$; $H(X) = \log |X|$ if and only if $p(x) = 1/|X|, \forall x \in X$.

Given two sets $X$ and $Y$ and a joint probability distribution $\{p(x,y)\}_{x \in X, y \in Y}$ on their cartesian product, the *conditional entropy* $H(X|Y)$, also called the equivocation of $X$ given $Y$, is defined as

$$H(X|Y) = -\sum_{y \in Y} \sum_{x \in X} p(y) p(x|y) \log p(x|y).$$

The conditional entropy can be written as

$$H(X|Y) = \sum_{y \in Y} p(y) H(X|Y=y)$$

where $H(X|Y=y) = -\sum_{x \in X} p(x|y) \log p(x|y)$ can be interpreted as the average uncertainty one has about which element of $X$ has been chosen when the choices are made according to the probability distribution $p(x|y)_{x \in X}$, that is, when it is known that the value chosen from the set $Y$ is $y$. From the definition of conditional entropy it is easy to see that

$$H(X|Y) \ge 0. \tag{2}$$

The entropy of the joint space $XY$ satisfies

$$H(XY) = H(X) + H(Y|X) = H(Y) + H(X|Y). \tag{3}$$

The *mutual information* between $X$ and $Y$ is defined by

$$I(X;Y) = H(X) - H(X|Y) \tag{4}$$

---

[2] All logarithms in this paper are of base 2

and enjoys the following properties:

$$I(X;Y) = I(Y;X), \qquad (5)$$

and

$$I(X;Y) \geq 0.$$

From which one gets

$$H(X) \geq H(X|Y). \qquad (6)$$

The *conditional mutual information* is defined by

$$I(X;Y|Z) = H(X|Z) - H(X|YZ). \qquad (7)$$

Notice that $H(X|ZY) = \sum_{y \in Y} p(y)H(X|Z, Y = y)$, where

$$H(X|Z, Y = y) = -\sum_{x,z} p(xz|y) \log p(x|yz).$$

When no ambiguity arises we will drop the comma in $H(X|Z, Y = y)$.

$I(X;Y|Z)$ satisfies three important properties,

$$I(X;Y|Z) \geq 0 \qquad (8)$$

$$I(X;Y|Z) = I(Y;X|Z) \qquad (9)$$

and

$$I(X;YZ) = I(X;Z) + I(X;Y|Z).$$

# 3  Secret Sharing Schemes

A secret sharing scheme permits a secret to be shared among $n$ participants in such a way that only qualified subsets of them can recover the secret, but any non-qualified subset has absolutely no information on the secret.

Given a set $P$, an *access structure* on $P$ is a family of subsets $A \subseteq 2^P$. The *closure* of a family of subsets $A \subseteq 2^P$, is defined as $closure(A) = \{A' : A \in A, A \subseteq A' \subseteq P\}$. A natural property for an access structure $A$ is that of being *monotone*, i.e., $A = closure(A)$.

Let $P$ be a set of participants, $\mathcal{A}$ be a monotone access structure on $P$ and $S$ be the set of secrets. Following the information-theoretic approach of [KaGrHe] and [Ko], we say that a Secret Sharing Scheme is a sharing of secrets among participants in $P$ such that

1. *Any qualified subset can reconstruct the secret.*
   For all $A \in \mathcal{A}$, $H(S|A) = 0$.

2. *Any non-qualified subset has absolutely no information on the secret.*
   For all $A \notin \mathcal{A}$, $H(S|A) = H(S)$.

**Remark 1.** Notice that $H(S|A) = 0$ means that each set of values of the shares in $A$ determines a unique value of the secret. In fact, by definition, $H(S|A) = 0$ implies that $\forall a \in A$ with $p(a) \neq 0$ $\exists s \in S$ such that $p(s|a) = 1$. Moreover, $H(S|A) = H(S)$ means that $S$ and $A$ are statistically independent, i.e., $\forall a \in A$ $\forall s \in S$, $p(s|a) = p(s)$ and therefore the knowledge of $a$ gives no information about the secret. Notice that the condition $H(S|A) = H(S)$ is equivalent to say that $\forall a \in A$ $H(S|A = a) = H(S)$.

Shares given to the participants are not necessarily to be taken from the same domain. For instance, let the set of participants be $P = \{A, B, C, D\}$ and consider the access structure $\mathcal{AS}$ consisting of the closure of the set $\left\{\{A, B\}, \{B, C\}, \{C, D\}\right\}$. Let the secret $s$ be a uniformly chosen $n$-bit string. A possible secret sharing scheme for $\mathcal{AS}$ consists of uniformly chosing 3 pairs of strings whose XOR give the secret $s$, that is such that $s = a \oplus b_1 = b_2 \oplus c_1 = c_2 \oplus d$ and giving shares $a$ to $A$, $b_1, b_2$ to $B$, $c_1, c_2$ to $C$ and $d$ to $D$. The size of the shares given to $B$ and $C$ is twice the size of the shares to $A$ and $D$, and the size of the secret itself, that is we have $H(B) = H(C) = 2H(A) = 2H(D) = 2H(S)$.

Karnin, Greene, and Hellman [KaGrHe] proved that in any threshold scheme any set $X_i$ from which the $i$-th share is taken satisfies $H(X_i) \geq H(S)$. What is the uncertainty on the shares for general access structures when other shares are known? Assume a set of participants $Y$ cannot determine the secret, but they could if another participant (or group of participants) $X$ would be willing to pool its own share. Intuitively, for general access structures, the uncertainty on the shares given to $X$ is at least as big as that on the secret itself, from the point of view of $Y$. Otherwise, the set of participants $Y$ would have some information on the secret and could decrease their uncertainty on $S$. This is formally stated and proved in the next lemma which constitutes an extension and a sharpening on Theorem 1 of Karnin, Greene and Hellman [KaGrHe].

**Lemma 3.1** *Let $Y \notin A$ and $X \cup Y \in A$. Then $H(X|Y = y) \geq H(S)$ for each possible value $y$ in $Y$.*

**Proof.** $I(X;S|Y = y)$ can be written either as $H(X|Y = y) - H(X|SY = y)$ or as $H(S|Y = y) - H(S|XY = y)$. Hence,

$$
\begin{aligned}
H(X|Y = y) &= H(X|SY = y) + H(S|Y = y) - H(S|XY = y) \\
&= H(X|SY = y) + H(S|Y = y) \\
&\geq H(S|Y = y) \\
&= H(S)
\end{aligned}
$$

The second line follows from the first, since $H(S|XY) = 0$ implies $H(S|XY = y) = 0$ for all $y$ such that $p(y) > 0$. □

By averaging on the elements $y \in Y$ we get that, in the same hypothesis of Lemma 3.1, it holds $H(X|Y) \geq H(S)$. Because of (6), we obtain that $H(X) \geq H(S)$, for each $X \subset P$, which is essentially Theorem 1 of [KaGrHe] generalized to monotone access structures.

Next lemma implies that the uncertainty on shares of participants, who cannot recover the secret, it cannot be decreased by the knowledge of the secret.

**Lemma 3.2** *If $X \cup Y \notin A$ then $H(Y|X) = H(Y|XS)$.*

**Proof.** The conditional mutual information $I(Y,S|X)$ between $Y$ and $S$ given $X$ can be written either as $H(Y|X) - H(Y|XS)$ or as $H(S|X) - H(S|XY)$. Hence, $H(Y|X) = H(Y|XS) + H(S|X) - H(S|XY)$. Because of $H(S|XY) = H(S|X) = H(S)$, for $X \cup Y \notin A$, we have $H(Y|X) = H(Y|XS)$. □

**Lemma 3.3** *Let $X, Y, Z \subset P$. If $X \cup Y \in A$ then $H(Z|XY) \leq H(Z|XS)$.*

**Proof.** The conditional entropy $H(ZS|XY)$ can be written either as $H(Z|XY) + H(S|XYZ)$ or as $H(S|XY) + H(Z|XYS)$. Since $X \cup Y \in A$ it follows $H(S|XY) = 0$ and $H(S|XYZ) = 0$. Hence, $H(Z|XY) = H(ZS|XY) = H(Z|XYS)$. Because of $I(Z;Y|XS) \geq 0$ one has $H(Z|XYS) \leq H(Z|XS)$ and the lemma follows. □

# 4   Bounds on the size of shares

Benaloh and Leichter [BeLe] gave the first example of an access structure for which any secret sharing scheme must give to some participant shares which are from a domain larger than that of the secret. The access structure they considered is $AS = closure\{\{A,B\},\{B,C\},\{C,D\}\}$. Recently, Brickell and Stinson [BrSt] showed that there are only two access structures with 4 participants which are the closure of a graph (i.e., the closure of a family whose elements are pairs of participants), satisfying above limitation. Such access structures are $AS$ and $AS2 = closure\{\{A,B\},\{B,C\},\{C,D\},\{B,D$ In this section we first give a lower bound on the entropy of the spaces from which the shares for the access structure $AS$ are taken. Then, we use this result to prove an analogous lower bound for $AS2$ and more general access structures.

A secret sharing scheme for $AS$ satisfies

1. $H(S|AB) = H(S|BC) = H(S|CD) = 0$.

2. $H(S|A) = H(S|B) = H(S|C) = H(S|D) = H(S|AC) = H(S|AD) = H(S)$.

We also have $H(S|BD) = H(S)$, but we will not make use of it. Now we state our lower bound.

**Theorem 4.1** *Any secret sharing scheme for $AS$ satisfies*

$$H(BC) \geq 3H(S).$$

**Proof.** From (4) we get that $H(B) = H(B|CA) + I(B;CA)$. From (7) and (9) we get that $H(B|CA) = H(S|CA) + H(B|CAS) = H(S) + H(B|CAS)$. Therefore, using formulae (4) and (3) we get

$$H(B) = H(S) + H(B|CAS) + H(A) + H(C|A) - H(A|B) - H(C|AB). \tag{10}$$

Consider now $I(BC;S)$ that can be written either as $H(BC) - H(BC|S) = H(BC) - H(B|S) - H(C|BS)$ or as $H(S) - H(S|BC) = H(S)$. We obtain

$$
\begin{aligned}
H(BC) &= H(S) + H(B|S) + H(C|BS) \\
&= H(S) + H(B) + H(C|BS) \quad \text{(from Lemma 3.2)}
\end{aligned}
$$

$$= H(S) + H(S) + H(B|CAS) + H(A) + H(C|A) - H(A|B) - H(C|AB)$$
$$+H(C|BS) \quad \text{(from (10))}$$
$$\geq 2H(S) + H(B|CAS) + H(A) + H(C|A) - H(A|B) \quad \text{(from Lemma 3.3)}$$
$$\geq 2H(S) + H(A) - H(A|B) + H(C|A) \quad \text{(from (2))}$$
$$\geq 2H(S) + H(C|A) \quad \text{(from (6))}$$
$$\geq 2H(S) + H(C|AD) \quad \text{(from (8))}$$
$$\geq 3H(S) \quad \text{(from Lemma 3.1)}.$$

$\Box$

The following corollary to Theorem 4.1 is immediate from (3) and (6).

**Corollary 4.1** *Any secret sharing scheme for $AS$ satisfies*

$$H(B) + H(C) \geq 3H(S).$$

A consequence of above corollary is that either $B$ or $C$ must have entropy at least $1.5H(S)$, that is 50% bigger than that of the secret. Recalling that the entropy of a set is a good approximation of the average number of bits needed to represent an element of the set, we get that there is a share whose size is at least 50% bigger than the secret size.

Benaloh and Leichter [BeLe] proved that for the access structure $AS$ it must hold either $|B| > |S|$ or $|C| > |S|$, where with $|S|$ we denote the number of different secrets and with $|B|$ ($|C|$) the number of different shares that can be given to $B$ ($C$). Then, Brickell and Stinson [BrSt] improved on [BeLe] proving that the number of possible shares either for $B$ or for $C$ must be at least $2|S| - 1$. Our Corollary 4.1 implies the following sharper lower bound.

**Corollary 4.2** *Suppose the secret is uniformly chosen in $S$. Any secret sharing scheme for $AS$ satisfies either $|B| \geq |S|^{1.5}$ or $|C| \geq |S|^{1.5}$.*

**Proof.** If the secret is uniformly chosen in $S$ we have that $H(S) = \log |S|$, and from Corollary 4.1 it follows $H(B) + H(C) \geq 3 \log |S|$. Hence, either $B$ or $C$ have entropy at least $1.5 \log |S|$. Assume $H(B) \geq 1.5 \log |S|$. From (1) we have $|B| \geq 2^{H(B)}$, and thus the number of different shares for $B$ must be greater than or equal to $2^{1.5 \log |S|}$, which implies that $|B| \geq |S|^{1.5}$. □

Notice that Corollary 4.1 gives a more general result, since it takes into account the probability distribution according to which the secret and the shares are chosen.

**Remark 2.** The bound given by Corollary 4.2 is the best possible. Indeed, consider the following secret sharing scheme for $\mathcal{AS}$. For a binary secret $s \in S = \{0,1\}$, uniformly choose 2 pairs of bits whose XOR give the secret $s$, that is such that $s = a \oplus b = c \oplus d$ and give share $a$ to the participant $A$, $bd$ to $B$, $c$ to $C$, and $d$ to $D$. It can be easily seen that this scheme meets all requirements for a secret sharing scheme, and that moreover $H(A) = H(C) = H(D) = H(S) = 1$ while $H(B) = 2$ and $H(BC) = 3H(S)$. If a 2-bit secret $s_0 s_1 \in \{0,1\}^2$ is to be shared, then the following scheme can be used. For $i = 0, 1$, uniformly choose bits $a_i, b_i, c_i, d_i$, such that $a_i \oplus b_i = c_i \oplus d_i = s_i$ and give share $a_0 a_1$ to $A$, $b_0 d_0 b_1$ to $B$, $c_0 c_1 a_1$ to $C$ and $d_0 d_1$ to $D$. This is a secret sharing scheme which satisfies $H(A) = H(D) = H(S) = 2$ and $H(B) = H(C) = 1.5 H(S) = 3$. The generalization to $n$-bit secrets, as well as to non-binary cases, is straightforward. In general, if $|S| = q^2$, $q$ integer greater than 2, the above procedure yields a scheme for which $|A| = |D| = q^2$ and $|B| = |C| = q^3 = (q^2)^{1.5}$.

Assume that all shares for participants are chosen from the same space $K$. As a consequence of Corollary 4.2 we get that the *information rate* $\log |S| / \log |K|$ (as defined in [BrSt]) for any secret sharing scheme for $\mathcal{AS}$ is at most $2/3$. The scheme above described has an information rate of exactly $2/3$ when $|S| = q^2$. Thus, the bound of $2/3$ is optimal for $\mathcal{AS}$ and settles a problem by [BrSt].

The bound given by Corollary 4.1 is the best possible for non-uniform distributions, as well. The construction of a secret sharing scheme which meets the bound with equality is a bit involved and will be given in the final version of the paper.

Our lower bound also holds for $\mathcal{AS}2$ which is the closure of the family

$$\{\{A,B\}, \{B,C\}, \{C,D\}, \{B,D\}\}.$$

It is easily seen that Theorem 4.1 also applies, since in the proof we did not make any use of the relation $H(S|BD) = H(S)$ (for $\mathcal{AS}2$ it holds $H(S|BD) = 0$). Hencefrom, the following theorem holds.

**Theorem 4.2** *Any secret sharing scheme for AS2 satisfies*

$$H(BC) \geq 3H(S) \quad and \quad H(BD) \geq 3H(S).$$

**Remark 3.** The bound given by Theorem 4.2 is best possible for uniform distributions. Indeed, consider the following secret sharing scheme for $\mathcal{AS}2$. For a binary secret $s \in S = \{0,1\}$, uniformly choose 2 pairs of bits whose XOR give the secret $s \in S$, that is such that $s = a \oplus b = c \oplus d$ and give share $a$ to participant $A$, $b$ to $B$, $ac$ to $C$, and $ad$ to $D$. This is a secret sharing scheme which satisfies $H(BC) = H(BD) = 3H(S)$. The scheme can be easily generalized to any non-binary space.

An immediate consequence of Theorem 4.2 is the following corollary.

**Corollary 4.3** *If the secret is uniformly chosen in $S$ then any secret sharing scheme for AS2 satisfies either*

$$|B| \geq |S|^{1.5},$$

*or*

$$|C| \geq |S|^{1.5} \quad and \quad |D| \geq |S|^{1.5}.$$

**Remark 4.** A close look to the proof of Theorem 4.1 reveals that exactly the same bound (i.e, $H(BC) \geq 3H(S)$) holds for any access structure $\Gamma$ for 4 participants $A, B, C$, and $D$, satisfying $\{AB\}, \{BC\}, \{ACD\} \in \Gamma$ and $\{AC\}, \{B\}, \{AD\} \notin \Gamma$. The minimal such structure is the closure of $\{\{AB\}, \{BC\}, \{ACD\}\}$, which has $|closure(\Gamma)| = 7$.

Finally, exploiting the structure of $\mathcal{AS}$, we can prove the following result.

**Theorem 4.3** *There is an access structure of $n \geq 5$ participants, for which any scheme requires a total entropy of*

$$\sum_{i=1}^{n} H(X_i) \geq (3n/2)H(S).$$

**Proof.** Consider the 'circular' access structure defined as the closure of the following set

$$\Big\{ \{X_1, X_2\}, \{X_2, X_3\}, ..., \{X_{n-1}, X_n\}, \{X_n, X_1\} \Big\}.$$

For each pair of set of shares $X_i$ and $X_{i+1}$, we have $H(X_i) + H(X_{i+1}) \geq 3H(S)$. Moreover, $H(X_1) + H(X_n) \geq 3H(S)$. Summing over all pairs we get $H(X_1) + H(X_n) + \sum_{i=1}^{n-1} H(X_i) + H(X_{i+1}) \geq 3nH(S)$. Hence, $\sum_{i=1}^{n} H(X_i) \geq (3n/2)H(S)$. ∏

# Acknowledgments

The authors would like to express their thanks to D. R. Stinson for his comments, and to C. Blundo for useful discussions about the tightness of the results.

# References

[BeLe] J. C. Benaloh and J. Leichter, *Generalized Secret Sharing and Monotone Functions*, Crypto 88, pp. 27-35.

[Bl]   G. R. Blakley, *Safeguarding Cryptographic Keys*, Proceedings AFIPS 1979 National Computer Conference, pp. 313-317, June 1979.

[BrDa] E. F. Brickell and D. M. Davenport, *On the Classification of Ideal Secret Sharing Schemes*, J. Cryptology, to appear.

[BrSt] E. F. Brickell and D. R. Stinson, *Some Improved Bounds on the Information Rate of Perfect Secret Sharing Schemes*, Crypto 90 (Published also as Research Report #106, May 1990, University of Nebraska).

[CsKo] I. Csiszár and J. Körner, *Information Theory. Coding theorems for discrete memoryless systems*, Academic Press, 1981.

[De]   D. Denning, *Cryptography and Data Security*, Addison–Wesley, Reading, MA, 1983.

[Ga]   R. G. Gallager, *Information Theory and Reliable Communications*, John Wiley & Sons, New York, NY, 1968.

[GoMiWi] O. Goldreich, S. Micali, and A. Wigderson, *How to Play Any Mental Game*, Proceedings of the 19th Annual ACM Symposium on Theory of Computing, 1987, New York, pp. 218–229.

[ItSaNi] M. Ito, A. Saito, and T. Nishizeki, *Secret Sharing Scheme Realizing General Access Structure*, Proc. IEEE Global Telecommunications Conf., Globecom 87, Tokyo, Japan, 1987, pp. 99–102.

[KaGrHe] E. D. Karnin, J. W. Greene, and M. E. Hellman, *On Secret Sharing Systems*, IEEE Trans. on Inform. Theory, vol. IT-29, no. 1, Jan. 1983, pp. 35-41.

[Ko]  S. C. Kothari, *Generalized Linear Threshold Schemes*, Crypto 84, pp. 231–241.

[Sham]  A. Shamir, *How to Share a Secret*, Communications of the ACM, vol. 22, n. 11, pp. 612-613, Nov. 1979.

[Shan]  C. E. Shannon, *The Mathematical Theory of Communication*, Bell. Syst. J., vol. 27, pp. 379–423, 623–656, July/Oct. 1948.

[Simm]  G.J. Simmons, *Robust Shared Secret Schemes or "How to be Sure You Have the Right Answer even though You don't Know the Question"*, Congressus Numerantium, vol. 8, pp. 215–248, 1989.

[Simm2]  G.J. Simmons, *The Geometry of Shared Secret Schemes*, Bulletin of the Institute of Combinatorics and its Applications (ICA), vol. 1, pp. 59–70, Jan. 1991.

# On Verification in Secret Sharing

Cynthia Dwork

IBM Almaden Research Center

650 Harry Road

San Jose, CA. 95120

dwork@almaden.ibm.com

## Abstract

Verifiable Secret Sharing (VSS) has proven to be a powerful tool in the construction of fault-tolerant distributed algorithms. Previous results show that Unverified Secret Sharing, in which there are no requirements when the dealer is faulty during distribution of the secret, requires the same number of processors as VSS. This is counterintuitive: verification that the secret is well shared out should come at a price. In this paper, by focussing on information leaked to *nonfaulty* processors during verification, we separate a certain strong version of Unverified Secret Sharing (USS) from its VSS analogue in terms of the required number of processors. The proof of the separation theorem yields information about communication needed for the original VSS problem. In order to obtain the separation result we introduce a new definition of secrecy, different from the Shannon definition, capturing the intuition that "information" received from faulty processors may not be informative at all.

# 1 Introduction

The $t$-resilient Verifiable Secret Sharing problem ($t$-VSS) was defined by Chor, Goldreich, Micali, and Awerbuch [4]. A solution to $t$-VSS is a protocol for a distributed system of $n$ processors allowing a distinguished *dealer* processor to irreversibly commit to a secret value that can be reconstructed with certainty at a later time, even if the dealer attempts to block the reconstruction. Specifically, if the dealer is nonfaulty until reconstruction then no set $F$ of up to $t$ faulty processors can learn anything about the secret before reconstruction, and the value reconstructed will indeed be the secret value of the dealer. Moreover, the members of $F$ cannot prevent reconstruction of the committed secret, even if the dealer is in $F$.

VSS and its applications have been widely studied in the literature [1, 2, 3, 6, 7, 8, 13]. In particular, Ben-Or, Goldwasser, and Wigderson showed that in a system of $n \geq 3t + 1$ processors, where $t$ is an upper bound on the number of faulty processors, any function of $n$ inputs can be computed in such a way that not only can the faulty processors not

J. Feigenbaum (Ed.): Advances in Cryptology - CRYPTO '91, LNCS 576, pp. 114-128, 1992.
© Springer-Verlag Berlin Heidelberg 1992

disrupt the computation, but they cannot learn any additional information about the inputs of the nonfaulty processors than that implied by their own inputs and the output of the function [2]. A similar, slightly weaker, result was obtained independently by Chaum, Crepeau, and Damgard [3]. In both these constructions, $t$-resilient VSS is used to share out the inputs to the function. The VSS protocols in [2, 8] differ from other VSS protocols in that they are error-free; secrecy is perfect (information-theoretic) and reconstruction never fails.[1] Dolev, Dwork, Waarts, and Yung [7] showed that the bound of $3t + 1$ processors for error-free $t$-VSS is tight, even in the presence of a broadcast channel. Moreover, the lower bound holds even for the easier problem of $t$-Unverified Secret Sharing ($t$-USS), a relaxation of $t$-VSS in which there are no requirements if the dealer is faulty during distribution of the secret. For the remainder of this paper we discuss only error-free protocols.

That $t$-USS and $t$-VSS should require exactly the same number of processors was puzzling. Error-free verification that the secret is well distributed seemed too powerful to come at no cost. Indeed, elementary arguments show that some communication among shareholders of a secret must take place in order to verify that a secret is well shared out. In this paper we obtain additional information about the structure of this communication. To do this, we define a very strong version of both VSS and its unverified analogue, and prove the separation for those problems in terms of the number of processors. By analyzing the proof of the separation result for the strong versions of the problems we obtain information about communication necessary during verification in any solution of the original $t$-VSS problem.

An interesting by-product of this work is the introduction of what we call *effectively perfect* secrecy. This new type of secrecy captures the intuition that, loosely speaking, "information" received from a faulty processor may not be information at all, since the faulty processor can "lie." In addition to being useful in obtaining the first separation result, we feel our definition of effectively perfect secrecy is an interesting step in trying to capture an appropriate notion of secrecy when the source of information is Byzantine.

The rest of this abstract is organized as follows. Section 2 contains formal definitions of several variants of secret sharing, of perfect secrecy, and of effectively perfect secrecy. Section 3 discusses some related results and applies one of these to our context. Section 4 contains the separation result and some of its implications for ordinary VSS. Discussion and open problems appear in Section 5.

---

[1] In some protocols secrecy is imperfect because it relies on public key cryptography; in others, reconstrution may fail because verification is performed using interactive proof systems techniques.

# 2 Definitions

We consider a completely synchronous distributed system of $n$ processors, $\{p_0, \ldots, p_{n-1}\}$, connected by a complete network of perfectly secure channels. Our definition of protocol is the standard one. Let $E$ be a finite field with a primitive $n$th root of unity $\omega$, such that $|E| > n$.

We assume the secrets are always elements of the finite field $E$. There is a fixed underlying probability distribution $\Pi$ on messages in $E$. *Information-theoretic (perfect) secrecy* says essentially that the best one can do at guessing a secret is to guess an element with maximal probability according to $\Pi$. We say a polynomial is of degree $\ell$ if it is of degree *at most $\ell$*.

Given a protocol $\mathcal{P}$, a processor executing $\mathcal{P}$ is a *disruptor* if it does not follow $\mathcal{P}$ correctly. It can misbehave by not choosing random values according to the distribution specified by $\mathcal{P}$, by failing to send specified messages, possibly sending arbitrary messages in their stead, and by making erroneous state transitions. A processor is a *gossip* if it follows $\mathcal{P}$ correctly but in addition sends extraneous messages labelled as gossip messages. Since the messages are labelled as extraneous, they are never confused with protocol messages. A processor is *pure* if it is neither disruptive nor a gossip. A processor is *faulty* if it is not pure.

A solution to the $(t, d)$-**Verifiable Secret Sharing** problem ($(t, d)$-VSS) is a pair of protocols $(\mathcal{P}_1, \mathcal{P}_2)$, called the *distribution* and *reconstruction* protocols, respectively. Let $p_0$ be a distinguished *dealer* processor with secret input $s$. If in $\mathcal{P}_1$ and $\mathcal{P}_2$ combined there are at most $t$ faulty processors (disruptors and gossips), *of which* at most $d$ are disruptors, then the following properties are required.

1. For every adversary strategy, if the adversary allows $p_0$ to remain pure until the beginning of execution of $\mathcal{P}_2$[2] then until that point no set of up to $t$ faulty processors has any information (in the information-theoretic sense) about the secret $s$. More precisely, for every adversary $\mathcal{A}$, for all pairs of messages $m, m' \in E$, and for all views $\mathcal{V}$ of the members of $F$, $\Pr\left[\mathcal{V} \mid \mathcal{A}, m\right] = \Pr\left[\mathcal{V} \mid \mathcal{A}, m'\right]$, where $F$ is the set of processors compromised by $\mathcal{A}$ and the probabilities are over all choices made by the processors and by the adversary.

2. Whether or not $p_0$ is pure until $\mathcal{P}_2$, the value obtained by executing $\mathcal{P}_2$ is completely

---

[2] $\mathcal{P}_2$ may begin long after $\mathcal{P}_1$ is completed, so the end of $\mathcal{P}_1$ is not the same as the beginning of $\mathcal{P}_2$. For most applications some secrets will be dealt out (using $\mathcal{P}_1$), some computations will be performed, and at some later time the secrets, or some functions of the secrets such as their sum, will be reconstructed (using $\mathcal{P}_2$).

determined by the end of $\mathcal{P}_1$, and remains unchanged regardless of the behavior of the disruptive processors.

3. If $p_0$ is nondisruptive throughout execution of $\mathcal{P}_1$ then the value obtained when $\mathcal{P}_2$ is executed is $s$, the true secret input of $p_0$.

When $t = d$ this is precisely the usual definition of $t$-resilient Verifiable Secret Sharing. The change is the addition of the category of "faulty gossips." These only affect secrecy and do not affect reconstructability. This point is subtle, and comes from the fact that we require perfect reconstructability.

Let $Q(\cdot)$ be a predicate, and let $\mathcal{P} = (\mathcal{P}_1, \mathcal{P}_2)$ be a VSS protocol. We say a coaliton of processors $L$ *prematurely learns* $Q(s)$ if in some execution $\xi$ of $\mathcal{P}$ in which $p_0$ has input $s$ and is pure until execution of $\mathcal{P}_2$, the members of $L$ do not have *implicit knowledge*[3] of $Q(s)$ before execution of $\mathcal{P}_1$ but they do have implicit knowledge of $Q(s)$ before $\mathcal{P}_2$.

A protocol solves the $(\ell, t, d)$-**Strong Verifiable Secret Sharing** problem $((\ell, t, d)$-SVSS), $\ell \geq t \geq d$, if in addition to solving $(t, d)$-VSS it satisfies the following conditions[4]:

1. If $p_0$, with input $s$, remains pure until the beginning of execution of $\mathcal{P}_2$, then no coalition $L$ of up to $\ell$ pure processors prematurely learns $Q(s)$ for any predicate $Q(\cdot)$.

2. If $p_0$, with input $s$, remains pure until the beginning of $\mathcal{P}_2$, then the protocol messages received by $L$ from the nondisruptive processors contain no information about $s$.

Since this definition is delicate, we give some intuition. Fix an execution of an $(\ell, t, d)$-SVSS protocol, and consider the histories of all pure processors until just before execution of $\mathcal{P}_2$. Then the first additional requirement says that if $p_0$ is pure at this point then, for every set $L$ of $\ell$ pure processors, the histories of the members of $L$ do not jointly have enough information to unambiguously determine anything about the secret not implicit in $\Pi$. Thus, even if members of $L$ were to "gossip" among themselves (in the colloquial sense), they would not prematurely learn anything about the secret. Since we think about what the members of the set $L$ could figure out if they were to pool their information about the execution, we generally talk about *coalitions* of size $\ell$. The second

---

[3] Implicit knowledge was defined by Halpern and Moses [11]. Roughly speaking, the definition says that at time $k$ in $\xi$, $L$ has implicit knowledge of a fact $\phi$ if and only if $\phi$ holds in all executions of the protocol in which the joint view of the members of $L$ is identical to their joint view at time $k$ of $\xi$.

[4] The bounds obtained are a function of $\max\{\ell, t\}$, $t$, and $d$. Thus, the case in which $\ell < t$ is somewhat degenerate, so we ignore it in this discussion.

additional requirement says that the partial information gained by $L$ necessarily comes from unreliable sources.

**Remark 1** *There exists an adversary strategy against the $(t, t)$-VSS protocol in [2] that guarantees that every pure processor other than the dealer prematurely learns the secret. Thus, the protocol in [2] does not solve even $(1, t, t)$-SVSS.*

To appreciate the significance of the remark, consider the problem of contract bidding. Let companies $X$, $Y$, and $Z$ be such that

1. Company $Z$ can beat any bid made by Company $X$.

2. Company $Y$ cannot match $X$'s bid.

3. Company $Y$ prefers that $Z$ will win the contract (rather than $X$).

4. Company $Z$ wishes to behave legally.

Suppose the bids are placed using 1-resilient verifiable secret sharing, and suppose further that "legal" behavior includes using any information gained during the distribution of secrets. If $X$ bids before $Z$ does, then, using the adversarial strategy mentioned in the remark, $Y$ can throw the contract to $Z$ by behaving in such a way that $Z$ learns $X$'s bid (and can therefore underbid $X$). Of course, $Y$ could always just tell $Z$ its share of $X$'s bid, but $Z$ might have no way of determining whether or not $Y$ is telling the truth. Precisely this point motivates the following discussion and definitions.

Although by definition a secret shared by $(\ell, t, d)$-SVSS enjoys perfect secrecy with respect to the faulty processors, and *some* secrecy with respect to small coalitions of pure processors (that is, coalitions of size at most $\ell$), it may not have *perfect* secrecy with respect to small coalitions. This is because some probabilistic information may be received from the faulty processors. To see how this might occur, let us say a faulty processor lies "convincingly" about its share of the secret, before reconstruction, if it announces a faulty share but no small coalition of pure processors can detect that the announced share is erroneous[5]. For example, in Shamir's scheme for sharing a secret [14], to ensure secrecy against a coalition of size $\ell$ the dealer chooses a polynomial $P$ of degree $\ell$ whose free term is the secret, and gives to the $i$th processor the "share" $P(i)$, $1 \leq i \leq n$. In this case it is very easy for a processor to lie convincingly to a coalition of $\ell$ nonfaulty

---

[5] It may be possible that, while small coalitions can not detect the fact that the announced share is erroneous, large coalitions of pure processors can do so; something like this is necessary so that faulty shares can be discarded during reconstruction of the secret.

procesors about its share: it simply chooses an arbitrary value and claims this is its share. Since every set of $\ell + 1$ points determines a polynomial of degree $\ell$ the lie is convincing (plausible).

If the probability is low that a faulty processor can lie convincingly to a small coalition of nonfaulty processors about its share of the secret, for example, if shares of the secret are certified with *check vectors* [13], then a plausible share announced by the faulty processor carries some informational content. In this case, continuing the example given above, if the faulty processor were to lie convincingly about its share of a degree $\ell$ polynomial by fortuitously managing to certify a false value, and if the values held by the coalition members together with this value from the faulty processor interpolate to yield a polynomial whose free term is, say, 5, then the coalition can conclude that almost surely the secret is 5. However, they will not *know*, in the sense of Halpern and Moses, that the secret is 5.

In some scenarios the curious parties have no interests in common with the disruptive parties. In this case, especially if the protocol is such that it is *easy* for the faulty processors to lie convincingly about their shares of the secret, it is not clear what it means to "learn" something from the faulty processors. We therefore define *Effectively Perfect SVSS*, in which we attempt to capture the intuition that information received from faulty processors may be of no use in determining the secret prematurely. As usual, we assume the existence of an adversary that controls the selection and behavior of faulty processors. The intuition to keep in mind is that we want a way of saying that even if the faulty processors truthfully announce their shares of the secret, no coalition of up to $\ell$ pure processors really learns anything about the secret, since the faulty processors could be lying convincingly about their shares.

A protocol $\mathcal{P} = (\mathcal{P}_1, \mathcal{P}_2)$ solves $(\ell, t, d)$-**Effectively Perfect SVSS** if in addition to solving $(\ell, t, d)$-SVSS it has the following properties.

1. For all adversaries $\mathcal{A}$ there exists an adversary $\mathcal{A}'$ such that, for all coalitions $L$ of at most $\ell$ pure processors, for every view $\mathcal{V}$ obtained by $L$ in some execution $\xi$ of $\mathcal{P}$ (before the start of $\mathcal{P}_2$) with adversary $\mathcal{A}$,

$$\Pr\left[\mathcal{V} \mid \mathcal{A}\right] \;=\; \Pr\left[\mathcal{V} \mid \mathcal{A}'\right]. \tag{1}$$

2. If the dealer is not compromised by $\mathcal{A}'$ before execution of $\mathcal{P}_2$, then for all legal messages $m'$

$$\Pr\left[\mathcal{V} \mid \mathcal{A}', m\right] \;=\; \Pr\left[\mathcal{V} \mid \mathcal{A}', m'\right]. \tag{2}$$

Here the notation $\Pr[\mathcal{V}\,|\mathcal{A}]$ denotes the probability that $L$ has view $\mathcal{V}$ given that the adversary is $\mathcal{A}$, where the probability distribution is over the choice of the secret as well as over the space of all coin tosses of all processors and of the adversary $\mathcal{A}'$. Similarly, the notation $\Pr[\mathcal{V}\,|\,\mathcal{A}',m]$ denotes the probability that $L$ has view $\mathcal{V}$ given that the adversary is $\mathcal{A}'$ and given that the secret dealt out is $m$, where the probability distribution is the space of all coin tosses of all processors and of the adversary $\mathcal{A}'$ (but not over choice of $m$).

The intuition is as follows. If $\Pr[\mathcal{V}\,|\mathcal{A}] = \Pr[\mathcal{V}\,|\,\mathcal{A}']$ then for all $L$ knows during $\xi$ (before execution of $\mathcal{P}_2$), the adversary is really $\mathcal{A}'$; if the adversary were really $\mathcal{A}'$ then since $\Pr[\mathcal{V}\,|\,\mathcal{A}',m] = \Pr[\mathcal{V}\,|\,\mathcal{A}',m']$ the secrecy would be perfect. Thus, if Equations 1 and 2 hold then secrecy is "effectively" perfect (see Remark 2). We quantify $m,m'$ over all legal messages, rather than over all elements of $E$, because it is possible that not all elements of $E$ are legal inputs to a given protocol.

**Remark 2** *The definition of effectively perfect secrecy is most interesting in a situation in which it is impossible to assign a probability distribution to the space of adversaries. In this case the definition implies that $L$ has no advantage in guessing the message over simply guessing according to the underlying probability distribution $\Pi$.*

A protocol solves $(\ell,t,d)$-**Perfect SVSS** if it solves $(\ell,t,d)$-SVSS and in addition secrecy with respect to any coalition of $\ell$ pure processors is perfect. More formally, for all adversaries $\mathcal{A}$, for all legal messages $m,m'$, for all coalitions $L$ of up to $\ell$ pure processors, and for every view $\mathcal{V}$ of $L$ before $\mathcal{P}_2$ in an execution in which the dealer remains pure until $\mathcal{P}_2$,
$$\Pr[\mathcal{V}\,|\,\mathcal{A},m] = \Pr[\mathcal{V}\,|\,\mathcal{A},m'].$$

**Remark 3** *An alternative definition for $(\ell,t,d)$-Perfect SVSS would be to take the probabilities over the choice of $\mathcal{A}$, and condition only on the secret. However, once again, we can think of no reasonable probability distribution on adversaries.*

For each of these types of Verified Secret Sharing we define a corresponding **Unverified** version by weakening the problem so that there are no requirements if the dealer is faulty during the execution of $\mathcal{P}_1$. In particular, as observed by MacEliece and Sarwate [12], solving $(t,d)$-Unverified Secret Sharing ($(t,d)$-USS) is essentially equivalent to constructing $d$-error-correcting codes with the constraint that no $t$ shares suffice to determine anything about the encoded value. This can be done using the $d$-error correcting BCH codes of length $t + 2d + 1$.

# 3  Related Work

As mentioned in the Introduction, secret sharing has been very widely studied. Simple secret sharing, resilient only to curious coalitions of $t$ gossips but to no disruptors, was defined by Shamir [14]. $t$-Verified Secret Sharing (what we are calling $(t,t)$-VSS) was defined by Chor, Goldwasser, Micali, and Awerbuch [4], whose original solution required many processors (as a function of $t$) and was not error-free. The introduction of zero-knowledge techniques [10], particularly in [9], yielded conceptually simple, elegant, and highly resilient small-error soutions to $t$-VSS requiring only $3t + 1$ processors (see also [5]). The $3t+1$-processor solution due to Chaum, Crepeau, and Damgard [3] enjoys perfect secrecy and requires no cryptographic assumptions, but has small probability of error. The first error-free solution to $t$-VSS was obtained by Ben-Or, Goldwasser, and Wigderson [2]. Their solution required only $3t + 1$ processors, which is optimal, even in the presence of a broadcast channel [7]. More precisely, the results in [2, 7] show that error-free $(t,d)$-VSS can be achieved with $t + 2d + 1$ processors, and this number is necessary even for the *unverified* version of the problem, in which there are no requirements if the dealer is faulty during the distribution protocol. Given a broadcast channel, Rabin and Ben-Or [13] achieved small-error $t$-VSS using only $2t + 1$ processors. Given *both* a broadcast channel and the ability to achieve *oblivious transfer*, Beaver and Goldwasser solve the problem in the presence of a faulty majority [1].

$(\ell, t, d)$-Strong Verifiable Secret Sharing was defined in [6]. The solution in that paper requires only $\max\{\ell, t\} + 2d + 1$ processors. In particular, when $\ell$, the size of the coalition of pure processors, equals $t$, the total number of faulty processors, strong verification incurs no additional cost in processors over $(t,d)$-*unverified* secret sharing. On the other hand, the paper also showed that if the secrecy with respect to coalitions of pure processors is required to be perfect then $\ell + t + 2d + 1$ processors are necessary and sufficient. We briefly review those arguments.

**Theorem 3.1** [6] *Any protocol for $(\ell, t, d)$-Perfect Strong Unverified Secret Sharing requires $\ell + t + 2d + 1$ processors. Moreover, this number of processors suffices even for $(\ell, t, d)$-Perfect Strong Verified Secret Sharing.*

**Proof:** By definition, any protocol for $(\ell + t, d)$-VSS guarantees perfect secrecy with respect to any set of $\ell + t$ players, even if $d$ of these are disruptive. Thus, such a protocol also solves $(\ell, t, d)$-SVSS in which the members of the curious coalition and the faulty processors number at most $\ell + d$ in total. The protocol in [7] for $(\ell + t, d)$-VSS[6] requires exactly $\ell + t + 2d + 1$ processors.

---

[6]based on the protocol for $(\ell + t, \ell + t)$-VSS in [2]

For necessity, suppose $n = \ell + t + 2d$ processors suffice for $(\ell, t, d)$-SVSS, and consider an adversary $\mathcal{A}$ that always compromises the $t$ processors $p_1 \ldots p_t$ (recall, the dealer is $p_0$), causing the compromised processors always to truthfully announce their shares in gossip messages. It is shown in [7] that any $n - 2d$ shares must be enough to reconstruct the secret. Thus, if $n = \ell + t + 2d$ then $\ell + t$ shares suffice. Clearly, for any two legal messages $m$ and $m'$, with this adversary the view of any coalition of $\ell$ pure processors when the secret message is $m$ does not occur with the same probability that they do when the message is $m'$, since the coalition has access to $\ell + t$ shares: its own $\ell$ shares plus the $t$ announced shares. This violates perfect secrecy. ∎

# 4 Separating Unverified Secret Sharing from Verifiable Secret Sharing

## 4.1 Separating the Strong Versions of the Problems

In this subsection we separate effectively perfect Strong Unverified Secret Sharing, in which there are no requirements if the dealer is faulty during the distribution protocol, from effectively perfect Strong Verifiable Secret Sharing. For simplicity, we take all parameters to be $t$. The full paper contains results for the general case. We abbreviate $(t, t, t)$-SVSS (respectively, $(t, t, t)$-SUSS) by $t$-SVSS (respectively, $t$-SUSS).

**Theorem 4.1** *Let $n = 4t$ and let $E$ be a field of at least $n + 1$ elements with a primitive $n$th root of unity $\omega$. Let $\Pi$ be the uniform probability distribution on $E$. There is an $n$-processor protocol for $t$-effectively perfect Strong Unverified Secret Sharing with message space $E$ and probability distribution $\Pi$.*

**Proof:** The protocol is trivial: given input $v$, the dealer chooses a random polynomial $f(\cdot) \in E(\cdot)$ of degree $2t - 1$ with free term $v$, and sends to each processor $p_i$, $0 \leq i < n$, (including itself) the value $f(\omega^i)$. The vector of shares is a codeword in the $t$-error correcting BCH code of length $4t$. To reconstruct the secret, agreement is run on the shares of all processors and the error-correction procedure for BCH codes is applied to retrieve $f$.

Let $\mathcal{A}$ be a disrupting adversary. Let $\xi$ be an execution of the dealing protocol with disrupting adversary $\mathcal{B}$ defined as follows. $\mathcal{B}$ simulates $\mathcal{A}$ precisely until $\mathcal{A}$ has compromised $t$ processors. If $\mathcal{A}$ compromises fewer than $t$ processors, or if $\mathcal{A}$ compromises the dealer, then $\mathcal{B}$ just simulates $\mathcal{A}$. Otherwise, let $D$ be the processors compromised by $B$ and let $q$ be compromised by $B$ no later than any other processor in $D$. Let $B$ choose uniformly at random an element $s_q \in_R E$. $B$ then simulates $A$ in an execution in which all processors in $D - \{q\}$ have the shares they actually received in $\xi$, but $q$ has value $s_q$.

The proof of effectively perfect secrecy rests on two claims, whose proofs are omitted for lack of space.

**Claim 4.1** *Let $\xi$ be an execution of the t-SUSS protocol with adversary $B$. Let $L$ be a set of $t$ processors pure in $\xi$ and not containing the dealer. Let $V$ be $L$'s view during $\xi$. Then $\Pr[V \mid B] = \Pr[V \mid A]$, where the probability space is over choice of secret as well as the random choices of all processors and of the adversary.*

**Claim 4.2** *Let $\xi$ be an execution of the t-SUSS protocol with adversary $B$, and let $L$ be a set of $t$ processors pure in $\xi$ and not containing the dealer. Let $V$ be $L$'s view during $\xi$. Then for all messages $m, m'$, if the dealer is not disrupted by $B$ then $\Pr[V \mid B, m] = \Pr[V \mid B, m']$, where the probability space is over all random choices of the processors and of $B$.*

Thus, the conditions of Equations 1 and 2 are satisfied. This completes the proof of the theorem. ∎

**Theorem 4.2** *t-Effectively Perfect Strong Verifiable Secret Sharing requires $4t + 1$ processors, for all $t \geq 2$.*

**Proof:** Suppose for the sake of contradiction that the theorem is false. Let $P = (P_1, P_2)$ be a protocol requiring only $n \leq 4t$ processors. Let adversary $A$ be as follows. In $P_1$, $A$ compromises a set $D$ of $t$ processors, chosen uniformly at random from the set of all $n - 1$ processors not containing the dealer. $A$ allows the execution to be failure-free; the point of compromising the processors is to give $A$ access to their message histories and random choices. Before execution of $P_2$ each processor in $D$ broadcasts its entire history during the execution of $P_1$. That is, each processor broadcasts its complete message history (sent and received), and all random choices made during the execution of $P_1$. For every coalition $L$ of at most $t$ pure processors, for all $m \neq m'$ and for all views $V$ of the members of $L$, $\Pr[V \mid A, m] \neq \Pr[V \mid A, m']$, since, together with the (truthful) history announced by $D$, the members of $L$ have $n - 2t$ shares, which by a result in [7] suffice to reconstruct the secret.

Now, let $A'$ be any disruptive adversary other than $A$. To satisfy the constraint that for all coalitions $L$ of up to $t$ pure processors, not containing the dealer, and for all views $\mathcal{V}$ of $L$, $\Pr[\mathcal{V} \mid A'] = \Pr[\mathcal{V} \mid A]$ (Equation 1), adversary $A'$ must choose the set $D$ with the same probability distribution as $A$, must never disrupt execution of $\mathcal{P}_1$ in a way detectable by any coalition of $t$ pure processors not containing the dealer, and must announce a supposed history of $D$ before execution of $\mathcal{P}_2$. Moreover, the members of $D$ must send the same message to every processor other than the dealer and other members of $D$, just as they would do under control of $A$; for if some member of $D$ were to send different messages to, say, $p$ and $q$, then the set $L = \{p, q\}$ would be able to distinguish $A'$ from $A$. This is where we use the condition $t \geq 2$.

Consider a particular execution $\xi$ of $\mathcal{P}_1$ with adversary $A'$. Let the processors be divided into four disjoint groups $R, S, T, W$, each of size at least 1 and at most $t$, where the dealer is in $T$ and the processors in $S$ have been compromised by $A'$. Let $\alpha, \beta, \tau, \delta$ be the histories, respectively, of $R, S, T, W$ at the end of $\xi$. We say $\xi$ *results in* $\alpha\beta\tau\delta$. Let $\gamma$ be the history announced by the members of $S$. Note that since $A$ always compromises exactly $t$ processors, $A'$ must do so as well, so $|S| = t$.

For $A'$ not to be distinguished from $A$ by $R$, for some vectors of histories $a_1, a_2$ there must exist a failure-free execution $E_R$ of $\mathcal{P}_1$ resulting in $\alpha\gamma a_1 a_2$. Similarly, for some $c_1, c_2$ there exists a failure-free execution $E_W$ resulting in $c_1\gamma c_2\delta$.

Since $R$ has history $\alpha$ in both $\xi$ and $E_R$, the messages exchanged between $R$ and $W$ are the same in $\xi$ as in $E_R$. Similarly, since $W$ has history $\delta$ in both $\xi$ and $E_W$, the messages exchanged between $R$ and $W$ are the same in $\xi$ as in $E_W$. Thus the messages exchanged between $R$ and $W$ are the same in executions $E_R$ and $E_W$. Since $S$ has history $\gamma$ in $E_W$ and $E_R$, the messages exchanged between $S$ and $W$ are the same in executions $E_R$ and $E_W$. For the same reason, messages exchanged between $S$ and $R$ are the same in executions $E_R$ and $E_W$.

Consider an execution of $\mathcal{P}_1$ with the following adversary $\mathcal{B}$. The processors in $T$ are faulty (including the dealer). They act toward the members of $R$ and $S$ as in execution $E_R$, while acting toward the members of $W$ as in execution $E_W$. At the end of $\mathcal{P}_1$, with the adversary following this strategy, the vector of histories is $\alpha\gamma * \delta$, where we have omitted the history of $T$ because these processors are faulty.

For histories $r, s, t, w$, let $\mathcal{P}_2(rstw)$ denote the outcome of $\mathcal{P}_2$ when the members of $R, S, T, W$ begin $\mathcal{P}_2$ in the states they would be in had they finished $\mathcal{P}_1$ with histories $r, s, t, w$, repectively, and were there to be no other faulty behavior in $\mathcal{P}_2$.

Let $v = \mathcal{P}_2(\alpha\gamma a_1 a_2)$. Since $E_R$ is failure-free and results in $\alpha\gamma a_1 a_2$, it must be the case that $\mathcal{P}_2(\alpha\gamma a_1 \delta) = v$, since otherwise, by choosing between $a_2$ and $\delta$, the members of $W$ could control the outcome of $\mathcal{P}_2$ after execution $E_R$ of $\mathcal{P}_1$. This implies that $\mathcal{P}_2(\alpha\gamma\tau\delta) = v$, since otherwise, after arranging an outcome $\alpha\gamma * \delta$ of $\mathcal{P}_1$, adversary $\mathcal{B}$ could control the outcome of $\mathcal{P}_2$ by choosing between $\tau$ and $a_1$ to determine its starting state in $\mathcal{P}_2$.

We now argue that $\mathcal{P}_2(\alpha\beta\tau\delta) = \mathcal{P}_2(\alpha\gamma\tau\delta)$ $(= v)$. This is because otherwise, after execution $\xi$ (which results in $\alpha\beta\tau\delta$ and in which only the members of $S$ are faulty), the members of $S$ could control the outcome of $\mathcal{P}_2$ by choosing between $\beta$ and $\gamma$. Thus, if $\mathcal{V}$ is the view of the members of $R$ after $\xi$ and after the members of $S$ have announced $\gamma$, then for all $v' \neq v$,

$$\Pr\left[\mathcal{V} \mid \mathcal{A}', v\right] \neq \Pr\left[\mathcal{V} \mid \mathcal{A}', v'\right].$$

This violates Equation 2 in the definition of effectively perfect secrecy. Thus, no adversary $\mathcal{A}'$ satisfying Equation 1 can also satisfy Equation 2. ∎

## 4.2 Implications for $t$-VSS

As we have seen, the distribution phase for $t$-USS requires only a single round of message exchange (the dealer sends a share to every player other than itself). An elementary hybrid argument shows that additional communication is required for the distribution phase of $t$-VSS. The proof of Theorem 4.2 yields information about the structure of this additional communication.

Let $n = 3t + 1$ and consider any $n$-processor protocol $\mathcal{P} = (\mathcal{P}_1, \mathcal{P}_2)$ for $t$-VSS (what we have been calling $(t, t)$-VSS). Let us emphasize certain points in the proof of Theorem 4.2.

1. $\alpha$ and $\gamma$ "fit," that is, there exists a failure-free execution of $\mathcal{P}_1$ that results in $\alpha\gamma a_1 a_2$, for some $a_1 a_2$. We defined $v$ to be $\mathcal{P}_2(\alpha\gamma a_1 a_2)$.

2. $\gamma$ and $\delta$ "fit."

3. $|S|, |T|, |W| \leq t$.

4. From these three points alone we concluded that the secret dealt out during $\xi$ was also $v$. For example, we did not need that $\gamma$ and $\tau$ fit, and we did not need to know $\tau$ or $\delta$.

Since we did not need that $\gamma$ and $\tau$ fit, the members of $S$ could be lying in $\gamma$ about their communication with the members of $T$. In particular, they could be lying about what they received from the dealer. However, since $\gamma$ fits $\delta$, the members of $S$ are not lying about their communication with $W$.

We obtained points (1) and (2) above from the definition of effectively perfect secrecy. Suppose we are given a failure-free execution of a distribution protocol in which the members of $R$ have history $\alpha$. Given $\alpha$, if we had any way of knowing that a history $\gamma$, fitting with $\alpha$, also fits the history of $W$, whatever that history may be, then we could determine the secret, provided the sizes of the sets $S, T, W$ satisfy condition (3). Thus, the proof of Theorem 4.2 shows that the secret is completely determined by $\alpha$ and the communication between the members of $S$ and $W$ during the distribution protocol. Since $|R| \le t$, $\alpha$ itself cannot hold any information about the secret. Thus there must exist some communication between $S$ and $W$. If we assume processors only communicate with explicit messages (and not via timeouts) this tells us a fair amount about the communication needed even in failure-free executions of the dealing protocol.

For example, if we choose $R$, $S$, and $T$ each to have size exactly $t$, then $W$ has size 1. The above discussion implies there must be communication between $S$ and $W$. Varying our choice of $W$ over all processors in $T$ other than the dealer we conclude $S$ must communicate with every processor not in $R \cup S$, except possibly the dealer. (Communication with the dealer can be argued separately.)

# 5   Discussion and Open Questions

This research was motivated by a desire to understand on an intuitive level precisely what must occur during verification that a secret is well distributed. By focussing on secrecy with respect to small coalitions of pure processors we were able to separate a strong version of Verified Secret Sharing from its Unverified analogue. To do this we introduced the notion of effectively perfect secrecy. As we saw in Section 4.2, examination of the proof of Theorem 4.2 yields information about the structure of communication during the distribution phase of any protocol for the original $t$-VSS problem. An example of the type of structure discovered was given in that section. More complete analysis remians to be performed.

We do not have a lower bound on processors needed for effectively perfect $(\ell, t, d)$-SUSS, nor even for effectively perfect $t$-SUSS (the case in which all three parameters are the same). The proof of Theorem 4.1 relies on the fact that every vector of $2t$ shares is in a sense equally probable, so the $t$ faulty players can always make up a vector of $t$ shares that fits with those shares held by the coalition of pure processors, *whoever may be in the coalition*. Interestingly, it is possible to show that if the faulty processors only wish to lie convincingly to a *particular* coaltion of pure gossips then it is possible to use polynomials of degree $t$ (rather than of degree $2t - 1$, as done in the proof of the Theorem), in which case $3t + 1$ processors suffice.

Although our bound on effectively perfect $t$-SVSS is tight, in the general case there is a gap between the lower bound of $\ell + 3d + 1$ processors for effectively perfect $(\ell, t, d)$-SVSS and the upper bound of $\ell + t + 2d + 1$.

**Acknowledgements** I am grateful to Stephen Ponzio for many hours of discussion. My original proof of effectively perfect secrecy for the protocol in Theorem 4.1 held only for static adversaries. Ponzio suggested the modification of $B$ used to prove the result for dynamic adversaries. Discussions with Joe Kilian and Larry Stockmeyer were also helpful; I thank them both.

# References

[1] D. Beaver, and S. Goldwasser, Multiparty Computation with Faulty Majority, *Proc. 30th Symp. on Foundations of Comp. Science*, pp. 468-473, 1989.

[2] M. Ben-Or, S. Goldwasser, and A. Wigderson, Completeness Theorems for Non-Cryptographic Fault-Tolerant Distributed Computation, *Proc. 20th Symp. on Theory of Computing*, pp. 1-10, 1988.

[3] D. Chaum, C. Crepeau, and I. Damgard, Multiparty Unconditionally Secure Protocols, *Proc. 20th Symp. on Theory of Computing*, 11-19, 1988.

[4] B. Chor, S. Goldwasser, S. Micali, and B. Awerbuch, Verifiable Secret Sharing and Achieving Simultaneity in the Presence of Faults, *Proc. 26 Symp. on Foundations of Computing*, pp. 383-395, 1985.

[5] B. Chor, and M. Rabin, Achieving Independence in Logarithmic Number of Rounds, *Proc. 6th Annual ACM Symp. on Principles of Distributed Computing*, pp. 260-268 (1987).

[6] C. Dwork, Strong Verifiable Secret Sharing, *to appear, Proc. 4th International Workshop on Distributed Algorithms (1990)*, Springer Verlag.

[7] D. Dolev, C. Dwork, O. Waarts, and M. Yung, Perfectly Secure Message Transmission, *Proc. 31st Annual Symposium on Foundations of Computer Science*, pp. 36-45 (1990).

[8] P. Feldman, and S. Micali, Optimal Algorithms for Byzantine Agreement, *Proc. 20th Symp. on Theory of Computing*, pp. 148-161, 1988.

[9] O. Goldreich, S. Micali, and A. Wigderson, How to Play Any Mental Game, *Proc. 19th Symp. on Theory of Computing*, pp. 218-229, 1987.

[10] S. Goldwasser, S. Micali, and C. Rackoff, The Knowledge Complexity of Interactive Proof-Systems, *Proc. 17th Annual ACM Symposium on Theory of Computing* (1985), pp. 291-304.

[11] J. Halpern and Y. Moses, Knowledge and Common Knowledge in a Distributed Environment, *JACM 37*(3), pp. 549-587, 1990.

[12] R. McEliece and D. Sarwate, On Sharing Secrets and Reed-Solomon Codes, *CACM 24*(9), pp. 583-584, 1981.

[13] T. Rabin, and M. Ben-Or, Verifiable Secret Sharing and Multiparty Protocols with Honest Majority, *Proc. 21st Symp. on Theory of Computing*, pp. 73-85, 1989.

[14] A. Shamir, How to Share a Secret, *CACM 22*, pp. 612-613, 1979.

# Non-Interactive and Information-Theoretic Secure Verifiable Secret Sharing

Torben Pryds Pedersen
Computer Science Department
Aarhus University, Denmark
tppedersen@daimi.aau.dk

## Abstract

It is shown how to distribute a secret to $n$ persons such that each person can verify that he has received correct information about the secret without talking with other persons. Any $k$ of these persons can later find the secret ($1 \leq k \leq n$), whereas fewer than $k$ persons get no (Shannon) information about the secret. The information rate of the scheme is $\frac{1}{2}$ and the distribution as well as the verification requires approximately $2k$ modular multiplications pr. bit of the secret. It is also shown how a number of persons can choose a secret "in the well" and distribute it verifiably among themselves.

## 1 Introduction

Secret sharing schemes were introduced independently in [Sha79] and [Bla79] and since then much work has been put into the investigation of such schemes (see [Sim90] for a list of references). The verifiable secret sharing schemes constitute a particular interesting class of these schemes as they allow each receiver of information about the secret (*share* of the secret) to verify that the share is consistent with the other shares.

Let the *dealer* be the person who has a secret and distributes it to $n$ *shareholders*, where $n > 0$. If the dealer trusts one of the shareholders completely, he could give the secret to this person and then avoid the troubles of having a secret sharing scheme. Thus in many applications the dealer does not trust the shareholders completely, and therefore it should be expected that (some of) the shareholders do not trust the dealer either. For this reason efficient verifiable secret sharing schemes are necessary in practice.

However, verifiable secret sharing has also turned out to be a useful tool in more theoretical work. In [BGW88] and [CCD88] unconditionally secure verifiable secret sharing schemes are constructed and used to design secure multi-party protocols. Unfortunately, these schemes are *interactive* — interaction between the participants is needed in order to verify the shares. Both of these schemes require that less than $\frac{n}{3}$ of the shareholders are dishonest. This is improved in [RB89], where a scheme with the same properties is presented, except that it allows less than $\frac{n}{2}$ dishonest participants. These three schemes

J. Feigenbaum (Ed.): Advances in Cryptology - CRYPTO '91, LNCS 576, pp. 129-140, 1992.
© Springer-Verlag Berlin Heidelberg 1992

all have the property that even an all powerful dealer cannot distribute incorrect shares (in [CCD88] and [RB89] there is an exponentially small error probability however).

In this paper, we are mainly interested in *non-interactive* verifiable secret sharing. In such a scheme only the dealer is allowed to send messages — in particular the shareholders cannot talk with each other or the dealer when verifying a share. This model is very suitable in practice as it allows distribution by mail for instance.

[Ben87] presented the first non-interactive verifiable secret sharing scheme, but it relied on the existence of a mutually trusted entity. In [Fel87] this entity is avoided by letting the dealer publish probabilistic encryptions of the polynomial used to compute the shares, and due to a homomorphism property of the encryption scheme verification of the shares is possible. This scheme is quite efficient, but after the distribution, the privacy of the secret depends on a computational assumption — such as the intractability of computing discrete logarithms.

The goal of this paper is to construct an efficient non-interactive scheme for verifiable secret sharing in which no (Shannon) information about the secret is revealed. [Ped91] presents a non-interactive verifiable secret sharing scheme which can be used for secrets, $s$, for which $g^s$ is known, where $g$ is the generator of a group. In this paper the scheme suggested in [Ped91] is modified in order to remove the assumption that $g^s$ is known beforehand. This results in a secret sharing scheme which is unconditionally secure for the dealer. However, in this scheme the dealer can succeed in distributing incorrect shares, if he can solve the discrete logarithm problem (see [BM84] for a formal definition). This property is inevitable as we shall see that it is impossible to construct a non-interactive secret sharing scheme in which no information about the secret is revealed and even a dealer with unlimited computing power cannot cheat. Thus this scheme is in some sense dual to that of [Fel87] (see Section 4.3).

The new secret sharing scheme is constructed by combining Shamir's scheme (see [Sha79]) with a commitment scheme, which is unconditionally secure for the committer and furthermore allows commitment to many bits simultaneously. This commitment scheme is a variant of a scheme proposed in [BCP].

After introducing some notation in Section 2, Section 3 describes the commitment scheme, and in Section 4 the secret sharing scheme is presented. As an application of this scheme, Section 5 shows how the shareholders can compute linear combinations of shared secrets and Section 6 concludes the paper.

# 2  Notation

Throughout this paper $p$ and $q$ denote large primes such that $q$ divides $p - 1$, $G_q$ is the unique subgroup of $\mathbb{Z}_p^*$ of order $q$, and $g$ is a generator of $G_q$. It can easily be tested if an element $a \in \mathbb{Z}_p^*$ is in $G_q$ since

$$a \in G_q \iff a^q = 1.$$

As any element $b \neq 1$ in $G_q$ generates the group, the discrete logarithm of $a \in G_q$ with respect to the base $b$ is defined and it is denoted $\log_b(a)$.

For any integer $x$ the length of the binary representation of $x$ is denoted $|x|$.

# 3   The Commitment Scheme

This section describes a commitment scheme, which is very similar to that of [BCP]. The only difference is in the choice of $g$ and $h$.

Let $g$ and $h$ be elements of $G_q$ such that nobody knows $\log_g h$. These elements can either be chosen by a trusted center, when the system is initialized, or by (some of) the participants using a coin-flipping protocol.

The committer commits himself to an $s \in \mathbb{Z}_q$ by choosing $t \in \mathbb{Z}_q$ at random and computing

$$E(s,t) = g^s h^t.$$

Such a commitment can later be opened by revealing $s$ and $t$. The following theorem is very easy to prove and shows that $E(s,t)$ reveals no information about $s$, and that the committer cannot open a commitment to $s$ as $s' \neq s$ unless he can find $\log_g(h)$.

**Theorem 3.1**
For any $s \in \mathbb{Z}_q$ and for randomly uniformly chosen $t \in \mathbb{Z}_q$, $E(s,t)$ is uniformly distributed in $G_q$.
If $s, s' \in \mathbb{Z}_q$ satisfies $s \neq s'$ and $E(s,t) = E(s',t')$, then $t \neq t' \bmod q$ and

$$\log_g h = \frac{s - s'}{t' - t} \bmod q.$$

Even though it will not be used in the following we mention that it is quite easy to prove one's ability to open two commitments as the same value without revealing this value. Let namely

$$\beta = E(s,t) \quad \text{and} \quad \beta' = E(s,t')$$

where $t \neq t'$. Anyone who knows an $r$ such that $\beta/\beta' = h^r$ can open $\beta$ as $s$ if and only if he can also open $\beta'$ as $s$. By revealing $r = t - t'$ it is therefore possible to prove equality of the contents of two commitments. Furthermore, $t - t'$ does not contain any information about $s$. It is not clear how to prove efficiently, that commitments to two different values really do contain different values. In particular, the proof of [BCC88] that two blobs contain different bits given a method of proving equality does not generalize to this commitment scheme.

Finally consider the efficiency of the commitment scheme. If $p$ and $q$ are constructed by first choosing $q$ and then determining $p$ as the first prime congruent to 1 mod $q$, heuristics show that $p \leq q(\log q)^2$ (see [Wag79]). Thus a commitment to $|q|$ bits requires at most $|q| + 2\log|q|$ bits. Furthermore, by first computing the product $gh$ a commitment to $s$ can be done in less than $2|q|$ multiplications modulo $p$ or less than two multiplications pr. bit of $s$. Thus the commitment scheme is quite efficient with respect to the size of commitments as well as the computation required.

# 4   Non-interactive Verifiable Secret Sharing

This section first defines verifiable secret sharing, and then the commitment scheme described above and the Shamir scheme are combined resulting in a non-interactive verifiable secret sharing scheme. Finally, the efficiency of the scheme is estimated.

## 4.1  Verification of Shares

Assume that a dealer, $D$, has a secret $s \in \mathbb{Z}_q$ and wants to distribute it among $n$ parties, $P_1, \ldots, P_n$, such that any $k$ of the shareholders can find $s$ if necessary, but less than $k$ shareholders get no (Shannon) information about $s$ (a $(k, n)$-threshold scheme). Shamir suggested that the dealer could do this by choosing a polynomial $f \in \mathbb{Z}_q[x]$ of degree at most $k - 1$ such that $f(0) = s$ and then give $P_i$ the share $f(i)$. $P_{i_1}, \ldots, P_{i_k}$ can later find $s$ from the formula for $f$:

$$f(x) = \sum_{j=1}^{k} (\prod_{l \neq j} \frac{x - i_j}{i_l - i_j}) f(i_j)$$

as

$$s = \sum_{j=1}^{k} (\prod_{l \neq j} \frac{i_j}{i_j - i_l}) f(i_j).$$

Our goal is to extend this scheme with a verification protocol, $VP$, such that any $k$ participants, who have (honestly) accepted their shares in $VP$ can find $s$. More formally $VP$ must satisfy:

**Definition 4.1**
A verification protocol, $VP$, takes place between the dealer and $P_1, \ldots, P_n$. It must satisfy the following two requirements:

1. If the dealer follows the distribution protocol and if the dealer and $P_i$ both follow $VP$, then $P_i$ accepts with probability 1.

2. For all subsets $S_1$ and $S_2$ of $\{1, \ldots, n\}$ of size $k$ such that all parties $(P_i)_{i \in S_1}$ and $(P_i)_{i \in S_2}$ have accepted their shares in $VP$ the following holds except with negligible probability in $|q|$: If $s_i$ is the secret computed by the participants in $S_i$ (for $i = 1, 2$) then $s_1 = s_2$.

A share is called *correct*, if it is accepted in $VP$.

Even though this definition allows any kind of interaction between the dealer and the participants we shall only be concerned with *non-interactive* verification protocols here. In this case the dealer sends extra information to each participant during the distribution, and in the verification protocol $P_i$ verifies that his secret share is consistent with this extra information.

Definition 4.1 does not refer to the secret when defining the correctness of a share. This is in accordance with the fact that no participant have any information about $s$ during the verification and therefore $s$ could be whatever the dealer claims. After the execution of the verification protocol the secret is defined as the value, which any $k$ participants with correct shares will find when combining their shares. If the dealer succeeds in distributing inconsistent shares, this is not well-defined, but Definition 4.1 guarantees that the dealer will be caught almost always when trying to cheat.

## 4.2  The Scheme

Let $g, h \in G_q$ be given such that the commitment scheme from Section 3 can be applied. By the fact that $\mathbb{Z}_q$ is a field, the dealer can distribute $s \in \mathbb{Z}_q$ as follows:

1. $D$ publishes a commitment to $s$: $E_0 = E(s,t)$ for a randomly chosen $t \in \mathbb{Z}_q$.

2. $D$ chooses $F \in \mathbb{Z}_q[x]$ of degree at most $k-1$ satisfying $F(0) = s$, and computes
   $s_i = F(i)$ for $i = 1, \ldots, n$.
   Let $F(x) = s + F_1 x + \ldots + F_{k-1} x^{k-1}$. $D$ chooses $G_1, \ldots, G_{k-1} \in \mathbb{Z}_q$ at random and
   uses $G_i$ when committing to to $F_i$ for $i = 1, \ldots, k-1$. $D$ broadcasts $E_i = E(F_i, G_i)$
   for $i = 1, \ldots, k-1$.

3. Let $G(x) = t + G_1 x + \ldots + G_{k-1} x^{k-1}$ and let $t_i = G(i)$ for $i = 1, \ldots n$. Then $D$
   sends $(s_i, t_i)$ secretly to $P_i$ for $i = 1, 2, \ldots, n$.

When $P_i$ has received his share $(s_i, t_i)$ he verifies that

$$E(s_i, t_i) = \prod_{j=0}^{k-1} E_j^{i^j} \qquad (*).$$

## Lemma 4.2
Let $S \subset \{1, \ldots, n\}$ be a set of $k$ participants such that $(*)$ holds for these $k$ parties. Then
these $k$ parties can find a pair $(s', t')$ such that $E_0 = g^{s'} h^{t'}$.

## Proof
Let $S \subseteq \{1, \ldots, n\}$ of size $k$ be given. The participants in $S$ first find the two unique
polynomials $F'$ and $G'$ of degree at most $k-1$ satisfying

$$\begin{aligned} F'(i) &= s_i \\ G'(i) &= t_i \end{aligned}$$

for $i \in S$. Now let $h = g^d$. Then

$$g^{F'(i) + dG'(i)} = E(s_i, t_i) = g^{s_i + dt_i}$$

for $i \in S$. Thus $(F' + dG')(x)$ is the unique polynomial of degree at most $k-1$ mapping
$i$ to $s_i + dt_i$. Let $E_j = g^{e_j}$. Then the polynomial

$$e(x) = \sum_{j=0}^{k-1} e_j x^j$$

satisfies $e(i) = s_i + dt_i$ for $i \in S$. Thus

$$e(x) = (F' + dG')(x)$$

and in particular

$$E_0 = g^{e(0)} = g^{F'(0) + dG'(0)} = g^{F'(0)} h^{G'(0)}.$$

Therefore it is sufficient to put $s' = F'(0)$ and $t' = G'(0)$. ∎

The members in $S$ do not have to find $F'$ in order to find the secret. It is more
efficient to use the formula

$$s = \sum_{i \in S} a_i s_i \qquad \text{where} \qquad a_i = \prod_{i \in S, i \neq i} \frac{i}{i-j}.$$

Note that they can also find $t$ by the formula

$$t = \sum_{i \in S} a_i t_i.$$

## Theorem 4.3

Under the assumption that the dealer cannot find $\log_g h$ except with negligible probability in $|q|$, the verification protocol satisfies Definition 4.1.

## Proof

It is not hard to see that $(*)$ will be satisfied for all participants if the dealer follows the protocol.

Let $S$ and $S'$ be two subsets of $\{1, \ldots, n\}$ of size $k$ such that all participants in $S$ and $S'$ have accepted their shares correctly. According to Lemma 4.2 the members of $S$ and $S'$ can find pairs $(s, t)$ and $(s', t')$, respectively, such that $E_0 = E(s, t) = E(s', t')$.

As the shares are consistent if and only if there is a polynomial, $f$, of degree at most $k - 1$ such that

$$f(i) = s_i \qquad \text{for } i = 1, 2, \ldots, n$$

the dealer can find the two sets $S$ and $S'$ as follows, if the shares are inconsistent:

1. Let $f$ be the unique polynomial of degree at most $k - 1$ such that $f(i) = s_i$ for $i = 1, 2, \ldots, k$.

2. Let $i = k + 1$.

3. If $i > n$ then stop (all shares are consistent).
   If $f(i) = s_i$ then put $i := i + 1$ and goto 3.
   Otherwise return the sets $S = \{1, 2, \ldots, k\}$ and $S' = \{1, 2, \ldots, k - 1, i\}$.

Thus, if the dealer has succeeded in distributing inconsistent shares, he can find $\log_g h$ by first finding $S$ and $S'$ as described above and then computing $\log_g h$ as in Theorem 3.1.
∎

As a consequence of Theorem 4.3 all the shares satisfying $(*)$ are consistent unless the dealer succeeds in finding $\log_g(h)$ *before* the last share has been sent.

The following theorem shows, that fewer than $k$ participants get no (Shannon) information about the secret. For any subset $S \subset \{1, \ldots, n\}$, $views_S$ denotes the messages, that the members of $S$ see:

$$views_S = (E_0, E_1, \ldots, E_{k-1}, (s_i, t_i)_{i \in S}).$$

## Theorem 4.4

For any $S \subset \{1, \ldots, n\}$ of size at most $k - 1$ and any $views_S$

$$Prob[D \text{ has secret } s \mid views_S] = Prob[D \text{ has secret } s]$$

for all $s \in \mathbb{Z}_q$.

## Proof

It is sufficient to prove the theorem in the case where $S$ has size $k - 1$. If $k - 1$ parties do not get any information about $s$ then neither does fewer than $k - 1$ parties.

Let $S = \{1, \ldots, k-1\}$ and let $views_S = (E_0, E_1, \ldots, E_{k-1}, (s_i, t_i)_{i=1,\ldots,k-1})$. For every $s \in \mathbb{Z}_q$ there is exactly one $t \in \mathbb{Z}_q$ such that $E_0 = E(s, t)$ and there is exactly one polynomial $F$ of degree at most $k-1$ satisfying

$$
\begin{aligned}
F(0) &= s \\
F(i) &= s_i \quad \text{for } i = 1, \ldots, k-1
\end{aligned}
$$

and exactly one polynomial $G$ of degree at most $k-1$ satisfying

$$
\begin{aligned}
G(0) &= t \\
G(i) &= t_i \quad \text{for } i = 1, \ldots, k-1
\end{aligned}
$$

Let $F(x) = s + F_1 x + \ldots + F_{k-1} x^{k-1}$ and $G(x) = t + G_1 x + \ldots + G_{k-1} x^{k-1}$. In order to show that $views_S$ does not contain any information about the secret it must be shown that $F$ and $G$ satisfies

$$
E(F_i, G_i) = E_i \quad \text{for } i = 1, \ldots, k-1,
$$

as this is true for the polynomials chosen by the dealer. As in the proof of Lemma 4.2 this follows from the fact that there is one and only one polynomial, $f$, of degree at most $k-1$ satisfying ($s_0 = s$, $t_0 = t$)

$$
g^{f(i)} = g^{s_i} h^{t_i}
$$

for $i = 0, 1, \ldots, k-1$ and the polynomial $F + dG$ satisfies this for $d = \log_g h$. ∎

## 4.3 Efficiency and Security

In this section, the computational requirements of the scheme are estimated and the scheme is compared to [Fel87].

First consider the size of the secret shares. The information rate (see [BD90]) is

$$
\frac{\text{size of secret}}{\text{size of share}} = \frac{1}{2}.
$$

Ignoring the time needed to evaluate $F(x)$ and $G(x)$ (this is reasonable as the polynomials are only evaluated on small arguments), the dealer has to compute $k$ commitments in order to verify a share. This requires less than $2|q|k$ multiplications modulo $p$ or approximately $2k$ multiplications pr. bit of the secret, if every element in $\mathbb{Z}_q$ can be chosen as the secret.

The verification requires $k-1$ exponentiations modulo $p$ and the computation of one commitment. This can be done in less than (again ignoring the computation of $i^j$ for $j = 1, \ldots, k-1$)

$$
2|q|(k-1) + 2|q| + (k-1) \approx (2|q| + 1)k
$$

multiplications. This is however, a pessimistic estimate as many of the exponents in the exponentiations are rather small (in particular, for $P_1$ they all equal 1).

The scheme presented here is in many respects similar to that of [Fel87], which works for any probabilistic encryption scheme in which a number of bits (say $l$) are encrypted as the "hard-core" bits of a one-way function with homomorphic properties. Specifically, it is suggested to use the function

$$x \mapsto g^x \qquad \text{for } x \in \mathbb{Z}_q^*$$

and encrypt $l = O(\log |q|)$ bits as $g^x$ where the $l$ bits in question are easy to compute from $x$. Using this scheme, the computational requirements when distributing an $l$-bits secret is very similar to the requirements in our scheme when distributing a $|q|$-bits secret (note that $|q| \approx 2^l$).

With respect to security the two schemes are dual to each other, because the encryption schemes used in [Fel87] only protects the secret under the assumption that the one-way function cannot be inverted. However, even an infinitely powerful dealer cannot distribute incorrect shares. In contrast, the new scheme protects the privacy of the secret unconditionally, but the correctness of the shares depends on a computational assumption.

Having these two secret sharing schemes it is natural to ask for a non-interactive scheme in which

- no information about the secret is revealed; and

- even an infinitely powerful dealer cannot compute inconsistent shares.

However, the following shows that such a scheme is impossible in the model which is used here. Let namely $b$ denote all the information which the dealer broadcasts in a non-interactive secret sharing scheme, and let $s_i$ be the secret share which is sent to $P_i$. Let $V(i, b, s_i)$ denote the verification predicate which $P_i$ computes in order to verify his share. Now consider $P_1, \ldots, P_{k-1}$ and assume that they have received correct shares. Let $S_k$ be the set of shares which $P_k$ can receive:

$$S_k(b) = \{s_k \mid V(k, b, s_k)\}.$$

As even an all powerful dealer cannot find inconsistent shares then $P_1, \ldots, P_{k-1}, P_k$ will find the same secret for any $s_k \in S_k$. This means that $P_1, \ldots, P_{k-1}$ can find the secret by guessing a secret share $s_k \in S_k$ and then combine their own shares with $s_k$.

In particular note that $S_k(b)$ is in $NP$ if $V$ can be computed in polynomial time. Therefore does $P_1, \ldots, P_{k-1}$ "only" need nondeterministic polynomial time in order to find the secret if the scheme is unconditionally secure for the shareholders. Similarly, a dishonest dealer can distribute inconsistent shares in nondeterministic polynomial time if the scheme reveals no information about the secret.

# 5  Computing on Shared Secrets

As mentioned in the introduction verifiable secret sharing is an important tool in the construction of secure protocols for multiparty computations. In particular both the construction in [BGW88] and [CCD88] utilize the fact that it is easy to compute linear combinations of shared secrets. In this section we show that this is also true if the secret sharing scheme presented here is used, and we present an application of this property.

## 5.1 Linear Combinations

Assume that two secrets $s'$ and $s''$ have been distributed as described in Chapter 4. In particular let $(s_i', t_i')$ and $(s_i'', t_i'')$ be $P_i$'s share of $s'$ and $s''$, respectively, and let $(E_0', E_1', \ldots, E_{k-1}')$ and $(E_0'', E_1'', \ldots, E_{k-1}'')$ be the broadcasted messages when the two secrets were distributed.

Each $P_i$ can compute $(E_0, E_1, \ldots, E_{k-1})$ corresponding to a verifiable distribution of $s = s' + s'' \bmod q$ as

$$E_j = E_j' E_j'' \qquad \text{for } j = 0, 1 \ldots k - 1.$$

Furthermore, $P_i$'s secret share, $(s_i, t_i)$, of $s$ is given by

$$\begin{aligned} s_i &= s_i' + s_i'' \bmod q \\ t_i &= t_i' + t_i'' \bmod q \end{aligned}$$

By insertion it is easy to see that if both $(s_i', t_i')$ and $(s_i'', t_i'')$ are correct shares (satisfy (*)) then $(s_i, t_i)$ is also a correct share of $s$; i.e.

$$g^{s_i} h^{t_i} = E_0 E_1^i \ldots E_{k-1}^{i^{k-1}}.$$

If, instead, $s$ is computed as $s = as' \bmod q$ for some $a \in \mathbb{Z}_q^*$, then $P_i$ can compute his share $(s_i, t_i)$ and $(E_0, E_1, \ldots, E_{k-1})$ as follows

$$\begin{aligned} E_j &= E_j^a \qquad \text{for } j = 0, 1, \ldots, k - 1 \\ s_i &= as_i' \bmod q \\ t_i &= at_i' \bmod q \end{aligned}$$

Again, it is easy to see that

$$g^{s_i} h^{t_i} = E_0 E_1^i \ldots E_{k-1}^{i^{k-1}}.$$

In both of the above cases Lemma 4.2 implies that any $k$ shareholders who have accepted their shares of $s'$ and $s''$ can find a pair $(s, t)$ such that

$$g^s h^t = E_0.$$

Furthermore, it is an immediate consequence of Theorem 4.4 that fewer than $k$ persons have no information about $s$ if $s'$ and $s''$ are distributed correctly.

## 5.2 Choosing an Anonymous Shared Secret

In [IS91] it was shown how to set up a secret sharing scheme without a mutually trusted authority, who knows the secret and distributes it. In this section we show how to achieve the same goal with verifiable secret sharing by demonstrating how $n$ participants can select a secret so that nobody knows it and distribute it verifiably among themselves in a $(k, n)$ secret sharing scheme. It is not hard to generalize the proposed method to let $l$ person $(k \le l \le n)$ select and distribute the secret.

Let $P_1, \ldots, P_n$ be the $n$ persons who want to choose a secret and distribute it among themselves and assume that each $P_i$ can make digital signatures. The protocol for $P_i$ is

1. Choose $s_{i0} \in \mathbb{Z}_q$ at random.

2. Distribute $s_{i0}$ verifiably among $P_1, \ldots, P_n$.
   Furthermore $P_i$ signs each secret share and sends the signature with the share.

3. Verify all the received shares. If a share is incorrect, $P_i$ publishes the share and its signature. Then $P_i$ stops.

4. Compute the share $(s_i, t_i)$ of $s = s_{10} + s_{20} + s_{n0}$ and the corresponding public information $(E_0, E_1, \ldots, E_{k-1})$ as described in Subsection 5.1.

It follows from the arguments in the previous subsection that

- $(s_i, t_i)$ is a correct share of $s$ if $P_i$ has accepted all shares correctly; and

- any $k$ participants can find a pair $(s', t')$ such that $E_0 = E(s', t')$.

We now show that $s$ is uniformly distributed in $\mathbb{Z}_q$, and that fewer than $k$ participants have no information about $s$.

**Theorem 5.1**
If $P_i$ chooses $s_{i0} \in \mathbb{Z}_q$ uniformly at random and at most $k - 1$ of the other parties cooperate, then $s$ is uniformly distributed in $\mathbb{Z}_q$.

**Proof**
Follows from the fact that no set of at most $k - 1$ participants (excluding $P_i$) get any information about $s_{i0}$. This implies that if at least one of the participants chooses $s_{i0}$ at random then

$$s = s_{10} + s_{20} + \ldots + s_{n0}$$

is uniformly chosen in $\mathbb{Z}_q$. ∎

As before let $views_S$ be the messages, which the participants in a subset $S$ of $\{1, \ldots, n\}$ see.

**Theorem 5.2**
For any $S \subset \{1, \ldots, n\}$ of size at most $k - 1$ and any $views_S$

$$Prob[s \text{ is chosen} \mid views_S] = \frac{1}{q}$$

for all $s \in \mathbb{Z}_q$, if the participants not in $S$ follow the protocol.

**Proof sketch**
Under the assumptions in the theorem it follows from Theorem 5.1 that each $s \in \mathbb{Z}_q$ is chosen with probability $\frac{1}{q}$.

Given $S \subset \{1, \ldots, n\}$ of size $k - 1$ and $views_S$. For any $s \in \mathbb{Z}_q$ there exists $q^{n-(k-1)-1} = q^{n-k}$ values of $(s_{j0})_{j \notin S}$ such that $s = \sum_{j=1}^n s_{j0}$, and as in the proof of Theorem 4.4 for each for these values of $s_{j0}$ $(j \notin S)$ there is exactly one value of $t_{j0}$ which gives the same messages from $P_j$. ∎

# 6 Conclusion

We have presented a non-interactive verifiable $(k,n)$-threshold scheme which is at least as efficient as earlier proposals. Unlike the schemes in [BGW88], [CCD88] and [RB89] this scheme protects the secret to be distributed unconditionally for any value of $k$ ($1 \leq k \leq n$), but the correctness of the shares depends on the assumption that the dealer cannot find discrete logarithms before the distribution has been completed. This result is optimal because in any non-interactive verifiable secret sharing scheme, which reveals no information about the secret, it is possible for a dishonest dealer to distribute inconsistent shares in nondeterministic polynomial time.

The information rate of the presented scheme is $\frac{1}{2}$ and the distribution of a secret in $\mathbb{Z}_q$ as well as the verification of a share requires at most $2\lfloor q/k \rfloor$ multiplications modulo $p$.

It was shown that it is very easy to compute linear combinations of shared secrets, and in particular it was demonstrated how, $l$ persons, $P_1, \ldots, P_l$, can select a secret democratically (without knowing the secret) and distribute it verifiably to $P_1, \ldots, P_l$, $P_{l+1}, \ldots, P_n$ in a $(k,n)$-threshold scheme.

# References

[BCC88] G. Brassard, D. Chaum, and C. Crépeau. Minimum disclosure proofs of knowledge. *Journal of Computer and System Sciences*, 37:156–189, 1988.

[BCP] J. Bos, D. Chaum, and G. Purdy. A voting scheme. Preliminary draft.

[BD90] E. F. Brickell and D. M. Davenport. On the classification of ideal secret sharing schemes. In *Advances in Cryptology - proceedings of CRYPTO 89*, pages 278 – 285, 1990.

[Ben87] J. C. Benaloh. Secret sharing homomorphisms: Keeping shares of a secret secret. In *Advances in Cryptology - proceedings of CRYPTO 86*, Lecture Notes in Computer Science, pages 251–260. Springer-Verlag, 1987.

[Bla79] G. R. Blakley. Safeguarding cryptographic keys. In *Proceedings AFIPS 1979 Nat. Computer Conf.*, pages 313 – 319, 1979.

[BM84] M. Blum and S. Micali. How to generate cryptographically strong sequences of pseudo-random bits. *SIAM Journal of Computation*, 13:850–864, 1984.

[BGW88] M. Ben-Or, S. Goldwasser, and A. Widgerson. Completeness theorems for non-cryptographic fault-tolerant distributed computation. In *Proceedings of the Twentieth Annual ACM Symposium on Theory of Computing*, pages 1–10, 1988.

[CCD88] D. Chaum, C. Crépeau, and I. Damgård. Multiparty unconditionally secure protocols. In *Proceedings of the Twentieth Annual ACM Symposium on Theory of Computing*, pages 11–19, 1988.

[Fel87] P. Feldman. A practical scheme for non-interactive verifiable secret sharing. In *Proceedings of the 28th IEEE Symposium on the Foundations of Computer Science*, pages 427 – 437, 1987.

[IS91]     I. Ingemarsson and G. J. Simmons. A protocol to set up shared secret schemes without the assistance of a mutually trusted party. In *Advances in Cryptology - proceedings of EUROCRYPT 90*, Lecture Notes in Computer Science, pages 266 – 282. Springer-Verlag, 1991.

[Ped91]    T. P. Pedersen. Distributed provers with applications to undeniable signatures, 1991. To appear in the proceedings of Eurocrypt'91.

[RB89]     T. Rabin and M. Ben-Or. Verifiable secret sharing and multiparty protocols with honest majority. In *Proceedings of the 21st Annual ACM Symposium on the Theory of Computing*, pages 73 – 85, 1989.

[Sha79]    A. Shamir. How to share a secret. *Communications of the ACM*, 22:612–613, 1979.

[Sim90]    G. J. Simmons. How to (really) share a secret. In *Advances in Cryptology - proceedings of CRYPTO 88*, Lecture Notes in Computer Science, pages 390 – 448. Springer-Verlag, 1990.

[Wag79]    S. S. Wagstaff Jr. Greatest of the least primes in arithmetic progression having a given modulus. *Mathematics of Computation*, 33(147):1073 – 1080, July 1979.

# Multiparty Secret Key Exchange Using a Random Deal of Cards[1]

(Extended Abstract)

Michael J. Fischer                  Rebecca N. Wright
Computer Science Department        Computer Science Department
Yale University                    Yale University
New Haven, CT 06520-2158           New Haven, CT 06520-2158
fischer-michael@cs.yale.edu        wright-rebecca@cs.yale.edu

## Abstract

We consider the problem of *multiparty secret key exchange*. A "team" of players $P_1$ through $P_k$ wishes to determine an $n$-bit secret key in the presence of a computationally unlimited eavesdropper, Eve. The team players are dealt hands of cards of prespecified sizes from a deck of $d$ distinct cards; any remaining cards are dealt to Eve. We explore how the team can use the information contained in their hands of cards to determine an $n$-bit key that is secret from Eve, that is, an $n$ bit string which each team player knows exactly but for which Eve's probability of guessing the key correctly is $1/2^n$ both before and after she hears the communication between the team players. We describe randomized protocols for secret key exchange that work for certain classes of deals, and we present some conditions on the deal for such a protocol to exist.

# 1   Introduction

An important problem of cryptography is the problem of *multiparty secret key exchange*. This can be viewed as a multiparty protocol between a group of players. At some point, a subset of $k \geq 2$ players $P_1$ through $P_k$ form a *team*. The rest of the players are considered eavesdroppers. The team players carry out randomized algorithms. Each player's random choices are private to that player. All communication is by public broadcast and is overheard by the eavesdroppers. The following scenario demonstrates a situation in which the need for secret key exchange might arise.

A certain government agency handles security of information on a "community of interest" basis. For each project within the agency, a group of people are chosen to work on the project. We call this group a team. Teams form and dissolve as various projects are started and completed. All communication regarding the project is intended to be shared with those on the team, and to be kept secret from those outside the team. However, the security of the various communication channels—the telephone, interoffice mail, electronic mail, and face-to-face communication—is not guaranteed. Hence, each team that forms would like to exchange a secret key, which it can then use as a part of

---

[1] This research was supported in part by National Science Foundation grant IRI-9015570.

J. Feigenbaum (Ed.): Advances in Cryptology - CRYPTO '91, LNCS 576, pp. 141-155, 1992.
© Springer-Verlag Berlin Heidelberg 1992

some cryptographic protocol to securely send all further communication regarding the project. Another place where this problem may arise is in a distributed system, for example a computer network linking a corporation's headquarters and branch offices.

Formally, the team wishes to determine a random $n$-bit sequence $S$ satisfying agreement, secrecy, and uniformity. *Agreement* is met if each team player knows $S$. *Secrecy* is met if the eavesdroppers' probability of guessing $S$ correctly is the same before and after hearing the communication between the team players. *Uniformity* requires that $S$ has equal probability of being any one of the $2^n$ possible $n$-bit sequences. Such a secret key is said to be *shared* by the team. Each team player has an output tape that is physically protected from the other players. An *n-bit secret key exchange protocol* is one in which each team player outputs the same $n$-bit sequence satisfying the secrecy and uniformity conditions. The output can then be used for a variety of cryptographic purposes, for example, as the key in private key cryptosystems (cf. [DH]).

We allow the eavesdroppers to be computationally unlimited, so standard cryptographic techniques based on computational difficulty cannot be used. In fact, a secret key exchange protocol is not possible without any further assumptions, for an eavesdropper can simulate any team player under all possible random choices and thereby learn $S$. Hence, we give the players secret initial information in the form of correlated random variables. While the value of each player's random variable is unknown to the other players, the distribution from which the random variables are chosen is publicly known. For any team that forms, the remaining players are assumed to collaborate against the team, possibly communicating among themselves via private channels. Thus we treat them as a single eavesdropper, Eve, who possesses the initial information of all of the non-team players. Note that because initial information is given to all players before the team forms, it is not possible to deny Eve all initial information. We would like to distribute the initial information in such a way that any team that forms can obtain a secret key.

Our framework is very general and admits the trivial solution in which each player is given *a priori* a secret key for each team to which the player might eventually belong. Any team that forms can use the corresponding preassigned secret key, but since there is an exponential number of possible teams, the amount of initial information is quite high. Also, the structure of the initial random information is rather complicated.

We desire instead correlated random variables that have a simple structure and a small amount of initial information. A familiar example of such correlated random variables is provided by ordinary card games in which players are dealt hands from a randomly shuffled deck of cards. By looking at her own cards, a player gains some information about the other players' hands. Namely, she learns a set of cards that appear in no other player's hand. Peter Winkler developed bidding conventions for the game of bridge whereby one player could send her partner secret information about her hand that was totally unrelated to the actual bid and completely undecipherable to the opponents, even though the protocol was known to them [Fl, Wi81a, Wi81b, Wi83]. Fischer, Paterson and Rackoff [FPR] carried this idea further, using deals of cards for secret bit transmission between two players. We consider secret key exchange protocols based on such card games in the remainder of this paper.

The problem of secret key exchange has been considered by others in the context of public key cryptography (cf. [DH, Me]). Impagliazzo and Rudich provide evidence that most of the standard techniques in cryptography cannot be used to construct a secret key exchange protocol from a one-way permutation [IR]. Our results are quite different in character from these, for we place no computational limitations on our participants. Thus, one-way permutations do not exist in our model, and one must rely on other assumptions, such as the existence of prior secret initial information as in this paper, in order to make the problem solvable. Furthermore, techniques such as those used by Maurer [Ma] will not work here since we require that the key obtained is *completely* secret from Eve and is known *exactly* to all the team players, as prescribed by the secrecy and agreement conditions.

In the remainder of the paper, we consider the situation in which a team has just formed, and investigate whether secret key exchange is possible. We use the following terminology. A *deck* $D$ is a finite set, whose elements we call *cards*; a *hand* is subset of $D$. Let $d$ be the size of the deck. The cards in the deck are known to all the players, as is the size of each player's hand, but the cards in each player's hand are private to that player. In an $(h_1, h_2, \ldots, h_k; e)$-*deal*, each team player $P_i$ is given a hand $H_i$ such that $H_i \subseteq D$ and $|H_i| = h_i$. Eve is dealt a hand $E$ such that $E \subseteq D$ and $e = |E| = d - \sum_{i=1}^{k} h_i$. The deal $\delta = (H_1, H_2, \ldots, H_k; E)$ is *legal* if $H_1, H_2, \ldots, H_k, E$ partition $D$. We call the description of the sizes of the hands, $\xi = (h_1, h_2, \ldots, h_k; e)$, the *signature*[2] of the deal, and call a deal having signature $\xi$ a $\xi$-*deal*. If all $k$ team players have the same hand size $h$ in a signature, we write $(h^k; e)$.

An $n$-bit secret key exchange protocol that always succeeds in obtaining an $n$-bit secret key for all legal $\xi$-deals is said to *work for* $\xi$. We also say such a protocol *performs n-bit secret key exchange for* $\xi$.

In Section 2, we describe a simple 1-bit secret key exchange protocol that works for all deals in which the team players' hands are sufficiently large relative to the size of

---

[2] This term is borrowed from algebra, and is not intended to have any connection to digital signatures.

the team and the size of Eve's hand. In Section 3, we present a protocol that improves on the first protocol in two ways. First, it establishes an $n$-bit secret key for arbitrary $n$. Second, it requires only that each team player hold an arbitrarily small fraction of the cards (assuming that the deck is sufficiently large). In Section 4, we present some necessary conditions on the deal for a secret key exchange protocol to exist. In Section 5, we show that the protocol presented in Section 2 is optimal for a natural class of related protocols.

# 2  A One-Bit Secret Key Exchange Protocol

We first consider a simple 1-bit secret key exchange protocol. We use the notion of a *key set* defined in [FPR]. A key set $K$ consists of two cards, one held by a team player $P$, the other held by a *different* team player $Q$. A key set $K = \{x, y\}$ is *opaque* if, given the information available to Eve, it is equally likely that $P$ holds $x$ and $Q$ holds $y$ or that $P$ holds $y$ and $Q$ holds $x$.

Once $P$ and $Q$ determine an opaque key set $K$ that they hold, they can use it to obtain a bit $r$ that is secret to Eve. Namely, they agree that $r = 0$ if $P$ holds $x$ and $r = 1$ if $P$ holds $y$, or vice versa. Thus $K$ acts as a 1-*bit secret channel*; that is, it allows $P$ and $Q$ to communicate a single bit secretly.

The structure of our protocol is as follows. We think of the team players as nodes of a graph. We connect two team players by an edge if the team players have a 1-bit secret channel between them. The goal of the protocol is to connect the team players. We obtain 1-bit secret channels by finding opaque key sets between pairs of team players until the team is connected. Then a designated player, say $P_1$, chooses a bit $s$ randomly. Using flooding on the 1-bit secret channels, $s$ is propagated to all the team players. Clearly $s$ satisfies agreement and uniformity. Secrecy is satisfied because each 1-bit channel preserves secrecy. Hence, $s$ is a 1-bit secret key.

We define the notion of a feasible player. Let each team player $P_i$ hold $h_i$ cards and let Eve hold $e$ cards. Then $P_i$ is *feasible* if $h_i > 1$, or if $h_i = 1$, $e = 0$, and $h_j > 1$ for all $j \neq i$. In the protocol that follows, we say a card $x$ is *discarded* from the deck if all team players agree to play as if $x$ is no longer part of the deck. Similarly, we say a team player $P$ *drops out* of the protocol if the team players agree to play as if $P$ were no longer part of the team. The protocol follows.

1. Let $P$ be the feasible player holding the smallest hand. (Ties are broken in favor of

the lower-numbered player.) If no player is feasible, then $P$ is the lowest-numbered player holding a non-empty hand, if any.

2. $P$ chooses a random card $x$ contained in her hand and a random card $y$ not in her hand and proposes $K = \{x, y\}$ as a key set by asking, "Does any team player hold a card in $K$?"[3]

3. If another team player $Q$ holds $y$, she knows that $K$ is a key set, so she *accepts* $K$ by announcing that she holds a card in $K$. The cards $x$ and $y$ are discarded. Whichever player of $P$ and $Q$ holds fewer cards exposes the remaining cards in her hand, which are discarded, and drops out of the protocol. The remaining team players go back to step 1 with the "new" deal.

4. If none of the team players holds $y$, then $K$ is *rejected*. In this case, $x$ and $y$ are discarded, and the players go back to step 1.

The execution of the protocol continues in this manner until either there are not enough cards left to complete steps 1 and 2, or until only one team player is left. In the first case, the protocol fails. In the second case, all the team players are connected by opaque key sets. To see this, note that every key set $K = \{x, y\}$ accepted in step 3 is opaque because it is equally likely to be proposed by $P$ in the symmetric deal where everything is the same except that $P$ holds $y$ and $Q$ holds $x$. Hence the team can obtain a 1-bit secret key by flooding as previously described. We call this protocol the SFP key set protocol (for smallest feasible player). An inductive argument shows the following.

**Theorem 2.1** *Let* $\xi = (h_1, ..., h_k; e)$. *Let* $h_i \geq 1$ *for* $1 \leq i \leq k$, *and* $\max h_i + \min h_i \geq k + e$. *Then the SFP key set protocol performs 1-bit secret key exchange for* $\xi$.

In Section 5 we consider protocols with different rules for choosing $P$ in step 1. We show there that the SFP key set protocol is optimal among all such key set protocols.

# 3   An $n$-Bit Secret Key Exchange Protocol

The SFP key set protocol has two limitations: it requires that the team hold more than half the cards in the deck, and it only provides a 1-bit secret key. Moreover, it is not obvious how to modify the protocol to overcome these limitations. For example, the

---

[3] In an abstract setting, $\{x, y\}$ is clearly the same as $\{y, x\}$. In an actual implementation, care must be taken that the communication of $\{x, y\}$ does not reveal which card came from $P$'s hand.

protocol cannot be repeated to obtain additional key bits since players drop out and expose their remaining cards during execution.

The first limitation is overcome in [FPR] for a team of two players. A 1-bit secret key exchange protocol is presented there that works when each team player holds any fixed fraction of the cards and the deck is sufficiently large. An analysis of that protocol establishes the following:

**Theorem 3.1** (Fischer, Paterson, Rackoff) *There is a 1-bit secret key exchange protocol* $\mathcal{P}$ *such that for all* $0 < \beta \leq 1/2$ *and* $d \geq \left(\frac{2}{\beta^2}\right) 2^{1/\beta}$, $\mathcal{P}$ *works for* $(\lfloor \beta d \rfloor, \lfloor \beta d \rfloor ; d - 2 \lfloor \beta d \rfloor)$.

We show how to use such a protocol to perform $n$-bit secret key exchange for teams of size $k$ and sufficiently large decks. Our construction is a general reduction of the $n$-bit, $k$-player problem for signature $\xi^* = (h^k; d - kh)$ to the 1-bit, 2-player problem for signature $\xi = (\lfloor h/2n \rfloor, \lfloor h/2n \rfloor ; d - 2 \lfloor h/2n \rfloor)$. Thus, given a protocol $\mathcal{P}$ that performs 1-bit secret key exchange for $\xi$, we construct a new protocol $\mathcal{P}^*$ that performs $n$-bit secret key exchange for $\xi^*$.

**Lemma 3.1** *Let* $n \geq 1$, $k \geq 2$ *and* $d \geq kh$. *Let* $\mathcal{P}$ *be a 1-bit secret key exchange protocol that works for*

$$\xi = \left( \left\lfloor \frac{h}{2n} \right\rfloor, \left\lfloor \frac{h}{2n} \right\rfloor ; d - 2 \left\lfloor \frac{h}{2n} \right\rfloor \right).$$

*Then there is a protocol* $\mathcal{P}^*$ *that performs* $n$-bit secret key exchange for $\xi^* = (h^k; d - kh)$.

Proof: Suppose $n$, $k$, $d$, $h$, $\mathcal{P}$, and $\xi$ satisfy the conditions of the lemma, and let $\xi^* = (h^k; d - kh)$. We construct an $n$-bit secret key exchange protocol $\mathcal{P}^*$ that works for $\xi^*$.

Assume the players are linearly ordered, say, by their indices. Two team players are said to be *neighbors* if they are adjacent in the ordering. $P_1$ is the leader and randomly chooses an $n$-bit string $S$ to be the secret key. Each pair of neighbors $P_i$ and $P_{i+1}$ uses $\mathcal{P}$ in sequence $n$ times to establish an $n$-bit secret key $B_i$ that they share, as described in detail below. When $P_i$ learns $S$ from $P_{i-1}$, she sends $E_i = S \oplus B_i$ to $P_{i+1}$ publicly. $P_{i+1}$ recovers $S$ by computing $E_i \oplus B_i$.

We now describe in detail how the one-time pads are established. Given a team player $P_i$, we say $P_{i+1}$ is the *right neighbor* of $P_i$ and $P_{i-1}$ is the *left neighbor* of $P_i$. Each player $P_i$ divides her hand into $2n$ parts, $H_i^1$ through $H_i^{2n}$, of size $\lfloor h/2n \rfloor$ and a (possibly empty) part containing her remaining cards. $P_i$ uses parts $H_i^1$ through $H_i^n$ to establish $B_i$ with her right neighbor, and she uses parts $H_i^{n+1}$ through $H_i^{2n}$ to establish $B_{i-1}$ with her left neighbor.

The $j^{\text{th}}$ bit of the one-time pad $B_i$ is gotten as follows. $P_i$ plays the role of player 1 in $\mathcal{P}$, pretending that the only cards she holds are those in $H_i^j$. $P_{i+1}$ plays the role of player 2 in $\mathcal{P}$, pretending that the only cards she holds are those in $H_{i+1}^{n+j}$. The other team players do not participate. We call the cards in $H_i^j \cup H_{i+1}^{n+j}$ the *current cards*. Both players pretend that Eve holds all but the current cards. Thus $P_i$ and $P_{i+1}$ execute $\mathcal{P}$ as if the deal were a $\xi$-deal. Since $\mathcal{P}$ is assumed to work for $\xi$, $P_i$ and $P_{i+1}$ obtain a shared secret bit, which they use for the $j^{\text{th}}$ bit of $B_i$.

Note that whenever a card $x$ not in the current cards is referenced, all players behave as if Eve holds $x$. If Eve does not hold $x$, she learns that $x$ does not lie in the current cards, but she learns nothing further about the location of $x$. Thus this process can be repeated, using each part of each team player's hand exactly once, to get all the one-time pads. ∎

We now apply Lemma 3.1 to families of 1-bit protocols.

**Theorem 3.2** *Let $n \geq 1$, $k \geq 2$, and let $f$ be a function on the reals. Suppose for every $0 < \beta \leq 1/4$ and every $d \geq f(\beta)$ that there is a 1-bit secret key exchange protocol $\mathcal{P}$ that works for $(\lfloor \beta d \rfloor, \lfloor \beta d \rfloor; d - 2 \lfloor \beta d \rfloor)$. Let $0 < \alpha \leq 1/k$, and let $d \geq f(\alpha/2n)$. Let $\mathcal{P}^*$ be the protocol constructed as in the proof of Lemma 3.1. Then $\mathcal{P}^*$ performs $n$-bit secret key exchange for $(\lfloor \alpha d \rfloor^k ; d - k \lfloor \alpha d \rfloor)$.*

**Proof:** Assume the hypotheses of the protocol, and assume we are given a deal of signature $\xi = (\lfloor \alpha d \rfloor^k ; d - k \lfloor \alpha d \rfloor)$. Let $h = \lfloor \alpha d \rfloor$ and let $\beta = \alpha/2n$. Since $\alpha \leq 1/k$, it follows that $d \geq k \lfloor \alpha d \rfloor = kh$ and $\beta \leq 1/4$. Also, since $n$ is an integer, $\lfloor \beta d \rfloor = \lfloor \alpha d/2n \rfloor = \lfloor \lfloor \alpha d \rfloor /2n \rfloor = \lfloor h/2n \rfloor$. Hence, $\mathcal{P}$ satisfies the conditions for Lemma 3.1. It follows from Lemma 3.1 that $\mathcal{P}^*$ performs $n$-bit secret key exchange for $(h^k; d - kh) = \xi$ as desired. ∎

The following corollary to Theorem 3.2 is immediate using Theorem 3.1, taking $f(\beta) = \left(\frac{2}{\beta^2}\right) 2^{1/\beta}$.

**Corollary 3.1** *Let $0 < \alpha \leq 1/k$. Suppose $d \geq 8 \left(\frac{n}{\alpha}\right)^2 2^{2n/\alpha}$. Then $\mathcal{P}^*$ performs $n$-bit secret key exchange for $(\lfloor \alpha d \rfloor^k ; d - k \lfloor \alpha d \rfloor)$.*

Unfortunately, the required deck size here grows exponentially in $n/\alpha$. Richard

Beigel [Be] has suggested an improved 1-bit two-player protocol in which the deck size appears to grow only polynomially in $1/\alpha$. Using such a protocol, our construction yields an $n$-bit team protocol for which the deck grows only polynomially in $n/\alpha$.

# 4 Lower Bound Results

In order to discuss lower bounds, we first define our model more precisely. We look at a synchronous distributed model of computation in which there is a *team* of $k$ players $P_1$ through $P_k$ and a passive eavesdropper, Eve. Let $\mathcal{P}$ be an $n$-bit secret key exchange protocol for $P_1$ through $P_k$. In each round of $\mathcal{P}$, each of the team players simultaneously broadcasts a message to all of the other players. All messages are overheard by Eve. Let $Z$ be the set of possible messages, and let $z_i \in Z$ be the message that each $P_i$ sends in the round. The $k$-tuple $(z_1, z_2, \ldots, z_k) \in Z^k$ is called a *statement* of $\mathcal{P}$. A sequence of statements is called a *conversation* of $\mathcal{P}$, denoted by $\tau_{\mathcal{P}}$. We assume each protocol $\mathcal{P}$ always terminates after some fixed number $t_{\mathcal{P}}$ of rounds. A conversation $\tau_{\mathcal{P}}$ is *complete* if $|\tau_{\mathcal{P}}| = t_{\mathcal{P}}$. As it will be clear from context which protocol is being discussed, we will omit the protocol subscripts.

The protocol run by each player $P_i$ is a randomized algorithm that determines the message for $P_i$ to send at each round based on her hand and the conversation so far. Specifically, let $\mathcal{H}_i$ be the set of possible hands for $P_i$. Let $H_i \in \mathcal{H}_i$, and let $\sigma$ be a conversation. A protocol for $P_i$ is a pair $(\mu_i, \mathcal{O}_i)$. If $\sigma$ is not complete, $\mu_i(H_i, \sigma)$ is a random variable over the message space $Z$, where $\Pr[\mu_i(H_i, \sigma) = z]$ is the probability that $P_i$ sends message $z$ at round $r+1$ given that $P_i$ holds hand $H_i$ and the conversation through round $r$ is $\sigma$. If $\sigma$ is complete, $\mathcal{O}_i(H_i, \tau) \in \{0, 1\}^n$ specifies $P_i$'s output value.

A *joint protocol* for players $P_1$ through $P_k$ consists of a set of protocols $(\mu_i, \mathcal{O}_i)$, where each $(\mu_i, \mathcal{O}_i)$ is a protocol for $P_i$. All the protocols $(\mu_i, \mathcal{O}_i)$ are known to each team player, as well as to Eve. Thus an $n$-bit secret key exchange protocol that works for $\xi$ is a joint protocol $\{(\mu_1, \mathcal{O}_1), \ldots, (\mu_k, \mathcal{O}_k)\}$ for the team players such that for all possible runs on each legal $\xi$-deal, if every team player $P_i$ plays according to $(\mu_i, \mathcal{O}_i)$, the team succeeds in obtaining an $n$-bit secret key. It is a straightforward exercise to modify the protocols we describe in English in this paper to fit this model.

We generalize a theorem of [FPR] to show that secret key exchange is not possible if the deal does not provide sufficient shared information. Throughout the remainder of this section, we fix a deck $D$ and a signature $\xi = (h_1, h_2, \ldots, h_k; e)$ such that $\sum_{i=1}^{k} h_i + e = |D|$.

Recall that a $\xi$-deal of a deck $D$ is a collection of $k+1$ hands $(H_1, \ldots, H_k; E)$ such that $|H_i| = h_i$ for $i \in \{1, \ldots, k\}$ and $|E| = e$, and recall that a deal is legal if the hands partition $D$. We sometimes use the term "general deal" to refer to a deal that is not necessarily legal. Let $\Delta'$ be the set of all (general) $\xi$-deals of $D$, and let $\Delta$ be the set of legal $\xi$-deals of $D$. Note that $\Delta \subseteq \Delta'$ and that a general deal $\delta$ is legal if and only if the hands in $\delta$ are pairwise disjoint.

A random legal deal is a uniformly distributed random variable over $\Delta$. A random general deal is a uniformly distributed random variable over $\Delta'$. Note that in both a random legal deal and in a random general deal, each hand $H_i$ is uniformly distributed over $\mathcal{H}_i$. The difference is that in a random general deal, the hands $H_1, \ldots, H_k$ are independent random variables, whereas in a random legal deal, they are correlated. Hence, only in a random legal deal does player $P_i$ get any information about the cards in other player's hands.

Let $\overline{\gamma}$ be the probability that a random general deal is also a legal deal. Intuitively, the smaller $\overline{\gamma}$ is, the more shared information the deal contains. The following theorem provides an upper bound on $\overline{\gamma}$ in order for $n$-bit secret exchange to be possible.

**Theorem 4.1** *Let $\xi$ and $\overline{\gamma}$ be as defined above, and let $n \geq 1$. If $\overline{\gamma} > 1/2^{k-1}$, then no protocol performs $n$-bit secret key exchange for $\xi$.*

**Proof (sketch):** Assume to the contrary that some $n$-bit secret key exchange protocol works for $\xi$ when $\overline{\gamma} > 1/2^{k-1}$. We may assume without loss of generality that $n = 1$. Using a somewhat involved probabilistic argument, we show that $|\Delta|/|\Delta'| \leq 1/2^{k-1}$, i.e., at most $1/2^{k-1}$ of all deals are legal. Since all deals are equally likely, it follows that $\overline{\gamma} \leq 1/2^{k-1}$, a contradiction. We conclude that no protocol performs 1-bit secret key exchange for $\xi$. ∎

The full proof is rather long and is omitted. (It may be found in [FW].) We remark that the theorem holds even for protocols in which Eve is not allowed to look at her hand. Thus, our theorem applies to a larger class of protocols than necessary. We do not know how to use Eve's ability to see her cards to improve this result.

**Corollary 4.1** *Let $n \geq 1$ and $2 \leq k \leq 8$. Then no protocol performs $n$-bit secret key exchange for $(1^k; 1)$.*

**Proof:** In these cases, $\overline{\gamma} = (k+1)!/(k+1)^k > 1/2^{k-1}$. ∎

For $k > 8, \overline{\gamma} = (k+1)!/(k+1)^k < 1/2^{k-1}$, so nothing can be concluded.

Theorem 4.1 says nothing about the $(1^k; 0)$ case. However, it is possible to show the following.

**Theorem 4.2** *Let* $n \geq 1$. *Then no protocol performs n-bit secret key exchange for* $(1, 1, 1; 0)$.

**Proof (sketch):** It is sufficient to show no protocol performs 1-bit secret key exchange for $(1, 1, 1; 0)$. To prove this, we look at properties of the possible conversations of a 1-bit secret key exchange protocol on $(1, 1, 1; 0)$-deals. Let $\tau$ be a complete conversation. We say that $\tau$ is *realizable* if there is some $\delta \in \Delta$ such that $\tau$ is a possible conversation of the protocol when the deal is $\delta$, and in this case we say $\delta$ is *consistent* with $\tau$. An output $v \in \{0, 1\}$ is *possible* given $\tau$ if there is some $\delta = (H_1, H_2, H_3) \in \Delta$ consistent with $\tau$ such that $v = \mathcal{O}_i(H_i, \tau)$ for each $i$.

Suppose $\mathcal{P}$ performs 1-bit secret key exchange for $(1, 1, 1; 0)$. We construct a tree of conversations as follows. The nodes of the tree are conversations, and the edges out of a node are labeled by possible next statements. Thus the interior nodes are partial conversations; leaf nodes are complete conversations. A conversation $\tau$ *passes through* a node $\sigma$ if $\tau$ extends $\sigma$. It can be shown that exactly two deals are consistent with each realizable conversation, and that both of the deals consistent with a realizable conversation have the same parity[4]. We say that the parity of a realizable conversation $\tau$ is the parity of the two deals consistent with $\tau$. We say a node is *single valued* if all conversations passing through it have the same parity. It is *multivalued* otherwise. We are now ready to derive a contradiction.

By the correctness of $\mathcal{P}$, all $(1, 1, 1; 0)$-deals must be possible initially. Thus the root of the tree is multivalued. Because only one conversation passes through any leaf node, all leaves are single valued. Hence there must be a multivalued node $\sigma$ having only single valued children. Thus there exist complete conversations $\tau_0$ and $\tau_1$ passing through $\sigma$ such that $\tau_0$ has parity 0 and $\tau_1$ has parity 1. It is then possible to construct an "interpolated" conversation passing through $\sigma$ that gives rise to a multivalued child, a contradiction. ∎

This proof is highly dependent on specific properties of the set of possible $(1, 1, 1; 0)$-deals, and does not generalize easily to larger teams. However, using an extension to the graph theoretical framework developed by Beaver, Haber and Winkler [BHW] to represent shared knowledge between two players, it is possible to show the following general result (cf. [FWW]).

---

[4] The parity of a $(1, 1, 1; 0)$-deal is the parity of the permutation describing it.

**Theorem 4.3** *Let $n \geq 1$, $k \geq 2$, and $e \geq 0$. Then no protocol performs n-bit secret key exchange for $(1^k; e)$ unless $n = 1, k = 2$, and $e = 0$.*

# 5  Key Set Protocols Revisited

Even for the simple case of $n = 1$, there is a large gap between signatures for which we have a secret key exchange protocol and signatures for which we have shown that no protocol exists. For example, $(2, 2, 2; 2)$ falls into this gap.

One approach to closing the gap is to modify the SFP key set protocol presented in Section 2. In step 1 of this protocol, a team player $P$, *the proposer*, is chosen. By considering different rules for choosing the proposer, we get a class of protocols. We call such a rule a *proposing rule*. We require a proposing rule to be a deterministic function of the current signature. We call the protocol that results from proposing rule $\mathcal{R}$ the $\mathcal{R}$ *key set protocol*. We call the class of all such protocols the class of key set protocols. By this definition, the SFP key set protocol results from the *smallest feasible player* proposing rule (SFP): If any team player is feasible, the feasible player with the smallest hand is chosen. (Ties are broken in favor of the lower-numbered player.) If no team player is feasible, the lowest-numbered team player holding a non-empty hand is chosen, if any.

Theorem 2.1 holds for any $\mathcal{R}$ key set protocol where $\mathcal{R}$ always chooses a feasible player if some team player is feasible. The converse, however, does not in general hold. For example, the signature $\xi = (3, 3, 2, 1; 1)$ does not satisfy the conditions of the theorem, but the SFP key set protocol works for $\xi$. We have been unable to find an exact characterization of the signatures for which the SFP key set protocol works. Nevertheless, it is possible to show that the SFP key set protocol is optimal for the class of key set protocols. By this we mean that for a signature $\xi$, if the $\mathcal{R}$ key set protocol works for $\xi$ for some $\mathcal{R}$, then the SFP key set protocol also works for $\xi$. To prove this we look at a simple combinatorial stick game between a team and an adversary. The stick game abstracts the important aspects of the key set protocol.

The stick game is a game between a team and an adversary. There are $k$ team piles, $P_1$ through $P_k$, and a pile $E$. Pile $P_i$ contains $h_i$ sticks, and pile $E$ contains $e$ sticks. The team always moves first. On the team's turn, the team designates a team pile $P_i$ containing at least one stick. On the adversary's turn, the adversary either removes one stick from $P_i$ and one from $E$ (allowed only when $e > 0$), or chooses another team pile $P_j$ such that $h_j > 0$, removes the smaller of $P_i$ and $P_j$ entirely, and removes one stick from the larger pile. Note that removing a pile is not the same as removing all the sticks in the pile. Play ends when there are one or zero team piles, in which case the team wins, or when there is no move available (either to the team or to the adversary), in which case the team loses. A configuration of the stick game can be described by the tuple $(h_1, \ldots, h_k; e; I)$, where $I$ specifies whether it is the team's turn $(T)$ or the adversary's turn $(A)$. We call the stick game starting from configuration $C$ the $C$ *stick game*.

A *strategy* for the team, or team strategy, is a function that, given a configuration of the stick game where it is the team's turn specifies the next team move. Similarly, an adversary strategy is a function that specifies the next adversary move. We say a configuration $C$ is *winning* if there is some team strategy $S$ such that if the team plays the $C$ stick game by strategy $S$, then the team wins regardless of the moves chosen by the adversary. We say $S$ is a *successful team strategy for* $C$. We call $S$ an *optimal team strategy* if it is a successful team strategy for every winning configuration $C$. We similarly define *optimal adversary strategy*.

The stick game is a finite game, since every adversary turn decreases the total number of sticks by at least two. Furthermore, it is a game of complete information, since the team and the adversary take turns and all information about the state is known to both the team and the adversary. Hence game theory tells us that every configuration is either winning or losing, and an optimal team strategy $S$ and an optimal adversary strategy $\mathcal{A}$ both exist [BCG].

We define a feasible pile in a stick game configuration exactly as we defined a feasible player in a signature, and we similarly define the SFP strategy for the team in the stick game. It is easy to see that a configuration in the stick game is winning for a given team strategy if and only if the key set protocol works for the corresponding signature when the team plays according to the corresponding proposing rule. Hence to show the optimality of the corresponding SFP key set protocol we need only show the optimality of the SFP stick game strategy.

We show this by a series of arguments known as strategy stealing arguments. We define $\text{size}((h_1, \ldots, h_k; e; I)) = k + e$. The strategy stealing arguments are by induction on $\text{size}(C)$. We construct configurations $C_1, \ldots, C_i$ and $C'_1, \ldots, C'_j$ as shown in Figure 1.

The configurations $C_1, \ldots$ are constructed by playing the $C_0$ stick game. We assume the team never makes a move that would take a winning configuration to a losing one, and we specify the adversary moves. Since an adversary move cannot take a winning configuration to a losing one, it follows that if $C_0$ is winning, then every $C_\ell$ is winning. Similarly, the configurations $C'_1, \ldots$ are constructed by playing the $C'_0$ stick game. We assume the adversary never makes a move on a losing configuration that results in a winning configuration, and we specify the team moves. It follows that if $C'_0$ is losing, then every $C'_\ell$ is losing, or conversely, if any $C'_\ell$ is winning, then $C'_0$ is winning. The

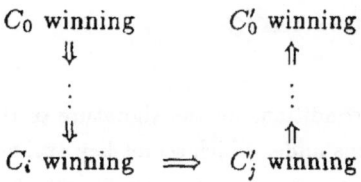

Figure 1: The strategy stealing argument.

construction terminates when we obtain $C_i$ and $C_j'$ for which we can show that if $C_i$ is winning then $C_j'$ is also winning.

A case by case analysis of possible adversary responses to each SFP team move enables us to prove the following. (A full proof appears in [FW]).

**Theorem 5.1** *The SFP strategy is an optimal team strategy for the stick game, and hence the SFP key set protocol is optimal for the class of key set protocols.*

Theorem 5.1 indicates that changing the proposing rule is not a sufficient modification to the key set protocol to close the gap described at the beginning of the section. However, there are other possible modifications to the key set protocol to consider. For example, one might allow the players to communicate in order to choose the proposer. This also does not close the gap, for we can show that the SFP key set protocol is optimal for the larger class of protocols this gives rise to. However, the optimality may fail if the proposed key set is allowed to be chosen non-randomly.

In the key set protocols described here, every time a key set is found, one of the team players discards all the cards in her hand and drops out of the protocol, except to wait to hear the secret bit. We do this in order to avoid getting more than one key set between any two players. It would be possible to consider key set protocols in which a team player only drops out when a team player in the same connected component of the key set graph is chosen to propose a key set. We suspect that this does not give the team additional power, and conjecture that Theorem 5.1 holds for this larger class of protocols.

Another possible modification to the key set protocol is to allow team players to discard only the key set cards and risk getting multiple key sets between two team players. It is an open question whether multiple key sets can be used (for example to "send" some of the cards in a player's hand to another player) to achieve 1-bit secret key exchange where no key set protocol of the class described in this paper succeeds.

# 6   Concluding Remarks

We have shown here some conditions on the signature of the deal that allow secret key exchange and some conditions under which secret key exchange is not possible. However, there is a large gap. There are many signatures for which we can neither give a secret key exchange protocol nor demonstrate the nonexistence of such a protocol.

As a future direction for this work, we intend to look at the concept of shared secret information between a team. We would like to develop a theory of shared secret information which can be applied to arbitrary correlated random variables. Specifically, can we quantify how many bits of shared secret information a deal contains for the team? How can we use this information to develop better protocols and tighter lower bounds on the signatures for which secret key exchange is possible? More generally, what other mechanisms besides deals from a common deck of cards give correlated random variables that can be used for secret key exchange?

Deals of cards have a small amount of initial information. However, deals of cards appear somewhat inefficient for secret key exchange, in that the number of secret bits the team can obtain is small in comparison to the number of cards they are dealt. Michael Rabin [Ra] suggests a protocol that uses private correlated random variables to solve another classical security problem, authentication. His method requires random variables that appear to contain more initial information than a deal of cards, but also appear to contain more shared secret information. We would like to use the theory of shared secret information suggested above to quantify the ratio of initial information to shared secret information, and to investigate upper and lower bounds on this ratio for secret key exchange protocols.

# 7   Acknowledgements

We thank Michael Merritt for his contribution to the proof of Lemma 3.1. We thank Peter Winkler for many helpful comments. We thank Nick Reingold for countless discussions, and for suggesting a simpler proof of a key lemma used in the full proof of Theorem 4.1.

# References

[BHW]  D. Beaver, S. Haber, and P. Winkler. On the Isolation of a Common Secret, preprint, Bellcore, 1991.

[Be]    R. Beigel. 1991. (Private communication.)

[BCG]   E. R. Berlekamp, J. H. Conway, and R. K. Guy. *Winning Ways*, Volume I, Academic Press Inc., London, 1982.

[DH]    W. Diffie and M. E. Hellman. New Directions in Cryptography. *IEEE Trans. Inform. Theory, IT-22, Vol. 6,* Nov. 1976, pp. 644–654.

[FPR]   M. J. Fischer, M. S. Paterson, and C. Rackoff. Secret Bit Transmission Using a Random Deal of Cards, *Distributed Computing and Cryptography*, American Mathematical Society, 1991, pp. 173–181.

[FWW]   M. J. Fischer, P. Winkler, and R. N. Wright. June 1990. (Private communication.)

[FW]    M. J. Fischer and R. N. Wright. Multiparty Secret Key Exchange Using a Random Deal of Cards, *Technical Report YALEU/DCS/TR-855*, Yale University, June 1991.

[Fl]    J. Flint. Cheating by Degrees, *The Times Saturday Review*, May 9, 1981.

[IR]    R. Impagliazzo and S. Rudich. Limits on the Provable Consequences of One-way Permutations, *Proc. 21st ACM Symposium on Theory of Computing*, May 1989, pp. 44–61.

[Ma]    U. M. Maurer. Perfect Cryptographic Security from Partially Independent Channels, *Proc. 23rd ACM Symposium on Theory of Computing*, May 1991, pp. 561–571.

[Me]    R. C. Merkle. Secure Communication over Insecure Channels, *Comm. ACM 21*, 4, April 1978, pp. 294–299.

[Ra]    M. Rabin. Cryptography Without Secrets. Presented at *DIMACS 1990 Workshop on Cryptography*, Princeton, NJ. October 1–4, 1990.

[Wi81a] P. Winkler. Cryptologic Techniques in Bidding and Defense, Parts I, II, III, and IV, *Bridge Magazine*, April—July, 1981.

[Wi81b] P. Winkler. My Night at the Cryppie Club, *Bridge Magazine*, August 1981, pp. 60–63.

[Wi83]  P. Winkler. The Advent of Cryptology in the Game of Bridge, *Cryptologia*, Vol. 7, No. 4, October 1983, pp. 327–332.

# Differential Cryptanalysis
## of
# Snefru, Khafre, REDOC-II, LOKI and Lucifer

(Extended Abstract)

*Eli Biham*        *Adi Shamir*

*The Weizmann Institute of Science*
*Department of Applied Mathematics and Computer Science*
*Rehovot 76100, Israel*

### Abstract

In [1,2] we introduced the notion of differential cryptanalysis based on chosen plaintext attacks. In [3,4] we described the application of differential cryptanalysis to Feal[13,12] and extended the method to known plaintext attacks. In this paper we apply differential cryptanalytic methods to the hash function Snefru[10] and to the cryptosystems Khafre[11], REDOC-II[6,7], LOKI[5] and Lucifer[8].

## 1   Introduction

The notion of differential cryptanalysis was introduced in [1,2,3,4]. In this paper differential cryptanalytic methods are applied to Snefru[10], Khafre[11], REDOC-II[6,7], LOKI[5] and Lucifer[8]. Due to space limitations only brief descriptions of the specific attacks can be given in this extended abstract. More extensive descriptions of the attacks will be given in the full paper.

Snefru[10] is a one way hash function suggested by Merkle as the Xerox secure hash function. In March 1990 a $1000 reward was offered to the first person to break the two-pass variant of Snefru by finding two messages which hash to the same value. A similar reward was later announced for breaking the four-pass variant of Snefru.

Khafre[11] is a fast software oriented cryptosystem suggested by Merkle. Although the number of rounds is not yet determined, the designer expects that almost all applications

J. Feigenbaum (Ed.): Advances in Cryptology - CRYPTO '91, LNCS 576, pp. 156-171, 1992.
© Springer-Verlag Berlin Heidelberg 1992

will use 16, 24 or 32 rounds.

REDOC-II[6,7] is a high speed confusion/diffusion/arithmetic cryptosystem suggested by Cryptech. REDOC-II has ten rounds, but even the one-round variant is claimed to be sufficiently strong since the round-function is very complicated. A reward of $5000 was offered for the best theoretical attack performed on the one-round variant and a reward of $20000 was offered for a practical known plaintext attack on the two-round variant.

LOKI[5] is a 64-bit key/64-bit block cryptosystem similar to DES which uses one twelve-bit to eight-bit S box based on irreducible polynomials in four S box entries. Two new modes of operation which convert LOKI into a hash function are defined.

Lucifer[8] is a S-P network cryptosystem designed by IBM prior to the design of DES. The variant of Lucifer with eight rounds has 128-bit blocks and 256-bit keys.

The main results described in this paper are:

Two-pass Snefru is easily breakable within three minutes on a personal computer. Our attack can find many pairs which hash to the same value and can even find several messages hashing to the same hashed value as a given message. The attack is also applicable to three-pass and four-pass Snefru with complexities which are much better than of the birthday attack. The attack is independent of the actual choice of the S boxes and one of its variants can even be used as a black box attack in which the choice of the S boxes is not known to the attacker.

Khafre with 16 rounds is breakable by a differential cryptanalytic chosen plaintext attack using about 1500 encryptions within about an hour on a personal computer. By a differential cryptanalytic known plaintext attack it is breakable using about $2^{38}$ encryptions. Khafre with 24 rounds is breakable by a chosen plaintext attack using about $2^{53}$ encryptions and using a differential cryptanalytic known plaintext attack it is breakable using about $2^{59}$ encryptions.

REDOC-II with one round is breakable by a differential cryptanalytic chosen plaintext attack using about 2300 encryptions within less than a minute on a personal computer. For REDOC-II with up to four rounds it is possible to find three bytes of the masks (created by 1280 byte key tables) faster than via an exhaustive search of the key. The three masks can even be found by a known plaintext attack.

LOKI with up to eleven rounds is breakable faster than exhaustive search by differential cryptanalytic attacks, either chosen plaintext or known plaintext attacks. We further show that every key of LOKI has 15 equivalent keys due to a key complementation property and thus the complexity of a known plaintext attack on the full 16-round version can be reduced to $2^{60}$. Another complementation property can reduce the complexity of a chosen plaintext attack by another factor of 16 to $2^{56}$. The two hash function modes of LOKI are shown to be insecure.

Lucifer with eight rounds is breakable within $2^{21}$ steps using 24 ciphertexts pairs.

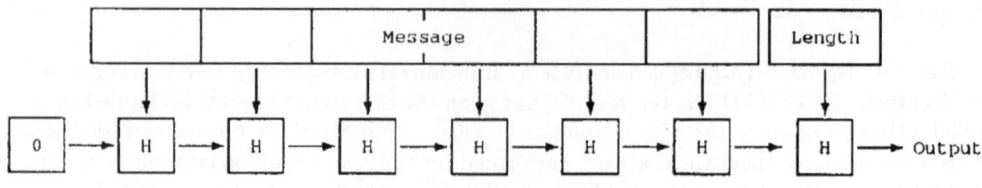

Figure 1: Outline of Snefru

# 2  Cryptanalysis of Snefru

Snefru[10] is designed to be a cryptographically strong hash function which hashes messages of arbitrary length into $m$-bit values (typically 128 bits). The messages are divided into $(512 - m)$-bit chunks and each chunk is mixed with the hashed value computed so far by a randomizing function H. The function H takes a 512-bit input and calculates an $m$-bit output. The new hashed value is the output of H. The outline of Snefru is given in figure 1.

The function H is based on a (reversible) 512-bit to 512-bit function E and returns a XOR combination of the first $m$ bits of the input and the last $m$ bits of the output of E. The function E randomizes the data in several passes. Each pass is composed of 64 randomizing rounds where in each one of them a different byte of the data is used as an input to an S box whose output word is XORed with the two neighboring words.

A cryptographically strong hash function is broken if two different messages which hash to the same value are found. In particular, we break Snefru by finding two different chunk-sized messages which hash to the same value, or in other words, finding two inputs of the function H which differ only in the chunk part and have the same output. Unless specified otherwise, we concentrate in the following discussion on two-pass Snefru with $m = 128$ (whose chunks are 384-bit long).

A universal attack on hash functions is based on the birthday paradox. If we hash about $2^{m/2}$ random messages ($2^{64}$ when $m = 128$) then with a high probability we find a pair of messages which hash to the same value. This attack is applicable to any hash function and is independent of its details.

For Snefru we designed a differential cryptanalytic attack which is also independent of the choice of the S boxes and can even be used when the hash function is viewed as a black box which hides the choice of the S boxes themselves from the attacker.

The basic attack is as follows: choose a random chunk-sized message and prepend the 128-bit zero vector (or any other 128-bit vector with the hash value from the previous chunk) to get the input of the function H. We create a second message from the first one by modifying the two bytes in the eighth and the ninth words which are used as inputs to

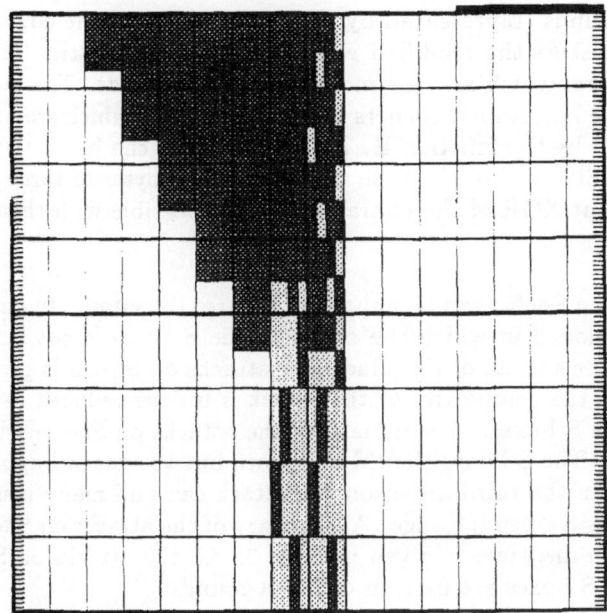

Figure 2: Graphic description of the characteristic

the S boxes at rounds 56 and 57 (the fourth use of these words). We hash both messages by the function H and compare the outputs of the two executions. A fraction of $2^{-40}$ of these pairs of messages are hashed to the same value. Therefore, by hashing about $2^{41}$ messages we can break Snefru.

In this attack we use a characteristic which differentiates only zero XOR values from non-zero XOR values and does not a priori fix the values of the non-zero XORs. In round 56 the byte from word eight is used to garble words seven and nine. In a fraction of about 1/256 of the pairs the garbled version of the byte in the ninth word cancels its chosen XOR between pairs. Therefore, for this fraction the XOR of this byte after round 56 is zero and the same values are XORed to the tenth word in both executions. The same values are used as inputs to the S boxes in both executions till the next time a byte of word seven is used at round 71. Round 71 garbles words six and eight by a different value for each execution and so does round 72 to words seven and nine. In a fraction of about 1/256 of the pairs the garbled version of the byte used as input to round 73 in the ninth word again cancels its previous XOR value. Therefore, for this fraction the XOR of this byte after round 72 is zero and the same values are XORed to the tenth word in both executions. The same values are used as inputs to the S boxes in both executions till the next time a byte of word six is used at round 86. The same cancellation should take place five times in rounds 56, 72, 88, 104 and 120. Therefore, the characteristic's probability is about $(1/256)^5 = 2^{-40}$. Each right pair with respect to this characteristic has zero XORs at the first $m$ bits of the input and at the last $m$ bits of the output and thus both messages are hashed to the same value. Figure 2 is a graphic description of the characteristic. In the figure each column represents a word of data and each row represents 16 rounds (represented by the thin lines along the edged). The gray area in the middle represents the modified words in the characteristic. The brighter gray area represets the bytes which are not modified in these words. The two black areas in the top-right and the bottom-left corners point to the words which are used in the calculation of the hash value by the function H. This same attack can break two-pass Snefru with $m$ up to 224 bits. Similar attacks with modification of bytes of three to seven consecutive words of the input XOR of the characteristic are possible with the same characteristic's probability.

The attacks on Snefru can be enhanced in three directions. In one direction black box attacks are developed in which the choice of the S boxes is not known to the attacker. A summary of the results of the black box attacks on Snefru is given in table 1. In the second direction the complexity of the attack is further reduced using the knowledge of the choice of the S boxes. A summary of the attacks on Snefru with known S boxes is given in table 2. The S boxes should be known but the general approach is independent of their choice. In the third direction the attack can find many messages which hash to the same value as a given message. A summary of the attacks on Snefru which find many partners of given messages is given in table 3. All the attacks on Snefru are applicable even if different S boxes are used in different rounds.

A personal computer implementation of this attack on two-pass Snefru finds a pair of messages within three minutes. It finds a partner of a given message in about an hour.

# 3   Cryptanalysis of Khafre

Khafre[11] is a software oriented cryptosystem with 64-bit blocks whose number of rounds (which should be a multiple of eight) is not yet determined. Each block is divided into two halves called the right half and the left half. In each round the lowest byte of the right half is used as index to an S box with 32-bit output. The left half is XORed with the output of the S box, the right half is rotated and the two halves are exchanged. The rotation is such that every byte is used once every eight rounds as an input to an S box. Before the first round and after every eighth round the data is XORed with 64-bit subkeys. These subkeys are the only way the key is involved in the cryptosystem.

The differential cryptanalysis of Khafre is based upon the observation that the number of output bits of an S box is more than twice the number of input bits. Therefore, given an output XOR of an S box in a pair, the input pair is (usually) unique and it is easy to find the two inputs. Moreover, there are about $(2^8)^2 /2 = 2^{15}$ possible input pairs for each S box, thus, only about $2^{-17}$ of the 32-bit values are possible output XORs of some pair.

A second observation is that there are characteristics in which only one even numbered round (or only one odd numbered round) has non-zero input XOR to the S box. The output XOR of this round in a right pair is easily derivable from the plaintext XOR and

| No. of passes | $m$ | Char prob | #mod bytes | Complexity of attack | Birthday complexity | Comments |
|---|---|---|---|---|---|---|
| 2 | 128–192 | $2^{-40}$ | 3 | $2^{20.5}$ | $2^{64}$–$2^{96}$ | |
| | 224 | | 2 | $2^{25}$ | $2^{112}$ | |
| | 128–192 | $2^{-40}$ | 4 | $2^{20.5}$ | $2^{64}$–$2^{96}$ | Alphanumeric |
| | 224 | | 2 | $2^{29}$ | $2^{112}$ | messages |
| 3 | 128 | $2^{-72}$ | 3 | $2^{49}$ | $2^{64}$ | |
| | 160 | | 2 | $2^{57}$ | $2^{80}$ | |

Table 1: Summary of the results of the black box attacks on Snefru

| No. of passes | $m$ | Char prob | #mod bytes | Complexity of attack | Birthday complexity | Comments |
|---|---|---|---|---|---|---|
| 2 | 128–192 | $2^{-40}$ | 4·1 | $2^{12.5}$ | $2^{64}$–$2^{96}$ | |
| | 224 | $2^{-56}$ | 2·3 | $2^{12.5}$ | $2^{112}$ | |
| | 128–192 | $2^{-40}$ | 4·1 | $2^{17}$ | $2^{64}$–$2^{96}$ | Alphanumeric |
| | 224 | | 2·1 | $2^{29}$ | $2^{112}$ | messages |
| 3 | 128–160 | $2^{-72}$ | 6·1 | $2^{28.5}$ | $2^{64}$–$2^{80}$ | |
| | 192 | $2^{-80}$ | 4·2 | $2^{28.5}$ | $2^{96}$ | |
| | 224 | $2^{-96}$ | 2·4 | $2^{33}$ | $2^{112}$ | |
| 4 | 128–192 | $2^{-160}$ | 4·4 | $2^{44.5}$ | $2^{64}$–$2^{96}$ | |
| | 224 | $2^{-112}$ | 2·2 | $2^{81}$ | $2^{112}$ | |

Table 2: Summary of the results of the attacks on Snefru with known S boxes

| No. of passes | $m$ | Char prob | #mod bytes | Complexity of attack | Brute force | Comments |
|---|---|---|---|---|---|---|
| 2 | 128–160 | $2^{-40}$ | 6·1 | $2^{24}$ | $2^{128}$–$2^{160}$ | |
| | 128–160 | | 6·1 | $2^{40}$ | $2^{128}$–$2^{160}$ | Black box |
| | 128–224 | $2^{-64}$ | 2·4 | $2^{24}$ | $2^{128}$–$2^{224}$ | |
| | 128–160 | $2^{-40}$ | 7·1 | $2^{32}$ | $2^{128}$–$2^{160}$ | Alphanumeric |
| | 128–160 | | 7·1 | $2^{40}$ | $2^{128}$–$2^{160}$ | Alphanumeric, black box |
| 3 | 128–224 | $2^{-96}$ | 2·4 | $2^{56}$ | $2^{128}$–$2^{224}$ | |
| 4 | 128–192 | $2^{-160}$ | 4·4 | $2^{88}$ | $2^{128}$–$2^{192}$ | |

Table 3: Summary of the results of the attacks which find partners of given messages

| Rnd | Left Half | | | | Right Half | | | | | Output XOR | | | |
|---|---|---|---|---|---|---|---|---|---|---|---|---|---|
| $\Omega_P$ | 0 | 0 | $A$ | 0 | 0 | 0 | $B$ | 0 | | | | | |
| 1 | 0 | 0 | $A$ | 0 | 0 | 0 | $B$ | 0 | $\rightarrow$ | 0 | 0 | 0 | 0 |
| 2 | $B$ | 0 | 0 | 0 | 0 | 0 | $A$ | 0 | $\rightarrow$ | 0 | 0 | 0 | 0 |
| 3 | $A$ | 0 | 0 | 0 | $B$ | 0 | 0 | 0 | $\rightarrow$ | 0 | 0 | 0 | 0 |
| 4 | 0 | $B$ | 0 | 0 | $A$ | 0 | 0 | 0 | $\rightarrow$ | 0 | 0 | 0 | 0 |
| 5 | 0 | $A$ | 0 | 0 | 0 | $B$ | 0 | 0 | $\rightarrow$ | 0 | 0 | 0 | 0 |
| 6 | 0 | 0 | 0 | $B$ | 0 | $A$ | 0 | 0 | $\rightarrow$ | 0 | 0 | 0 | 0 |
| 7 | 0 | 0 | 0 | $A$ | 0 | 0 | 0 | $B$ | $\rightarrow$ | $C$ | $D$ | $E$ | $A^\dagger$ |
| 8 | 0 | 0 | $B$ | 0 | $C$ | $D$ | $E$ | 0 | $\rightarrow$ | 0 | 0 | 0 | 0 |
| 9 | $D$ | $E$ | 0 | $C$ | 0 | 0 | $B$ | 0 | $\rightarrow$ | 0 | 0 | 0 | 0 |
| 10 | $B$ | 0 | 0 | 0 | $D$ | $E$ | 0 | $C$ | $\rightarrow$ | $F \oplus B^\ddagger$ | $G$ | $H$ | $I$ |
| 11 | 0 | $C$ | $D$ | $E$ | $F$ | $G$ | $H$ | $I$ | $\rightarrow$ | $J$ | $K$ | $D \oplus L^\ddagger$ | $E^\dagger$ |
| 12 | $I$ | $F$ | $G$ | $H$ | $J$ | $M^0$ | $L$ | 0 | $\rightarrow$ | 0 | 0 | 0 | 0 |
| 13 | 0 | $J$ | $M^0$ | $L$ | $I$ | $F$ | $G$ | $H$ | $\rightarrow$ | $N$ | $P \oplus J^\ddagger$ | $Q$ | $L^\dagger$ |
| 14 | $G$ | $H$ | $I$ | $F$ | $N$ | $P$ | $R^0$ | 0 | $\rightarrow$ | 0 | 0 | 0 | 0 |
| 15 | $R^0$ | 0 | $N$ | $P$ | $G$ | $H$ | $I$ | $F$ | $\rightarrow$ | $S$ | $T$ | $U$ | $P^\dagger$ |
| 16 | $H$ | $I$ | $F$ | $G$ | $V$ | $T$ | $W^0$ | 0 | $\rightarrow$ | 0 | 0 | 0 | 0 |
| $\Omega_T$ | $T$ | $W^0$ | 0 | $V$ | $H$ | $I$ | $F$ | $G$ | | | | | |

Table 4: A characteristic of Khafre

the ciphertext XOR. Given this output XOR we can discard most of the wrong pairs by the first observation, leaving only a small fraction of about $2^{-17}$ of them.

The characteristics of Khafre are described by templates which choose between zero XORs and non-zero XORs. Each right pair may have its own value of the non-zero XORs. The characteristic described in table 4 is used as an example of the cryptanalysis of Khafre with 16 rounds. Each value 0 describes a byte which has equal values in both executions of the encryptions of the pair (zero XOR). Each letter denotes a XOR value which is not zero. A letter with a superscript $^0$ denotes a XOR value which can be either zero or non-zero. The exact values of the non-zero XOR values vary for every right pair. The superscript $^\dagger$ means that the byte of the output XOR must be equal to the corresponding byte of the left half in order to cause the input XOR byte of the S box in the next round to be zero. Each occurrence of $^\dagger$ causes a reduction of the probability of the characteristic by $\frac{1}{255}$. The superscript $^\ddagger$ means that the byte of the output XOR must not be equal to the corresponding byte of the left half in order to prevent a zero value in the corresponding byte in the next round, so that it can become zero in one of the following rounds, after XORing with another non-zero value. Each occurrence of $^\ddagger$ causes a reduction of the probability of the characteristic by $\frac{254}{255}$. Therefore, the probability of this characteristic is $\left(\frac{1}{255}\right)^4 \cdot \left(\frac{254}{255}\right)^3 \approx 2^{-32}$. The input XOR $\Omega_P$ of the characteristic has two degrees of freedom: each one of $A$ and $B$ can have 255 possible values. Therefore, the characteristic points to $255^2 \approx 2^{16}$ possible plaintext XORs. Using this characteristic we can break Khafre with 16 rounds using about $2^{34}$ pairs.

| Rounds | Char prob | Pairs needed | Chosen plaintexts | Known plaintexts |
|--------|-----------|--------------|-------------------|------------------|
| 16 | $2^{-16}$ | $3 \cdot 2^{16}$ | 1536 | $2^{37.5}$ |
| 24 | $2^{-56}$ | $2^{60}$ | $2^{53}$ | $2^{58.5}$ |

Table 5: Summary of the results of the attacks on Khafre

Differential cryptanalytic attacks can be converted to known plaintext attacks[3,4]. This attack can be converted to a known plaintext attack using about $2^{41.5}$ plaintext/ciphertext pairs. In such an attack, the $2^{41.5}$ plaintexts can form $(2^{41.5})^2/2 = 2^{82}$ pairs. Since there are only $2^{64}$ possible plaintext XORs (the block size is 64 bits), about $2^{82}/2^{64} = 2^{18}$ pairs occur with each plaintext XOR. There are about $2^{16}$ usable input XORs of the characteristic and thus we get about $2^{16} \cdot 2^{18} = 2^{34}$ candidate pairs which can be used to break khafre with 16 rounds.

A summary of the best results we obtained for 16-round Khafre and 24-round Khafre is given in table 5 which describes the number of pairs needed for the attack, the number of chosen plaintexts needed, and the number of known plaintexts needed. Note that these complexities are independent of the actual choice of the S boxes, although the S boxes themselves should be known. The attacks are applicable even if different S boxes are used in different rounds. Our personal computer implementation of the chosen plaintext attack on 16-round Khafre takes about an hour.

# 4  Cryptanalysis of REDOC-II

REDOC-II[6,7] is a ten-round cryptosystem with 70-bit blocks (arranged as ten bytes of seven bits). Each round contains six phases: (1) First variable substitution, (2) Second variable substitution, (3) First variable key XOR, (4) Variable enclave, (5) Second variable key XOR and (6) Variable permutation.

An important property of the enclave tables is that they are linear operations in terms of addition which can be described as the product of a fixed matrix with the current vector of bytes. By modifying only upper bits in the input, only upper bits in the output are modified. Moreover, the linear modification table of the upper output bits by the upper input bits uniquely identifies the enclave table used. This property can even be used in the variable enclave phase. The left half of the input with two of the bytes of the right half affect the choice of the enclave tables used in this phase. However, three of the bytes of the right half do not affect the choice of the enclave tables (in the first round they are the eighth, ninth and the tenth bytes), and thus the modifications of the upper bits of the output are linear functions of the modifications of the upper bits of the input. Note that since we XOR the left half with the right half as the last step in the variable enclave phase we get a symmetric modification in both halves and therefore, an even number of modified upper bits.

In this attack we use the following characteristic:

| After Phase | Data XOR | | | | | | | | | | |
|---|---|---|---|---|---|---|---|---|---|---|---|
| $\Omega_P$ | 0 | 0 | 0 | 0 | 0 | 0 | 0 | $A$ | 0 | 0 | |
| First Subst | 0 | 0 | 0 | 0 | 0 | 0 | 0 | $B$ | 0 | 0 | For some $B$ |
| Second Subst | 0 | 0 | 0 | 0 | 0 | 0 | 0 | 64 | 0 | 0 | with probability about 1/128 |
| Key XOR | 0 | 0 | 0 | 0 | 0 | 0 | 0 | 64 | 0 | 0 | |
| Enclave | $C$ | 0 | $D$ | $E$ | $F$ | $C$ | 0 | $D$ | $E$ | $F$ | with probability about 1/2 |
| Key XOR | $C$ | 0 | $D$ | $E$ | $F$ | $C$ | 0 | $D$ | $E$ | $F$ | |
| Permutation | Some permutation of $C$,0,$D$,$E$,$F$,$C$,0,$D$,$E$,$F$ | | | | | | | | | | |
| $\Omega_T$ | Some permutation of $C$,0,$D$,$E$,$F$,$C$,0,$D$,$E$,$F$ | | | | | | | | | | |

where $A, B \in \{1, \ldots, 127\}$ and $C, D, E, F \in \{0, 64\}$ (not all of them zero). In total this characteristic has probability about $\frac{1}{256}$. The ciphertext XOR has 60 zero bits (six in each byte) and the XORed value of the uppermost bits is zero as well. Similar characteristics exist in which the difference is at the ninth and tenth bytes rather than at the eighth byte. Differences in more than one of these three bytes is also possible with smaller probabilities, but if the difference is the same in all the differing bytes and the values of all the differing bytes in the plaintexts are equal then the probability stays about $\frac{1}{256}$.

Given sufficiently many pairs encrypted by one-round REDOC-II with the plaintext differences specified in the characteristics we can discard (almost) all the wrong pairs by verifying that the 61 bits of the ciphertext XORs (60 + 1) are really zero. Only a negligible fraction of $2^{-61}$ of the wrong pairs may remain. In practice, only right pairs remain.

For each of the $16 \cdot 16 = 256$ possible values of the masks of the substitution phases we count the number of pairs whose differing byte after the two substitutions resulting from the masks differ only by the uppermost bit. For each one of the 128 possible values of the mask of the permutation phase we count the number of pairs whose ciphertext XOR permuted by the resulting inverse permutation is symmetric and has zeroes in the second and the seventh bytes. The right values of these mask bytes are likely to be the ones counted most frequently and thus can be identified. This attack needs about 1000 pairs and finds three masks of the processed key.

The attack can be enhanced by using structures of 32 encryptions with identical nine bytes and whose tenth byte gets 32 different values. In such a structure there are 496 pairs. There are only 128 possible differences after the second substitution and thus there are about four pairs which differ only by one uppermost bit after the substitution phases. These four pairs use the same enclave tables and thus with probability about half the structure contains four right pairs, and with probability about half does not contain any right pair. Using three such structures with identical eight bytes, 32 plaintexts differ at the ninth byte, 32 differ at the tenth byte and 32 differ at both the ninth and the tenth bytes with equal values in both bytes in each plaintext, we are guaranteed to have at least one structure whose choosing byte of the second key XOR has no difference and thus to have about four right pairs. This enhanced attack needs only 96 chosen plaintexts and their corresponding ciphertexts. REDOC-II with up to four rounds is also vulnerable to this attack. The attack can again be converted to a known plaintext attack. Chosen

| Rnds | Char prob | Pairs needed | Chosen plains | Chosen ciphers | Known plains | Comments |
|------|-----------|--------------|---------------|----------------|--------------|----------|
| 1 | $2^{-8}$ | – | 2300 | .. | – | All masks + key tables |
| 1 | $2^{-8}$ | 1000 | 96 | 40 | $2^{35.5}$ | Three masks |
| 2 | $2^{-29}$ | $2^{31}$ | $2^{25}$ | $2^{24}$ | $2^{46}$ | Three masks |
| 3 | $2^{-50}$ | $2^{52}$ | $2^{46}$ | $2^{45}$ | $2^{56.5}$ | Three masks |
| 4 | $2^{-71}$ | $2^{73}$ | $2^{67}$ | $2^{66}$ | $2^{67}$ | Three masks |

Table 6: Summary of the results of the attacks on REDOC-II

ciphertext attacks on these variants which find the three masks are also possible and need about a third of the data compared to the chosen plaintext attacks.

A summary of the results on REDOC-II is given in table 6.

The three masks of the substitution and the permutation phases of the one-round variant can be found within less than a second on a personal computer using 96 encryptions. A more complicated attacking program on one-round REDOC-II (which cannot be described in this extended abstract) finds all the masks and all the key tables in about a minute using about 2300 encryptions with more than 90% success rate. Using about 3900 encryptions the success rate becomes better than 99%.

# 5 Cryptanalysis of LOKI

LOKI[5] is a 64-bit key/64-bit block cryptosystem similar to DES which uses one twelve-bit to eight-bit S box (based on irreducible polynomials) replicated four times in each round. The expansion and the permutation are replaced by new choices and the initial and final transformations are replaced by XORs with the key. The bit permutations in the key scheduling are replaced by rotations and the subkeys become 32-bit long. The XOR of the input of the $F$ function with the key is done before the expansion and therefore neighboring S boxes receive common bits. Two new modes of operation which convert LOKI into a hash function are defined.

The pairs XORs distribution table of the larger S box of LOKI has much smaller probabilities than the ones of DES (average $\frac{1}{256}$ and maximum $\frac{1}{64}$). However, it is possible to have non-zero XORs in the inputs of two S boxes resulting with the same output, whereas in DES this requires at least three S boxes. We have found the following two-round iterative characteristic with probability $\frac{118}{2^{20}} \approx 2^{-13.12}$ (this probability is calculated using the observation that two neighboring S boxes have four common input bits, otherwise we get slightly smaller probability):

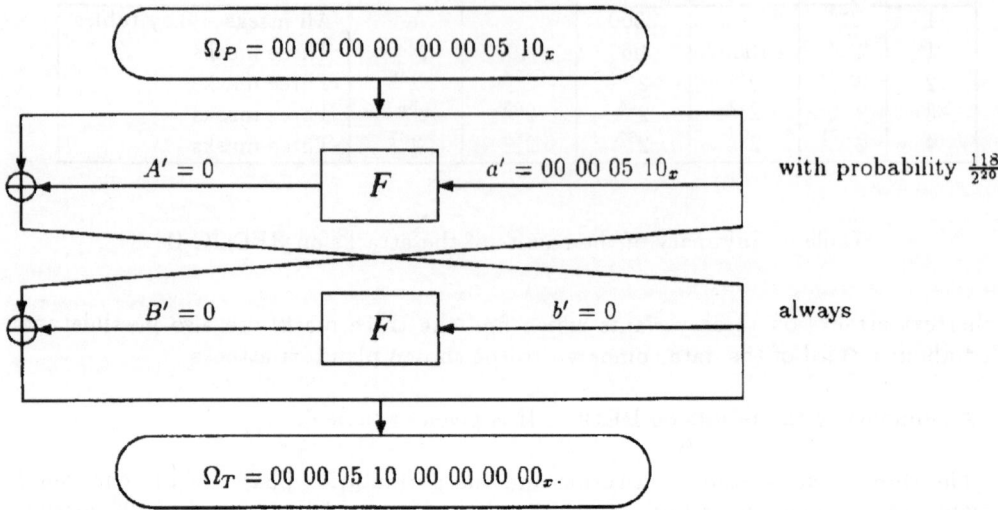

$\Omega_P = 00\ 00\ 00\ 00\ \ 00\ 00\ 05\ 10_x$

$A' = 0$      $F$      $a' = 00\ 00\ 05\ 10_x$     with probability $\frac{118}{2^{20}}$

$B' = 0$      $F$      $b' = 0$     always

$\Omega_T = 00\ 00\ 05\ 10\ \ 00\ 00\ 00\ 00_x.$

This characteristic can be iterated to nine rounds with probability about $2^{-52.5}$ and to eleven rounds with probability about $2^{-65.5}$. Since all the four S boxes of LOKI are the same and all the output XORs in this characteristic are zero, there are three similar characteristics in which the XOR pattern is rotated by units of eight bits. There is another eight-round iterative characteristic in which only non-replicated bits of some S box are different and the outputs differ only by one bit. This characteristic is:

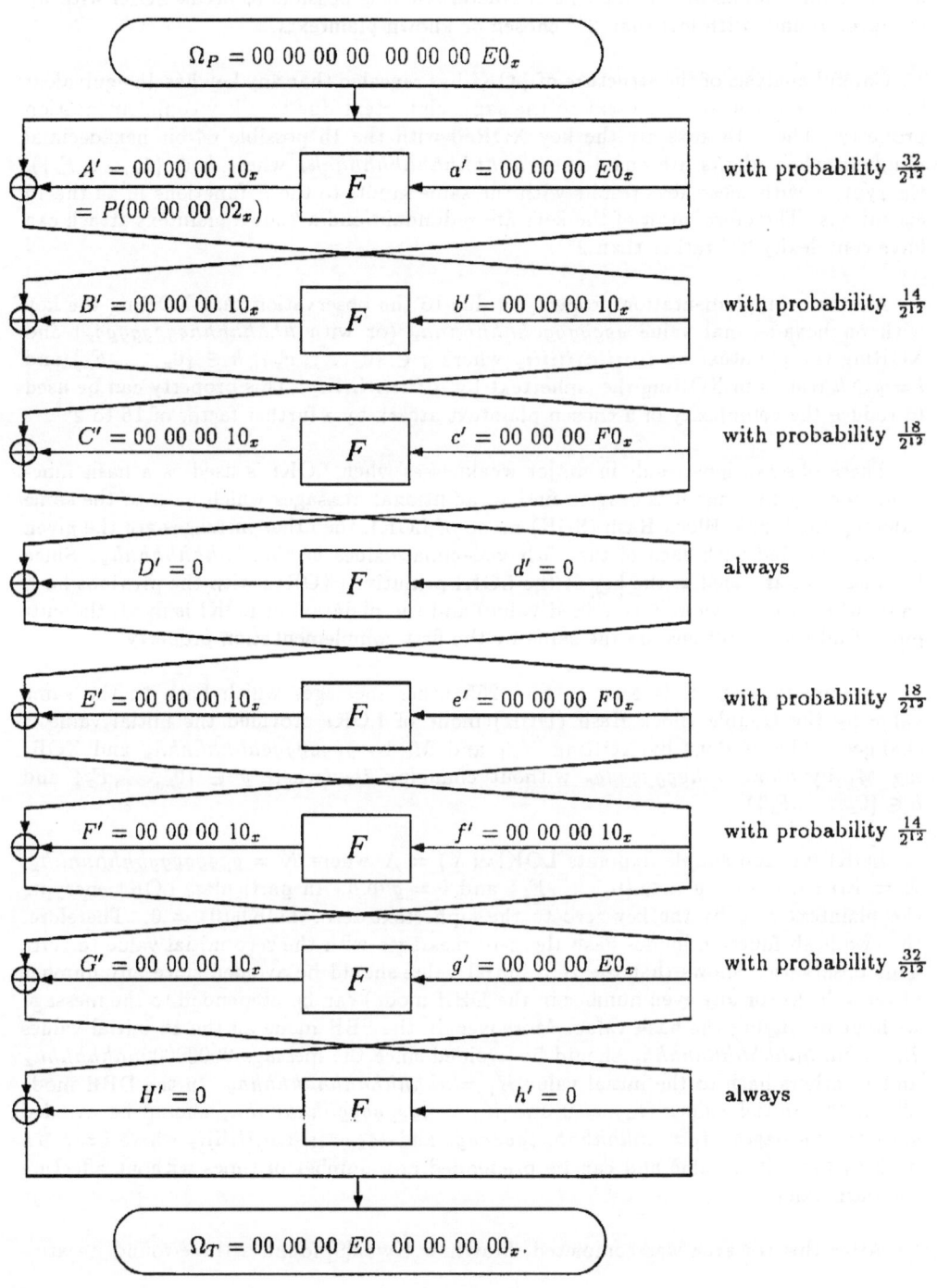

$$\Omega_P = 00\ 00\ 00\ 00\ \ 00\ 00\ 00\ E0_x$$

$A' = 00\ 00\ 00\ 10_x$  $F$  $a' = 00\ 00\ 00\ E0_x$  with probability $\frac{32}{2^{12}}$
$= P(00\ 00\ 00\ 02_x)$

$B' = 00\ 00\ 00\ 10_x$  $F$  $b' = 00\ 00\ 00\ 10_x$  with probability $\frac{14}{2^{12}}$

$C' = 00\ 00\ 00\ 10_x$  $F$  $c' = 00\ 00\ 00\ F0_x$  with probability $\frac{18}{2^{12}}$

$D' = 0$  $F$  $d' = 0$  always

$E' = 00\ 00\ 00\ 10_x$  $F$  $e' = 00\ 00\ 00\ F0_x$  with probability $\frac{18}{2^{12}}$

$F' = 00\ 00\ 00\ 10_x$  $F$  $f' = 00\ 00\ 00\ 10_x$  with probability $\frac{14}{2^{12}}$

$G' = 00\ 00\ 00\ 10_x$  $F$  $g' = 00\ 00\ 00\ E0_x$  with probability $\frac{32}{2^{12}}$

$H' = 0$  $F$  $h' = 0$  always

$$\Omega_T = 00\ 00\ 00\ E0\ \ 00\ 00\ 00\ 00_x.$$

This iterative characteristic has probability about $2^{-46}$ and its extension to nine rounds has the same probability. Using this characteristic it is possible to break LOKI with up to eleven rounds with less than $2^{64}$ chosen or known plaintexts.

Careful analysis of the structure of LOKI has revealed that any key has 15 equivalent keys which encrypt any plaintext to the same ciphertext due to a key complementation property. These 15 keys are the key XORed with the 15 possible 64-bit hexadecimal numbers whose digits are equal (i.e., $hhhhhhhhhhhhhhhh_x$ where $h \in \{1_x, \ldots, F_x\}$). Encryption with these keys results with the same inputs to the $F$ functions in all the 16 executions. Therefore, most of the keys are redundant and a known plaintext attack can have complexity $2^{60}$ rather than $2^{64}$.

Another complementation property is due to the observation that XORing the key with an hexadecimal value $gggggggghhhhhhhh_x$ (or with $hhhhhhhhgggggggg_x$) and XORing the plaintext by $iiiiiiiiiiiiiiii_x$ where $g \in \{0_x, \ldots, F_x\}$, $h \in \{0_x, \ldots, F_x\}$ and $i = g \oplus h$ results in XORing the ciphertext by $iiiiiiiiiiiiiiii_x$. This property can be used to reduce the complexity of a chosen plaintext attack by a further factor of 16 to $2^{56}$.

These observations result in major weaknesses when LOKI is used as a hash function. For any message it is easy to find 15 additional messages which hash to the same value by the Single Block Hash (SBH) mode of LOKI: the other messages are the given message XORed with each of the 15 hexadecimal values $hhhhhhhhhhhhhhhh_x$. Since the messages are used as the key of the LOKI primitive (XORed with the previous hash value which can be viewed as a fixed value) and the plaintext of LOKI is fixed, the outputs of all the executions are the same by the first complementation property.

For any message it is easy to find 255 other messages which hash to the same value by the Double Block Hash (DBH) mode of LOKI provided the initial value is changed. This is done by XORing $H_{-1}$ and $M_2$ by $gggggggghhhhhhhh_x$ and XORing $M_1$ by $hhhhhhhhgggggggg_x$ without changing $H_0$ (where $g \in \{0_x, \ldots, F_x\}$ and $h \in \{0_x, \ldots, F_x\}$).

LOKI has 256 simple fixpoints $\text{LOKI}_K(X) = X$ where $K = gggggggghhhhhhhh_x$, $X = iiiiiiiiiiiiiiii_x$, $g, h \in \{0_x, \ldots, F_x\}$ and $i = g \oplus h$. In particular, LOKI encrypts the plaintext zero by the key zero to the ciphertext zero: $\text{LOKI}_0(0) = 0$. Therefore, the two hash function modes hash the zero messages with the zero initial value to zero. This observation shows that the zero initial value should be avoided since any number of zero-blocks (or any even number in the DBH mode) can be prepended to the message without modifying the hash value. Moreover, in the SBH mode all the 16 initial values $H_0 = hhhhhhhhhhhhhhhh_x$ should be avoided since the message $00000000hhhhhhhh_x$ and 15 others hash to the initial value $H_1 = hhhhhhhhhhhhhhhh_x$. In the DBH mode all the 256 initial values $H_{-1} = 0$ and $H_0 = gggggggghhhhhhhh_x$ should be avoided since the messages $M_1 = hhhhhhhhgggggggg_x$ and $M_2 = iiiiiiiiiiiiiiii_x$ where $i = g \oplus h$ hash to the initial value and can be prepended any number of times without affecting the hash value.

After this research was completed, Matthew Kwan[9] found a three-round iterative

| Input | Output of $S_0$ | Output of $S_1$ | Equal bits |
|-------|-----------------|-----------------|------------|
| 0000 | 0100 | 1111 | .1.. |
| 0001 | 0001 | 1100 | ..0. |
| 0010 | 1110 | 1000 | 1..0 |
| 0011 | 1000 | 0010 | .0.0 |
| 0100 | 1101 | 0100 | .10. |
| 0101 | 0110 | 1001 | .... |
| 0110 | 0010 | 0001 | 00.. |
| 0111 | 1011 | 0111 | ..11 |
| 1000 | 1111 | 0101 | .1.1 |
| 1001 | 1100 | 1011 | 1... |
| 1010 | 1001 | 0011 | .0.1 |
| 1011 | 0111 | 1110 | .11. |
| 1100 | 0011 | 1010 | .01. |
| 1101 | 1010 | 0000 | .0.0 |
| 1110 | 0101 | 0110 | 01.. |
| 1111 | 0000 | 1101 | ..0. |

| Input | Equal bits |
|-------|------------|
| .000 | .1.. |
| 0.00 | .1.. |
| 001. | ...0 |
| .110 | 0... |
| 10.0 | ...1 |
| 110. | .0.. |

Table 7: Output bits that are equal for both S boxes (left table)

Table 8: Output bits that are equal for both S boxes and two input values (right table)

characteristic of LOKI with probability $2^{-14.4}$ which can be use to break LOKI with up to 14 rounds. He also found many more fixpoints of LOKI.

# 6   Cryptanalysis of Lucifer

Lucifer[8] is a substitution/permutation network cryptosystem designed by IBM prior to the design of DES. In Lucifer the input of the S boxes is the bit permuted output of the S boxes of the previous round. The input of the S boxes of the first round is the plaintext itself. A key bit is used to choose the actual S box at each entry out of two possible four-bit to four-bit invertible S boxes.

Given an input of an S box the outputs of the two possible S boxes are known. Each output bit may be equal in the two S boxes or may be different. Usually only one or two output bits are equal in the two S boxes. In few cases one output bit is equal in all the four output values obtained when two input values differing by one bit (for example $8_x$ and $A_x$) enter the two possible S boxes. In particular, there are pairs for which three output bits are equal and the fourth bit differ when using different S box.

For the sake of concreteness, we use the third and fourth lines of S1 of DES as the S boxes $S_0$ and $S_1$ of Lucifer. Other choices of the S boxes give similar results. Table 7 describes the S boxes and the equal bits of the outputs of the two S boxes. We see that eleven inputs cause two equal bits, four cause one equal bit and one input does not cause any equal bit. Table 8 describes the equal bits of two input values which differ by one bit using both S boxes. A binary notation is used in the tables.

By consulting these tables we can create many plaintexts whose particular (chosen) bit at an interior round has a chosen fixed value, regardless of the choice of the key. We can also create pairs of plaintexts which differ in a later round only at a particular bit. Lucifer with eight rounds can be attacked using the encryptions of such plaintexts. The attack on Lucifer with 128-bit blocks with eight rounds needs about 24–30 encryptions and takes about $2^{21}$ steps. Its personal computer implementation requires a few seconds with almost 100% success rate.

Another variant of Lucifer which is described in [14] is more similar to DES. Its variant with eight rounds is weaker than the eight-round variant of Lucifer described in [8].

# References

[1] Eli Biham, Adi Shamir, *Differential Cryptanalysis of DES-like Cryptosystems (extended abstract)*, Advances in cryptology, proceedings of CRYPTO 90, 1990.

[2] Eli Biham, Adi Shamir, *Differential Cryptanalysis f DES-like Cryptosystems*, Journal of Cryptology, Vol. 4, No. 1, 1991, to appear.

[3] Eli Biham, Adi Shamir, *Differential Cryptanalysis of Feal and N-Hash (extended abstract)*, Advances in cryptology, proceedings of EUROCRYPT 91, 1991.

[4] Eli Biham, Adi Shamir, *Differential Cryptanalysis of Feal and N-Hash*, in preperation.

[5] Lawrence Brown, Josef Pieprzyk, Jennifer Seberry, *LOKI - A Cryptographic Primitive for Authentication and Secrecy Applications*, Advances in cryptology, proceedings of AUSCRYPT 90, pp. 229–236, 1990.

[6] Michael C. Wood, technical report, Cryptech inc., Jamestown, NY, July 1990.

[7] Thomas W. Cusick, Michael C. Wood, *The REDOC-II Cryptosystem*, Advances in cryptology, proceedings of CRYPTO 90, 1990.

[8] H. Feistel, *Cryptography and Data Security*, Scientific American, Vol. 228, No. 5, pp. 15–23, May 1973.

[9] Matthew Kwan, private communications.

[10] Ralph C. Merkle, *A Fast Software One-Way Hash Function*, Journal of Cryptology, Vol. 3, No. 1, pp. 43-58, 1990.

[11] Ralph C. Merkle, *Fast Software Encryption Functions*, Advances in cryptology, proceedings of CRYPTO 90, 1990.

[12] Shoji Miyaguchi, Akira Shiraishi, Akihiro Shimizu, *Fast Data Encryption Algorithm Feal-8*, Review of electrical communications laboratories, Vol. 36, No. 4, pp. 433–437, 1988.

[13] Akihiro Shimizu, Shoji Miyaguchi, *Fast Data Encryption Algorithm Feal*, Advances in cryptology, proceedings of EUROCRYPT 87, pp. 267–278, 1987.

[14] Arthur Sorkin, *Lucifer, a Cryptographic Algorithm*, Cryptologia, Vol. 8, No. 1, pp. 22–41, January 1984.

A KNOWN PLAINTEXT ATTACK OF FEAL-4 AND FEAL-6

Anne TARDY-CORFDIR and Henri GILBERT
Centre National d'Etudes des Télécommunications (CNET)
PAA/TSA/SRC
38-40 rue de la République
92131 Issy les Moulineaux
FRANCE

Abstract

*We present new results on the cryptanalysis of the FEAL-N blockcipher. As a matter of fact, almost all the attacks of this cryptosystem published so far are chosen plaintext attacks [3,4,5,7], except the announcement in [7] of a non-differential known plaintext attack of FEAL-4 which requires about 100000 plaintext blocks. We describe known plaintext attacks of FEAL-4 and FEAL-6, which require about 1000 and 20000 plaintext blocks respectively and are based on correlations with linear functions. Using similar methods, we have also found more recently an improved attack on FEAL-4, which requires only 200 known plaintext blocks.*

## 1 The FEAL-N cryptosystem

FEAL-N is an N-round blockcipher proposed by NTT [1,2]. The standard version FEAL-8 is well suited for a fast software execution. So far, chosen plaintext attacks of FEAL-4 [3,4] and FEAL-8 [5] and chosen plaintext attacks that break FEAL-N faster than an exhaustive search for any $N \leqslant 31$ [7] have been published. [7] contains also some bounds on the extension of differential attacks to known plaintext attacks, and the announcement of a non-differential known plaintext attack on FEAL-4, which requires about 100000 plaintext blocks.

In this paper we present known plaintext attacks of FEAL-4 and FEAL-6. These attacks are statistical in nature, and require a limited number of ciphertext blocks and the corresponding plaintext (about 1000 blocks for the attack of FEAL-4 described here, about 200 blocks for an improved attack of FEAL-4, and about 20000 blocks for the attack of FEAL-6). There are no particular constraints on the plaintext.

J. Feigenbaum (Ed.): Advances in Cryptology - CRYPTO '91, LNCS 576, pp. 172-182, 1992.
© Springer-Verlag Berlin Heidelberg 1992

We are using the following notations :

- If X represents a 32-bit word $(x_{31}, x_{30}, \ldots, x_0)$, $X_0$ is the byte $(x_{31}, x_{30}, \ldots, x_{24})$; $X_1$ is the byte $(x_{23}, x_{22}, \ldots, x_{16})$, etc; we also write : $X = (X_0, X_1, X_2, X_3)$;
- If X and Y are two binary strings of equal length, $X \oplus Y$ represents the bitwise xor between X and Y;
- If B represents the byte $(b_7, b_6, b_5, b_4, b_3, b_2, b_1, b_0)$, the byte $(b_5, b_4, b_3, b_2, b_1, b_0, b_7, b_6)$ is denoted by ROT2(B); the byte $(b_6, b_5, b_4, b_3, b_2, b_1, b_0, 0)$ is denoted by SH1(B);
- If $B_1$ and $B_2$ are two bytes, the byte $B_1 + B_2$ represents the sum modulo 256 of the numbers represented by $B_1$ and $B_2$, using the usual binary convention (low weight bit right). We also define the ternary operator SBOX : $SBOX(B_1, B_2, \epsilon) = ROT2(B_1 + B_2 + \epsilon)$ where $\epsilon \in \{0,1\}$.

The FEAL-N algorithm can be divided in two components : the key schedule and the data randomizer.

We do not need here to consider the detail of the key schedule : let us only say that the key schedule transforms the 64-bit secret key into an expanded key composed of the 2N+16 bytes $K_0, K_1, \ldots, K_{2N+15}$.

The data randomization can be split into the three following steps :

## The initial step
We start with a 64-bit word $(I^0, I^1)$ as input. Then we compute a new 64-bit word $(X^0, X^1)$ defined by :

$$X^0 = I^0 \oplus (K_{2N}, K_{2N+1}, K_{2N+2}, K_{2N+3})$$
$$X^1 = X^0 \oplus I^1 \oplus (K_{2N+4}, K_{2N+5}, K_{2N+6}, K_{2N+7})$$

## The main step
The 64-bit word $(X^0, X^1)$ is taken as the input to an N round Feistel scheme. Rounds are numbered from 0 to N-1. At round i, a new 32-bit word $X^{i+2}$ is produced, given by the equation :

$$X^{i+2} = f_i(X^{i+1}) \oplus X^i$$

The function $f_i$ is defined by :
$$\{0,1\}^{32} \to \{0,1\}^{32}$$
$$X = (X_0, X_1, X_2, X_3) \mapsto Y = (Y_0, Y_1, Y_2, Y_3)$$

where :
$$Y_1 = SBOX(X_0 \oplus X_1 \oplus K_{2i}, X_2 \oplus X_3 \oplus K_{2i+1}, 1),$$
$$Y_0 = SBOX(X_0, Y_1, 0),$$
$$Y_2 = SBOX(Y_1, X_2 \oplus X_3 \oplus K_{2i+1}, 0),$$
$$Y_3 = SBOX(Y_2, X_3, 1)$$

The function $f_i$ is one to one and depends only on the two expanded key bytes $K_{2i}$ and $K_{2i+1}$. In the (usual) 64-bit representation of the Feistel scheme, the output of round i is the 64 bit word $(X^{i+1}, X^{i+2})$;

**The final step**

The 64-bit word $(X^N, X^{N+1})$ is taken as input to the final step. The 64-bit ciphertext block $(O^0, O^1)$ is defined by :

$$O^0 = X^{N+1} \oplus (K_{2N+8}, K_{2N+9}, K_{2N+10}, K_{2N+11})$$
$$O^1 = X^N \oplus X^{N+1} \oplus (K_{2N+12}, K_{2N+13}, K_{2N+14}, K_{2N+15})$$

## 2 Principle of the attack

Our attack is a statistical variant of the well known "meet in the middle" method. It is based on two kinds of relations :

(1) It uses some key-independent statistics which involve the plaintext and an intermediate block of the FEAL-N data randomizer (say the block $X^{N-1}$, which appears as an input to the last round of the Feistel scheme).

(2) In addition, the deciphering algorithm provides a key-dependent relation between this intermediate block and the ciphertext.

An exhaustive search for the value optimizing the agreement between the a priori expected statistics (1) and the statistics deduced from the ciphertext (2) provides the part of the expanded key involved in (2). The knowledge of this part of the expanded key can be generally used for the derivation of an additional part of the expanded key, based on further statistics of the form (1), etc... A full attack consists of the stepwise derivation of the entire expanded key.

The main difficulty of such an attack is (1), i.e. finding key-independent statistics. In order to obtain such statistics, our attack uses extensively the fact that in [0,255] considered as an 8-dimensional vector space over GF(2) the SBOX operator is nearly linear.

## 3 A linear approximation of the FEAL S-boxes.

We must find a good linear approximation of the S-box operator. Also we must find a good approximation of the two following operations in [0,255] :
- addition : $(B,B') \mapsto (B+B') \mod 256$
- addition and successor : $(B,B') \mapsto (B+B'+1) \mod 256$
We are led to study the addition in $\mathbb{N}$.

For $n \in \mathbb{N}^*$, $f_n$ denotes the following boolean function :

$$\{0,1\}^{2n+2} \rightarrow \{0,1\}$$
$$(x_n, \ldots, x_0, y_n, \ldots, y_0) \mapsto z_n$$

where $z_{n+1} z_n z_{n-1} \ldots z_0$ is the binary representation of the sum in $\mathbb{N}$ of the two numbers $x$ and $y$ represented by $x_n x_{n-1} \ldots x_0$ and $y_n y_{n-1} \ldots y_0$ respectively.

**Proposition**

For every $n \in \mathbb{N}^*$ a best linear approximation of $f_n$ is the function $\tilde{f}_n$ defined by :

$$\{0,1\}^{2n+2} \rightarrow \{0,1\}$$
$$(x_n, \ldots, x_0, y_n, \ldots, y_0) \mapsto x_n \oplus x_{n-1} \oplus y_n$$

and $\qquad d(f_n, \tilde{f}_n) = \frac{1}{4} \cdot 2^{2n+2}$ $\qquad$ (i)

**Proof**

We first state (i). Our proof is basically the same as the one contained in [8], where (i) and similar relations are mentioned. On $\Omega = \{0,1\}^{2n+2}$ equipped with the uniform probability we define the boolean random variable $c_k$ ($1 \leq k \leq n$) of a sample $(x_n, \ldots, x_0; y_n, \ldots, y_0)$ as the left carry generated by adding the numbers $x_{k-1} \ldots x_0$ and $y_{k-1} \ldots y_0$. For instance $c_1(1;1)=1$ and $c_1(1;0)=0$. We also define the random variable $c_0 = 0$.

$\Pr_{(x,y)} \in \Omega \ \{f_n(x,y) \neq \tilde{f}_n(x,y)\}$
$\quad = \Pr_\Omega \{x_n \oplus y_n \oplus c_n \neq x_n \oplus x_{n-1} \oplus y_n\}$
$\quad = \Pr_\Omega \{x_{n-1}=1 \wedge c_n=0\} + \Pr_\Omega \{x_{n-1}=0 \wedge c_n=1\}$
$\quad = \Pr_\Omega \{x_{n-1}=1 \wedge y_{n-1}=0 \wedge c_{n-1}=0\}$
$\quad + \Pr_\Omega \{x_{n-1}=0 \wedge y_{n-1}=1 \wedge c_{n-1}=1\}$
$\quad = \Pr_\Omega \{x_{n-1}=1\} . \Pr_\Omega \{y_{n-1}=0\} . \Pr_\Omega \{c_{n-1}=0\}$
$\quad + \Pr_\Omega \{x_{n-1}=0\} . \Pr_\Omega \{y_{n-1}=1\} . \Pr_\Omega \{c_{n-1}=1\}$
$\quad$ (we are using the fact that for $\epsilon$, $\epsilon'$, $\epsilon'' \in \{0,1\}$ the events $\{x_{n-1}=\epsilon\}$, $\{y_{n-1}=\epsilon'\}$ and $\{c_{n-1}=\epsilon''\}$ are independent)
$\quad = \frac{1}{4} \cdot (\Pr_\Omega \{c_{n-1}=0\} + \Pr_\Omega \{c_{n-1}=1\}) = \frac{1}{4}$

Thus (i) is proved.

The fact that $\tilde{f}_n$ is a best linear approximation of $f_n$ is a consequence of (i). Let $L$ be any affine boolean function on $\{0,1\}^{2n+2}$ other than $\tilde{f}_n$. We have :

$$d(\tilde{f}_n, L) = \frac{1}{2} \cdot 2^{2n+2} \text{ (ii)}$$

From (i) (ii) and the triangular inequality :

$$d(\tilde{f}_n, L) \leq d(\tilde{f}_n, f_n) + d(f_n, L) \text{ we deduce :}$$

$$d(f,L) \geq \frac{1}{4} \cdot 2^{2n+2} \text{ Q.E.D.}$$

**Note** : of course the function $\hat{f}_n$ defined in replacing $x_{n-1}$ by $y_{n-1}$ in the expression of $\tilde{f}_n$ is also a best linear approximation of $f_n$.

The above proposition suggests the following linear approximation for the addition :

$$B + B' \simeq B \oplus B' \oplus SH1(B') \quad (a)$$

(for each of the 8 bit positions in a byte, the equality between the bit at the left and the bit at the right of $\simeq$ holds with a probability of at least 0.75 ). Similarly we are led to the following approximation for the addition and successor operation :

$$B + B' + 1 \simeq B \oplus B' \oplus SH1(B') \oplus 1 \qquad (b)$$

Our attack uses a keyless linear approximation of the encryption scheme obtained by omitting the expanded key and by replacing the S-boxes with their linear approximation derived from (a) and (b). If $X^n$ denotes one of the intermediate variables of the encryption scheme, the corresponding value obtained by replacing the encryption scheme with its keyless linear approximation will be denoted by $\tilde{X}^n$.

## 4 The attack of FEAL-4

### 4.1 Statistics

The attack of FEAL-4 uses key-independent statistics which involve the intermediate variable $X^3$ and the plaintext. The following diagram shows the relation between the bytes $X_0^3$ and $X_1^3$ and the bytes $X_0^2$, $X_0^1$ and $X_1^1$.

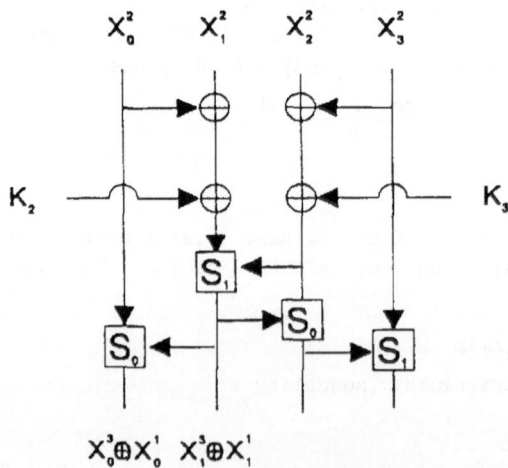

In using the explicit expression of the left S-box $S_0$ in the above diagram, we obtain the relation :

$$X_0^3 \oplus X_0^1 = ROT2 (X_0^2 + (X_i^3 \oplus X_i^1 )).$$

Now by using the linear approximation of the addition of Section 3 we obtain :

$$X_0^3 \oplus X_0^1 \simeq ROT2(X_0^2 \oplus X_i^3 \oplus X_i^1 \oplus SH1(X_i^3 \oplus X_i^1 )).$$

We call $\varphi$ the function defined by :

$$\varphi(X^n) = X_0^n \oplus ROT2(X_i^n \oplus SH1(X_i^n )).$$

We can restate the above relation :

$$\varphi(X^3) \simeq ROT2(X_0^2) \oplus \varphi(X^1) \quad (R)$$

We studied the statistics of the byte $\varphi(X^3) \oplus ROT2(\tilde{X}_0^2) \oplus \varphi(\tilde{X}^1)$, where $\tilde{X}_0^2$ and $\tilde{X}^1$ are keyless linear approximations of $X_0^2$ and $X^1$ obtained as explained in Section 3. These statistics are summarized in Table 1. They are key-independent, i.e. for each bit position the absolute value of the deviation from 0.5 is independent of the key. They are non uniform and express a correlation between a function of $X^3$ (the term $\varphi(X^3)$) and a function of the plaintext (the two last terms), so they are of the desired form.

| bit number | average value |
|:----------:|:-------------:|
| 0 | 0.578 |
| 1 | 0.580 |
| 2 | 0.667 |
| 3 | 0.413 |
| 4 | 0.373 |
| 5 | 0.434 |
| 6 | 0.377 |
| 7 | 0.572 |

Table 1 : Statistics obtained with 10000 blocks.
Only the absolute value of the deviation from 0.5 is significant.

## 4.2 Derivation of the expanded key

The relation between the bytes $X_0^3$ and $X_i^3$ (which are needed for computing the expression $\varphi(X^3) \oplus ROT2(\tilde{X}_0^2) \oplus \varphi(\tilde{X}^1)$) and the 64-bit ciphertext block $(0^0, 0^1)$ is illustrated in the diagram hereafter :

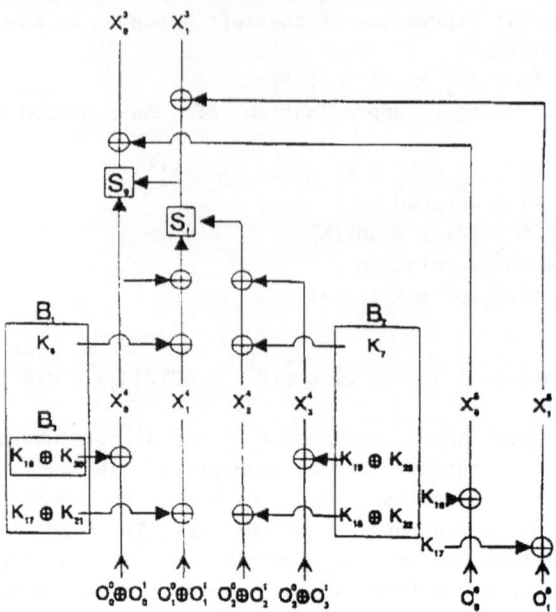

This diagram shows that $X_0^3$ and $X_1^3$ can be calculated up to the unknown constants $K_{16}$ and $K_{17}$ using only the three unknown combinations $B_1$, $B_2$ and $B_3$. A more careful analysis shows that $\varphi(X^3)$ can be calculated up to an unknown constant byte using only the 7 lowest weight bits of $B_1$, $B_2$ and $B_3$ and the bit $B_1[7] \oplus B_2[7]$, i.e. 22 unknown keybits.

The procedure for testing a value of the 22 unknown bits is the following :

- for each plaintext block we calculate $\text{ROT2}(\tilde{X}_0^2) \oplus \varphi(\tilde{X}^1)$. This is done only once;
- for each ciphertext sample we calculate $\varphi(X^3)$ up to a constant, using the assumed value of the 22 keybits;
- we assign to that 22 keybits value a "criterion value" : the sum of the absolute values of the deviation from 0.5 of the average of each bit of the byte $\varphi(X^3) \oplus \text{ROT2}(\tilde{X}_0^2) \oplus \varphi(\tilde{X}^1)$ (this byte is calculated up to an unknown constant which has no effect on the criterion value).

We select the value of the 22 keybits for which that criterion value is maximal. In fact if the 22 keybits value is not the correct one, the calculated $\varphi(X^3)$ has no sense and each bit of the studied byte has an average value close to 0.5.

Experiments prove that this test leads to the correct value of the 22 keybits with only 1000 plaintext blocks and the corresponding ciphertext (we obtained some good results even with only 300 blocks). In order to improve the computation time, we searched appropriately selected parts of the keybits first. With this improved method, only an half of hour computing time of a SUN4 workstationwas needed for deriving the correct 22 keybits from 1000 blocks.

Once the first 22 unknown keybits have been derived, new key-independent statistics must be used for deriving further unknown keybits. This process is quite similar to the derivation of the expanded key in the chosen plaintext attack of [5]. We restricted our experiments to the beginning of the derivation, but there is no substantial difficulty in continuing this derivation.

## 5 The attack of FEAL-6

### 5.1 Statistics
We must now find key-independent statistics which involve the intermediate variable $X^5$ .

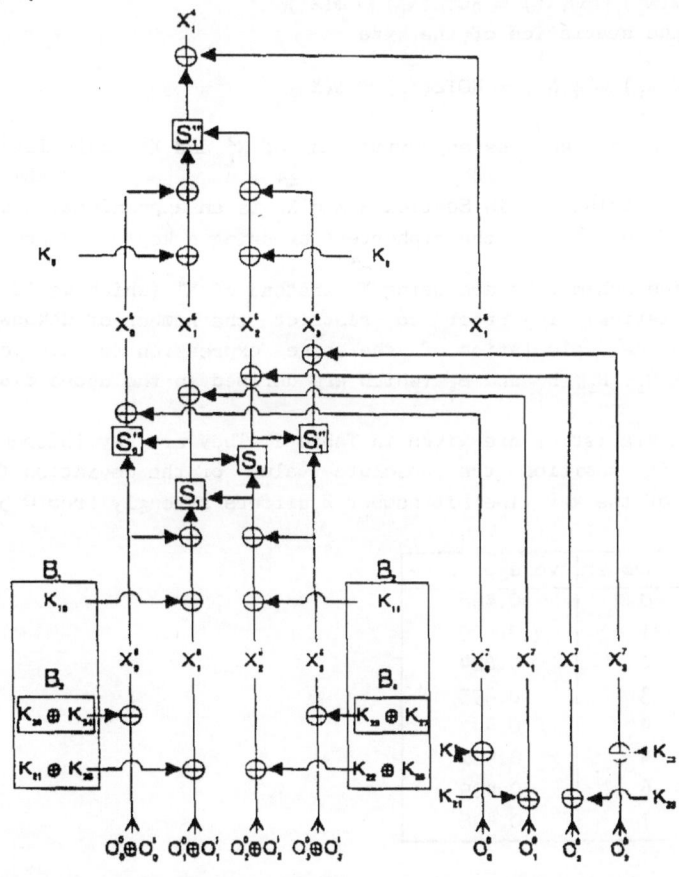

In the previous Section we have used the approximate relation :
$$ROT2(X_0^{i+1}) \simeq \varphi (X^{i+2}) \oplus \varphi(X^i) \quad (R)$$
For the attack of FEAL-6 we are using another similar approximate relation. Instead of $\varphi$ it involves a new function denoted by $\psi$, which is defined by :
$$\psi(X^i) = X_0^i \oplus X_1^i \oplus ROT2(SH1(X_1^i)) \oplus X_2^i$$
We have the following approximate relation :
$$ROT2(X_1^{i+1}) \simeq \psi(X^i) \oplus \psi(X^{i+2}) \quad (\mathfrak{R})$$
We can prove that the bits number 2 of the left and right bytes of $(\mathfrak{R})$ are strictly equal :
$$ROT2(X_1^{i+1})[2] = \psi(X^i)[2] \oplus \psi(X^{i+2})[2]$$
For the other bit positions, the correlations expressed by $(\mathfrak{R})$ are very low.

From the relations :
$$ROT2(X_1^2) \simeq \psi(X^3) \oplus \psi(X^1) \quad \text{and}$$
$$ROT2(X_1^4) \simeq \psi(X^3) \oplus \psi(X^5)$$
we deduce :
$$ROT2(X_1^2) \oplus \psi(X^1) \simeq ROT2(X_1^4) \oplus \psi(X^5)$$
We studied the statistics of the byte :
$$ROT2(\tilde{X}_1^2) \oplus \psi(\tilde{X}^1) \oplus ROT2(\tilde{\tilde{X}}_1^4) \oplus \psi(X^5)$$
where $\tilde{X}_1^2$ and $\tilde{X}^1$ are keyless approximations of $X_1^2$ and $X^1$ calculated from the plaintext as explained in Section 3 and $\tilde{\tilde{X}}_1^4$ is an approximation of $X_1^4$ which is derived from $X^5$ and the ciphertext by using a keyless approximation of the decryption scheme. We are using $\tilde{\tilde{X}}_1^4$ instead of $X_1^4$ (which would have given better statistics) in order to restrict the number of unknown keybytes involved in the calculation of the above expression to only four unknown combinations $B_1$, $B_2$, $B_3$ and $B_4$ (which are defined in the above diagram).

The obtained statistics are given in Table 2. They are key independent, i.e. for each bit position the absolute value of the deviation from 0.5 is independent of the key. The bit number 2 differs strongly from 0.5.

| bit number | average value |
|:---:|:---:|
| 0 | 0.498 |
| 1 | 0.499 |
| 2 | 0.624 |
| 3 | 0.493 |
| 4 | 0.497 |
| 5 | 0.501 |
| 6 | 0.499 |
| 7 | 0.496 |

Table 2 : Statistics obtained with 100000 blocks
Only the absolute values of the deviations from 0.5 are significant

## 5.2 Derivation of the expanded key

The attack method is similar to the one used for FEAL-4. We show the very beginning of the attack, i.e. the procedure for the test of a value of $B_1$ and $B_2$ (more precisely for the test of the 7 lowest weight bits of $B_1$ and $B_2$ and of the bit $B_1[7] \oplus B_2[7]$, i.e. 15 bits) :

- for each plaintext block we calculate $ROT2(\overset{\sim 2}{X_0})$ and $\psi(\overset{\sim 1}{X})$ . This is done once only;
- for each ciphertext block we calculate $X_1^5$ and $X_2^5$ up to the unknown constants $K_{21}$ and $K_{22}$, using $B_1$ and $B_2$. We calculate then approximate values of $X_0^5$ and $X_3^5$ from $X_1^5$, $X_3^5$ and the ciphertext , using a keyless linear approximation of the left and right S-boxes in the first round of the decryption scheme. We also calculate $\overset{\approx 4}{X_0}$ from the obtained approximate value of $X^5$ and the ciphertext, using a keyless linear approximation of the second round of the decryption scheme (all the calculations are represented in the diagram of Section 5.1);
- we assign to $B_1$ and $B_2$ a criterion value : the absolute value of the average deviation from 0.5 of the obtained approximate value of the bit $ROT2(\overset{\sim 2}{X_1})[2] \oplus \psi(\overset{\sim 1}{X})[2] \oplus ROT2(\overset{\approx 4}{X_1})[2] \oplus \psi(X^5)[2]$ .
We finally select the value of the 15 unknown bits for which the criterion value is maximal.

The experiments of this attack made with 20000 plaintext blocks and the corresponding ciphertext led to the correct value of the 15 keybits. The derivation of these 15 bits took approximately 10 hours computation time on a SUN4 workstation (using a non optimised Pascal program). We did not experiment the whole continuation of the derivation of the expanded key, but there is no substantial difficulty in continuing the derivation.

Partial experiments of a similar attack based on the function $\varphi$ of Section 4 showed that it should be possible to reduce the number of blocks required to a few thousands, at the expense of increasing the number of unknown keybits in the first step of the attack. This other attack requires an exhaustive search of the four bytes $B_1$, $B_2$, $B_3$ and $B_4$ with 3000 blocks; its full test was not within the reach of our computer.

## 6 Improved results on FEAL-4

The above attack on FEAL-6 suggested us an improvement to the FEAL-4 attack described in Section 4. The new attack is entirely based on the approximate relation $(\mathfrak{R})$, as for the FEAL-6 attack. It requires about 200 plaintext blocks. According to our experiments, the derivation of the first 12 unknown keybits takes 20 seconds on a SUN4 workstation. Our estimate of the time required for the entire key derivation is a few minutes.

## 7 Conclusion

The attacks presented here are an example of the use of correlations with linear functions for the cryptanalysis of blockciphers. They belong, together with the differential attacks [4,5,6,7], to a broader family of statistical attacks. They use approximate relations in the same way as differential cryptanalysis uses caracteristics [6]. The relations (R) and (ℜ) are similar to eight one-round caracteristics each (one for each bit position), and the statistics used for the attack of FEAL-4 and FEAL-6 are similar to 2-rounds caracteristics and 4-rounds caracteristics respectively. A known plaintext attack of the standard version FEAL-8 would require an efficient 6-rounds approximate relation. We do not know whether such relations can be found.

## 8 Acknowledgements

The authors wish to thank Marc Girault and Janice Bell for their discerning remarks and valuable suggestions on the early version of this work, and François Allègre for generously cooperating to improve the presentation of the results.

REFERENCES

[1] A. Shimizu, S. Miyaguchi, "Fast Data Encipherment Algorithm FEAL". Advances in Cryptology - Eurocrypt 87, Lecture Notes in Computer Science, Vol 304, Springer Verlag, 1988.
[2] S. Miyaguchi, "News on Feal cipher", talk at the Rump session, Crypto'90, 1990.
[3] Bert Den Boer, "Cryptanalysis of FEAL", Advances in Cryptology - Eurocrypt 88, Lecture Notes in Computer Science, Vol 330, Springer Verlag, 1989.
[4] S. Murphy, "The Cryptanalysis of Feal-4 with 20 Chosen Plaintexts", Journal of Cryptology Vol2 N°3, 1990.
[5] H. Gilbert , G. Chassé, "A Statistical Attack of the FEAL-8 Cryptosystem", Proceedings of Crypto'90.
[6] E. Biham, A. Shamir, "Differential Cryptanalysis of DES-like Cryptosystems", Proceedings of Crypto'90.
[7] E. Biham, A. Shamir, "Differential Cryptanalysis of Feal and N-Hash", extended abstract, Proceedinds of Eurocrypt'91.
[8] W. Meier, O. Staffelbach, "Correlation Properties of Combiners with Memory in Stream Ciphers", to appear in the Journal of Cryptology.

# A switching closure test to analyze cryptosystems

(Extended abstract)

**Hikaru Morita**     **Kazuo Ohta**     **Shoji Miyaguchi**

NTT Laboratories

NTT R&D Center (Room 309A), 1-2356 Take Yokosuka Kanagawa 238-03 Japan

Phone: +81-468-59-2514     FAX: +81-468-59-3858     E-mail: morita@sucaba.ntt.jp

## Abstract

The closure test MCT (meet-in-the-middle closure test) was introduced to analyze the algebraic properties of cryptosystems [KaRiSh]. Since MCT needs a large amount of memory, it is hard to implement with an ordinary meet-in-the-middle method. As a feasible version of MCT, this paper presents a switching closure test SCT which based on a new memoryless meet-in-the-middle method. To achieve the memoryless method, appropriate techniques, such as expansion of cycling detection methods for one function into a method for two functions and an efficient intersection search method that uses only a small amount of memory, are used in an extremely effective manner.

## 1. Introduction

There are two approaches in cryptography to analyzing the security levels of cryptosystems. The first is to develop unique attacks for each cryptosystem. This utilizes the idiosyncrasies of each cryptosystem. The second approach is to analyze cryptosystems to find their features such as algebraic or statistical structures; the cryptosystems are regarded as black-box functions. The latter approach is important because you can accumulate knowledge of cryptosystems with a common framework.

Even if you find the statistical structure of a cryptosystem, you do not automatically know of a useful method to attack the cryptosystem. To find the algebraic structure of cryptosystems in general, Kaliski et al. [KaRiSh] proposed two closure tests: CCT (cycling closure test) and MCT (meet-in-the-middle closure test). These tests can detect features such as algebraic closure. Moreover, Kaliski et al. also proposed two cryptattack methods based on the algebraic features. CCT experiments performed by Kaliski et al. detected that DES is not closed.

Generally, both CCT and MCT can determine if a cryptosystem is closed or not. If a cryptosystem is closed, they give the same results "Fail", which means the cryptosystem might be breakable. However, if a cryptosystem is not closed, you cannot be sure that they will give the same results "Pass" because it isn't known whether CCT and MCT can detect the same algebraic structure or not. Our interest was that MCT might prove to be a fertile avenue for cryptographic research. MCT offers the possibility of extracting information from a not-closed cryptosystem that would allow the cryptosystem to be broken. Moreover, a cryptosystem may fail under MCT even if it passes CCT.

J. Feigenbaum (Ed.): Advances in Cryptology - CRYPTO '91, LNCS 576, pp. 183-193, 1992.
© Springer-Verlag Berlin Heidelberg 1992

CCT needs (operation) time of $O\left(\sqrt{|K|}\right)$ and a small amount of (memory) space where $|K|$ is the size of key space $K$ of the cryptosystem. However, MCT needs space and time of $O\left(\sqrt{|K|}\right)$. No feasible method to achieve the meet-in-the-middle strategy, which MCT uses, has been proposed because the strategy needs a lot of memory.

In this paper, we present a switching closure test (SCT) as a feasible version of MCT by using a memoryless method. Up to now, though the memoryless method has been applied to collision search [QuDe], this paper applies it for the first time to a closure test for cryptosystems. Section 2 gives the background of our research. Section 3 shows the procedures of SCT. Section 4 describes a feasibility study that confirms SCT performance. The paper is concluded in Section 5.

## 2. Background
### 2.1 What is a closure structure?
The below explanation of closure structure follows [KaRiSh].

Let us denote a cryptosystem $\Pi = (K, M, C, E)$, where $K$, $M$, $C$ are key space, message space, and ciphertext space, respectively and $E : K \times M \to C$ is a transformation such that, for $k \in K$, the mapping $E_k = E(k, \cdot)$ is invertible.

### [Definition 1]
$\Pi = (K, M, C, E)$ is closed if and only if its set of encryption transformations, $\left\{ E_k \middle| k \in K \right\}$ is closed under functional composition, i.e., for every two keys $i, j \in K$ there exists a key $k \in K$ such that $E_j E_i = E_k$.

Kaliski et al. presented two closure tests, MCT and CCT, for determining if a cryptosystem is closed or not. If the cryptosystem passes either test, then it is not closed with high probability. Though CCT was implemented in [KaRiSh], no feasible method has been presented to achieve MCT, because it uses $O\left(\sqrt{|K|}\right)$ operation time and $O\left(\sqrt{|K|}\right)$ memory space.

MCT is based on the following property which is satisfied by closed cryptosystems.

### [Property 1]
Let $\Pi = (K, M, C, E)$ satisfy $M = C$, the number of $\left\{ E_k \middle| k \in K \right\}$ be $m$, and $k \in K$ be any key. If $\Pi = (K, M, M, E)$ is closed, then there are exactly $m$ pairs of keys $(i, j)$ such that $E_j E_i = E_k$.

## 2.2 Meet-in-the-middle closure test (MCT) [KaRiSh]
MCT works as follows: given $\Pi = (K, M, M, E)$, pick any key $k \in K$ and search for keys $a, b \in K$ such that $E_k = E_b E_a$. To search for them, you use a standard "meet-in-the-middle" strategy. The MCT procedure is shown in Fig. 2.1.

Suppose that a pair $(p, c)$ is given where $c = E_k(p)$. If $\Pi$ is closed, then property 1 above means that there are $m$ pairs $(i, j)$ among all $m^2$ key pairs satisfying $E_j E_i = E_k$.

Therefore, the probability of a match between $\{E_i(p)\}$ and $\{E_j^{-1}(c)\}$ is $r_1 r_2 \dfrac{m}{m^2}$, where $r_1$ is the number of elements of $\{E_i(p)\}$ and $r_2$ is the number of elements of $\{E_j^{-1}(c)\}$. If $\Pi$ is closed, $m = O(|K|)$, and $r_1 r_2 = O(m)$, then we can find a pair $(i, j)$ such that $E_j E_i = E_k$ with high probability.

If there is no match in MCT under the condition $r_1 r_2 = O(m)$, you can conclude that the cryptosystem is not closed with confidence. Note that MCT requires $r_1$ operations of $E_i(p)$, $r_2$ operations of $E_j^{-1}(c)$ and at least $r_1$ or $r_2$ memory space. If $r_1 = r_2$, which is optimal from the standpoint of operation number, $r_1 = r_2 = O(\sqrt{m})$.

input: a cryptosystem $\Pi = (K, M, M, E)$ and integer control parameters $r_1$, $r_2$, $l$.

Step 1. Pick $k \in K$ and $p_1, p_2, \cdots, p_l \in M$ at random.

    For $i = 1$ to $l$, compute $c_i = E(k, p_i)$.

    Let $p = p_1$ and $c = c_1$.

Step 2. For $i = 1$ to $r_1$ and $j = 1$ to $r_2$, select $a_i, b_j \in K$ at random

    and compute $x_i = E(a_i, p)$ and $y_j = E^{-1}(b_j, c)$.

Step 3. Sort triples $(x_i, a_i, "A")$ for $1 \le i \le r_1$

    and $(y_j, b_j, "B")$ for $1 \le j \le r_2$ on the first components.

Step 4. For each "match" $x_i = y_j$ with $1 \le i \le r_1$ and $1 \le j \le r_2$,

    if $E_k = E_{b_j} E_{a_i}$, then return ("Match found").

    (To test if $E_k = E_{b_j} E_{a_i}$, statistically verify that $c_h = E(b_j, E(a_i, p_h))$ for all $1 \le h \le l$.)

Step 5. return("No match found").

## Fig. 2.1 Meet-in-the-middle closure test (MCT) procedure

## 2.3 Related Work

The meet-in-the-middle strategy is effective in cryptography [DiHe, QuDe].

In [DiHe], this strategy is used to find a key pair $(k_1, k_2)$ from a pair $(p, c)$ in the double-encryption cryptosystem, where $c = E(k_2, E(k_1, p))$. If an exhaustive key search is used, $O(|K|^2)$ operations are needed. If a meet-in-the-middle strategy is applied, only $O(|K|)$ operations and $O(|K|)$ memory space are required.

Quisquater et al. developed the meet-in-the-middle technique with $O(\sqrt{|K|})$ operations without memory. The technique was applied to find collisions of hash functions [QuDe].

Collision is not a problem for a hash function since collision is only based on the hash-function's randomness. On the other hand, if a pair of keys $(k_1, k_2)$ is found for a cryptosystem by using MCT, it implies that the cryptosystem is vulnerable.

# 3. Switching closure test (SCT) procedure

This section introduces the memoryless procedure needed to make the ordinary meet-in-the-middle method feasible and shows how to apply the procedure to a closure test.

## 3.1 Memoryless meet-in-the-middle procedure

We propose the memoryless meet-in-the-middle procedure in Fig. 3.1. In the procedure, the period-length search required by Steps 2 and 6, is given in Paragraph (1). The intersection-point search of Steps 3 and 7 is described in Paragraph (2). If the random function $h$ is defined as shown in Paragraph (3), the intersection-point search can be expanded into the collision-point search for a meet-in-the-middle method.

input: a function $h(x)$ switching $f(x)$ or $g(x)$ and an integer control parameter $t$.

Step 1. Pick $x_0^{(i)} \in M$ for $i = 1, 2, \cdots, t$ at random.

Step 2. $i = 1$.

Search period - length $\lambda$ for sequence $S^{(i)}$ started from $x_0^{(i)}$.

(where $S^{(i)} = \{x_0^{(i)}, x_1^{(i)}, \cdots\}$)

Step 3. Search for an intersection point in the sequence $S^{(i)}$.

Step 4. If the intersection point found is the collision point in $S^{(i)}$ where $f(x)$ and $g(y)$ meet

then return$(x, y)$.

Step 5. $i = i + 1$.

Step 6. Search period - length $\lambda$ for the sequence $S^{(i)}$ started from $x_0^{(i)}$

and check that the new sequence $S^{(i)}$ meets the previous sequnces

$\{S^{(1)}, S^{(2)}, S^{(3)}, \cdots, S^{(i-1)}\}$.

Step 7. Search for a new intersection point in $S^{(i)}$ or between $S^{(i)}$ and $S^{(j)}$ ($1 \le j \le i - 1$).

If the intersection point found is the collision point in $S^{(i)}$ or between $S^{(i)}$ and $S^{(j)}$

where $f(x)$ and $g(y)$ meet, then return$(x, y)$.

Step 8. Go to Step 5.

## Fig. 3.1 Memoryless meet-in-the-middle procedure

## (1) Period-length search [Kn, SeSzYa]

If the random function $h$ generates values $x$, the "Birthday Paradox" states that the random sequence $S = \{x_0, x_1, \cdots\}$ has a period whose length is $O(\sqrt{|X|})$, where $x_{i+1} = h(x_i)$ and $|X|$ shows the size of $X$ space. When the sequence $\{x_0, x_1, \cdots\}$ is plotted on directed graphs, it can be drawn as shown in Fig.3.2 (a).

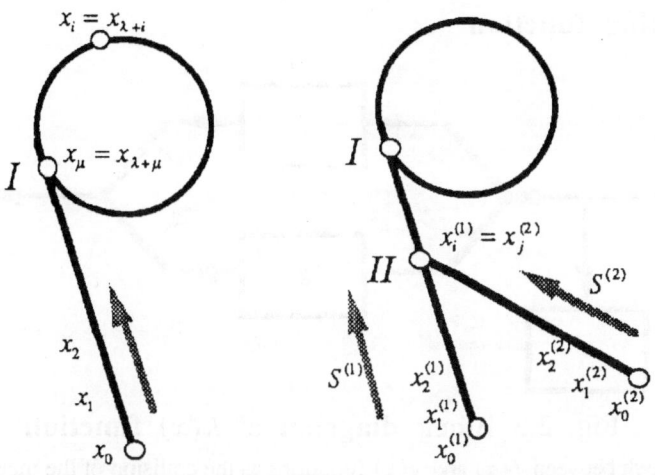

(a) Original sequence    (b) Two sequences
contains Point I    meet at Point II

Fig. 3.2 Sequences on directed graphs

Methods to find period-length $\lambda$ have been developed in the design of a random generator [Kn, SeSzYa]. The methods compare two values $x_i$ and $x_j$ $(i \neq j)$ to determine $x_i = x_{\lambda+i}$. We based our memoryless meet-in-the-middle procedure on these methods.

## (2) Intersection search

There are two kind of intersection points as shown in Fig.3.2. Point I is represented by

$$x_\mu = h\big(x_{\mu-1}\big), \quad x_{\lambda+\mu} = h\big(x_{\lambda+\mu-1}\big),$$

where $x_\mu = x_{\lambda+\mu}$, $x_{\mu-1} \neq x_{\lambda+\mu-1}$.

Point I is shown as the junction between a loop and a leader in Fig.3.2 (a). Point II in Fig.3.2 (b) is represented by $x_i^{(1)} = h\big(x_{i-1}^{(1)}\big)$ and $x_j^{(2)} = h\big(x_{j-1}^{(2)}\big)$ where $x_i^{(1)} = x_j^{(2)}$ and $x_{i-1}^{(1)} \neq x_{j-1}^{(2)}$ where the superscripts distinguish values of Sequences $S^{(1)}$ and $S^{(2)}$. To find Point II, sequences starting from two different initial values $x_0^{(1)}$ and $x_0^{(2)}$ are needed. It is known that graphs of the random function $h$ tend to have one giant loop (or component) and a few large leaders (or trees) [FlOd].

In brief, to find Point I, after the period-length $\lambda$ is determined, pairs, $(x_0, x_\lambda)$, $(x_1, x_{\lambda+1})$, $\cdots$, $(x_i, x_{\lambda+i})$ are compared until $x_\mu = x_{\lambda+\mu}$ is found. However, this procedure is inefficient because you need $\mu$ comparisons and $2\mu$ operations of the function $h$. Therefore, to overcome this inefficiency, we have developed techniques that require only $O\big(\log_2(\mu)\big)$ operations. The techniques will be presented in the full paper version. The same approach is used to find Point II.

## (3) Switching function

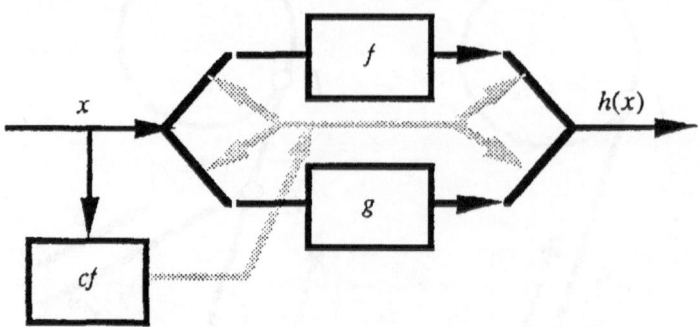

### Fig. 3.3 Block diagram of $h(x)$ function

To find the match between $f(x)$ and $g(x)$ functions as the collision of the meet-in-the-middle procedure, let's define $h(x)$ as a switching-type function of $f(x)$ or $g(x)$ conditionally defined as

$$h(x) = \begin{cases} f(x) & \text{if } cf(x) \text{ is true,} \\ g(x) & \text{if } cf(x) \text{ is false,} \end{cases}$$

where $cf(x)$ is a conditional function which generates true or false with 50-% probability for each value $x$.

The intersection points found in Paragraph (2) are expected to contain collision points between $f$ and $f$ with 25 %, between $g$ and $g$ with 25 %, and between $f$ and $g$ with 50 %. The intersection points between $f$ and $g$ mean the collision points between two different functions $f$ and $g$. Consequently, the meet-in-the-middle procedure succeeds for two different functions.

## 3.2 Closure test for cryptography functions
### (1) How to apply to a closure test

The SCT procedure is presented in Fig. 3.4. If SCT detects an $x$ and $y$ pair that satisfies $E(x, p) = E^{-1}(y, c)$ for any $(p, c)$, the cryptosystem fails in SCT. On the other hand, if SCT doesn't detect any $x$ and $y$ pair several times, the cryptosystem passes.

input:  functions $f(x) \equiv E(x,p)$ and $g(x) \equiv E^{-1}(x,c)$ and integer control parameter $l,t$.

Step 1. Pick $k \in K$ and $p_1, p_2, \cdots, p_l \in M$ at random.

   For $i = 1$ to $l$, compute $c_i = E(k, p_i)$.

   Set $p = p_1, c = c_1$.

Step 2. Call Memoryless Meet - in - the - middle procedure $(f,g,t)$,

   then get $(x,y)$ at the collision point.

Step 3. If $E_k = E_y E_x$, then return ("Match found")

   (To test if $E_k = E_y E_x$, statistically verify $c_h = E(y, E(x, p_h))$ for all $1 \le h \le l$.)

Step 4. return("No match found").

## Fig. 3.4 Switching closure test (SCT) procedure

Since we want to find key pairs $(k_1, k_2)$ instead of the real secret key $k$ for any plaintext and ciphertext pair $(p,c)$ where $c = E(k_2, E(k_1, p))$ and $c = E(k,p)$, a meet-in-the-middle method is used to find pairs of $x$ and $y$ which make $E(x,p) = E^{-1}(y,c)$. In the SCT procedure in Fig. 3.4, SCT verifies that $E(x,p) = E^{-1}(y,c)$ for any $(p,c)$. To simplify the explanation, we omit functions $F_E$ and $F_D$ from Fig. 3.4. More precisely, the $f$ and $g$ functions are defined as shown in Fig. 3.5.

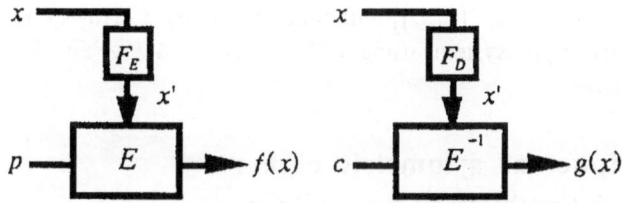

## Fig. 3.5 Definitions of $f$ and $g$

## (2) Strategies & probability to detect closure structure

We have devised two strategies to increase the intersection points in SCT after the first period-length and intersection-point searches. In Strategy #1, an intersection search is carried out from another start point for the same plaintext and ciphertext pair. Strategy #2 is to carry out an intersection search for another plaintext and ciphertext pair. Therefore, Strategy #2 employs both period-length and intersection searches and always finds the Point I in Fig. 3.2.

   If a cryptosystem is closed, their probability of success can be assessed from the analysis given in Section 2.2. If, finally, $r_1$ values of $f$ and $r_2$ values of $g$ have been generated by the $h$ function, their probability is approximately given by

$$1 - \exp\left(-\frac{r_1 r_2}{m}\right),$$

where there are $m$ kinds of independent transformations. In Strategy #1, if $r_1'$ values of $f$ and $r_2'$ values of $g$ newly appear, its probability becomes

$$1 - \exp\left(-\frac{(r_1 + r_1')(r_2 + r_2')}{m}\right),$$

because Strategy #1 replaces $r_1$ and $r_2$ with $(r_1 + r_1')$ and $(r_2 + r_2')$, respectively. On the other hand, in Strategy #2, if $r_1'$ and $r_2'$ values also newly appear, its probability becomes

$$1 - \exp\left(-\frac{r_1 r_2 + r_1' r_2'}{m}\right),$$

because the first and second searches are independent.

Strategy #2 needs more operations than #1. Strategy #1 has a higher probability of success than #2 if $r_1'$ and $r_2'$ have the same values for both strategies. However, Strategy #2 can be efficiently implemented on parallel processing hardware. Therefore, Strategy #2 is better for hardware implementations.

## 4. Feasibility study

This section explains the SCT's detectability of closure property for both symmetric and asymmetric ciphers. Moreover, we will show that SCT yields a known-plaintext attack against closed cryptosystems. In the case of a symmetric cipher, if you find the key pair $(k_1, k_2)$ from $(p, c)$ using SCT, where $c = E(k, p)$ and $E_k = E_{k_2} E_{k_1}$, then you can decipher any ciphertext $c'$ by $E^{-1}\left(k_1, E^{-1}(k_2, c')\right)$ without a secret key $k$. However, is it impossible to attack asymmetric cryptosystems using SCT? In Section 4.2 we attack a small model of an RSA cryptosystem.

### 4.1 Caesar cipher as symmetric cipher

The definition of the Caesar cipher is given as shown;

$$E(k, p) = p + k \bmod n,$$

$$E^{-1}(k, c) = c - k \bmod n.$$

We define functions, $f$, $g$, $cf$, respectively as;

$$f(x) \quad = p + x \bmod n,$$

$$g(x) \quad = c - x \bmod n,$$

$$cf(x) \quad = (\text{true if } x \text{ is "odd", false if } x \text{ is "even"}).$$

At first, $(p, c) = (5, 2)$, and $n = 11$ are given. Though a secret key $k = 8$ is kept secret, Fig. 4.1 is drawn by SCT. If you start from $x_0^{(1)} = 1$ or $x_0^{(2)} = 0$, you find a loop with $\lambda = 3$ or $\lambda = 2$ without the collision point. If you start from $x_0^{(3)} = 4$, you find a loop with $\lambda = 4$ with the collision point $f(9) = g(10)$. Since you can verify $f(9) = g(10)$ for all other plaintext and ciphertext pairs $(p, c) = (6, 3), (7, 4), (8, 5), \cdots$, the Caesar cipher fails in SCT.

The Caesar cipher is shown to be broken in SCT because plaintext values $p'$ can be calculated from ciphertext values $c'$ by using $p' = E^{-1}(9, E^{-1}(10, c'))$.

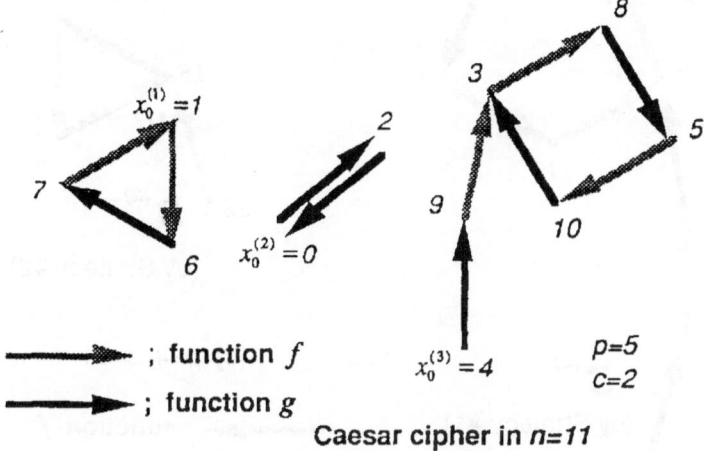

; function $f$

; function $g$

$x_0^{(3)} = 4$

$p=5$
$c=2$

Caesar cipher in $n=11$

## Fig. 4.1 Caesar cipher

## 4.2 RSA cryptosystem as asymmetric cipher

This section presents a feasibility study for a small version of RSA [RiShAd]. In this model, the relation of parameters is:

$$E(k_e, p) = p^{k_e} \bmod n,$$

$$E^{-1}(k_d, c) = c^{k_d} \bmod n$$

$$(k_e k_d = 1 \bmod L, n = pq, L = \mathrm{LCM}(p-1, q-1)).$$

Thus, we can define functions, $f$, $g$, $cf$, respectively as;

$$f(x) = p^x \bmod n,$$

$$g(x) = c^x \bmod n,$$

$$cf(x) = (\text{true if } x > \frac{n}{2}, \text{ false if } x \le \frac{n}{2}).$$

At first, $n = 33$, $k_e = 3$, and $(p,c) = (13,19)$ are given. Though secret values $(k_d = 7, L = 10)$ are kept secret, Fig. 4.2 is drawn by SCT. If you search from the initial value 18, you find period-length $\lambda = 5$ and a collision of $f(18) = f(28)$. Since SCT cannot find the collision of $f$ and $g$, you know that the collision is wrong.

In Strategy #1, the intersection search is carried out on the same plane from another start point 12. Then, you can find the collision of $f(19) = g(13)$ which is right for all pairs $(p,c)$. On the other hand, in Strategy #2, the intersection search is carried out on another plane for $(p,c) = (4,31)$ from another start point 22. You find the right collision of $f(22) = g(4)$. Thus, RSA fails in SCT.

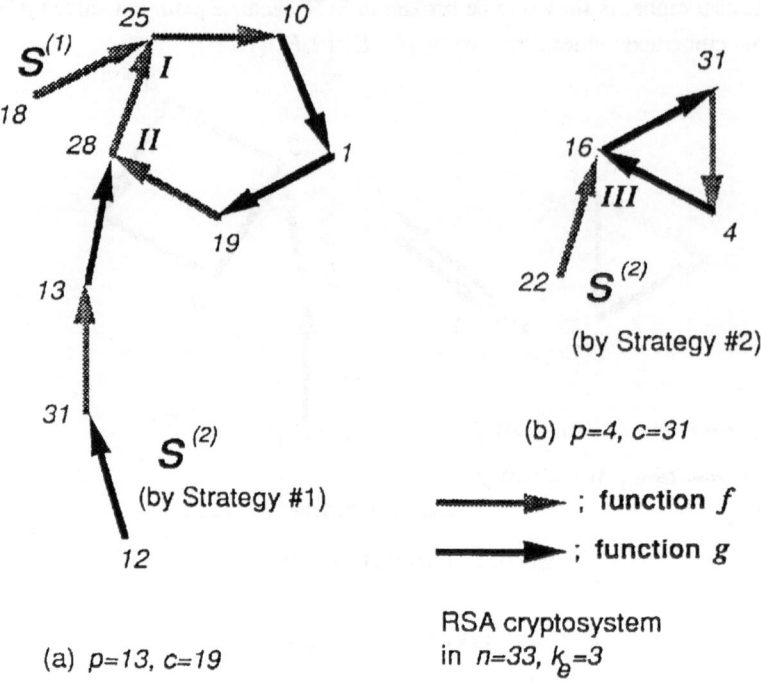

**Fig. 4.2 Small model of RSA**

Though RSA is an asymmetric cipher, it has one idiosyncrasy that allows it to be broken. If the right collision of $f(x) = g(y)$ is found, $x = k_e y \bmod L$ must be right. Therefore, since you can know a multiple of $L$, the composite number $n$ can be factorized by using the multiple [Mi]. In the above example, $22 = 3 \times 4 \bmod 10$. However, since commercial RSA schemes use $n$ greater than $2^{500}$, SCT would need more than $2^{250}$ operations; RSA is not menaced by SCT.

## 5. Conclusion

A switching closure test SCT based on a new memoryless meet-in-the-middle procedure has been proposed as a feasible version of MCT. To achieve the memoryless procedure, several techniques, the most important of which are expansion of cycling detection methods for one function into a method for two functions and an efficient intersection search by using a small amount of memory, are effectively used. Moreover, feasibility studies using a Caesar cipher and a small model of an RSA cryptosystem have been presented.

We intend to apply SCT to various kinds of cryptosystems.

# References

[DiHe] W. Diffie and M. E. Hellman: "Exhaustive Cryptanalysis of the NBS Data Encryption Standard," Computer, 10, 6, pp.74-84, June 1977.

[FlOd] P. Flajolet and A. M. Odlyzko: "Random Mapping Statistics," Advances in Cryptology-EUROCRYPT'89, Proceedings, pp.329-354, Springer-Verlag, 1990.

[KaRiSh] B. S. Kaliski Jr., R. L. Rivest, and A. T. Sherman: "Is the Data Encryption Standard a Group? (Results of Cycling Experiments on DES)," J. Cryptology, 1, 1, pp.3-36, 1988.

[Kn] D. E. Knuth: Exercise 3.1 No. 7, "The Art of Computer Programming 2nd ed. (Seminumerical Algorithms)," Addison-Wesley, 1981.

[Mi] G. L. Miller: "Riemann's hypothesis and tests for primality," J.Computer and System Science, 13, pp.300-317, 1976.

[QuDe] J.-J. Quisquater and J.-P. Delescaille: "How Easy is Collision Search. New Results and Applications to DES," Advances in Cryptology-CRYPTO'89, Proceedings, pp.408-413, Springer-Verlag, 1990.

[RiShAd] R. L. Rivest, A. Shamir, and L. Adleman: "A Method of Obtaining Digital Signatures and Public Key Cryptosystems," Comm. of ACM, pp.120-126, Feb. 1978.

[SeSzYa] R. Sedgewick, T. G. Szymanski, and A. C. Yao: "The Complexity of Finding Cycles in Periodic Functions," SIAM J. Comp., 11, 2, pp.376-390, May 1982.

# An Attack on the Last Two Rounds of MD4

Bert den Boer
Philips Crypto B.V.
P.O. Box 218
5600 MD Eindhoven
The Netherlands

Antoon Bosselaers
ESAT Laboratory, K.U. Leuven
Kard. Mercierlaan 94
B-3001 Heverlee
Belgium
bosselaers@esat.kuleuven.ac.be

## Abstract

In [Rive90] the MD4 message digest algorithm was introduced taking an input message of arbitrary length and producing an output 128-bit message digest. It is conjectured that it is computationally infeasible to produce two messages having the same message digest, or to produce any message having a given prespecified target message. In this paper it is shown that if the three round MD4 algorithm is stripped of its first round, it is possible to find for a given (initial) input value two different messages hashing to the same output. A computer program implementing this attack takes about 1 millisecond on a 16 Mhz IBM PS/2 to find such a collision.

# 1 Introduction

The MD4 Message Digest Algorithm, by Ronald L. Rivest and RSA Data Security, Inc., is intended for file hashing: it accepts arbitrarily large inputs and produces an output of 128 bits. It is conjectured that it is computationally infeasible to produce two messages having the same message digest, or to produce any message having a given prespecified target message digest. The MD4 algorithm is designed to be quite fast on 32-bit machines.

An interesting topic of investigation is how these claims relate to the number of rounds of MD4, and whether they hold for a weaker version of the algorithm, stripped of its first or last round. The latter was considered by Ralph Merkle [Merk90], who showed that skipping the last round jeopardizes the strength of the system: for 99.99% of all initial values it is possible to find two message differing in only 3 bits, which are hashed to the same output value. We derived an algorithm for it and wrote a computer program implementing the attack. The program takes less than a millisecond on a 16 Mhz IBM PS/2 to find such a collision. Next, we investigated whether by skipping the first round one would also be able to produce a collision of messages. It will be shown that it is indeed possible for MD4 stripped of its first round to find for a given (initial) input value two different messages hashing to the same output.

In Section 2 a short description of MD4 is given. In Section 3 the attack on the last

J. Feigenbaum (Ed.): Advances in Cryptology - CRYPTO '91, LNCS 576, pp. 194-203, 1992.
© Springer-Verlag Berlin Heidelberg 1992

two rounds is explained, and an example collision for MD4 skipping the first round is given. The possibility to extend this attack to the full three round algorithm is briefly discussed.

# 2 Short description of MD4

Below only a general description of the MD4 message digest algorithm is given. For a detailed description the reader is referred to [Rive90]. In this description a *byte* is defined as an 8-bit quantity and a *word* as a 32-bit quantity. A sequence of bits can be interpreted as a sequence of bytes, where each consecutive group of 8 bits is interpreted as a byte with the *high*-order bit of each byte listed first. Similarly, a sequence of bytes can be interpreted as a sequence of words, where each consecutive group of 4 bytes is interpreted as a word with the *low*-order byte given first. The input and output of MD4 is considered to be a sequence of bytes, not words, but the internal operations of the algorithm are word oriented.

The MD4 recipe for a $b$-bit message consists of the following steps:

1. **Append padding bits and the message length:** a single "1" bit, $l - 1$ zero bits ($1 \leq l < 512$) and the 64-bit representation of $b \bmod 2^{64}$ are appended to the message such that the length $b + l + 64$ of the extended message is a multiple of 512. The 64 bits containing the message length are appended as two 32-bit words, *low*-order word first in accordance with the previous conventions. The (new) message is now represented as a sequence $M[0], M[1], \ldots, M[n-1]$ of $n$ words, where $n$ is a multiple of 16 (because $32 \cdot n = b + l + 64 \equiv 0 \bmod 512$).

2. **Initialize a 4-word buffer $(A, B, C, D)$:**

   $A = 67452301; B = \text{EFCDAB89}; C = 98\text{BADCFE}; D = 10325476.$

   (32-bit constants in hexadecimal notation, high-order digits first)

3. **Process the message in 16-word blocks:**

   ```
   for i = 0 to (n/16) − 1 do
      begin
         for j = 0 to 15 do
            X[j] = M[16i + j];
         (AA, BB, CC, DD) = (A, B, C, D);
         Round 1;
         Round 2;
         Round 3;
   ```

$$A = A + AA;$$
$$B = B + BB;$$
$$C = C + CC;$$
$$D = D + DD;$$

      end;

**4. The output is the 4-word buffer $(A, B, C, D)$.**

Figure 2 shows the outline of step 3 of MD4, without the feedforward.

# 3  Description of the attack on the last two rounds

Each of the three rounds of MD4 consists of 16 elementary operations on the 4-word buffer $(A, B, C, D)$. Let $(A_i, B_i, C_i, D_i)$ denote the value of $(A, B, C, D)$ after $i$ elementary operations. In this section only the last two rounds of MD4 are considered. The elementary operations are therefore numbered relative to the beginning of the second round. It will be shown that it is possible to find for a given input two different 16-word message blocks hashing to the same output. The underlying observation is that the 8 message words $X[1]$, $X[5]$, $X[9]$, $X[13]$, $X[2]$, $X[6]$, $X[10]$ and $X[14]$ used in the elementary operations 5 till 12 are the same as those used in the elementary operations 21 till 28. In other words the *same* 8 message words are used in the middle 8 elementary operations of the second and third round. A similar observation applies for the 8 message words $X[0]$, $X[4]$, $X[8]$, $X[12]$, $X[3]$, $X[7]$, $X[11]$ and $X[15]$ used in the first 4 (elementary operations 1 till 4 and 17 till 20) and last 4 (elementary operations 13 till 16 and 29 till 32) elementary operations of the second and third round. The latter 8 message words $X[0]$, $X[4]$, $X[8]$, $X[12]$, $X[3]$, $X[7]$, $X[11]$ and $X[15]$ are given the same value in the two 16-word message blocks. Consequently $(A_4, B_4, C_4, D_4)$ has the same value for both messages. If $(A_{12}, B_{12}, C_{12}, D_{12})$ is equal for both messages, then $(A_{20}, B_{20}, C_{20}, D_{20})$ will be equal too, and if $(A_{28}, B_{28}, C_{28}, D_{28})$ has the same value for both messages, both messages are hashed to the same output value. The two message blocks only differ in the remaining 8 words $X[1]$, $X[5]$, $X[9]$, $X[13]$, $X[2]$, $X[6]$, $X[10]$ and $X[14]$ used in the middle 8 elementary operations of the last two rounds. The two alternatives for these message words are precisely chosen in such a way that the 4-word buffer $(A, B, C, D)$ has two alternatives after 8 and 24 elementary operations (this is halfway the second and third round), but the same value for both messages after 12 and 28 elementary operations. Hence we have two different messages and a single input value, which are hashed to the same output value. This situation is illustrated in Figure 1, where every dot represents a different value of the buffer $(A, B, C, D)$.

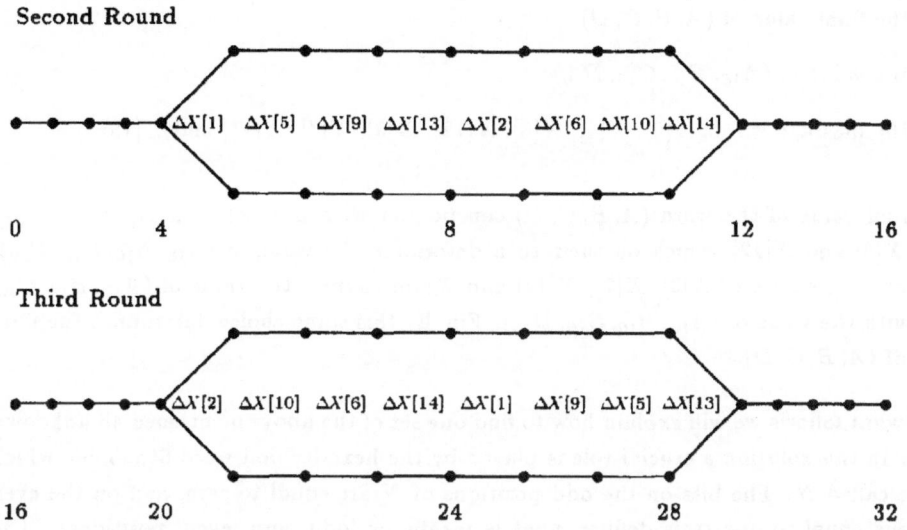

Figure 1: Outline of the attack on the last two rounds

The problem we are confronted with is the following. We have to solve 32 equations (twice the middle 8 elementary operations of each round, one for each alternative of the input) with unknowns:

- the value of $(A_4, B_4, C_4, D_4)$

- two alternatives of $(A_8, B_8, C_8, D_8)$

- the value of $(A_{12}, B_{12}, C_{12}, D_{12})$

- the value of $(A_{20}, B_{20}, C_{20}, D_{20})$

- two alternatives of $(A_{24}, B_{24}, C_{24}, D_{24})$

- the value of $(A_{28}, B_{28}, C_{28}, D_{28})$

- two alternatives for the message words $X[2]$, $X[6]$, $X[10]$, $X[14]$, $X[1]$, $X[5]$, $X[9]$ and $X[13]$

Altogether there are 48 unknown words. Once we found a solution for this problem, we are left with 16 equations (the first and last 4 elementary operations of each round) with 16 unknowns:

- the final value of $(A, B, C, D)$

- the value of $(A_{16}, B_{16}, C_{16}, D_{16})$

- the message words $X[0]$, $X[4]$, $X[8]$, $X[12]$, $X[3]$, $X[7]$, $X[11]$ and $X[15]$

An initial value of the word $(A, B, C, D)$ can be met with precisely one choice of $X[0]$, $X[4]$, $X[8]$ and $X[12]$, which on their turn determine the value of $(A_{16}, B_{16}, C_{16}, D_{16})$. Precisely one choice of $X[3]$, $X[7]$, $X[11]$ and $X[15]$ couples the value of $(A_{12}, B_{12}, C_{12}, D_{12})$ with the value of $(A_{16}, B_{16}, C_{16}, D_{16})$. Finally this same choice determines the final value of $(A, B, C, D)$.

In what follows we will explain how to find one set of the above mentioned 48 unknown words. In this solution a crucial role is played by the hexadecimal word 55555555, which will be called $N$. The bits on the odd positions of $N$ are equal to zero, and on the even positions equal to one (this defines what is meant by 'odd' and 'even' positions). The number $N$ has the following interesting property: any rotation in any direction over an odd number of bits yields $2N$ (or $\overline{N}$). It is precisely this property of $N$ which is used to find a solution for the problem we are left with. We will first introduce some notation:

| | |
|---|---|
| $\overline{A}$ | denotes the bit wise complement of $A$. |
| $A \& B$ | denotes the bit wise AND of the words $A$ and $B$. |
| $A \ll s$ | denotes the shifting of $A$ to the left by $s$ bit positions. |
| $A \lll s$ | denotes the circularly shifting (rotating) of $A$ to the left by $s$ bit positions. |
| $A \ggg s$ | same as above, but to the right. |
| $A_0^N$ | denotes a word with following two alternatives: the bits of $A_0^N$ on the even positions are all equal to one for the first alternative (denoted by $A^N$), and all equal to zero for the second alternative (denoted by $A_0$), i.e. $A_0^N \& N$ equals either $N$ or 0. The bits on the odd positions of $A_0^N$ can be chosen freely, but are equal for both alternatives. |
| $A^N$, $A_0$ | are the two alternatives of the word $A_0^N$. |
| $A_N^0$ | denotes similarly a word with following two alternatives: the bits of $A_N^0$ on the even positions are all equal to zero for the first alternative (denoted by $A^0$), and all equal to one for the second alternative (denoted by $A_N$), i.e. $A_N^0 \& N$ equals either 0 or $N$. The bits on the odd positions of $A_N^0$ can be chosen freely, but are equal for both alternatives. |
| $A^0$, $A_N$ | are the two alternatives of the word $A_N^0$. |

The solution consists of the following 5 steps:

**step 1** Choose the value of $(A, B, C, D)$ equal to

- $(A_N^0, B_N^0, C_N^0, D_N^0)$ after 8 elementary operations,
- $(A_0^N, B_0^N, C_0^N, D_0^N)$ after 24 elementary operations.

The 128 $(= 2 \cdot 4 \cdot 16)$ bits on the odd positions of one alternative of these words can be chosen freely. The bits on the odd positions of the other alternative are of course the same. Note that the even positions after 8 and 24 elementary operations are the complement of each other. This results in 32 equations: the middle 8 elementary equations of the last two rounds, each with 2 alternatives.

$$A_N^0 = (A_4 + g(B_4, C_4, D_4) + X^i[1] + E2) \lll gs1 \qquad (1)$$
$$D_N^0 = (D_4 + g(A_N^0, B_4, C_4) + X^i[5] + E2) \lll gs2 \qquad (2)$$
$$C_N^0 = (C_4 + g(D_N^0, A_N^0, B_4) + X^i[9] + E2) \lll gs3 \qquad (3)$$
$$B_N^0 = (B_4 + g(C_N^0, D_N^0, A_N^0) + X^i[13] + E2) \lll gs4 \qquad (4)$$

$$A_{12} = (A_N^0 + g(B_N^0, C_N^0, D_N^0) + X^i[2] + E2) \lll gs1 \qquad (5)$$
$$D_{12} = (D_N^0 + g(A_{12}, B_N^0, C_N^0) + X^i[6] + E2) \lll gs2 \qquad (6)$$
$$C_{12} = (C_N^0 + g(D_{12}, A_{12}, B_N^0) + X^i[10] + E2) \lll gs3 \qquad (7)$$
$$B_{12} = (B_N^0 + g(C_{12}, D_{12}, A_{12}) + X^i[14] + E2) \lll gs4 \qquad (8)$$

$$A_0^N = (A_{20} + h(B_{20}, C_{20}, D_{20}) + X^i[2] + E3) \lll hs1 \qquad (9)$$
$$D_0^N = (D_{20} + h(A_0^N, B_{20}, C_{20}) + X^i[10] + E3) \lll hs2 \qquad (10)$$
$$C_0^N = (C_{20} + h(D_0^N, A_0^N, B_{20}) + X^i[6] + E3) \lll hs3 \qquad (11)$$
$$B_0^N = (B_{20} + h(C_0^N, D_0^N, A_0^N) + X^i[14] + E3) \lll hs4 \qquad (12)$$

$$A_{28} = (A_0^N + h(B_0^N, C_0^N, D_0^N) + X^i[1] + E3) \lll hs1 \qquad (13)$$
$$D_{28} = (D_0^N + h(A_{28}, B_0^N, C_0^N) + X^i[9] + E3) \lll hs2 \qquad (14)$$
$$C_{28} = (C_0^N + h(D_{28}, A_{28}, B_0^N) + X^i[5] + E3) \lll hs3 \qquad (15)$$
$$B_{28} = (B_0^N + h(C_{28}, D_{28}, A_{28}) + X^i[13] + E3) \lll hs4 \qquad (16)$$

In each block of four equations there is now one equation with only 2 unknowns: (4), (5), (12) and (13). Going up or down within each block (up in the first and third, down in the other two) one encounters equations with more and more unknowns. The route to follow is quite obvious now: solve the equations with only 2 unknowns by making a free choice for one of them, and work your way up (or down) the other equations, solving them for the remaining unknowns.

**step 2** Choose $X^1[1]$, $X^1[2]$, $X^1[5]$, $X^1[10]$, $X^1[13]$ and $X^1[14]$. This gives, in addition to the 128 bits of step 1, another 192 bits of freedom. Equations (4), (5), (12) and (13) yield $B_4$, $A_{12}$, $B_{20}$ and $A_{28}$ respectively, as well as the alternative message words $X^2[13]$, $X^2[2]$, $X^2[14]$ and $X^2[1]$. The choices for $X^1[5]$ and

$X^1[10]$ are not used until step 5. The two alternatives of $X[6]$ and $X[9]$ are fixed by the choices we already made, as will become clear in the following three steps.

**step 3** If a majority ($g$) or an exor ($h$) function has two fixed inputs and one input with an alternative then the bits on the even positions of the fixed inputs are taken equal. This means that the bits on the even positions of the pairs $(B_4, C_4)$, $(A_{12}, D_{12})$, $(B_{20}, C_{20})$ and $(A_{28}, D_{28})$ are per pair taken equal.

The two alternatives for the equations (7) and (10) contain the unknowns $C_{12}$, $D_{20}$ and two alternatives for $X[10]$, in addition to the unknowns $D_{12}$ and $C_{20}$. By reversely rotating these four equations by the right amount and subtracting them from each other, the first four unknowns drop out leaving one equation in the unknowns $D_{12}$ and $C_{20}$. We do the same with the first alternative of the equations (6) and (11). The unknown alternative $X^1[6]$ drops out, resulting in another equation in the unknowns $D_{12}$ and $C_{20}$. If we denote the two alternatives of equation ($i$) by ($i$a) and ($i$b), we obtain the following set of 2 equations:

$$((7a) \ggg gs3) - ((7b) \ggg gs3) - (((10a) \ggg hs2) - ((10b) \ggg hs2))$$

$$((6a) \ggg gs2) - ((11a) \ggg hs3)$$

or

$$h(A^N, B_{20}, C_{20}) - h(A_0, B_{20}, C_{20}) + g(D_{12}, A_{12}, B^0) - g(D_{12}, A_{12}, B_N) = N$$
$$(D_{12} \ggg gs2) + C_{20} =$$
$$(C^N \ggg hs3) + D^0 + g(A_{12}, B^0, C^0) - h(D^N, A^N, B_{20}) + E2 - E3$$

where only the lefthand sides contain the unknowns $D_{12}$ and $C_{20}$. The choice mentioned in the beginning of this step gives a solution for this set of 2 equations. For, the first equation holds if the bits on the even positions of $C_{20}$ are taken equal to those of $B_{20}$, and the even bits of $D_{12}$ equal to those of $A_{12}$. The remaining 16 bits of $D_{12}$ and $C_{20}$ can then easily be solved from the second equation, as explained in the next step. An analogous set of 2 equations in the unknowns $C_4$ and $D_{28}$ can be derived in the same way from equations (2) and (15), and (3) and (14). This set can be easily solved under the same conditions.

**step 4** Since $gs2$ is odd, the left term of the second equation in the previous step can be written as the sum of two variables $DC$ and $CD$:

$$(D_{12} \ggg gs2) + C_{20} = DC + CD$$

where

$$DC = (D_{12} \ggg gs2) \,\&\, \overline{N} + C_{20} \,\&\, N$$
$$CD = (D_{12} \ggg gs2) \,\&\, N + C_{20} \,\&\, \overline{N}$$

$DC$ contains on the odd bit positions the known bits of $D_{12}$ and on the even bit positions the known bits of $C_{20}$, and $CD$ contains, respectively on the even and odd bit positions, the yet unknown bits of $D_{12}$ and $C_{20}$, which can now easily be found. An analogous method, based on the oddness of $hs2$, yields the remaining unknown bits of $C_4$ and $D_{28}$.

**step 5** This step is no more than an exercise with blanks.

- (6) or (11) yields two alternatives of $X[6]$
- (7) and (8) yield $C_{12}$ and $B_{12}$, respectively
- (10) and (9) yield $D_{20}$ and $A_{20}$, respectively
- (3) or (14) yields two alternatives of $X[9]$
- (15) and (16) yield $C_{28}$ and $B_{28}$, respectively
- (2) and (1) yield $D_4$ and $A_4$, respectively

The only condition imposed by the attack on the constants of equations (1) to (16) is that all the values of the rotation constants must be odd.

One can (easily) proof that the difference between two messages produced in this way is constant and equal to

$$0 \quad -2N \quad 2N \quad 0 \quad 0 \quad -2N \quad 2N \quad 0 \quad 0 \quad -N \quad N \quad 0 \quad 0 \quad -N \quad N \quad 0$$

where every number stands for a 32-bit word. A program has been written implementing this attack. With this program it takes about 1 millisecond on a 16 Mhz IBM PS/2 to find such a collision. As an example, the following pair of 512-bit messages (written as 16 32-bit words, in hexadecimal notation) produces a collision for MD4, as described in Section 2 and using only the last two rounds in the third step of the recipe:

Message 1:
72A3B049 213AE143 D954E8C9 50BD4CB5 25A3A0B3 C79B12BE 029B6AE9 091A6156
75B5516B DA420FD6 0A6854EB 758F514D 9EA01345 0F796EAC DB54B645 4089373B

Message 2:
72A3B049 CBE58BED 2EAA3E1F 50BD4CB5 25A3A0B3 7245BD68 57F0C03F 091A6156
75B5516B 2F97652B B512FF96 758F514D 9EA01345 64CEC401 85FF60F0 4089373B

Common Message Digest:
E259F484 488AE67F B01E240C 497301A3

To produce such a pair of messages one has altogether 320 bits of freedom. It is conceivable that this freedom can be used to produce identical intermediate values and different 512-bit message blocks, producing a collision for the entire algorithm. In addition one could also use the extra freedom of $X[0]$, $X[4]$, $X[8]$ and $X[12]$ (or of $X[3]$, $X[7]$, $X[11]$ and $X[15]$). However, this does not result in an attack on the complete three round algorithm, since in that case the initial value is not dealt with.

# References

[Rive90]  R. L. Rivest, "The MD4 Message Digest Algorithm", Abstracts Crypto '90, pp. 281-291.

[Merk90]  R. Merkle, personal communication.

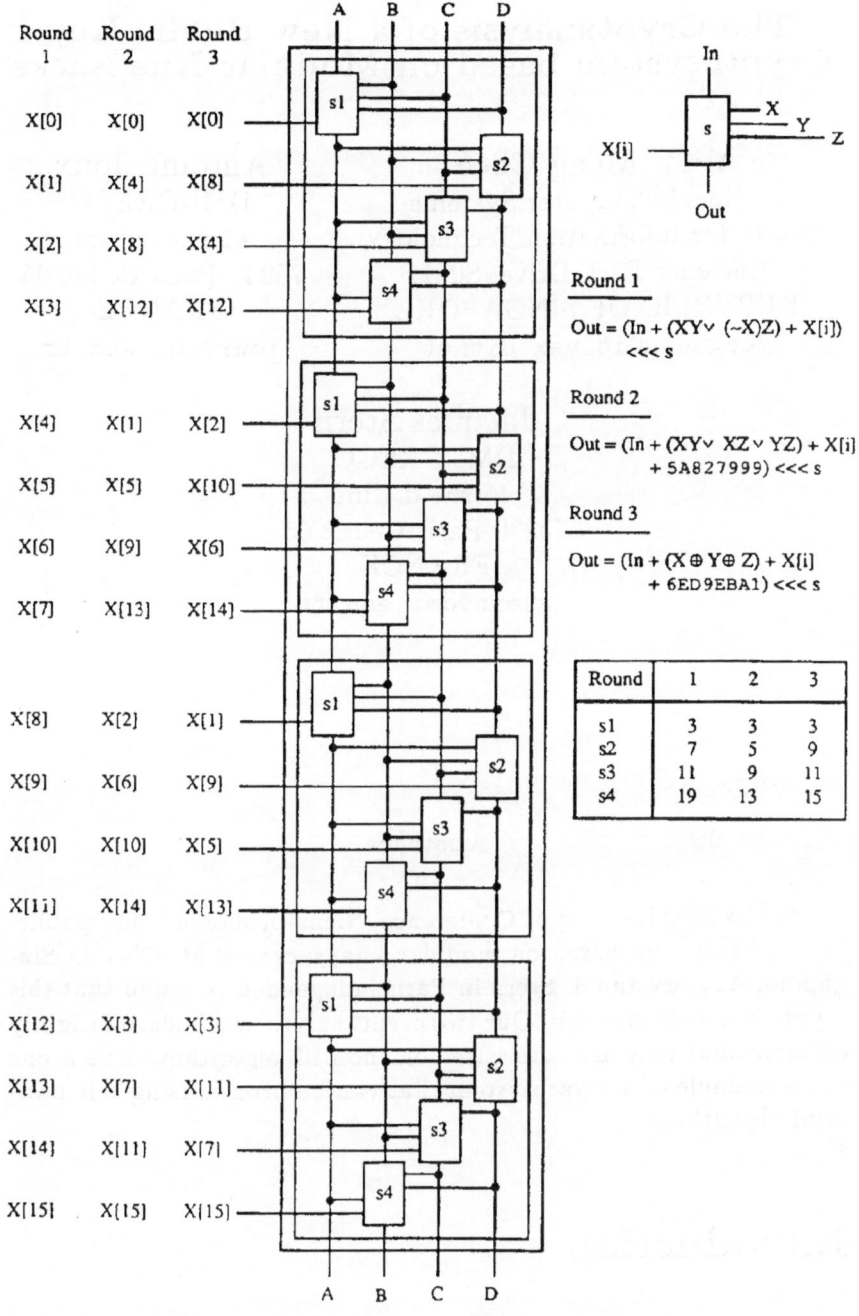

Figure 2: Outline of MD4 (without feedforward)

# The Cryptanalysis of a New Public-Key Cryptosystem based on Modular Knapsacks

Yeow Meng Chee
National Computer Systems
Center for Information Technology
73 Science Park Drive, S0511
REPUBLIC OF SINGAPORE
yeowmeng@itivax.bitnet

Antoine Joux
DMI-GRECC
45 rue d'Ulm
75230 Paris Cedex 05
FRANCE
joux@dmi.ens.fr

Jacques Stern
DMI-GRECC
45 rue d'Ulm
75230 Paris Cedex 05
FRANCE
stern@dmi.ens.fr

## Abstract

At the 1990 EuroCrypt Conference, Niemi proposed a new public-key cryptosystem based on modular knapsacks. Y.M. Chee in Singapore, A. Joux and J. Stern in Paris independently found that this cryptosystem is insecure. Our two cryptanalytic methods are slightly different, but they are both based on the LLL algorithm. This is one more example of a cryptosystem that can be broken using this powerful algorithm.

# 1 Introduction

Let $p$ be a prime and denote by $\mathbf{Z}/p\mathbf{Z}$ the field of integers modulo $p$. Unless otherwise stated, all vectors shall be assumed to be column vectors. The MODULAR KNAPSACK problem is defined as follows:

J. Feigenbaum (Ed.): Advances in Cryptology - CRYPTO '91, LNCS 576, pp. 204-212, 1992.
© Springer-Verlag Berlin Heidelberg 1992

## MODULAR KNAPSACKS

INSTANCE: A prime $p$, a matrix $E \in (\mathbf{Z}/p\mathbf{Z})^{n \times m}$ and a vector $c \in (\mathbf{Z}/p\mathbf{Z})^n$.
QUESTION: Is there a vector $x \in \{0,1\}^m$ such that $Ex = c$ over $\mathbf{Z}/p\mathbf{Z}$ ?
The MODULAR KNAPSACK problem is a decision problem that is NP-complete in the strong sense, even under the restriction $m = 2n$ [Nie91].
The related NP-hard algorithmic problem is considered here: Find a vector $x \in \{0,1\}^m$ that satisfies $Ex = c$ over $\mathbf{Z}/p\mathbf{Z}$ when one exists.

At the 1990 EuroCrypt Conference, Niemi proposed a new public-key cryptosystem based on this problem [Nie91]. Y.M. Chee in Singapore, A. Joux and J. Stern in Paris independently discovered that this cryptosystem is insecure. The purpose of this paper is to present our cryptanalysis on Niemi's cryptosystem. Our attacks are based on the LLL algorithm [LLL82]. This is one more example of a cryptosystem that can be broken using this powerful algorithm (see [Adl83, Ste87, ST91]).

## 2   The Proposed Cryptosystem

We briefly review Niemi's public-key cryptosystem in this section. The basic idea is a notion of absolute values in $\mathbf{Z}/p\mathbf{Z}$. The *absolute value* $|g|$ of $g \in \mathbf{Z}/p\mathbf{Z}$ is the minimum of the least non-negative residues modulo $p$ of the two integers $g$ and $-g$. We call $g$ *k-small* if $|g| \le k$ and $g$ *k-large* if $|g| \ge \lceil p/2 \rceil - k$. We typically speak of *small* and *large* numbers, thus leaving $k$ unfixed. The construction of the cryptosystem is as follows. Fix a prime $p$, and positive integers $n$ and $k \ll p$. We randomly select matrices $C, D, S \in (\mathbf{Z}/p\mathbf{Z})^{n \times n}$ with $k$-small entries, a non-singular matrix $R \in (\mathbf{Z}/p\mathbf{Z})^{n \times n}$, and a diagonal matrix $\Delta \in (\mathbf{Z}/p\mathbf{Z})^{n \times n}$ with $k$-large entries. The public information is $p$ and the $n \times 2n$ matrix $E = (\,A \quad B\,)$, where

$$A = R^{-1}(\Delta - SC), \tag{1}$$

$$B = -R^{-1}SD. \tag{2}$$

The private key is $R$. The matrices $C, D, S$, and $\Delta$ should also be kept secret but they are not needed after the initial construction. The message space is $\mathcal{M} = \{x \in \{0,1\}^{2n}\}$, and the ciphertext space is $\mathcal{C} = \{c \in (\mathbf{Z}/p\mathbf{Z})^n\}$. The encryption function is $\mathcal{E} : \mathcal{M} \to \mathcal{C}$ defined by $\mathcal{E}(x) = Ex$, arithmetic being done modulo $p$.

To decrypt a ciphertext $c$, we compute $l = Rc$. From (1) and (2) we can show that

$$(\Delta \quad 0)\, x = l + S\,(C \quad D)\, x.$$

Since the entries of $C$, $D$, and $S$ are $k$-small and $x \in \{0,1\}^{2n}$, the entries of $S\,(C \quad D)\,x$ should be small as well. Hence, $\Delta_{i,i} x_i = l_i + \alpha_i$ for some small $\alpha_i$, $1 \leq i \leq n$. It follows that our decryption rule is:

$$x_i = \begin{cases} 0, & \text{if } l_i \text{ is small;} \\ 1, & \text{if } l_i \text{ is large;} \end{cases}$$

for $1 \leq i \leq n$. The bits $x_i$, $n+1 \leq i \leq 2n$ can be obtained by solving the matrix equation

$$Bx^{(2)} = c - Ax^{(1)},$$

where $x^{(1)} = (x_1, \ldots, x_n)^T$ and $x^{(2)} = (x_{n+1}, \ldots, x_{2n})^T$. This can easily be done since we have $n$ equations in $n$ unknowns.

The decryption rule for $x_i$, $1 \leq i \leq n$, does not always yield the correct plain bits since its correctness depends on the size of the entries of $S\,(C \quad D)\,x$. Niemi restricts himself to the case $S = I$, where $I$ denotes the identity matrix, and claims that in this case, the sufficient condition to ensure correct decryption is $p > 4kn$. Niemi also claims that $k = 1$ is a good choice.

In the sequel, we show how the plaintext can be recovered from the ciphertext without the knowledge of the secret key $R$.

## 3 The Cryptanalytic Principle

An *integer lattice* $\mathcal{L}$ of dimension $m$ is an additive subgroup of $\mathbf{Z}^n$ that contains $m$ linearly independent vectors over $\mathbf{R}^n$ (hence $m \leq n$). An *ordered basis* $(v_1, \ldots, v_m)$ of a lattice $\mathcal{L}$ of dimension $m$ is a list of elements of $\mathcal{L}$ such that $\mathcal{L} = \mathbf{Z}v_1 \oplus \mathbf{Z}v_2 \oplus \cdots \oplus \mathbf{Z}v_m$. We represent an ordered basis of an $m$-dimensional lattice $\mathcal{L}$ by the $n \times m$ *basis matrix*

$$V = (v_1 \quad v_2 \quad \cdots \quad v_m),$$

whose columns are the basis vectors. A lattice with basis matrix $V$ is simply denoted by $\mathcal{L}(V)$.

The main idea behind the attacks we are going to describe is the following. It is well-known that the LLL algorithm [LLL82] is a polynomial time algorithm designed to find a short (non-zero) vector in an integer lattice. More precisely, if the dimension of the lattice is $n$, then the LLL algorithm can find a vector in the lattice whose length is no more than $2^{(n-1)/2}$ times the length of the shortest vector in the lattice. In particular, if the length of the shortest vector in the lattice is $2^{(n-1)/2}$ times smaller than that of the other vectors, then the LLL algorithm will find the shortest vector. In practice, the LLL algorithm is much more effective and finds vectors whose lengths are much smaller than that gauranteed by the theoretical bound; and other algorithms exist, that are even more powerful [ScE91]. In our attacks, we transform the problem of finding the plaintext to that of finding short vectors in certain lattices. Then we show that the short vector is much shorter than the average short vectors. This gives heuristical evidence that the short vector can be found in polynomial time.

# 4 The Attack of Y.M. Chee

An observer of Niemi's cryptosystem who sees a ciphertext $c$, and has knowledge of public information $p$ and $E$, can recover the corresponding plaintext by solving for a vector $x \in \{0,1\}^{2n}$ in the matrix equation $Ex = c$ over $\mathbf{Z}/p\mathbf{Z}$. The equivalent problem over $\mathbf{Z}$ is to find $x \in \{0,1\}^{2n}$ such that

$$( E \quad -pI ) \begin{pmatrix} x \\ y \end{pmatrix} = c, \tag{3}$$

for some $y \in \mathbf{Z}^n$.

**Lemma 4.1** *Let $\mathcal{L}$ be the lattice with basis matrix $V = \begin{pmatrix} I & 0 \\ M & -c \end{pmatrix}$. Then $Mu = \lambda c$ for some $\lambda \in \mathbf{Z}$ if and only if $\begin{pmatrix} u \\ 0 \end{pmatrix} \in \mathcal{L}$.*

**Proof:** The lattice $\mathcal{L}$ contains a vector $\begin{pmatrix} u \\ 0 \end{pmatrix}$ if and only if there exist some integer $\lambda$ and integral vector $v$ such that

$$\begin{pmatrix} u \\ 0 \end{pmatrix} = \begin{pmatrix} I & 0 \\ M & -c \end{pmatrix} \begin{pmatrix} v \\ \lambda \end{pmatrix} = \begin{pmatrix} v \\ Mv - \lambda c \end{pmatrix} \iff Mu = \lambda c.$$

It is easy to see that Lemma 4.1 implies that solving for $x \in \{0,1\}^n$ satisfying (3) for some $y \in \mathbf{Z}^n$ is equivalent to finding a vector of the form $\begin{pmatrix} u \\ 0 \end{pmatrix}$, first $2n$ components of $u$ being either 0 or 1, in the lattice $\mathcal{L}$ with basis matrix

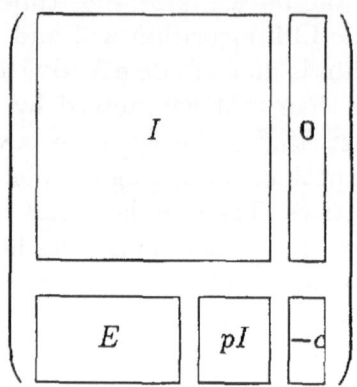

such that the first $2n$ components of $u$ constitutes a $\{0,1\}$-vector $x$ satisfying $Ex = c$. Since the first $2n$ components of $u$ is either 0 or 1, $\begin{pmatrix} u \\ 0 \end{pmatrix}$ is a reasonably short vector in $\mathcal{L}$. Given an ordered basis of a lattice, the LLL algorithm computes another ordered basis, containing relatively short vectors, for the lattice. This new ordered basis is called a *reduced basis*. Our hope is that by running the LLL algorithm on the lattice $\mathcal{L}$, the vector $\begin{pmatrix} u \\ 0 \end{pmatrix}$ we are looking for appears in the reduced basis. Unfortunately, because the last $n$ components of $u$ may be large, such a vector is often too long to appear in any reduced bases. In order to remedy this situation, we adopt the following strategy.

Let

$$\epsilon_{i,j} = (\underbrace{0,\ldots,0}_{i-1}, -2^{j-1}p, 0, \ldots, 0)^T,$$

for $1 \le i \le n$. Then $x \in \{0,1\}^{2n}$ satisfies (3) for some $y \in \mathbf{Z}^n$ if and only if $x$ satisfies

$$( E \quad \epsilon_{1,1} \quad \cdots \quad \epsilon_{1,j_1} \quad \epsilon_{2,1} \quad \cdots \quad \epsilon_{2,j_2} \quad \cdots \quad \epsilon_{n,1} \quad \cdots \quad \epsilon_{n,j_n} ) \begin{pmatrix} x \\ y \end{pmatrix} = c, \quad (4)$$

for some $y \in \mathbf{Z}^{j_1+j_2+\cdots+j_n}$, where $j_i > 0$ for all $1 \le i \le n$. Let $s_i = \sum_{j=1}^{2n} E_{i,j}$ denote the sum of all entries in row $i$ of $E$. It is easy to see that if we choose $j_i = \lceil \log_2(s_i/p) \rceil$, $1 \leq i \leq n$, then $x$ satisfies (4) for some $y \in \{0, \pm 1\}^{j_1 + j_2 + \cdots + j_n}$.

We now consider a new lattice with the $(3n + \sum_{i=1}^{n} j_1) \times (2n + 1 + \sum_{i=1}^{n} j_i)$ basis matrix

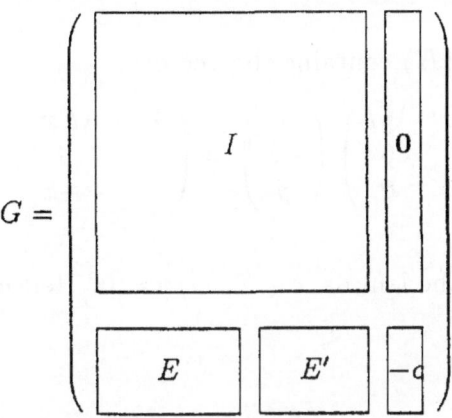

$$G =$$

where $E' = ( \epsilon_{1,1} \quad \cdots \quad \epsilon_{1,j_1} \quad \epsilon_{2,1} \quad \cdots \quad \epsilon_{2,j_2} \quad \cdots \quad \epsilon_{n,1} \quad \cdots \quad \epsilon_{n,j_n} )$. It follows from previous discussions that we are looking for a vector $\begin{pmatrix} u \\ 0 \end{pmatrix} \in \mathcal{L}(G)$ such that its first $n$ components consitutes a $\{0, 1\}$-vector $x$ satisfying $Ex = c$. There exists such a vector whose components are either 0, or $\pm 1$. This short vector very often appears in the reduced basis of $\mathcal{L}(G)$.

# 5 The Attack of A. Joux and J. Stern

Given a ciphertext $c$ and public information $p$ and $E$, we choose a large scaling factor $\lambda$ and define:

$$H =$$

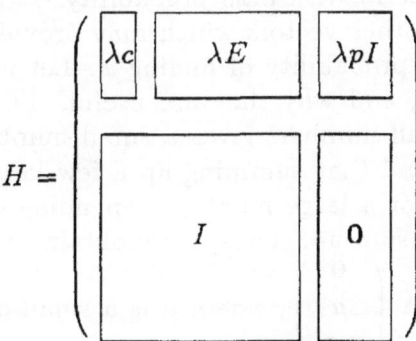

**Lemma 5.1** *If $x \in \mathbf{Z}^{2n}$ satisfies (3) for some $y \in \mathbf{Z}^n$, then* $\begin{pmatrix} 0 \\ 1 \\ -x \end{pmatrix}$ *is a vector in the lattice $\mathcal{L}(H)$.*

**Proof:** The lattice $\mathcal{L}(H)$ contains the vector

$$\begin{pmatrix} \lambda c & \lambda E & \lambda p I \\ 1 & 0 & 0 \\ 0 & I & 0 \end{pmatrix} \begin{pmatrix} 1 \\ -x \\ y \end{pmatrix} = \begin{pmatrix} \lambda c - \lambda E x + \lambda p y \\ 1 \\ -x \end{pmatrix}.$$

By the hypothesis of the lemma, $c - Ex + py = 0$. Hence $\begin{pmatrix} 0 \\ 1 \\ -x \end{pmatrix}$ is a vector in $\mathcal{L}(H)$. $\blacksquare$

As a consequence of Lemma 5.1, we see that if $x \in \{0,1\}^{2n}$ is the plaintext corresponding to a ciphertext $c$, then $v(x) = \begin{pmatrix} 0 \\ 1 \\ -x \end{pmatrix}$ is a short vector in the lattice $\mathcal{L}(H)$. In fact,

$$\|v(x)\|^2 = \|x\|^2 + 1 \le 2n + 1.$$

Let us now discuss the other short vectors in $\mathcal{L}(H)$. Since $\lambda$ is large, the first $n$ components of the first vector of the reduced basis for $\mathcal{L}(H)$ will almost surely all be zero. A random vector of this form has average length $\sqrt{(2n+1)(p^2-1)/12}$. This shows that with $p = 4kn$, $v(x)$ is approximately $2kn/\sqrt{3}$ times shorter than an average vector with first $n$ components all zero. This provides heuristical evidence that the vector $v(x)$ appears in the reduced basis for $\mathcal{L}(H)$ with high probability. It is also interesting to remark that there are other vectors which may provide a decryption of $c$, since they increase the probability of finding $x$. Let us explain informally what these vectors are, and why they are useful. First, we can say that summing up a few small numbers gives a small number (with a different constant $k$ of course) and that summing up a few large numbers can give either a small number or a large number, depending on the parity of the number of numbers we sum up. Thus, if we obtain in the reduced basis a short vector of the form $\begin{pmatrix} 0 \\ \mu \\ -x' \end{pmatrix}$, where $\mu$ is a small odd number, we can write $E(\mu x - x') = 0$ and thus, if $\mu x - x'$ is small enough, we can infer that the first $n$ components of this vector are all even, and therefore that the first $n$ components of $x$ and $x'$ have the same parity.

# 6   Conclusion

The previous sections gave heuristical evidence that Niemi's proposed public-key cryptosystem is not secure. We would like to remark that it gets less and less secure. The reason for this is that a recent improvement of attacks against low-density knapsacks [CLJ91] can be used to improve the attacks described here. The idea is to replace the identity part of the basis matrices as described in [CLJ91]. We plan to carry out systematic experiments with this improved version.

**Acknowledgement.** The first named author would like to thank K. H. Lim for helpful discussions.

# References

[Adl83]   L. Adleman. *On Breaking the Iterated Merkle-Hellman Public Key Cryptosystem*, in: Advances in Cryptology, Proceedings of CRYPTO '82, Plenum Press, New York, 1983, 303–308.

[CLJ91]   A. J. Coster, B. LaMacchia, A. Joux, A. Odlyzko, C. P. Schnorr and J. Stern. *Improved Low-Density Subset Sum Algorithms*, to appear.

[LLL82]   A. K. Lenstra, H. W. Lenstra Jr. and L. Lovász. *Factoring Polynomials with Rational Coefficients*, Mathematische Annalen **261** (1982), 515–534.

[Nie91]   V. Niemi. *A New Trapdoor in Knapsacks*, in: Advances in Cryptology, Proceedings of EUROCRYPT '90, Lecture Notes in Computer Science **473**, Springer-Verlag, Berlin, 1991, 405–411.

[ScE91]    C. P. Schnorr, M. Euchner. *Lattice Basis Reduction: Improved Practical Algorithms and Solving Subset Sum Problems*, in: Proceedings of the FCT'91, Lecture Notes in Computer Science, Springer-Verlag, Berlin, to appear.

[Sha82]    A. Shamir. *A Polynomial-Time Algorithm for Breaking the Basic Merkle-Hellman Cryptosystem*, in: Proceedings of the 23rd IEEE Symposium on Foundations of Computer Science, IEEE, New York, 1982, 145–152.

[Ste87]    J. Stern. *Secret Linear Congruential Generators are Not Cryptographically Secure*, in: Proceedings of the 28th IEEE Symposium on Foundations of Computer Science, IEEE, New York, 1987, 421–426.

[ST91]     J. Stern and P. Toffin. *Cryptanalysis of a Public-Key Cryptosystem Based on Approximations by Rational Numbers*, in: Advances in Cryptology, Proceedings of EUROCRYPT '90, Lecture Notes in Computer Science **473**, Springer-Verlag, Berlin, 1991, 313–317.

# A One-Round, Two-Prover, Zero-Knowledge Protocol for NP

Dror Lapidot
Department of Applied Math.
The Weizmann Institute of Science
Rehovot, Israel
drorl@wisdom.bitnet

Adi Shamir
Department of Applied Math.
The Weizmann Institute of Science
Rehovot, Israel
shamir@wisdom.bitnet

### Abstract

The model of zero knowledge multi prover interactive proofs was introduced by Ben-Or, Goldwasser, Kilian and Wigderson. A major open problem associated with these protocols is whether they can be executed in parallel. A positive answer was claimed by Fortnow, Rompel and Sipser, but its proof was later shown to be flawed by Fortnow who demonstrated that the probability of cheating in $n$ independent parallel rounds can be exponentially higher than the probability of cheating in $n$ independent sequential rounds. In this paper we use refined combinatorial arguments to settle this problem by proving that the probability of cheating in a parallelized BGKW protocol is at most $1/2^{n^{1/9}}$, and thus every problem in NP has a one-round two prover protocol which is perfectly zero knowledge under no cryptographic assumptions.

# 1 Introduction

In [GMW] Goldreich, Micali and Wigderson show that under the assumption that one way functions exist, every NP language has a computational zero knowledge interactive proof system. They prove it by giving a sequential zero knowledge protocol for an NP-complete statement. Results in [F2] and [BHZ] imply that if perfect zero-knowledge interactive proof-systems for NP exist (i.e. which do not rely on the fact that the verifier is polynomial time bounded), then the polynomial time hierarchy would collapse to its second level. This provides strong evidence that it will be very hard to show that NP has perfect zero-knowledge interactive proofs. As a result, considerable effort was devoted in the last few years to the design of alternative models in which it would be possible to solve the problems of perfect zero-knowledge proofs for NP, zero-knowledge proofs for NP without intractability assumptions, and zero-knowledge proofs for NP in a constant number of rounds.

Feige and Shamir [FS] solved the problem of zero-knowledge argument (namely, when the prover is polynomially bounded) for NP in a constant number of rounds, under the assumption that one-way functions exist. The counterpart problem with respect to an unbounded prover has been solved by Goldreich and Kahan [GK] under the assumption that claw-free functions exist. The problem of perfect zero knowledge was solved for

J. Feigenbaum (Ed.): Advances in Cryptology - CRYPTO '91, LNCS 576, pp. 213-224, 1992.
© Springer-Verlag Berlin Heidelberg 1992

some special cases: Brassard, Crepeau and Yung [BCY] show the existence of parallel perfect zero knowledge arguments for NP under the Certified Discrete Log Assumption (or alternatively, under a generalization of this assumption), and Bellare, Micali and Ostrovsky [BMO] exhibit perfect zero-knowledge proofs for Quadratic residuosity and graph isomorphism in 5 rounds.

Ben-Or, Goldwasser, Kilian and Wigderson [BGKW] suggested the novel concept of multi-prover zero-knowledge interactive proof system for NP, solved the perfect zero-knowledge problem by exhibiting a *sequential* two-prover protocol which achieves this aim, and remarked that the *parallel* execution of their protocol is also a perfect zero-knowledge proof system with a single round under a weak definition which requires only a constant probability of cheating. Fortnow, Rompel and Sipser [FRS] claimed a similar result under the stronger definition which requires a negligible probability of cheating, but their proof of soundness was later shown to be faulty by Fortnow [F1], and no alternative parallel protocol is currently known to be sound in this strong sense. Moreover, there are some examples of protocols (see [F1] and (4.1) here) for which the probability of cheating in their parallel version is known to be exponentially better than in their sequential version.

In this paper we solve this open problem: we prove the soundness of the *parallel* two prover zero knowledge interactive proof for $NP$ suggested by Ben-Or, Goldwasser, Kilian and Wigderson in [BGKW]. As a first step we describe a simpler one-round two-prover interactive proof for Hamiltonicity, and prove that it is sound, complete and perfect zero knowledge under no intractability assumptions. We then show that the same techniques can be applied to the original [BGKW] protocol.

In section 2 we give some definitions. In section 3 we present our simplified parallel protocol for Hamiltonicity, and prove its correctness in section 4. In section 5 we prove that our protocol is also a perfect zero knowledge proof of knowledge, which can extract an actual witness from any sufficiently successful pair of provers.

# 2  Definitions

**Definition 1:**
Let $L$ be an NP-language. We say that $L$ has a two-prover interactive proof system if there exists an interactive BPP machine $V$ (the verifier) capable of interacting with two other machines $P_1$ and $P_2$ (the provers). The provers can cooperate and choose a common strategy before the interaction with the verifier starts, but are isolated from each other during the execution of the protocol. The protocol has to satisfy the following conditions:

1. $\exists P_1, P_2 \quad \forall x \in L$   the probability that $V$ accepts $x$ is overwhelming.

2. $\forall P_1, P_2 \quad \forall x \notin L$, the probability that $V$ accepts $x$ is negligible.

**Definition 2:**
Let $(P_1, P_2, V)$ be a two-prover interactive proof system for $L$. Let $View_{P_1,P_2,V}(x)$ denote the verifier's view during the protocol (namely the sequence of messages exchanged between the verifier and the provers along with the private random bits of $V$). This is a probability space taken over the coin tosses of $V$ and the random tapes of $(P_1, P_2)$. We say that two-prover interactive protocol $(P_1, P_2, V)$ is perfect zero knowledge for $V$ if there exists a BPP machine $M$ such that $M(x) = View_{P_1,P_2,V}(x)$. We say that $L$ has a two-prover perfect zero-knowledge proof system if there exist independent provers $P_1$, $P_2$ such that for all BPP verifiers $\hat{V}$, there exists a probabilistic Turing machine $M$ such that for all $x \in L$, $M(x) = View_{P_1,P_2,\hat{V}}(x)$ and $M(x)$ terminates in expected polynomial time.

**Definition 3:** Let $H$ be a $t \times t$ matrix of zeroes and ones (which can be thought of as an adjacency matrix of a directed graph). We say that $H$ is exactly Hamiltonian if there is exactly a single 1 in every row and in every column, and these $t$ ones define a permutation with a single cycle.

**The Basic Step of Proofs of Hamiltonicity (with a single prover):**
Let $A$ and $B$ be two $t \times t$ random matrices of zeroes and ones whose pointwise $XOR$ $A \oplus B = H$ is a random exactly Hamiltonian matrix. Denote by $S$ the Hamiltonian cycle on $t$ nodes whose adjacency matrix is $H$. Assume now that an honest prover wants to use $H$ in order to prove to $V$ the Hamiltonicity of some graph $G$ with $t$ nodes, and assume that only the prover knows $A$, $B$ and $H$ but $V$ is convinced that $H$ is exactly Hamiltonian. Let $\pi$ be a permutation that maps $S$ onto the Hamiltonian cycle of $G$ (i.e. $\pi(S) \subseteq G$). $P$ sends $V$ the permutation $\pi$ and the values of all the entries in $\pi(A)$ and $\pi(B)$ which do not correspond to edges in $G$. $V$ accepts the proof iff all the revealed pairs $((\pi(A)_{i,j}, \pi(B)_{i,j})$ such that $(i,j)$ is non-edge in $G$) are $(0,0)$ or $(1,1)$. $P$'s proof implies that the $t$ ones that remain unrevealed in $\pi(H)$ correspond to edges of $G$, and thus $G$ contains a Hamiltonian cycle.

Informally, this protocol is zero knowledge since all the verifier gets is a collection of (pairs of equal) random bits and a random permutation, and both things can be simulated in random polynomial time.

# 3   The Two Prover Protocol

Let $(P_1, P_2, V)$ denote the two-prover protocol which receives as input the graph $G = (V, E)$, $|V| = t$ and tries to prove its Hamiltonicity. Let $P_1$ and $P_2$ share two random $t \times t$

matrices $A$ and $B$ such that $A \oplus B = H$, where $H$ is a random $t \times t$ exactly Hamiltonian matrix, and assume that $P_1$ has a witness for this statement on his auxiliary tape. The basic two prover protocol (**BP**) of Hamiltonicity is:

- $V$ randomly and independently chooses two bits $b_1$ and $b_2$. He sends $b_1$ to $P_1$ and $b_2$ to $P_2$.

- If $b_1 = 0$ then $P_1$ sends $A$ and $B$ to $V$, otherwise he executes the basic step of the previous section.

- If $b_2 = 0$ then $P_2$ sends $A$ to $V$, otherwise he sends $B$ to $V$.

- According to $b_1$ $V$ either checks that $A \oplus B$ is exactly Hamiltonian or checks that the basic step was done correctly, and in both cases he verifies the consistency of the revealed entries with $P_2$'s response. $V$ accepts iff these checks are successful.

The full protocol $FP_n$ is a one-round protocol which consists of $n$ *parallel* independent executions of BP, where $n$ is a security parameter.

In the next two sections we prove that $FP_n$ is a perfect zero knowledge interactive proof for Hamiltonicity, and that it is also a perfect zero knowledge proof of knowledge, which directly gives the following theorems:

**Theorem 1:** *Every language in NP has a two prover perfect zero knowledge interactive proof of membership in one round without making any intractability assumptions.*

**Theorem 2:** *Every language in NP has a two prover perfect zero knowledge interactive proof of knowledge in one round without making any intractability assumptions.*

# 4    Correctness

Our first goal is to prove that the parallel protocol $FP_n$ is a perfect zero knowledge proof for Hamiltonicity.

**Completeness:** $P_1$ (which is either infinitely powerful or polynomial time bounded with knowledge of a Hamiltonian cycle in $G$) can determine the permutation $\pi$ of the basic step and perform the protocol. Notice that unlike the [BGKW] protocol, only $P_1$ has to know the actual input graph, while $P_2$ should only know its size $t$.

**Zero-Knowledge:** We construct a probabilistic polynomial time simulator $M$ which without knowledge of a cycle in $G$ can give a response to every $2n$-bit query of $V$ which is perfectly indistinguishable from the answers of the real provers. This simulation can be easily carried out because $b_1$ and $b_2$ are chosen by $V$ before it gets any messages from the provers, and thus $M$ can use them in choosing $A$ and $B$. If $b_1 = 0$ then $M$ sends $V$ two random $t \times t$ 0/1 matrices whose $XOR$ is an exactly Hamiltonian matrix and according to $b_2$ he sends $V$ one of these matrices. If $b_1 = 1$, $M$ randomly chooses a 0/1 matrix $A$ and a permutation $\pi$, simulates $P_1$'s basic step (with the pair $(A, A)$ and $\pi(G)$) and sends $A$ as a simulation of $P_2$. It is easy to verify that this simulation is perfectly indistinguishable from a real execution, which means that our protocol is perfect zero-knowledge.

The main difficulty (and therefore the motivation of this paper) is how to prove the soundness.

## 4.1   Where is The Problem?

Consider first the basic protocol BP. It is easy to see that simultaneous success of $(P_1, P_2)$ in answering the four possible requests of $V$ implies the Hamiltonicity of $G$. Moreover, one can verify that the probability of cheating (when $G$ is not Hamiltonian) is at most 3/4, and thus the probability of cheating in $n$ sequential independent executions of BP is at most $(\frac{3}{4})^n$.

We would like to get the same result with respect to parallel executions but its falsehood is the motivation of this paper. Fortnow [F1] constructed a (somewhat artificial) two prover protocol that accepts all inputs with probability 1/2 such that there exists a strategy for the parallel execution of two rounds which causes the verifier to accept all inputs with probability 3/8. We now show that this problem can in fact arise in our protocol by showing that if $G$ is not Hamiltonian then the probability of cheating in $FP_2$ is greater than $(\frac{3}{4})^2$. We demonstrate this fact by specifying a strategy for cheating $(P_1, P_2)$ which succeeds in 10 out of the 16 possible requests of $V$.

Let $(X, Y)$ and $(Z, W)$ be two pairs of $t \times t$ 0/1 matrices such that $X \oplus Y$ and $Z \oplus W$ are exactly Hamiltonian matrices. Let $\hat{W}$, $\hat{X}$ and $\hat{Y}$ be sets of $t^2 - |E(G)|$ entries of $W, X, Y$, respectively, which correspond to non-edges in $\psi(G)$ for some arbitrary permutation $\psi$. Let $b_{i,j}$ ($1 \le i, j \le 2$) be the bit sent by $V$ to $P_i$ in the $j$'th round, and $A_{i,j}$ be the corresponding answer of $P_i$.

The strategy is:

Instructions for $P_1$:

| $b_{1,1}$ | $b_{1,2}$ | $A_{1,1}$ | $A_{1,2}$ |
|-----------|-----------|-----------|-----------|
| 0 | 0 | $(X, Y)$ | $(Z, W)$ |
| 0 | 1 | $(X, Y)$ | $(\hat{W}, \hat{W})$ and $\psi$ |
| 1 | 0 | $(\hat{Y}, \hat{Y})$ and $\psi$ | $(Z, W)$ |
| 1 | 1 | $(\hat{X}, \hat{X})$ and $\psi$ | $(\hat{W}, \hat{W})$ and $\psi$ |

Instructions for $P_2$:

| $b_{2,1}$ | $b_{2,2}$ | $A_{2,1}$ | $A_{2,2}$ |
|---|---|---|---|
| 0 | 0 | X | W |
| 0 | 1 | X | W |
| 1 | 0 | Y | Z |
| 1 | 1 | Y | W |

It is easy to check that the following matrix represents the successful executions of $FP_2$ whenever the provers follow the above strategy:

|    | 00 | 01 | 10 | 11 |
|----|----|----|----|----|
| 00 | 0  | 1  | 0  | 1  |
| 01 | 1  | 1  | 0  | 1  |
| 10 | 1  | 0  | 1  | 0  |
| 11 | 1  | 1  | 1  | 0  |

In this matrix the pairs at the top are the $(b_{1,1}, b_{1,2})$ requests, those on the left are the $(b_{2,1}, b_{2,2})$ requests, and the ten 1-entries represent the successful executions in which $V$ accepts the provers' messages. Since all the choices of $b_{i,j}$ quadruples are equally likely, the cheating $(P_1, P_2)$ succeed with probability $\frac{10}{16}$ (which is greater than $(\frac{3}{4})^2$). A simple extension of this strategy to $n$ parallel rounds (which succeeds with probability $(\frac{10}{16})^{n/2} > (\frac{3}{4})^n$) demonstrates the difficulty of proving the soundness of parallel executions by using standard techniques. In the next subsection we show how to overcome this problem.

## 4.2 The Proof of Soundness.

Our main theorem uses novel techniques to show that the parallel protocol is sound, by proving that the probability of cheating decreases exponentially fast:

**Theorem 3:** *If $G$ is not Hamiltonian then*

$$\forall(\hat{P}_1, \hat{P}_2) \ Pr\{FP_n \ succeeds\} < \frac{1}{2^{n/9}}$$

*where the probability is taken over the coin tosses of $V$.*

**Proof:** Without loss of generality we can assume that $\hat{P}_1$ and $\hat{P}_2$ are deterministic, and use their best strategy against the particular verifier $V$. Denote by $\sigma$ a random $n$-bit string sent by $V$ to $\hat{P}_2$, and by $\tau$ a random $n$-bit string sent by $V$ to $\hat{P}_1$. Let $\sigma_k$ ($\tau_k$) be the $k$'th bit of $\sigma$ ($\tau$). For each $\sigma$ denote by $A_\sigma$ the set of all those $\tau$'s for which $FP_n$ succeeds on $(\sigma, \tau)$. We prove the theorem by proving that if:

$$Pr\{FP_n \ succeeds\} \geq \frac{1}{2^{n/9}}$$

then there exists a successful quadruple, i.e. $(\sigma', \sigma'', \tau', \tau'')$ such that $FP_n$ succeeds on each one of the following pairs: $(\sigma', \tau')$, $(\sigma', \tau'')$, $(\sigma'', \tau')$, $(\sigma'', \tau'')$, and there exists $1 \leq k \leq n$ such that:

$$\sigma'_k \neq \sigma''_k \quad \text{and} \quad \tau'_k \neq \tau''_k .$$

**Lemma 4:** The existence of a successful quadruple implies the Hamiltonicity of $G$.
**Proof:** Assume that $(\sigma', \sigma'', \tau', \tau'')$ is a successful quadruple and without loss of generality assume that for some $1 \leq k \leq n$

$$\sigma'_k = 0, \ \sigma''_k = 1, \ \tau'_k = 0, \ \tau''_k = 1.$$

We concentrate now on the answers of the provers at the $k$'th stage of the parallel protocol: As a response for $\sigma'$, $P_1$ sends $V$ the $0/1$ $t \times t$ matrices $A$ and $B$, where $H = A \oplus B$ is an exactly Hamiltonian matrix. The success of the executions implies that $P_2$ sends $A$ as a response to $\tau'$, and $B$ as a response to $\tau''$. It also implies that while executing the basic step in response to $\sigma''$, $P_1$ sends a permutation $\pi$ and pairs of equal bits which are identical to their counterparts in $P_2$'s matrices, and thus identical also to their counterparts in $P_1$'s answer on $\sigma'$ (i.e. $A$ and $B$). Therefore, by executing this protocol just against $P_1$ on $\sigma'$ and on $\sigma''$ we can extract the Hamiltonian cycle (HC) in $G$ by concentrating on his answers at the $k$'th stage, and comparing the adjacency matrix of $\pi(G)$ to $H = A \oplus B$. ∎

The existence of a successful quadruple was shown to contradict the assumption that $G$ is not Hamiltonian. Note that the condition on $k$ is essential, since in the concrete matrix demonstrated at the end of section 4.1 there are several quadruples $\sigma', \sigma'', \tau', \tau''$ which define four successful executions, but we cannot extract the witness since none of them satisfies the condition on $k$. For example: $\sigma' = (01)$, $\sigma'' = (11)$, $\tau' = (00)$, $\tau'' = (01)$ define four successes but there is no index $1 \leq k \leq 2$ on which $\sigma'$ differs from $\sigma''$ and $\tau'$ differs from $\tau''$ simultaneously.
**Definition:** We say that $\sigma$ is good if

$$|A_\sigma| \geq \frac{2^n}{2 \cdot 2^{n/9}} .$$

**Lemma 5:** If $Pr\{FP_n \text{ succeeds}\} \geq \frac{1}{2^{n/9}}$ then there exist at least $\frac{2^n}{2 \cdot 2^{n/9}}$ good $\sigma$'s.
**Proof:** The provers are deterministic, therefore there are at least $(2^{2n}/2^{n/9})$ $2n$-bit strings for which $(P_1, P_2)$ succeed. Therefore trivially by applying an elementary counting argument we get the result. ∎

Denote by $T$ the set of all the good $\sigma$'s ($|T| \geq \frac{2^n}{2 \cdot 2^{n/9}}$). Our goal now is to show that it is possible to choose a set $S \subseteq T$ of $4 \cdot 2^{n/9}$ good $n$-bit strings $\sigma$'s such that every two strings in $S$ differ from each other in more than $9n/40$ bits.
**An algorithm for choosing $S$:**
*BEGIN*

- $S \longleftarrow \phi$.

- Repeat $4 \cdot 2^{n/9}$ times: Choose an arbitrary good $n$-bit string $\sigma$ in $T$, add it to $S$, and remove from $T$ all the strings which differ from $\sigma$ in less than $9n/40$ bits.

*END*

**Lemma 6:** *This algorithm cannot stop prematurely.*

**Proof:** First we have to notice that the total number of $n$-bit strings $x = (x_1, x_2, \ldots, x_n)$ for which $\sum_{i=1}^{n} x_i < \frac{9n}{40}$ is less than:

$$9n/40 \begin{pmatrix} n \\ 9n/40 \end{pmatrix} < \frac{2^n}{2^{11n/48}}$$

for all sufficiently large $n$.

Therefore for each $n$-bit string there are at most $\frac{2^n}{2^{11n/48}}$ strings which differ from it in less than $9n/40$ bits. Therefore the validity of the following inequality implies the success of the algorithm:

$$4 \cdot 2^{n/9}(1 + \frac{2^n}{2^{11n/48}}) \leq \frac{2^n}{2 \cdot 2^{n/9}} \leq |T|. \qquad \blacksquare$$

**Lemma 7:** *There exist $\sigma', \sigma'' \in S$, such that:*

$$|A_{\sigma'} \bigcap A_{\sigma''}| \geq \frac{2^n}{10 \cdot 2^{2n/9}}.$$

**Proof:** According to the inclusion exclusion formula we have:

$$\sum_{\sigma \in S} |A_{\sigma}| - \sum_{\sigma', \sigma'' \in S} |A_{\sigma'} \bigcap A_{\sigma''}| \leq 2^n.$$

If the Lemma is not true then we get:

$$4 \cdot 2^{n/9} \cdot \frac{2^n}{2 \cdot 2^{n/9}} - \frac{4^2 \cdot 2^{2n/9}}{2} \cdot \frac{2^n}{10 \cdot 2^{2n/9}} \leq 2^n.$$

which is false. $\qquad \blacksquare$

Denote by $\sigma'$ and $\sigma''$ two strings in $S$ for which:

$$|A_{\sigma'} \bigcap A_{\sigma''}| \geq \frac{2^n}{10 \cdot 2^{2n/9}}.$$

We showed that every two strings in $S$ differ from each other in at least $9n/40$ bits, and in particular these two $\sigma', \sigma''$ have this property. Denote by $I$ the set of $9n/40$ indices in which $\sigma'$ differs from $\sigma''$. Choose an arbitrary $\tau' \in A_{\sigma'} \bigcap A_{\sigma''}$. There are exactly $\frac{2^n}{2^{9n/40}}$

$n$-bit strings which are identical to $\tau'$ on each of the indices of $I$. Therefore the total number of strings in the intersection which are identical to $\tau'$ on each of the indices of $I$ is bounded by:

$$\frac{2^n}{2^{9n/40}} < \frac{2^n}{10 \cdot 2^{2n/9}} \leq |A_{\sigma'} \bigcap A_{\sigma''}|.$$

Therefore there exists $\tau'' \in A_{\sigma'} \bigcap A_{\sigma''}$ which differs from $\tau'$ in at least one of the indices of $I$, and we have thus found a successful quadruple. ∎

**Remarks:**

1. Recent improvements of the analysis (obtained independently by Peleg, Alon and Feige [Fe]) reduced the upper bound on the probability of cheating and extended the analysis to other protocols based on constant-size queries.

2. The same technique of successful quadruples can be used to prove the soundness of the original [BGKW] protocol. The analysis is slightly more complicated due to their use of three valued "bits" as messages, and will be given in the full version of this extended abstract.

# 5  The Protocol is a Proof of Knowledge.

In this section we prove that our protocol for Hamiltonicity is also a perfect zero knowledge proof of knowledge. We follow the definition suggested by Feige, Fiat and Shamir in [FFS].

**Definition:**
Let $(P_1, P_2, V)$ be a two-prover perfect zero knowledge interactive proof system for an NP-language $L$ such that $P_1$ and $P_2$ are probabilistic polynomial time bounded. We say that $(P_1, P_2, V)$ is an interactive proof of knowledge if there exists an interactive probabilistic machine $T$ (knowledge extractor with complete control over $(\hat{P}_1, \hat{P}_2)$ ) such that for all $(\hat{P}_1, \hat{P}_2)$ and for all input $x$, if $V$ accepts the proof (that $x \in L$) with non negligible probability, then the output produced by $T$ at the end of polynomially many executions of $(\hat{P}_1, \hat{P}_2, T)$ on input $x$ is a witness for $x \in L$ and $T$ terminates in expected polynomial time. More formally:

$$\exists T \; \forall(\hat{P}_1, \hat{P}_2) \; \forall x \; \forall a \; \exists b \; \exists N \; \forall n > N$$

$$Pr\{(\hat{P}_1, \hat{P}_2, V) \; succeeds \; on \; x\} > 1/n^a \implies$$

$$Pr\{output \; of \; (\hat{P}_1, \hat{P}_2, T) \; on \; x \; is \; a \; witness \; for \; x\} = 1$$

*and the expected running time of $T$ is $O(n^b)$, where the probability is taken over the coin tosses of $V$.*

**Theorem 8:** $FP_n$ is a perfect zero knowledge interactive proof of knowledge for Hamiltonicity.

**Proof:** Without loss of generality we can assume that $P_1$ and $P_2$ are deterministic. Therefore the probability space consists of all the (equally likely) $2n$-bit strings which $V$ may send to $(P_1, P_2)$, and at least $2^{2n}/n^a$ of them result in successful executions.

Due to the same argument (and using the same notation) of the previous section we conclude that there exist at least $2^n/2n^a$ $\sigma$'s whose $|A_\sigma| \geq 2^n/2n^a$, and call them good $\sigma$'s.

**Lemma 9:** *For every set $\hat{S}$ of $4n^{2a}$ good $\sigma$'s there exist $\sigma', \sigma'' \in \hat{S}$ such that:*

$$|A_{\sigma'} \bigcap A_{\sigma''}| \geq 2^n/(2n^a)^3.$$

**Proof:** As in the proof of Lemma 7, the first two terms of the inclusion exclusion formula trivially give the result. ∎

We now specify the knowledge extractor $T$: Choose a random set $\hat{S}$ of $4n^{2a}$ good $\sigma$'s. This step can be performed by an expected polynomial number of statistical experiments of the following type: randomly choose an $n$-bit string $\sigma$; for this string choose independently polynomially many random $n$-bit strings ($\tau$'s), execute the protocol for each such pair $(\tau, \sigma)$ and estimate the probability of success with respect to this $\sigma$.

Choose an arbitrary pair $\sigma', \sigma'' \in \hat{S}$ which satisfies Lemma 9 (there are only $O(n^{4a})$ pairs for which we have to execute statistical experiments). Choose an arbitrary $n$-bit string in $A_{\sigma'} \bigcap A_{\sigma''}$, and call it $\tau'$.

Notice the following crucial point: In order to choose $\hat{S}$, we randomly choose *polynomially many* $n$-bit strings, each one by $n$ unbiased and independent coin tosses, and thus every two chosen strings differ from each other in at least $n/3$ bits with overwhelming probability. In particular, the $\sigma', \sigma''$ chosen from $\hat{S}$ satisfy this property with overwhelming probability. Denote by $J$ the set of indices on which $\sigma'$ differs from $\sigma''$ ($|J| \geq n/3$). The same argument used in the proof of *Theorem* 1 yields that almost all the strings in $A_{\sigma'} \bigcap A_{\sigma''}$ differ from $\tau'$ in at least one of the indices of $J$, therefore we can easily choose a string in this intersection which has this property, and call it $\tau''$.

Now all $T$ has to do in order to extract the Hamiltonian cycle in $G$ is to execute the protocol $FP_n$ against $(P_1, P_2)$ on the following four pairs:
$(\tau', \sigma'), (\tau', \sigma''), (\tau'', \sigma'), (\tau'', \sigma'')$, and use Lemma 4. To complete the proof, we can execute in parallel an exhaustive search for a witness to handle the negligible probability that the main procedure fails to find a witness. ∎

# 6 Acknowledgments

We are grateful to Uri Feige for pointing out the parallelization problem, and for interesting discussions and helpful comments on this work.

# References

[BCY] G. Brassard, C. Crepeau, M. Yung. *Everything in NP can be argued in perfect zero knowledge in a bounded number of rounds*, Proceedings of 16th ICALP (1989).

[BMO] M. Bellare, S. Micali and R. Ostrovsky. *Perfect Zero-Knowledge in Constant Rounds*, Proceedings of the 22nd annual ACM Symposium on Theory of Computing (1990), 482–493.

[BGKW] M. Ben-Or, S. Goldwasser, J. Kilian, A. Wigderson. *Multi-Prover Interactive Proofs: How to Remove Intractability Assumptions*. Proceedings of the 20th annual ACM Symposium on Theory of Computing (1988), 113–131.

[BHZ] R. Boppana, J. Hastad and S. Zachos. *Does CoNP Have Short Interactive Proofs?*, Information Processing Letters **25** 2 (1987), 127–132.

[F1] L. Fortnow. *Complexity Theoretic Aspects of Interactive Proof Systems*, Ph.D. Thesis, MIT/LCS/TR-447, (1989).

[F2] L. Fortnow. *The Complexity of Perfect Zero-Knowledge*, Proceedings of the 19th annual ACM Symposium on Theory of Computing (1987), 204–209.

[Fe] U. Feige. *On the Success Probability of the Two Provers in One-Round Proof Systems*, Proceedings of the 6th Structure in Complexity Theory Conference (1991), IEEE.

[FFS] U. Feige, A. Fiat and A. Shamir. *Zero Knowledge Proofs of Identity*, Proceedings of the 19th annual ACM Symposium on Theory of Computing (1987), 210–217.

[FRS] L. Fortnow, J. Rompel and M. Sipser. *On the Power of Multi-Prover Interactive Protocols*, Proceedings of the 3rd Structure in Complexity Theory Conference (1988), 156–161.

[FS] U. Feige and A. Shamir. *Witness Indistinguishable and Witness Hiding Protocols*, Proceedings of the 22th annual ACM Symposium on Theory of Computing (1990), 416–426.

[GK] O. Goldreich and A. Kahan, private communication (1990).

[GMW]   O. Goldreich, S. Micali and A. Wigderson. *Proofs that Yield Nothing But their Validity and a Methodology of Cryptographic Protocol Design*, Proceedings of the 27th Symposium on Foundations of Computer Science (1986), IEEE, 174–187.

[GMR]   S. Goldwasser, S. Micali, and C. Rackoff. *The Knowledge Complexity of Interactive Proofs*, Proceedings of the 17th annual ACM Symposium on Theory of Computing (1985), 291–304.

# Interactive Proofs with Space
# Bounded Provers

Joe Kilian *
NEC Research Institute
Princeton, NJ 08540

Ronitt Rubinfeld †
Department of Computer Science
Princeton University
Princeton, NJ 08544

## Abstract

Recent results in interactive proof systems [12][13] [1] seem to indicate that it is easier for a prover in a single prover interactive proof system to cheat the verifier than it is for a prover in a multiple prover interactive proof system. We show that this is not the case for a single prover in which all but a fixed polynomial of the prover's space is erased between each round. One consequence of this is that any multiple prover interactive protocol in which the provers need only a polynomial amount of space can be easily transformed into a single prover interactive protocol where the prover has only a fixed polynomial amount of space. This result also shows that one can easily transform checkers [5] into adaptive checkers [7] under the assumption that the program being checked has space bounded by a fixed polynomial.

# 1   Introduction

Recent results in complexity theory have shown that IP=PSPACE [12][13] and that MIP=NEXPTIME [1]. This gives reason to believe that there is a significant difference in the power of a single prover interactive proof system versus the power of multiple prover interactive proof systems, i.e. that since the multiple provers are constrained to be consistent with each other, they cannot cheat the verifier as easily, and thus more difficult languages can have such proof systems. It has been shown that the same set of

*Supported by an NSF fellowship while at MIT.
†Supported by DIMACS, NSF-STC88-09648.

J. Feigenbaum (Ed.): Advances in Cryptology - CRYPTO '91, LNCS 576, pp. 225-231, 1992.
© Springer-Verlag Berlin Heidelberg 1992

languages is accepted by the following three types of interactive proof systems: multiple prover systems, single prover systems where the prover is constrained to answer according to functions that are fixed in advance, and single prover systems in which the memory of the prover gets wiped out between each question (i.e. the prover has no memory of the conversation) [9][3].

One might conjecture that allowing the prover in a single prover system to have partial memory of the conversation could increase his ability to cheat substantially, thus decreasing the power of the system. We show that this is *not* the case: that if there is an interactive protocol against a prover that does not remember anything between questions, then for any $s$ it can be modified into an interactive protocol that works against a prover that remembers $s$ bits between questions. The running time of the new protocol is polynomial in the running time of the old protocol and $s$. Note that the IP prover need only remember the history of the conversation between rounds, which is a polynomial number of bits (however, here the polynomial is chosen after the protocol is decided upon rather than before).

This result has the following application to cryptography: it shows that two prover protocols for identification implemented by two credit cards can be implemented by a single credit card, as long as the credit card is guaranteed to have a limited amount of memory.

The results in this paper apply to program result checking as well [5] [7]. They show how to transform a checker that works assuming that the program is a *fixed* function, into an adaptive checker which instead assumes only that the program has polynomial space at its disposal. This is interesting because it allows one to assume that the checker works even if hardware faults evolve over time, or in the case that the software is written such that running the program on certain inputs may have unintended side effects on the program's future behavior.

A somewhat related result in [10] shows how to self-correct [6] some functions from space bounded tested programs. This result applies only to functions which are polynomials, and does not show how to give program result checkers for those functions.

# 2 Definitions

We informally describe the following modifications of definitions of interactive proof systems and IP given in [11]:

DEFINITION 2.1 *A s-space, t-round Interactive Protocol $(A, B)$ is a pair of turing machines (TM) $(A, B)$ which share an input tape (read only). Both have a private read/write work tape and read-only random tape. There are two communication tapes: one which $B$ has write-only access to, and $A$ has read-only access to, and one which $A$ has write-only access to, and $B$ has read-only access to. We think of the first tape as containing messages sent to, or "questions" asked of $A$, and the second as messages sent to, or "answers" to $B$. The machines take $t$ turns being active with $B$ going first. Before each message to $A$, all but the first $s$ bits of $A$'s private work tape are erased. $A$ is computationally unbounded and $B$ is polynomial time bounded.*

DEFINITION 2.2 *Let $L \subset \{0, 1\}^*$. We say that $L$ has a $s$-space $t$-round interactive proof system (IPS) if there exists a TM $V$ such that*

1. *There is a TM $P$ s.t. $(P, V)$ is a s-space t-round interactive protocol and for all $x \in L$ s.t. $|x|$ is sufficiently large, $Pr[V accepts] > 2/3$ (when probabilities are over coin tosses of $P$ and $V$).*

2. *For all TM's $P'$ s.t. $(P', V)$ is a s-space t-round interactive protocol and for all $x \notin L$ s.t. $|x|$ is sufficiently large, $Pr[V accepts] < 1/3$ (when probabilities are over coin tosses of $P'$ and $V$).*

*We say that $(P, V)$ is a $s$-space $t$-round interactive proof system for $L$.*

Define $IP(s, t) = \{L | L$ *has an s-space t-round interactive proof system*$\}$

We may think of $P$ as deterministic, giving optimal answers to maximize the probability that $V$ accepts.

# 3 Main Theorem

**Theorem 1** *If $L \in IP(0, t)$, then for all $s$, $L \in IP(s, O(st))$.*

**Proof:** We show that if there is a 0-space, $t$-round interactive protocol for $L$ then we can construct an $s$-space $O(st)$-round interactive protocol for $L$.

The 0-space, $t$-round protocol for $L$ can be run $O(s)$ times in order to reduce the error probability from $\frac{1}{3}$ to $\frac{1}{6}2^{-s}$. Call the resulting low error protocol $C_P^V$, and let

$C_P^V(w, r) = (x_1, y_1, \ldots, x_m, y_m)$ denote the $m$-round conversation between verifier $V$ and prover $P$, where $w$ is the input, $r$ is the random string used by the verifier, the $x_i$'s are the "questions" sent by the verifier to the prover, and the $y_i$'s are the "answers" sent by the prover to the verifier (note that $m$ is $O(st)$).

Let $\Phi(w, r, C_P^V(w, r))$ be the function which the verifier evaluates after the conversation in order to decide whether to accept or reject $w$.

Let $\tilde{P}$ denote any prover that can remember $s$ bits between questions.

We are now ready to present the protocol:

**$s$-space $O(st)$-round interactive protocol:**
On input $w$:
1. Run protocol $C_{\tilde{P}}^V(w, r) = (x_1, y_1, \ldots, x_m, y_m)$. If $\Phi(w, r, C_{\tilde{P}}^V(w, r)) = $ "REJECT" then reject and halt.
2. Do $3m$ times:
    Pick $i \in_R [1, m]$
    Verifier asks question $x_i$ and receives answer $\hat{y}_i$.
    If $y_i \neq \hat{y}_i$ then reject and halt.
3. Accept $w$.

**Proof of Correctness of $s$-space $O(st)$-round protocol:** If $w \in L$, then it is obvious from our assumption that $L \in IP(0, t)$ that there is a prover $P$ which can only remember $s$ bits after every question such that $Pr_r[\Phi(w, r, C_P^V(w, r)) = $ "ACCEPT"$] \geq 2/3$.

To prove the theorem for the case when $w$ is not in $L$, we need to show that no prover that can remember $s$ bits is likely to fool the verifier into accepting $L$.

We first note that any space $s$ prover $\tilde{P}$ can be viewed as a collection of $2^s$ functions in the following manner: consider a deterministic finite state automaton with $2^s$ states, where each state $i$ is labeled with function $P^i$. The transitions between functions are labeled by all the possible questions that a verifier could ask of the prover. Then the prover is at one of the $2^s$ states, and whenever the verifier asks a question, the prover answers the question according to the function which labels the state, and goes to a new state according to the transition function applied to the current state and the question just asked by the verifier.

For fixed $i$, we say that $r$ is $P^i$-*bad for* $w$ if $\Phi(w, r, C_{P^i}^V(w, r)) = $ "ACCEPT" (where the prover $P^i$ is the prover which answers according to function $P^i$). Since $C_{P^i}^V$ is a

0-space interactive protocol for $L$ with error $\leq \frac{1}{6}2^{-s}$, we know that $r$ is $P^i$-bad with the same probability. We say that $r$ is $\tilde{P}$-*bad for* $w$ if there is an $i$ such that $r$ is $P^i$-bad for $w$. Since there are only $2^s$ $P^i$'s, $Pr[r \text{ is } \tilde{P} - bad \text{ for } w] \leq 2^s \cdot \frac{1}{6}2^{-s} = \frac{1}{6}$.

For each $r$, one of the following three cases must hold

1. $\Phi(w, r, C_{\tilde{P}}^V(w, r)) =$ "REJECT", in which case the verifier rejects.

2. $r$ is $\tilde{P}$-bad for $w$. By the above reasoning, this case happens with probability $\leq 1/6$.

3. $\Phi(w, r, C_{\tilde{P}}^V(w, r)) =$ "ACCEPT", but $r$ is not $\tilde{P}$-bad for $w$. Thus for all $i$,

$$\Phi(w, r, C_{P^i}^V(w, r) = (a_1, b_1), \ldots, (a_m, b_m)) = \text{"REJECT"}.$$

Then for all $i$, there is a $j$ such that $x_j = a_j$ but $y_j \neq b_j$ (since the conversations cannot be the same, and the verifier follows the same algorithm, the first difference must come from the prover). Therefore, no matter which state the prover is in during a loop of Step 2 of the protocol, the probability that a question is asked for which the answer $y_j \neq \hat{y}_j$ is at least $1/m$. After $3m$ times, the probability that the verifier will not reject is at most $e^{-3}$.

Thus, if $w$ is not in $L$, the verifier will reject with probability at least $1 - \frac{1}{6} - e^{-3} \geq 2/3$.

∎

# 4   Bounding the Power of an $s$-space Prover.

The transformation used in the proof of Theorem 1 works only for deterministic provers, since a legitimate probabilistic prover might cause the verifier to reject in Step 2 by giving inconsistent answers to its questions. One can replace any probabilistic prover with an "optimal" deterministic prover, but this new prover may have much greater computational requirements. Hence, such a simple fix will not allow us to carry over our results to program result checking.

However, we can use the general idea used in the proof of Theorem 1 to directly bound the advantage of an $s$-space bounded prover over a 0-space bounded prover. Our theorem is as follows:[1]

---

[1] This result was independently discovered by Lund (personal communication).

**Theorem 2** *Suppose that in an interactive protocol $(P, V)$ the prover's memory is partially erased at most $t$ times. Let $P_s$ be a prover that is allowed to remember $s$ bits between partial erasures, and let $P_0$ be an optimal prover that is not allowed to remember any bits between erasures. Then, for all $x$,*

$$\frac{Pr[(P_s, V) \ accepts \ x]}{Pr[(P_0, V) \ accepts \ x]} \leq 2^{st}.$$

**Proof:** We assume without loss of generality that $P_s$ is deterministic, and denote by $p$ the probability that $(P_s, V)$ accepts $x$. We now construct a 0-space bounded prover $P_0$ such that $(P_0, V)$ will accept $x$ with probability at least $2^{-st}p$. $P_0$ works exactly as does $P_s$, except that whenever its memory is (totally) erased it sets the first $s$ bits of its memory to a random $s$-bit string.

Suppose that $(P_s, V)$ accepts when $V$ uses $r$ as its random input. It suffices to show that $(P_0, V)$ will accept with probability $2^{-st}$ when $V$ uses $r$ as its random input. Let $S_i^r$ denote the contents of the first $s$ bits of $P_s$'s memory after the $i$th (partial) memory erasure. With probability $2^{-st}$, it will be the case that for each $i$, $1 \leq i \leq t$, $P_0$ will fill its memory with $S_i^r$ after the $i$th memory erasure. Whenever this happens, the behavior of $P_0$ will be identical to that of $P_s$, and $V$ will accept. Thus, $(P_0, V)$ will accept with probability at least $2^{-st}$ whenever $(P_s, V)$ accepts, and the theorem follows. ∎

Thus, any protocol which achieves a sufficiently low probability of error, using sufficiently few memory erasures, is automatically robust against an $s$-space bounded prover, without modification. Therefore, given an interactive proof system robust against 0-space bounded provers, using only $t$ memory erasures, one needs only to reduce the error probability to less than $\frac{1}{3} \cdot 2^{-st}$, while preserving the total number of memory erasures.

# 5   Acknowledgments

We would like to thank Dick Lipton for suggesting the problem. We would also like to thank Uri Feige, Shafi Goldwasser, Diane Hernek, Hugo Krawczyk and Mike Luby for very extensive and helpful discussions on this subject, and for helpful comments on the writeup.

# References

[1] Babai, L., Fortnow, L., Lund, C., "Non-Deterministic Exponential Time has Two-

Prover Interactive Protocols", Technical Report 90-03, University of Chicago, Dept. of Computer Science. Also in *Proceedings of the 31st Annual Symposium on Foundations of Computer Science,*, 1990.

[2] Ben-Or, M., Goldwasser, S., Kilian, J., and Wigderson, A., "Efficient Identification Schemes Using Two Prover Interactive Proofs", *Advances in Cryptology - CRYPTO '89*, Springer-Verlag.

[3] Ben-Or, M., Goldwasser, S., Kilian, J., and Wigderson, A., "Multi-Prover Interactive Proofs: How to Remove Intractability Assumptions", *Proc. 20th ACM Symposium on Theory of Computing*, 1988, pp. 113-131.

[4] Blum, M., "Designing programs to check their work", Submitted to *CACM*.

[5] Blum, M., Kannan, S., "Program correctness checking ... and the design of programs that check their work", *Proc. 21st ACM Symposium on Theory of Computing*, 1989.

[6] Blum, M., Luby, M., Rubinfeld, R., "Self-Testing/Correcting Programs with Applications to Numerical Problems", *Proc. 22nd ACM Symposium on Theory of Computing*, 1990.

[7] Blum, M., Luby, M., Rubinfeld, R., "Program Result Checking against Adaptive Programs and in Cryptographic Settings", *Distributed Computing and Cryptography*, DIMACS Series in Discrete Mathematics and Theoretical Computer Science, Vol. 2, 1991.

[8] Feige, U., "NEXPTIME has Two-Provers One-Round Proof Systems With Exponentially Small Error Probability", Manuscript.

[9] Fortnow, L., Rompel, J., Sipser, M., "On the Power of Multi-Prover Interactive Protocols", Proc. $3^{rd}$ Structure in Complexity Theory Conference, 1988, pp. 156-161.

[10] Gemmell, P., Lipton, R., Rubinfeld, R., Wigderson, A., "Self-Testing/Correcting for Polynomials and for Approximate Functions", *Proceedings of 23rd ACM STOC*, 1991.

[11] Goldwasser, S., Micali, S., Rackoff, C., The Knowledge Complexity of Interactive Proof Systems", *SIAM J. Comput.*, 18(1),1989, pp. 186-208.

[12] Lund, C., Fortnow, L., Karloff, H., Nisan, N., "Algebraic Methods for Interactive Proof Systems", *Proceedings of the 31st Annual Symposium on Foundations of Computer Science,*, 1990.

[13] Shamir, Adi, "IP=PSPACE", *Proceedings of the 31st Annual Symposium on Foundations of Computer Science, 1990*.

# Functional Inversion and Communication Complexity

## Shang-Hua Teng[*]

Xerox Corporation
Palo Alto Research Center
3333 Coyote Hill Road
Palo Alto, California 94304

### Abstract

In this paper, we study the relation between the multi-party communication complexity over various communication topologies and the complexity of inverting functions and/or permutations. In particular, we show that if a function has a *ring-protocol* or a *tree-protocol* of communication complexity bounded by $H$, then there is a circuit of size $O(2^H n)$ which computes an inverse of the function. Consequently, we have proved, although inverting $NC^0$ Boolean circuits is $NP$–complete, planar $NC^1$ Boolean circuits can be inverted in $NC$, and hence in polynomial time. In general, $NC^k$ planar boolean circuits can be inverted in $O(n^{log^{(k-1)} n})$ time. Also from the ring-protocol results, we derive an $\Omega(n \log n)$ lower bound on the VLSI area to layout any one-way functions. Our results on inverting boolean circuits can be extended to invert algebraic circuits over finite rings.

One significant aspect of our result is that it enables us to compare the communication power of two topologies. We have proved that on some topologies, no one-way function nor its inverse can be computed with bounded communication complexity.

## 1 Introduction

One of the most fundamental questions in cryptanalysis is to characterize the class of permutations (or functions) whose inverse can be computed in polynomial time or by a polynomial size circuit [1, 10, 12, 16]. Much research in theoretically cryptography has been centered around finding the weakest possible cryptographic assumptions required in implementing major primitives [11, 4]. However, progress on characterizing permutations with small inversion circuits is very slow [12].

In this paper, we study the relation between multi-party communication complexity over various communication topologies and the complexity of inverting permutations and functions We show some nontrivial classes of permutations whose inverse can be computed efficiently.

In particular, we show that if a function has a *ring-protocol* or a *tree-protocol* of communication complexity bounded by $H$, then there is a circuit of size $O(2^H n)$ which computes an inverse of the function. Consequently, we have proved, although inverting $NC^0$ Boolean circuits is $NP$–complete, planar $NC^1$ Boolean circuits can be inverted in $NC$, and hence in polynomial time. In general,

---

[*]This work was supported in part by National Science Foundation grant DCR-8713489. Part of this work was done while the author was at School of Computer Science, Carnegie Mellon University, Pittsburgh, PA 15213.

$NC^k$ planar boolean circuits can be inverted in $O(n^{log^{(k-1)}n})$ time. Also from the ring-protocol results, we derive an $\Omega(n \log n)$ lower bound on the VLSI area to layout any one-way functions. Our results on inverting boolean circuits can be extended to invert algebraic circuits over finite rings.

One significant aspect of our result is that it enables us to compare the communication power of two topologies. We have proved that on some topologies, no one-way function nor its inverse can be computed with bounded communication complexity.

## 2   Definitions

Let $B = \{0,1\}$, i.e., the field $ZF(2)$. Let $f : B^n \to B^m$ be a *boolean mapping* from $B^n$ to $B^m$. The mapping $f$ is a permutation if $m = n$ and $f$ is a *bijection*. A function $g : B^m \to B^n$ is an *inverse* of $f$ if for all $y \in B^m$, $f(g(y)) = y$ whenever $g(y)$ is defined. In this paper, let $B_{n,m}$ denote the set of all boolean mappings from $B^n$ to $B^m$.

A *Boolean circuit* is a directed acyclic graph whose nodes have indegree either 0 or 2. A node of indegree 0 is labeled with a variable, or with a boolean constant. A node with indegree 2 is labeled with a boolean function of 2 inputs. A node with a variable label is called an *input node* and the one with outdegree 0 is called an *output node*. We assume that each boolean circuit is *reduced* in the sense that no two input nodes share the same label. Each circuit $C$ with $n$ input nodes and $m$ output nodes defines, in a natural way, a function, denoted by $f_C$, from $B^n$ to $B^m$.

A circuit $C$ *computes* a function $f$ if $f_C = f$. A circuit $C'$ is an *inversion circuit* of $f$ if $C'$ computes an inverse of $f$.

The non-uniform and uniform versions of the *inversion problem* are defined as follows.

**Definition 2.1 (Inversion Problem)**

- **(Non-uniform)** *Is there a polynomial size circuit that computes an inverse of a given function* $f \in B_{n,m}$?

- **(Uniform)** *Given a circuit or (a straight line program) that computes a given function $f$, construct an inversion circuit (with size bounded by a predefined function in $n$ and $m$) of $f$.*

## 3   Communication Complexity

For each function $f \in B_{n,m}$, we write $f : 2^X \to 2^Y$, where $X$ denotes the set of $n$ inputs and $Y$ the set of outputs.

### 3.1   Two Party Communication Complexity

Suppose there are two processors in the system. For each partition $(X_1, X_2)$ of $X$, processor 1 receives the values of variables in $X_1$ and processor 2 receives the values of variables in $X_2$. The *two party communication complexity* of $f$ with respect to the partition $(X_1, X_2)$, denoted by $C_f(X_1, X_2)$, is the number of bits the processors, using an optimal protocol, have to exchange, in the worst case, in order to jointly compute the values of all outputs of $f$ [17, 13].

Notice that an optimal protocol for computing $f$ with respect to the partition $(X_1, X_2)$ also induces a natural partition of $Y$ into $(Y_1, Y_2)$ such that in the protocol, processor $i$ is responsible to compute the values of all variables in $Y_i$, $(i \in \{1, 2\})$.

Let $\mathcal{P}(X)$ denote the set of all partitions of $X$ and $S_n$ the set of all permutations from $\{1, ..., n\}$ to $\{1, ..., n\}$. For each $\pi \in S_n$, let

$$\mathcal{P}_\pi(X) = \{(\{x_{\pi(1)}, ..., x_{\pi(k)}\}, \{x_{\pi(k+1)}, ..., x_{\pi(n)}\}) : 1 \leq k \leq n\}.$$

**Definition 3.1 (Two Party Communication Complexity)** *The* symmetric communication complexity *of a function $f \in \mathcal{B}_{n,m}$, denoted by $SC(f)$, is defined to be*

$$SC(f) = \max_{(X_1, X_2) \in \mathcal{P}(X)} C_f(X_1, X_2).$$

*The* permutational communication complexity *of a function $f \in \mathcal{B}_{n,m}$, denoted by $PC(f)$, is defined to be*

$$PC(f) = \min_{\pi \in S_n} \max_{(X_1, X_2) \in \mathcal{P}_\pi(X)} C_f(X_1, X_2).$$

It is easy to see that for all function $f$, $PC(f) \leq SC(f)$.

## 3.2 Multi-Party Communication Complexity

A *communication topology* of $N$ nodes is a graph $G = (V, E)$ with $V = \{p_0, ..., p_{N-1}\}$ and $E \subset V \times V$, where $V$ models the set of processors and $G$ models the underlying communication network.

Each processor $p_i$ is a Turing machine which has an input tape, an output tape and a work tape. Each edge of $G$ models the communication channel between processors sited at its two ends. The whole system forms a computing device where each processor has some information, called *input* of the processor, and the processors want to jointly compute their respective share of outputs which are functions of all the inputs.

The computation is guided by a *distributed protocol* $\mathcal{P}$ which is a set of rules specifying the order and content of messages sent from one processor to another. We assume that all processors have unlimited computing power and the local computation is free. We only charge for the bits transmitted from one processor to the others. One major goal in the field of distributed computing is to design a distributed protocol to compute a given function that minimizes the maximum number of bits one processor has to receive, to send, or both.

For each topology $G$ and protocol $\mathcal{P}$, let $\phi_G(\mathcal{P}, p_i)$ and $\psi_G(\mathcal{P}, p_i)$ denote, respectively, the maximum number of bits $p_i$ has to receive and send in the worst case. Let $\omega_G(\mathcal{P}, p_i) = \phi_G(\mathcal{P}, p_i) + \psi_G(\mathcal{P}, p_i)$.

A distributed protocol $\mathcal{P}$ *computes* a function $f \in \mathcal{B}_{n,m}$ if there is an $N$-partition $(X_0, ..., X_{N-1})$ of $X$ and $(Y_0, ..., Y_{N-1})$ of $Y$, where processor $p_i$ receives an assignment $x_i$ of $X_i$ as its input, such that after running protocol $\mathcal{P}$, $p_i$ computes $y_i$ with $y = f(x)$, where $y = (y_0, ..., y_{N-1})$.

For each function, there is a trivial protocol with null communication cost, i.e., the one which assigns all inputs and all outputs to a single processor. In order to avoid this triviality, we only concern ourselves the set of *balanced protocols*,

**Definition 3.2 (Balanced–Protocols)** *A partition $(X_0, ..., X_{N-1})$ of $X$ is $H$-balanced if for all $0 \leq i \leq N - 1$, $|X_i| \leq H$. A protocol $\mathcal{P}$ for a function $f : 2^X \to 2^Y$ is $H$-balanced if its input–partition is $H$-balanced.*

Let $\mathcal{P}_{G,H}(f)$ denote the set of all $H$-balanced protocols that compute $f : 2^X \to 2^Y$,

**Definition 3.3 (Balanced Communication Complexity)** *For each function* $f : 2^X \to 2^Y$, *define*[1]

$$\Phi_{G,H}(f) = \min_{\mathcal{P} \in \mathcal{P}_{G,H}(f)} \max_i \phi_G(\mathcal{P}, p_i)$$

Notice that if the balanced communication complexity of a function $f$ is small, then $f$ can be computed by a circuit of small size (The proof of the following lemma will appear in the full paper).

**Proposition 3.1** *For each graph* $G$, *for each* $H \in \mathcal{R}^+$, *each function* $f : 2^X \to 2^Y$ *can be computed by a circuit of size* $O\left(2^{H + \Phi_{G,H}(f)} n\right)$. □

The topology of communication networks play an important role in designing communication-efficient protocols. The set of communication topologies studied in this paper includes cliques, mesh, planar graphs, rings, and trees. The corresponding protocols are respectively called, *ideal protocols, mesh protocol, planar protocols, ring protocols*, and *tree protocols*.

# 4 Communication Topologies and Functional Inversion

In this section, we examine the communication power of various topologies including rings, meshes, trees, and cliques. We show that no one-way function (permutation) can be computed on a ring or a tree with bounded information exchange between neighbors.

## 4.1 Rings

We now prove that if a function $f$ can be computed by an $H$-balanced ring-protocol with communication complexity $\Phi_H(f)$, then there is a circuit of size $O(2^{H + \Phi_H(f)})$ which computes an inverse of $f$.

Let $\mathcal{P}$ be an $H$-balanced ring-protocol which computes $f$ with communication complexity $\Phi_H(f)$; let $(X_0, \ldots, X_{N-1})$ be the $H$-balanced partition induced by $\mathcal{P}$ on inputs and $(Y_0, \ldots, Y_{N-1})$ the partition on outputs; and let $l_i$ and $r_i$ be the number of bits the processor $i$ sends to processor $i - 1$ and $i + 1$, respectively. For simplicity, all '+' and '-' (on index) in this section are modulo $N$. Let $h = H + \Phi_H(f)$. By definition, we have $l_i + r_i \leq h$.

Let $U_i = (u_{i,1}, ..., u_{i,l_i})$ and $V_i = (v_{i,1}, ..., v_{i,r_i})$ denote the set of variables whose values processor $i$ sends to processor $i - 1$ and $i + 1$ respectively, in the protocol $\mathcal{P}$.

Notice that the protocol $\mathcal{P}$ defines a natural function $f_i$ associated with processor $i$, from $(X_i \cup V_{i-1} \cup U_{i+1})$ to $(Y_i \cup U_i \cup V_i)$. Because $f_i$ has only $O(h)$ bit inputs, $f_i$ is computable by a circuit of size $O(2^h)$ (see Lemma 3.1). Let $C_i$ be such a circuit computing $f_i$.

---

[1] We can also define:

$$\Psi_{G,H}(f) = \min_{\mathcal{P} \in \mathcal{P}_{G,H}(f)} \max_i \psi_G(\mathcal{P}, p_i)$$

$$\Omega_{G,H}(f) = \min_{\mathcal{P} \in \mathcal{P}_{G,H}(f)} \max_i \omega_G(\mathcal{P}, p_i).$$

We now define for each $y \in \mathcal{B}^m$ a digraph $G_y$ with the property that $G_y$ is not acyclic iff there exists $x \in \mathcal{B}^n$ such that $f(x) = y$.

For each output $y \in \mathcal{B}^m$, let $M_i$ and $T_i$ be $2^{l_i} \times 2^{r_{i-1}} \times 2^{l_{i+1}} \times 2^{r_i}$ matrices whose entries are defined as follows.

For each $i : 0 \le i \le t - 1$, for each assignment $u_i, v_{i-1}, u_{i+1}, v_i$ to $U_i, V_{i-1}, U_{i+1}, V_i$.

- If there is an assignment $x_i$ to $X_i$, such that $f_i(x_i, v_{i-1}, u_{i+1}) = (y_i, u_i, v_i)$, then $T_i[u_i, v_{i-1}, u_{i+1}, v_i] = X_i$ and $M_i[u_i, v_{i-1}, u_{i+1}, v_i] = 1$;
- If there is no such assignment, $M_i[u_i, v_{i-1}, u_{i+1}, v_i] = 0$;

We now define the digraph $G_y = (V, E)$ as

$$V = \bigcup_{i=0}^{N-1} (\{i\} \times \mathcal{B}^{l_i} \times \mathcal{B}^{r_{i-1}})$$

$$E = \{((i, u_i, v_{i-1}), (i+1, u_{i+1}, v_i)) | M_i[u_i, v_{i-1}, u_{i+1}, v_i] = 1\}$$

**Lemma 4.1** $G_y$ is not acyclic iff there exists $x \in \mathcal{B}^n$ such that $f(x) = y$.

**Proof:** Suppose that there exists $x \in \mathcal{B}^n$ such that $f(x) = y$. Since $f$ can be computed by an $H$-balanced ring-protocol with communication complexity $\Phi_H(f)$ as above, there are $x_i$, $u_i$, and $v_i$ such that $(y_i, u_i, v_i) = f_i(x_i, v_{i-1}, u_{i+1})$, and hence, $((i, u_i, v_{i-1}), (i+1, u_{i+1}, v_i))$ is an edge in $G_y$. Thus $(0, u_0, v_{N-1}), (1, u_1, v_0), \ldots, (N-1, u_{N-1}, v_{N-2}), (0, u_0, v_{N-1})$ forms a cycle in $G_y$.

On the other hand, since each simple cycle in $G_y$ contains exactly one node from

$$\{i\} \times \mathcal{B}^{l_i} \times \mathcal{B}^{r_{i-1}}.$$

Hence each simple cycle of $G_y$ is of the form

$$(0, u_0, v_{N-1}), (1, u_1, v_0), \ldots, (N-1, u_{N-1}, v_{N-2}), (0, u_0, v_{N-1}).$$

By definition of $G_y$, there exists $x_i$, such that $(y_i, u_i, v_i) = f_i(x_i, v_{i-1}, u_{i+1})$, and therefore $f(x) = y$.
□

We now show how to invert $f$, given $C_i$.

**Inputs:** $y \in \mathcal{B}^m$.

- compute the matrices $M_i$ and $T_i$ for $0 \le i \le N$ using $C_i$;
- construct the digraph $G_y$, using $M_i$'s;
- if $G_y$ has no cycle, then output that there is no $x$ such that $f(x) = y$;
- otherwise, compute a cycle of $G_y$ $(0, u_0, v_{N-1}), \ldots, (N-1, u_{N-1}, v_{N-2}), (0, u_0, v_{N-1})$, and output $x = (x_0, \ldots, x_{N-1})$, where $x_i = T_i[u_i, v_{i-1}, u_{i+1}, v_i]$.

It is easy to check that the above algorithm runs in time $O(2^h n)$. Let $C$ be a circuit that simulates the above algorithm, we have,

**Theorem 4.1** For each $f \in \mathcal{B}_{n,m}$, if there is an $H$-balanced ring-protocol computing $f$ with communication complexity $\Phi_H(f)$, then there is a circuit of size $O(2^{H+\Phi_H(f)} n)$ which computes an inverse of $f$.
□

We say a function $f \in \mathcal{B}_{n,m}$ is $h$-ring-partitionable if it can be computed by an $H$-ring protocol such that $H + \Phi_H(f) \le h$.

**Corollary 4.1** If $f$ is $O(\log n)$-ring-partitionable, then there is a polynomial size circuit computing an inverse of $f$. Hence, there is no one-way function which is $O(\log n)$-ring-partitionable.
□

## 4.2 Trees

We now show that if a function $f$ can be computed by an $H$-balanced tree-protocol with communication complexity $\Phi_H(f)$, then there is a circuit of size $O(2^{H+\Phi_H(f)}n)$ which computes an inverse of $f$.

Without loss of generality, we can assume that trees are rooted. But in the tree-protocol, each node can communicate with any of its neighbor (children and parent). For simplicity of the presentation, we further assume that the trees are binary, i.e., each node has at most two children. Our results can be extended to any bounded degree tree.

Let $\mathcal{P}$ be an $H$-balanced tree-protocol computing $f$ with communication complexity $\Phi_H(f)$; let $(X_0, \ldots, X_{N-1})$ be the $H$-balanced partition induced by $\mathcal{P}$ on inputs and $(Y_0, \ldots, Y_{N-1})$ be the partition on outputs. For each node $i$ in a given tree, let $p(i)$, $lc(i)$, $rc(i)$, be its parent, left child, and right child, respectively. Let $c(i)$ be a child of $i$. Let $p_i$, $l_i$ and $r_i$ be the number of bits the processor $i$ sends to processors $p(i)$, $lc(i)$, and $rc(i)$, respectively. Let $h = H + \Phi_H(f)$. By definitions, we have $p_i + l_i + r_i \leq h$.

We now reduce the inversion problems to the following *consistency problem* on trees.

A *labeled tree* is a 3-tuple $(T, F, Z)$ where $T$ is a rooted tree with $N$ nodes $\{0, .., N-1\}$, $Z = \{Z_0, \ldots, Z_{N-1}\}$, and $G = \{g_0, \ldots, g_{i-1}\}$. Each node $i$ in $T$ is associated with a set $Z_i$ of $k_i$ boolean variables and a $(k_i + k_{p(i)} + k_{lc(i)} + k_{rc(i)})$-place boolean function $g_i$ which only depends on variables with node $i$ and with neighbors of node $i$. An assignment to variables in $Z$ *satisfies* $g_i$, if the value of $g_i$ is 1 under this assignment.

**Definition 4.1 (Consistency Problem on Trees)** *Given a labeled tree* $(T, G, Z)$, *compute an assignment of* $Z$ *which satisfies all functions* $g_i$, $0 \leq i \leq N-1$.

The consistency problem on trees can be solved in $O(2^{\max_i(k_i)}n)$ time by RAKE operation [9, 8, 2]. Recently, the author gave an optimal $O(\log n)$ time algorithm for this problem when $(\max_i k_i)$ is a constant [14].

Let $U_i = (u_{i,1}, \ldots, u_{i,l_i})$, $V_i = (v_{i,1}, \ldots, v_{i,r_i})$, and $W_i = (w_{i,1}, \ldots, w_{i,r_i})$ denote the set of variables of whose values processor $i$ sends to processors $p(i)$, $lc(i)$, and $rc(i)$, respectively, in the protocol $\mathcal{P}$. Notice that the protocol $\mathcal{P}$ defines a natural function $f_i$ associated with processor $i$, from $X_i \cup U_{p(lc(i))} \cup U_{p(rc(i))} \cup W_{c(p(i))}$ to $Y_i \cup U_i \cup V_i \cup W_i$. Because $f_i$ has only $O(h)$ bits inputs, $f_i$ is computable by a circuit of size $O(2^h)$ (see Lemma 3.1). Let $C_i$ be such a circuit computing $f_i$.

Now, let $Z_i = X_i \cup U_i \cup V_i \cup W_i$ and let $g_i$ be a function from $(X_i \cup U_{p(lc(i))} \cup U_{p(rc(i))} \cup W_{c(p(i))} \cup U_i \cup V_i \cup W_i)$ to $B$ such that $g_i$ has value 1 if

$$(y_i \cup U_i \cup V_i \cup W_i) = f_i(X_i \cup U_{p(lc(i))} \cup U_{p(rc(i))} \cup W_{c(p(i))}).$$

¿From the above discussion, we have the following lemma (the proof will appear in the full paper).

**Lemma 4.2** *for each* $y \in B^m$, *for each assignment* $x$ *to* $X$, *there is an assignment,* $u_i$ *to* $U_i$, $v_i$ *to* $V_i$, *and* $w_i$ *to* $W_i$ *satisfying all* $g_i$ *iff* $f(x) = y$.

Therefore, for each $y \in B^m$, in $O(2^h n)$ time, we can, using the algorithm for consistency problem on trees, compute an $x \in B^n$, such that $f(x) = y$ (if such an $x$ exists). Let $C$ be a circuit that simulates the above algorithm, we have,

**Theorem 4.2** *For each $f \in \mathcal{B}_{n,m}$, if there is an $H$-balanced tree-protocol computing $f$ with communication complexity $\Phi_H(f)$, then there is an inversion circuit of size $O(2^{H+\Phi_H(f)}n)$ for $f$.* □

We say a function $f \in \mathcal{B}_{n,m}$ is $h$-tree-partitionable if it can be computed by an $H$-tree-protocol such that $H + \Phi_H(f) \leq h$.

**Corollary 4.2** *If $f$ is $O(\log n)$-tree-partitionable, then there is a polynomial size circuit computing an inverse of $f$. Hence, there is no one-way function which is $O(\log n)$-tree-partitionable.* □

## 4.3 Cliques

In the above two subsections, we show that if the balanced communication complexity (on trees or rings) of a function is small, then there exists a small size circuit computing an inverse of the function. Of course, the results depend critically on the topology of the communication networks. To what topology can our results be extended? We first observe that our result can be extended to $O(\log n)$ by $n$ meshes (the proof will appear given in the full paper).

**Theorem 4.3** *For each $f \in \mathcal{B}_{n,m}$, if there is an $H$-balanced mesh-protocol on the $O(\log n) \times n$ mesh computing $f$ with communication complexity $\Phi_H(f)$, then there exists a circuit of size $O(2^{H+\Phi_H(f)}n^2)$ which computes an inverse of $f$.* □

It is remain open whether the similar result exists for an $n$ by $n$ mesh.

We now show, it is unlikely to extend the results to all topologies with bounded degree. We say a function $f \in \mathcal{B}_{n,m}$ is $k$-partitionable if there is a $k$-balanced protocol on an $n$-clique with communication complexity $\Phi_H(f)$ bounded above by $k$.

**Theorem 4.4** *If[2] $NP \neq P$, there is a 6-partitionable function $f$ such that no polynomial size circuit computes an inverse of $f$.* □

**Proof:** This theorem follows simply from the following lemma.

**Lemma 4.3 (Garey and Johnson)** *The SAT problem, in which each clause contains at most 3 variables or the negation of variables and each variable or its negation is in at most three clause, is $NP$-complete.* □

**Corollary 4.3** *If $NP \neq P$, there is a 6-partitionable function $f$ which is neither $O(\log n)$-ring partitionable, nor $O(\log n)$-tree partitionable.* ■

Similarly, we have,

**Corollary 4.4** *If $NP \neq T(2^{polylog})$, there is a 6-partitionable function $f$ which is neither polylog-ring partitionable nor polylog-tree partitionable.* □

---

[2]In this paper, the notation of $NP \neq P$ denote that there is an NP function which can not be computed by a polynomial size circuit.

# 5 Inverting Planar Circuits

A boolean circuit $C$ is *planar* if (1) the underlying graph of $C$ is planar and (2) all inputs are on the same face of the underlying graph, (this face is called the *input face*).

We now show the relationship between the depth of a planar boolean circuit and the balanced communication complexity (on ring) of the function it computes.

**Lemma 5.1** *If a function $f \in \mathcal{B}_{n,m}$ can be computed by a planar circuit of depth $d$, then $f$ is $O(d)$-ring-partitionable.*

**Proof:** Without loss of generality, we can assume that $C$ is embedded on the surface of a cylinder with the input face at the bottom if the cylinder (see Figure 1).

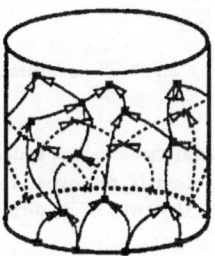

Figure 1: Embedding Planar Circuits on a Cylinder

Since the height of $C$ is $d$, $C$ has a $(1/3, 2/3)$-separator of size $d$ [6, 7] that $(1/2, 2/3)$-splits the inputs (See Figure 2).

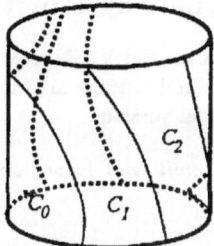

Figure 2: Partition of a Circuit by a $h$-separator

By recursively applying the separator partition, we can partition the circuit into $n'$ components, $C_0, \ldots, C_{n'-1}$, each contains at most $h$-inputs. We say two components are neighbors, if they share some nodes which are removed during the partition. From the construction above, it follows that each component has at most two neighbors. Moreover, no pair of neighbors share more than $d$ nodes which are removed, and hence, without loss of generality, we assume $C_i$ has neighbor $C_{i-1}$ and $C_{i+1}$. Therefore, we have an $d$-balanced ring-protocol with $n'$ nodes, where the processor on node $i$ evaluates the component $C_i$ and communicates with processor on node $i - 1$ and $i + 1$ to evaluate the nodes on the separator. Clearly, the communication complexity $\Phi_H(f)$ is bounded by $O(d)$. □

**Theorem 5.1** *If $f$ can be computed by a planar circuit of depth $d$, then an inverse of $f$ can be computed by a circuit of size $O(2^d n)$.* □

A function $f \in \mathcal{B}^{n,m}$ is $NC^k$-computable if $f$ can be computed by an $O((\log n)^k)$-depth circuit of polynomial size. It is $NC^k$-planar-computable if it can be computed by a $O((\log n)^k)$-depth planar circuit of polynomial size.

**Corollary 5.1** *If $NP \neq P$, then there is an $NC^0$ function which can not be computed by an $NC^1$ planar circuit.* □

Combining with a result of Hastad [3],

**Corollary 5.2** *if $P \neq NC^1$, then there is an $NC^0$ permutation which can not be computed by an $NC^1$ planar circuit.* □

Note that in the definition of the planar circuit, it is crucial to impose the restriction all inputs are on the same face. When this restriction is removed, the class of resulting circuits is called *general planar circuits*. The computational power of general planar circuit is greater than planar circuit (the proof will appear in the full paper).

**Theorem 5.2** *If $NP \neq P$, there is a function $f$ computable by a general planar circuit with constant depth and polynomial size, whose inverse is not computable by any polynomial size circuit.* □

# 6 Area Requirement of One-way Functions

In this section, we prove a lower bound on the VLSI area requirement of one-way functions in Thompson model [15, 5] where all inputs and outputs are on the boundary of the Thompson grid. We can prove (the proof will be in the final version)

**Theorem 6.1** *If a function $f$ has a circuit with layout area $A$, then there is a circuit of size $O(2^{A/n})$ computing an inverse of $f$.* □

**Corollary 6.1** *For all one-way functions $f$, the area required to layout $f$ is at least $\Omega(n \log n)$.* ∎

# 7 Final Remarks

All results presented in the above section are stated in the non-uniform form. Similar uniform version of the results can be proven. We also consider the parallel complexity of inverting boolean circuits. Those results will be included in the full paper. One interesting question remain open is to what topology can our upper bound result be extended. In particular, it is interesting to know whether similar results can be obtained on $n$ by $n$ meshes.

Finally, we have also obtained some results that relates the two-party communication complexity to the complexity of inverting permutations. Those results will be included in the final version of the paper.

Acknowledgments We would like to thank Alan Frieze, Merrick Furst, Hillel Gazit, Manpreet Khaira, Zhi-Li Zhang for helpful discussions.

# References

[1] R. Boppana and J. Lagarias. One-way functions and circuit complexity. In *Proc. Struc. in Compl. Theory, Lect. Notes. in Computer Science.*, 1986.

[2] H. Gazit, G. L. Miller, and S.-H. Teng. Optimal tree contraction in the EREW Model, In *Current Computations edited by S. K. Tewsburg, B. W. Dickinson, and S. C. Schwartz"*, pages 139–156. 1988.

[3] J. Hastad. *Computational Limitations for Small Depth Circuits.* The MIT Press, 1986.

[4] R. Impagliazzo and S. Rudich. Limits on the provable consequence of one-way permutations. In *Proceedings of the 21st Annual ACM Symposium on Theory of Computing*, pages 44–61. 1989.

[5] Frank Thomson Leighton. *Complexity Issues in VLSI.* Foundations of Computing. MIT Press, Cambridge, MA, 1983.

[6] R.J. Lipton and R.E. Tarjan. A separator theorem for planar graphs. *SIAM J. of Appl. Math.*, 36:177–189, April 1979.

[7] G. L. Miller. Finding small simple cycle separators for 2-connected planar graphs. In *Proceedings of the 16th Annual ACM Symposium on Theory of Computing*, pages 376–382, 1984.

[8] G. L. Miller and J. H. Reif. Parallel tree contraction and its applications. In *26th Symposium on Foundations of Computer Science*, pages 478–489, 1985.

[9] J. Pearl. *Heuristics: Intelligent Search Strategies for Computer Problem Solving.* Addison Wesley, 1984.

[10] R. Rivest, A. Shamir, and L. Adleman. A method for obtaining digitial signatures and public–key cryptosystems. *CACM*, 21(2):120–126, 1978.

[11] J. Rompel. One-way functions are necessary and sufficient for secure signatures. In *Proceedings of the 22th Annual ACM Symposium on Theory of Computing*, pages 387–394. 1990.

[12] C. Sturtivant and Z.-L. Zhang. Efficiently inverting bijections given by straight line programs. In *31st Annual Symposium on Foundations of Computer Science*, pages 327–334. 1990.

[13] M. Szegedy. Functions with bounded symmetric communication complexity and circuit with mod $m$ gates. In *Proceedings of the 22th Annual ACM Symposium on Theory of Computing*, pages 278–286. 1990.

[14] S. H. Teng. Fast parallel algorithms for tree-based constraint satisfaction problems. Manuscript, Carnegie Mellon University, 1990.

[15] C. D. Thompson. *A Complexity Theory for VLSI.* PhD thesis, Carnegie-Mellon University, Department of Computer Science, 1980.

[16] A. C.-C. Yao. Theory and application of trapdoor functions. In *23th Annual Symposium on Foundations of Computer Science*, pages 80–91. IEEE, 1982.

[17] A. C.-C. Yao. Some complexity questions related to distributive computing. In *Proceedings of the 11st Annual ACM Symposium on Theory of Computing*, pages 209–213. ACM, 1979.

# The Use of Interaction in Public Cryptosystems.
(extended abstract)

Steven Rudich

School of Computer Science
Carnegie Mellon University
rudich@cs.cmu.edu

### Abstract

For every k, we construct an oracle relative to which secret agreement can be done in k passes, but not in k-1. In particular, for k=3, we get an oracle relative to which secret agreement is possible, but relative to which trapdoor functions do not exist. Thus, *unlike* the case of private cryptosystems, there is no black box reduction from a k-pass system to a k-1 pass system. Our construction is natural– suggesting that real-world protocols could trade higher interaction costs for an assumption strictly weaker than the existence of trapdoor functions. Finding a complexity theoretic assumption necessary and sufficient for public cryptosystems to exist is one of the important open questions of cryptography. Our results make clear the possibility that this question is impossible to answer because it contains a false hidden assumption: the existence of a 2-pass public cryptosystem follows from the existence of a k-pass system. The question should really be a family of questions: given k find an assumption equivalent to the existence of a k-pass public cryptosystem.

# 1 Introduction

An important project in cryptography is to classify protocols according to the complexity theoretic assumptions that are necessary and sufficient to guarantee their existence. This classification not only lends a structure and coherence to the field, but bases the viability of cryptography on the most general possible assumptions (as opposed to those involving specific problems such as factoring). An excellent example of this type of result is that private-key cryptography (under any reasonable definition) is possible if and only if one-way functions exist[ILL89, IL89]. This example leads one to seek a corresponding result for public cryptosystems (being able to send a secret message to a person with whom you share no secret information). Researchers, however, have been unsuccessful in finding a natural, complexity-theoretic assumption that is equivalent to the existence of public cryptosystems. We shed new light on the difficulty of this problem; in the process, we solve some of the main open problems posed in "A Basic Theory of Public and Private Cryptosystems"[Rac88].

Following Rackoff's example, we consider private-key cryptography as the ability to send secret messages to a person with whom you share a secret string; public cryptosys-

J. Feigenbaum (Ed.): Advances in Cryptology - CRYPTO '91, LNCS 576, pp. 242-251, 1992.
© Springer-Verlag Berlin Heidelberg 1992

tems as the ability to send secret messages to a person with whom you share no secret information. In neither type of cryptography, do we include a constant bound on the number of rounds of interaction as part of the definition. Thus, we call it "public cryptography" and not "public-key cryptography" as defined by [DH76]. (From now on, we measure the amount of interaction in terms of passes rather than rounds, e.g., Alice to Bob to Alice is two passes, but only one round.) Although all known protocols for public cryptosystems[DH76, RSA78, GM84] can be easily altered to use no more than two passes, there is no a priori reason to suspect this will always be so. We consider secret agreement as the ability to agree on a secret bit with a person with whom you share no secret information. Under our definitions, secret agreement and public cryptosystems are equivalent; if one is possible so is the other. We will use them interchangeably.

We show that for any $k \geq 2$ there exists an oracle relative to which public cryptosystems are possible in k passes, but not in k-1 passes. Furthermore, the internal structure of the oracle is not an unnatural construct achieved through diagonalization: *it uses a random function which shares features with the discrete-logarithm problem, used by Diffie and Hellman[DH76] in their original protocol for public-key cryptography.* Our result applies directly to Rackoff's problem of finding "a convincing example where extra passes appear to help" achieve secure public cryptosystems. In contrast, Rackoff's problem for private-key cryptography was resolved oppositely. It has been shown that a k-pass private-key cryptosystem exists if and only if a one pass private-key cryptosystem exists[ILL89, IL89]; furthermore, these results have the form of standard *black box* reductions. Our result rules out any black box reduction for public cryptosystems. We think this difference is counter-intuitive. Our oracle is natural and is intended to reflect real world cryptography.

Black box reductions are quite natural to cryptography. Unlike the situation in complexity theory, a black box reduction from A to B is the preferred result. This is because cryptographers ultimately want to implement their work. The reductions should be effective, simple, and modular, e.g., black box. Thus, cryptographers seek other kinds of reductions only as a last resort. Black box reductions are the only type possible when assumption A is physical (e.g., envelopes).

Setting $k = 3$, we get an oracle, $\Gamma$, relative to which three pass public cryptosystems exist, but two pass systems do not. Oracles separations of this kind rule out the black box arguments used in all known cryptographic reductions among protocols which pass information from one party to another (as opposed to zero-knowledge protocols). One interpretation of this result is that the existence of public cryptosystems is not provably equivalent to any complexity-theoretic assumption that in turn implies the existence of a 2-pass cryptosystem. For example, all the notions of a "trapdoor" function or "trapdoor" permutation appearing in the literature[DH76, RSA78, Yao82] imply the existence of a 2-pass public-key cryptosystem. Thus, relative to $\Gamma$, public cryptosystems are possible, but trapdoor functions do not exist; trapdoor functions are not a necessary consequence of public cryptosystems. In the other direction, previous work by Impagliazzo and Rudich[IR89] has shown similar evidence that the existence of a one-way permutation is not sufficient for the existence of public cryptosystems. Combining these results, we are at a loss for a good candidate for a complexity-theoretic assumption characterizing the nature of public cryptography. Perhaps the requirements of public cryptosystems have no natural expression in complexity theory (again, in contrast to private-key cryptography).

The usual protocol design philosophy minimizes the amount of interaction. However, current public cryptosystems are based on specific number theoretic problems (e.g. factoring, discrete-log) which might someday be broken. Our results suggest that public cryptosystems could trade higher amounts of interaction for weaker assumptions less likely to be broken. In particular, we justify the following open problem: Find a 3-pass system based on an assumption which seems to be weaker than the existence of trapdoor functions.

The proof requires a very precise analysis of the information possessed by Alice and Bob at each step. After concluding that the flow of information in a two pass protocol has a restricted form, we show any protocol with this form is insecure. This requires extending the techniques in [IR89].

# 2    Overview of the oracle for three passes versus two

The oracle is inspired by the Diffie–Hellman protocol[DH76]: Alice picks a prime $p$ and a random $a < p$. Alice picks a random $x$, Bob picks a random $y$. Alice sends $a, p$, and $a^x \bmod p$. Bob sends $a^y \bmod p$. Alice computes $(a^y)^x \bmod p$. Bob computes $(a^x)^y \bmod p$. Both parties arrive at the same result. The eavesdropper, Eve, has only seen $a, p, a^x \bmod p$, and $a^y \bmod p$; the only known way for Eve to compute $a^{xy}$ is to compute the discrete-log. The salient feature of this protocol is that commutativity allows Alice and Bob to arrive at the same result by a different calculation.

The oracle will contain two random functions, $\xi$ and $DH$. Function $\xi$ takes an input and returns a random string three times its length. With probability 1, $\xi$ is a 1-1 function for sufficiently large input strings. (Moreover, $\xi$ is the same "annihilating" function defined by Kurtz, Mahaney, and Royer[KMR89]. We will use this fact later.) The function $DH$ is designed to maintain the following property: $DH(x, \xi(y \cdot \xi(x))) =$

$DH(y, \xi(x \cdot \xi(y)))$. ($\cdot$ means concatenation.) Apart from this property, $DH$ is a random function, i.e. we know the above pair is equal to the same random bit. (We also include a PSPACE-complete portion of the oracle to insure that protocols which do not use the random functions portion of the oracle are not secure. For example, we want to be sure no two-pass protocol based on factoring or discrete-log could be secure.)

Using this oracle the following three pass protocol is secure: Alice picks a random $x$, Bob picks a random $y$. Alice sends $\xi(x)$. Bob sends $\xi(y)$ and $\xi(y \cdot \xi(x)))$. Alice sends $\xi(x \cdot \xi(y)))$. Alice computes $DH(x, \xi(y \cdot \xi(x)))$. Bob computes $DH(y, \xi(x \cdot \xi(y)))$. They both arrive at the same result.

Why is there no 2-pass protocol relative to this oracle? The precise answer is quite technical. Very generally, we show that no two pass protocol can use the oracle to arrive at the same result by different calculations, i.e., the queries to the oracle that turn out to be useful are exactly those that both parties query. Once this is shown we can use the techniques developed in [IR89] to break the protocol.

More precisely, a *dual pair* is a pair of queries to the $DH$ portion of the oracle having the form $\{(x, \xi(y \cdot \xi(x))), (y, \xi(x \cdot \xi(y)))\}$. The fact that $\xi$ is 1-1 (for suff. large inputs) insures that any two distinct dual pairs are disjoint (for suff. large inputs). A protocol *hits* a dual pair if each query in the pair is made by at least one of the participants. We show that at the moment a two pass protocol hits a dual pair, one of the two participants has already queried both $x$ and $y$. Thus, he/she can calculate both members of the dual pair. This means that one of the two calculations is the same as the one done by his/her partner (in the language of [IR89], an intersection query). The oracle is not being used to arrive at the same result by a different calculation from one's partner. The situation is not substantively different from using a random function oracle with a PSPACE-complete oracle. It has already been shown that relative to such an oracle secure secret agreement (public cryptosystems) is impossible[IR89].

# 3 Notation and definitions

We will abbreviate probabilistic polynomial-time Turing machine with the notation $PPTM$. We use the notation *poly* to refer to some polynomial function. Thus, we can use the freewheeling arithmetic *poly* $*$ *poly* $=$ *poly*. By $x \cdot y$ we mean the concatenation of the strings $x$ and $y$. The three oracle $PPTMs$ (alice, Bob, and Eve) which we will consider will all have access to the same fixed oracle.

A *secret agreement protocol* is a pair of oracle $PPTMs$ called Alice and Bob. Each machine has a set of private tapes: a random-bit tape, an input tape, two work tapes, and a secret tape. In addition, they have a common communication tape that both can read and write. A run of the protocol is as follows: Alice and Bob both start with the same integer parameter $l$ written in unary on their input tapes; Alice and Bob run, communicating via the common tape; Alice and Bob both write a bit on their secret tapes. Alice and Bob run in time polynomial in $l$. ($l$ is often called the *security parameter*.) If this bit is the same, Alice and Bob are said to *agree*. It should be noted that a protocol which can agree on a bit can be run multiple times to agree on a string; we will consider only protocols which agree on a single bit. The entire history of the writes to the communication tape is called *the conversation*. $\alpha(l)$ will denote the probability that Alice and Bob agree on the same bit.

An oracle $PPTM$ Eve *breaks* a secret agreement protocol if Eve, given only $l$ and the conversation, can guess the bit with probability greater than $1/2 + 1/poly(l)$. Eve can only use time bounded by a polynomial in $l$. A protocol is *secure* if no Eve can break it.

# 4 Construction of the oracle for $k = 3$

Let $\xi$ be a random function which takes any input string to a string of independent random bits three times the length of the input string. Let $\mu$ be random function from unordered pairs of strings to a random bit. To any particular choice of $\xi$ and $\mu$ we can associate a binary function $DH$ defined by the following property (assuming $\xi$ is 1-1):

$$DH(p, \xi(q \cdot \xi(p))) = DH(q, \xi(p \cdot \xi(q))) = \mu(\{p, q\})$$

$DH$ is undefined everywhere else. Of course, $\xi$ might not be 1-1. But with probability one, $\xi$ fails to be 1-1 for finitely many inputs[KMR89]. So with probability one, $DH$ is well defined for sufficiently large inputs; we can make all the small inputs evaluate to zero.

We construct a random $\Gamma$ as follows. Pick a random $\xi$ and $\mu$. Now construct an oracle with three parts:

- The function $\xi$.
- The function $DH$ which is associated with $\xi$ and $\mu$.
- A PSPACE-complete oracle.

By the above remarks, we know that with probability one, $\Gamma$ is well defined. It is important to note that when we say with probability one over random $\Gamma$, we mean over random $\xi$ and $\mu$. This should not be confused with saying that $\Gamma$ is a random oracle. The results in this paper are not being proved relative to a random oracle.

# 5 A three pass public cryptosystem

We can use $\Gamma$ to acheive a three pass public cryptosystem which we call the *natural cryptosystem* associated with $\Gamma$. The following is a protocol for Alice and Bob to agree on a random bit:

Alice and Bob agree on a security parameter $l$. Alice picks a random $x$ of length $l$, Bob picks a random $y$ of length $l$. Alice sends $\xi(x)$. Bob sends $\xi(y)$ and $\xi(y \cdot \xi(x)))$. Alice sends $\xi(x \cdot \xi(y)))$. Alice computes $DH(x, \xi(y \cdot \xi(x)))$. Bob computes $DH(y, \xi(x \cdot \xi(y)))$. They both arrive at the same result.

**Theorem 5.1** *The natural cryptosystem associated with $\Gamma$ is correct and secure with probability one. (If Eve asks a polynomially bounded number of oracle queries, not even infinite computational power will help her guess their secret bit with probability greater than $1/2 + poly(l)/2^l$.)*

**Proof:** The protocol is clearly correct as long as $\Gamma$ is well defined. This happens with probability one.

For the security of the protocol it suffices to argue that knowing the conversation, i.e., $\xi(y)$, $\xi(x)$, $\xi(x \cdot \xi(y)))$, and $\xi(y \cdot \xi(x)))$, does not reveal any information about $x$ or $y$. The proof is standard and we omit it here. ∎

# 6 Three passes are required

In this section we argue that three passes are required for secure secret agreement relative to a random $\Gamma$.

## 6.1 Defining knowledge about the oracle.

It is possible to formalize the notion of an oracle $TM$ knowing certain facts about a random $\Gamma$. We say an oracle $TM$ $T$ *tried* $q$ at a certain point in its computation if it makes a query to $\Gamma$ of the form: $\xi(*q*)$, $DH(*,q)$, or $DH(q,*)$ where $*$ is any string. We say a protocol tried $q$ if either Alice or Bob tried $q$. We say a protocol queries a *dual pair* involving $p$ and $q$ if the protocol has made the queries: $DH(p,\xi(q \cdot \xi(p)))$ and $DH(q,\xi(p \cdot \xi(q)))$.

**Lemma 6.1** *With probability one, over random $\Gamma$, for any oracle PPTM $T$ using $\Gamma$, for sufficiently large $n$ and any string $q$ of length greater than or equal to $n$, the probability (over random tapes of $T$) that $T(n)$ tried $\xi(q)$ at time $t$ without having queried $\xi(q)$ at a time prior to $t$ is bounded by $poly(n)/2^n$.*

Proof description: The proof of lemma 3.4 in [KMR89] already proves the above result for a random oracle $\xi$ (as opposed to $\Gamma$). Their proof techniques can be generalized to $\Gamma$ because the $DH$ portion of the oracle that can be queried without first querying $\xi(q)$ is independent from $\xi(q)$.

This theorem can be equally well applied to protocols rather than to individual machines; a protocol can be simulated by a single $PPTM$.

## 6.2 Two pass protocols have restricted form

**Lemma 6.2** *Any run of a secret agreement which satisfies the following two properties must make at least three passes: 1) The protocol queries some dual pair involving $p$ and $q$, when neither party has tried both $p$ and $q$. 2) The protocol never tries $\xi(q)$ without first having queried $\xi(q)$.*

**Proof:** Suppose Alice made the query $DH(p,\xi(q \cdot \xi(p)))$ and Bob made the query $DH(q,\xi(p \cdot \xi(q)))$. Thus, Alice tried $p$, but not $q$. Bob tried $q$, but not $p$. The protocol tried $\xi(q \cdot \xi(p))$. By property 2, someone queried $\xi(q \cdot \xi(p))$; it must be Bob since it wasn't Alice who tried $q$. Thus, Bob tried $\xi(p)$. Symmetrically, Alice tried $\xi(q)$.

We can now reason about who tried what first. For example, before the protocol tried $\xi(p)$ it must have queried $\xi(p)$ (property 2). Thus either Alice or Bob queried $\xi(p)$; it must have been Alice lest Bob have tried both $p$ and $q$ (contradicting property 1). Thus Alice tried $p$ before Bob tried $\xi(p)$.

Alice tried $\xi(q \cdot \xi(p))$, but did not make that particular query lest Alice have already tried $q$. By property 1, that query was made previously. It must have been made by Bob. Before Bob could have made it, Bob must have tried $\xi(p)$. Thus, Bob tried $\xi(p)$ before Alice tried $\xi(q \cdot \xi(p))$.

Summarizing more succinctly: By property 2 and the definition of trying, Alice tried $p$ before Bob tried $\xi(p)$ before Bob queried $\xi(q \cdot \xi(p))$ before Alice tried $\xi(q \cdot \xi(p))$. Symmetrically, Bob tried $q$ before Alice tried $\xi(q)$ before Bob tried $\xi(p \cdot \xi(q))$. Alice and Bob are both involved in two separate passes. There must have been at least three passes in all.  ∎

We say a protocol has *restricted form* if, with probability one, over random $\Gamma$, for sufficiently large $n$, the protocol will have probability greater than $1 - poly(n)/2^n$ of having a run in which each time the protocol queries a dual pair involving $p$ and $q$ of length greater than $n$, at least one of the two parties has tried both $p$ and $q$.

Combining lemmas 6.1 and 6.2 we get the following result:

**Lemma 6.3** *Any two pass protocol has restricted form.*

## 6.3  Two pass protocols can be broken by Eve

**Lemma 6.4** *With probability one, over random $\Gamma$, any protocol of restricted form can be broken by Eve.*

Proof description: In previous work by Impagliazzo and Rudich[IR89], it is shown that no protocol is secure relative to an oracle with just the $\xi$ and PSPACE-complete portions. Intuitively, a protocol of restricted form just can't make any other use of the $DH$ portion of the oracle besides extracting random bits from it; thus, such a protocol is no more secure than it would be using only the $\xi$ portion of the oracle.

[IR89] rely on the notion of an *intersection query*, a query to the oracle that is made by both Alice and Bob. They show that if Eve has figured out all the intersection queries that occurred before a given time, then Eve has a high probability of figuring out the next intersection query. By maintaining this inductive procedure Eve can figure out the final intersection query, namely, the secret itself.

If a protocol using $\Gamma$ has restricted form, we can assume without loss of generality when the protocol queries a dual pair the party that tried both $p$ and $q$ (with high probability one of the parties tried this, unless the queries are very short and clearly useless) can ask both queries in the dual pair. Thus, Alice and Bob will intersect on this dual pair. Using the techniques Impagliazzo and Rudich, it can be shown that Eve can use the same inductive procedure on the intersection queries.

# 7 Putting it together

Combining lemmas 5.1 and 6.3 with the above theorem we get:

**Theorem 7.1** *With probability one over random* $\Gamma$*, a three pass public cryptosystem exists, but a two pass system does not.*

**Corollary 7.1** *There exists an oracle relative to which public cryptosystems exist, but trapdoor functions do not.*

This corollary should be contrasted with the result in [IR89] stating the existence of an oracle relative to which one-way permutations exists, public cryptosystems do not.

To generalize the oracle construction to $k > 3$, we simply have to change the definition of the $DH$ function portion of the oracle. For example, for $k = 4$, $DH$ is defined by the following property:

$$DH(p, \xi(q \cdot \xi(p \cdot \xi(q)))) = DH(q, \xi(p \cdot \xi(q \cdot \xi(p)))) = \mu(\{p, q\})$$

The proof techniques in this paper remain unaffected.

We get:

**Theorem 7.2** *For any* $k \geq 2$*, there exists an oracle relative to which k pass public cryptosystems are possible, but k-1 pass systems do not.*

# 8 Acknowledgments

I would like to thank Charlie Rackoff, Jim Mcinness, and Russell Impagliazzo for helpful discussions.

# References

[DH76] W. Diffie and M. E. Hellman. New directions in cryptography. *IEEE Transactions on Information Theory*, IT-22:644–654, 1976.

[GM84] S. Goldwasser and S. Micali. Probabilistic encryption. *Journal of Computer and System Sciences*, 28:270–299, 1984.

[IL89] R. Impagliazzo and M. Luby. One-way functions are essential for complexity based cryptography. In *Proceedings of the 30th Annual Symposium on Foundations of Computer Science*, IEEE, 1989.

[ILL89] R. Impagliazzo, L. Levin, and M. Luby. Pseudo-random number generation from one-way functions. In *Proceedings of the 21st Annual Symposium on Theory of Compu ting*, ACM, 1989.

[IR89] R. Impagliazzo and S. Rudich. Limits on the provable consequences of one-way permutations. In *Proceedings of the 21st Annual Symposium on Theory of Compu ting*, ACM, 1989.

[KMR89] S. Kurtz, S. Mahaney, and J. Royer. The isomorphism conjecture fails relative to a random oracle. In *Proceedings of the 21st Annual Symposium on Theory of Compu ting*, ACM, 1989.

[Rac88] Charles Rackoff. A basic theory of public and private cryptosystems. In *Proceedings of Advances in Cryptography*, CRYPTO, 1988.

[RSA78] R. Rivest, A. Shamir, and L. Adelman. A method for obtaining digital signatures and public-key cryptosystems. *Communications. ACM.*, 21(2):120–126, Feb 1978.

[Yao82] A.C. Yao. Theory and applications of trapdoor functions. In *Proceedings of the 23rd Annual Symposium on Foundations of Computer Science*, pages 80–91, IEEE, 1982.

# New Public-Key Schemes Based on Elliptic Curves over the Ring $Z_n$

Kenji Koyama*
Ueli M. Maurer[†]
Tatsuaki Okamoto[‡]
Scott A. Vanstone[§]

**ABSTRACT**   Three new trapdoor one-way functions are proposed that are based on elliptic curves over the ring $Z_n$. The first class of functions is a naive construction, which can be used only in a digital signature scheme, and not in a public-key cryptosystem. The second, preferred class of function, does not suffer from this problem and can be used for the same applications as the RSA trapdoor one-way function, including zero-knowledge identification protocols. The third class of functions has similar properties to the Rabin trapdoor one-way functions. Although the security of these proposed schemes is based on the difficulty of factoring $n$, like the RSA and Rabin schemes, these schemes seem to be more secure than those schemes from the viewpoint of attacks without factoring such as low multiplier attacks. The new schemes are somewhat less efficient than the RSA and Rabin schemes.

## 1   Introduction

In their seminal 1976 paper [3], Diffie and Hellman introduced the concept of a trapdoor one-way function (TOF). A TOF is a function that is easy to evaluate but infeasible to invert, unless a secret trapdoor is known, in which case the inversion is also easy. Although no realisation of a TOF was proposed in [3], Diffie and Hellman observed that such a function would allow the construction of digital signature schemes and public-key cryptosystems, two concepts that they introduced.

The first implementation of a TOF was proposed by Rivest, Shamir and Adleman in 1978 [21]. Its security relies on the difficulty of factoring a composite number $n$. Some other implementations [20, 4] of TOFs have been proposed based on the difficulty of factoring and discrete logarithms. From another direction, one of the recent topics in the field of elliptic curves is their applicability to cryptography. The points of an elliptic curve $E$ over a *finite field* form an abelian group, and hence the group $E$ can be used to implement analogs of the Diffie-Hellman key exchange scheme and the ElGamal public key cryptosystem, as explained in [9]. The security of these analogous systems rests on the difficulty of the discrete logarithm problem on an elliptic curve.

*NTT Laboratories, Sanpeidani, Inuidani, Seikacho, Kyoto, 619-02, Japan
[†]Princeton University, Princeton, NJ 08544, USA; Supported by Omnisec AG, Switzerland
[‡]NTT Laboratories, Yokosuka-shi, Kanagawa 238-03, Japan
[§]University of Waterloo, Ontario, N2L 3G1, Canada

J. Feigenbaum (Ed.): Advances in Cryptology - CRYPTO '91, LNCS 576, pp. 252-266, 1992.
© Springer-Verlag Berlin Heidelberg 1992

In this paper, we propose new TOFs (or public-key cryptographic schemes) based on elliptic curves over a *ring* $Z_n$. The security of these TOFs depends on the difficulty of factoring $n$. Although these schemes are less efficient than the RSA and Rabin schemes, our schemes seem to be more secure from the viewpoint of some attacks that do not use factoring such as low multiplier attacks. In this case, even when the RSA system can be broken without factoring the modulus, our schemes seem to remain secure.

We begin with a brief review of the basic definitions and facts about elliptic curves over a finite field. In Section 3, we show some properties of elliptic curves over a ring, which are used in the succeeding sections. Section 4 proposes a naive construction of the TOF (Type 0 scheme) based on elliptic curves over a ring, but which can be used only in a digital signature scheme, and not in a public-key cryptosystem. In Sections 5 and 6, we propose the Type 1 and Type 2 schemes respectively based on the elliptic curve over a ring, and discuss their properties. Section 7 discusses the security of the proposed schemes, and Section 8 discusses their performance.

## 2 Elliptic Curves over a Finite Field

Let $K$ be a field of characteristic $\neq 2, 3$, and let $a, b \in K$ be two parameters satisfying $4a^3 + 27b^2 \neq 0$. An elliptic curve over $K$ with parameters $a$ and $b$ is defined as the set of points $(x, y)$ with $x, y \in K$ satisfying the equation

$$y^2 = x^3 + ax + b,$$

together with a special element denoted $\mathcal{O}$ and called the point at infinity. We will mainly be interested in elliptic curves over the finite field $\mathbf{F}_p$ with $p$ elements, for some prime $p$. Such a curve will be denoted $E_p(a, b)$. What makes elliptic curves interesting in cryptography is the fact that an addition operation on the points of an elliptic curve can be defined that makes it into an abelian group. This addition operation, which has but its name in common with the ordinary addition of integers, is described in the following.

Let $E$ be an elliptic curve, and let $P$ and $Q$ be two points on $E$. The point $P + Q$ is defined according to the following rules. If $P = \mathcal{O}$, then $-P = \mathcal{O}$, and $P + Q = Q$ (i.e., $\mathcal{O}$ is the neutral element of $E$). Let $P = (x_1, y_1)$ and $Q = (x_2, y_2)$. If $x_1 = x_2$ and $y_1 = -y_2$, then $P + Q = \mathcal{O}$ (i.e., the negative of the point $(x, y)$ is the point $(x, -y)$). In all other cases the coordinates of $P + Q = (x_3, y_3)$ are computed as follows. Let $\lambda$ be defined as

$$\lambda = \begin{cases} \dfrac{y_2 - y_1}{x_2 - x_1} & \text{if } x_1 \neq x_2 \\ \dfrac{3x_1^2 + a}{2y_1} & \text{if } x_1 = x_2. \end{cases}$$

(When $P + Q \neq \mathcal{O}$, then the denominator is always non-zero and thus the quotient is defined.) The resulting point $P + Q = (x_3, y_3)$ is defined by

$$x_3 = \lambda^2 - x_1 - x_2$$
$$y_3 = \lambda(x_1 - x_3) - y_1.$$

Clearly, the first equation is equivalent to $x_3 = \lambda^2 - 2x_1$ when $P = Q$. All computations are in the field over which $E$ is defined. In particular, when the field is $\mathbf{F}_p$, all computations are modulo $p$.

Let $\#E_p(a, b)$ denote the order (i.e., the number of points) of the elliptic curve $E_p(a, b)$. It is well-known that $\#E_p(a, b) = p + 1 + t$ where $|t| \leq 2\sqrt{p}$ for every elliptic curve over $\mathbf{F}_p$. Every value of $t$ within the given bounds is taken for some pair $(a, b)$, but this fact will not be used in this paper. There exists a polynomial-time algorithm due to Schoof [22] for computing the order of an elliptic curve, but this algorithm is quite impractical for large $p$. It is known that $E_p(a, b)$ is either cyclic or the product of two cyclic groups. In the latter case, $E_p(a, b) \cong \mathbf{Z}_{N_1} \times \mathbf{Z}_{N_2}$ where $N_1 \cdot N_2 = \#E_p(a, b)$, where $N_2$ divides $N_1$ and where $N_2$ also divides $p - 1$. We refer to [9] for a more detailed introduction to elliptic curves, and to [8] for some further cryptographically useful properties of elliptic curves.

For some special classes of elliptic curves the order and group structure is easily determined. The following well known two lemmas illustrate this point.

**Lemma 1.** *Let $p$ be an odd prime satisfying $p \equiv 2 \pmod 3$. Then, for $0 < b < p$, $E_p(0, b)$ is a cyclic group of order*

$$\#E_p(0, b) = p + 1.$$

**Proof.** We first prove that $\#E_p(0, b) = p + 1$. When $p \equiv 2 \pmod 3$ then the mapping $x \mapsto x^3$ is a permutation on $\mathbf{F}_p$. Hence for every $b$ there are exactly $(p - 1)/2$ numbers $x \in \mathbf{F}_p$ for which $x^3 + b$ is a quadratic residue, and for each such $x$ there are two points on $E_p(0, b)$, viz., the points $(x, \pm\sqrt{x^3 + b})$. Together with the points $(\sqrt[3]{-b}, 0)$ and $\mathcal{O}$ there are $p + 1$ points on $E_p(0, b)$. To prove that $E_p(0, b)$ is cyclic (see also [8]), suppose it is not. Then $E_p(0, b) \cong \mathbf{Z}_{N_1} \times \mathbf{Z}_{N_2}$ where $N_1 N_2 = p + 1$ and $N_2$ divides $p - 1$. Hence $N_2 = 2$ and $N_1$ is even. Then the group $\mathbf{Z}_{N_1} \times \mathbf{Z}_2$ must have four elements $P$ for which $-P = P$. However, there are exactly two points, $P = \mathcal{O}$ and $(\sqrt[3]{(-b)}, 0)$ for which $-P = P$, since the only points $P$ on $E_p(0, b)$ for which $-P = P$ are the points $(x, y)$ with $y = 0$. This contradiction implies $E_p(0, b)$ is cyclic. $\square$

**Lemma 2.** *Let $p$ be a prime satisfying $p \equiv 3 \pmod 4$. Then, for $0 < a < p$, we have*

$$\#E_p(a, 0) = p + 1.$$

*Moreover, $E_p(a, 0)$ is cyclic if $a$ is a quadratic residue modulo $p$ and $E_p(a, 0) \cong \mathbf{Z}_{(p+1)/2} \times \mathbf{Z}_2$ otherwise.*

**Proof.** Let $f(x) = x^3 + ax$. $f(x)$ is an odd function, i.e., $f(-x) = -f(x)$. The condition $p \equiv 3 \pmod 4$ implies that for every $s \in \mathbf{Z}_p^*$, exactly one of the two numbers $s$ or $-s$ is a quadratic residue modulo $p$. This follows from the fact that $(p - 1)/2$ is odd and thus $-1$ is a quadratic non-residue modulo $p$. Consider the $(p - 1)/2$ pairs $[x, -x]$ for $0 < x \leq (p - 1)/2$. For every such pair, either $f(x) = f(-x) = 0$ or $f(x)$ is a quadratic residue or $f(-x)$ is a quadratic residue. In either of the three cases, there exist 2 point on $E_p(a, b)$ associated with the pair $[x, -x]$, viz., $(\pm x, 0)$, $(x, \pm\sqrt{f(x)})$ or $(-x, \pm\sqrt{-f(x)})$, respectively. Together with $(0, 0)$ and $\mathcal{O}$ the total number of points on $E_p(a, b)$ is $p + 1$. The proof of the last claim is similar to the proof given for Lemma 1. $\square$

# 3   Elliptic Curves over a Ring

We now consider elliptic curves over the ring $\mathbf{Z}_n$, where $n$ is an odd composite squarefree integer. (An alternative notation for $\mathbf{Z}_n$ used in the literature is $\mathbf{Z}/n\mathbf{Z}$.) Similar to the definition of $E_p(a, b)$, an elliptic curve $E_n(a, b)$ can be defined as the set of pairs $(x, y) \in \mathbf{Z}_n^2$ satisfying $y^2 \equiv x^3 + ax + b \pmod{n}$, together with a point $\mathcal{O}$ at infinity. An addition operation on $E_n(a, b)$ can be defined in the same way as the addition operation on $E_p(a, b)$, simply by replacing computations in $\mathbf{F}_p$ by computations in $\mathbf{Z}_n$. However, two problems occur. The first problem is that because the computation of $\lambda$ requires a division which in a ring is defined only when the divisor is a unit, the addition operation on $E_n(a, b)$ is not always defined. The second problem, which is related to the first is that $E_n(a, b)$ is not a group. It would therefore seem impossible to base a cryptographic system on $E_n(a, b)$. In the following we present a natural solution to these problems.

For the sake of simplicity, let $n = pq$ in the sequel be the product of only two primes as in the RSA system. Moreover, the addition operation on $E_n(a, b)$ described above, whenever it is defined, is equivalent to the (componentwise defined) group operation on $E_p(a, b) \times E_q(a, b)$. By the Chinese Remainder Theorem, every element $c$ of $\mathbf{Z}_n$ can be represented uniquely as a pair $[c_p, c_q]$ where $c_p \in \mathbf{Z}_p$ and $c_q \in \mathbf{Z}_q$. Thus every point $P = (x, y)$ on $E_n(a, b)$ can be represented uniquely as a pair $[P_p, P_q] = [(x_p, y_p), (x_q, y_q)]$ where $P_p \in E_p(a, b)$ and $P_q \in E_q(a, b)$, with the convention that $\mathcal{O}$ is represented by $[\mathcal{O}_p, \mathcal{O}_q]$, where $\mathcal{O}_p$ and $\mathcal{O}_q$ are the points at infinity on $E_p(a, b)$ and $E_q(a, b)$, respectively. By this mapping, all elements of $E_p(a, b) \times E_q(a, b)$ are exhausted except the pairs of points $[P_p, P_q]$ for which exactly one of the points $P_p$ and $P_q$ is the point at infinity. Note that the addition operation on $E_n(a, b)$ described above is undefined if and only if the resulting point, when interpreted as an element of $E_p(a, b) \times E_q(a, b)$, is one of these special points.

It is important to note that when all prime factors of $n$ are large, it is extremely unlikely that the sum of two points on $E_n(a, b)$ is undefined. In fact, if the probability of the addition operation being undefined were non-negligible, then the very execution of a computation on $E_n(a, b)$ would be a feasible factoring algorithm, which is assumed not to exist. Therefore, the first problem will cause no difficulties in practice.

The second problem, that $E_n(a, b)$ is not a group, can be solved by the following lemma. That is, although we cannot use the properties of a finite group directly, we can use a property of $E_n(a, b)$ which is similar to that of a finite group. The following lemma can be easily obtained from the Chinese Remainder Theorem.

**Lemma 3.** *Let $E_n(a, b)$ be an elliptic curve such that $\gcd(4a^3 + 27b^2, n) = 1$ and $n = pq$ $(p, q: \text{prime})$. Let $N_n$ be $\operatorname{lcm}(\#E_p(a, b), \#E_q(a, b))$. Then, for any $P \in E_n(a, b)$, and any integer $k$,*

$$(k \cdot N_n + 1) \cdot P = P \text{ over } E_n(a, b).$$

We should note that it is possible to define an elliptic curve over a ring so that the resulting structure is a group. For our purposes, this is unnecessary.

# 4 Naive Construction of TOF Based on Elliptic Curves over a Ring

In this section, we show a naive construction of TOFs (Type 0 scheme) which are based on elliptic curves over a ring. These TOFs can be used only in a digital signature scheme, and not in a public-key cryptosystem. The shortcomings of the TOFs of this section are elliminated in the Type 1 and 2 schemes shown in following sections.

A digital signature scheme based on $E_n(a, b)$ can be set up as follows. The signer Alice chooses two primes $p$ and $q$ (or, more generally, a set of two or more distinct primes) and two parameters $a$ and $b$ satisfying $\gcd(4a^3 + 27b^2, n) = 1$, where $n = pq$. She then computes the orders of the elliptic curves $E_p(a, b)$ and $E_q(a, b)$ (for example using Schoof's algorithm [22]), chooses a public encryption multiple $e$ relatively prime to both $\#E_p(a, b)$ and $\#E_q(a, b)$, and computes the secret decryption multiple $d$ according to

$$d \equiv e^{-1} \pmod{\mathrm{lcm}(\#E_p(a, b), \#E_q(a, b))}.$$

Alice releases as public parameters $n, a, b$ and $e$. When she later wants to sign a message $M$ she associates a point $P = (x, y) \in E_n(a, b)$ with $M$ in a publicly-known way (see below) and computes the point $Q = (s, t)$ on $E_n(a, b)$ according to

$$Q = (s, t) = d \cdot P.$$

The signature for the message $M$ is the pair $(s, t)$, which can be checked by computing

$$P = (x, y) = e \cdot Q$$

on $E_n(a, b)$ and extracting the message $M$ from $(x, y)$ (because $(ed) \cdot P = P$ from Lemma 3).

Here, given a message $M$, a point $(x, y)$ on $E_n(a, b)$ can efficiently be associated with $M$. $M$ is first padded with sufficient redundancy, for instance by appending zero's to $M$, resulting in $M'$. $x$ is defined as the smallest integer greater or equal to $M'$ such that $x^3 + ax + b$ is a quadratic residue modulo $n$, and $y$ is defined as one of the square roots modulo $n$ of this number.

The shortcomings of this scheme are as follows:
(1) Schoof's algorithm [22] to compute $\#E_p(a, b)$ and $\#E_q(a, b)$ is infeasible for large $p$.
(2) The signature is roughly twice as long as the original message $M$.
(3) This scheme cannot be used for a public-key cryptosystem, since knowledge of the trapdoor is required to create a point on $E_n(a, b)$, which corresponds to a plaintext.

This scheme may be advantageous in some circumstances. It does allow digital signature without the possibility of encryption.

# 5 Basic TOF Based on Elliptic Curves over a Ring

In this section, we propose a new TOF (Type 1 scheme) that is based on elliptic curves over a ring. It overcomes the three shortcomings of the Type 0 scheme. For simplicity, we show a protocol for a public-key cryptosystem based on elliptic curves as described in Lemma 1. We can easily construct a public-key cryptosystem in the case of Lemma 2, and digital signature schemes, although we omit a description.

**Step 0 (Key Generation)** User U chooses large primes $p$ and $q$ such that

$$p \equiv q \equiv 2 \pmod 3.$$

U computes the product $n = pq$, and $N_n = \mathrm{lcm}(\#E_p(0, b), \#E_q(0, b)) = \mathrm{lcm}(p + 1, q + 1)$.

U chooses an integer $e$ which is coprime to $N_n$, and computes an integer $d$ such that

$$ed \equiv 1 \pmod{N_n}.$$

Summarizing, U's secret key is $d$, $(p, q, \#E_p(0, b), \#E_q(0, b), N_n)$, and U's public key is $n, e$.

**Step 1 (Encryption)** A plaintext $M = (m_x, m_y)$ is an integer pair, where $m_x \in \mathbf{Z}_n$, $m_y \in \mathbf{Z}_n$. Let $M = (m_x, m_y)$ be a point on the elliptic curve $E_n(0, b)$, where $b$ is determined by $m_x$ and $m_y$.

Sender A encrypts the point $M$ by encryption function $\mathbf{E}(\cdot)$ with the receiver's public key $e$ and $n$ as

$$C = \mathbf{E}(M) = e \cdot M \text{ over } E_n(0, b),$$

and sends a ciphertext pair $C = (c_x, c_y)$ to a receiver B.

**Step 2 (Decryption)** Receiver B decrypts a point $C$ by decryption function $\mathbf{D}(\cdot)$ with his secret key $d$ and public key $n$ as

$$M = \mathbf{D}(C) = d \cdot C \text{ over } E_n(0, b).$$

**[Notes]**

1. In the case of Lemma 1, the minimum possible value of $e$ is 5 because $2|N_n$ and $3|N_n$. In the case of Lemma 2, the minimum possible value of $e$ is 3 because $2|N_n$.

2. For elliptic curves, the addition formula is independent of $a$ and $b$, and the doubling formula is independent of $b$. Thus, the above protocol does not require computation of the value $b = y^2 - x^3 \bmod n$. If Lemma 2 is adopted, for the addition formula the sender S must compute $a$ such that $a = (m_y^2 - m_x^3)/m_x \bmod n$, and the receiver R must compute $a$ such that $a = (c_y^2 - c_x^3)/c_x \bmod n$.

3. This scheme has the interesting property that it is not defined on a single group but on a large class of groups, all with the same order. The curve to be used is determined by the plaintext to be transmitted.

# 6 Rabin-type Generalization

## 6.1 Protocol

We propose another TOF (Type 2 Scheme) also based on elliptic curves over a ring, which is the Rabin-type generalization of the basic TOF (Type 1 scheme). The Type 2 scheme also overcomes the three deficiencies of the Type 0 scheme. For simplicity, we described the protocol for a public-key cryptosystem based on elliptic curves described in Lemma 1.

**Step 0 (Key Generation)** User U chooses large primes $p$ and $q$ such that

$$p \equiv q \equiv 2 \pmod 3.$$

U computes the product $n = pq$, and the orders $N_p = \#E_p(0, b) = p + 1$ and $N_q = \#E_q(0, b) = q + 1$.

Summarizing, U's secret key is $p$, $q$, $N_p$, $N_q$, and U's public key is $n$.

**Step 1 (Encryption)** A plaintext $M = (m_x, m_y)$ is an integer pair, where $m_x \in \mathbf{Z}_n$, $m_y \in \mathbf{Z}_n$. Let $M = (m_x, m_y)$ be a point on the elliptic curve $E_n(0, b)$, where $b$ is determined by $m_x$ and $m_y$.

Sender A encrypts the point $M$ by doubling on the elliptic curve $E_n$ with the receiver's public key $n$ as

$$C = 2 \cdot M \text{ over } E_n(0, b),$$

and sends a ciphertext pair $C = (c_x, c_y)$ to a receiver B.

**Step 2 (Decryption)** Receiver B computes $M_p \in E_p(0, b)$ and $M_q \in E_q(0, b)$ from $C_p = (c_x \bmod p, \; c_y \bmod p) \in E_p(0, b)$ and $C_q = (c_x \bmod q, \; c_y \bmod q) \in E_q(0, b)$ such that

$$C_p = 2 \cdot M_p \text{ over } E_p(0, b), \quad C_q = 2 \cdot M_q \text{ over } E_q(0, b),$$

by using a halving algorithm, which is described in Section 6.2.

B computes $M = (m_x, m_y) \in E_n$ from $M_p = (m_{px}, m_{py}) \in E_p(0, b)$ and $M_q = (m_{qx}, m_{qy}) \in E_q(0, b)$ using the Chinese Remainder Theorem.

**[Notes]**

1. Since both $N_p$ and $N_q$ are even, 2 is not coprime to $N_p$, $N_q$ and $N_n$.

2. The Type 2 scheme has the drawback that there is 4:1 ambiguity in the decrypted messages, as is true for the original Rabin scheme.

3. In decryption based on a halving formula, the algorithm for finding a non-double point requires an exact expression of the elliptic curve. Thus, the receiver B must compute $b$ such that $b = c_y^2 - c_x^3 \bmod n$.

## 6.2 Halving Algorithm

In general, points on $E_p(a, b) : y^2 = x^3 + ax + b \bmod p$ can be separated into 2 classes, as integers in $\mathbf{Z}_p$ are classified into quadratic residue and quadratic non-residue modulo $p$.

**Definition** If $P = 2 \cdot X$ over $E_p(a, b)$ for some point $X$ on the curve $E_p(a, b)$, then we call point $P$ a *double point*, where we denote the set of all double points by $DP_p$. If $P \neq 2 \cdot X$ over $E_p(a, b)$ for any point $X$, then we call point $P$ a *non-double point*, where we denote the set of all non-double points by $NDP_p$. $\square$

Double points and non-double points are distinguishable by using the following three lemmas, when the group structure of $E_p(a, b)$ is known.

**Lemma 4.** Assume that $E'$ is a cyclic subgroup of $E_p(a, b)$ having the maximum order $N'$. Let $P$ be in $E'$, and $N'$ be even. Then

$$P \in DP_p \text{ if and only if } N'/2 \cdot P = \mathcal{O} \text{ over } E_p(a, b),$$

**Lemma 5.** Assume that $E'$ is a cyclic subgroup of $E_p(a, b)$ with the maximum order $N'$. Let $\alpha$ be the cardinality of $DP_p$ in $E'$. Then

$$\alpha = \begin{cases} N'/2, & \text{if } N' \text{ is even;} \\ N', & \text{if } N' \text{ is odd.} \end{cases}$$

**Lemma 6.** Assume that $E_p(a,b)$ has the group structure $\mathbf{Z}_{(p+1)/2} \times \mathbf{Z}_2$. Let $E'$ be a cyclic subgroup of $E_p(a,b)$ with the maximum order $(p+1)/2$ and let $Q$ be a point in this subgroup. Then

$$P \in DP_p \text{ and } P \in E' \text{ if and only if } e_{(p+1)/2}(P,Q) = 1 \text{ and } (p+1)/4 \cdot P = \mathcal{O} \text{ over } E_p(a,b),$$

where $e_{(p+1)/2}$ is the Weil pairing function [8, 19]. Note that $(p+1)/2$ is always even.

Next, consider a halving algorithm on elliptic curve $E_p(a,b)$ which outputs a half point of a given point over $E_p(a,b)$.

The algorithm of Adleman, Manders and Miller [1, 11] for computing a square root mod $p$ is easily adapted to a halving algorithm in $E_p(a,b)$. For completeness we describe the result.

**Theorem 7.** There exists an expected polynomial time algorithm which, given an odd prime $p$, an elliptic curve $E_p(a,b)$ in the case of Lemma 1 or 2, $N_p$, and a point $Q \in DP_p$ as inputs, will output a half point of $Q$ over $E_p(a,b)$.

The proof of Theorem 7 is a direct consequence of the following algorithm.

**Halving Algorithm on Elliptic Curve for Type 2 scheme**
  Input: $p$ (prime), $E_p(a,b)$, $N_p$, $Q$ $(= 2 \cdot H) \in E_p(a,b)$.
  Step 1. Compute an odd $c$, and $h$ such that $N_p = 2^h c$.
  Step 2. Choose random point $T$ such that $T \in NDP_p$ and $T$ is in the maximum
          cyclic subgroup including $Q$.
  Step 3. Set $Y = Q$, $H = (c+1)/2 \cdot Q$ over $E_p(a,b)$.
  Step 4. Find the least $k$ such that $(2^k c) \cdot Y = \mathcal{O}$ over $E_p(a,b)$.
  Step 5. If $k = 0$ then output $H$; else set

$$Y = Y - 2^{h-k} \cdot T \text{ over } E_p(a,b), \quad H = H - 2^{h-k-1} \cdot c \cdot T \text{ over } E_p(a,b)$$

   and go to step 4.
  Output: $H$.

An algorithm for finding a non-double point $T$ is derived from Lemmas 4 and 6 as follows:

**Algorithm 1 for Finding a Non-Double Point ($E_p(a,b)$: cyclic)**
  Input: $p$ (prime), $E_p(a,b)$, $N_p$.
  Step 1. Choose a random point $T = (t_x, t_y)$ on the curve.
  Step 2. If $T$ is a non-double point, that is, $N_p/2 \cdot T \neq \mathcal{O}$ over $E_p(a,b)$,
            then output $T$; else go to step 1.
  Output: $T = (t_x, t_y) \in NDP_p$.

**Algorithm 2 for Finding a Non-Double Point ($E_p(a,0) \cong \mathbf{Z}_{(p+1)/2} \times \mathbf{Z}_2$)**
  Input: $p$ (prime), $E_p(a,0)$, $N_p$, $Q \in E_p(a,0)$.
  Step 1. Choose a random point $T = (t_x, t_y)$ on the curve $E_p(a,0)$ such that
            $e_n(Q,T) = 1$.
  Step 2. If $T$ is a non-double point, that is, $(p+1)/4 \cdot T \neq \mathcal{O}$ over $E_p(a,0)$,
            then output $T$; else go to step 1.

Output: $T$ such that $T = (t_x, t_y) \in NDP_p$, and $T \in E'$, where $E'$ is a cyclic subgroup of $E_p(a, 0)$ with the maximum order of $(p + 1)/2$ which includes point $Q$.

There exists a polynomial time general algorithm for finding a point on the elliptic curve [9]. In case 1, for any $y \in Z_p$, the point $((y^2 - b)^{1/3}, y)$ is on the curve. Since $3 \nmid p - 1$, the value of $(y^2 - b)^{1/3}$ can be easily computed by $(y^2 - b)^\beta \bmod p$, where $3\beta \equiv 1 \bmod (p - 1)$. In case 2, for any $x \in Z_p$, the point $(x, (x^3 + ax)^{1/2})$ is on the curve. Since $p = 4k + 3$ ($k$ : integer), the value of $(x^3 + ax)^{1/2}$ can be easily computed by $(x^3 + ax)^{k+1} \bmod p$.

# 7 Security

The security of the proposed Type 1 scheme and Type 2 scheme over elliptic curves is based on the difficulty of factoring $n$. In this section, we discuss the security of these schemes from various viewpoints.

## 7.1 Solving the Order

The original RSA and Rabin schemes can be broken if one can determine order of the multiplicative groups. It is known that finding $\phi(n) = (p - 1)(q - 1)$ is computationally equivalent to factoring $n$. That is, the former is polynomially reducible to the latter, and vice versa. In our proposed schemes (Types 1 and 2 in the cases of Lemmas 1 and 2), a similar relationship holds.

**Theorem 8.** *Let $N_n$ be $\mathrm{lcm}(\#E_p(a, b), \#E_q(a, b)) = \mathrm{lcm}(p + 1, q + 1)$. Finding $N_n$ is computationally equivalent to factoring the composite number $n$.*

## 7.2 Finding the Secret Key

The security of the original RSA scheme is also based on the difficulty of finding the secret exponent key. The security of the Type 1 scheme is also based on the difficulty of finding the secret multiplier key $d$. We have the following relationship.

**Theorem 9.** *Solving a secret key $d$ from public keys $e$ and $n$ is computationally equivalent to factoring a composite number $n$.*

## 7.3 Complete Breaking

*Completely breaking* Type 1 and 2 schemes means to recover both $m_x$ and $m_y$ from any ciphertext pair $(c_x, c_y)$ and the public keys. It is well known that completely breaking the original Rabin cryptosystem is as hard as factoring the composite $n$ used as the modulus. For the Type 2 scheme, we have the following theorem.

**Theorem 10.** *Completely breaking the Type 2 scheme is computationally equivalent to factoring $n$.*

Proof: It is clear that if once the factors of $n$ are known, plaintext $(m_x, m_y)$ can easily be computed from ciphertext $(c_x, c_y)$ and public keys $(a, n)$. Conversely, if there is an Algorithm A1, given $P$ on $E_n(a, b)$ ($E_n(0, b)$ or $E_n(a, 0)$), to output $Q$ satisfying $P = 2 \cdot Q$ with non-negligible probablity, then we can construct an expected polynomial-time algorithm B to factor $n$, using A1 as an oracle. First, B chooses a random point $R = $

$(r_x, r_y)$ $(r_x, r_y \in \mathbf{Z}_n)$, and multiplies it by 2, asks A1 to halve this point, and B obtains $R'$ satisfying $P = 2 \cdot R'$ with non-negligible probablity. Then B computes $R_0 = R - R'$. Since $2 \cdot R_0 = \mathcal{O}$, and $R_0$ over $E_p(a, b)$ ($R_0$ over $E_q(a, b)$) is $\mathcal{O}_p$ ($\mathcal{O}_q$), then $R_0$ is an undefined point with probability $1/2$. If $R_0$ is undefined, B can compute a non-trivial factor of $n$ by the extended Euclidean algorithm used for division modulo $n$. Clearly, the expected running time of B is polynomial-time in $\log n$.  $\square$

In the Type 1 scheme, the equivalence between completely breaking this scheme and factoring $n$ is *not* known. This situation is the same as the original RSA scheme.

## 7.4  Homomorphism Attacks and Their Countermeasures

The encryption-decryption functions $E(\cdot)$ and $D(\cdot)$ for Type 1 and 2 schemes are homomorphic for addition as

$$E(M_1 + M_2) = E(M_1) + E(M_2) \quad \text{and} \quad D(M_1 + M_2) = D(M_1) + D(M_2),$$

for any points $M_1$ and $M_2$ on the *same* elliptic curve. This kind of homomorphic property is the basis for some attacking methods proposed [7] against the original RSA and Rabin schemes.

The probability that randomly chosen integer pairs $M_1$ and $M_2$ are on the same elliptic curve is as negligiblly small. Thus, passive attacks using homomorphism seem to be ineffective against Type 1 and 2 schemes.

Consider an active attack (a chosen-plaintext attack) using homomorphism. Suppose an attacker $A$ wants to make a victim $B$ sign a plaintext $M = (m_x, m_y)$ without $B$'s consent. $A$ generates another message $M'$ with $B$'s public keys $(e_B, n_B)$ and random integer $r$,

$$M' = M + e_B \cdot (r \cdot M) \text{ over } E_{n_B},$$

and sends $M'$ to B. B makes a signature $S'$ for $M'$ with his secret key $d_B$:

$$S' = d_B \cdot M' = d_B \cdot (M + e_B \cdot (r \cdot M)) \text{ over } E_{n_B}.$$

Then, $A$ computes a signature $S$ for $M$ from $S'$ by

$$S = S' - r \cdot M \text{ over } E_{n_B}.$$

Using this technique, $A$ can forge $B$'s signatures without $B$'s secret key. To counter this attack, a randomization of a plaintext with a hashing function h should be applied before the application of the function D. This method is similar to that required for the original RSA scheme.

## 7.5  Isomorphism Attacks and Their Countermeasures

**Definition**  Let $n = pq$ ($p, q$: prime), and $E_n^1$ and $E_n^2$ be elliptic curves such that

$$E_n^1 : \ y^2 = x^3 + a_1 x + b_1 \bmod n, \quad E_n^2 : \ y^2 = x^3 + a_2 x + b_2 \bmod n.$$

$E_n^1$ and $E_n^2$ are isomorphic if there exist $u_p \in \mathbf{Z}_p^*$ and $u_q \in \mathbf{Z}_q^*$ such that

$$a_2 \equiv u_p^4 a_1 \bmod p, \quad b_2 \equiv u_p^6 b_1 \bmod p,$$

$$a_2 \equiv u_q^4 a_1 \bmod q, \quad b_2 \equiv u_q^6 b_1 \bmod q.$$

Then the following isomorphic property of the elliptic curves over a ring is shown by using the property of the elliptic curves over a finite field and the Chinese Remainder Theorem.

**Lemma 11.** Let $E_n^1$ and $E_n^2$ be elliptic curves such that

$$E_n^1: \; y^2 = x^3 + a_1 x + b_1 \bmod n, \quad E_n^2: \; y^2 = x^3 + a_2 x + b_2 \bmod n.$$

Let $M_1 = (m_{1x}, m_{1y})$, $C_1 = (c_{1x}, c_{1y}) \in E_n^1$ and $M_2 = (m_{2x}, m_{2y})$, $C_2 = (c_{2x}, c_{2y}) \in E_n^2$ where

$$C_1 = e \cdot M_1 \text{ over } E_n^1, \quad C_2 = e \cdot M_2 \text{ over } E_n^2.$$

Then the following statements are equivalent:

(i) $E_n^1$ and $E_n^2$ are isomorphic.

(ii) $a_2 \equiv u^4 a_1 \bmod n, \quad b_2 \equiv u^6 b_1 \bmod n \quad \exists u \in \mathbf{Z}_n^*. \hfill (1)$

(iii) $c_{2x} \equiv u^2 c_{1x} \bmod n, \quad c_{2y} \equiv u^3 c_{1y} \bmod n \quad \exists u \in \mathbf{Z}_n^*. \hfill (2)$

(iv) $m_{2x} \equiv u^2 m_{1x} \bmod n, \quad m_{2y} \equiv u^3 m_{1y} \bmod n \quad \exists u \in \mathbf{Z}_n^*. \hfill (3)$

If $C_1$, $C_2$ and $M_1$ satisfying congruence (2) are given, then $M_2$ can be easily found by computing congruence (3). Notice that it is easy to check whether or not congruence (2) holds. If $M_1$ and $M_2$ are randomly chosen, then the probability that there exists $u$ satisfying congruence (2) is a negligibly small $1/n$ for large $n$. Thus, passive attacks using isomorphism seem to be difficult for Types 1 and 2 schemes.

Consider an active attack (a chosen-plaintext attack) based on the isomorphic property of the elliptic curves. Suppose an attacker $A$ wants to make a victim $B$ sign a plaintext $M = (m_x, m_y)$ without $B$'s consent. $A$ generates another message $M'$ with $B$'s public key $n_B$ and random integer $u$:

$$M' = (u^2 m_x \bmod n_B, \; u^3 m_y \bmod n_B),$$

and sends $M'$ to $B$. $B$ makes a signature $S' = (s_x', \; s_y')$ for $M'$ with his secret key $d_B$:

$$S' = d_B \cdot M' \text{ over } E_{n_B}'.$$

Then, $A$ computes a signature $S = (s_x, \; s_y)$ for $M$ from $S'$ by

$$S = (s_x, \; s_y) = (u^{-2} s_x' \bmod n_B, \; u^{-3} s_y' \bmod n_B).$$

Note that the curve $E_{n_B}$ containing points $(M, S)$ and the curve $E_{n_B}'$ containing points $(M', S')$ are isomorphic. Using this technique, $A$ can forge $B$'s signatures without $B$'s secret key. To counter this attack, the same technique described in Section 7.4 can be applied.

An attacker may try to forge a signature by using both homomorphism and isomorphism shown above. However, such combined attacks can also be prevented by randomization with the hash function h.

## 7.6 Security for Low Multiplier Attack

Hastad [6] showed a low exponent attack on the original RSA and Rabin schemes when the same message is encrypted with several distinct moduli. He considered the problem of solving systems of congruences $P_i(m) \equiv 0 \pmod{n_i}$ $i = 1, ..., k$, where $P_i$ are polynomial of degree $e$ and the $n_i$ are distinct relatively prime numbers and $m < \min n_i$. He proved that if $k > \frac{e(e+1)}{2}$, then $m$ can be recovered in polynomial time. Thus, he pointed out that enciphering linearly related messages with the RSA scheme with low exponent or the Rabin scheme is insecure. For the original RSA scheme, let $c = m^e \bmod n$, $c_i = m_i^e$ mod $n_i$, and $n = n_1 \cdot n_2 \cdots n_k$. In Hastad's algorithm, $c$ is first obtained from $c_i$ using the Chinese Remainder Theorem. Next, $m$ can be efficiently calculated from $c = m^e$ (with neglecting $n$), provided that $m^e < n$. For our proposed Types 1 and 2 schemes, let $C = e' \cdot M$ over $E_n(a, b)$, $C_i = e' \cdot M$ over $E_{n_i}$, where $C = (c_x, c_y)$, $M = (m_x, m_y)$, $C_i = (c_{ix}, c_{iy})$. The value of $(c_x, c_y)$ is also obtained from $(c_{ix}, c_{iy})$. However, it is difficult to solve $(m_x, m_y)$ from $(c_x, c_y)$ because $c_x$ and $c_y$ are expressed by *rational* equations in $m_x$ and $m_y$. Since the rational equations include divisions modulo $n$, if we transform the rational form relation into the polynomial form relation, the size of the coefficient of the polynomial form is of the order of $n$'s size. Therefore, it seems impossible to solve the rational or polynomial form relation by neglecting modulus $n$. Thus, even if the multiplier $e'$ is small, a Hastad-like attack does not seem to work against the elliptic curve cryptosystems.

# 8 Performance

An elliptic curve addition $P_1 + P_2$ on $E_n(a, b)$ requires one division, one squaring operation and one general multiplication in $Z_n$ when $P_1 \neq P_2$, and an extra squaring when $P_1 = P_2$. (The much faster additions and subtractions in $Z_n$ are neglected for the sake of simplicity). Surprisingly, as opposed to $Z_n$ where squaring can be performed faster than a general multiplication, doubling a point on an elliptic curve is computationally more costly than adding two different points. This means that in order to compute a multiple $c \cdot P$ of a point $P$, an irregular addition chain for $c$ avoiding doubling operations should be used. When neglecting the fact that squaring in $Z_n$ can be implemented somewhat faster than a general multiplication, elliptic curve addition and doubling operations require about 2 and 3 multiplications in $Z_n$ and one division in $Z_n$, respectively.

Division in $Z_n$ can be implemented by the generalized Euclidean algorithm for computing greatest common divisors. The most efficient algorithm for computing multiplicative inverses, however, is that invented by Massey [17], which is a generalization of Stein's algorithm [25]. However, a division in $Z_n$ seems to be less efficient than a multiplication in $Z_n$.

On the other hand, if we calculate the addition on $E_n(a, b)$ in homogeneous coordinates, we can avoid the division in $Z_n$ (except the final stage of the addition chain), although we must perform more multiplications.

Let $P_1 = (x_1, y_1, z_1) \in E_p(a, b)$, $P_2 = (x_2, y_2, z_2) \in E_p(a, b)$, and suppose that $P_1, P_2 \neq \mathcal{O}$, $P_1 \neq P_2$ and $P_1 \neq -P_2$. The addition formula [9] for $E_p(a, b)$ to find $P_3 = P_1 + P_2 =$

$(x_3, y_3, z_3)$ is given by

$$\begin{cases} x_3 = v\{z_2(u^2 z_1 - 2v^2 x_1) - v^3\} \mod p, \\ \\ y_3 = z_2(3uv^2 x_1 - v^3 y_1 - u^3 z_1) + uv^3 \mod p, \\ \\ z_3 = v^3 z_1 z_2 \mod p, \end{cases}$$

where $u = y_2 z_1 - y_1 z_2 \mod p$, $v = x_2 z_1 - x_1 z_2 \mod p$.
The doubling formula [9] for $E_p(a, b)$ to find $P_3 = 2 \cdot P_1$ is given by

$$\begin{cases} x_3 = 2y_1 z_1 (w^2 - 8x_1 y_1^2 z_1) \mod p, \\ \\ y_3 = 4y_1^2 z_1 (3wx_1 - 2y_1^2 z_1) - w^3 \mod p, \\ \\ z_3 = 8y_1^3 z_1^3 \mod p, \end{cases}$$

where $w = 3x_1^2 + az_1^2 \mod p$.

One addition over $E_n(a, b)$ requires 12 multiplications in $Z_n$, and one doubling over $E_n(a, b)$ requires 10 multiplications in $Z_n$, if $a = 0$.

Therefore, in the affine coordinates, the computation required for our scheme (Scheme 1) is about $(2 + c)$ times as much as that for the RSA scheme, where $c$ is the ratio of the computation amount of division in $Z_n$ to that of multiplication in $Z_n$. On the other hand, in the homogeneous coordinates, the computation required for encryption with our scheme is about 11 times as much as that for the RSA scheme. Since in our elliptic curve system a message consists of two elements of $Z_n$ compared to only one in the RSA system, the computation speed of our scheme is about $2/(2 + c)$ or $1/6$ of the speed of RSA.

# 9 Conclusions

We have proposed new public key cryptosystems based on elliptic curves modulo $n$, where $n$ is a product of two large primes. Furthermore, we have given some analysis of the security of these systems. For the proposed Type 1 scheme, the master key concept [10] and the blind signature concept [2] are similarly applicable (using the combined techniques of Sections 7.4 and 7.5).

# Acknowledgements

We would like to thank Martin Benninger, Burt Kaliski, Neal Koblitz, Alfred Menezes, Pierre Schmid, and Hiroki Shizuya for helpful discussions and for their support.

# References

[1] L. Adleman, K. Manders, and G. Miller, "On taking roots in finite fields", *20th FOCS*, Vol. 20, 1977, pp.175-178 (1977).

[2] D. Chaum, "Blind signatures for untraceable payments", Proc. of Crypto'82, pp.199-203 (1982).

[3] W. Diffie and M.E. Hellman, "New directions in cryptography, IEEE Transactions on Information Theory," Vol. 22, No. 6, pp. 644-654 (1976).

[4] T. El-Gamal, "A public key cryptosystem and a signature scheme based on the discrete logarithm", IEEE Transactions on Information Theory, Vol. 31, No. 4, pp. 469-472 (1985).

[5] S. Goldwasser and J. Kilian, "Almost all primes can be quickly certified", Proc. of the 18th Annual ACM Symposium on the Theory of Computing, pp. 316-329 (1986).

[6] J. Hastad, "On using RSA with low exponent in a public key network", Proc. of Crypto'85, pp.403-408 (1985).

[7] W. Jonge and D. Chaum, "Attacks on some RSA signatures", Proc. of Crypto'85, pp.18-27 (1985).

[8] B.S. Kaliski, "A pseudo-random bit generator based on elliptic logarithms", Proc. of Crypto'86, pp. 84-103 (1987).

[9] N. Koblitz, A Course in Number Theory and Cryptography, Berlin: Springer-Verlag, (1987).

[10] K. Koyama, "A Master Key for the RSA public-key cryptosystem", I.E.C.E. Trans.(D), J-65, 2, pp.163-170 (1982).

[11] E. Kranakis, Primality and Cryptography, Stuttgart: Teubner, and New York: John Wiley & Sons, (1986).

[12] A.K. Lenstra, H.W. Lenstra, M.S. Manasse and J.M. Pollard, "The number field sieve", Proc. of STOC'90, pp.564-572 (1990).

[13] A.K. Lenstra and M.S. Manasse, "Factoring with two large primes", Proc. of EURO-CRYPT'90, pp.72-82 (1991)

[14] H.W. Lenstra, "Factoring integers with elliptic curves", Annals of Mathematics, Vol. 126, pp. 649-673 (1987).

[15] U.M. Maurer, "Fast generation of RSA-moduli with almost maximal diversity", Proc. of EUROCRYPT'89, pp. 636-647 (1990).

[16] U.M. Maurer and Y. Yacobi, "Non-interactive public-key cryptography", to appear in Proc. Eurocrypt '91.

[17] J.L. Massey, "Cryptography - fundamentals and applications (Copies of transparencies)", Advanced Technology Seminars, Zurich, Switzerland, (1988).

[18] G.L. Miller, "Riemann's hypothesis and tests for primality", J. Comput. System Sci. Vol.13, pp.300-317, (1976).

[19] A.J. Menezes, T. Okamoto, S.A. Vanstone, "Reducing Elliptic Curve Logarithms to Logarithms in a Finite Field", Proc. of STOC'91, pp.80-89 (1991).

[20] M.O. Rabin, "Probabilistic algorithm for testing primality", Journal on Number Theory, Vol. 12, pp. 128-138 (1980).

[21] R.L. Rivest, A. Shamir, and L. Adleman, "A method for obtaining digital signatures and public-key cryptosystems", Communications of the ACM, Vol. 21, No. 2, pp. 120-126 (1978).

[22] R. Schoof, "Elliptic curves over finite fields and the computation of square roots mod $p$", Mathematics of Computation, Vol. 44, No. 170, pp. 483-494 (1985).

[23] J.H. Silverman, *The Arithmetic of Elliptic Curves*, Springer-Verlag, (1986).

[24] G. Simmons and M. Norris, "Preliminary comments on the M.I.T public key cryptosystem", Cryptologia, Vol. 1, No. 4, pp. 406-414 (1977).

[25] J. Stein, "Computational problems associated with Racah algebra", J. Comp. Phys., Vol. 1, pp. 397-405 (1961).

# Efficient Algorithms for the Construction of Hyperelliptic Cryptosystems

Tatsuaki Okamoto†       Kouichi Sakurai‡

†NTT Laboratories
Nippon Telegraph and Telephone Corporation
1-2356, Take, Yokosuka-shi, Kanagawa-ken, 238-03 Japan
‡Information Systems and Electronics Development Laboratory
Mitsubishi Electric Corporation
5-1-1, Ofuna, Kamakura, 247 Japan

## Abstract

The jacobian of hyperelliptic curves, including elliptic curves as a special case, offers a good primitive for cryptosystems, since cryptosystems (discrete logarithms) based on the jacobians seem to be more intractable than those based on conventional multiplicative groups. In this paper, we show that the problem to determine the group structure of the jacobian can be characterized to be in NP ∩ co-NP, when the jacobian is a non-degenerate type ("non-half-degenerate"). We also show that the hyperelliptic discrete logarithm can be characterized to be in NP ∩ co-NP, when the group structure is non-half-degenerate. Moreover, we imply the reducibility of the hyperelliptic discrete logarithm to a multiplicative discrete logarithm. The extended Weil pairing over the jacobian is the key tool for these algorithms.

# 1   Introduction

The finite abelian groups play an important role in constructing many public-key cryptosystems and error correcting codes. The most typical member of the finite abelian groups is the multiplicative group of a finite field, and the first public-key cryptosystem (key-distribution system) was constructed on a multiplicative group [DH]. However, since the structure of multiplicative groups is very simple, certain special techniques [Odl, Cop1, Cop2] were developed that could attack some cryptosystems (or their discrete logarithms) based on multiplicative groups. On the contrary, the jacobians of hyperelliptic curves, including elliptic curves as a special case, offer a rich source of "naturally occuring" (more complex) finite abelian groups, and cryptosystems based on the jacobians seem to be more intractable than those based on multiplicative groups [Mil1, Kob1, MOV].

In order to use the jacobians for cryptosystems, we should determine their group structures and the intractability of their related cryptosystems (discrete logarithms). As for the group structure, Miller has shown an efficient algorithm of determining the structure of an *elliptic curve group*, using an oracle of factoring. As for the intractability of the discrete logarithm of the *elliptic curve*, it has been known that some specific elliptic discrete

J. Feigenbaum (Ed.): Advances in Cryptology - CRYPTO '91, LNCS 576, pp. 267-278, 1992.
© Springer-Verlag Berlin Heidelberg 1992

logarithms are as tractable as multiplicative discrete logarithms [MOV]. Thus it remained open whether these results about *elliptic curves* could be extended to *hyperelliptic curves*.

The hyperelliptic discrete logarithm has been characterized from the viewpoint of structural computational complexity [SIS]. According to their result, the hyperelliptic discrete logarithm was characterized as more intractable than the multiplicative discrete logarithm. More precisely, they have shown that a problem corresponding the hyperelliptic discrete logarithm is in NP ∩ co-AM, while a problem corresponding the multiplicative discrete logarithm is in NP ∩ co-NP. However, it remained open whether the problem corresponding to the hyperelliptic discrete logarithm is in NP ∩ co-NP.

In this paper, we extend the above results of elliptic curves to derive similar results for the *hyperelliptic curves*; we show that the problem to determine the group structure of the jacobian can be characterized to be in NP ∩ co-NP, when the jacobian is a non-degenerate type ("non-half-degenerate"), and show that some specific *hyperelliptic* discrete logarithms are as tractable as multiplicative discrete logarithms. Moreover, we partially solve the above-mentioned open problem regarding the characterization of the hyperelliptic discrete logarithms; we show that the problem corresponding the hyperelliptic discrete logarithm is in NP ∩ co-NP, when the group structure is non-half-degenerate. Note that this result does not state that the hyperelliptic discrete logarithm is as tractable as the multiplicative discrete logarithm. (The above result is only a characterization from the viewpoint of structural computational complexity.)

The extended Weil pairing defined over hyperelliptic curves plays an essential role throughout this paper. So, first, in section 3, we define the extended Weil pairing and introduce an efficient algorithm to compute the extended Weil pairing. Then, in section 4, we show that the problem corresponding to the group structure of the non-half-degenerate jacobian is in NP ∩ co-NP. Section 5 shows that the problem corresponding to the non-half-degenerate hyperelliptic discrete logarithm is in NP ∩ co-NP, and that some specific *hyperelliptic* discrete logarithms are as tractable as multiplicative discrete logarithms.

# 2 Hyperelliptic Curves and the Jacobian

This section briefly introduces the notions regarding the jacobians of hyperelliptic curves. For more detail, refer to [Kob2, Lan, Sil]

Let $K$ be an arbitrary field, and let $\overline{K}$ denote its algebraic closure. Let $C$ be a hyperelliptic curve of genus $g$ over $K$, whose equation is of the form $v^2 + h(u)v = f(u)$, where $h(u)$ is a polynomial of degree at most $g$ and $f(u)$ is a monic polynomial of degree $2g + 1$. Here $f$ and $h$ have coefficients in $K$, and we assume that the curve has no singular point.

Let $L$ be a field containing $K$. An $L$-point $P$ denotes an infinite point $O$ or $P_{x,y}$ where $(x \in L, y \in L)$ is a solution of the hyperelliptic curve equation. If $\sigma$ is an automorphism of $L$ over $K$, we let $P^{\sigma}$ denote $P_{\sigma(x),\sigma(y)}$ and $O^{\sigma}=O$.

A divisor is a finite formal sum of $\overline{K}$-points $D = \sum m_i P_i$. We define the degree of $D$ to be the integer $\sum m_i$. The divisors form an additive group $\boldsymbol{D}$, in which the divisors of degree 0 form a subgroup $\boldsymbol{D}^0$. Given $D = \sum m_i P_i \in \boldsymbol{D}$, we define $D^+ = \sum_{m_i>0} m_i P_i$. We say that $D \geq 0$ if $D = D^+$. Given two divisors $D_1 = \sum m_i P_i$ and $D_2 = \sum n_i P_i$ in $\boldsymbol{D}^0$, we define $\gcd(D_1, D_2) \in \boldsymbol{D}^0$ to be $(\sum \min(m_i, n_i) P_i)$.

We define the order of a polynomial function $p(u, v)$ with coefficients in $\overline{K}$ at a point $P \in C$, denoted $\operatorname{ord}_P p$, as follows:

(1) Assume $P = P_{x,y}$ is a finite point. $p(u, v)$ can be reduced to the form $\bar{p}(u, v) = (u - x)^{r_0}(a_0(u) - b_0(u)v)$, where $(u - x)$ does not divide both $a_0$ and $b_0$. Let $r = r_0$ if $P \neq \bar{P}$ and $r = 2r_0$ if $P = \bar{P}$. Then, $\mathrm{ord}_{P_{x,y}}p = r$ if $a_0(x) - b_0(x)y \neq 0$, else, it equals to $r$ plus the exponent of the highest power of $(u - x)$ which divides $a_0(u)^2 + h(u)a_0(u)b_0(u) - f(u)b_0(u)^2$.

(2) If $P = O$, then $\mathrm{ord}_O P = - \max(2\deg a, 2g + 1 + 2\deg b)$.

To any $p(u, v)$ such that $\bar{p} \neq 0$, we associate the divisor $\mathrm{div}(p) = \sum (\mathrm{ord}_P p)P \in \boldsymbol{D}^0$. By rational function on $C$ we mean a ratio of the form $p(u, v)/q(u, v)$ with $\bar{q} \neq 0$. $K(C)$ denotes the rational function field of curve $C$ over field $K$. A divisor of the form $\mathrm{div}(p/q) = \mathrm{div}(p) - \mathrm{div}(q) \in \boldsymbol{D}^0$ is called principal. The quotient group $\boldsymbol{D}^0/\boldsymbol{P}$ is called the jacobian $\boldsymbol{J}$ of the curve $C$, where $\boldsymbol{P}$ is the subgroup of principal divisors. $O$ denotes the identity element of $\boldsymbol{J}$, which is the element corresponding to $\boldsymbol{P}$. When two divisors $D_1$ and $D_2$ are in the same element of $\boldsymbol{J}$, $D_1$ is said to be *linearly equivalent* to $D_2$ and we denote $D_1 \sim D_2$. Then, there exists a rational function $f$ such that $D_1 = D_2 + \mathrm{div}(f)$.

The support of a divisor $D = \sum m_i P_i$ is the set of points $P \in C$ for which $m_i \neq 0$. Now let $f \in \overline{K}(C)$ be a function such that $\mathrm{div}(f)$ and $D$ have disjoint supports. Then, we define $f(D) = \prod f(P_i)^{m_i}$.

We associate to $D$ the set of functions $L(D) = \{f \in \overline{K}(C) \mid \mathrm{div}(f) \geq -D\} \cup \{0\}$. $L(D)$ is a finite dimensional $\overline{K}$-vector space, and we denote its dimension $l(D)$.

Every $D \in \boldsymbol{D}^0$ can be uniquely represented as an element of $\boldsymbol{J}$ by a reduced divisor $D_1 = \sum m_i P_i - (\sum m_i)O$ with $\sum m_i \leq g$. This result follows from the Rieman-Roch theorem. We denote $(P), (Q)$ as the reduced divisors of $P, Q \in J[m]$, and we also denote $(D)$ as the reduced divisor such that $(D) \sim D$, where $D$ is a divisor.

A semireduced divisor $D = \sum m_i P_i - (\sum m_i)O$ can be uniquely represented as the gcd of two divisors of functions of the form $a(u)$ and $b(u) - v$, where $a(u) = \prod(u - x_i)^{m_i}$ and $b(u)$ is the unique polynomial of degree $< \deg a(u)$ such that $b(x_i) = y_i$ for each $i$ and $b(u)^2 + h(u)b(u) - f(u)$ is divisible by $a(u)$. A divisor $D$ represented in the form $\gcd(a(u), (b(u) - v))$ is abbreviated $D = \mathrm{div}(a, b)$. $D$ is reduced if and only if $\deg a \leq g$.

# 3  Extension of the Weil Pairing

The Weil pairing was originally defined over elliptic curves by A. Weil [Sil]. Lang generalized the Weil pairing over the abelian varieties [Lan]. In this section, we define the extended Weil pairing on the jacobian of the hyperelliptic curves, which is a specific class of Lang's generalization, and show an expected polynomial time algorithm of computing the extended Weil pairing. We have two different ways to define the extended Weil pairing. One is suitable for the efficient computation of the pairing, and the other is suitable for proving some properties, although these definitions are equivalent. Here, we only show the definition that is suitable for the efficient computation of the pairing.

## 3.1  Definition of the extended Weil pairing

**Definition 3.1** *Let $C$ be a hyperelliptic curve defined over $\overline{K}$, and $\boldsymbol{J}$ be the Jacobian on $C$ ($\boldsymbol{J} = \boldsymbol{D}^0/\boldsymbol{P}$). Let $\boldsymbol{J}[m]$ be $\boldsymbol{D}^0[m]/\boldsymbol{P}$ and $\mu_m$ be the set of m-th roots of the unity, where $\boldsymbol{D}^0[m] = \{D \mid D \in \boldsymbol{D}^\circ \text{ and } mD \in \boldsymbol{P}\}$ and the characteristic of $K$ is prime to $m$.*

First, we define a function $w_m$

$$w_m : D^0[m] \times D^0[m] \to \mu_m$$

as follows; Let $X, Y \in D^0[m]$, and we assume $X, Y$ are disjoint supports. Since $X$ and $Y$ have order $m$, there are functions $f_X, f_Y \in \overline{K}$ such that $\mathrm{div}(f_X) = mX$ and $\mathrm{div}(f_Y) = mY$. Then we define

$$w_m(X, Y) := f_X(Y)/f_Y(X).$$

Then, we define a pairing (the extended Weil pairing)

$$e_m : J[m] \times J[m] \to \mu_m$$

as follows: Let $P, Q \in J[m]$, and $A$ and $B$ be divisors over $C$ such that $A \in P$ and $B \in Q$ and they have disjoint supports. Since $A, B \in D^0[m]$, we can define $w_m(A, B)$. Then we define

$$e_m(P, Q) = w_m(A, B).$$

We will show an efficient algorithm based on the above definition.

## 3.2 Miller's algorithm

This subsection introduces Miller's algorithm (algorithm 1 in [Mil2]), which is used in the extended Weil pairing algorithm.

### Algorithm 1 (Miller's Algorithm) :

**Input** A hyperelliptic curve $C$ with genus $g$, and a divisor $A \in D^0$

**Output** A function $f$, and a reduced divisor $B$ such that $A = B + \mathrm{div}(f)$

**Step 1** Rewrite the divisor $A = a_1 P_1 + a_2 P_2 + \ldots + a_k P_k$ as a sum of reduced divisors $a_1(P_1 - O) + a_2(P_2 - O) + \ldots + a_k(P_k - O)$.

**Step 2** Calculate a basis for the space $L(3gO)$ in the form $f_1, \ldots, f_d$ where $\mathrm{ord}_O f_1 > \mathrm{ord}_O f_2 > \mathrm{ord}_O > \ldots > \mathrm{ord}_O f_d$. (There is a one-to-one correspondence between reduced divisors and integral ideals of the ring of functions whose only poles are at $O$. Each ideal can be represented by means of the Grobner basis.)

**Step 3** For each reduced divisor $(P_i - O)$, use doubling and addition repeatedly to compute a reduced divisor $B$ and a function $f$ such that $a_1(P_1 - O) + \ldots + a_k(P_k - O) = B + \mathrm{div}(f)$. This computation can be done by repeatedly using the following primitive computation: given two reduced divisors $P$ and $Q$, compute a reduced divisor $R$ and a function $h$ such that $P + Q = R + \mathrm{div}(h)$. The following substeps show this computation.

**Step 3-1** Find a function $s \in L(3gO - P^+ - Q^+)$, where $P = P^+ - gO, Q = Q^+ - gO$.

**Step 3-2** Set $S = \mathrm{div}(s) + 3gO - P^+ - Q^+$.

**Step 3-3** Find a function $t \in L(2gO - S)$, and set $T = \mathrm{div}(t) + 2gO - S$. Here $R = T - gO$, and $h = s/t$.

**Step 4** Output $B$ and $f$.

## 3.3 Extended Weil pairing algorithm

Here, we show an expected polynomial time algorithm for computing the extended Weil pairing. The Weil pairing is defined over two elements $P, Q$ in $J[m]$. However, in order to calculate the value of $e_m(P, Q)$ in an algorithm, $P, Q$ must be given explicitly (or in a polynomial-size expression). Any element in $J[m]$ can be uniquely represented by a *reduced divisor* from the Riemann-Roch theorem. Therefore, the reduced divisor is the best explicit representation of an element of $J[m]$.

**Algorithm 2 (Extended Weil pairing):**
Input   $(P), (Q)$ such that $P, Q \in J[m]$
Output   $e_m(P, Q)$
Step 1   Select two reduced divisors $T$ and $U$ over $C$ randomly.
Step 2   Compute $((P) + T)$ and $((Q) + U)$. For this computation, we use Cantor's (Koblitz's) algorithm [Can, Kob2].
Step 3   Set $A = ((P) + T) - T$, and $B = ((Q) + U) - U$. (Note that $A - (P)$ is in $P$, and that $gO$ of $((P) + T)$ and $gO$ of $T$ are cancelled in $A$.)
Step 4   Compute functions $f_A$ and $f_B$. For this computation, we use Algorithm 1 (Miller's algorithm).
Step 5   Compute $f_A(B)$ and $f_B(A)$. If either $f_A(B)$ or $f_B(A)$ is zero or undefined, then return to 1. Otherwise, compute $f_A(B)/f_B(A)$ as $e_m(P, Q)$.

**Lemma 3.2** *Algorithm 2 is performed in expected polynomial time in $\log q$.*

**Proof:**

Let $1 = a_1, \ldots, a_t = m$ be an addition chain, which is used to compute functions $f_A$ and $f_B$. $T$ and $U$ both have $M^g$ candidates, where $M$ is the number of $K$-points of curve $C$ (note that $M$ is not the number of $J$). We define a bad pair $(T, U)$ such that $A$ (consists of at most $2g$ support points) is disjoint from $(a_i(Q + U))^+$ (consists of at most $g$ support points) and $(a_i U)^+$ (consists of at most $g$ support points), and $B$ (consists of at most $2g$ support points) is disjoint from $(a_i(P + T))^+$ (consists of at most $g$ support points) and $(a_i T)^+$ (consists of at most $g$ support points). Therefore, the failure probability at step 5 of the above algorithm is at most $8tgM^{g-1}/M^{2g} = 8tg/M^{g+1}$. Hence, this failure probability is $O(g(\log q)/2^{(g+1)(\log q)})$ (or negligible). Thus, this algorithm is expected polynomial time in $\log q$. (The expected number of rounds from step 1 to 5 is almost 1.)   ¶

Similarly, the extended Weil pairing can be computed in non-deterministic polynomial time.

## 3.4 Correctness of the definition

In this subsection, we show that the extended Weil pairing satisfies some properties that are needed for the intended applications.

**Lemma 3.3** *$w_m$ is well-defined.*

**Lemma 3.4** *Let $P, P', Q, Q' \in D^0[m]$ such that $P - P'$ (resp. $Q - Q'$) $\in P$. Then*

$$w_m(P', Q) = w_m(P, Q), \qquad w_m(P, Q') = w_m(P, Q).$$

Lemma 3.4 implies that $w_m$ induces a natural pairing $e_m$ over $J[m] \times J[m]$. Therefore the definition that $e_m(P, Q) = w_m(A, B)$ makes sense.

Next we investigate some properties of $e_m$.

**Theorem 3.5**

*(1)  For any elements $P, Q \in J[m]$,*

$$e_m(P, Q) \in \mu_m.$$

*(2)  Alternating: For any elements $P, Q \in J[m]$,*

$$e_m(P, Q) = e_m(P, Q)^{-1}.$$

*(3)  Bilinear: For any elements $P_1, P_2, Q \in J[m]$,*

$$e_m(P_1 + P_2, Q) = e_m(P_1, Q)e_m(P_2, Q),$$

$$e_m(P, Q_1 + Q_2) = e_m(P, Q_1)e_m(P, Q_2).$$

*(4)  Identity: For any element $P \in J[m]$, $e_m(P, P)$ is 1.*

*(5)  Non-degeneracy: If $e_m(P, Q) = 1$ for all $P \in J[m]$, then $Q = O$.*

# 4  Complexity of Determining Hyperelliptic Group Structure

This section shows that the problem to determine the group structure of a jacobian $J$ over $F_q$ can be characterized to be in NP ∩ co-NP, when $J$ is "non-half-degenerate".

Let $J$ be a jacobian over a field $F_q$ with group structure $Z_{n_1} \times Z_{n_2} \times \ldots \times Z_{n_{2g}}$, (simply we write $(n_1, n_2, \ldots, n_{2g})$), where $n_i \geq 1$ $(1 \leq i \leq 2g)$, and $n_j$ divides $n_i$ when $n_j < n_i$. (This comes from the property of finite abelian groups.) The maximal order of an element in $J$ is $n_1$.

$(G_1, G_2, \ldots, G_{2g})$ be a *canonical generating tuple* for the abelian group of $J$, if every element $X \in J$ can be written uniquely as

$$X = a_1 G_1 + \ldots + a_g G_{2g},$$

where $0 \leq a_i < n_i$ and $n_i = \mathrm{Ord}(G_i)$. ($\mathrm{Ord}(G_i)$ denotes the order of $G_i$.)

$< G_1, \ldots, G_r >$ denotes the subgroup generated from $G_1, \ldots, G_r$. Note that $\langle G_1, G_2 \rangle$ and $\langle n_1, n_2 \rangle$ are used for denoting a paired property of the group structure (see Lemma 4.1 for the definition of "paired canonical generating tuple").

**Lemma 4.1** *Let $J$ be a jacobian over a field $F_q$ and $(G_1, G_2, \ldots, G_{2g})$ ( $\mathrm{Ord}(G_i) = n_i$ ) be a canonical generating tuple of $J$, where $n_{2i} \leq n_{2i-1}$ (but the other greater or smaller relations are not fixed). Let $h_i$ $(i = 1, \ldots, g)$ be the homomorphism*

$$h_i : X \in J_q[n_{2i-1}] \mapsto e_{n_{2i-1}}(G_{2i-1}, X),$$

and $f_i$ $(i = 1, \ldots, g)$ be the homomorphism

$$f_i : J_q[n_{2i-1}] \;\rightarrow\; J_q[n_{2i-1}]/ < G(J_q[n_{2i-1}]) - G_{2i} >,$$

where $J_q[n]$ denotes $\{P \mid P \in J \wedge nP = O\}$, and $G(J_q[n_{2i-1}])$ denotes $\{G_j \mid n_j$ devides $n_{2i-1}\}$.

Then there exists a canonical generating tuple $(G_1, G_2, \ldots, G_{2g})$ such that for all elements $P, Q \in J_q[n_{2i-1}]$,

$$h_i(P) = h_i(Q) \quad \textit{if and only if} \quad f_i(P) = f_i(Q).$$

The canonical generating tuple satisfying the above property is written as $(\langle G_1, G_2 \rangle, \langle G_3, G_4 \rangle, \ldots, \langle G_{2g-1}, G_{2g} \rangle)$ and is called a paired canonical generating tuple. Here, $(\langle n_1, n_2 \rangle, \langle n_3, n_4 \rangle, \ldots, \langle n_{2g-1}, n_{2g} \rangle)$ denotes its group structure. Without loss of generality, we assume that $n_{2(i+j)-1} \leq n_{2i-1}$ $(i = 1, \ldots, g-1; j = 1, \ldots, g-i)$.

**Proof:**

We will show that we can construct a paired canonical generating tuple $(\langle G_1, G_2 \rangle, \langle G_3, G_4 \rangle, \ldots, \langle G_{2g-1}, G_{2g} \rangle)$ such that $f_i(P) = f_i(Q)$ (or $P - Q \in < G(J_q[n_{2i-1}]) - G_{2i} >$) if and only if $e_{n_{2i-1}}(G_{2i-1}, P) = e_{n_{2i-1}}(G_{2i-1}, Q)$.

Let $J[n_1]$ be defined over the algebraic closure field $\overline{F}_q$ (see subsection 3.1), of which $J$ is a subgroup. Since the group structure of $J[n_1]$ is $(n_1)^{2g}$, there exist elements $\gamma_2, \ldots, \gamma_{2g}$ such that $(G_1, \gamma_2, \ldots, \gamma_{2g})$ is a canonical generating tuple for $J[n_1]$, and $G_i = (n_1/n_i)\gamma_i$ $(i = 2, \ldots, 2g)$.

First, we will prove it when $i = 1$. An element $P \in J$ whose order is the maximaum order, $n_1$, is selected, and set $G_1 = P$. Next, since $h_1$ is a linear map with the kernel, $\mathrm{Ker}(h_1)$, of co-dimension 1, there exists an element $\gamma_2 \in J[n_1]$ such that $\mathrm{Ord}(\gamma_2) = n_1$ and $\gamma_2 \notin \mathrm{Ker}(h_1)$ (or $e_{n_1}(G_1, \gamma_2) \neq 1$). Therefore, when $(G_1, \gamma_2, \ldots, \gamma_{2g})$ is a canonical generating tuple for $J[n_1]$, $< G_1, \gamma_3, \ldots, \gamma_{2g} > \in \mathrm{Ker}(h_1)$. Then, a canonical generating tuple for $J$, $(G_1, G_2, \ldots, G_{2g})$ is determined by $G_i = (n_1/n_i)\gamma_i$ $(i = 2, \ldots, 2g)$.

Next, we will show that for all elements $P, Q \in J_q[n_1]$,

$$h_1(P) = h_1(Q) \quad \textit{if and only if} \quad f_1(P) = f_1(Q).$$

(If)  Suppose that $f_1(P) = f_1(Q)$. Then by the definiton, there exists an integer $c$ such that $P - Q = c_1 G_1 + c_3 G_3 + \cdots c_{2g} G_{2g}$. Using bilinearity and the identity of the extended Weil pairing, and the above mentioned property of the map $h_1$,

$$
\begin{aligned}
e_{n_1}(G_1, P) &= e_{n_1}(G_1, Q + c_1 G_1 + c_3 G_3 + \cdots c_{2g} G_{2g}) \\
&= e_{n_1}(G_1, Q)e_{n_1}(G_1, G_1)^{c_1} e_{n_1}(G_1, G_3)^{c_3} \cdots e_{n_1}(G_1, G_{2g})^{c_{2g}} \\
&= e_{n_1}(G_1, Q).
\end{aligned}
$$

(Only if)  Suppose $f_1(P) \neq f_1(Q)$. Then there exists integers $c_1, c_2, \ldots c_{2g}$ such that $P - Q = c_1 G_1 + c_2 G_2 + c_3 G_3 + \cdots c_{2g} G_{2g}$, where $c_2 G_2 \neq O$.

$$
\begin{aligned}
e_{n_1}(G_1, P) &= e_{n_1}(G_1, Q + c_1 G_1 + c_2 G_2 + \cdots c_{2g} G_{2g}) \\
&= e_{n_1}(G_1, Q)e_{n_1}(G_1, G_1)^{c_1} e_{n_1}(G_1, c_2 G_2) \cdots e_{n_1}(G_1, c_{2g} G_{2g}) \\
&= e_{n_1}(G_1, Q)e_{n_1}(G_1, c_2 G_2).
\end{aligned}
$$

Therefore, if $e_{n_1}(G_1, c_2 G_2) \neq 1$, then the proof of this (Only if) part is completed.

Next, we will prove that $e_{n_1}(G_1, c_2 G_2) \neq 1$. From the nongeneracy of the Weil pairing, $c_2 G_2$ is $O$ if and only if, for all elements $X = a_1 G_1 + a_2 \gamma_2 + \cdots a_{2g} \gamma_{2g}$ in $J[n_1]$ $(0 \leq a_i < n_1)$,

$$e_{n_1}(c_2 G_2, X) = 1.$$

Then,

$$
\begin{aligned}
e_{n_1}(c_2 G_2, X) &= e_{n_1}(c_2 G_2, a_1 G_1 + a_2 \gamma_2 + \cdots a_{2g} \gamma_{2g}) \\
&= e_{n_1}(c_2 G_2, G_1)^{a_1}.
\end{aligned}
$$

Hence, for all elements $X \in J[n_1]$, $e_{n_1}(c_2 G_2, X) = 1$ if and only if $e_{n_1}(c_2 G_2, G_1) = 1$. Therefore, $c_2 G_2$ is $O$ if and only if $e_{n_1}(c_2 G_2, G_1) = 1$. By the condition, $c_2 G_2$ is not $O$, so $e_{n_1}(c_2 G_2, G_1) \neq 1$.

Hence the proof has been completed when $i = 1$. We can easily prove it sequentially when $i = 2, 3, \ldots, g$ in the same manner as $i = 1$, by considering the subgroup $< G_{2i-1}, G_{2i}, \ldots, G_{2g} >$ in place of $J$. ¶

From the above lemma, when $(\langle G_1, G_2 \rangle, \langle G_3, G_4 \rangle, \ldots, \langle G_{2g-1}, G_{2g} \rangle)$ is a *paired* canonical generating tuple, $\mathrm{Ord}(e_{n_{2i-1}}(G_{2i-1}, G_{2i})) = n_{2i}$, and $e_{n_{2i-1}}(G_{2i-1}, G_j) = 1$ $(j \neq 2i)$. Then, we can say that the $g$ subgroups $< G_1, G_2 >, < G_3, G_4 >, \ldots, < G_{2g-1}, G_{2g} >$ are independent, in the sense that the extended Weil pairing of elements from two different subgroups is always 1.

**Definition 4.2** *Let $J$ be a jacobian over $F_q$ with a paired canonical generating tuple, $(\langle G_1, G_2 \rangle, \ldots, \langle G_{2g-1}, G_{2g} \rangle)$. $J$ is half-degenerate if there exist at least two cyclic subgroups, $< G_{2i-1} \neq O, G_{2i} = O >$, (or there exits at least two $i$'s $\in \{1, 2, \ldots, g\}$ such that $G_{2i-1} \neq O$ and $G_{2i} = O$). $J$ is non-half-degenerate if it is not half-degenerate, (or there exits at most one $i \in \{1, 2, \ldots, g\}$ such that $G_{2i-1} \neq O$ and $G_{2i} = O$).*

**Lemma 4.3** *Let $J$ be a jacobian over a field $F_q$ with group structure $(\langle n_1, n_2 \rangle, \langle n_3, n_4 \rangle, \ldots, \langle n_{2g-1}, n_{2g} \rangle)$. Then, $q - 1$ divisible by $n_{2i}$ $(i = 1, \ldots, g)$.*

**Proof:**

Let $(\langle G_1, G_2 \rangle, \langle G_3, G_4 \rangle, \ldots, \langle G_{2g-1}, G_{2g} \rangle)$ be a *paired* canonical generating tuple of the abelian group of $J$. Consider the multiplicative group $M_i$ $(i = 1, \ldots, g)$ consisting of values $e_{n_{2i-1}}(G_{2i-1}, X)$ where $X$ ranges over the elements of $J_q[n_{2i-1}]$. This forms a multiplicative group from the bilinearity and identity of the extended Weil pairing, and the size of $M_i$ is $n_{2i}$ from Lemma 4.1. Since the values $e_{n_{2i-1}}(G_{2i-1}, X)$ are in the finite field $F_q$, group $M_i$ is a subgroup of the multiplicative group $F_q^*$. Consequently, the size of group $F_q^*$ is divisible by the size $M_i$, so $q - 1$ is divisible by $n_{2i}$. ¶

**Lemma 4.4** *Let $J$ be a jacobian over a field $F_q$. Assume that $J$ is non-half-degenerate. Then the group structure of $J$ is $(\langle n_1, n_2 \rangle, \langle n_3, n_4 \rangle, \ldots, \langle n_{2g-1}, n_{2g} \rangle)$, if and only if there exists $2g$-tuple $(\langle P_1, P_2 \rangle, \langle P_3, P_4 \rangle, \ldots, \langle P_{2g-1}, P_{2g} \rangle)$ such that, for all $i = 1, \ldots, g$,*

$$\mathrm{Ord}(P_j) = n_j \quad (j = 1, \ldots, 2g),$$

$$\mathrm{Ord}(e_{n_{2i-1}}(P_{2i-1}, P_{2i})) = n_{2i},$$

$$e_{n_{2i-1}}(P_{2i-1}, P_j) = 1 \quad (j \neq 2i; \; j \in \{1, \ldots, 2g\}),$$

$$e_{n_{2i}}(P_{2i}, P_j) = 1 \quad (j \neq 2i - 1; \; j \in \{1, \ldots, 2g\}),$$

$$N = n_1 \cdot \ldots \cdot n_{2g},$$

*where $P_1, \ldots, P_{2g}$ be elements of $J$, and $N$ be the number of elements of $J$.*

**Proof:**

(Only if) Suppose that the group structure of $J$ is $(\langle n_1, n_2 \rangle, \ldots, \langle n_{2g-1}, n_{2g} \rangle)$. Then, clearly there exists a generating tuple $(P_1, \ldots, P_{2g})$ which satisfies the above conditions.

(If) Suppose that there exists $2g$-tuple $(P_1, \ldots, P_{2g})$ which satisfies the above conditions. From Lemma 4.1, $e_{n_{2i-1}}(P_{2i-1}, P_j) = 1$ $(j \neq 2i)$ and $e_{n_{2i}}(P_{2i}, P_j) = 1$ $(j \neq 2i-1)$ implies that $P_j$ $(j \neq 2i-1, 2i)$ is not included in subgroup $< P_{2i-1}, P_{2i} >$, if $P_{2i-1} \neq O$, $P_{2i} \neq O$ and $P_j \neq O$. From the assumption that $J$ is non-half-degenerate, there exists at most one $i \in \{1, \ldots, g\}$ such that $P_{2i-1} \neq O$ and $P_{2i} = O$. Therefore, the condition implies that each non-identity subgroup $< P_{2i-1}, P_{2i} >$ is independent from the other non-identity subgroups, and each subgroup has the structure $(n_{2i-1}, n_{2i})$, where non-identity subgroup $< P_{2i-1}, P_{2i} >$ denotes the subgroup such that $< P_{2i-1}, P_{2i} > \neq O$ (or $P_{2i-1} \neq O$). Therefore, $N = n_1 \cdot \ldots \cdot n_{2g}$ results in $(\langle P_1, P_2 \rangle, \ldots, \langle P_{2g-1}, P_{2g} \rangle)$ being a paired canonical generating tuple. This concludes that the group structure is $(\langle n_1, n_2 \rangle, \ldots, \langle n_{2g-1}, n_{2g} \rangle)$. ¶

Then we show the main result of this section. The following theorem shows that a membership problem regarding the problem to determine the group structure of a jacobian is in NP ∩ co-NP, when the jacobian is non-half-degenerate.

**Definition 4.5** *HESTR is a language, or membership problem such that*

$HESTR = \{ \langle C, g, q, (m_1, \ldots, m_{2g}) \rangle \mid$ *the group structure of the jacobian $J$ of curve $C$,* $(\langle n_1, n_2 \rangle, \ldots, \langle n_{2g-1}, n_{2g} \rangle)$, *satisfies* $n_i \geq m_i$, $(1, \ldots, 2g)$. $\}$,

*where $C$ is a hyperelliptic curve with genus $g$ defined over $F_q$ ($q$ is a prime power), $m_i$ is a positive integer.*

**Theorem 4.6** *HESTR is in NP ∩ co-NP, when $J$ is non-half-degenerate.*

**Proof:**

If a nondeterministic machine shows a witness that $(\langle n_1, n_2 \rangle, \ldots, \langle n_{2g-1}, n_{2g} \rangle)$ is the group structure of $J$, the witness is used for both HESTR and the complement of HESTR. When $J$ is non-half-degenerate, the witness is $(P_1, P_2, \ldots, P_{2g})$ which satisfies the conditions of Lemma 4.4, factors of the number of the elements of $J$, $N$, and appropriate reduced divisors $T$ and $U$ for computing the extended Weil pairing value (see Algorithm 2). Then, from Lemma 4.4, a poly-time machine can check the group structure using the extended Weil paring and factoring (for checking orders). Here, the poly-time machine can compute $N$ by Pila's algorithm [Pil]. (Note that $(P_1, P_2, \ldots, P_{2g})$ is a generating tuple of this group.) Since the extended Weil pairing can be computed in polynomial-time by using appropriate $T$ and $U$, HESTR is in NP ∩ co-NP. ¶

Theorem 4.6 can be written as follows, using the notion of the promise problem [ESY]: Let $(Q_1, R_1)$ be a promise problem such that $Q_1$ is the promise that $J$ is non-half-degenerate, and $R_1$ is the property that HESTR is true. Then $(Q_1, R_1)$ is in NPP ∩ co-NPP, and $(Q_1, R_1)$ has a solution in NP ∩ co-NP.

Note that generally the fact that $(Q, R)$ is in NPP ∩ co-NPP does not imply that $(Q, R)$ has a solution in NP ∩ co-NP (see [ESY]). However, $(Q_1, R_1)$ above has a solution in NP ∩ co-NP, since the witness of $R_1$ can also be the witness of $Q_1$ (or $Q_1$ is in NP), while generally promise $Q$ is not in NP.

# 5   Complexity of Hyperelliptic Discrete Logarithm

This section introduces two results about the difficulty of the hyperelliptic discrete logarithm; one is the characterization of the problem from the viewpoint of the structural complexity theory. This improves on the result of [SIS]. The other is the reduction of the hyperelliptic curve discrete logarithms to the conventional multiplicative discrete logarithms, which is an extension of the result by [MOV].

## 5.1   Discrete logarithms over the Jacobians

**Definition 5.1** *Let $P \in J$ over $F_q$ be an element of maximum order $n_1$, and let $R \in J$. The hyperelliptic curve logarithm problem is the following: Given $P$ and $R$, determine the unique integer $l$, $0 \le l \le n_1 - 1$, such that $R = lP$, provided that such an integer exists.*

**Definition 5.2** *HEDL is a language, or membership problem such that*

$$HEDL = \{\langle C, g, q, P, R, l_0 \rangle \mid \text{ there exists } l \text{ such that } l \le l_0 \text{ and } R = lP. \},$$

*where $C$ is a hyperelliptic curve with genus $g$ over $F_q$ and $P \in J$ over $F_q$ be an element of maximum order $n_1$, and let $R \in J$.*

## 5.2   HEDL is NP ∩ co-NP when non-half-degenerate

**Theorem 5.3** *HEDL is NP ∩ co-NP, when $J$ is non-half-degenerate.*

**Proof:**

When $< C, g, q, P, R, l_0 >$ is in HEDL, then integer $l$ that satisfies $R = lP$ and $l \le l_0$ is the witness for the input in HEDL. Clearly the computation of $R = lP$ and $l \le l_0$ is deterministic polynomial time. Therefore, HEDL is in NP.

There are two cases in which $< C, g, q, P, R, l_0 >$ is not in HEDL. One is the case where there exists $l'$ such that $R = l'P$ and $l' \not\le l_0$. The other case is where $l$ does not exist such that $R = lP$. In the former case, $l'$ is the witness for the input not in HEDL. In the latter case, when $J$ is non-half-degenerate, the group structure, its witness, $(P_1, \ldots, P_{2g})$ etc., (Theorem 4.6), and a vector $(a_1, \ldots, a_{2g})$ such that $P = P_1$ and $R = a_1 P_1 + \cdots + a_{2g} P_{2g}$ are the witness for the input not in HEDL. This is because $l$ does not exist such that $R = lP$ if and only if there exists $i$ such that $a_i \ne 0$ and $i \ne 1$. Here, Theorem 4.6 guarantees the existence of the witness for the group structure for HEDL, when $J$ is non-half-degenerate. Therefore, HEDL is in co-NP. ¶

Similarly to Theorem 4.6, Theorem 5.3 can be written as follows, using the notion of the promise problem [ESY]: Let $(Q_1, R_2)$ be a promise problem such that $Q_1$ is the promise that $J$ is non-half-degenerate, and $R_2$ is the property that HEDL is true. Then $(Q_1, R_2)$ is in NPP ∩ co-NPP, and $(Q_1, R_2)$ has a solution in NP ∩ co-NP.

## 5.3   Reducing hyperelliptic logarithms to multiplicative logarithms

**Definition 5.4** *Let $J$ be a jacobian over $F_q$ with a paired canonical generating tuple, $(\langle G_1, G_2 \rangle, \ldots, \langle G_{2g-1}, G_{2g} \rangle)$, and its group structure be $(\langle n_1, n_2 \rangle, \ldots, \langle n_{2g-1}, n_{2g} \rangle)$. Let*

$(\langle G_1, \gamma_2 \rangle, \ldots, \langle \gamma_{2g-1}, \gamma_{2g} \rangle)$ be the paired canonical generating tuple of $J[n_1]$, where $G_i = (n_1/n_i)\gamma_i$ $(i = 2, \ldots, 2g)$. Then, $J^{(i)}[n_1]$ denotes $< \gamma_{2i-1}, \gamma_{2i} >$.

## Algorithm 3 (Reduction of HEDL) :

**Input** An element $P \in J$ over $F_q$ of maximum order $n_1$, and $R \in J$.

**Output** An integer $l$ such that $R = lP$.

**Step 1** Determine the smallest integer $k$ such that $J(F_{q^k})$ includes $J^{(1)}[n_1]$, where $P$ is the first element, $G_1$, of the paired canonical generating tuple of $J[n_1]$.

**Step 2** Find $Q \in J(F_{q^k})$ such that $\alpha = e_{n_1}(P, Q)$ has order $n_1$.

**Step 3** Compute $\beta = e_{n_1}(R, Q)$

**Step 4** Compute $l$, the discrete logarithm of $\beta$ to the base $\alpha$ in $F_{q^k}$.

Note that the output of the above algorithm is correct since

$$\beta = e_{n_1}(R, Q) = e_{n_1}(lP, Q) = e_{n_1}(P, Q)^l = \alpha^l.$$

*Remark:* Similar to algorithm 2 of [MOV], the above algorithm is incomplete as we do not provide methods for determining $k$, or for finding the point $Q$. In the final version of this paper, we will show algorithms to find $k$ and $Q$ for some specific hyperelliptic curves.

# 6 Conclusion

In this paper, we have shown that the problem to determine the group structure of the jacobian can be characterized to be in NP $\cap$ co-NP, when the jacobian is non-half-degenerate. Moreover, we have shown that the hyperelliptic discrete logarithm can be characterized to be as tractable as the multiplicative discrete logarithm from the viewpoint of structural computational complexity, when the jacobian is non-half-degenerate. It is an open problem to eliminate the condition of non-half-degeneracy for the jacobian in our results.

# Acknowledgments

Authors would like to sincerely thank Neal Koblitz for pointing out serious mistakes in the abstract version of this paper and for invaluable suggestions. We also would like to thank Joan Feigenbaum for introducing us to Neal Koblitz, and her kind support. We wish to thank Hiroki Shizuya for his useful suggestions and discussions. We also thank Toshiya Itoh for his sending us several useful documents. The first author would like to thank Kenji Koyama, Alfred Menezes and Scott Vanstone for their useful discussions.

# References

[Can] D. Cantor, "Computing in the Jacobian of a Hyperelliptic Curve", *Math. Comp.*, 48, pp.95–101 (1987).

[Cop1] D. Coppersmith, "Fast evaluation of logarithms in fields of characteristic two", *IEEE Transactions on Information Theory*, **IT-30**, 587–594 (1984).

[Cop2] D. Coppersmith, A. Odlyzko and R. Schroeppel, "Discrete logarithms in $GF(p)$", *Algorithmica*, 1 (1986), 1-15.

[DH] W. Diffie and M. E. Hellman, "New Directions in Cryptography", *IEEE Transactions on Information Theory*, Vol.IT-22, No.6, pp.644–654 (1976).

[ElG] T. ElGamal, "A subexponential-time algorithm for computing discrete logarithms over $GF(p^2)$", *IEEE Transactions on Information Theory*, **IT-31**, pp.473–481 (1985).

[ESY] S. Even, A.L. Selman and Y. Yacobi, "The Complexity of Promise Problems with Applications to Public-Key Cryptography", *Information and Control*, **61**, pp.159–173 (1984).

[Ful] W. Fulton, "Algebraic Curves," Benjamin, New York, 1969.

[Kal] B. Kaliski, "A pseudorandom bit generator based on elliptic logarithms", *Advances in Cryptology: Proceedings of Crypto '86*, Lecture Notes in Computer Science, **293**, Springer-Verlag, pp.84–103 (1987).

[Kob1] N. Koblitz, "Elliptic Curve Cryptosystems", *Math. Comp.*, 48, pp.203–209 (1987).

[Kob2] N. Koblitz, "Hyperelliptic Cryptosystems", *Journal of Cryptology*, Vol.1, pp.139–150 (1989).

[Knu] D. Knuth, The Art of Computer Programming, Vol. 2. Reading, MA: Addison-Wesley, 1981.

[Lan] S. Lang, Abelian Varieties, Interscience, New York, 1959.

[MOV] A.J. Menezes, T. Okamoto, S.A. Vanstone, "Reducing Elliptic Curve Logarithms to Logarithms in a Finite Field", *Proc. of STOC'91*, pp.80–89 (1991).

[Mil1] V. Miller, "Uses of elliptic curves in cryptography", *Proc. of Crypto '85*, pp.417–426 (1986).

[Mil2] V. Miller, "Short programs for functions on curves", unpublished manuscript, 1986.

[Odl] A. Odlyzko, "Discrete logarithms and their cryptographic significance", *Proc. of Eurocrypt '84*, pp.224–314, (1985).

[Pil] J. Pila, "Frobenius Maps of Abelian Varieties and Finding Roots of Unity in Finite Fields", *PhD Thesis of Stanford Univ.*, (1988)

[Sch1] R. Schoof, "Elliptic curves over finite fields and the computation of square roots mod $p$", *Mathematics of Computation*, 44, pp.483–494 (1985).

[Sch2] R. Schoof, "Nonsingular plane cubic curves over finite fields", *Journal of Combinatorial Theory*, A 46, pp.183–211 (1987).

[Sil] J. Silverman, *The Arithmetic of Elliptic Curves*, Springer-Verlag, New York, 1986.

[SIS] H. Shizuya, T. Itoh, K.Sakurai, "On the Complexity of Hyperelliptic Discrete Logarithm Problem", to appear in *Proc. of Eurocrypt '91*.

# CM–CURVES WITH GOOD CRYPTOGRAPHIC PROPERTIES

Neal Koblitz

Dept. of Mathematics GN-50

University of Washington

Seattle, WA 98195, U.S.A.

koblitz@math.washington.edu

## Abstract

Our purpose is to describe elliptic curves with complex multiplication which in characteristic 2 have the following useful properties for constructing Diffie–Hellman type cryptosystems: (1) they are nonsupersingular (so that one cannot use the Menezes–Okamoto–Vanstone reduction of discrete log from elliptic curves to finite fields); (2) the order of the group has a large prime factor (so that discrete logs cannot be computed by giant-step/baby-step or the Pollard rho method); (3) doubling of points can be carried out almost as efficiently as in the case of the supersingular curves used by Vanstone; (4) the curves are easy to find.

# 1  Introduction

In Atkin's version of the Goldwasser–Kilian primality test ([1], [9]) one starts with a quadratic imaginary field $K = \mathbf{Q}(\sqrt{-D})$ and then constructs an elliptic curve over a finite field which is the reduction of an elliptic curve with complex multiplication by $K$. This idea can also be applied to the search for elliptic curves which are suitable for the type of cryptosystem described in [3], [8]. As in the primality test, we are looking for elliptic curves whose number of points is equal to a large prime number times a small factor. However, unlike in the primality test, where the curves are defined over very large prime fields, our curves will be defined over small fields. Moreover, we shall be interested in an additional property of the curves, the property of having a small trace of Frobenius. In particular, we shall study curves over small fields of characteristic 2 for which the trace of the Frobenius map is $\pm 1$, i.e., for which the complex multiplication field is $\mathbf{Q}(\sqrt{-D})$ for $D = 2^{k+2} - 1$ a Mersenne number. Such curves lend themselves to particularly efficient computation, since the doubling of points (more precisely, multiplying points by $2^k$) can be speeded up when this condition holds.

J. Feigenbaum (Ed.): Advances in Cryptology - CRYPTO '91, LNCS 576, pp. 279-287, 1992.
© Springer-Verlag Berlin Heidelberg 1992

# 2  Anomalous curves

An elliptic curve $E$ defined over the field $\mathbf{F}_q$ of $q$ elements will be called "anomalous" if the trace of the Frobenius map (the map $(x, y) \mapsto (x^q, y^q)$) is equal to 1. Equivalently, an "anomalous" curve over $\mathbf{F}_q$ is one for which the number of $\mathbf{F}_q$-points is equal to $q$.[1] On an anomalous elliptic curve $E$ over $\mathbf{F}_q$, the Frobenius map $\varphi$ satisfies the characteristic equation $T^2 - T + q = 0$.

We shall also be interested in the "twist" $\widetilde{E}$ of $E$, whose Frobenius satisfies $T^2 + T + q = 0$ (the number of $\mathbf{F}_q$-points on $\widetilde{E}$ is $q + 2$). By the "$n$-twist" $\widetilde{E}_n$ of $E$ we mean the twist of the curve $E$ regarded as a curve over the extension field $\mathbf{F}_{q^n}$ (thus, $\widetilde{E}_1 = \widetilde{E}$). If $q$ is odd and $E$ has equation $y^2 = x^3 + bx + c$, then $\widetilde{E}_n$ has equation $\beta y^2 = x^3 + bx + c$, where $\beta \in \mathbf{F}_{q^n}$ is a nonsquare; if $q$ is even, then the equations are a little different, as we shall see in the examples below. If $n = 2^r n_0$ with $n_0$ odd, then $\widetilde{E}_n$ can be defined over the smaller field extension $\mathbf{F}_{q^{2^r}}$, and its Frobenius map $(x, y) \mapsto (x^{q^{2^r}}, y^{q^{2^r}})$ satisfies the equation $T^2 + aT + q^{2^r} = 0$, where $a$ is the trace of the complex number $\left((1 + \sqrt{1 - 4q})/2\right)^{2^r}$.

The most important case for practical implementation is $q = 2^k$. In that case, the computation of $\varphi : (x, y) \mapsto (x^{2^k}, y^{2^k})$ on an $\mathbf{F}_{2^{kn}}$-point is accomplished by a shift operation of negligible time. Thus, if we want to multiply a point $P$ by $2^k$ on an anomalous curve, the fastest way to do this is to use the identity $\varphi^2 - \varphi + 2^k = 0$, i.e., $2^k P = \varphi(P) - \varphi^2(P)$, since instead of $k$ additions of points we need only perform one. (On the twisted curve $\widetilde{E}$, one analogously has $2^k P = -\varphi(P) - \varphi^2(P)$.)

The greater efficiency obtained if one can double points by taking squares in $\mathbf{F}_{2^n}$ was first realized by Menezes and Vanstone [6], who were working with curves defined over $\mathbf{F}_2$ whose Frobenius map has trace 0, i.e., satisfies the relation $T^2 + 2 = 0$. In that case, since $2P = -\varphi^2(P)$, no addition of points is required, i.e., doubling of points is "free." However, curves with 0 trace of Frobenius are supersingular. In [7] it was shown that the discrete log problem on a supersingular elliptic curve reduces to the discrete log problem in the multiplicative group of a finite field of about the same size. That is, supersingular elliptic curve cryptosystems are now known to be no more secure than the original Diffie–Hellman cryptosystem in a small extension of the underlying finite field. For this reason we shall keep away from curves whose Frobenius map $\varphi$ has trace 0. The anomalous curves — those for which $\varphi$ has trace 1 — are the "next best thing."

In general, for given $q$ the equation of an anomalous elliptic curve over $\mathbf{F}_q$ can be found

---

[1] The term "anomalous" was introduced by Barry Mazur in a different context: given an elliptic curve $E$ over a number field, he calls a prime "anomalous" for $E$ if the Frobenius of $E$ at that prime has trace 1.

by finding $\mathbf{F}_q$-roots of the modular equation corresponding to the complex multiplication field $\mathbf{Q}(\sqrt{1-4q})$, as explained in [4]. However, in our examples we shall be concerned only with small $q$, for which an equation for $E$ can be found quickly by trial and error.

**Theorem.** *Let $E$ be an anomalous elliptic curve defined over $\mathbf{F}_q$, and let $\widetilde{E}$ be its twist.*

(a) *If $P$ is an $\mathbf{F}_{q^n}$-point on $E$ (or $\widetilde{E}$), then the multiple $qP$ can be computed with a single addition of points (together with shift operations for the computation of $x \mapsto x^q$ in a normal basis of $\mathbf{F}_{q^n}$).*

(b) *In the special case $q = 2$, any of the multiples $2^l P$ for $l \le 4$ can be computed with a single addition of points.*

**Proof.** Part (a) follows from the above discussion.

(b) In the case $q = 2$, at first it might seem that an anomalous curve has no advantage, because computing $2P = P + P$ takes only one addition of points anyway. However, if we use the relation $T - T^2 = 2$ satisfied by $\varphi$, iterate and simplify, we obtain the following polynomial identities satisfied by the map $\varphi$ (which is defined on the $\mathbf{F}_{2^n}$-points of $E$ by $P_{(x,y)} \mapsto P_{(x^2,y^2)}$):

$$4 = 2T - 2T^2 = (T - T^2)T - 2T^2 = -T^3 - T^2$$

$$8 = 4 \cdot 2 = (-T^3 - T^2)(T - T^2) = -T^3 + T^5$$

$$16 = 4^2 = T^6 + 2T^5 + T^4 = T^6 + (T - T^2)T^5 + T^4 = -T^7 + 2T^6 + T^4 =$$

$$= -T^7 + (T - T^2)T^6 + T^4 = T^4 - T^8.$$

(The analogous formulas on the twist $\widetilde{E}$ are obtained from these by replacing $T$ by $-T$.) Thus, in computing $kP$, any string of $l \le 4$ zeros can be handled with a single addition of points, as claimed.

Roughly speaking, if one uses $k$'s of small Hamming size, one gets doubling of points "almost 3/4 for free." If $E$ has equation $y^2 + xy = f_3(x)$ for $f_3(x) \in \mathbf{F}_2[x]$ of degree 3 (an explicit equation will be given below), and if $P = P_{(x,y)}$ is an $\mathbf{F}_{2^n}$-point, then the above binomials in $T$ lead to simple formulas for $2^l P$, $l \le 4$, for example: $8 P_{(x,y)} = P_{(x^8,x^8+y^8)} + P_{(x^{32},y^{32})}$.

Alternately, as Victor Miller pointed out to me, for $k$ arbitrary it is efficient to write

$k$ to the base 16 and precompute $k_0 P$ for $1 \leq k_0 < 16$. Then if one uses the last formula above to compute $16^j P$, it is easy to see that on the average the number of additions of points is less than $1/3$ of the expected number of additions of points required with the repeated doubling method based on the binary expansion of $k$.

# 3 Number of points

Let $E$ be an anomalous curve over $\mathbf{F}_q$, and let $\widetilde{E}_n$ be its $n$-twist. Then there is a simple relationship between the number $N_n$ (resp. $\widetilde{N}_n$) of $\mathbf{F}_{q^n}$-points on $E$ (resp. on $\widetilde{E}_n$) and the root $\alpha = (1 + \sqrt{1 - 4q})/2$ of the characteristic polynomial $T^2 - T + q$. Namely, $N_n = |\alpha^n - 1|^2$, $\widetilde{N}_n = |\alpha^n + 1|^2$. This leads to a very simple algorithm for computing $N_n$ and $\widetilde{N}_n$: first compute the Fibonacci–type sequence $a_n$ given by $a_0 = 2$, $a_1 = 1$, $a_{n+1} = a_n - q \, a_{n-1}$ for $n \geq 1$; then $N_n = q^n + 1 - a_n$ and $\widetilde{N}_n = q^n + 1 + a_n$.

Once we have an anomalous curve $E$ defined over $\mathbf{F}_q$, we want to find an extension field $\mathbf{F}_{q^n}$ such that the number $N_n$ of $\mathbf{F}_{q^n}$-points on $E$ or the number $\widetilde{N}_n$ of $\mathbf{F}_{q^n}$-points on $\widetilde{E}_n$ is divisible by a large prime (say, of at least 30 digits). Because $N_n = |\alpha^n - 1|^2$ and $\widetilde{N}_n = |\alpha^n + 1|^2$, it follows that $N_{n_1} | N_n$ whenever $n_1 | n$ and $\widetilde{N}_{n_1} | \widetilde{N}_n$ whenever $n/n_1$ is an odd integer. So if $N_n$ (resp. $\widetilde{N}_n$) is to be a product of a small factor and a large prime, we must take $n$ equal to a prime (resp. equal either to a prime or else to a prime times a very small power of 2).

# 4 Examples defined over $\mathbf{F}_2$

Here we consider the anomalous curve $E : y^2 + xy = x^3 + x^2 + 1$ over $\mathbf{F}_2$ and its twist $\widetilde{E} : y^2 + xy = x^3 + 1$, which have complex multiplication by $\mathbf{Q}(\sqrt{-7})$. For certain prime $n$ one has $N_n = 2 \cdot \text{prime}$ (or $\widetilde{N}_n = 4 \cdot \text{prime}$). Here is a table of all values of $N_n/2$ and $\widetilde{N}_n/4$ for $n < 200$ which are prime (actually, probable prime, since I verified primality using *Mathematica*) and which are of at least 30 digits:

$N_{101}/2 = 1\ 26765\ 06002\ 28230\ 88614\ 28085\ 08011$

$N_{107}/2 = 81\ 12963\ 84146\ 06692\ 18285\ 10322\ 12511$

$N_{109}/2 = 324\ 51855\ 36584\ 26701\ 48744\ 86564\ 61467$

$N_{113}/2 = 5192\ 29685\ 85348\ 27627\ 89670\ 38334\ 67507$

$N_{163}/2 =$ 5846 00654 93236 11672 81474 17535 98448 34832 91185 74063

$\widetilde{N}_{103}/4 =$ 2 53530 12004 56459 53586 25300 67069

$\widetilde{N}_{107}/4 =$ 40 56481 92073 03335 60436 34890 37809

$\widetilde{N}_{131}/4 =$ 6805 64733 84187 69269 32320 12949 34099 85129

Thus, for example, the number of points on the curve $y^2 + xy = x^3 + 1$ over $\mathbf{F}_{2^{131}}$ (a field which according to the table in [11] has an optimal normal basis) is divisible by a 39-digit probable prime. (The field $\mathbf{F}_{2^{113}}$ also has an optimal normal basis.)

# 5 Examples defined over $\mathbf{F}_4$, $\mathbf{F}_8$ and $\mathbf{F}_{16}$

I. We consider the curve $E : y^2 + xy = x^3 + \gamma$, where $\gamma \in \mathbf{F}_4$ satisfies $\gamma^2 = \gamma + 1$, and its twist $\widetilde{E} : y^2 + xy = x^3 + \gamma x^2 + \gamma$. The curves $E$ and $\widetilde{E}$ have complex multiplication by $\mathbf{Q}(\sqrt{-15})$. For certain prime $n$ one has $N_n = 4 \cdot$prime or $\widetilde{N}_n = 6 \cdot$prime. Here is a table of all probable prime values of at least 30 digits of $N_n/4$ and $\widetilde{N}_n/6$ for $n < 100$:

$N_{67}/4 =$ 54445 17870 73501 54153 44659 58609 44105 99059

$N_{79}/4 =$ 91 34385 23331 81432 38773 05730 45979 44745 23653 03319

$\widetilde{N}_{59}/6 =$ 55384 49982 43714 94566 50574 99908 87769

Note that the fields $\mathbf{F}_{4^{67}}$ and $\mathbf{F}_{4^{79}}$ have optimal normal bases [11].

II. We consider the curve $E : y^2 + xy = x^3 + \gamma$, where $\gamma \in \mathbf{F}_8$ satisfies $\gamma^3 = \gamma + 1$, and its twist $\widetilde{E} : y^2 + xy = x^3 + x^2 + \gamma$. The curves $E$ and $\widetilde{E}$ have complex multiplication by $\mathbf{Q}(\sqrt{-31})$. For certain prime $n$ one has $N_n = 8 \cdot$prime or $\widetilde{N}_n = 10 \cdot$prime. Here is a table of all probable prime values of at least 30 digits of $N_n/8$ and $\widetilde{N}/10$ for $n < 66$:

$N_{37}/8 =$ 324 51855 36584 26723 11495 75723 35741

$\widetilde{N}_{47}/10 =$ 27 87593 14981 63278 92689 03181 39617 36218 74561

$\widetilde{N}_{59}/10 =$ 191 56194 26082 36107 29479 33791 57473 18375 04813 70807 01777

III. Finally, we return to the curve $E : y^2 + xy = x^3 + x^2 + 1$ in §4, and consider its 4-twist $\tilde{E}_4 : y^2 + xy = x^3 + \gamma x^2 + 1$, where $\gamma \in \mathbf{F}_{16}$ is an element with absolute trace 1. Since the 4-th power of $\alpha = (1 + \sqrt{-7})/2$ is $(1 - 3\sqrt{-7})/2$, it follows that $E$ regarded over $\mathbf{F}_{16}$ is also anomalous. (The fact that the same curve is anomalous over both $\mathbf{F}_2$ and $\mathbf{F}_{16}$ is to be expected, because the complex multiplication fields $\mathbf{Q}(\sqrt{1 - 2^{k+2}})$ are the same when $k = 1$ and $k = 4$, since $\sqrt{-63} = 3\sqrt{-7}$.) For certain $n$ equal to 4 times a prime, one has $\tilde{N}_n = \tilde{N}_4 \cdot \text{prime} = 18 \cdot \text{prime}$. There is one case for $n < 200$ when $\tilde{N}_n/18$ is a prime of more than 30 digits:

$$\tilde{N}_{148}/18 = 1982\ 28846\ 20916\ 10945\ 91407\ 67798\ 27981\ 11637\ 92081$$

The field $F_{2^{148}}$ happens to have an optimal normal basis [11].

In summary, the above elliptic curves all give rise to Diffie–Hellman type cryptosystems which are secure at our present level of knowledge and technology. The examples in §4 have the additional feature that, when computing a multiple $kP$, any string of $\leq 4$ zeros in the binary representation of $k$ can be handled with only a single addition of points. In the case of the examples in §5.I (respectively, §5.II, §5.III) a string of 2 (resp. 3, 4) zeros in $k$ can be handled with a single addition of points.

# 6 Some aspects of efficient implementation

**Balanced binary expansion.** As noted in [10], one can take advantage of the fact that subtracting points on an elliptic curve is as easy as adding. For example, instead of computing $15P$ as $P + 2(P + 2(P + 2P))$, it is more efficient to compute $2(2(2(2P))) - P$. This is different from exponentiation in a finite field, where it would take longer to compute $\left(\left(\left(a^2\right)^2\right)^2\right)^2 / a$ than $a\left(a\left(a \cdot a^2\right)^2\right)^2$, because division takes much longer than multiplication.

Suppose you want to compute $kP$. The following algorithm, which is equivalent to the second algorithm in [10], will give $k$ as a sum of a minimal number of powers of 2 with coefficients $\pm 1$: move from right to left in the binary expansion of $k$, replacing each sequence of two or more 1-bits $11 \cdots 11$ by $100 \cdots 0$-1. We shall call the result the "balanced binary expansion" of $k$. For example, for $k = 3895$ we move from the binary to the balanced binary expansion as follows:

$$
\begin{array}{ccccccccccccc}
 & 1 & 1 & 1 & 1 & 0 & 0 & 1 & 1 & 0 & 1 & 1 & 1 \\
 & 1 & 1 & 1 & 1 & 0 & 0 & 1 & 1 & 1 & 0 & 0 & -1 \\
 & 1 & 1 & 1 & 1 & 0 & 1 & 0 & 0 & -1 & 0 & 0 & -1 \\
1 & 0 & 0 & 0 & -1 & 0 & 1 & 0 & 0 & -1 & 0 & 0 & -1
\end{array}
$$

The balanced binary expansion of an arbitrary $k$ is likely to have more sequences of several 0's than its binary expansion. In fact, it is simple to show that on the average $2/3$ of a number's balanced binary digits are 0. Thus, when we are computing on the anomalous curves in §4, the easy step of converting $k$ to balanced binary will generally enable us to compute $kP$ faster, because of the circumstance that any string of $\leq 4$ zeros can be handled with a single addition of points. For example, to compute $15P = 16P - P$ requires only 2 additions of points.

In a Diffie–Hellman type key exchange, where one multiplies points by randomly generated $r$-bit integers $k$, one could limit oneself to $k$ of Hamming size $\leq s$, where $s \ll r$. If the binary expansion is used, there are $\sum_{j \leq s} \binom{r}{j}$ such $k$; whereas if we use the balanced binary expansion, then there are almost $\sum_{j \leq s} 2^j \binom{r}{j}$ different $k$ of Hamming size $\leq s$. (We say "almost" because not all sequences of digits can occur; but most do occur when $s \ll r$.)

The following is an even more efficient key exchange procedure. It is based on a suggestion of Hendrik Lenstra.

**Base-$\varphi$ expansion.** Again suppose that we are working in the group of $\mathbf{F}_{2^n}$-points of the anomalous $\mathbf{F}_2$-curve $E : y^2 + xy = x^3 + x + 1$ or its twist $\widetilde{E} : y^2 + xy = x^3 + 1$. Then on $E$ the Frobenius map $\varphi : (x, y) \mapsto (x^2, y^2)$ is the element $\pi = (1 + \sqrt{-7})/2$ of the endomorphism ring $\mathbf{Z}[(-1 + \sqrt{-7})/2]$ (on $\widetilde{E}$ it is $\pi = (-1 + \sqrt{-7})/2$). In the key exchange protocol, instead of choosing a random $r$-bit positive integer $n$ whose balanced binary expansion has Hamming size $\leq s$, each player now chooses a linear combination $n$ of the $\varphi^j$, $0 \leq j < r$, with coefficients $c_j = 0$ or $\pm 1$, such that $\leq s$ of the coefficients are nonzero. Then computing $nP = \sum c_j \varphi^j(P)$ requires only $\leq s - 1$ additions of points, and we have recaptured the efficiency of working with supersingular curves.

One could also compute arbitrary multiples $nP$, where now $n \in \mathbf{Z}$, by representing $n$ "to the base $\varphi$." Namely, since $\varphi = (\pm 1 + \sqrt{-7})/2$ is an element of norm 2 in the Euclidean domain $\mathbf{Z}[(1 + \sqrt{-7})/2]$, any element of the ring — in particular, $n$ — has a unique representation in the form $\sum \epsilon_j \varphi^j$, where $\epsilon_j \in \{0, 1\}$.

We can also obtain a "balanced $\varphi$-expansion" of $n$ as follows. Recall that $\varphi$ satisfies $\varphi(1 - \varphi) = 2$ on $E$ (it satisfies $-\varphi(1 + \varphi) = 2$ on $\widetilde{E}$). We shall work on $E$ (the argument for

$\widetilde{E}$ is analogous with the $\varphi$-expansion replaced by the $(-\varphi)$-expansion). Write $n = n_0 + 2n_1 + 2n_2$, where $n_0 \in \{0, 1\}$ and $n_2$ is the part of the $\varphi$-expansion of $(n - n_0)/2$ consisting of all runs of $\geq 2$ consecutive 1-bits. Note that $2(1 + \varphi + \varphi^2 + \cdots + \varphi^{j-1}) = \varphi - \varphi^{j+1}$. Hence we replace each sequence of $j \geq 2$ consecutive 1-bits $11 \cdots 11$ in the expansion of $n_2$ by $-1\,000 \cdots 10$ in the expansion of $2n_2$.

But unfortunately, expressing an arbitrary $n$ as a balanced $\varphi$-expansion will not necessarily be more efficient than using its balanced binary expansion. This is because the $\varphi$-expansion of $n$ has approximately twice as many bits as the binary expansion. The following example illustrates why the base $\varphi$ does not generally have an advantage over the base 2.

**Example.** Consider the group of $\mathbf{F}_8$-points of $E : y^2 + xy = x^3 + x^2 + 1$, which has order 14. Suppose we want to compute $10P$. Using the binary expansion, we take $2(P + 4P)$, which requires 3 additions. Since the base-$\varphi$ expansion of 5 is 100101, computing $10P = (\varphi^5 + \varphi^2 + 1)2P$ also requires 3 additions. Note that if we happen to know that $\varphi$ acts as $-3$ on the $\mathbf{F}_8$-points of $E$, and so $10 = \varphi^2 + 1$, then we can compute $10P$ with a single addition of points. However, in the general case of $\mathbf{F}_{2^n}$-points it is not clear how to obtain a $\varphi$-expansion of $n$ that is much shorter than the one that comes from the Euclidean algorithm in the ring $\mathbf{Z}\left[(1 + \sqrt{-7})/2\right]$.

**Acknowledgments.** I would like to thank Hendrik Lenstra, Andrew Odlyzko, and Scott Vanstone for helpful conversations.

# References

[1]   S. Goldwasser, J. Kilian, Almost all primes can be quickly certified, *Proceedings of the 18th ACM Symp. Theory of Computing* (1986), 316-329.

[2]   N. Koblitz, *A Course in Number Theory and Cryptography*, Springer-Verlag, 1987.

[3]   N. Koblitz, Elliptic curve cryptosystems, *Math. of Computation*, **48** (1987), 203-209.

[4]   A. K. Lenstra and H. W. Lenstra, Jr., Algorithms in number theory, in: *Handbook of Theoretical Computer Science*, Vol. A, *Algorithms and Complexity*, ed. by j. van Leeuwen, Amsterdam: Elsevier (1990), 673-715.

[5]   A. Menezes and S. A. Vanstone, Isomorphism classes of elliptic curves over finite fields of characteristic 2, *Utilitas Mathematica*, **38** (1990), 135-154.

[6] A. Menezes and S. A. Vanstone, Elliptic curve cryptosystems and their implementation, to appear in *J. Cryptology*.

[7] A. Menezes, T. Okamoto, and S. A. Vanstone, Reducing elliptic curve logarithms to logarithms in a finite field, *Proceedings of the 23rd ACM Symp. Theory of Computing*, 1991.

[8] V. Miller, Use of elliptic curves in cryptography, *Advanced in Cryptology – Crypto '85*, Springer-Verlag, 1986, 417-426.

[9] F. Morain, Implementation of the Goldwasser–Kilian–Atkin primality testing algorithm, preprint.

[10] F. Morain and J. Olivos, Speeding up the computations on an elliptic curve using addition-subtraction chains, *R.A.I.R.O. Technical Informatics and Applications*, **24** (1990), 531-543.

[11] R. C. Mullin, I. M. Onyszchuk, S. A. Vanstone, and R. M. Wilson, Optimal normal bases in GF($p^n$), *Discrete Appl. Math.*, **22** (1988/89), 149-161.

# A New ID-Based Key Sharing System

Shigeo TSUJII
Dept. of Electrical and Electronic Eng.
Tokyo Institute of Technology

Jinhui CHAO
Dept. of Electrical and Electronic Eng.
Tokyo Institute of Technology
jchao@ss.titech.ac.jp

## Abstract

Non-interactive ID-based key sharing schemes are convenient in practice since they do not need preliminary communication. However, they are vulnerable to entities conspiracy. This paper proposes a new ID-based non-interactive key sharing scheme with high security against conspiracy of entities.

# 1 Background

This paper addresses the ID information based key sharing systems in secret communication. The ID-based key sharing scheme seems originally appeared in Blom's work [1]. This interesting idea, however, really began to attract a great deal of attention only after Shamir in 1984 proposed explicitly the concept of an ID-based system [2]. Since then, active researches have been observed, especially in Japan, to develop concrete ID-based key sharing schemes.

ID-based key sharing scheme can be categorized into interactive and non-interactive ones. The interactive schemes require preliminary communication between entities before they share their common key [3]. On the other hand, there is no need of any preliminary communication in non-interactive schemes.

In this paper, we consider the non-interactive schemes. Researches have been continuing in this field, which include T.Matsumoto and H.Imai [4], H.Tanaka [5], S.Tsujii et al [6], [7]. T.Harada and N.Matsuzaki [8] etc.. However, the non-interactive schemes suffered from the conspiracy problem. In other words, if a certain number of entities show each other their secrets given by the trusted center, they maybe able to reveal the center secrets or to forge the common secret keys between some other entities. We define "threshold of conspiracy" as the minimum number of entities in order to reveal the center secrets in such way. (Recently, another key distribution method is proposed by Y. Murakami, S.Kasahara [10][11] and a little later by U.M.Maurer and Y.Yacobi [12], which is also discussed in [13] .)

J. Feigenbaum (Ed.): Advances in Cryptology - CRYPTO '91, LNCS 576, pp. 288-299, 1992.
© Springer-Verlag Berlin Heidelberg 1992

Thus, to find a non-interactive ID-based scheme has been a challenging problem for the researchers in this field.

Despite of extensive efforts on this subject, all the non-interactive schemes proposed so far are unable to extend their threshold beyond the number of secret parameters in the center. Therefore, it has been skeptical about whether there exist schemes without conspiracy threshold.

In this paper, a novel non-interactive key sharing schemes is presented. It is believed to be highly secure in the sense that it is free from the conspiracy problem.

# 2 Center algorithm priori to key sharing

A trusted center prepares four kinds of information, in addition to processing of ID information as followings:

1. Publicized information common to all entities;

2. Center secret information common to all entities;

3. Center secret information for each entity;

4. Entity secret information for key sharing.

## 2.1 ID information pre-processing

The center chooses an one-way function and transforms the $l$-bit ID vectors to $n$-bit random vectors, then publicizes them to all the entities.

$$h(\cdot) \quad : \quad \text{Hash function which converts} l - \text{bit sequence of original}$$
$$\text{ID vector of an entity to an} - \text{bit random sequence.}$$

$$ID_A, ID_B \quad : \quad \text{Modified ID vector of entities A and B as images of}$$
$$\text{the original ID vectors of A and B under} \quad h(\cdot).$$

$$ID_A = (a_1, a_2, \ldots, a_n)^t \quad a_k \in GF(2);$$
$$ID_B = (b_1, b_2, \ldots, b_n)^t \quad b_k \in GF(2);$$

We also need the binary complement of the ID vectors

$$ID_A^c = (a_1^c, a_2^c, \ldots, a_n^c)^t \qquad a_k^c : \quad \text{binary complement of} \quad a_k;$$
$$ID_B^c = (b_1^c, b_2^c, \ldots, b_n^c)^t \qquad b_k^c : \quad \text{binary complement of} \quad b_k.$$

## 2.2 Publicized information common to all entities

The center publicizes a composite number $N$, which is determined as follows.

$$
\begin{aligned}
N &= P \cdot Q \cdot R \cdot T \\
P &= \quad 2p + 1 \qquad \text{80digits (250bit)} \\
Q &= \quad 2q + 1 \qquad \text{80digits (250bit)} \\
R &= \quad 2r + 1 \qquad \text{80digits (250bit)} \\
T &= \quad 2t + 1 \qquad \text{80digits (250bit)}
\end{aligned}
$$

Here $P$, $Q$, $R$ and $T$ are Sophie-Germain primes, and $p$, $q$, $r$, $t$ are primes. We assume that it is difficult to factorize $pq$ and $rt$.

## 2.3 Center Secret information common to all entities

The center specifies the following parameters and keeps them for its secrets.

$$
\begin{aligned}
(1) \qquad & \lambda(N) &=& \; 2pqrt \\
(2) \qquad & X, Y &:& \; n \times n \quad \text{nonsingular symmetric matrices;} \\
& X &=& \; (x_{ij}), \quad x_{ij} = x_{ji}, \quad x_{ij} \in Z_{\lambda(N)} \\
& Y &=& \; (y_{ij}), \quad y_{ij} = y_{ji}, \quad y_{ij} \in Z_{\lambda(N)} \\
& x_i &:& \; \text{i-th row vector of } X; \\
& y_i &:& \; \text{i-th row vector of } Y; \\
(3) \qquad & g &:& \; \text{a maximum generator in } Z_N^*;
\end{aligned}
$$

Here, $Z_N^*$ stands for the set of the elements in $Z_N$ which are relatively prime to $N$ or the unit group of $Z_N$. The maximum generator is a generator in the unit group of $Z_N$ with the maximum order, or its order equals the Carmichael function $\lambda(N)$.

## 2.4 Center secrets for each entities

For notational simplicity, we define a scalar product operation "$\otimes$" between vectors and vectors with a matrix.

<u>Definition</u>: An exponential-product of a row vector $u$ and a column vector $v$ is defined as

$$u \bigotimes v = \prod_{k=1}^{n} u_k^{v_k} \tag{1}$$

where
$$v = (v_1, \ldots, v_n)^t, \quad v_k \in Z \tag{2}$$
$$u = (u_1, \ldots, u_n), \quad u_k \in Z \tag{3}$$

The product of a $n \times n$ matrix $U$ and a column vector $v$ are defined as

$$U \bigotimes v = (u_1 \bigotimes v, \ldots, u_n \bigotimes v)^t \tag{4}$$

$$= (\prod_{j=1}^{n} u_{1j}^{v_j}, \ldots, \prod_{j=1}^{n} u_{nj}^{v_j})^t \tag{5}$$

where
$$U = (u_1^t, \ldots, u_n^t)^t \tag{6}$$
$$u_i = (u_{i1}, \ldots, u_{in}), i = 1, \ldots, n \tag{7}$$

are the row vectors of $U$. The center computes the following secrets for each entity, e.g. A;

(1)
$$\alpha_{Akj} \in Z_{\lambda(N)}^* \quad (1 \le j \le n, \quad k = 1, 2) \tag{8}$$

$$\alpha_{Ak} = \prod_{j=1}^{n} \alpha_{Akj} \mod \lambda(N) \tag{9}$$

$$c_{Aj} = (c_{A2}, \ldots, c_{An}), \quad c_{Aj} \in Z_{\lambda(N)}^* \tag{10}$$

$$\beta_{Ak1j} \in Z_{\lambda(N)}^* \quad (2 \le j \le n) \tag{11}$$

where $\quad \alpha_{A1j}\beta_{A21j} = \alpha_{A2j}\beta_{A11j} \tag{12}$

$$\beta_{Ak2j} = c_{Aj}\beta_{Ak1j} \quad (2 \le j \le n) \tag{13}$$

$$\beta_{Aki} = \prod_{j=1}^{n} \beta_{Akij} \mod \lambda(N) \tag{14}$$

here $\beta_{Aki1}$ are chosen to satisfy

$$\alpha_{A1}^{-1}\beta_{A1i} + \alpha_{A2}^{-1}\beta_{A2i} = 0 \mod \lambda(N) \tag{15}$$
$$(i = 1, 2 \quad k = 1, 2)$$

(2)
$$s_{A1} = (s_{A11}, \ldots, s_{A1n}) \tag{16}$$

$$= (X \otimes ID_A)^T \tag{17}$$

$$= (\prod_{j=1}^{n} x_{1j}^{a_j}, \ldots, \prod_{j=1}^{n} x_{nj}^{a_j}) \mod \lambda(N) \tag{18}$$

$$s_{A2} = (s_{A21}, \ldots, s_{A2n}) \tag{19}$$

$$= (Y \otimes ID_A)^T \tag{20}$$

$$= (\prod_{j=1}^{n} y_{1j}^{a_j}, \ldots, \prod_{j=1}^{n} y_{nj}^{a_j}) \quad \text{mod } \lambda(N) \tag{21}$$

$$s_{Aij} \in \mathbf{Z}_{\lambda(N)} \tag{22}$$

## 2.5 Individual secrets for each entities

The center then delivers to entity A through a secure channel the following individual secret data matrices.

(1)  $\quad G_{Ak} = g^{\alpha_{Ak}^{-1}} \quad (\text{mod } N) \tag{23}$

(2)  $\quad \boldsymbol{D}_{Ak} = [\, d_{Ak}(i,j)\,], \quad k = 1, 2; \quad i = 1, 2; \quad j = 1, \ldots, n \tag{24}$

with row vectors as

$$d_{Ak1} = (\, d_{Ak}(1,1), \ldots, d_{Ak}(1,n)\,)$$
$$d_{Ak2} = (\, d_{Ak}(2,1), \ldots, d_{Ak}(2,n)\,)$$

$$d_{Ak}(i,j) = 2pq \,\alpha_{Akj}\, s_{Aij} + \tau t\, \beta_{Akij} \tag{25}$$

Notice that $d_{Ak}(i,j)$ is not computed with modulo arithmetics, e.g. mod $\lambda(N)$, but with the arithmetics over the integer ring. This is required in order to keep $\lambda(N)$ secret as explained in section 5. Thus $d_{Ak}(i,j)$ may take larger values. The increase of the length, however, is no more than twice, so it will cause little problem when fast modular exponentiation algorithms are used.

# 3 Common Key Generation

When key sharing is required between entity A and B, A computes the following parameter (we call it the key kernel) over the integer ring $\mathbf{Z}$, (since the Carmichael function is unknown for all entities).

$$H_{ABk} = (d_{Ak1} \bigotimes ID_B) \cdot (d_{Ak2} \bigotimes ID_B^c)$$

$$= \prod_{j=1}^{n} d_{Ak}(1,j)^{b_j} \prod_{j=1}^{n} d_{Ak}(2,j)^{b_j} \tag{26}$$

and calculates the key to entity B as

$$K_{AB} = G_{A1}^{H_{AB1}} \cdot G_{A2}^{H_{AB2}} \quad \text{mod } N. \tag{27}$$

At the same time, B calculates also his key kernel over the integer ring $\mathbf{Z}$

$$H_{BAk} = (d_{Bk1} \bigotimes ID_A) \cdot (d_{Bk2} \bigotimes ID_A^c) \tag{28}$$

and the key to entity A

$$K_{BA} = G_{B1}^{H_{BA1}} \cdot G_{B2}^{H_{BA2}} \quad \mathrm{mod}\ N. \tag{29}$$

We note that the key kernels for A and B are not the same. However, we will show that the keys produced from the key kernels between A and B are equal. Since

$$
\begin{aligned}
H_{ABk} &= (2pq)^n \alpha_{Ak} S_{AB} + \prod_{j=1}^{n} rt\beta_{Akb;j} + l\lambda(N) \\
&= (2pq)^n \alpha_{Ak} S_{AB} + (rt)^n \beta_{ABk} + l\lambda(N) \tag{30}
\end{aligned}
$$

Here, 
$$\beta_{ABk} := \prod_{j=1}^{n} \beta_{Akb;j} \tag{31}$$

$$
\begin{aligned}
S_{AB} &= s_{A1} \bigotimes ID_B \cdot s_{A2} \bigotimes ID_B^c \\
&= (X \bigotimes ID_A)^t \bigotimes ID_B \cdot (Y \bigotimes ID_A^c)^t \bigotimes ID_B^c \\
&= \prod_{i=1}^{n}\prod_{j=1}^{n} x_{ij}^{b;a_j} \prod_{i=1}^{n}\prod_{j=1}^{n} y_{ij}^{b_i^c a_j^c} \quad \mathrm{mod}\ \lambda(N), \tag{32}
\end{aligned}
$$

As shown at the end of this section, entity A will exponentiate $d_{Ak}(i,j)$ to $G_{Ak}$ to calculate $K_{ABk}$. The last term in Eq.(31) will vanish during these processes despite that A does not know $\lambda(N)$. In the sequel,

$$
\begin{aligned}
K_{ABk} &= G_{Ak}^{H_{ABk}} \\
&= g^{\alpha_{Ak}^{-1}[\alpha_{Ak}(2pq)^n S_{AB} + (rt)^n \beta_{ABk}]} \\
&= g^{[(2pq)^n S_{AB} + \alpha_{Ak}^{-1} \beta_{ABk}(rt)^n]} \quad (\mathrm{mod}\ N) \tag{33} \\
K_{AB} &= G_{A1}^{H_{AB1}} \cdot G_{A2}^{H_{AB2}} \\
&= g^{[(2pq)^n S_{AB} + \alpha_{A1}^{-1} \beta_{AB1}(rt)^n]} \\
&\quad \cdot g^{[(2pq)^n S_{AB} + \alpha_{A2}^{-1} \beta_{AB2}(rt)^n]} \\
&= g^{[2(2pq)^n S_{AB} + (\alpha_{A1}^{-1}\beta_{AB1} + \alpha_{A2}^{-1}\beta_{AB2})(rt)^n]} \\
&= g^{2(2pq)^n S_{AB}} \quad (\mathrm{mod}\ N), \tag{34}
\end{aligned}
$$

The last equality is derived as follows. We assume $b_1 = 1$, but we can prove it by the same way in the case of $b_1 = 0$. Since

$$\beta_{AB1} = \beta_{A11} \cdot \prod_{j=2}^{n} c_{Aj}^{b_j^c}, \qquad \beta_{AB2} = \beta_{A21} \cdot \prod_{j=2}^{n} c_{Aj}^{b_j^c}$$

Thus 
$$
\begin{aligned}
\alpha_{A1}^{-1}\beta_{AB1} + \alpha_{A2}^{-1}\beta_{AB2} &= (\alpha_{A1}^{-1}\beta_{A11} + \alpha_{A2}^{-1}\beta_{A21}) \prod_{j=2}^{n} c_{Aj}^{b_j^c} \\
&= 0 \quad \mathrm{mod}\ \lambda(N)
\end{aligned}
$$

due to the condition equation (15).

On the other hand,

$$
\begin{aligned}
H_{BAk} \quad (\mathrm{mod}\ \lambda(N)) &= (2pq)^n \alpha_{Bk} S_{BA} + \prod_{j=1}^{n} rt\beta_{Bka_jj} \\
&= (2pq)^n \alpha_{Bk} S_{BA} + (rt)^n \beta_{BAk} \quad \mathrm{mod}\ \lambda(N) \quad (35) \\
S_{BA} &= s_{B1} \bigotimes ID_A \cdot s_{B2} \bigotimes ID_A^c \\
&= (X \bigotimes ID_B)^t \bigotimes ID_A \cdot (Y \bigotimes ID_B^c)^t \bigotimes ID_A^c \\
&= \prod_{i=1}^{n}\prod_{j=1}^{n} x_{ij}^{a_ib_j} \prod_{i=1}^{n}\prod_{j=1}^{n} y_{ij}^{a_i^c b_j^c} \quad \mathrm{mod}\ \lambda(N), \quad (36)
\end{aligned}
$$

$$(37)$$

$$
\begin{aligned}
K_{BA} &= G_{B1}^{H_{BA1}} \cdot G_{B2}^{H_{BA2}} \\
&= g^{[2(2pq)^n S_{BA} + (\alpha_{B1}^{-1}\beta_{BA1} + \alpha_{B2}^{-1}\beta_{BA2})]} \\
&= g^{2(2pq)^n S_{BA}} \quad (\mathrm{mod}\ N), \quad (38)
\end{aligned}
$$

Considering that $X$ and $Y$ are symmetric, $(x_{ij} = x_{ji})$, $(y_{ij} = y_{ji})$,

$$
S_{AB} = S_{BA} \quad \mathrm{mod}\ \lambda(N) \quad (39)
$$

$$
\text{thus,} \quad K_{AB} = K_{BA} \quad \mathrm{mod}\ N \quad (40)
$$

is obviously satisfied.

In fact, the entities have no knowledge of $\lambda(N)$. Thus, entity A can only compute the exponent of $K_{ABk}$, $\prod_{j=1}^{n} d_{Ak}(1,j)^{b_j} \prod_{j=1}^{n} d_{Ak}(2,j)^{b_j^c}$ over the integer ring, which may result in some very large number. A practical way for entity A to obtain $K_{AB}$ is as follows. Notice that $g^{\lambda(N)} = 1\ \mathrm{mod}\ N$, then we can calculate

$$
K_{ABk} = ((((G_{A1}^{d_{Ak}(1,1)^{b_1}})^{d_{Ak}(2,1)^{b_1^c}})^{d_{Ak}(1,2)^{b_2}})^{d_{Ak}(2,2)^{b_2^c}})^{\cdots} \quad \mathrm{mod}\ N
$$

# 4 A Working Example

The following dummy example will facilitate the understanding of the above scheme. For simplicity, no large prime factors are included in $N$. First the center prepares the following parameters.

Let $n = 3$,

$$ID_A = (1, 0, 1)^t$$

$$ID_B = (0, 1, 1)^t$$

$$N = 5 \cdot 7 \cdot 11 \cdot 23 = 8855$$

$$\lambda(N) = 2 \cdot 2 \cdot 3 \cdot 5 \cdot 11 = 660$$

$$g = 17$$

$$X = \begin{pmatrix} 29 & 23 & 7 \\ 23 & 13 & 17 \\ 7 & 17 & 19 \end{pmatrix}$$

$$Y = \begin{pmatrix} 29 & 7 & 17 \\ 7 & 19 & 31 \\ 17 & 31 & 13 \end{pmatrix}$$

The center secrets for entities A and B are set as

| | | | |
|---|---|---|---|
| $s_{A1} = (203, 391, 133)$ | | $s_{B1} = (13, 17, 11)$ |
| $s_{A2} = (493, 217, 221)$ | | $s_{B2} = (29, 29, 23)$ |
| $c_A = (7, 19)$ | | $c_B = (13, 17)$ |
| $\alpha_{A1} = (29, 17, 31)$ | | $\alpha_{B1} = (161, 221, 323)$ |
| $\alpha_{A2} = (13, 19, 23)$ | | $\alpha_{B2} = (117, 589, 403)$ |
| $\alpha_{A1} = 143$ | | $\alpha_{B1} = 133$ |
| $\alpha_{A1}^{-1} = 487$ | | $\alpha_{B1}^{-1} = 397$ |
| $\alpha_{A2} = 401$ | | $\alpha_{B1} = 557$ |
| $\alpha_{A2}^{-1} = 581$ | | $\alpha_{B1}^{-1} = 173$ |

| | | | |
|---|---|---|---|
| $\beta_{A11} = (29, 19, 23)$ | | $\beta_{B11} = (13, 19, 29)$ |
| $\beta_{A12} = (31, 463, 437)$ | | $\beta_{B12} = (37, 247, 493)$ |
| $\beta_{A21} = (29, 17, 13)$ | | $\beta_{B21} = (29, 23, 19)$ |
| $\beta_{A22} = (361, 119, 247)$ | | $\beta_{B12} = (381, 299, 323)$ |

Also, the center delivers the following individual data to the entity A.

$$G_{A1} = 7213$$

$$G_{A2} = 5397$$

$$D_{A1} = \begin{pmatrix} 72239 & 80809 & 50741 \\ 173269 & 69733 & 106247 \end{pmatrix}$$

$$D_{A2} = \begin{pmatrix} 33263 & 90083 & 37423 \\ 96763 & 56021 & 74581 \end{pmatrix}$$

Based on these data and the ID information of entity B, entity A calculates the key kernel and $K_{AB}$,

$$H_{ABk} = (2pq)^3 \alpha_{Ak} x_{21} x_{23} x_{31} x_{33} y_{12} + (rt)^3 \prod_{j=1}^{3} \beta_{Akb_j j} \tag{41}$$

$$K_{AB} = g^{(2pq)^3 x_{21} x_{23} x_{31} x_{33} y_{12}} \quad \text{mod } 8855 \tag{42}$$

At the same time, entity B receives his individual data matrix

$$G_{B1} = 822$$
$$G_{B2} = 4352$$
$$D_{B1} = \begin{pmatrix} 56743 & 62041 & 75239 \\ 43447 & 176149 & 118999 \end{pmatrix}$$
$$D_{B2} = \begin{pmatrix} 42619 & 51653 & 113449 \\ 30951 & 150737 & 158009 \end{pmatrix}$$

Entity B then calculates the key kernel and key to entity A as

$$H_{BAk} = (2pq)^3 \alpha_{Bk} x_{12} x_{13} x_{32} x_{33} y_{21} + (rt)^3 \prod_{j=1}^{3} \beta_{Bka_j j} \tag{43}$$

$$K_{BA} = g^{(2pq)^3 x_{12} x_{13} x_{32} x_{33} y_{21}} \quad \text{mod } 8855 \tag{44}$$

Note the second terms in $H_{AB}$ and $H_{BA}$ are eliminated during generation process of common keys in the sequel. Thus, the common key

$$K_{AB} = K_{BA} = 246 \quad \text{mod } 8855 \tag{45}$$

is obtained between A and B.

# 5  Security Consideration Against Conspiracy

## 5.1  Condition required to break the scheme

We consider the conditions for a conspired group of entities to attack any particular entity X or to forge the common keys between X and other entities.

In fact, among the center secrets, $X$, $Y$ and $\lambda(N) = 2pqrt$, only $rt$ may be revealed under the following conspiracy attacks.

Suppose that a conspiracy group consists of three members A,B,C. They can produce key kernels $H_{AB}, H_{BC}, H_{CA}$ by simulating the key sharings between A and B, B and C, also C and A. This circle of key sharings can also be formed in the reverse order, when the conspirators have $H_{AC}, H_{CB}, H_{BA}$. If they took the products of each triples of the key kernels, the difference $H_{AB}H_{BC}H_{CA} - H_{AB}H_{BC}H_{CA}$ will be a multiple of $rt$. By choice of several different triples of conspirators to obtain more multiples of $rt$, the $rt$ can be found as the GCD of these quantities. (We sometime call these kinds of attack as "loop attack").

Once the $rt$ is revealed, each conspirator Z can know about $pq\alpha_{Zkj}S_{Zij}$ (mod $rt$) by taking modulo $rt$ on $d_{Zk}(i,j)$. By solving a system of linear equations, $X$, $Y$ (mod $rt$) and $pq$ (mod $rt$) can also be obtained.

However, to forge the common keys of entity X requires values of $p,q$ or $\lambda(N)$, which cannot be derived from $pq$ (mod $rt$). In conclusion, the integrity of the proposed scheme lies on the difficulty to find $\lambda(N)$ .

## 5.2   Consideration on the Carmichael function

Now we address the possibility of revealing Carmichael function $\lambda(N)$ or $pq$ in the following three situations.

First, we suppose that entity A tries to find $pq$ or $\lambda(N)$ from its individual data matrices $D_{Ak}$. Notice that the first and second terms of

$$d_{Ak}(i,j) = pq\alpha_{Akj}S_{Aij} + rt\beta_{Akij}$$

contain different parameters at different rows and columns, no one can eliminate the second terms in $d_{Ak}(i,j)$ in order to reach the first terms which contains $pq$.

Besides, these quantities are calculated over the integer ring without any modulo $\lambda(N)$ operations involved. Therefore, it is impossible to fabricate two different integers which are congruent modulo $\lambda(N)$. i.e., $\lambda(N)$ cannot be found by a single entity himself.

Also, the parameters in each elements of the individual data matrices are distinct for different entities. Thus, even a number of entities conspired together, there is no way to find $pq$, since the system of equations to solve these parameters always contain more unknowns than the number of the equations.

Secondly, we assume the attack is conducted by A using its key kernels to a group of entities B, C, D, $\cdots$, $H_{AB}, H_{AC}, H_{AD}, \cdots$. Since the second term in

$$H_{AB} = (2pq)^n \alpha_A S_{AB} + (rt)^n \beta_{ABk} + l\lambda(N)$$

is also different for different pairs of entities, it can not be removed by subtraction. Thus, the information on $pq$ will not be separated out.

Besides, numerous entities, e.g. A, B, C may conspire together by using their key kernels to implement a loop attack. If the products such as $H_{AB}H_{BC}H_{CA}$ and $H_{AC}H_{CB}H_{BA}$ had same values over $Z_{\lambda(N)}$, or congruent modulo $\lambda(N)$, they would reveal $\lambda(N)$. In our setting, however, $H_{AB}H_{BC}H_{CA}$ and $H_{AC}H_{CB}H_{BA}$ always have different values, thus nothing about $\lambda(N)$ can be revealed.

Thirdly, we consider the situations when the conspired entities show each others their common keys, e.g. $K = g^{(2pq)^n S_{AB}} \bmod N$, etc. Since the discrete logarithm problem is computationally difficult, and factorization of N are unknown to them, the scheme will remain secure under such attacks.

# 6 Conclusion

We have shown a new ID-based non-interactive key sharing scheme. It is designed to clear out all kinds of approaches used until now to break out the center secrets or implement attack to an arbitrary entity in existing non-interactive ID-based schemes. Thus, it is considered to be highly secure against the conspiracy attacks by any group of entities.

**Acknowledgment:** The authors wish to thank for Professor Hatsukazu Tanaka of Kobe University for stimulating discussions with him, and Mr. Genichi Nishio of Tokyo Institute of Technology for his helpful suggestions.

# References

[1] R. Blom " Non-public key distribution," Proceeding of Crypto'82, pp.231-236, 1982.

[2] A. Shamir "Identity-based cryptosystem and signature scheme," Proceeding of Crypto'84, pp.47-53, 1984.

[3] E. Okamoto, K. Tanaka " Key distribution system based on identification information," IEEE Journal on Selected Areas in Communications, Vol.7, No.4, pp.481-485, May, 1989.

[4] T. Matsumoto, H. Imai " On the key predistribution system: A practical solution to the key distribution problem ," Proceeding of Crypto'87, pp.185-193, 1987.

[5] H. Tanaka, " A realization scheme for the identity-based cryptosystem," Proceeding of Crypto'87, pp.340-349, 1987.

[6] S. Tsujii, T.Itoh, " ID-based cryptosystem based on the discrete logarithm problem," IEEE Journal on Selected Areas in Communications, Vol.7, No.4, pp.467-473, May, 1989.

[7] S. Tsujii, T.Itoh, " ID-based cryptosystem using discrete logarithm problem," *Electronics Letters*, Vol.23, No.24, pp.1318-1320, Nov. 1987. May, 1989.

[8] . Harada, Matsuzaki "An ID-based key sharing scheme without preliminary communication," IEICE Japan Tech. Rep. ISEC89-38, Dec. 1989

[9] H. Tanaka "Identity-based non-interactive common- information generation and its application to cryptosystems," Proceeding of Symposium on Cryptography and Information Security, SCIS91, Japan, Dec. 1990.

[10] Y. Murakami, S. Kasahara "An ID-based key distribution system," IEICE Japan Tech. Rep. ISEC90-26, Sept. 1990.

[11] Y. Murakami, S. Kasahara "The discrete Logarithm problem under a composite modulus," IEICE Japan Tech. Rep. ISEC90-42, Dec. 1990.

[12] U. M. Maurer, Y. Yacobi "Non-interactive public key cryptography," Proceeding of EUROCRYPT'91, 1991.

[13] T.Matsumoto, H.Imai "On the security of some key sharing schemes (Part 2)" IEICE Japan Tech. Rep. ISEC90-28, 1990.

# Pseudo-random Generators from One-way Functions

Michael Luby
International Computer Science Institute
Berkeley, California, U.S.A.

**Abstract**

One of the basic primitives in cryptography and other areas of computer science is a pseudo-random generator. The usefulness of a pseudo-random generator is demonstrated by the fact that it can be used to construct a private key cryptosystem that is secure even against chosen plaintext attack. A pseudo-random generator can also be used to conserve random bits and allows reproducibility of results in Monte Carlo simulation experiments. Intuitively, a *pseudo-random generator* is a polynomial time computable function $g$ that stretches a short random string $x$ into a much longer string $g(x)$ that "looks" just like a random string to *any* polynomial time adversary that is allowed to examine $g(x)$.[1] Thus, a pseudo-random number generator can be used to efficiently convert a small amount of true randomness into a much longer string that is indistinguishable from a truly random string of the same length to any polynomial time adversary.

On the other hand, there seem to be a variety of natural examples of another basic primitive; the one-way function. Intuitively, a function $f$ is *one-way* if: (1) given any $x$, $f(x)$ can be computed in polynomial time; (2) given $f(x)$ for a randomly chosen $x$, it is not possible on average to find an inverse $x'$ such that $f(x') = f(x)$ in polynomial time. It has not been proven that there are any one-way functions, but there are a number of problems from number theory, coding theory, graph theory and combinatorial theory that are candidates for problems that might eventually be proven to be one-way functions.

We show how to construct a pseudo-random generator from *any* one-way function. The journal version of this work (in preparation) is the combination of the results announced in the conference papers [ILL, Impagliazzo Levin Luby] and [H, Håstad].

# References

[1] Impagliazzo, R., Levin, L. and Luby, M, "Pseudo-random number generation from one-way functions", 21$^{rst}$ *STOC*, 1989, pp 12-24.

[2] Håstad, J. "Pseudo-Random Generators under Uniform Assumptions", 22$^{nd}$ *STOC*, 1990, pp 395-404.

---

[1]This should be contrasted with the classical definition of a pseudo-random generator. A classical pseudo-random generator is required to pass a particular set of statistical tests, but does not necessarily satisfy the more general requirement that it pass all polynomial time tests. This is a particularly important distinction in the context of cryptography, where the adversary must be assumed to be as malicious as possible, with the only restriction on tests being computation time.

# NEW RESULTS ON PSEUDORANDOM PERMUTATION GENERATORS BASED ON THE DES SCHEME

Jacques PATARIN

INRIA Domaine de Voluceau BP 105 78153 Le Chesnay Cedex France

J. Feigenbaum (Ed.): Advances in Cryptology - CRYPTO '91, LNCS 576, pp. 301-312, 1992.
© Springer-Verlag Berlin Heidelberg 1992

# NEW RESULTS ON PSEUDORANDOM PERMUTATION GENERATORS BASED ON THE DES SCHEME

## Abstract

We denote by $\psi^k$ the permutation generator based on the DES Scheme with $k$ rounds where the $S$ boxes are replaced by random independant functions. We denote by $|P_1 - P_1^*|$, (respectively $|P_1 - P_1^{**}|$), the probability of distinguishing such a permutation from a random function (respectively from a random permutation) by means of a distinguishing circuit that has $m$ oracle gates.

In 1988, M. Luby and C. Rackoff [1] proved that

$$\forall k \geq 3, |P_1 - P_1^*| \leq \frac{m(m-1)}{2^n}.$$

At Eurocrypt 90, J. Pieprzyk wondered at the end of his paper [4] if that inequality could be improved. This is the problem we consider here. In particular, such an improvement could greatly reduce the length of the keys used in a "direct" application of these theorems to a cryptosystem.

Our main results will be :

1. For $\psi^3$ and $\psi^4$ there is no really tighter inequality than $|P_1 - P_1^*| \leq \frac{m(m-1)}{2^n}$.

2. However for $\psi^5$ (and then for $\psi^k, k \geq 5$), there is a much tighter inequality than Luby - Rackoff's one. For example for $\psi^6$, $|P_1 - P_1^*|$ and $|P_1 - P_1^{**}|$ are $\leq \frac{12m}{2^n} + \frac{18m^3}{2^{2n}}$.

3. When $m$ is very small ($m = 2$ or $3$ for example) it is possible to have an explicit evaluation of the effects of the number of rounds $k$ on the "better and better pseudorandomness" of $\psi^k$.

# 1 Notations and definitions

**Definitions 1**
- $I_n$ is the set $\{0, 1\}^n, n \in \mathbf{N}$.

- For $a, b \in I_n$, $[a, b]$ will be the string of length $2n$ of $I_{2n}$ which is the concatenation of $a$ and $b$.

- If $A$ and $B$ are two sets, $A^B$ will be the set of all functions from $B$ to $A$.

- The set of all functions from $I_n$ to $I_n$ is $F_n$. So $F_n = I_n^{I_n}$.

- The set of all permutations from $I_n$ to $I_n$ is $B_n$, so $B_n \subset F_n$.

- o is the composition of functions.

- $E_0$ is the number of elements of $F_n$. So $E_0 = (2^n)^{2^n} = 2^{n \cdot 2^n}$.

- $f^2$ is $f \circ f$.

**Definition 2** Let $f_1$ be a function from $I_n$ to $I_n$, and let $L$, $R$, $S$, and $T$ be elements of $I_n$. Then by definition : $\Psi(f_1)$ is the function from $I_{2n} \rightarrow I_{2n}$ such that:

$$\forall (L,R) \in I_n^2, \ \Psi(f_1)[L,R] = [S,T] \iff \begin{cases} S = R \\ T = L \oplus f_1(R) \end{cases},$$

where $\oplus$ is the bitwise addition modulo 2.

This can be represented by the diagram

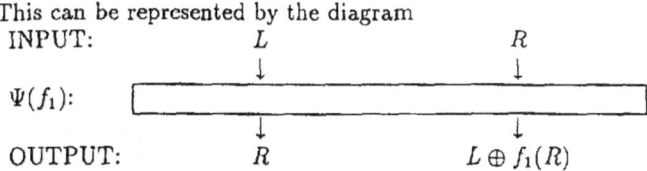

INPUT:      $L$                    $R$

$\Psi(f_1)$:

OUTPUT:     $R$            $L \oplus f_1(R)$

Note that $\Psi(f_1)$ is a permutation $I_{2n} \rightarrow I_{2n}$.

**Definition 3** Let $f_1, f_2, \ldots, f_k$ be $k$ functions from $I_n$ to $I_n$. $\Psi(f_1,\ldots,f_k)$ is the permutation from $I_{2n}$ to $I_{2n}$ defined by:

$$\Psi(f_1,\ldots,f_k) = \Psi(f_k) \circ \cdots \circ \Psi(f_2) \circ \Psi(f_1),$$

where $\circ$ is the composition of functions. For example we have for $\psi(f_1, f_2, f_3, f_4)$ :

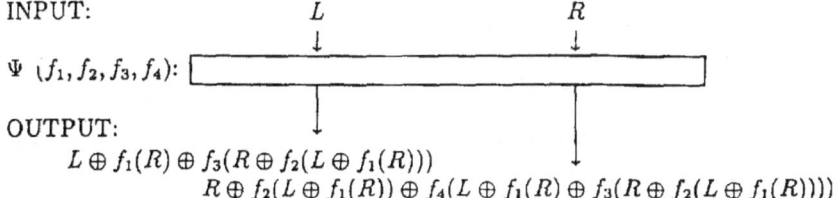

INPUT:                    $L$                    $R$

$\Psi(f_1, f_2, f_3, f_4)$:

OUTPUT:

$$L \oplus f_1(R) \oplus f_3(R \oplus f_2(L \oplus f_1(R)))$$
$$R \oplus f_2(L \oplus f_1(R)) \oplus f_4(L \oplus f_1(R) \oplus f_3(R \oplus f_2(L \oplus f_1(R))))$$

**Remark:**
$\Psi(f_1,\ldots,f_k)$ is in fact a $k$ *iteration DES Scheme* where the S-boxes are replaced by the functions $f_1,\ldots,f_k$.

**Definition 4** We will use the notation $\psi^k$ to say that we are considering a permutation $\psi(f_1,\ldots,f_k)$, where $f_1,\ldots,f_k$ are $k$ independant function randomly chosen in $F_n$.

We will assume that the definitions of permutation generator, distinguishing circuit, random oracle, pseudorandom permutation generator, and super pseudorandom permutation generator are known. These definitions can be found in [1] for example.

**Definition 5** Let $\phi$ be a distinguishing circuit. We will denote by $\phi(f)$ its output (1 or 0) when its oracle gates are given the values of the function $f$.
We will denote by $P_1$ the probability that $\phi(f) = 1$ when $f_1,\ldots,f_k$ are $k$ functions randomly chosen in $F_n$, and $f = \psi(f_1,\ldots,f_k)$.

So : $P_1 = \dfrac{\text{Number of } (f_1, \ldots, f_k) \text{ such that } \phi(\psi(f_1, \ldots, f_k)) = 1}{E_0^k}$.

We will denote by $P_1^*$ the probability that $\phi(f) = 1$ when $f$ is randomly chosen in $F_{2n}$.

Then : $P_1^* = \dfrac{\text{Number of functions } f \in F_{2n} \text{ such that } \phi(f) = 1}{(2^{2n})^{(2^{2n})}}$.

And we will denote by $P_1^{**}$ the probability that $\phi(f) = 1$ when $f$ is randomly chosen in $B_{2n}$.

Then : $P_1^{**} = \dfrac{\text{Number of permutations } f \in B_{2n} \text{ such that } \phi(f) = 1}{(2^{2n})!}$.

Notice that $P_1$ depends on $k$ and $\phi$, and that $P_1^*$ depends on $\phi$.
A distinguishing circuit has only normal oracle gates. To insist on this, we will use sometimes the expression "normal distinguishing circuit" for "distinguishing circuit". A "super distinguishing circuit" has normal and inverse oracle gates. (See [1] for precise definitions).

**Definition 6** Let $\phi$ be a super distinguishing circuit.
We will define $\phi(f), P_1$ and $P_1^{**}$ exactly as for normal distinguishing circuit.

Notice that here $P_1^*$ is not defined. This is because an inverse oracle gate is just defined with permutations.

**Definition 7** Let $\sigma$ be the permutation such that :
$\forall (L, R) \in I_n^2, \sigma[L, R] = [R, L]$. ($\sigma$ "swaps" the left and the right parts). $\sigma \in B_{2n}$.
Then for all functions $f_1, \ldots, f_k$ of $F_n$ we have : $\psi(f_1)^{-1} = \sigma \circ \psi(f_1) \circ \sigma$.
And : $\psi(f_1, \ldots, f_k)^{-1} = \sigma \circ \psi(f_k, \ldots, f_1) \circ \sigma$.

In [1], M. Luby and C. Rackoff proved that for $\psi^3$ (or for $\psi^k, k \geq 3$), for any normal distinguishing circuit $\phi$ with $m$ oracle gates, $|P_1 - P_1^*| \leq \dfrac{m(m-1)}{2^n}$.

The aim of this paper is to find conditions on $k$ under which such an inequality can significantly be improved. In paragraph 6 we will give an example of J. Pieprzyk which shows why such an improvement can be interesting.

## 2  The case $m = 2$

Here we will just consider distinguishing circuits with two oracle gates. Of course this case is less important than the cases where $m$ is large. ($m$ large will be subject of paragraphs 3,4 and 5). But when $m$ is very small ($m = 0, 1, 2$ or $3$) it is possible to study the problem completely, and to obtain the exact maximum values of $|P_1 - P_1^*|$ and $|P_1 - P_1^{**}|$, and this is done for each $k$. Then this case will show with high precision how our generator of permutations "better and better pseudorandom" becomes when the number of rounds increases.

**Remark:**
For $m = 0$ and $m = 1$ we have $|P_1 - P_1^*| = 0$ if $k \geq 2$. So the real problem begins when $m \geq 2$.

Let $L_1, R_1, L_2, R_2, S_1, T_1, S_2, T_2$ be elements of $I_n$ such that $(L_1, R_1) \neq (L_2, R_2)$ and $(S_1, T_1) \neq (S_2, T_2)$.

The key property is that, we are able to find the exact number $H$ of $k$-tuples of functions $(f_1, \ldots, f_k)$ such that :

$\forall i, 1 \leq i \leq m, \psi^k(f_1, \ldots, f_k)[L_i, R_i] = [S_i, T_i]$ when $m$ is very small ($m = 2$ here). Then, the values $H$ will give us the maximum of $|P_1 - P_1^*|$ and $|P_1 - P_1^{**}|$.

For $m = 2$ an explicit calculation gives the values $H$. (The proof is by induction on $k$).
For an even $k$ these values are :

**Theorem 2.1** Let $a_0 = \dfrac{1}{1 - \frac{1}{2^{2n}}} \cdot \dfrac{E_0^k}{2^{4n}}$, where $E_0 = 2^{n \cdot 2^n}$.

Then when $k$ is even and $k \geq 2$, we have :

**Case 1 :** $R_1 \neq R_2$ and $S_1 \neq S_2$. Then $H = a_0 \left( 1 - \dfrac{1}{2^{kn}} \right)$.

**Case 2 :** $R_1 \neq R_2, S_1 = S_2$ and $R_1 \oplus R_2 \neq T_1 \oplus T_2$.
or : $R_1 = R_2, S_1 \neq S_2$ and $S_1 \oplus S_2 \neq L_1 \oplus L_2$

Then $H = a_0 \left( 1 - \dfrac{1}{2^{(\frac{k}{2}-1)n}} - \dfrac{1}{2^{(\frac{k}{2})n}} + \dfrac{1}{2^{(k-1)n}} \right)$.

**Case 3 :** $R_1 \neq R_2, S_1 = S_2$ and $R_1 \oplus R_2 = T_1 \oplus T_2$
or : $R_1 = R_2, S_1 \neq S_2$ and $S_1 \oplus S_2 = L_1 \oplus L_2$

Then $H = a_0 \left( 1 + \dfrac{1}{2^{(\frac{k}{2}-2)n}} - \dfrac{1}{2^{(\frac{k}{2}-1)n}} - \dfrac{2}{2^{\frac{kn}{2}}} + \dfrac{1}{2^{(k-1)n}} \right)$.

**Case 4 :** $R_1 = R_2$ and $S_1 = S_2$

Then $H = a_0 \left( 1 - \dfrac{1}{2^{(k-2)n}} \right)$.

When $k$ is odd and $k \geq 3$, calculation of $H$ is also possible. There are then five cases. (See [3] for details).

The values of $H$ will give us the maximum of $|P_1 - P_1^*|$ and the maximum of $|P_1 - P_1^{**}|$.
We will denote this numbers by $|P_1 - P_1^*|_{\max}$ and $|P_1 - P_1^{**}|_{\max}$.

We find (for $m = 2$) :

| | $\|P_1 - P_1^*\|_{\max}$ | approximate value of $\|P_1 - P_1^{**}\|_{\max} \simeq$ |
|---|---|---|
| $\psi^1$ | $1 - \dfrac{1}{2^{3n}}$ | $1 - \dfrac{1}{2^{3n}}$ (The exact value is : $1 - \dfrac{1}{2^{3n} - 2^n}$) |
| $\psi^2$ | $1 - \dfrac{1}{2^n}$ | $1 - \dfrac{1}{2^n}$ |
| $\psi^3$ | $\dfrac{1}{2^n} - \dfrac{1}{2^{2n}}$ | $\dfrac{1}{2^n}$ |
| $\psi^4$ | $\dfrac{1}{2^n} - \dfrac{1}{2^{2n}}$ | $\dfrac{1}{2^n}$ |
| $\psi^5$ | $\dfrac{2}{2^{2n}} - \dfrac{2}{2^{3n}}$ | $\dfrac{1}{2^{2n}}$ |
| $\psi^6$ | $\dfrac{1}{2^{2n}} + \dfrac{1}{2^{3n}} - \dfrac{2}{2^{4n}}$ | $\dfrac{1}{2^{2n}}$ |
| $\psi^7$ | $\dfrac{1}{2^{2n}} + \dfrac{1}{2^{4n}} - \dfrac{2}{2^{5n}}$ | $\dfrac{1}{2^{3n}}$ |
| $\psi^8$ | $\dfrac{1}{2^{2n}}$ | $\dfrac{1}{2^{3n}}$ |
| $\psi^k, k \geq 8$ | $\dfrac{1}{2^{2n}}$ | $\dfrac{1}{2^{(\frac{k}{2}-1)n}}$ for $k$ even $\qquad$ $\dfrac{1}{2^{(\frac{k}{2}-\frac{1}{2})n}}$ for $k$ odd |

$\forall k \geq 8, \|P_1 - P_1^*\|_{\max} = \dfrac{1}{2^{2n}}.$

$\|P_1 - P_1^*\|_{\max} \nrightarrow 0$ because $\psi^k(f_1, \ldots, f_k)$ is a permutation so $(L_1, R_1) \neq (L_2, R_2) \Rightarrow (S_1, T_1) \neq (S_2, T_2)$.

But we have :

$$\|P_1 - P_1^{**}\| \overset{k \to +\infty}{\Longrightarrow} 0.$$

## Conclusion

When $m = 2$ we can obtain the exact values of $\|P_1 - P_1^*\|_{\max}$ and $\|P_1 - P_1^{**}\|_{\max}$ for all $k$. (See [3] for the exact values of $\|P_1 - P_1^{**}\|_{\max}$).

For $m = 2$, the result of M. Luby and C. Rackoff says that $\forall k \geq 3, \|P_1 - P_1^*\|_{\max} \leq \dfrac{2}{2^n}$.

This gives us a good minoration for $\psi^3$ and $\psi^4$ (because then the exact value of $\|P_1 - P_1^*\|_{\max}$ is $\dfrac{1}{2^n}$), but for $k \geq 5$, $\|P_1 - P_1^*\|_{\max} \leq \dfrac{2}{2^{2n}}$. So, for $k \geq 5$ and $m = 2$, it is indeed possible to improve the result of M. Luby and C. Rackoff.

This lets us hope that we can improve this result for other values of $m$ as well.

Another important result that we obtain is that $|P_1 - P_1^{**}| \xrightarrow{k \to +\infty} 0$, and when $k$ is large the rate of convergence is about $2^{\frac{kn}{2}}$. (It is possible to see this directly in the expressions of $H$ that we have given). So we have an explicit evaluation of the effects of the number of rounds $k$ on the "better and better pseudorandomness" of $\psi^k$, when $m = 2$.

# 3 General properties of $P_1, P_1^*$ and $P_1^{**}$

We will always denote by $m$ the number of oracle gates, by $k$ the number of rounds $\psi$ that we use in $\psi^k$, and by $n$ the integer such that the permutations that we are considering are in $B_{2n}$.

**Definition 8** When $m, k$ and $n$ are fixed, we will denote by $|P_1 - P_1^*|_{\max}$ the smallest real number such that :
for all normal distinguishing circuit that has $m$ oracle gates, we have : $|P_1 - P_1^*| \leq |P_1 - P_1^*|_{\max}$.
So $|P_1 - P_1^*|_{\max}$ is less or equal than 1, and it depends on $m, k$ and $n$.
And we will define $(P_1 - P_1^*)_{\max}$ and $(P_1^* - P_1)_{\max}$ in the same way.

**Definition 9** When $m, k$ and $n$ are fixed, we will denote by $|P_1 - P_1^{**}|_{\max}$ the smallest real number such that :
for all super distinguishing circuits that have $m$ oracle gates, we have : $|P_1 - P_1^{**}| \leq |P_1 - P_1^{**}|_{\max}$.
We define $(P_1 - P_1^{**})_{\max}$ and $(P_1^{**} - P_1)_{\max}$ in the same way.
Now we will see some example of the properties of these values.
(See [3] for the proofs).

**Theorem 3.1** *There is always a distinguishing circuit such that* $|P_1 - P_1^*| = |P_1 - P_1^*|_{\max}$ *and there is always a super distinguishing circuit such that* $|P_1 - P_1^{**}| = |P_1 - P_1^{**}|_{\max}$.

**Theorem 3.2** $(P_1 - P_1^*)_{\max} = (P_1^* - P_1)_{\max} = |P_1 - P_1^*|_{\max}$.

**Theorem 3.3** $(P_1 - P_1^{**})_{\max} = (P_1^{**} - P_1)_{\max} = |P_1 - P_1^{**}|_{\max}$.

**Theorem 3.4** *When $m$ increases (and $k$ and $n$ are fixed), $|P_1 - P_1^*|_{\max}$ and $|P_1 - P_1^{**}|_{\max}$ increase.*

**Theorem 3.5** *When $k$ increases (and $m$ and $n$ are fixed), $|P_1 - P_1^*|_{\max}$ and $|P_1 - P_1^{**}|_{\max}$ decrease.*

## Remarks

1. Theorem 3.5 is very important because it shows that when the number of rounds $k$ increases, the random properties of $\psi^k$ can just be better. But notice that this is due to the fact that all the $f_1, \ldots, f_k$ are **independant** function randomly chosen in $F_n$. For example $\psi(f, f, f, f^2)$ is pseudo-random (as claimed in [4]), but if one adds a round $\psi(f^2)$, we obtaint $G = \psi(f^2, f, f, f, f^2)$. And this one is not pseudo-random. This is because it is its own inverse if left and right halves of inputs and outputs are swapped : $G^{-1} = \sigma \circ G \circ \sigma$. So if $g$ is a permutation such that $g[L, R] = [S, T]$ by testing if $g[T, S] = [R, L]$ it is possible to know if $g$ is probably a permutation of $G$ or not.

2. The decrease is not necessarily strict for $|P_1 - P_1^*|_{\text{max}}$ as we have seen for $m = 2$.

**Theorem 3.6** *For all normal distinguishing circuit with $m$ oracle gates, $|P_1^* - P_1^{**}| \le \dfrac{m(m-1)}{2.2^{2n}}$.*

**Remark:**
This shows that if $m$ is not of order $2^n$, it is not possible to distinguish a random permutation from a random function with a high probability. The converse of this property is well known : it is indeed possible to distinguish with a high probability a random permutation of $B_{2n}$ from a random function of $F_{2n}$ when $m$ is of order $2^n$. (This is "the birthday paradox").

**Theorem 3.7** *It is possible to distinguish a random permutation from a permutation $\psi^k$ with a high probability when $m$ is of order $2^n$. (k is fixed here, the number of oracle gates is limited by $m$, but the number of computations to analyse these $m$ values is not limited).*

**Idea of the proof**

There are a lot of different ways to prove this theorem 3.7. The simplest is perhaps to see that it is a consequence a Shannon's theorem : the secret key should be at least as great as that of the known plaintext.
It is possible to use this theorem here because we suppose that there is no limit on the amount of computation that a circuit can do to analyse its $m$ values.
Then, if real random functions $f_1, \ldots, f_k$ of $F_n$ are the secret key, the length of the key is about $k.n.2^n$ bits. And with $m$ oracle gates, $m.2n$ bits will be known.
So if $m > \dfrac{k.2^n}{2}$, it is possible to find a circuit $\phi$ with $m$ normal oracle gates such that $|P_1 - P_1^{**}|$ is not negligible. (But $\phi$ will eventually do a lot of computations).

**Theorem 3.8** *If $m, n$ and $k$ are $\ge 2$, then $|P_1 - P_1^*|_{\text{max}} \ne 0$ and $|P_1 - P_1^{**}|_{\text{max}} \ne 0$.*
*This a consequence of theorem 3.4 and of the values that we have found for $m = 2$ in paragraph 2.*

**Conclusion**

When $m$ is small compared to $\sqrt{2^n}$, and $k \ge 3$, Luby and Rackoff's property shows that it is not possible to distinguish a permutation $\psi^k$ from a random function (or a random permutation) with $m$ normal oracle gates and with a high probability. But when $m$ is of order $2^n$, it is possible to distinguish a permutation $\psi^k$ from a random permutation and from a random function, and to distinguish a random permutation from a random function.
So the problem is now : what will happen when $m$ is between $\sqrt{2^n}$ and $2^n$ ? This is what we will try to see now.

# 4 $\psi^3$ and $\psi^4$ when $m \ge 0(2^{\frac{n}{2}})$

We will see that when $m \ge 0(2^{\frac{n}{2}})$, it is possible to distinguish the permutations $\psi^3$ and $\psi^4$ from random permutations.

**Proof for $\psi^3$**

Let $\phi$ be the following distinguishing circuit : $\phi$ will analyse a function $f$ of $F_{2n}$ like this :

1. $\phi$ chooses $m$ distinct $R_i, 1 \leq i \leq m$, and chooses $m$ values $L_i$ arbitrarily in $I_n, 1 \leq i \leq m$.

2. $\phi$ asks for the values $[S_i, T_i] = f([L_i, R_i]), 1 \leq i \leq m$.

3. $\phi$ counts the number $N$ of equalities of the form $R_i \oplus S_i = R_j \oplus S_j, i < j$.

4. Let $N_0$ be the expectation of $N$ when $f$ is a random permutation, and $N_1$ be the expectation of $N$ when $f$ is a $\psi^3(f_1, f_2, f_3)$.
   Then $N_1 \simeq 2N_0$, because when $f$ is a $\psi^3(f_1, f_2, f_3)$, $R_i \oplus S_i = f_2(L_i \oplus f_1(R_i))$ so $f_2(L_i \oplus f_1(R_i)) = f_2(L_j \oplus f_1(R_j)), i < j$, if $L_i \oplus f_1(R_i) \neq L_j \oplus f_1(R_j)$ and $f_2(L_i \oplus f_1(R_i)) = f_2(L_j \oplus f_1(R_j))$ or if $L_i \oplus f_1(R_i) = L_j \oplus f_1(R_j)$.

So if $\phi$ gives 1 as output when $N$ is closer to $N_1$ and 0 as output when $N$ is closer to $N_0$, $\phi$ will have a $|P_1 - P_1^{**}|$ close to 1 when $N_0$ is greater than 1, that is to say when $m \geq 0(2^{\frac{n}{2}})$.

**Conclusion :** For $\psi^3$, there is a converse to Luby-Rackoff's property. It is possible to distinguish with a good probability the permutations $\psi^3$ from random permutations with $m$ oracle gates, if and only if $m$ is of order $\sqrt{2^n}$.

Notice also that here the $m$ values $[R_i, L_i]$ chosen can be chosen randomly in $I_n$. In terms of cryptography this means that it is possible to use a "known plaintext attack" (we don't have to use a "chosen plaintext attack").

**Proof for $\psi^4$**

This time, we take $R_i = 0$ (or $R_i$ constant), and we count the number $N$ of equalities of the form $S_i \oplus L_i = S_j \oplus L_j, i < j$. In fact, when $f = \psi(f_1, f_2, f_3, f_4)$, then $S_i \oplus L_i = f_3(f_2(L_i \oplus f_1(0))) \oplus f_1(0)$. So the probability of such an equality is about the double in this case than in the case where $f$ is a random permutation (because if $f_2(L_i \oplus f_1(0)) = f_2(L_j \oplus f_1(0))$ this equality holds, and if $\beta_i = f_2(L_i \oplus f_1(0)) \neq f_2(L_j \oplus f_1(0)) = \beta_j$ but $f_3(\beta_i) = f_3(\beta_j)$, this equality also holds).

**Conclusion :** For $\psi^4$, as for $\psi^3$, there is a converse to Luby-Rackoff's property. It is possible to distinguish with a good probability the permutations $\psi^3$ and $\psi^4$ from random permutations with $m$ oracle gates, if and only if $m$ is of order $\sqrt{2^n}$. We will see that this will not be true for $\psi^k, k \geq 5$.

Notice that for $\psi^4$ we have used a "chosen plaintext attack" (because all the $R_i$ are constant). And it is possible to prove that this is necessary if $m$ is of order $\sqrt{2^n}$. (See [3]).

# 5 Properties of $\psi^5$ and $\psi^6$

For $\psi^6$, we have proved the following theorem. (See [3] for the demonstration).

**Theorem 5.1** *For $\psi^6$ and for all super distinguishing circuit with $m$ oracles gates, we have :*
$$|P_1 - P_1^{**}| \leq \frac{18m}{2^n} + \frac{12m^3}{2^{2n}}.$$

The main idea in proving this theorem is to evaluate the number $H$ of $k$-tuples of functions $(f_1, \ldots, f_k)$ such that : $\forall i, 1 \leq i \leq m, \psi^k(f_1, \ldots, f_k)[L_i, R_i] = [S_i, T_i]$. Here $k = 5$ or $6$, the $[L_i, R_i], 1 \leq i \leq m$, are $m$ pairwise distinct elements of $I_{2n}$, and the $[S_i, T_i], 1 \leq i \leq m$ are also $m$ pairwise distinct elements of $I_{2n}$. ("Pairwise distinct" means that if $i \neq j$, then $L_i \neq L_j$ or $R_i \neq R_j$).(See [3] for a complete proof).

This theorem shows that it is not possible to distinguish with a good probability a random permutation from a permutation $\psi^k, k \geq 6$, if $m$ is not at least of order $2^{\frac{2n}{3}}$. We will give in the next paragraph an exemple of an application of this result.

For $\psi^5$, we have just proved the following theorem.

**Theorem 5.2** *For $\psi^5$ and for all normal distinguishing circuit with $m$ oracles gates, $|P_1 - P_1^*|$ is negligible when $n$ is large if $m$ is not at least of order $2^{\frac{2n}{3}}$.*

**Remark:**
The theorems 5.1 and 5.2 show that $\psi^5$ and $\psi^6$ are really sensibly better permutation generators than $\psi^3$ and $\psi^4$. And we have strong presumption (see [3]) that the properties of $\psi^5$ and $\psi^6$ are even better.
For example, it is probable that this conjecture holds :

**Conjecture**
For $\psi^5$, or perhaps $\psi^6$ or $\psi^7$, and for any distinguishing circuit with $m$ oracle gates we have :
$|P_1 - P_1^*| \leq \frac{30m}{2^n}$. (The number 30 is just an example).
If this conjecture is true (and it is probably true), it shows that in fact when $k \geq 5$, $m$ should be of order $2^n$ to distinguish a permutation $\psi^k$ from a random function (or a random permutation).

# 6 Example of application

We will now see an example given by J. Pieprzyk at the end of his talk at Eurocrypt'90.
This is just an example and there are a lot of different (and clever) ways to use the results on pseudorandom permutations. (In general a pseudorandom function generator is used and not real random functions as we will do). But this example is instructive, and this was the example that we had in mind when we decided to work in an improvement of the inequalities.

## The problem

Suppose that you want to use the results in a direct way, that is to say with $k$ real random functions $f_1, \ldots, f_k$ of $F_n$ which are the secret key. Then your secret key will be $k.n.2^n$ bits long. And suppose that you want that the permutation $\psi(f_1, \ldots, f_k)$ is not distinguishable from a random permutation with a good probability for all distinguishing circuit with $m \leq 10^9$. Notice that if this property holds, then to distinguish $\psi(f_1, \ldots, f_k)$ from a random permutation with a good probability it is necessary to do at least $10^9$ computations. Then, what will be the length of the secret key ?

• If you use Luby-Rackoff's property : for $\psi^3, |P_1 - P_1^*| \leq \dfrac{m^2}{2^n}$, then since $m \simeq 2^{30}$, you will take $n \simeq 64$, so the length of the key is $3.64.2^{64}$ bits. This is of course too much !

• If you use Pieprzyk's property : $\psi(f, f, f, f^2)$ is pseudorandom, then you will divided "at best" the length of the key by 3, and the length is of course still too much. (We say "at best" because in fact the inequality of $|P_1 - P_1^*|$ is worse in this case : see the paragraph 7).

• If you use our property for $\psi^6$ : $|P_1 - P_1^*| \leq \dfrac{12m}{2^n} + \dfrac{18m^3}{2^{2n}}$, then since $m \simeq 2^{30}$, you will take $n \simeq 48$, so the length of the key is $6.48.2^{48}$ bits. This is still too much ! But ... we have divided the length of the key by 40000.

• And in fact, if the conjecture of paragraph 5 is true, it is probably possible to take $n \simeq 32$ for $\psi^6$.

Then the length of the key will be $6.32.2^{32}$ bits. Of course this is still a lot, but because of Shannon's theorem there is no hope to reduce the length of the key by much more (if you are considering that the distinguishing circuits are not limited in the amount of computation that they can perform to analyse their $m$ values).

## 7 Remark for $\psi(f, f, f, f^2)$

When $f$ is a random function of $F_n$, $\psi(f, f, f, f^2)$ is a pseudo random permutation of $B_{2n}$. But there is a little mistake in one of the the the proofs of J. Pieprzyk : his lemma 4.1 page 145 of [4] is wrong. (And then the inequality obtained for this generator is worse).
For example, let $\phi$ be this normal distinguishing circuit, which has only one oracle gate. $\phi$ will test like this a function $F$ of $I_{2n} \rightarrow I_{2n}$.

1. $\phi$ chooses an element $R$ of $I_n$ (for example $R = 0$) and take $L = 0$.

2. $\phi$ asks for the value $F[0, R] = [S, T]$.

3. If $R = S = T$, then $\phi$ gives the output 1. If not, $\phi$ gives the output 0.

**Evaluation of $P_1 = P_r[C_{2n}(\psi(f, f, f, f^2))]$.** (This is the notation of J. Piepzryk).
If $F = \psi(f, f, f, f^2)$, we have : $\begin{cases} S = f(R) \oplus f(R \oplus f^2(R)) \\ T = R \oplus f^2(R) \oplus f^2(S). \end{cases}$

$P_1$ is the probability that $R = S = T$ when $f$ is randomly chosen in $F_n$.
But here (this will not be the case for $\psi^4(f, f, f, g)$) if $R = S$ we will have necessarily $T = R$.
So $P_1 = \dfrac{1}{2^n}$.

Evaluation of $Q_1 = P_r[C_{2n}(\psi(f, f, f, g))]$ (This is the notation of J. Pieptryk).

If $F = \psi(f, f, f, g)$, we have : $\begin{cases} S = f(R) \oplus f(R \oplus f^2(R)) \\ T = R \oplus f^2(R) \oplus g(S). \end{cases}$

$Q_1$ is the probability that $R = S = T$ when $f$ and $g$ are randomly and independently chosen in $F_n$.
So $Q_1 = \dfrac{1}{2^{2n}}$.

Then, $|P_1 - Q_1| = \dfrac{1}{2^n} - \dfrac{1}{4^n}$, which is not smaller than $\dfrac{9}{4^n}$ for all $n$, as was mentioned in lemma 4.1. of [4].
An other problem of $\psi(f, f, f, f^2)$ is that this generator is not super pseudo random. (see [3]).

# 8  Conclusion

We have seen that $\psi^k$, for $k \geq 5$, is an "exponentially" better pseudorandom permutation generator than $\psi^3$ and $\psi^4$. This improvement of the properties of $\psi^k$ when $k \geq 5$ is a new result, and it holds for small values of $m$ as for great values of $m$.

# References

[1] M. Luby and Ch. Rackoff, *How to construct pseudorandom permutations from pseudorandom functions*, SIAM Journal and Computing, 17(2) : 373-386, April 1988.

[2] J. Patarin, *Pseudorandom permutations based on the DES Scheme*, Proceedings of EUROCODE'90.

[3] J. Patarin, *Etude des générateurs de permutations basés sur le Schéma du D.E.S.*, Thèse. To be publish in September 1991, INRIA, Domaine de Voluceau, Le Chesnay, France.

[4] J. Pieprzyk, *How to construct pseudorandom permutations from Single Pseudorandom Functions*, EUROCRYPT'90, Århus, Denmark, May 1990.

[5] Y. Zheng, T. Matsumoto and H. Imai, *Impossiblility and optimality results on constructing pseudorandom permutations*, Abstract of EUROCRYPT'89, Houthalen, Belgium, April 1989.

# Faster Modular Multiplication
# by Operand Scaling

Colin D. Walter

Computation Department, U.M.I.S.T.,

PO Box 88, Sackville Street, Manchester M60 1QD, U.K.

e-mail: cdw@sa.co.umist.ac.uk

Key Words: *Modular Multiplication, Fast Computer Arithmetic, Digital Arithmetic Methods, RSA Algorithm, Cryptography.*

## Abstract

There are a number of techniques known for speeding up modular multiplication, which is the main arithmetic operation in RSA cryptography. This note shows how to gain speed by scaling the modulus. Resulting hardware is limited only by the speed of addition[1]. Detailed analysis of fan out shows that over existing methods the speedup is potentially as much as two-fold. This is because the addition and fan out can now be done in parallel. Of course, in RSA the modulus can be chosen to need no scaling, so that most of the minor extra costs are eliminated.

---

[1] J.-J. Quisquater informed me at the conference that he had spoken on a similar technique for software in the rump session at EUROCRYPT '90, but nothing appears in the Proceedings.

J. Feigenbaum (Ed.): Advances in Cryptology - CRYPTO '91, LNCS 576, pp. 313-323, 1992.
© Springer-Verlag Berlin Heidelberg 1992

# 1 Introduction

One of the motivations for studying fast modular multiplication is its use in cryptography, including the RSA algorithm [5]. That algorithm provides potentially the most widely useful system as it appears to be arbitrarily secure. However, its arithmetic intensity requires dedicated hardware if it is to be used in a real-time system working with bulk data.

A number of techniques are already known for improving the speed of hardware for modular multiplication of integers. These are surveyed in, for example, Eldridge & Walter [3]. Most can be combined without difficulty with the modification suggested here, and so our contribution is presented in terms of the essential, basic techniques described by Brickell [2]. Fundamental there is the use of a truncated partial product and truncated modulus to determine, with sufficient accuracy, the correct multiple of the modulus to subtract during each of the repeated addition cycles that perform the multiplication. This had been used for some time in the case of real number division, being reported on by, for example, Atkins [1] and Taylor [6] in cases of number representations with radix greater than 2. In a recent paper [4], Ercegovac and Lang show how improve this technique for division by scaling both numerator and divisor by the same amount in order to obtain known, fixed, most significant digits for the divisor. With these digits known, the hardware logic for deciding the multiple of the divisor to subtract is much simpler. So the clock may be run faster and the quotient obtained more quickly. A similar procedure works for modular multiplication by scaling the modulus, and we present the details for this here.

As in the case of division, the speed-up consequent from this technique derives from the reduced complexity of the hardware logic for deciding the multiple of the divisor to subtract from the dividend. Analysis by Eldridge and Walter in [3] of logic for the usual modular multiplication algorithm shows that, as with division (see [6]), this complexity normally determines the critical path length in the hardware, and so the clock speed and overall time.

The overheads entailed by employing the technique here are minimal. Initially, scaling of the modulus would probably be done by software. In the case of the RSA algorithm the same modulus is used over and over again, so that scaling done once for all is very cheap. During computation the registers need to be a digit or so larger, which affects the chip area only marginally. Also one or two more iterations of the main loop need to be done. This hardly affects the time at all. After the loop, the result may be too large and a few extra subtractions of the original modulus may be necessary. This is potentially the most expensive overhead as the original modulus may need to be reloaded or kept in a further register. Overall, the hardware is almost the same as before, with slightly adjusted parameters, except for the improved logic mentioned above. The gain in efficiency against the minor overheads is worked out in detail in this paper, with encouraging results.

# 2  Overview of the Algorithm

We begin by noting that fast modular multiplication is usually done by repeated cycles involving shifting and addition, as in ordinary multiplication, together with a simultaneous modular subtraction. Thus, each cycle also needs to predict the multiple of the modulus to subtract in the next cycle.

Suppose we represent numbers with radix $r$. If we wish to calculate the residue $R$ of $(A \times B) \bmod M$, or indeed the integer quotient $Q = (A \times B) \ div \ M$, then, with some detail yet to be explained, the basis of the algorithm in [2] is the following:

```
Type  Index      =  0..MaxIndex ;
      Register   =  Array[Index] of Digit ;

Procedure ModMult( A, B, M : Register ;  Var R, Q : Register ) ;
```
{ Pre-Conditions : $M_{min} \leq M \leq M_{max}$  and $A, B \geq 0$ }
{ Post-Conditions: $A \times B = Q \times M + R$  and $Top(R) \leq L$   }

```
Var   J  : Index ;

      Function Quotient(ToprR,TopM : Int) : Digit ;
```
      { Post-Condition : $Quotient \approx (ToprR) \ div \ TopM$ }
      Begin ... End ;

```
Begin { ModMult }
      R := 0 ;  Q := 0 ;
      For J := MaxIndex DownTo 0 do
      Begin { Loop Invariant: Top(R) ≤ L  and  R ≥ 0 }
            Q[J] := Quotient(Top(r*R),Top(M)) ;
            R    := r*R + A[J]*B - Q[J]*M ;
      End ;
End ; { ModMult }
```

It is fairly straightforward to see that the output satisfies $A \times B = Q \times M + R$. For speed, the quotient digits are generated by only considering the topmost digits of the partial product $R$ and the modulus $M$. These are extracted by the function $Top$, which truncates a fixed number (usually most) of the lowest digits. By allowing the digits of $Q$ to lie in a sufficiently wide range, the accumulating partial product can be kept fairly small, being bounded through some fixed $L$. Appropriate choices make $R$ less than $2M$, but not necessarily less than $M$. So the final output may fail to be the least non-negative residue of $A \times B$ modulo $M$, but it is easy to subtract an extra $M$ to obtain $(A \times B) \bmod M$, if necessary. The precise conditions required for undefined constants such as $L$ are given in [7]. Such detail is not needed here, although we look at $L$ in section 4.

# 3   Scaling the Modulus

Let $q$ be the number of the most significant digits of the modulus $M$ which the function $Quotient$ needs and suppose $M$ has a standard, non-redundant representation, i.e. digits in the range $0..r-1$. Assume inputs are shifted as necessary to give the modulus exactly $m$ digits, so that the hardware function $Top$ just truncates the $m - q$ least significant digits of both $M$ and the partial product $R$. We want to scale the modulus $M$ by a factor $f$ such that $fM$ has its $q$ most significant digits fixed, say, to $M_{fix}$.

The revised algorithm uses $fM$, with an appropriate shift, in place of $M$. One benefit of this is that $Quotient$ is easier to calculate because it no longer depends on any digits of $Top(M)$, as they are fixed. This saves minimal hardware area, but, more importantly, shortens the cycle time of each iteration. In particular, if *Quotient* is performed by doing $div\ (Top(M)+1)$ and $M_{fix} = r^q - 1$ then the implied integer division is by $r^q$ and can be done just by shifting. The penalties of the technique include the pre-calculation of $f$ and $fM$ (which may be needed in non-redundant form), an increase in register lengths by the number of digits in $f$, and, if necessary, up to $2f$ final subtractions of $M$ from the output, which may otherwise be nearly as large as $2fM$.

Let us now show how to calculate $f$. Suppose $fM$ has $p$ non-redundant digits. Then, for the $q$ most significant digits of $fM$ to be $M_{fix}$, $f$ must satisfy

$$M_{fix} \ \leq \ r^{q-p}fM \ < \ M_{fix}+1$$

This is equivalent to demanding that $f$ lie in the real interval

$$[\ r^{p-q}M_{fix}/M \ , \ r^{p-q}(M_{fix}+1)/M \ [$$

This must be of length at least 1 in order that it always contain an integer which can be chosen as the value of $f$. The condition for this is $M \leq r^{p-q}$, in other words, $fM$ has at least $q$ more digits than $M$. Ideally, $p$ should be picked minimally. Thus, $f$ could be calculated by brute force using

$$f \ = \ (\ r^m \times (M_{fix}+1) - 1\ )\ div\ M \qquad \text{with} \quad p = m + q \qquad\qquad (*1)$$

A more efficient approach may be desirable, one which derives $f$ from a truncated value of $M$. Suppose $q'$ digits of $M$ are needed to find such an $f$. Let $Top'$ be the function that provides these. From the property $r^{m-q'}Top'(M) \leq M < r^{m-q'}(Top'(M)+1)$ we can approximate the ends of the interval above to obtain the strict sub-interval

$$[\ r^{p-q}M_{fix}\ /\ r^{m-q'}Top'(M)\ , \ r^{p-q}(M_{fix}+1)\ /\ r^{m-q'}(Top'(M)+1)\ ]$$

This has length at least 1 precisely when

$$Top'(M) \times (\ Top'(M)+1\ ) \quad \leq \quad r^{p-m+q'-q}(\ Top'(M) - M_{fix}\ )$$

By viewing this as a quadratic in $Top'(M)$, it is most difficult to satisfy at the extreme of the range $[r^{q'-1}, r^{q'} - 1]$ which is furthest from the turning point $(r^{p-m+q'-q} - 1)/2$. Unfortunately, for $p = m + q$ it does not hold when $Top'(M) = r^{q'} - 1$, and so we need to increase $p$ to $p = m + q + 1$. Then the lower limit $r^{q'-1}$ is the harder to satisfy and we require

$$r^{q'-1} \times (\ r^{q'-1} + 1\ ) \quad \leq \quad r^{q'+1} \times (\ r^{q'-1} - M_{fix}\ )$$

or, equivalently,

$$M_{fix} \quad < \quad r^{q'-1} \ - \ r^{q'-3}\ .$$

Since $M_{fix} < r^q$, this will always hold by taking $q' = q + 2$, (and usually when $q' = q + 1$). Thus a solution which yields $f$ from only the topmost digits of $M$ is given by

$$f \quad = \quad (r^{q'+1}(M_{fix}+1))\ div\ (Top'(M)+1) \quad \text{with} \quad p = m+q+1 \quad \text{and} \quad q' = q+2 \qquad (*2)$$

To summarise the results of this section, we begin by choosing a suitable $M_{fix}$ with $q$ digits which would make computation of $Quotient$ easy if $M_{fix}$ were given by $Top$ applied to the modulus. Next we replace the modulus $M$ by $fM$ where $f$ is as defined in either $(*1)$ or $(*2)$. Lastly, when running the modular multiplication algorithm with the new modulus, perform extra subtractions of the original modulus as necessary after the main loop to obtain the least non-negative residue. This can be done with about $q + 2$ shifts and subtractions of digit multiples of the original modulus because $(*1)$ and $(*2)$ yield $f \leq r^{q+1}$ and $f \leq r^{q+2}$ respectively in the worst cases.

# 4   Solutions for Radix 2

Now let us look at the saving in computational time by seeing how the hardware is affected in the case of radix 2. Assume that $M$ has already been replaced by $fM$ and shifted, so that $Top(M) = M_{fix}$. Suppose also that $M$ is in usual non-redundant binary form. However, let $R$ have digits from $0..2$. Speed is obtained mainly by using this redundant representation in order to curtail carry propagation to only one or two places during the addition. This enables digit operations for addition to be carried out in parallel. One choice for $Quotient$ which is discussed in [7] is

$$Quotient(Topr\,R, Top\,M) \;=\; Topr\,R\ div\ (Top\,M{+}1)$$

A sensible choice for $M_{fix}$ is therefore $2^q - 1$ so that $div$ can be performed simply by shifting. A value for $q$ which makes the algorithm work now has to be determined.

The loop invariant for the addition cycle must be preserved. So $Top(R) \le L$ must imply the condition

$$Top(\ 2R + A[J]{\times}B - (Top(2R)\ div\ 2^q){\times}M\ ) \;\le\; L \qquad (*3)$$

since the left side is the value of $Top(R)$ for the next iteration. A scheme following the lines of Brickell [2] computes $(A{\times}B)\ mod\ M$ as $((SA{\times}B)\ mod\ SM)\ div\ S$ for some shift factor $S$, with $Top$ truncating appropriately more digits. Here $S$ is chosen sufficiently large for the input $A[J]{\times}B$ not to affect any of the thus-redefined top digits in the value of $R$ to which it contributes. So, that term may be ignored. Now, looking at top digits only,

$$
\begin{aligned}
2R &- (Top(2R)\ div\ 2^q){\times}M \\
&< \ (\ Top(2R) + 1\ )2^{m-q} - (\ Top(2R)\ div\ 2^q\ ){\times}(2^m - 2^{m-q}) \\
&= \ \{\ Top(2R) - 2^q(Top(2R)\ div\ 2^q)\ \}{\times}2^{m-q} + 2^{m-q} + (Top(2R)\ div\ 2^q){\times}2^{m-q} \\
&= \ (\ Top(2R)\ mod\ 2^q\ ){\times}2^{m-q} + 2^{m-q} + (\ Top(2R)\ div\ 2^q\ ){\times}2^{m-q}
\end{aligned}
$$

Applying $Top$ to this, and noting the strictness of the inequality, ensures the condition ($*3$) is met if

$$Top(2R) \bmod 2^q \quad + \quad Top(2R) \operatorname{div} 2^q \quad \leq \quad L \qquad (*4)$$

Here $R$ may equal $M$. Thus $Top(R)$ may be at least as great as $Top(M) = 2^q - 1$. Hence $Top(2R) = 2^{q+1} - 1$ is possible, and for this the inequality requires $L \geq 2^q$. We will show that ($*4$) is satisfied by taking $L = 2^q$ and $q \geq 2$. So suppose this is the value of $L$ and that $Top(R) \leq L$. As digits of $R$ are at most 2, we have $Top(2R) \leq 2Top(R) + 2$ when the multiplication is done by shifting. Thus $Top(2R) \leq 2L + 2 = 2^{q+1} + 2$. The left side of ($*4$) is a saw-tooth function of $Top(2R)$, with increasing maxima before each multiple of $2^q$. So ($*4$) is satisfied if it holds at the last value, when $Top(2R) = 2^{q+1} + 2$, and at the previous maximum, when $Top(2R) = 2^{q+1} - 1$. Both are easily seen to satisfy the inequality if $q \geq 2$, confirming the validity of the choice for $L$. The output conveniently satisfies $R < 2M$ because $Top(R) \leq L < 2L-2 = 2Top(M) \leq Top(2M)$ and similarly $Q[J] \leq 2$ because $Top(2R) \operatorname{div} (Top(M)+1) \leq (2L+2) \operatorname{div} L = 2$.

There are no solutions at all for $q \leq 1$. Larger values of $q$ progressively simplify the hardware, but each increase by 1 costs an extra digit position in registers, an extra addition cycle, and another final subtraction of a shifted digit multiple of the original modulus.

# 5   Improved Circuits for Radix 2

Now recall that hardware clock speed is limited by the longest path in the circuit from input to output. The length of the shortest possible clock cycle is approximately the sum of delay times associated with the gates on such a path. This in turn is roughly proportional to the number of such gates. In [3], Figure 2, there is a circuit for implementing the software addition cycle with a delay carry adder. This uses the same redundant number system assumed at the start of the previous section to allow parallel digit operations. Generating the new value for $R$ as well as the *Quotient* digit for the next iteration results in a critical path length of 11 XOR gates compared with the 6 needed for calculating a typical output digit. However, like the clock signals, the *Quotient* digit needs to be broadcast subsequently to each place in the adder. We will assume the technology requires a tree 5 gates deep to do this for a 512 to 1024 bit modulus. Then the correct multiple of $M$ can be selected ready for the next iteration using two more gates. If we preferentially broadcast to the topmost inputs first (2 gates) then the path length at the top end is actually $11+2+2 = 15$ gates, whilst that for a typical output digit is $6+5+2 = 13$ gates.

If the *Quotient* digit were to be computed earlier, then the fanning out of this information could be overlapped with the current addition to reduce the critical path length closer to the theoretical minimum of 6, which is the number of gates for finding a typical output digit in the adder. We now show how scaling the modulus makes this possible.

Suppose we take $q \geq 2$. Then the most significant digit of $R$ has index at most $m$ because $R < 2M$. Indeed, if a suffix $i$ denotes the digit coefficient of $2^i$ in a number representation, then $R_m = 0$ or 1. This bound on $R$ determines the size of registers as needing $m+1$ digits. So the subtraction of $Q_J \times M$ might be implemented here by adding $Q_J$ times the complement $(2^{m+1}-1) - M$ together with an initial carry $Q_J$ at the bottom end and ignoring an overflow of $Q_J \times 2^{m+1}$. Call this input $M^*$, and assume that the inherent non-zero digit multiples are obtained by shifting so that its digits are bits. Then, because $M_{fix} = 2^q - 1$ gives $M_m = 0$ and $M_i = 1$ for $m-1 \geq i \geq m-q$, the topmost digits of $M^*$ satisfy $M_m^* = 0$ or 1, and $M_i^* = 0$ for $m-1 \geq i > m-q$. The initial carry does not propagate up the adder more than a couple of places, and so it does not affect the top digits. Finally, $Q_J$ has the simple formula $2R_m + R_{m-1}$.

Now take $q = 4$. The top end of the delay carry adder simplifies to the typical bit slice illustrated in Figure 1 because the most significant digits of input $A_J \times B$ are 0. Using the various bit values just described, consequent simplifications to the bit slice yield most of the top end of Figure 1. However, once $R$ is computed, part of the next addition cycle can be performed on its topmost digits to convert them nearer to non-redundant form. This is illustrated in that part of the figure below the dotted line which marks the end of one iteration of the software algorithm proved above. Enough has been done there to remove the possibility that $R_{m-4} = 2$, i.e. $(2R)_{m-3} = 2$, which explains the other simplification to the input.

The advantage of starting part of the next iteration is that the quotient digit can be calculated earlier in the cycle. Here it appears after a maximum of 3 gates, rather than the 11 noted above: a substantial reduction. Since it is actually computed earlier than a typical digit output from lower down the adder, it is clearly possible after further modifications to fan out this information in parallel with the addition rather than sequentially after it, thereby reducing the critical path length to that of the adder (6 here). This requires a lot of the top digit calculations to be considerably advanced, but it would enable chips using scaling to run at about double the speed of others with the only significant cost being an extra register to hold $M^*$. To build such a circuit is just tedious development and we omit the details.

Finally, we consider how to add surrounding detail to Figure 1 without trying to advance the quotient digit computations still further. If all the topmost input bits needed for calculating the quotient digit are already in position at the start of a clock cycle, then generating the same inputs for the next cycle requires 3 gates for the quotient digit, 2 for fanning it out and 2 for selecting digits for $M^*$: a total of 7. Let us use 5 gates to completely disseminate the new quotient digit to all digit positions. So this makes a total depth of $3+5 = 8$ gates at the top end. The main part of a 512- to 1024-bit adder then just needs a depth of 2 gates for selecting $M^*$ as well as the 6 gates of the adder itself. This makes the critical path length just 8, compared to 15 without modulus scaling. Counting 2 gates as the equivalent of the set-up and hold times for registers, the hardware presented here should be able to be run at about $(15+2)/(8+2)$ times the speed of comparable hardware without a scaled modulus, i.e. 70% faster.

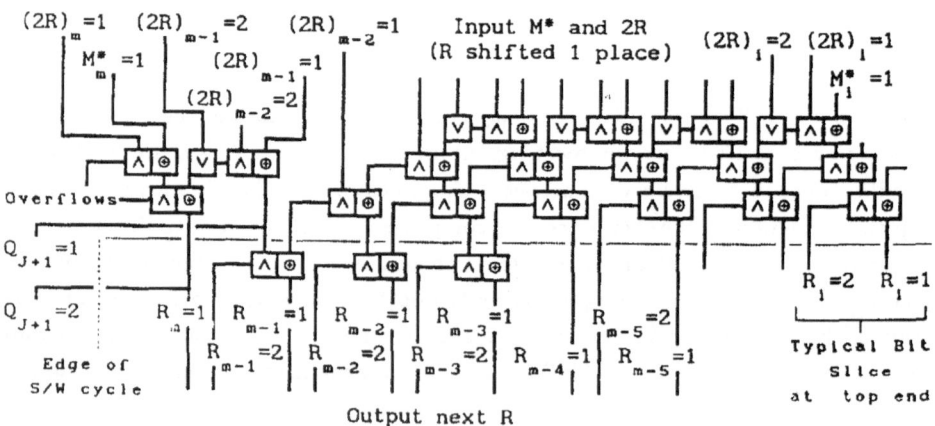

Figure 1. Adder for radix 2 when $q = 4$ and $M_{fix} = 15$.

# 6 Final Detail and Conclusions

We have shown how to scale the modulus for modular multiplication to potentially double the speed of hardware, giving sufficient detail to achieve a speedup factor of 70%. The cost for radix 2 involved 4 extra bit positions in registers and consequently 4 extra clock cycles - less than 1% in space or time for typical RSA applications. For the full doubling of speed an extra register holding $M^*$ is required. Further penalties are slight. They concern pre- and post- processing. Initial scaling is cheap when the modulus is much used as it is done once for all. The output is bounded by $2fM$, where $f$ is the scaling factor. Hence $M$ needs to be loaded and subtracted as necessary. However, in RSA cryptography this does not need to be done until decryption, and it can be avoided entirely by choosing a modulus which needs no scaling.

# References

[1] D. E. Atkins, Higher Radix Division using Estimates of the Divisor and Partial Remainders, IEEE Trans. Comp., vol. C-17, 1968, pp. 925-934.

[2] E. F. Brickell, A Fast Modular Multiplication Algorithm with Application to Two Key Cryptography, Advances in Cryptology (Proceedings of CRYPTO 82) ed. Chaum et al., Plenum, 1983, pp. 51-60.

[3] S. E. Eldridge and C. D. Walter, Montgomery's Algorithm for Fast Modular Multiplication, IEEE Trans. Comp., to appear.

[4] M. D. Ercegovac and T. Lang, Simple Radix-4 Division with Operands Scaling, IEEE Trans. Comp., vol. 39, 1990, pp. 1204-8.

[5] R. L. Rivest, A. Shamir and L. Adleman, A Method of Obtaining Digital Signatures and Public Key Cryptosystems, Comm. ACM, vol. 21, 1978, pp. 120-126.

[6] G. S. Taylor, Radix 16 SRT Dividers with overlapped Quotient Selection Stages, Proc. IEEE 7th Symp. Comp. Arith., 1985, pp. 64-73.

[7] C. D. Walter, Fast Modular Multiplication using 2-Power Radix, Intern. J. Computer Maths., vol. 39, 1991, pp. 21-28.

# Universal Electronic Cash

Tatsuaki Okamoto        Kazuo Ohta

NTT Laboratories
Nippon Telegraph and Telephone Corporation
1-2356, Take, Yokosuka-shi, Kanagawa-ken, 238-03 Japan

## Abstract

This paper proposes the first ideal untraceable electronic cash system which solves the most crucial problem inherent with real cash and all previous untraceable electronic cash systems. The main advantage of the new system is that the customer can subdivide his cash balance, $C$ (dollars), into many pieces in any way he pleases until the total value of all subdivided piece equals $C$. This system can be implemented efficiently. In a typical implementation, the data size of one piece of electronic cash is less than 100 bytes regardless of the face value of piece, the computation time for each transaction is several seconds, assuming the existence of a Rabin scheme chip. The security of this scheme relies on the difficulty of factoring.

# 1   Introduction

Electronic cash is one of the most important applications of modern cryptology because an electronic money (cash) system will be widely installed in the near future; smart cards will become electronic wallets storing electronic cash. The security of real cash heavily depends on physical properties such as the difficulty of reproducing bills and coins. The security of electronic cash systems cannot depend on any physical condition, but must be guaranteed by mathematics. Here, cryptographic techniques are essentially used to guarantee security. Then, information itself has a value, and electronic cash can be transfered through networks.

What then is the ideal cash system? The criteria describing the ideal cash system are as follows:

(a) *Independence*: The security of electronic cash cannot depend on any physical condition. Then the cash can be transfered through networks.

(b) *Security*: The ability to copy (reuse) and forge the cash must be prevented.

(c) *Privacy (Untraceability)*: The privacy of the user should be protected. That is, the relationship between the user and his purchases must be untraceable by anyone.

(d) *Off-line payment*: When a user pay the electronic cash to a shop, the procedure between the user and the shop should be executed in an off-line manner. That is, the shop does not need to be linked to the host in user's payment procedure.

J. Feigenbaum (Ed.): Advances in Cryptology - CRYPTO '91, LNCS 576, pp. 324-337, 1992.
© Springer-Verlag Berlin Heidelberg 1992

(e) *Transferability*: The cash can be transfered to other users.

(f) *Dividability*: One issued piece of cash worth value $C$ (dollars) can be subdivided into many pieces such that each subdivided piece is worth any desired value less than $C$ and the total value of all pieces is equivalent to $C$.

Several electronic cash systems have been proposed by [Ch, Da, PW, EGY, OkOh2, CFN, OkOh1]. The security of the electronic cash system by [EGY] depends on a physical condition. Therefore, [EGY] does not satisfy criterion (a). There are two types of electronic cash systems satisfying criteria (a), (b) and (c); *on-line untraceable* electronic cash systems, and *off-line untraceable* electronic cash systems.

Some *on-line untraceable* electronic cash systems have been proposed by [Ch, Da, PW], which satisfy criteria (a) through (f) except criterion (d). However, the on-line cash systems are not practical from the viewpoints of turn-around-time, communication cost, and database-maintainance cost. Therefore, the off-line cash systems are preferable from the practical viewpoint, although they are technically difficult to construct.

An *off-line untraceable* electronic cash system satisfying criteria (a), (b), (c) and (d) was firstly proposed by [CFN], based on the cut-and-choose methodology and a collision free one-way function technique. An electronic cash system satisfying criteria (a), (b), (c), (d) and (e) was then proposed by [OkOh1]. In [OkOh1], the disposable zero-knowledge authentication scheme is used in place of the collision free function technique in [CFN].

In [OkOh1], an electronic coupon ticket system was also proposed, in which one piece of electronic cash can be subdivided into many pieces whose values are all equivalent. In this system, however, if a customer pays for an article with cents, the store receives an enormous number of one-cent electronic coupon tickets from the customer (for example, when the price of the article is $356.27, the store receives 35627 electronic coupon tickets, where the data size of each ticket is several kilobytes. So, the store receives about 200 megabytes of data for purchasing just one article.) Therefore, no electronic cash system satisfying criterion (f) as well as the other criteria (a) through (e) has been proposed so far.

It must be noted that even the real cash system cannot satisfy criterion (f). This is the reason why we must hold many bills and coins in our wallets. On the other hand, other typical exchange systems such as bank notes and credit cards do not satisfy criteria (a) and (c). Prepaid cards such as telephone cards do not satisfy criterion (a), although they almost satisfy critria (b) through (f). Therefore, we do not have the ideal cash system so far, either electronic or real.

In this paper, we propose the first electronic cash system that satisfies all six criteria. That is, this system is the first version of the ideal cash system. Moreover, the new system is more efficient and practical than any previous system even if we restrict the comparison to the two criteria (a) through (d).

Our scheme uses the cut-and-choose methodology as all previous schemes. The new key techniques of our scheme are the square root molulo $N$ ($N$ is the Williams integer), and the hierarchical structure table. The former is used mainly for criteria (a) through (e) (or in place of the techniques such as the collision free function [CFN], and disposable zero-knowledge authentication [OkOh1]. The latter combined with the former is used for criterion (f), where the hierarchical structure table corresponds to the structure of the cash system.

This paper is constructed as follows: First, in section 2, we will introduce the background of the key techniques including the number theoretic conventions, and the hierarchical structure table of the cash system. In section 3, we will propose the basic version of our electronic cash system. Section 4 explains how electronic credits can be transfered to another customer. Section 5 estimates the properties of the electronic cash system.

# 2 Preparations

## 2.1 Number Theoretic Conventions

**Definition 2.1** $N$ is called the Blum integer [Bl] if $N = PQ$ ($P, Q$ are prime) and $P = 3$ (mod 4), and $Q = 3$ (mod 4).
$N$ is called the Williams integer [W] if $N = PQ$ ($P, Q$ are prime) and $P = 3$ (mod 8), and $Q = 7$ (mod 8). Note that the Williams interger is a specific type of the Blum integer. So, the Williams integer has all properties of the Blum integer.

Let $(x/N)$ denote the Jacobi symbol, when $N$ is a composite number, and denote the Legendre symbol, when $N$ is a prime. When $N = PQ$ ($P, Q$ are prime), we can classify $Z_N^*$ into four classes; $Z_{(1,1)} = \{x \in Z_N^* \mid (x/P) = 1, (x/Q) = 1\}$ $Z_{(1,-1)} = \{x \in Z_N^* \mid (x/P) = 1, (x/Q) = -1\}$, $Z_{(-1,1)} = \{x \in Z_N^* \mid (x/P) = -1, (x/Q) = 1\}$, and $Z_{(-1,-1)} = \{x \in Z_N^* \mid (x/P) = -1, (x/Q) = -1\}$.

Clearly, $Z_{(1,1)}$ denotes the set of quadratic residue intergers in $Z_N^*$. Hereafter, we often write $QR_N$ as $Z_{(1,1)}$, and $QNR_N$ as the other classes.

**Proposition 2.2** Let $N$ be the Blum integer, and $x \in QR_N$. Then, for any integer $t$ ($1 \leq t$), there are four values $y_1, y_2, y_3, y_4$ such that $y_i^{2^t} \equiv x$ (mod $N$) and that $y_1 \in Z_{(1,1)}$, $y_2 \in Z_{(1,-1)}$, $y_3 \in Z_{(-1,1)}$, $y_4 \in Z_{(-1,-1)}$.
In addition, $y_1 \equiv -y_4$ (mod $N$), $y_2 \equiv -y_3$ (mod $N$), $(y_1/N) = (y_4/N) = 1$, and $(y_2/N) = (y_3/N) = -1$.

The above proposition immediately implies that four values of $2^t$-th root $y$ of $x$ can be uniquely determined by two bit information; one is whether $(y/N) = 1$ or $-1$, and the other is whether $y < N/2$ or not. In other words, when $y < N/2$, there are two values of $y$, one of which is $(y/N) = 1$ and the other is $(y/N) = -1$.

$x^{1/2^t}$ mod $N$ ($1 \leq t$) can be computed efficiently (in expected polynomial time) from $x, P, Q$ [R, Ber], and $(y/N)$ can also be computed efficiently from $y$ and $N$, while to compute $x^{1/2^t}$ mod $N$ from $x$ and $N$ is as difficult as factoring $N$ [R].

**Proposition 2.3** Let $N = PQ$ be the Williams integer. Then, for any $x \in Z_N^*$, either one of $x, -x, 2x$ and $-2x$ is in $QR_N$. In addition, when $ax \in QR_N$ ($a$ is either $1, -1, 2$, or $-2$), $bx$ is not in $QR_N$ ($b \neq a$, and $b$ is either $1, -1, 2,$ or $-2$).

The above proposition is easily proven by the following result;

$$(-1/P) = -1, (-1/Q) = -1, (2/P) = -1, (2/Q) = 1.$$

**Definition 2.4** Let $N$ be the Williams integer, and $x \in QR_N$.

$$[x^{1/2^t} \bmod N]_{QR} = y$$

such that $y^{2^t} = x \bmod N$ and $y \in QR_N$. $(1 \le t)$

$$[x^{1/2^t} \bmod N]_1 = y'$$

such that $y'^{2^t} = x \bmod N$, $(y'/N) = 1$ and $0 < y' < N/2$. $(1 \le t)$

$$\cdot [x^{1/2^t} \bmod N]_{-1} = y''$$

such that $y''^{2^t} = x \bmod N$, $(y''/N) = -1$ and $0 < y'' < N/2$. $(1 \le t)$
Let $N$ be the Williams integer, and $z \in Z_N^*$.

$$< z >_{QR} = dz \bmod N$$

such that $d \in \{\pm 1, \pm 2\}$ and $dz \bmod N \in QR_N$.

$$< z >_1 = d'z \bmod N$$

such that $d' \in \{1, 2\}$ and $(d'z/N) = 1$.

$$< z >_{-1} = d''z \bmod N$$

such that $d'' \in \{1, 2\}$ and $(d''z/N) = -1$.

From the properties of the Williams number (and the Blum number), each value of $y, y', y''$, $d, d', d''$ is uniquely determined respectively.

## 2.2 Hierarchical Structure Table

In our cash system, the hierarchical structure table plays an important role because it allows the issued electronic bill $C$ to be subdivided into many pieces such that each subdivided piece is worth any desired value less than $C$ and the total value of all pieces is equivalent to $C$.

The hierarchical structure table is a tree of $t$ levels, in which each node has two sons, the unique root node exists at the top of the tree. So, there are $2^{i-1}$ nodes at the $i$-th level.

Here, we show the significance of the tree in our cash system. For easy understanding, we use a simple example, where the tree has three levels, and the value of the issued bill $C$ is \$100. The nodes of the $i$-th level correspond to $\$100/2^{i-1}$. So, the customer can use the bill in \$25 increments, since the nodes of the bottom level (the third level) correspond to \$25 (see Figure 1).

We give two restrictions to the usage of the bill with relating to the tree as follows:

1. The value corresponding to a node, $N$, is the total of the values corresponding to nodes that are the direct sons of $N$.

2. When a node (the corresponding value) is used, all descendant nodes and all ancestor nodes of this node cannot be used.

3. No node can be used more than once.

We show the case when customer Alice uses \$75 first and then uses \$25. When she uses \$75, she must use node $\Gamma_{00}$ (\$50), and node $\Gamma_{010}$ (\$25). From the above restrictions, only $\Gamma_{011}$ (\$25) can be used after the use of $\Gamma_{00}$ and $\Gamma_{010}$ (see Figure 2).

More generally, if Alice wants to use a bill worth \$1000 by the cent, she would need a hierarchical structure table of 17 levels ($\log_2 100000 \approx 16.5$). She would then use about 8 nodes in average (minimum: one node; maximum: 16 nodes) in order to pay by the cent for each purchase (e.g., \$334.36 payment).

Moreover, in our concrete cash scheme that will be shown in the following sections, we need two hierarchical structure tables ($\Gamma$ table and $\Lambda$ table); $\Gamma$ table is used to realize the first restriction, and $\Lambda$ table to realize the second restriction. $\Gamma$ table and $\Lambda$ table have the same structure such that they are trees with the same topology (or the same number of layers), and that $\Gamma_{j_1 \dots j_t}$ and $\Lambda_{j_1 \dots j_t}$ both correspond to the same position node ($\text{Node}_{j_1 \dots j_t}$) of the money structure table. In the example of Figures 1 and 2, $\Gamma_{00}$ and $\Lambda_{00}$ correspond to the same position node, the left node of \$50, of the money structure table.

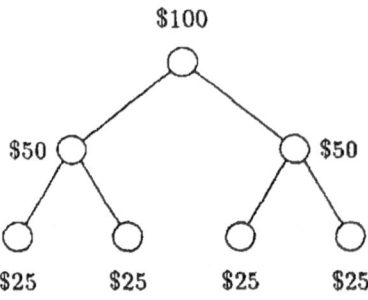

Figure 1: Hierarchical Structure Table (Money Structure)

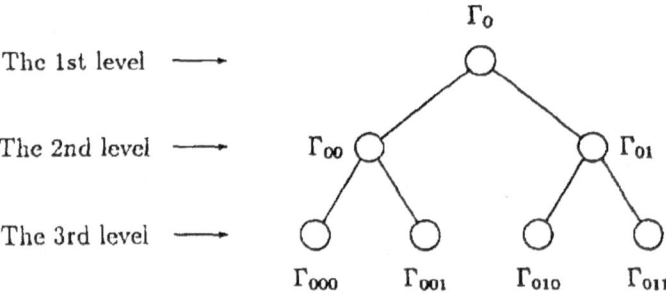

Figure 2: Hierarchical Structure Table ($\Gamma$ Table)

# 3  Basic Universal Electronic Cash Scheme

In this section, we introduce the basic universal electronic cash scheme which satisfies the five criteria ((a) through (f) except (e)(Transferability)).

## 3.1  Protocol

### Protocol 1 (Basic universal electronic cash):

For blind digital signatures[Ch], bank $A$ has generated keys of the RSA scheme; $(e_A, n_A; d_A)$, $(e'_A, n'_A; d'_A)$, $(e''_A, n''_A; d''_A)$, ..., where $(e_A, n_A)$, $(e'_A, n'_A)$, ... are public keys, and $d_A, d'_A, \ldots$ are the corresponding secret keys. $A$ has published $(e_A, n_A)$, $(e'_A, n'_A)$, $(e''_A, n''_A)$, ..., where $(e_A, n_A)$ corresponds to the *electronic license* that $A$ issues, and $(e'_A, n'_A)$, $(e''_A, n''_A)$, ... correspond to the value of the *electronic bill* that $A$ issues. For example, $100 corresponds to $(e'_A, n'_A)$, and $500 corresponds to $(e''_A, n''_A)$, etc. Bank $A$ also sets the security parameter $K = O(|n_A|) = O(|n'_A|) = \ldots$ (for example, $K = 40$).

$A$ has also published three randomized hash functions, $f_\Gamma, f_\Lambda, f_\Omega$, to generate the hierarchical structure tables, $\Gamma$ table and $\Lambda$ table. Here, the function values are assumed to distribute uniformly (for example, the universal hash functions [CW], and pseudo-random generator). Note that the one-wayness or collision-freeness is not required for these functions.

Customer $P$ has a bank account number $ID_P$ and has generated the key of the RSA scheme, $(e_P, n_P; d_P)$, and published $(e_P, n_P)$ for digital signatures.

**Note 1:**  Any multiple blind digital signature [OkOh1] can be used in place of the RSA scheme for bank $A$ above. For example, the blind digital signature scheme based on the Fiat-Shamir signature scheme [OkOh2] can be used for this purpose. Moreover, any digital signature scheme can be used in place of the RSA scheme for customer $P$ above. For example, [FOM] can be used for this purpose.

**Note 2:**  The secure exchange problem is out of the scope of this paper. For example, $A$ and $P$ exchange electronic cash and withdrawal, $P$ and $V$ exchange payment and articles, and $V$ and $A$ exchange payment history and credit. The secure exchange problem can be practically solved by the usage of digital signature schemes. More secure but less efficient solutions for this problem has been shown in [EGL].

### Part I.

When a customer $P$ opens an account at bank $A$, $A$ issues an electronic license $B = \{B_i \mid 1 \le i \le K/2\}$ to use the electronic cash of bank $A$. (Precisely, the electronic license is $(B, \{I_i, N_i\}, L)$. For simplicity, however, we simply call it $B$.) To get $B$, $P$ conducts the following protocol with $A$. This procedure is executed *only once* when $P$ opens the account, unless $P$ uses the electronic cash invalidly.

**Step 1:**  Customer $P$ chooses a random value $a_i$, and the Williams integers $N_i$ with two large prime factors $P_i, Q_i$ ($N_i = P_i Q_i$), where $P_i \equiv 3 \pmod 8$ and $Q_i \equiv 7 \pmod 8$, for $i = 1, \ldots, K$.

**Step 2:**  $P$ forms and sends $K$ blind candidates $W_i (i = 1, \ldots, K)$ to bank $A$.

$$W_i = r_i^{e_A} g(I_i \parallel N_i) \bmod n_A \quad \text{for } 1 \le i \le K,$$

where $r_i \in Z_{n_A}$ is a random integer, $g$ is an appropriate one-way hash function, and

$$S_i = ID_P \parallel a_i \parallel (g(ID_P \parallel a_i))^{d_P} \bmod n_P,$$
$$= S_{1,i} \parallel S_{2,i},$$
$$I_{1,i} = S_{1,i}^2 \bmod N_i, \quad I_{2,i} = S_{2,i}^2 \bmod N_i,$$
$$I_i = I_{1,i} \parallel I_{2,i}.$$

Here, $\parallel$ denotes the concatenation.

**Step 3:** $A$ chooses a random subset of $K/2$ blind candidates indices $U = \{i_j\}, 1 \le i_j \le K$ for $1 \le j \le K/2$ and transmits it to $P$.

**Step 4:** $P$ displays the $a_i, P_i, Q_i, (g(ID_P \parallel a_i))^{d_P} \bmod n_P, ID_P, r_i$ for all $i$ in $U$, then $A$ checks them. If they are not valid, $A$ halts this protocol. To simplify notations, we will assume that $U = \{K/2 + 1, K/2 + 2, \ldots, K\}$.

**Step 5:** $A$ gives $P$

$$(\prod_{i=1}^{K/2} W_i)^{d_A} \bmod n_A.$$

**Step 6:** $P$ can then extract the electronic license $B = (\prod_{i=1}^{K/2} g(I_i \parallel N_i))^{d_A} \bmod n_A$.

## Part II.

When customer $P$ wants bank $A$ to issue an electronic bill worth \$100, $C$, which corresponds to $(e'_A, n'_A)$, $P$ conducts the following protocol with $A$.

**Step 1:** $P$ chooses a random value $b$, forms and sends $Z$ to $A$.

$$Z = r^{e'_A} g(B \parallel b) \bmod n'_A,$$

where $r \in Z_{n'_A}$ is a random integer.

**Step 2:** $A$ gives $Z^{d'_A} \bmod n'_A$ to $P$ and charges $P$'s account \$100.

**Step 3:** $P$ can then extract the electronic bill $C = (g(B \parallel b))^{d'_A} \bmod n'_A$.

## Part III.

To pay a shop $V$ a certain amount of money, $P$ and $V$ proceed as follows:

First, for easy understanding, we will show a simple example of this protocol, when $P$ pays \$75 to $V$ based on the hierarchical structure table of three levels, as was shown in subsection 2.2. Here, we assume that $P$ has received \$100 bill $C$ from Bank $A$ in Part II.

**Step 1:** As the preliminary stage of Part III, $P$ computes the value of $\Gamma_{i,0}$ $(i = 1, \ldots, K/2)$ as follows:

$$\Gamma_{i,0} = < f_\Gamma(C \parallel 0 \parallel N_i) >_{QR}.$$

(See Subsection 2.1 for the notation of $<>_{QR}$.)

**Step 2:** When $P$ decides to pay \$75, first $P$ computes $X_{i,00}$ (corresponding to \$50) and $X_{i,010}$ (corresponding to \$25) $(i = 1, \ldots, K/2)$ as follows:

$$X_{i,00} = [\Gamma_{i,0}^{1/4} \bmod N_i]_{-1}$$

$$X_{i,010} = [(\Omega_{i,0}^2 \Gamma_{i,0})^{1/8} \bmod N_i]_{-1}.$$

Here, $\Omega_{i,0} = < f_\Omega(C \parallel 0 \parallel N_i) >_1$.
$P$ sends $(I_i, N_i, X_{i,00}, X_{i,010})$ $(i = 1, \ldots, K/2)$ and $(B, C)$ to $V$.

**Note:** The above calculation of $X_{i,00}$ and $X_{i,010}$ is based on the following algorithm:

$$X_{i,00} = [\Gamma_{i,00}^{1/2} \bmod N_i]_{-1},$$

$$X_{i,010} = [\Gamma_{i,010}^{1/2} \bmod N_i]_{-1},$$

where

$$\Gamma_{i,00} = [\Gamma_{i,0}^{1/2} \bmod N_i]_{QR}$$

$$\Gamma_{i,01} = [\Omega_{i,0}\Gamma_{i,0}^{1/2} \bmod N_i]_{QR}$$

$$\Gamma_{i,010} = [\Gamma_{i,01}^{1/2} \bmod N_i]_{QR}$$

Here, summarizing the algorithm, first, the $\Gamma$ table of the correponding nodes $(\Gamma_{i,00}, \Gamma_{i,010})$ are calculated, then the square roots of these values in $QNR$ (these Jacobi symbol values are $-1$) are $X_{i,00}$ and $X_{i,010}$.

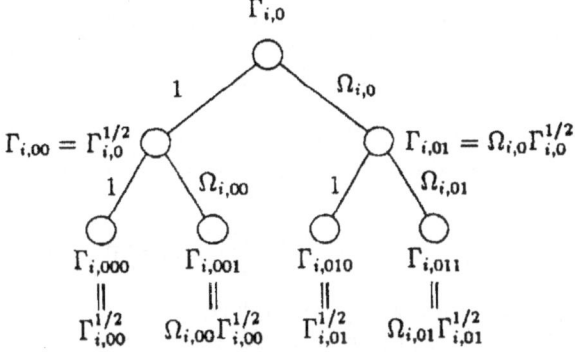

Figure 3: Node Values of $\Gamma$ Table (Three Layer Example)

**Step 3:** $V$ verifies the validity of the signatures $B$ for $\{(I_i, N_i)\}$, and $C$ for $B$. $V$ computes $\Omega_{i,0}$, $f_\Gamma(C \parallel 0 \parallel N_i)$ then verifies the validity of $X_{i,00}$ and $X_{i,010}$ $(i = 1, \ldots, K/2)$ such that

$$(X_{i,00}/N_i) = (X_{i,010}/N_i) = -1,$$

$$X_{i,00}^4 = d_i f_\Gamma(C \parallel 0 \parallel N_i) \bmod N_i$$

$$X_{i,010}^8 = d_i \Omega_{i,0}^2 f_\Gamma(C \parallel 0 \parallel N_i) \bmod N_i,$$

where $d_i \in \{\pm 1, \pm 2\}$ $(i = 1, \ldots, K/2)$. If they are valid, $V$ selects random bits, $E_{i,00}$, $E_{i,010} \in \{0, 1\}$ $(i = 1, \ldots, K/2)$, and sends them to $P$. Otherwise $V$ halts this protocol.

**Step 4:** $P$ computes

$$Y_{i,00} = [\Lambda_{i,00}^{1/2} \bmod N_i]_{(-1)^{E_{i,00}}},$$

$$Y_{i,010} = [\Lambda_{i,010}^{1/2} \bmod N_i]_{(-1)^{E_{i,010}}},$$

and sends $(Y_{i,00}, Y_{i,010})$ $(i = 1, \ldots, K/2)$ to $V$. Here,

$$\Lambda_{i,00} = < f_\Lambda(C \parallel 00 \parallel N_i) >_{QR},$$

$$\Lambda_{i,010} = < f_\Lambda(C \parallel 010 \parallel N_i) >_{QR}.$$

**Step 5:** $V$ verifies that

$$(Y_{i,00}/N_i) = (-1)^{E_{i,00}}, (Y_{i,010}/N_i) = (-1)^{E_{i,010}},$$

$$Y_{i,00}^2 = d_i' f_\Lambda(C \parallel 00 \parallel N_i) \bmod N_i,$$

$$Y_{i,010}^2 = d_i''' f_\Lambda(C \parallel 010 \parallel N_i) \bmod N_i,$$

where $d_i', d_i''' \in \{\pm 1, \pm 2\}$ $(i = 1, \ldots, K/2)$. If verification succeeds, $V$ accepts $P$'s messages as \$75 from electronic bill $C$.

Next, we show the protocol of Part III in general cases. Here, we assume that $\Gamma$ table has more than $t$ levels, and that the node corresponding to the value of $P$'s payment to $V$ is $\Gamma_{j_1 \ldots j_t}$ (and $\Lambda_{j_1 \ldots j_t}$), where $j_1, \ldots, j_t \in \{0,1\}$. Usually, there are several nodes which correspond to the payment (e.g., in the above simple example, two nodes form $P$'s \$75 payment). Then, the following protocol of each node must be executed simultaneously, in the same manner as the above protocol, which has two nodes.

**Step 1:** This preliminary stage of Part III is the same as the above protocol.
**Step 2:** When $P$ determines the node, $\Gamma_{j_1 \ldots j_t}$ (and $\Lambda_{j_1 \ldots j_t}$), corresponding to the payment, $P$ computes $X_{i,j_1 \ldots j_t}$,

$$X_{i,j_1 \ldots j_t} = [(\Omega_{i,j_1 \ldots j_{t-1}}^{2^{t-1} j_t} \Omega_{i,j_1 \ldots j_{t-2}}^{2^{t-2} j_{t-1}} \cdots \Omega_{i,0}^{2 j_2} \Gamma_{i,0})^{1/2^t} \bmod N_i]_{-1},$$

where $\Omega_{i,j_1 \ldots j_t} = < f_\Omega(C \parallel j_1 \parallel \cdots \parallel j_t \parallel N_i) >_1$.
$P$ sends $(I_i, N_i, X_{i,j_1 \ldots j_t})$ $(i = 1, \ldots, K/2)$ and $(B, C)$ to $V$.
**Note:** The above calculation of $X_{i,j_1 \ldots j_t}$ is based on the following algorithm:

$$X_{i,j_1 \ldots j_t} = [\Gamma_{i,j_1 \ldots j_t}^{1/2} \bmod N_i]_{-1},$$

where

$$\Gamma_{i,j_1 \ldots j_{t+1}} = [\Omega_{i,j_1 \ldots j_t}^{j_{t+1}} \Gamma_{i,j_1 \ldots j_t}^{1/2} \bmod N_i]_{QR}.$$

**Step 3:** $V$ verifies the validity of the signatures $B$ for $\{(I_i, N_i)\}$, and $C$ for $B$. $V$ computes $\Omega_{i,j_1 \ldots j_t}$ (if $j_{t+1} = 1$) then verifies the validity of $X_{i,j_1 \ldots j_t}$ $(i = 1, \ldots, K/2)$ such that

$$(X_{i,j_1 \ldots j_t}/N_i) = -1,$$

$$X_{i,j_1 \ldots j_t}^{2^t} = d_i \Omega_{i,j_1 \ldots j_{t-1}}^{2^{t-1} j_t} \Omega_{i,j_1 \ldots j_{t-2}}^{2^{t-2} j_{t-1}} \cdots \Omega_{i,j_1}^{2 j_2} f_\Gamma(C \parallel 0 \parallel N_i) \bmod N_i,$$

where $d_i \in \{\pm 1, \pm 2\}$ $(i = 1, \ldots, K/2)$. If they are valid, $V$ selects random bits, $E_{i,j_1 \ldots j_t} \in \{0,1\}$ $(i = 1, \ldots, K/2)$, and sends them to $P$. Otherwise $V$ halts this protocol.

**Step 4:** $P$ computes

$$Y_{i,j_1\cdots j_t} = [\Lambda^{1/2}_{i,j_1\cdots j_t} \bmod N_i]_{(-1)^{E_{i,j_1\cdots j_t}}}.$$

Here,

$$\Lambda_{i,j_1\cdots j_t} = <f_\Lambda(C \parallel j_1 \parallel \cdots \parallel j_t \parallel N_i) >_{QR}.$$

**Step 5:** $V$ verifies that

$$(Y_{i,j_1\cdots j_t}/N_i) = (-1)^{E_{i,j_1\cdots j_t}},$$

$$Y^2_{i,j_1\cdots j_t} = d'_i f_\Lambda(C \parallel j_1 \parallel \cdots \parallel j_t \parallel N_i) \bmod N_i,$$

where $d'_i \in \{\pm 1, \pm 2\}$ $(i = 1, \ldots, K/2)$. If verification succeeds, $V$ accepts $P$'s messages as payment of the amount due.

**Note:** To prevent bank $A$ from crediting an invalid shop's account in Part III, we can enhance the protocol as follows: Here, we simply write $E_i$ as $E_{i,j_1\cdots j_t}$. $V$ selects a random value $E'_i$, and sends $V$'s identity $ID_V$, time $T$, and $E'_i$ $(i = 1, \ldots, K/2)$ to $P$ in place of sending $E_i$. $V$ computes $(E_1, \ldots, E_{K/2}) = h(ID_V \parallel T \parallel E'_1 \cdots E'_{K/2})$, where $h$ is a one-way function whose output is uniformly random. $P$ also computes $E_i$ $(i = 1, \ldots, K/2)$.

## Part IV.

For bank $A$ to credit $V$'s account by the appropriate amount, $V$ sends the history of Part III of this protocol, $H$, to $A$, which credits $V$'s account. After checking the validity of $H$, bank $A$ must store $H$ in its database. If $A$ finds an invalid payment, $A$ reveal the secret information $S_i$ of costumer $P$ who is responsible for the invalid payment from $H$ and the related history.

**(End of Protocol 1)**

**Note 1:** Since bank $A$ has already known $K/2$ pieces of $S_i$ in Part I (e.g., $S_{K/2+1}, \ldots, S_K$), $(K/2+1)$ pieces of $S_i$ shown by $A$ are the evidence of the invalid payment by a customer.

**Note 2:** Bank $A$ can store $H$ with dividing it into two parts, $H_1$ and $H_2$. $H_1$ is used to check the invalid payment, and $H_2$ is to compute $S_i$ when $A$ finds an invalid payment. $H_1$ consists of the hashed value of $C$ and the nodes corresponding to the payment. Here, the hashed value of $C$ is the searching key in the database, and $H_1$ can be very short (e.g, 10 bytes). On the other hand, $H_2$ is almost same as $H$, and is pointed from $H_1$. Therefore, $H_1$ can be stored in a database which is easy of access, while $H_2$ can be stored in a device such as a magnetic tape and a laser disk, which is not easy of access but has big capacity. $H_1$ and $H_2$ (especially $H_2$) can be stored in a distributed manner.

## 3.2 Correctness

Here, we show briefly that Protocol 1 satisfies the five criteria of (a)*Independence*, (b)*Security*, (c)*Privacy*, (d)*Off-line payment*, and (f)*Divisibility*. Among them, criteria (a) and (d) are clearly satisfied. Therefore, we show that the other three criteria are satisfied.

- *Privacy:* First, if the customer accurately follows the protocol, even the coalition of bank $A$ and store $V$ cannot get any knowledge about the identity of $P$ with non-negligible probability, assuming that factoring is difficult for $A$ and $V$.

- *Dividability:* As shown in Subsection 2.2, if three restrictions on the usage of the hierarchical structure table are satisfied, then the dividability condition is satisfied. (In the next item (security), we will show that the second and third restrictions are securely realized. The first restriction can be clearly realized as a protocol.) Then, when $R$ is the ratio of the value of an electronic bill, $C$, (e.g, \$1000) to the minimum unit of payment (e.g., 1 cent), then the processing and communication amounts for payment are in proportion to $\log_2 R$.

- *Security:* First, we show that the third restriction of the hierarchical structure table (Subsection 2.2) is securely realized. If customer $P$ uses any part of $C$ (any node of the hierarchical structure table of $C$) more than once, bank $A$ can obtain the identity of $P$ with overwhelming probability, since the Williams integer $N$ can be factored in polynomial-time from $[x^{1/2} \bmod N]_1$ and $[x^{1/2} \bmod N]_{-1}$, and since $V$ challenges $P$ randomly using $\Lambda$ table, along with the cut-and-choose methodology. Next, we show that the second restriction of the hierarchical structure table (Subsection 2.2) is securely realized. Here, for easily understanding, we use the simple example, where the value of $C$ is \$100, and $P$ pays \$75 to $V$ (Figure 1, 2, and 3). Note that the cut-and-choose methodology is also implicitly crucial in assuring correctness, although we omit a detailed explanation here (roughly, thanks to this methodology, we can assume that $I_i, N_i$ are correctly generated).

  First, we show that the first restriction is satisfied: that is, when nodes $\Gamma_{00}, \Gamma_{010}$ are used, then all descendant and ancestor nodes of these nodes, $\Gamma_0, \Gamma_{000}, \Gamma_{001}$, and $\Gamma_{01}$, cannot be used. When $\Gamma_{00}$ is used, $P$ sends $X_{i,00} = [\Gamma_{i,00}^{1/2} \bmod N_i]_{-1}$ $(i = 1, \ldots, K/2)$ to $V$ (finally to $A$). Then, if $P$ uses $\Gamma_{000}$, $P$ sends $X_{i,000} = [\Gamma_{i,000}^{1/2} \bmod N_i]_{-1}$ $(i = 1, \ldots, K/2)$. Since $[\Gamma_{i,00}^{1/2} \bmod N_i]_1 = X_{i,000}^2 \bmod N_i$, $A$ can factor $N_i$ from $X_{i,00}$ and $X_{i,000}^2 \bmod N_i$ (then, the identity of $P$ is revealed). Similarly, if $\Gamma_0$ or $\Gamma_{001}$ is used with $\Gamma_{00}$, or if $\Gamma_0$ or $\Gamma_{01}$ is used with $\Gamma_{010}$, then the identity of $P$ is revealed. Therefore, when $\Gamma_{00}, \Gamma_{010}$ are used, then $\Gamma_0, \Gamma_{000}, \Gamma_{001}$, and $\Gamma_{01}$, cannot be used, with concealing the identity of $P$.

  Finally, we show the necessity of $\Omega$, using a simple example. Assume that $\Omega_{i,j_1\cdots j_t}$ is a constant value, e.g., 3. Then, in Figure 3, $\Gamma_{01} = 3(\Gamma_0)^{1/2}$, where we omitt the suffix of $i$ and $\bmod N_i$, for simplicity. So, when a customer uses the nodes of $\Gamma_{00}$ and $\Gamma_{01}$, he opens the values of $X_{00} = (\Gamma_0)^{1/4}$ and $X_{01} = (3(\Gamma_0)^{1/2})^{1/2} = 3^{1/2}(\Gamma_0)^{1/4}$, where the jacobi symbol values of $X_{00}$ and $X_{01}$ are $-1$. Then, the shop can obtain $3^{1/2}$ by calculating $X_{01}/X_{00}$, where the jacobi symbol of this value is 1. The same situation occurs when the customer uses the nodes of $\Gamma_{000}$ and $\Gamma_{001}$, and so on. Therefore, suppose that a customer uses $\Gamma_{000}, \Gamma_{001}, \Gamma_{010}$, and $\Gamma_{0110}$, whose usage is valid. (So, he opens $X_{000}, X_{001}, X_{010}$, and $X_{0110}$.) Then, the shop can calculate $A = 3^{1/2}$ by $X_{001}/X_{000}$, and also calculate the value of $X_{011}$ by $AX_{010}$. Therefore, the shop can factor $N$ by using the values of $X_{011}$ and $(X_{0110})^2$, where the jacobi symbol of $X_{011}$ is $-1$ and that of $(X_{0110})^2$ is 1. Thus, the shop can know the customer's ID, although the customer uses the nodes validly.

# 4 Transferable Universal Electronic Cash

In this section, we propose an electronic cash scheme satisfying the criterion of (e) *Transferability* in addition to the other five criteria.

## Protocol 2. (Transferable universal electronic cash)

This protocol is constructed based on Protocol 1. To simplify the description of this protocol, we suppose an example similar to that in Section 3, where $C$ is worth \$100, customer $P_1$ who has spent \$75 transfers the remaining \$25 to customer $P_2$, and $P_2$ uses \$25 at shop $V$.

### Part I.

When customers $P_1$ and $P_2$ open their accounts at bank $A$, $A$ issues electronic licenses $B^{(j)}$ to a customer $P_j$ $(j = 1, 2)$. Hereafter, in this protocol, $x^{(j)}$ means $x$ of $P_j$, where variable $x$ follows the definition in Protocol 1.

### Part II.

Suppose that customer $P_1$ has bank $A$ issue an electronic bill worth \$100, $C$.

### Part III.

To transfer $C$ to another customer $P_2$, $P_1$ and $P_2$ proceeds as follows:
(Step 1) $P_2$ takes the role of $V$ in Protocol 1 as $P_1$ pays shop $P_2$ \$25 (corresponding to node $\Gamma_{011}$) (Part III of Protocol 1).
(Step 2) $P_1$ sends certification $T$ that denotes the transfer of $C$ from $P_1$ to $P_2$. For example, $P_1$ sends a (Rabin scheme) digital signature $T = (< g(C \parallel 011 \parallel B^{(2)} >_{QR})^{1/2} \bmod N_1^{(1)}$.

### Part IV.

To pay shop $V$ \$25, $P_2$ and $V$ proceed as follows:
(Step 1) $P_2$ sends the history of Part III of this protocol, $H^{(1)}$, to $V$. $V$ checks the validity of $H^{(1)}$.
(Step 2) $P_2$ follows Part III of Protocol 1 with shop $V$ to pay $C$. Here, $P_2$ sends $V$ messages corresponding to nodes $\Gamma_{011}^{(2)}$ and $\Lambda_{011}^{(2)}$.

### Part V.

To have bank $A$ credit $V$'s account by \$25, $V$ sends the history of Part IV of this protocol, $H^{(2)}$, to $A$, which credits $V$'s account. Bank $A$ must store $H^{(2)}$ in its database.

(End of Protocol 2)

# 5 Performance Estimation

We will briefly explain an example of the new cash system implementation. Here we assume that $K = 40$, $|N_i|$ is 64 bytes, and the hierarchical structure table has 17 levels. We also assume that a bank issues a piece of cash worth \$1000 to customer Alice. Alice can disburse her cash in any way she pleases until the total expended equals \$1000. Then, she uses just 64 bytes of data for the electronic bill ($C$) worth \$1000 and her proper data (electronic license, $B$) is about several kilobytes. Thus the total amount of data is small enough to be stored on typical smart cards. When she buys several articles (e.g., the total payment for them is \$334.36) at a store, her card transmits only 20 kilobytes on average. The computation time for generating the data representing the payment (e.g., \$334.36) that will be sent to the store is about several seconds, assuming the existence of a Rabin scheme chip of 30 Kbps (kilo-bit per second). If the value of the payment is known in advance, the computation for the payment can be executed in advance.

# 6 Conclusion

In this paper, we have proposed the first ideal untraceable electronic cash system, The customer can subdivide his cash balance, $C$ (dollars), into many pieces in any way he pleases until the total value of all subdivided piece equals $C$. A smart card equipped with a Rabin scheme chip and the distributed database system for a bank to store $H_1$ and $H_2$ should be implemented efficiently to realize the universal electronic cash system. From a theoretical viewpoint, it remains open to construct an unconditionally untraceable universal electronic cash system.

# Acknowledgments

Authors wish to thank A. Herzberg, S. Kurihara, K. Sakurai and A. Shamir for their useful discussions.

# References

[Ber]   E.R.Berlekamp, "Factoring Polynomials over Large Finite Fields," Math. Comp., Vol.24, No.111, pp.713-735 (1970)

[Bl]   M.Blum, "Coin flipping by telephone", IEEE, COMPCON, pp.133-137 (1982)

[Ch]   D.Chaum, "Security without Identification: Transaction Systems to Make Big Brother Obsolete," Comm. of the ACM, 28, 10, pp.1030-1044 (1985)

[CFN]   D.Chaum, A.Fiat and M. Naor, "Untraceable Electronic Cash," Proc. of Crypto'88, pp.319-327 (1988)

[CW]   J.L.Carter and M.N.Wegman, "Universal Classes of Hash Functions," Journal of Computer and System Sciences, 18, pp.143-154 (1979)

[Da]   I.B.Damgård, "Payment Systems and Credential Mechanisms with Provable Security Against Abuse by Individuals," Proc. of Crypto'88, pp.328-335 (1988)

[EGL]   S.Even, O.Goldreich, A.Lempel: "A Randomized Protocol for Signing Contracts", Proc. of Crypto'82, pp.205-210 (1982)

[EGY]   S.Even, O.Goldreich, Y.Yacobi: "Electronic Wallet", Proc. of Crypto'83, pp.383-386 (1983)

[FOM]   A.Fujioka, T.Okamoto, S.Miyaguchi: "ESIGN: An Efficient Digital Signature Implementation for Smart Cards", to appear in Proc. of Eurocrypt'91

[H]   B.Hayes, "Anonymous One-Time Signatures and Flexible Untraceable Electronic Cash," Proc. of Auscrypt'90, pp.294-305 (1990)

[OkOh1]   T.Okamoto, and K.Ohta "Disposable Zero-Knowledge Authentications and Their Applications to Untraceable Electronic Cash," Proc. of Crypto'89, pp.481-496 (1989)

[OkOh2] T.Okamoto, and K.Ohta "Divertible Zero-Knowledge Interactive Proofs and Commutative Random Self-Reducible," Proc. of Eurocrypt'89 (1989)

[PW] B.Pfitzmann, M.Waidner, "How to Break and Repair a "Provably Secure" Untraceable Payment System," to appear in Proc. of Crypto'91

[R] M.O.Rabin, "Digitalized Signatures and Public-Key Functions as Intractable as Factorization," Tech. Rep., MIT/LCS/TR-212, MIT Lab. Comp. Sci., (1979)

[W] H.C.Williams, "A Modification of the RSA Public-Key Encryption Procedure," IEEE Trans. on Information Theory, Vol.IT-26, No.6, pp.726-729 (1980)

# How to Break and Repair a "Provably Secure" Untraceable Payment System

## (Extended Abstract)

Birgit Pfitzmann[1], Michael Waidner[2]

## Abstract

On Crypto '88, an untraceable payment system with provable security against abuse by individuals was presented by Damgård. We show how to break the untraceability of that system completely.

Next, an improved version of the system is presented. We also augment the system by security for the individuals against loss of money, and we introduce the possibility of receipts for payments. Finally, whereas all this concerned an on-line system, we present a similar construction for untraceable electronic cash.

## 1 Introduction

We start with a brief overview over untraceable payment systems. Then we give an overview over the rest of the paper.

### 1.1 Untraceable payment systems in general

The main characteristic of untraceable payment systems is that, like with conventional cash, the system operator (normally called "bank") cannot completely observe the payment behaviour of the individuals. Also, payer and payee may want to be untraceable by each other, or at least one of them. The need for such untraceable payments was discussed, e.g., in [Chau_85].

The first system of this kind, with several variants, was presented in [Chau_83, Chau_85], and in more detail in [Chau_89]. Common characteristics of all the variants are:

---

[1] Institut für Informatik, Universität Hildesheim, Samelsonplatz 1, W-3200 Hildesheim, FRG; fax +49-5121-860475; phone +49-5121-883-739;
e-mail pfitzb@infhil.uucp (via unido.informatik.uni-dortmund.de).
[2] Institut für Rechnerentwurf und Fehlertoleranz, Universität Karlsruhe, Postfach 6980, W-7500 Karlsruhe 1, FRG; fax +49-721-370455; phone +49-721-608-4024;
e-mail waidner@ira.uka.de.

---

J. Feigenbaum (Ed.): Advances in Cryptology - CRYPTO '91, LNCS 576, pp. 338-350, 1992.
© Springer-Verlag Berlin Heidelberg 1992

- They work for on-line payments, i.e. the bank is needed within each payment.
- They assume that individuals have normal non-anonymous bank accounts, but money can be withdrawn from one account (in a form called "electronic coin") and deposited into another account in a way that the bank cannot trace from whom to whom the money was passed.
- The untraceability is unconditional. (Of course, suitable circumstances must be assumed: Enough coins of the same denomination must always have been withdrawn.)
- Different payments are unlinkable. The contrary would be that for several payments, it could be observed that they were made by the same person (although not by whom). Linkability may be dangerous, because it facilitates deanonymization. For instance, if an individual makes linkable payments to several organizations, and is personally known to one of them, they all can put their information together. And even if the individual is originally known to none of them, they may compare their information about the untraceable individuals' spending behaviour with the bank's information about when and how much money each real person withdrew and thus find out who is who.
- The security against abuse by individuals, in particular that they cannot make up coins themselves, or deposit coins twice, relies on a form of RSA.

The variants differ in who is untraceable by whom and in the degree of security against fraud, also by the bank, that they offer. (An efficiency improvement was presented in [Chau3_90].)

Other variants of payment systems achieve even more untraceability by eliminating the fixed accounts (but this may not always be desired, e.g., for taxing), or enable provable security against abuse on the basis of any signature scheme at the cost of a slight decrease in untraceability, or guarantee receipts for payments [BüPf_89].

Untraceable off-line payments exist, too [ChFN_90, CBHM_90]. Their security is necessarily a bit smaller than that of on-line systems can be: In on-line systems, one can prevent individuals from spending the same money twice, whereas in off-line systems, one can only detect this afterwards. (Note that all these systems do not assume the existence of tamper-proof devices.) Thus there is a risk that the individual has no money to pay back; but this risk is also accepted with some non-digital payment systems. Again, the untraceability is unconditional, whereas the security relies on a form of RSA.

On Crypto '88, an untraceable payment system with provable security against abuse by individuals was introduced [Damg_90]. This system should mostly have the same characteristics as the basic system from [Chau_89] (on-line, fixed accounts, unconditional untraceability, but not of the payee against a collusion of payer and bank, unlinkability), but additionally, the security against fraud by individuals should be provably as hard as a well-known cryptographic assumption. The price paid is that this system is far less efficient than all the systems mentioned above. Security against fraud by the bank is not considered. The cryptographic assumption is stated as "claw-free permutation pairs and a trap-door one-way function exist"; actually, the underlying protocol from [ChDG_88] assumes quadratic residuosity, but a construction of a similar protocol on the stated assumptions has been sketched by the same authors [Damg_91].

(Later, an efficient untraceable payment system, again with the same characteristics as the basic system from [Chau_89], but based on the Fiat-Shamir-scheme instead of RSA, was introduced in [OkOh_90]. Security against fraud by the bank is not considered there, either. Off-line systems on similar assumptions are contained in [OkOh1_90, OkOh_91]. However, some of the efficiency in these systems is gained by making payments linkable.)

## 1.2   Overview over this paper

We first show that Damgård's payment system is not untraceable at all (§2). This section also contains a description of that system. (Note that [Damg_90] also contains a credential system; we do not break that.)

In §3, we present a way to repair the untraceability, while maintaining security against abuse by individuals on the same assumptions as in [Damg_90].

In §4, we add measures to ensure security against fraud by the bank (on the even weaker assumption of any signature scheme). This is a highly desirable property for a payment system anyway; and in particular, if the clients want unconditional security against the bank being curious (or its employees, or the programmers or operators of its computers), they might also appreciate some security against losing their money. We also introduce the option of a secure exchange of a receipt for the payment.

In §5, we sketch extensions to other variants of on-line payment systems, in particular, one with maximal untraceability. We also mention how to make clients unconditionally secure against fraud. In §6, we sketch a provably secure untraceable off-line payment system. The paper ends with a warning (§7).

## 2   Breaking the Untraceability of Damgård's Payment System

We first describe the payment system as far as we need it (§2.1). Then we show why unconditional untraceability was claimed for it, and why this does not hold (§2.2).

## 2.1 Description of the system

The basic idea of Chaum's payment systems is that electronic coins are numbers of a special form, with an RSA-signature by the bank. Untraceability is achieved by having the bank sign the coin in a blinded form. Before passing the coin to the payee, the payer takes the "blinding factor" off and obtains a coin that is still signed by the bank, but unconditionally unlinkable to its previous form.

The basic idea of Damgård's system is to use a provably secure signature scheme in the sense of [GoMR_88] instead of RSA. By definition, a local transformation of one signature into a different one is not possible in such schemes. Instead, "blind signing" is performed by a two-party computation protocol between the client $A$ (Alice) and the bank:

Protocol: For a withdrawal, $A$ chooses a random number $R$ as a coin number. They perform the two-party protocol from [ChDG_88] on the signing function, where $A$ enters $R$ as her private input and the bank its secret key $SK$; they use the version of the protocol where $A$'s input is unconditionally hidden. The output, i.e. the bank's signature on $R$, is opened to $A$ only.

To spend the coin, $A$ hands $R$ and the signature to the payee $C$ (Chris), who passes it to the bank. If the coin has not been deposited before (the bank keeps a list of coin numbers to check this), it deposits the money to $C$'s account.

## 2.2 How to trace all payments

We show that the system described above is not untraceable at all: Neither does the theorem proved about it contain what untraceability means in the real world, nor can real untraceability be proved about the system in general, nor is the system secure when it is, as suggested, used with the particular signature schemes from [BeMi_88].

Problem with the theorem: Untraceability in [Damg_90] is said to follow immediately from Theorem 3, which states that during the withdrawal protocol, the bank obtains no information in the Shannon sense about the number $R$ it signs, i.e. the coin number. (And this theorem is true.) Thus, when the coin is deposited, the bank does not recognize it.

However, during the deposit, not only the number $R$, but also the signature on it is shown. Hence the theorem should contain that the bank does not obtain any information about the signature either. (Thus the actual flaw in [Damg_90] is in the middle of p. 332, in the sentence saying that Theorem 3 is sufficient for Condition 2.)

Problem with the actual systems: First consider the signature scheme from [BeMi_88]. There, each signature is a list, and the $i$-th signature issued with respect to a certain key is a list of length $i$. Thus, for each $i$, the bank only needs to store which individual withdrew the $i$-th coin, say Alice. Later, when another individual, say Chris, deposits a coin where the signature is a list of length $i$, the bank knows that Chris received this coin from Alice. Hence there is no untraceability at all.

Since list-like authentication is a rather special and inefficient case, consider the efficient signature scheme from [GoMR_88], too. There, tree-authentication is used. Thus, the number $i$ of a signature can be derived from its position in the tree. (Of course, the signature is passed on without the tree, but for each part of the signature, one can see whether it is a left or right child of its parent.) Therefore, the same attack is possible, and there is no untraceability either.

**Problem with the general system:** In most provably secure signature schemes, the signer's input is not just the key; in particular, the schemes are not memory-less. As long as the input changes from one signature to the next, information may leak through into the signatures. Thus, in general, signature schemes with memory are unsuitable.

More generally, even if the input were only the secret key, security is not trivial: The bank might try to use different secret keys for different signatures. It is not excluded that several secret keys lead to valid signatures. If the resulting signatures are different, the bank can later see which secret key a deposited coin was signed with. Thus it need only store which key it used when which individual withdrew coins, and untraceability is lost.

## 3 Repairing the Untraceability

We repair the untraceability in a way that is applicable to any provably secure signature scheme: During the deposit, the signature is not shown. Instead, the payer $A$ proves in zero-knowledge that she has it. Similar ideas can be found in the credential system in [Damg_90] and in §2.1 of [Chau_90]. In contrast to [Chau_90] (where blind RSA-signatures are used), one still needs the two-party protocol to issue the signature: Not only the existence of any signature must be proved, but of one on a coin number that has not been deposited before; hence the coin number must be shown in the deposit. Therefore, it must be hidden during the withdrawal. Thus the protocol is:

**Withdrawal:** Like in §2.1.

**Deposit:** A priori, the participants must have agreed upon an encoding of the signatures so that they are of equal length. Now $A$ tells the payee $C$ the coin number $R$. $C$ tells $R$ and his account number to the bank. Finally, $A$ gives the bank a computationally convincing perfect zero-knowledge proof (or: argument) that she knows the bank's signature on $R$.

Proof (Sketch): Untraceability: By definition of perfect zero-knowledge, the bank and $C$ obtain no more knowledge than the coin-number $R$, and that this is one of the coins a signature was given on (more precisely: that $A$ knows a value passing the signature test). Thus, if all honest clients test each signature that they receive during a withdrawal with exactly this test, the coin can correspond to any of the previous withdrawals, since the bank does not obtain any information about the coin number during those.

The security against abuse by individuals is obviously unchanged from [Damg_90] as long as the cryptographical assumption for the soundness of the zero-knowledge proof holds. This can be the same assumption as for the two-party computation.

**Alternative:** Another way to repair the system is to restrict oneself to memory-less and deterministic provably secure signature schemes. Such schemes exist, see [Gold_87]; the construction can also be applied to obtain a signature scheme based on any one-way permutations [NaYu_89]. Now the secret key of the bank is fixed by commitments (unconditionally committing), and within the two-party signing protocol, it is checked that the key entered fits these commitments. The protocol from [ChDG_88] guarantees unconditional correctness of the output for deterministic computations, if the participant who unconditionally hides his secrets, i.e. $A$, is honest. Thus the output is a deterministic function of the coin-number and the commitments. Hence no information can leak into the signature. (Note that the commitments would be unnecessary if the signature test admitted just one signature; but this is not the case with the signature schemes considered.)

# 4  Security for individuals against fraud

In this section, we make the payment system provably secure for all parties for the case considered in [Damg_90]. Thus, in particular, payer and bank can trace the payee. All the measures in Sections 4, 5, and 6 are only sketched in this extended abstract.

**Tasks:** No security against fraud by the bank is guaranteed in [Damg_90]. (This has not been claimed, thus it is not a mistake; but it is nevertheless a desirable property.)

In particular, the bank can always claim that a coin with a particular number has been deposited before and can therefore not be deposited now. Then the bank can keep this money to itself. For the basic untraceable payment system by Chaum, this problem has already been considered at least in [Chau_89, BüPf_89].

Additionally, one should make the withdrawals secure.

If payer and payee do not trust each other, one must also take care about receipts.

Secure deposits: This problem can be solved in a conceptually simpler way than in the efficient systems: Before a withdrawal, A chooses a new key pair (PK, SK) of the signature scheme used, and uses PK as the coin number. (Thus this number can be regarded as a pseudonym of the possessor of the coin.) Now A can uniquely designate that she wants to spend the coin, and to whom, by signing a corresponding message with SK. The bank confirms the deposit for C by a signed message containing his account number and the coin number.

Proof (sketch): If the bank refuses to accept a coin, one needs a court, where the protocol is repeated. (This can also be an arbiter within the network, via whom all the messages are sent in this case.) First A repeats the zero-knowledge proof that she has the bank's signature on her coin, with the bank acting as the verifier. With the proof systems used, the court can check if the bank must be convinced. Also, A's deposit order is tested with PK. If the bank now claims that the coin has already been deposited, it can only claim that this has been to C's account, since it is cryptographically hard to forge A's signature on a different deposit order. Now the court asks the bank to give C the signature confirming the deposit again. Even if the coin had already been deposited (i.e. if it was not the bank who tried to cheat, but A and C), this does not give C additional money, since he just receives the same signature again. (The bank need not even store the exact signature if one defines that only one deposit confirmation per account number and coin number is valid.)

However, in this protocol, C had to tell A his account number. If C wants to be untraceable by A, unless the bank helps A, one can proceed as follows: Suppose C is known to A under a pseudonym $C_A$, and his account number is $C_B$. Then A signs that she gives the coin to $C_A$ (and hands this to C), and C signs (using a key pair whose-public key is part of $C_A$) that he deposits this money on the account $C_B$.

Secure withdrawals: The bank might also just claim that all the money of a client has already been withdrawn. (This problem is omitted in [Chau_89], too. However, in such a system, it can easily be solved by having the payer sign an order for each withdrawal.)

Here, where the withdrawal is a two-party computation, both bank and payer must sign each message of the protocol. (The payer's public key for this purpose must be established together with the account number.) Then in the case of a dispute, the whole withdrawal can be reconstructed by a court.

Receipts: In a system guaranteeing payer untraceability only, this is easy: A requires a receipt after the payment is completed. If C refuses this, A complains to the bank, who signs a receipt instead. (And if the bank refuses, too, one needs a court again.) In the case where C should normally be untraceable, the bank must use the pseudonym $C_A$ in the receipt, not $C_B$: Otherwise A may falsely claim that C refused a receipt, just to find out C's account number.

# 5 More General On-line Payments

We first sketch a payment system with maximal untraceability, and provable security against fraud for all parties. Then we show a variant with maximal untraceability if fixed accounts are required. We also note that feasible versions of these systems can be obtained with blind RSA-signatures.

**Maximal untraceability and provable security:** Assume that both $A$ and $C$ want to be untraceable and secure against fraud even if the other one colludes with the bank. (The bank, however, is still known to everybody.) We first assume there are no fixed accounts (like with cash, where the bank cannot see how much money participants receive and spend either).

Pseudonyms are public keys in the secure signature scheme used. (When someone chooses a pseudonym, of course they choose the complete key pair.) A sentence like "someone sends a message under his pseudonym $X$" means that the message is signed with the secret key corresponding to $X$, and that the recipient checks this. Also note (although this has implicitly been used all the time) that people can be addressed under pseudonyms, either because they are anonymously meeting in a shop, or, more likely, on an underlying network offering untraceability (see, e.g., [Chau_81, Chau_88]).

Assume that $A$ is known to $C$ under a pseudonym $A_C$, and $C$ to $A$ as $C_A$. Also assume that $A$ owns a coin of a certain denomination under a pseudonym $A_B$, i.e. she possesses a signature of the bank on $A_B$.

1. $C$ chooses a new pseudonym $C_B$ for this payment. $A$ and $C$, under their normal pseudonyms $A_C$ and $C_A$, tell each other their pseudonyms $A_B$ and $C_B$, and what kind of transfer they wish.
2. $A$, under the pseudonym $A_B$, tells the bank to transfer this coin to $C_B$. To prove that she owns a coin under this pseudonym indeed, she proves in perfect zero-knowledge that she knows the signature of the bank on $A_B$.
3. The bank checks that the coin has not been deposited before. Then it sends signed messages confirming the transfer of a coin from $A_B$ to $C_B$ to $A$ and $C$ (under their pseudonyms $A_B$ and $C_B$). (If the bank refuses, it can be forced by a court, since it is not anonymous; if the court is an arbiter within the network, $A$ and $C$ can appeal under their pseudonyms $A_B$ and $C_B$.)
4. $C$, under the pseudonym $C_A$, sends a receipt of the payment from $A_C$ to $A$.

If $C$ refuses, $A$ can use the bank's confirmation from Step 3, together with C's message from Step 1, instead, because they prove that money was transferred from $A_B$ to $C_B$, and that $C_B$ is another pseudonym of $C_A$, chosen for such a payment.

If $C$ wishes, $A$ can also send him a confirmation of the payment, indicating just the pseudonyms $A_C$ and $C_A$. A refusal can be treated as with the receipt.

5. Now $C$ transfers his coin to a pseudonym unknown to $A$. For this, he chooses a new pseudonym $C'_B$ and executes the withdrawal protocol with the bank (see §2.1) with $C'_B$ as the coin number, and all messages signed under the pseudonym $C_B$.

When $C$ wants to spend the coin he has just received, he uses $C'_B$ as $A_B$.

The untraceability is maximal since during the transfer, nobody obtains any information (in the Shannon sense) about a pseudonym of anybody else that will ever be used again, or has ever been used before.

Cryptographical security holds as before.

**Variant with fixed accounts:** If one wants to force each participant to use a fixed account (e.g. for taxing), but keep the mutual anonymity, one can split Step 5 into a deposit into C's account, and a subsequent withdrawal:

5a. $C$ transfers his coin to a new pseudonym $C'_B$ as above.
5b. $C$ deposits the coin on his account, i.e. he sends a message including the account number under the pseudonym $C'_B$, and proves that he knows a signature on $C'_B$.
5c. Now he withdraws the money again, i.e. he executes the withdrawal protocol using a third pseudonym $C''_B$ as the coin number, signing everything under his real name.

To distinguish coins that have just been received, and those that have been deposited in an account already, the bank must use different signatures in Step 5a and 5c.

**Feasible RSA-versions:** The two systems just described can also easily be implemented with blind RSA-signatures. Of course, the provable security is lost, but the systems become far more efficient. We sketch this for the system with maximal untraceability: In Step 2, the RSA-signature on $A_B$ is shown directly. Instead, $C_B$ is chosen right at the beginning as a blinded version of $C'_B$. Thus instead of Step 5, $C$ can locally unblind the signature received on $C_B$ to obtain one on $C'_B$. In this form, these systems are already contained in [PWP_87].

**Unconditional security?** Since one makes the clients unconditionally untraceable, one might also like to make them unconditionally secure against fraud. As far as signatures are only exchanged between a client and the bank, this can easily be achieved if the clients use signatures where signers are unconditionally secure [PfWa_91, BlPW_91]. Thus it works immediately as long as no receipts are needed.

If one wants to consider receipts between clients, too, or to make the bank unconditionally secure, too, one would need unconditionally secure signatures

[ChRo_90]. Since signatures need not be transferred in our case, the original version can be used. However, with these signatures, a client cannot locally choose a new public key. Hence many steps of the protocol would become multi-party computations.

# 6 Off-line Payments

The main problem with off-line payments is that digital money can be copied, thus someone may spend the same money several times if there is no on-line bank to check that they don't. This must be detected afterwards, so that the culprit must pay the money back (if he can be found and has enough money). At first look, this seems difficult to achieve when the payer is untraceable. However, the problem was solved in [ChFN_90] using an interactive payment protocol that achieves a very high probability ($1-2^{-k}$ for a security parameter $k$) that someone can be traced after spending money twice. We adapt that idea.

Now, however, we need that signatures can be passed from the payee $C$ to the bank later, thus we need the withdrawal according to the alternative in §3.

The bank keeps one counter for each individual $A$, counting the coins that $A$ has withdrawn.

1. Before the withdrawal of the $v$-th coin, $A$ computes a signature $S$ on the message "I have cheated with coin $v$" with her standard key and keeps it to herself. (Of course, the message can be coded much shorter.) She also chooses a pseudonym $A_v$ for this coin (i.e. the public key of a new key pair), and $k$ random numbers $r_i$ of the length of $S$. Now she computes unconditionally hiding commitments $x_i$ on $r_i$ and $y_i$ on $S+r_i$ and forms the coin number
$$R := ((x_1, y_1), \dots, (x_k, y_k), A_v).$$

2. $A$ and the bank use a two-party protocol to get $R$ signed by the bank as in the remark in §3; within this protocol, it is additionally checked that $R$ is of the proper form (i.e. $A$ must enter the information used to construct $R$ as additional secret inputs). The result of this check is made visible to the bank. Apart from that, $R$ is kept unconditionally secret as above.

3. When $A$ pays the coin to $C$, she hands $R$ and the signature to $C$, and signs the payment under the pseudonym $A_v$. For each index $i$, $C$ may choose whether $A$ must open $x_i$ or $y_i$.

4. To deposit the coin, $C$ passes the complete information received from $A$ to the bank. When $A$ paid the same coin to two honest participants, with high probability there will be an index $i$ such that $A$ has opened both $x_i$ and $y_i$, i.e. shown $r_i$ and $S+r_i$. Hence $S$ can be computed and $A$ punished.

Measures against a collusion of $A$ and $C$ can be taken as in [ChFN_90].

# 7 Outlook

Using the brute force method of applying digital signatures and general multi- (or at least two-)party protocols, one can probably invent lots of other variants of payment system quickly. Apart from proving that the security of such systems can be based on rather weak assumptions, an advantage may be that most of these systems are conceptually simpler than their more practical counterparts; i.e. they may more easily convince a general public that it is possible to combine untraceability and security. However, since they are not very efficient at present, we stop that here.

**Warning:** Although we claimed that all our systems are unconditionally untraceable and provably secure, one should be careful. The security definitions we sketched were on the same level of abstractness as the previous one, which turned out to be partially wrong. Thus people would be wise not to be too convinced (even if ours are correct, as we hope), since obviously a wrong definition on this level can seem ok for quite a while. Hence one should look for definitions independent of the particular payment system considered, something like: "A payment system is an $x$-tuple of algorithms *pay, receive* ... such that ... honest participants never lose money except if they execute *pay* ... ". This is, however, a rather daunting task. (For instance, what is "money" in the general case, and how does one treat the case where a court is needed in between?) Some steps in that direction have been taken in [WaPf_85, ChEv_87], but the former for a simple value exchange problem, the latter rather for a credential mechanism, and both only with algebraic models of cryptographic primitives.

# Acknowledgements

We are happy to thank *Andreas Pfitzmann* for helpful discussions and *Ivan Damgård* and *Tatsuaki Okamoto* for helpful letters.

# References

BeMi_88    Mihir Bellare, Silvio Micali: How to sign given any trapdoor function; 20th Symposium on Theory of Computing (STOC) 1988, ACM, New York 1988, 32-42.

BlPW_91    Gerrit Bleumer, Birgit Pfitzmann, Michael Waidner: A Remark on a Signature Scheme where Forgery can be Proved; Eurocrypt '90, LNCS 473, Springer-Verlag, Berlin 1991, 441-445.

BüPf_89    Holger Bürk, Andreas Pfitzmann: Digital Payment Systems Enabling Security and Unobservability; Computers & Security 8/5 (1989) 399-416.

CBHM_90    David Chaum, Bert den Boer, Eugène van Heijst, Stig Mjølsnes, Adri Steenbeek: Efficient offline electronic checks; Eurocrypt '89, LNCS 434, Springer-Verlag, Berlin 1990, 294-301.

Chau_81    David Chaum: Untraceable Electronic Mail, Return Addresses, and Digital Pseudonyms; Communications of the ACM 24/2 (1981) 84-88.

Chau_83    David Chaum: Blind Signatures for untraceable payments; Crypto '82, Plenum Press, New York 1983, 199-203.

Chau_85    David Chaum: Security without Identification: Transaction Systems to make Big Brother Obsolete; Communications of the ACM 28/10 (1985) 1030-1044.

Chau_88    David Chaum: The Dining Cryptographers Problem: Unconditional Sender and Recipient Untraceability; Journal of Cryptology 1/1 (1988) 65-75.

Chau_89    David Chaum: Privacy Protected Payments – Unconditional Payer and/or Payee Untraceability; SMART CARD 2000: The Future of IC Cards, Proc. of the IFIP WG 11.6 International Conference; North-Holland, Amsterdam 1989, 69-93.

Chau_90    David Chaum: Showing credentials without identification: Transferring signatures between unconditionally unlinkable pseudonyms; Auscrypt '90, LNCS 453, Springer-Verlag, Berlin 1990, 246-264.

Chau3_90   David Chaum: Online cash checks; Eurocrypt '89, LNCS 434, Springer-Verlag, Berlin 1990, 288-293.

ChDG_88    David Chaum, Ivan Bjerre Damgård, Jeroen van de Graaf: Multiparty Computations ensuring privacy of each party's input and correctness of the result; Crypto '87, LNCS 293, Springer-Verlag, Berlin 1988, 87-119.

ChEv_87    David Chaum, Jan-Hendrik Evertse: A secure and privacy-protecting protocol for transmitting personal information between organizations; Crypto '86, LNCS 263, Springer-Verlag, Berlin 1987, 118-167.

ChFN_90    David Chaum, Amos Fiat, Moni Naor: Untraceable Electronic Cash; Crypto '88, LNCS 403, Springer-Verlag, Berlin 1990, 319-327.

ChRo_90    David Chaum, Sandra Roijakkers: Unconditionally Secure Digital Signatures; Crypto '90, 11-15 August 1990, Abstracts, 209-217.

Damg_90    Ivan Bjerre Damgård: Payment Systems and Credential Mechanisms with Provable Security Against Abuse by Individuals; Crypto '88, LNCS 403, Springer-Verlag, Berlin 1990, 328-335.

Damg_91    Ivan Bjerre Damgård: Private communication, Brighton, April 10th 1991.

Gold_87    Oded Goldreich: Two Remarks Concerning the Goldwasser-Micali-Rivest Signature Scheme; Crypto '86, LNCS 263, Springer-Verlag, Berlin 1987, 104-110.

GoMR_88   Shafi Goldwasser, Silvio Micali, Ronald L. Rivest: A Digital Signature Scheme Secure Against Adaptive Chosen-Message Attacks; SIAM J. Comput. 17/2 (1988) 281-308.

NaYu_89   Moni Naor, Moti Yung: Universal One-way Hash Functions and their Cryptographic Applications; 21st STOC, ACM, New York 1989, 33-43.

OkOh_90   Tatsuaki Okamoto, Kazuo Ohta: Divertible zero-knowledge interactive proofs and commutative random self-reducibility; Eurocrypt '89, LNCS 434, Springer-Verlag, Berlin 1990, 134-149.

OkOh1_90  Tatsuaki Okamoto, Kazuo Ohta: Disposable zero-knowledege authentications and their applications to untraceable electronic cash; Crypto '89, LNCS 435, Springer-Verlag, Heidelberg 1990, 481-496.

OkOh_91   Tatsuaki Okamoto, Kazuo Ohta: Universal Electronic Cash; Crypto '91, Santa Barbara, CA, 11.-15. August 1991, Abstracts, 8.7-8.13.

PfWa_91   Birgit Pfitzmann, Michael Waidner: Fail-stop Signatures and their Application; Securicom 91, Paris 1991, 145-160.

PWP_87    Birgit Pfitzmann, Michael Waidner, Andreas Pfitzmann: Rechtssicherheit trotz Anonymität in offenen digitalen Systemen; Computer und Recht 3/10,11,12 (1987) 712-717, 796-803, 898-904; Revision: DuD 14/5-6 (1990) 243-253, 305-315.

WaPf_85   Michael Waidner, Andreas Pfitzmann: Betrugssicherheit trotz Anonymität. Abrechnung und Geldtransfer in Netzen; Proc. Datenschutz und Datensicherung im Wandel der Informationstechnologien, IFB 113, Springer-Verlag, Berlin 1985, 128-141; Revision: DuD /1 (1986) 16-22.

# Practical Quantum Oblivious Transfer

Charles H. Bennett
*IBM Research* [*]

Gilles Brassard [†]
*Université de Montréal* [‡]

Claude Crépeau [†]
*École Normale Supérieure* [§]

Marie-Hélène Skubiszewska
*Université Paris–Sud*

## Abstract

We describe a protocol for *quantum oblivious transfer*, utilizing faint pulses of polarized light, by which one of two mutually distrustful parties ("Alice") transmits two one-bit messages in such a way that the other party ("Bob") can choose which message he gets but cannot obtain information about both messages (he will learn his chosen bit's value with exponentially small error probability and may gain at most exponentially little information about the value of the other bit), and Alice will be entirely ignorant of which bit he received. Neither party can cheat (ie deviate from the protocol while appearing to follow it) in such a way as to obtain more information than what is given by the description of the protocol. Our protocol is easy to modify in order to implement the All-or-Nothing Disclosure of one out of two string messages, and it can be used to implement bit commitment and oblivious circuit evaluation without complexity-theoretic assumptions, in a way that remains secure even against cheaters that have unlimited computing power. Moreover, this protocol is practical in that it can be realized with available opto-electronic apparatus while being immune to any technologically feasible attack for the foreseeable future.

---

[*] IBM T. J. Watson Research Laboratory, Yorktown Heights, New York, NY 10598, USA. e-mail: bennetc@watson.ibm.com.

[†] Supported in part by Canada's NSERC.

[‡] Département IRO, Université de Montréal, C.P. 6128, succursale "A", Montréal (Québec), Canada H3C 3J7. e-mail: brassard@iro.umontreal.ca.

[§] Département de Mathématiques et d'Informatique, École Normale Supérieure, 45 rue d'Ulm, 75230 Paris CEDEX 05, France. e-mail: crepeau@dmi.ens.fr.

[¶] Laboratoire de Recherche en Informatique, Université Paris–Sud, Bâtiment 490, 91405 Orsay, France. e-mail: skubi@dec.prl.com.

J. Feigenbaum (Ed.): Advances in Cryptology - CRYPTO '91, LNCS 576, pp. 351-366, 1992.
© Springer-Verlag Berlin Heidelberg 1992

# 1   Introduction and history

Quantum cryptography was initiated by Stephen Wiesner more than two decades ago [30]. Over the years, a large number of theoretical applications of quantum physics to cryptography have been discovered: unforgeable bank notes and multiplexing channel [30], unforgeable subway tokens [5], self-winding one-time pad [4], key distribution [3], oblivious transfer [13], coin flipping [3, 8], and bit commitment [8]. Recently, much excitement was created [29, 18, 14, 26, 15, 28, etc.] when the success of a first experimental prototype was reported for the quantum key distribution protocol [1]. Until now, not only was this prototype the first physical realization of a quantum cryptographic protocol, but key distribution was the only quantum protocol ever proposed that could in fact be implemented reasonably with available technology. Even then, the prototype is not entirely convincing because it achieves secure key exchange over the distance of 32 centimeters!

In this paper, we extend the applicability of quantum cryptography by describing a new protocol for oblivious transfer that is practical in the sense that it can be realized with available opto-electronic apparatus while being immune to any technologically feasible attack for the foreseeable future, regardless of the computing power available to would-be cheaters. Techniques similar to those explained here can also be used to overcome the lack of tolerance to errors apparently inherent to the quantum bit commitment protocol of [8]. In this paper, we only concentrate on the new quantum oblivious transfer protocol, and leave it for the reader to figure out how these techniques apply to the bit commitment protocol. A major advantage of these protocols over the already-feasible key distribution is that bit commitment and oblivious transfer make perfect sense over a short distance.

Previous quantum protocols have been proposed for both these tasks, but either they leaked too much information [30], or they could not have been implemented in practice because they required one party to generate pure single-photon light pulses [3] or because they could not tolerate errors due to detector noise [13, 8].

Before we proceed, let us recall the purpose of Oblivious Transfer (OT). In Rabin's original OT [27], Alice sends a one-bit message to Bob, which he receives with probability 50%, while receiving nothing otherwise. Bob finds out whether or not he received Alice's bit, but Alice remains totally ignorant about this. Neither Alice nor Bob can influence the probability 50% of success. The related notion of 1-out-of-2 Oblivious Transfer ($\binom{2}{1}$–OT) was subsequently [1] invented by Even, Goldreich and Lempel [16]. In this scenario, Alice and Bob, play the following game. Alice starts with two one-bit messages of her choosing. The purpose of the protocol is for Alice to transmit the messages to Bob in such a way that he can choose to receive either one of them (learning its value with exponentially small error probability) but cannot obtain significant partial information on both [2], while Alice remains entirely ignorant of which of the two messages he received. It is shown in [11] that $\binom{2}{1}$–OT and Rabin's OT are equivalent in the sense that either one can be

---

[1] In fact, what Wiesner called "multiplexing channel" as early as the late 1960's [30] is essentially what we now call 1-out-of-2 oblivious transfer (of messages rather than single bits), but his protocol leaked partial information on both messages and could be subverted by a receiver who lied about the quantum efficiency of his detectors. Thus, it can be said that the original inventor of oblivious transfer is Wiesner and that the current paper, which fixes the shortcomings of Wiesner's protocol, is making quantum cryptography go full circle.

[2] More precisely, if $b_0, b_1$ are Alice's bits and $\Delta$ is the data Bob received through the protocol, then at least one of $H(b_0|\Delta, b_1)$ or $H(b_1|\Delta, b_0)$ should be exponentially close to 1.

implemented from a primitive that implements the other. Therefore, at least from a theoretical point of view, it does not matter which of these two protocols we achieve. The Quantum OT protocol described in this paper implements directly $\binom{2}{1}$-OT, which is preferable from a practical point of view.

Although OT might seem to be a bizarre idea at first, it is now well-known [22, 12] that it is a very useful primitive for building up interesting protocols, such as two-party oblivious circuit evaluation (by which Alice owns a secret $x$, Bob owns a secret $y$, and both of them compute the value of $f(x, y)$ for an agreed upon function $f$, in such a way that Alice learns nothing about $y$ and Bob learns nothing about $x$, except for what can be inferred from one's private input and the public value of $f(x, y)$).

Our new quantum OT protocol is described in Section 2, after a brief review of the main features of quantum physics. Section 3 reviews two fundamental mathematical tools that are useful in order to implement quantum OT in practice and prove its security. Section 4 describes the only possible cheating strategies under the technologically reasonable assumptions that light pulses cannot be stored for a significant length of time. Moreover, Section 4 proves, under this assumption, that our quantum OT protocol cannot be cheated by either party. Finally, Section 5 addresses more sophisticated attacks, which are completely infeasible at present or with any foreseeable technology: pulse storing and coherent measurements. It is shown how to overcome the first of these attacks, but nothing is known about the unconditional security of our protocol against the second attack (which is even more unreasonable than the first, technologically speaking). Nevertheless, even this second attack (or in fact *any* attack consistent with quantum physics) can be thwarted from a computational point of view under the assumption that one-way functions exist.

Let us emphasize that all known classical (ie *non*-quantum) protocols for OT allow at least one among Alice or Bob to cheat without risk of detection if she or he can break an unproved cryptographic assumption of some sort. Moreover, classical OT protocols necessarily offer the opportunity for one party to attempt cheating *off-line*, which means that these protocols fail even if the cryptographic assumption can only be broken at the cost of spending days of computing time on a supercomputer. More importantly, they can fail *retroactively* if the appropriate algorithmic breakthrough is discovered years after the protocol has taken place, as long as the cheating party has kept a transcript of the execution of the protocol. In contrast, the basic quantum OT protocol fails against pulse storing *only* if the attack is carried out *on-line*, while the protocol is taking place. In particular, better technology in the future would not compromise the security of OTs carried out today. Similarly, the computational version of our scheme (assuming the existence of one-way permutations), which is secure against arbitrary technology but not arbitrary computing power, must be cheated on-line if it is to be cheated at all.

# 2 Method

This section describes a quantum oblivious transfer protocol implementable under realistic physical conditions and assumptions similar to those used in the quantum key distribution protocol of [2]. In particular we assume that the quantum transmission consists of series of very dim pulses of coherent or incoherent polarized light rather than individual photons (which are harder to generate), that the receiver attempts to detect the pulses by noisy, imperfectly quantum-efficient detectors such as photomultiplier tubes, and, as stated in the introduction, that the pulses cannot be stored for a significant length of time, so the receiver must measure each pulse before the next one arrives or else lose the opportunity of measuring it at all.

The quantum transmission used in the protocol uses light pulses of four canonical polarizations: horizontal, vertical, $45°$-diagonal, and $135°$-diagonal, henceforth denoted $H$, $V$, $P$, and $Q$ respectively. As is well known, rectilinear ($H$ and $V$) photons can be reliably distinguished by one type of measurement, while diagonal ($P$ and $Q$) photons can be reliably distinguished by another type of measurement; but the uncertainty principle of quantum physics decrees that a random outcome results, and all information is lost, if one attempts to measure the rectilinear polarization of a diagonal photon, or vice versa. More generally, if a $\phi$-polarized photon is subjected to a polarization measurement along axis $\theta$, it behaves like a $\theta$-polarized photon with probability $\cos^2(\phi - \theta)$ and like a $(\theta + 90°)$-polarized photon with the complementary probability $\sin^2(\phi - \theta)$. Such a measurement can be performed by using a $\theta$-oriented piece of birefringent material such as calcite to split the incoming light beam into two beams (polarized at $\theta$ and $\theta + 90°$), then directing these beams into two sensitive photon detectors such as photomultiplier tubes. A pair of polarization states, such as $H$ and $V$, or $P$ and $Q$, that can be reliably distinguished by some measurement is called a *basis*; we will use polarization states $H$ and $V$ to represent the bits 0 and 1 respectively in the rectilinear basis, and $P$ and $Q$ to represent the same bits in the diagonal basis.

At first it would seem that Rabin's OT could be achieved quite simply by having Alice send Bob a single photon encoding the bit to be obliviously transferred in one of the two canonical bases (rectilinear or diagonal), chosen randomly by Alice. Bob would then randomly choose a basis in which to measure the photon, and finally Alice would tell him the correct basis. At that point Bob would have a half chance of having received Alice's bit in the correct basis, and a half chance of knowing he had spoiled it, but Alice would not know which occurred. This simple protocol is inadequate because its probability of success would be seriously affected by inefficiency or noise in Bob's detectors, and because it would allow Bob to get too much partial information about Alice's bit all the time by measuring in a basis intermediate between rectilinear and diagonal, say $\theta = 22\frac{1}{2}°$.

A protocol for achieving $\binom{2}{1}$-OT based on the above idea was proposed by Crépeau and Kilian [13], but it was impractical because it failed dramatically in a realistic setting in which transmission errors may occur and dim light pulses are used rather than single photons. The more complicated protocol below is free from these disadvantages. The first step is necessary to adjust the protocol to the physical limitations of Bob's detection apparatus, but it may be skimmed at first reading, being somewhat peripheral to the main idea of the protocol. (The dark count rate $d$ is a detector's probability of registering a count during a time slot when no photons are incident on it, and the quantum efficiency $q$ is the excess probability, above $d$, of registering a count when one photon is incident on the detector; a typical photomultiplier tube might have $d = 10^{-5}$ and $q = 25\%$.) Let $b_0$ and $b_1$ be Alice's bits and let $c$ be Bob's choice (ie Bob wishes to obtain $b_c$).

1. Bob tells Alice the quantum efficiency $q$ and dark count rate $d$ of his detectors. If these values are satisfactory (see below), Alice next tells Bob the intensity $\mu$ of light pulses she will be using, the fraction $a$ of these pulses she will expect him to detect successfully, and the bit error rate $\varepsilon$ she will be willing to correct in his data to compensate for his dark counts and other noise sources. She also decides on a security parameter $N$ used below, which she communicates to Bob. Alice and Bob agree on a linear binary error-correcting code capable of correcting with very high probability $N$-bit words transmitted with expected error rate $\varepsilon$ (see Section 3.1).

   More precisely, $a$ would normally be set to $1 - e^{-(\mu q + 2d)} \approx \mu q$, the Poisson probability of detecting 1 or more photons (or dark counts) in a pulse of intensity $\mu$, but might be set lower to allow for attenuation in the optical path between Alice and Bob. Similarly $\varepsilon$ would normally be set to $d/a \approx d/\mu q$, the expected error rate from dark counts in Bob's two detectors, but might be set higher to compensate for other noise sources. Alice's choice of $\mu$ is guided by the need to simultaneously set $a \approx \mu q$ high enough and $\varepsilon \approx d/\mu q$ low enough that a cheating Bob, whose detectors were in fact far less noisy and more efficient than he claimed, would not gain a significant advantage from the brighter pulses and more voluminous check information he had thus induced Alice to send. In Section 4.3 it is shown that safe oblivious transfer can be achieved when $H(2\varepsilon) < \frac{1}{2} - (1 - e^{-\mu} - \mu e^{-\mu})/2a$, where $H$ is the *entropy* function [3]. If this condition cannot be met, Alice aborts the protocol.

   Finally, Alice and Bob engage in a *test run* in which Alice sends pulses of intensity $\mu$ in a prearranged sequence of polarizations, and Bob, reading each pulse in the correct basis, verifies that he can indeed detect the pulses with probability greater than $a$ and error rate less than $\varepsilon$.

2. Alice sends Bob a random sequence of $2N/a$ faint pulses of the four canonical polarizations.

3. Bob randomly decides for each pulse whether to measure it in the rectilinear or diagonal basis, and records the basis and measurement result in a table whenever (with probability approximately $a$) a pulse is detected. Therefore Bob should successfully receive roughly $2N$ pulses. If he receives a few more, he ignores the excess; if he receives a few less, he completes his table by making a few random guesses, so that it has exactly $2N$ entries. Bob then reports to Alice the arrival times of all $2N$ pulses he committed himself to have received, but not the bases he used or his measurement results.

4. Alice tells Bob the bases she used to send each of the pulses he received.

5. Bob partitions his pulses into two sets of $N$ pulses each: a "good" set consisting (as much as possible) of pulses he received in the correct basis, and a "bad" set consisting (as much as possible) of pulses he received in the wrong basis. He tells Alice the addresses of the two sets, but he does not tell her which is the good set and which is the bad set. At this point, Bob shares with Alice a word (ie an $N$-bit string) corresponding to his good set of measurements (with an expected error rate

---

[3] The entropy function is defined as $H(p) = p \lg \frac{1}{p} + (1 - p) \lg \frac{1}{1-p}$.

not greater than $\varepsilon$); he shares nothing (or nearly nothing since he may have received slightly more than $N$ bits in the correct basis) with her with respect to his bad set of measurements provided that he faithfully followed the protocol. Alice does not know which word she shares with Bob. (It may well be that Bob did not quite receive $N$ good pulses because of statistical fluctuations in the number of pulses received — which could be less than $2N$ — and in the proportion of pulses that he measured in the correct basis — which could be slightly under $\frac{1}{2}$. However, when $N$ is large enough, the errors that this might create in his good set are negligible compared to the expected errors due to noise.)

6. Using the error-correcting code chosen at step 1, Alice computes the syndromes of the words corresponding to each set, and she sends them to Bob over an error-free channel. Given this data, Bob should be able to recover the original word corresponding to his good set but not that corresponding to his bad set.

   Furthermore, Alice computes a random subset parity for each set, and tells Bob the addresses defining these random subsets, but not the resulting parities. At this point, Bob knows one of these parities exactly, while knowing nothing (or nearly nothing) about the other parity, and he knows which parity he knows. Of course, Alice knows both parities, but she does not know which one Bob knows. Let $x_0$ and $x_1$ denote these parity bits, and let $\hat{c}$ denote which one Bob knows.

7. Bob tells Alice whether or not $c = \hat{c}$. (This is the very first time in the protocol that $c$ enters into play.)

8. If $c = \hat{c}$, Alice gives $x_0 \oplus b_0$ and $x_1 \oplus b_1$ to Bob (in this prescribed order), otherwise she gives him $x_0 \oplus b_1$ and $x_1 \oplus b_0$. From this, Bob extracts $b_c$.

**Theorem:** Let $\Delta$ be the data Bob obtains from the protocol. At least one of $\mathbf{H}(b_0|\Delta, b_1)$ or $\mathbf{H}(b_1|\Delta, b_0)$ is exponentially close (in $N$) to 1. Regardless of what happens, Alice learns nothing.

**Proof:** The rest of this paper constitutes the proof of this theorem. The main idea is that Alice uses an error-correcting code to give Bob enough side information to correct the errors in the good set but not the bad set, then hashes each set down to a single bit in such a way that Bob's residual information on the bit corresponding to his bad set is negligibly small.

**Note:** Because privacy amplification [7] can be used to distill more than one bit, it is easy to modify the protocol so that $b_0$ and $b_1$ are $k$–bit messages rather than single bits, in effect implementing directly the two-message version of ANDOS, the all-or-nothing-disclosure-of-secrets of [9].

# 3 Review of useful tools

Two fundamental tools will be needed in order to allow the honest Bob to receive bit $b_c$ while preventing a cheating Bob from learning something about both bits: concatenated codes and privacy amplification.

## 3.1 Concatenated codes

One major problem in making our protocol work in practice is that we need to furnish Bob with information by which he can correct the small error rate of the good pulses (due to dark counts and other unavoidable noise), and do so with reasonable decoding effort and exponentially small (in $N$) residual error probability; while at the same time preventing him (except with exponentially small probability of success) from correcting all the errors in a set containing a significant proportion of pulses received in wrong bases, even with unlimited decoding effort. A concatenated code [17] combining a Reed-Solomon (RS) code [23] and a random linear binary code of exponentially smaller size is an appropriate choice for this purpose.

Such codes offer exponentially small residual error probability, while allowing information to be transmitted through a noisy binary symmetric channel efficiently at a rate $R(\varepsilon) \leq 1 - \mathrm{H}(2\varepsilon)$ Their decoding may be accomplished efficiently by Berlekamp's algorithm for the RS-code and by a brute-force search for the random linear code (the brute-force search takes exponential time in the size of the random linear code, but this is efficient since this code is chosen to be exponentially smaller than the RS-code).

Recall that to each binary linear error-correcting code is associated a *parity check matrix* $H$ so that a word $b$ is a codeword if and only if $Hb^{\mathsf{T}}$ is the zero vector. For an arbitrary word $b$, the value of $Hb^{\mathsf{T}}$ is called the *syndrome* of $b$. Our use of error-correcting codes is somewhat nonstandard. Instead of sending a codeword into the (noisy) quantum channel, Alice sends a random word. To allow efficient decoding by Bob, she also sends him the corresponding syndrome over a noiseless channel. It is easy to see that this does not alter Bob's decoding effort, and it has the advantage of facilitating the use of privacy amplification (see below).

The fact that these codes can also prevent Bob (except with exponentially small probability of success) from correcting the errors in a set containing a significant proportion of pulses received in wrong bases, even with unlimited decoding effort, is far more complicated to demonstrate. We sketch in Section 4.2 that whatever set of (canonical or noncanonical) bases Bob uses at step 3 to get his data and whatever partition he chooses at step 5, the additional information provided to him by Alice does not enable him to correct the errors in both sets, or even gain partial information about more than one of Alice's bits (except with exponentially small probability).

## 3.2 Privacy amplification

Privacy amplification is a tool developed in [7] for distilling a short very secret string from a longer partly-secret one. Here, we need only a rather simple special case of this technique. Let $x$ denote a string of length $N$ about which Bob knows only $k$ parity bits [4], where $k < N$. A special case of Theorem 10 in [7, p. 224] says that if a random subset of the bits of $x$ is chosen, the probability that Bob has any information about its parity is less than $2^{-(N-k-1)}/\ln 2$.

---

[4] A parity bit about $x$ is the exclusive-or of an arbitrary subset of the bits of $x$. In particular, physical bits and check bits generated by linear error-correction codes, such as the syndrome of $x$, are parity bits.

In particular, consider the case in which Bob already knows $t$ bits of $x$ and consider a security parameter $s$. If no more than $N - t - s - 1$ additional parity bits are given to Bob as the syndrome of $x$ with respect to a linear code, the expected amount of information he has on the parity of a random subset of $x$ is less than $2^{-s}/\ln 2$. (This is a conservative estimate since it is likely that the check bits would not be entirely independent from the bits previously known.) Therefore, if Bob knows a proportion $\gamma < 1 - \mathbf{H}(2\varepsilon)$ of the bits of $x$ before receiving the syndrome, and if enough check bits are provided to correct a proportion $\varepsilon$ of errors, then the probability that Bob knows anything about the parity of a random subset of the bits of $x$ remains arbitrarily small provided that $x$ is sufficiently long.

# 4 Various cheats and how to overcome them

Let us first notice that there is very little that Alice can do in order to cheat the quantum OT protocol of Section 2. Obviously, she can cheat at step 8 by telling Bob the complement of what she should. However, this does not count as genuine cheating since in this case an OT will have been carried out, except that the bit transferred will not have been what it should have (nothing can prevent this type of cheating unless Alice has to commit to her bits before the start of the protocol — an entirely different problem known as *verifiable* oblivious transfer [12]).

What *would* count as a genuine success in cheating for Alice would be if she could determine (or at least get an indication about) which of her bits was of interest to Bob (ie the value of $c$). But notice that Bob does not say anything that involves $c$ until step 7. Moreover, $\hat{c}$ is purely random and information-theoretically hidden from Alice because she cannot tell which of Bob's sets was the good set [5]. Therefore, telling Alice at step 7 whether or not $c = \hat{c}$ does not reveal any information about $c$ either. Thus, it is information-theoretically impossible for Alice to cheat, regardless of her computing power and available technology, provided that Bob faithfully follows his protocol.

Nevertheless, there *is* one thing that Alice can attempt in the hope that Bob will goof: she can use garbage for one of the two syndromes she sends at step 6. The point is that Bob would have no way of detecting such behaviour if she sends garbage in relation to his bad set (which he does not even try to correct). Therefore, *if Bob complains*, she learns that this must be because she chose to send garbage for the good set. In itself, this cheat would not pay off because Bob would catch Alice in the act of cheating before she had any chance to learn something: Bob's choice $c$ is not used in the protocol until step 7, after Alice is asked to send her syndromes. However, if Bob does *not* complain, Alice might infer that she picked the bad set — since otherwise, she may think, he *would* have complained! This is more serious because in this case the protocol will continue and Alice will learn Bob's choice $c$, and moreover Bob will not even be aware of this leakage. Of course, each time Alice gambles on this, she runs a 50% chance of being caught, but it may be worthwhile since it could be that even one undetected success is enough to tell Alice a great deal. There is an easy way out for Bob: if he discovers that Alice has cheated, he stoically shuts his mouth and continues as if nothing had happened. (Once

---

[5] This is why we had to use *noninteractive* reconciliation, such as that provided by error-correcting codes, rather than the *interactive* reconciliation protocols of [6, 2].

aware of Alice's dishonesty, he takes whatever actions are necessary to counter her plans, but he must do so discreetly.) If Alice knows that this will be Bob's behaviour, she knows that she cannot hope to learn anything from cheating, and thus she may not even attempt it. Potential harm caused by this kind of cheating behaviour from Alice can also be prevented mathematically rather than psychologically. The protocol used in [13] to reduce $\binom{2}{1}$–OT to so-called $\alpha$–$\binom{2}{1}$–OT can be used here to ensure that Alice cannot gain information on Bob's choice except with exponentially small probability, and that she is almost certain to be caught in the act (before gaining any information) if she even tries.

In sharp contrast, several cheating strategies are available for Bob to attempt creating two good sets at step 5, or at least two sets so that he learns something about both of Alice's bits. We shall now demonstrate that, regardless of Bob's strategy, there is at least one set that would result in Bob learning at most an exponentially small bias on the corresponding bit of Alice. Without loss of generality, we shall concentrate on *symmetric* strategies, ie cheating strategies that favour neither of the sets formed by Bob. Indeed, any asymmetric strategy would reduce Bob's advantage about one of Alice's bits, and would therefore be less good if Cheating Bob's goal is to learn something about both bits.

## 4.1   The standard attack

Let us first consider the easy case in which Bob does *not* cheat at step 3. In such a case, Bob's only symmetric strategy would be to select about $N/2$ good bits (and thus $N/2$ bad bits) in each set. As a result, Bob knows only about half of the bits in each set. As long as the number of check bits sent by Alice at step 6 for each set is less than $N/2$, it follows that Bob knows less than $N$ parity bits about each set. Hence, privacy amplification applies to conclude that Bob's expected information on the parities of both random subsets chosen by Alice at step 8 are vanishingly small. Therefore, this attack is futile whenever $\mathbf{H}(2\varepsilon) < \frac{1}{2}$, ie $\varepsilon < 5.501\%$, as we have seen in Section 3.2.

To be technically exact, one should consider the case in which Bob is more lucky than average at step 3 and gets more than $N$ good bits. The number $L$ of good bits follows a Binomial$(2N, 1/2)$. Therefore, the standard deviation of $L/2$ is $\sqrt{N/8}$. This implies that the probability that $L/2$ exceeds $N/2 + 5\sqrt{N/8}$ is about one in two million. Moreover, one should also take account of the privacy amplification parameter $s$ (cf Section 3.2). Setting $s = 21$ makes Bob's probability of knowing the parity of a random subset less than about one in two million as well. Therefore, if the code's syndromes are of length less than $N/2 - 5\sqrt{N/8} - 22$ bits, the probability that Bob succeeds at cheating is no better than one in a million. In practice, this means that $\varepsilon$ should be somewhat smaller than 5.501% for Alice to accept to play the game, but that the threshold probability tends to 5.501% as $N$ tends to infinity. In our analysis of the other, more sophisticated, attacks, we shall be somewhat sloppy and determine $\varepsilon$ as if Bob did not get more information than average. A more careful analysis will be provided in the final paper.

## 4.2 The Breidbart attack

An obvious way in which Bob can cheat is by measuring Alice's pulses in bases other than rectilinear or diagonal. The most extreme such strategy would be for him to measure each pulse in the so-called *Breidbart basis* [5], which is angle $22\frac{1}{2}^{\circ}$, precisely half-way between the canonical bases. When he does this, Bob obtains each of Alice's bits with probability $\beta = \cos^2 22\frac{1}{2}^{\circ} = (2 + \sqrt{2})/4 \approx 85.3553\%$. Note that knowing a bit with probability $\beta$ yields only $1 - \mathbf{H}(\beta) \approx 0.399$ bit of information in the sense of Shannon, whereas a legitimate measurement in a canonical basis yields an expected 0.5 bit of Shannon information. Nevertheless, it could happen that Breidbart measurements are more useful in the presence of additional check bit information and/or more resistant to privacy amplification.

It turns out that this is not so: no measurement can do better than the legitimate measurements in canonical bases. We now sketch the proof of this claim. Due to space limitation we cannot give a complete proof, which will appear in the journal version of this paper. Rather, we restrict our attention to the situation in which Bob performs only Breidbart measurements[6]. We analyse the volume of check bits that Alice can give to Bob without compromising the secrecy of her two bits. First we make a few legitimate simplifications of the situation we want to analyze. The following scenario summarizes the situation.

- We assume that the quantum channel is error free (this only makes Bob more powerful).

- Alice sends Bob a bit string $b = b_1, b_2, ..., b_N$.

- Bob receives it as $b' = b'_1, b'_2, ..., b'_N$ through a binary symmetric channel which transmit bits correctly with probability $\beta$ (from the Breidbart measurements).

- Alice reveals the syndrome $S_b = Hb^{\top}$ to Bob, where $H$ is the $K \times N$ parity check matrix of the linear code considered ($K$ is the syndrome length).

- Alice picks a random subset $I$ of $\{1, 2, ..., N\}$ and announces it to Bob.

- Bob wants to approximate $z = \bigoplus_{i \in I} b_i$.

Let the actual number of errors in Bob's data be $D$ (out of $N$ bits). To simplify the analysis, assume that the exact value of $D$ is revealed to Bob by God. We are about to prove Bob's inability to cheat even when provided with this additional information, which of course implies the same in the real world (since he could elect not to use the information even if provided). As long as $K \leq 3N/5$, we now show that, except with exponentially small probability, Bob will have an exponential number of equally likely candidates for Alice's original string $b$. Therefore, privacy amplification applies to conclude that his information on $z$ is vanishingly small. In contrast, any value of $K$ larger than $N/2$ would have allowed Bob to guess $z$ with good probability if his information had been obtained

---

[6] *A priori*, it could be that the best strategy for Bob is a mixed strategy in which he measures some pulses in the Breidbart basis, some in canonical bases, and perhaps some others in yet other bases.

by use of measurements in canonical bases (in which case Bob would know half the bits of $b$ exactly and would have no information on the other half).

For any positive $\delta < 1 - \beta$, except with exponentially small probability (as a function of $N$), for all large enough $N$,

$$N/2 < N - D < (\beta + \delta)N .$$

Moreover, the number of words at Hamming distance $D$ from $b'$ is $\binom{N}{D}$, which is thus lower-bounded by

$$\binom{N}{D} > \binom{N}{(\beta + \delta)N} .$$

Using the approximation [23]

$$\frac{2^{\mathbf{H}(\lambda)N}}{\sqrt{8N\lambda(1 - \lambda)}} \leq \binom{N}{\lambda N} \leq \frac{2^{\mathbf{H}(\lambda)N}}{\sqrt{2\pi N\lambda(1 - \lambda)}} ,$$

we get the lower bound

$$\binom{N}{D} > \frac{2^{\mathbf{H}(\beta + \delta)N}}{\sqrt{N}}$$

because $8\lambda(1 - \lambda) \leq 1$ precisely when $\lambda \geq \beta$ (or $\lambda \leq 1 - \beta$).

We want to obtain a lower bound on the number of words at distance $D$ from $b'$ that have $b$'s syndrome since those are the only candidates for $b$ in the eyes of Bob. Unfortunately, we cannot simply divide the above lower bound on $\binom{N}{D}$ by $2^K$, which is the number of syndromes, because there is no reason *a priori* to believe that all the syndromes are equally represented among the words at distance $D$ from $b'$. Let $M$ stand for $\binom{N}{D}/2^K$. Let $N_D(x, y)$ be the number of words with syndrome $y$ at distance $D$ from a fixed word $w$ with syndrome $x$ (this function is well defined because its value is independent of the specific choice of $w$; moreover, $N_D(x, y) = N_D(\bar{0}, x \oplus y) = N_D(y, x)$). Provided that $K \leq 3N/5$, we now show that $N_D(S_{b'}, S_b)$ is exponentially large except with exponentially small probability, where the probability is taken over all choices of $b'$ at distance $D$ from $b$. More precisely, we now show that $N_D(S_{b'}, S_b) \geq 2^{-r}M$ with probability at least $1 - 2^{-r}$ for any security parameter $r > 0$.

Starting from word $b$, each syndrome $s$ occurs $N_D(S_b, s)$ times among the words at distance $D$ from $b$. Therefore syndrome $s$ has probability $N_D(S_b, s)/\binom{N}{D} = N_D(s, S_b)/\binom{N}{D}$ of being selected, ie of being that of the actual $b'$. Thus, any syndrome $s$ for which $N_D(s, S_b) < 2^{-r}M$ (which would be bad because it would mean less uncertainty for Bob) has probability of occurrence less than $(2^{-r}M)/\binom{N}{D} = \frac{1}{2^K}2^{-r}$. Even if all but one syndrome were in that category, their collective probability would still be less than $2^{-r}$. This establishes the claim that $N_D(S_{b'}, S_b) \geq 2^{-r}M$, except with probability less than $2^{-r}$.

Putting this together with our lower bound on $\binom{N}{D}$, we conclude that, except with probability less than $2^{-r}$ and provided that $N/2 < N - D < (\beta + \delta)N$,

$$N_D(S_{b'}, S_b) \geq 2^{-r}M = \frac{\binom{N}{D}}{2^K}2^{-r} > \frac{2^{\mathbf{H}(\beta + \delta)N - K - r}}{\sqrt{N}} .$$

Let $\rho$ and $\nu$ be two arbitrary positive constants such that $\rho + \nu < \mathbf{H}(\beta + \delta) - \frac{K}{N}$, which is always possible provided that $K < 3N/5$ and $\delta$ is small enough. Setting $r = \rho N$ yields the final result that $N_D(S_{b'}, S_b) > 2^{\nu N}/\sqrt{N}$, which is exponentially large in $N$, except with probability less than $2^{-\rho N} + \text{Prob}[N - D \geq (\beta + \delta)N \text{ or } D \geq N/2]$, which is exponentially small in $N$.

At this point one can invoke the privacy amplification theorem [7] of [7] and say that the residual information about $z = \bigoplus_{i \in I} b_i$ is exponentially small in $N$ because Bob has exponentially many candidates from which to choose $b$. This completes the argument from which we conclude that canonical measurements would have been more useful to Bob since they would allow Cheating Bob to recover both of Alice's messages easily if she were willing to supply as many as $K = 3N/5$ check bits in her syndromes (see Section 4.1).

The analysis for all possible canonical and noncanonical measurements is somewhat similar to what we just presented but much more complicated. From now on we assume that Bob makes his measurements in the canonical bases, because he would gain less information otherwise.

## 4.3 Beamsplitting

Another way by which Bob can cheat involves step 3 again. The idea is to capitalize on the fact that the pulses sent by Alice at step 2 are not pure single-photon states. Recall that Alice's pulses are sent with an expected $\mu$ photon per pulse, where $\mu$ is significantly smaller than 1. More precisely, a perfectly efficient photo-counter would count for each pulse a number of photons that follows a Poisson distribution with mean $\mu$. In particular, there is a probability $\xi = 1 - e^{-\mu} - \mu e^{-\mu} \approx \mu^2/2$ that a pulse would give rise to a multiple count. We shall assume conservatively that whenever a multiple count is obtained, Bob learns Alice's bit with certainty [8].

It is now important to remember that Honest Bob's detectors have less than perfect efficiency. Recall that Bob's counting efficiency, denoted by $a$, was determined at step 1 and that the number of pulses sent by Alice at step 2 is $M = T/a$, where $T = 2N$ is the number of pulses that Bob must receive successfully. But now consider the case of Cheating Bob, whose photodetectors are in fact perfect. Such a Bob can obtain Alice's bit with certainty for the entire set of $M\xi = T\xi/a$ multiple-count pulses, and he would report success on those at step 3. Assuming that $\xi < a$ —otherwise, Alice would have aborted the protocol at step 1— Bob still has to report success on an additional $(1 - \xi/a)T$ pulses, which he chooses randomly among the single-count pulses, which he read (according to the honest protocol) in random canonical bases.

---

[7] To be technically exact, one needs Lemma 9 rather than Theorem 10 from [7] in this case.

[8] In principle, though not with present technology, he could do this by analyzing the photon number state of the original pulse without spoiling its polarization, then separating all two-photon pulses into two single photons and measuring one in each canonical basis. After hearing the correct basis from Alice at step 4, he would know which measurement was relevant and thus learn Alice's bit with certainty. In practice, he could learn Alice's bit with probability 75% for double-count pulses by a much simpler apparatus in which a half-silvered mirror is used to split the beam into two parts, one measured rectilinearly and one diagonally. If two counts were obtained in such an apparatus, Bob would be able, after hearing the correct basis from Alice, to determine her bit accurately except when (with probability 25%) both counts had occurred in the wrong-basis half of the apparatus, in which case he would know that he failed to learn anything about Alice's bit.

As a result, Bob knows $T\xi/a$ bits from beamsplitting and about half of the remaining $(1 - \xi/a)T$ bits from "honest" behaviour, for a total of $\gamma T$ bits, where $\gamma = \frac{1}{2} + \xi/2a$. This is $(1 + \xi/a)$ times more bits than the $T/2$ that he would have expected to know had he not taken advantage of multiple-count pulses. In this case, the symmetric cheating strategy consists of splitting the $T = 2N$ bits in two sets of size $N$ so that he knows a proportion $\gamma$ of the bits in each set. From here, the analysis is similar to that of the standard attack (Section 4.1), except that Bob knows a larger fraction of the bits of whichever set is chosen by Alice. Therefore, this cheat will be thwarted provided that $H(2\varepsilon) < 1 - \gamma = \frac{1}{2} - \xi/2a$.

This completes the formal demonstration of the main theorem (Section 2), under the reasonable assumption that Bob must measure each pulse before the next one arrives or else lose the opportunity of measuring it at all: the protocol is safe, even against cheaters having access to unlimited computing power, because step 1 makes sure that $H(2\varepsilon) < \frac{1}{2} - \xi/2a$. The closer to this value is $\varepsilon$, the more pulses will have to be received successfully by Bob at step 3 in order to take account of expected statistical deviations, as explained in Section 4.1. (It is according to this consideration that Alice chooses the value of $N$ at step 1.)

As a numerical example, consider the case in which the efficiency of Honest Bob's photodetectors is $q = 25\%$, and assume that Alice sends her pulses at intensity $\mu = 0.05$. In this case, ignoring dark counts and attenuation in the optical channel, Bob's expected counting efficiency would be $a = 1 - e^{-\mu q} \approx 1.242\%$, $\xi \approx 0.1209\%$, $\gamma \approx 54.87\%$, and therefore expected error rates $\varepsilon$ up to about 4.725% on the legitimate use of the quantum channel can be tolerated. If errors are due only to dark counts, this implies that one expected dark count every 2000 time slots can be tolerated, which is entirely reasonable with current technology.

# 5 More sophisticated attacks

In principle, the quantum OT protocol described in Section 2 could be subjected to more sophisticated attacks, which are possible in principle although infeasible at present or in the foreseeable future. The first of these attacks, *pulse storing*, can be overcome at the cost of making the protocol more complicated, although it would remain possible to implement it with current technology. The second attack, *coherent measurements*, may be impossible to counter, but it is even more unrealistic than the first one.

## 5.1 Pulse storing

Instead of measuring the pulses at step 3, Bob could merely pretend to do so, while in fact storing all the pulses he pretended to detect in a lossless delay line. Then, after Alice has announced the sending bases at step 4, he could measure them in the correct bases — which he now knows— using a perfectly efficient detector. He would then be able to present Alice with two "good" sets of bits, and thus obtain both $b_0$ and $b_1$. In order to mount such an attack, it is clear that Bob needs to be able to keep the pulses' polarization for an arbitrary long time (because Alice might suspect Bob of attempting this attack and thus wait for a while before step 4) and that he must have perfect or near-perfect photo-detection. However, even *this* would not be sufficient. Bob's additional difficulty is that he must tell Alice as early as step 3 which pulses he claims to have successfully measured. But recall that the pulses are so dim that even a perfectly efficient apparatus would detect only about a fraction $\mu$ of them. No technology is available or foreseeable for determining whether the pulse would be detected (formally, measuring the number-state of the pulse) without in fact attempting to detect it, which would spoil it!

Even if we grant Bob the technology necessary to perform this attack, there is a conceptually easy fix to the OT protocol. First of all, Alice would send $3N/a$ pulses at step 2, allowing roughly $3N$ of them to be successful if Bob is honest. Then, before step 4, Bob would use a bit commitment scheme to commit to each of the bases used for his successful measurements as well as to the bits thus obtained. Still before step 4, Alice would select a random subset of $N$ reported successes, and ask Bob to open his commitments for those. This allows Alice to check that Bob's commitments are correct (subject to error rate $\varepsilon$) when his committed basis is correct and that his commitments are uncorrelated to the correct bits when his basis is incorrect. Not only does this prove to Alice that Bob measured the pulses before step 4, but also that he did not measure them in noncanonical bases (such as the Breidbart basis).

But of course, one may ask which commitment scheme should be used? Obviously, we would lose most of the benefit from quantum cryptography if we used a scheme that is merely computationally secure. Fortunately, *quantum* bit commitment schemes exist [3, 8]. Even though the schemes presented in [3, 8] are technologically unreasonable, as mentioned in the introduction, the techniques used in the current paper can be used also to modify the scheme of [8] in order to render it feasible with current technology.

## 5.2   Coherent measurements

So far, we have limited Bob to measuring pulses one at a time, and combining the classical results of these measurements with information subsequently obtained from Alice. The formalism of quantum mechanics allows a more general kind of measurement, which is even more infeasible than pulse storing. Such a measurement would treat the entire sequence of $M$ pulses sent during step 2 as a single $2^M$-state quantum system, cause it to interact coherently with an intermediate quantum system of comparable complexity, maintain the phase coherence of the intermediate system for an arbitrarily long time, then finally measure the intermediate system in a way depending on the information provided by Alice at step 4.

In the light of the previous section, avoiding this attack appears easy. Indeed the fix we just showed for pulse storing will also apply to this kind of attack. Unfortunately, the bit commitment scheme of [8] is also susceptible to coherent measurements (although in the case of that scheme the receiver will be Alice, which means that *she* will be the one who can potentially cheat). Alternatively, we could use the bit commitment scheme implicit in [3], but *it* is susceptible to an attack related to the Einstein–Podolsky–Rosen paradox (in addition to requiring the use of single-photon pulses, which are hard to generate in practice). As a consequence, it is not known whether our protocols can be made unconditionally secure against all possible attacks consistent with quantum physics.

Nevertheless, an interesting protocol results if we are satisfied with computational security. Indeed, it is well-known that computationally secure bit commitments are possible under the assumption that one-way functions exist [20, 19, 24]. Therefore, quantum physics provides for an OT protocol that is computationally secure against unrestricted technology (including the ability to perform coherent measurements) under the sole assumption that one-way functions exist. This is interesting because Impagliazzo and Rudich have proved that one-way functions are not sufficient to implement OT in the classical (ie non-quantum) model [21]. Moreover, under the assumption that one-way permutations [25] or one-way group actions [10] exist, it is possible to accomplish a quantum OT protocol that will leak no additional information to either party unless the computational assumption is broken *on-line*, while the protocol is taking place. In contrast, all classical OT protocols are susceptible to off-line cheating: at least one party has complete information (in the sense of Shannon) on the other party's secret.

# Acknowledgements

We are greatly indebted to Ivan Damgård for his many valuable comments. We thank also Silvio Micali for pointing out that computational complexity based quantum cryptography is interesting since it allows to build oblivious transfer around one-way functions.

# References

[1] Bennett, C. H., F. Bessette, G. Brassard, L. Salvail and J. Smolin, "Experimental quantum cryptography", *Advances in Cryptology — Eurocrypt '90 Proceedings*, April 1990, Springer-Verlag, pp. 253-265.

[2] Bennett, C. H., F. Bessette, G. Brassard, L. Salvail and J. Smolin, "Experimental quantum cryptography", *Journal of Cryptology*, Vol. 5, no. 1, 1992, to appear.

[3] Bennett, C. H. and G. Brassard, "Quantum cryptography: Public key distribution and coin tossing", *Proceedings of IEEE International Conference on Computers, Systems, and Signal Processing*, Bangalore, India, December 1984, pp. 175-179.

[4] Bennett, C. H., G. Brassard and S. Breidbart, "Quantum cryptography II: How to re-use a one-time pad safely even if $\mathcal{P} = \mathcal{NP}$", unpublished manuscript available from the authors, November 1982.

[5] Bennett, C. H., G. Brassard, S. Breidbart and S. Wiesner, "Quantum cryptography, or unforgeable subway tokens", *Advances in Cryptology: Proceedings of Crypto '82*, August 1982, Plenum Press, pp. 267-275.

[6] Bennett, C. H., G. Brassard and J.-M. Robert, "How to reduce your enemy's information", *Advances in Cryptology — Crypto '85 Proceedings*, August 1985, Springer-Verlag, pp. 468-476.

[7] Bennett, C. H., G. Brassard and J.-M. Robert, "Privacy amplification by public discussion", *SIAM Journal on Computing*, Vol. 17, no. 2, April 1988, pp. 210-229.

[8] Brassard, G. and C. Crépeau, "Quantum bit commitment and coin tossing protocols", *Advances in Cryptology — Crypto '90 Proceedings*, August 1990, Springer-Verlag, to appear.

[9] Brassard, G., C. Crépeau and J.-M. Robert, "Information theoretic reductions among disclosure problems", *Proceedings of 27th IEEE Symposium on the Foundations of Computer Science*, October 1986, pp. 168-173.

[10] Brassard, G. and M. Yung, "One-way group actions", *Advances in Cryptology — Crypto '90 Proceedings*, August 1990, Springer-Verlag, to appear.

[11] Crépeau, C., "Equivalence between two flavours of oblivious transfers (abstract)", *Advances in Cryptology: Proceedings of Crypto '87*, August 1987, Springer-Verlag, pp. 350–354.

[12] Crépeau, C., "Verifiable disclosure of secrets and application", *Advances in Cryptology: Proceedings of Eurocrypt '89*, April 1989, Springer-Verlag, pp. 181–191.

[13] Crépeau, C. and J. Kilian, "Achieving oblivious transfer using weakened security assumptions", *Proceedings of 29th IEEE Symposium on the Foundations of Computer Science*, October 1988, pp. 42–52.

[14] Deutsch, D., "Quantum communication thwarts eavesdroppers", *New Scientist*, 9 December 1989, pp. 25–26.

[15] Ekert, A., "La mécanique quantique au secours des agents secrets", *La recherche*, No. 233, June 1991, pp. 790–791.

[16] Even, S., O. Goldreich and A. Lempel, "A randomized protocol for signing contracts", *Advances in Cryptology: Proceedings of Crypto '82*, August 1982, Plenum Press, pp. 205–210.

[17] Forney, G. D., *Concatenated Codes*, The M.I.T. Press, 1966.

[18] Gottlieb, A., "Conjugal secrets — The untappable quantum telephone", *The Economist*, Vol. 311, no. 7599, 22 April 1989, p. 81.

[19] Håstad, J., "Pseudo-random generation under uniform assumptions", *Proceedings of the 22nd Annual ACM Symposium on Theory of Computing*, May 1990, pp. 395–440.

[20] Impagliazzo, R., L. A. Levin and M. Luby, "Pseudo-random generation from one-way functions", *Proceedings of the 21st Annual ACM Symposium on Theory of Computing*, May 1989, pp. 12–24.

[21] Impagliazzo, R. and S. Rudich, "Limits on the provable consequences of one-way permutations", *Proceedings of the 21st Annual ACM Symposium on Theory of Computing*, May 1989, pp. 44–61.

[22] Kilian, J., "Founding cryptography on oblivious transfer", *Proceedings of the 20th Annual ACM Symposium on Theory of Computing*, May 1988, pp. 20–31.

[23] MacWilliams, F. J. and N. J. A. Sloane, *The Theory of Error-Correcting Codes*, North-Holland, 1977.

[24] Naor, M., "Bit commitment using pseudo-randomness", *Advances in Cryptology — Crypto '89 Proceedings*, August 1989, Springer-Verlag, pp. 128–136. To appear in *Journal of Cryptology*, Vol. 4, no. 2, 1991.

[25] Naor, M., R. Ostrovsky, R. Venkatesan and M. Yung, "Perfect zero-knowledge arguments for NP can be based on general complexity assumptions", Manuscript available from the authors, 1991.

[26] Peterson, I., "Bits of uncertainty: Quantum security", *Science News*, Vol. 137, 2 June 1990, pp. 342–343.

[27] Rabin, M. O., "How to exchange secrets by oblivious transfer", Technical Memo TR-81, Aiken Computation Laboratory, Harvard University, 1981.

[28] Stewart, I., "Schrödinger's catflap", News and Views, *Nature*, Vol. 353, 3 October 1991, pp. 384–385.

[29] Wallich, P., "Quantum cryptography", *Scientific American*, Vol. 260, no. 5, May 1989, pp. 28–30.

[30] Wiesner, S., "Conjugate coding", manuscript written *circa* 1970, unpublished until it appeared in *Sigact News*, Vol. 15, no. 1, 1983, pp. 78–88.

# Exploiting Parallelism
# in Hardware Implementation of the DES

Albert G. Broscius
Distributed Systems Lab
Dept. of CIS
Univ. of Pennsylvania
Phila PA, 19104-6389 USA
broscius@cis.upenn.edu

Jonathan M. Smith
Distributed Systems Lab
Dept. of CIS
Univ. of Pennsylvania
Phila, PA, 19104-6389 USA
jms@cis.upenn.edu

### Abstract

The Data Encryption Standard algorithm has features which may be used to advantage in parallelizing an implementation. The kernel of the algorithm, a single round, may be decomposed into several parallel computations resulting in a structure with minimal delay. These rounds may also be computed in a pipelined parallel structure for operations modes which do not require cryptext feedback. Finally, system I/O may be performed in parallel with the encryption computation for further gain. Although several of these ideas have been discussed before separately, the composite presentation is novel.

# 1  Introduction

[1] The Data Encryption Standard (DES) is probably the most widely used publicly available secret-key algorithm. Since its introduction by the National Bureau of Standards (NBS) in 1977[FIPS46], DES implementations have improved greatly in encryption rate. Yet, typical computer communication rates have also increased significantly during the same period. Today's high-performance computer networks extend still further the encryption bandwidth needed for adequate performance of secure systems [Giga90]. Thus, we examine means to increase the throughput of a DES implementation to satisfy these demands.

We discuss parallel approaches for several levels of an implementation. At the lowest level, the kernel of the algorithm can be split into several parallel computations for increased speed. By generating subkeys one cycle in advance, the time required can be effectively overlapped with the use of the subkey in the rest of the round operation. An additional overlap can be made of the two stages of exclusive-or (XOR) gates at the expense of increased complexity and gate-count.

One level upward in the hierarchy, the use of multiple round implementations can

---

[1] This research was supported by NSF and DARPA through the Corporation for National Research Initiatives, and by Bellcore through Project DAWN.

increase computation bandwidth if the DES mode of operation chosen does not require feedback of ciphertext. Of the official modes[FIPS81], this requirement rules out all but the Electronic Code Book (ECB) method. Unfortunately, ECB is known to be susceptible to plaintext frequency-analysis based attacks since multiple identical input blocks result in the same output cryptext block. We discuss in section 3 of this paper a proposed operating method [Feldmeier91] that resists this attack yet does not require feedback of ciphertext.

Finally, at the system level, the processing of I/O concurrent with DES computation provides for continuous operation of the encryption unit. In addition to this buffering, the use of Direct Memory Access (DMA) for encryption allows the host processor to continue other work concurrently with the ongoing encryption.

# 2 Algorithm Kernel

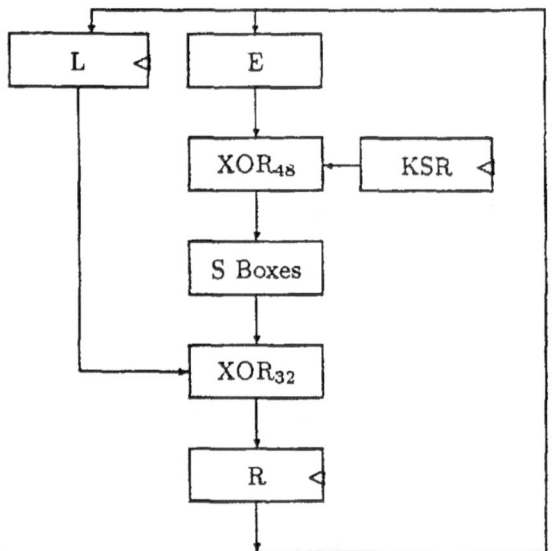

Figure 1: Simple Implementation of Algorithm Kernel

| Shift1 | Shift2 | XOR#1 | S Boxes | XOR#2 | Reg. Load |
|--------|--------|-------|---------|-------|-----------|

Figure 2: Timing Diagram for Circuit of Fig. 1

The kernel of the DES algorithm consists of four operations: key generation, key mixing, substitution table lookup and data mixing between the $R$ and $L$ words. This kernel is repeated for sixteen iterations with only one key generation parameter dependent on iteration number. This single parameter specifies one or two shifts of the circular registers from which the current key is derived.

A straightforward implementation of the kernel is depicted in Fig.1. The box labeled $KSR$ represents the circular shift registers which hold the key data. These are to be clocked either once or twice depending on the iteration number. Once the key has been shifted, the key-mixing box denoted $XOR_{48}$ outputs the modulo 2 sum of the key data with the extended $R$ data after a propagation delay interval. The $S$ $Boxes$ then begin their access time delay interval before output of their results. The box marked $XOR_{32}$ then begins mixing in data from the $L$ register. After a propagation delay of an XOR gate, data are ready at the input to the $R$ register. Once a register setup-time has passed, the $R$ and $L$ registers may be clocked once. A register propagation delay later, the cycle may begin once more.

Timing analysis reveals that the critical timing path results from two shifts of the key registers, the keying XOR array, the S Box table lookup, the R-L mixing XOR array, plus the register loading delays. A simplified timing diagram is shown in Fig. 2. The critical path timing defines the limiting rate at which round computation may proceed. Assuming these delays are minimal, the only way to improve the critical path timing is to modify the circuit so that these sequential processes become concurrent. We will now examine several ways to achieve this concurrency.

## 2.1   Key Parallelism

Separating the key generation from the remaining three stages of the algorithm kernel can reduce the critical path timing. This approach saves delay by updating the key shift register in anticipation of the next iteration simultaneous with the remaining operations in the current iteration. An additional key latch is introduced to buffer the key value for the current iteration on the input to the key-mixing XOR stage as shown in Fig. 3.

This key parallelism was suggested by Diffie and Hellman [Diffie77] in their timing approach for the proposed DES key-search device. They did not include the additional key latch but instead relied on strict control of key shift timing with respect to the overall R-L clock timing to prevent a race condition. Our introduction of the key latch allows greater tolerance in clock provision by ensuring that the key data input to the key-mixing XOR cannot change during the iteration cycle.

Later, a different key-parallel approach incorporating a multiplexer (MUX) was used

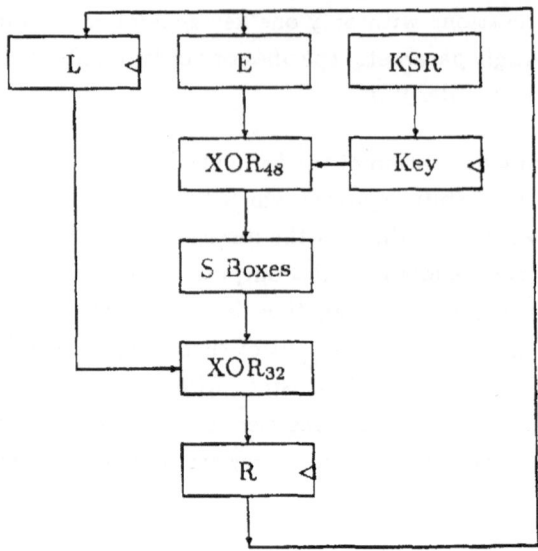

Figure 3: Pipelined Key Generation Algorithm Kernel

|        | Shift1  | Shift2 | Key Latch |
|--------|---------|--------|-----------|
| XOR#1  | S Boxes | XOR#2  | Reg. Load |

Figure 4: Timing Diagram for Circuit of Fig. 3

| | | | MUX Latch |
|---|---|---|---|
| XOR#1 | S Boxes | XOR#2 | Reg. Load |

Figure 5: Timing Diagram for Circuit of Fig. 4

by Fairfield et al [Fair84]. Their MUX approach allowed either one or two shifts in either the encryption or decryption direction to be performed in one clocking operation. Additionally, a key loading operation could be selected by the multiplexer. This shortens the time required for the key generation somewhat since the MUX propagation delay is likely to be much lower than a full key shift cycle. More importantly, since the key shift register (KSR) no longer generates intermediate results, as it did when two shifts were required for a given iteration, the extra key latch introduced above to prevent race conditions is no longer necessary so the block diagram reverts to that of Fig.1. A simplified timing diagram for this arrangement is shown in Fig. 5.

## 2.2   XOR Rearrangement

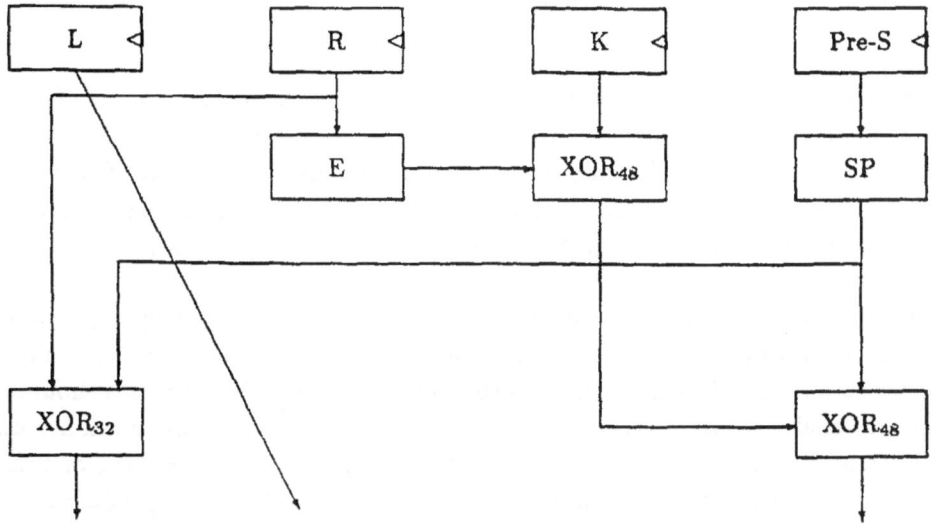

Figure 6: Block Diagram of Datapath with Single XOR Delay in Critical Path

Since the XOR summation is a bitwise linear operation, the order in which XOR operations are performed does not alter their algebraic correctness. Thus, these operations may be grouped (or associated) in any order whatsoever without changing the final results of the combined operations.

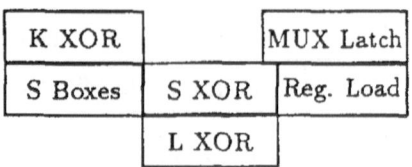

Figure 7: Timing Diagram for Circuit of Fig. 6

If we remove the labeling of R and L in a pair of consecutive rounds of the DES, we observe that there are two stages of XORs, where the second follows the first directly with only the E expansion separating the two. Since E may be commuted with the XOR at the cost of additional bits in the XOR array, we may combine the 48-bit XOR and the 32-bit XOR into a single 48-bit XOR, which would remain in the critical timing path, and a 48-bit XOR which would be computed concurrent with the previous S Box table lookup operation. This transformation also requires the addition of a 32-bit XOR array since the $R$ value is no longer produced in the critical timing path.

# 3 Multi-Round Parallelism

Using multiple stages in parallel limits the computation of feedback modes of encipherment. Since a parallel implementation begins processing subsequent blocks before completion of a current block's encryption, modes that use the cryptext of a prior block cannot be computed at the full bandwidth that a feedforward mode can achieve. Three of the four modes defined by the NBS for use of the DES require feedback.

A feedforward operation mode proposed by Feldmeier and McAuley appears to overcome the weaknesses of ECB. Their modified ECB mode of operation combines a sequence number with each plaintext block using the XOR operation. This approach should thwart frequency-analysis style attacks since multiple instances of a plaintext block are mapped to different cryptext elements. Using a 64 bit sequence number, cycling of this space would take place in $2^{67}$ bytes of a data stream. This mode allows independent processing of data elements by avoiding the interdependence of subsequent encryption operations found in feedback modes.

An intermediate alternative between feedback and feedforward modes is the use of multiple interleaved chains. The degree of interleaving can be chosen to allow for as much bandwidth gain through parallelism as needed.

373

## 3.1 Pipeline

L, R, and K Inputs from Previous Stage

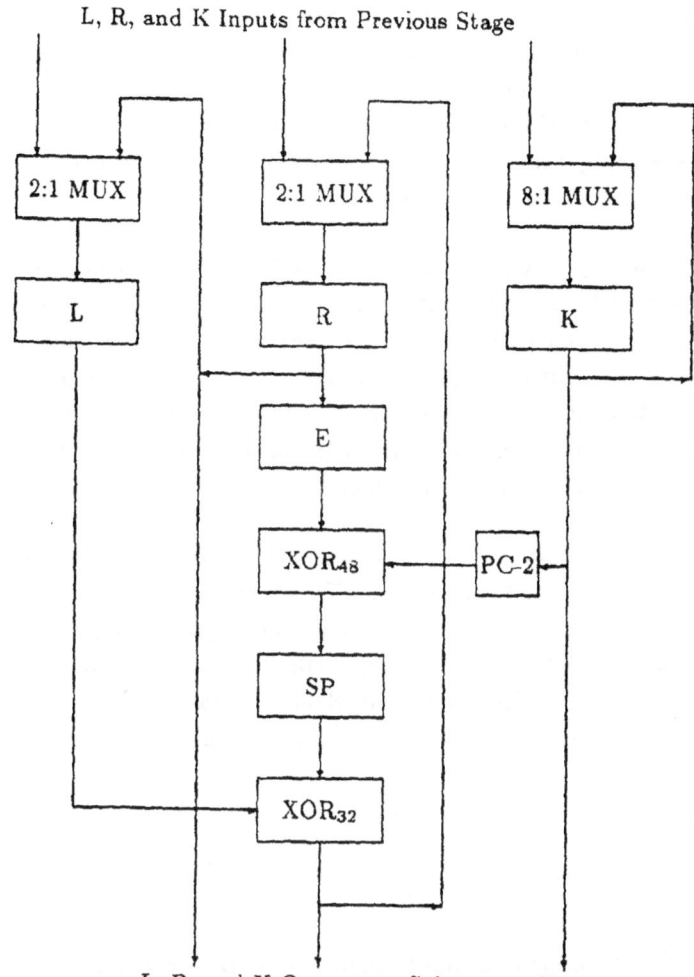

L, R, and K Outputs to Subsequent Stage

Figure 8: Pipeline Segment for DES with Key Transport

The parallel computation elements may each be configured to implement a fraction of the rounds in a pipeline approach or each element may operate independently in a computation farm approach which we discuss in section 3.2. A pipeline of elements may be configured from two, four, eight or sixteen round implementations. Each element would operate on a 64-bit block for an equal number of cycles needed to partition the algorithm computation. Thus, a two round pipeline would execute eight cycles on each of the processors in the pipeline. Similarly, a four round pipeline would execute four cycles on each processor.

When keying needs to be updated frequently, the pipeline style allows a matching of the datapath flow with a parallel keypath. In this way, data blocks are accompanied by their key throughout the computation. Switching keys between successive datablocks without flushing the pipeline is made possible since the key and data streams are synchronized. Each stage of the pipeline has the structure depicted in Fig. 8. Note that the 8:1 key MUX actually selects between four different shifted versions of either the current key or the input key from the previous stage.

For infrequent key changes, the tradeoff in keying interconnection may not be worthwhile as compared to maintaining separate key registers for each stage of the pipeline. Each round would then maintain its own key load (shadow) register in this approach. The standard's key shifting sequence would be partially executed on each stage. Since a partial execution of the key schedule would not result in a complete cycling of the keytext, the key would be reloaded from the shadow register when it had completed its share of the computation on a data block.

A limitation of the pipeline approach is the bandwidth ceiling imposed by the number of rounds in the algorithm, sixteen. This means that a single pipeline of processors cannot provide more than sixteen times the encryption bandwidth of a single processor. Additionally, the pipeline suffers in scalability since the number of stages possible is restricted to be a factor of sixteen. This deficit is most notable when considering an upgrade of a pipeline: to gain any increase in bandwidth requires a doubling in computation resources.

## 3.2 Computation Farm

Instead of a pipeline approach, multiple devices may be configured as a computation farm with each given subsequent plaintext elements to process. This configuration allows for smooth increase in available encryption bandwidth since the number of rounds used need not be a power of two as in the case of the pipeline parallelism.

Managing the farm requires logic similar to that used in FIFO buffers. A counter to keep track of the next available processor and the last busy processor are required. A generalized depiction of the interconnection is shown in Fig.9, using an Input Manager and Output Manager to coordinate operations.

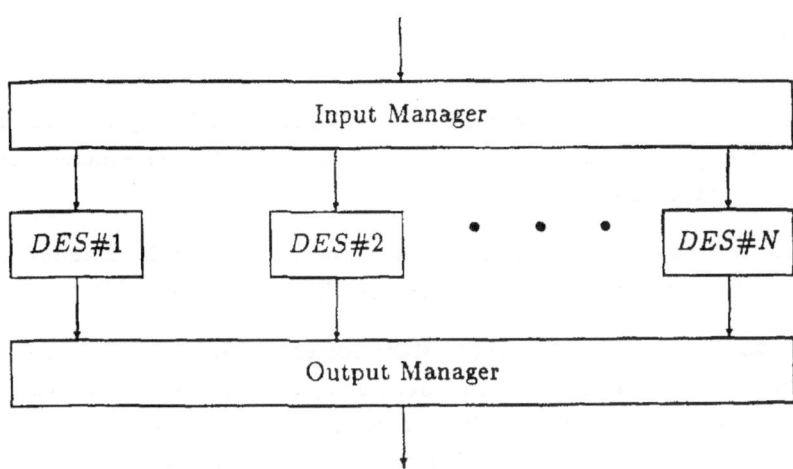

Figure 9: Computation Farm Block Diagram

# 4  System-Level Parallelism

To maintain constant throughput rates requires careful consideration of the encryption system's interface or input/output section. Overlap of the input, output and encryption processes of subsequent text blocks provides high throughput [Ver88]. Similarly, DMA support decouples the host processor from the encryption function to allow CPU processing of other tasks to proceed in parallel with the encryption request[Anderson87].

# 5  Conclusion

Parallel aspects of the DES may be exploited at three levels: within the algorithm kernel, through duplication of the algorithm kernel, and in the encryption processor I/O design. Consideration of operation mode also impacts the maximum performance attainable – nonstandard or hybrid operations modes should be studied further as a means of increasing bandwidth without compromising security.

As part of our work with the Aurora network testbed [Giga90], we have developed a DES board [Broscius91] using SSI TTL and MSI PALs using the MUX key register approach. Testing of the wirewrapped prototype indicated an encryption rate of 93 Mbps. Further work on a DMA interface to the MicroChannel interface bus of the IBM RS/6000 is planned. However, recent announcement by VLSI Technology of their VM007 encryption processor [VLSI91] with 192 Mbps performance obsoletes our discrete approach and will most likely be used in our final version.

# References

[Anderson87] David P. Anderson and P. Venkat Rangan, *High-Performance Interface Architectures for Cryptographic Hardware*, EUROCRYPT '87 Proceedings, Springer-Verlag, Amsterdam, 1987

[Broscius91] Albert G. Broscius, *Hardware Analysis and Implementation of the NBS Data Encryption Standard*, MSE Thesis, CIS Dept., Univ. of Penn., May 1991

[Davio83] Marc Davio, Yvo Desmedt, Marc Fosseprez, Rene Govaerts, Jan Hulsbosch, Patrik Neutjens, Philippe Piret, Jean-Jacques Quisquater, Joos Vandewalle and Pascal Wouters, *Analytical Characteristics of the DES* Advances in Cryptology: Proceedings of CRYPTO 83, Plenum Press, New York, 1984

[Denning82] Dorothy Denning, *Cryptography and Data Security* , Addison-Wesley (1982)

[Diffie77] Whitfield Diffie and Martin E. Hellman, *Exhaustive Cryptanalysis of the NBS Data Encryption Standard* , IEEE Computer Vol. 10 No. 6, June 1977 pp. 74-84

[Fair84] R.C.Fairfield, A. Matsuevich and J. Plany, *An LSI Digital Encryption Processor*, Advances in Cryptology: Proceedings of CRYPTO 84, Springer-Verlag, New York, 1985

[FIPS46] National Bureau of Standards, *Federal Information Processing Standard #46: The Data Encryption Standard*

[FIPS81] National Bureau of Standards, *Federal Information Processing Standard #81: Operational Modes of the DES*

[Feldmeier91] Anthony McAuley and David C. Feldmeier, *Minimizing Protocol Ordering Constraints to Improve Performance* , Submitted for publication, Available via anonymous *ftp* from Internet host *thumper.bellcore.com*

[Giga90] Anonymous, *Gigabit Network Testbeds* , IEEE Computer, Vol. 23 No. 9

[Ver88] Ingrid Verbauwhede, Frank Hoornaert, Joos Vandewalle and Hugo de Man, *Security and Performance Optimization of a New DES Data Encryption Chip* , IEEE Journal of Solid State Circuits Vol. 23, No. 3, pp. 647-656, June 1988

[VLSI91] VLSI Technology, Inc., *VM007 Data Encryption Processor* , Tempe, AZ 1991

# Foundations of Secure Interactive Computing

Donald Beaver *

AT&T Bell Laboratories

### Abstract.

The problem of secure multiparty computation is usually described as follows: each of $n$ players in a network holds a private input $x_i$. Together they would like to compute a function $F(x_1, \ldots, x_n)$ without revealing the inputs, even though no particular player can be trusted. Attempts to contrive formal definitions for the problem have treated properties of the solution separately (correctness, privacy, etc.), giving an *ad hoc* collection of desirable properties and varied definitions that do not support clear or comparable proofs.

We propose a clear, concise, and unified definition for security and reliability in interactive computations. We develop a reduction called *relative resilience* that captures all desired properties at a single blow. Relative resilience allows one to classify and compare arbitrary protocols in terms of security and reliability, in the same way that Turing reductions allow one to classify and compare algorithms in terms of complexity. Security and reliability reduce to a simple statement: a protocol for $F$ is *resilient* if it is as resilient as an *ideal* protocol in which a trusted host is available to compute $F$. Relative resilience captures the notions of security and reliability for a wide variety of interactive computations, including zero-knowledge proof systems, Byzantine Agreement, oblivious transfer, two-party oblivious circuit evaluation, among others.

*Relative resilience* provides modular proof techniques that other approaches lack: one may compare a sequence of protocols ranging from the real-world protocol to the ideal protocol, proving the relative resilience of each successive protocol with greater clarity and less complexity. Folk theorems about the "transitivity" of security and the security of concatenated protocols are now provable; and the proofs reveal that such folk theorems fail under subtle conditions that have previously gone unnoticed. The conciseness[1] and modularity of our definitions and proof techniques provide great clarity in designing and reasoning about protocols and have already lead to provably secure protocols that are significantly more efficient than those appearing in the literature.

*This research was supported in part under NSF grant CCR-870-4513 at Harvard University, and by an AT&T Bell Laboratories postdoctoral fellowship. Contact: Donald Beaver, 313 Whitmore, Penn State Univ., State College, PA 16802; (814) 863-0147; beaver@cs.psu.edu.

[1]We have developed our definitions with great care and precision, and we believe them well-suited to culling a meaningful 15-page abstract. A full version is available on request (see also [2, 4]).

# 1 Introduction

The purpose of cryptographic research, especially in the theoretical domain, is threefold:

1. to develop new techniques for secure communication and computation;
2. to investigate and improve efficiency;
3. to provide proofs of security.

Whether it address secure communication, reliable file storage, operating system security, or computations performed on private data, cryptographic research must provide clear and provable results. Without clarity, efficiency and implementation are impossible; without proofs, as a long history of broken systems shows, no system can be relied upon without fear.

We investigate and define the nature of security for interactive computations, in which results need to be computed based on values supplied by two or more participants. The results must satisfy an intuitive idea of correctness, and often are required to preserve the privacy of certain information (*eg.* the input values).

Typically, an interactive computation is described as a *multiparty protocol*: $n$ players, each holding a private input $x_i$, wish to compute some function $F(x_1, \ldots, x_n)$ without revealing anything about the inputs than what is computable solely from learning $F(x_1, \ldots, x_n)$. The results should be robust against an adversary who attacks the protocol, gaining information from some players and perhaps even causing faulty messages to be sent. A well-known example is the *secret ballot,* in which the participants compute the sum of their votes without revealing how any individual voted. An adversary might choose or learn some of the votes, but it should not learn anything more than the overall tally and the choices of the players it corrupts.

A wide variety of network models (private channels, broadcast, oblivious transfer), computational complexity assumptions, and adversarial powers is examined in the literature [27, 19, 8, 11, 5, 24, 2]. The purpose of this paper, however, is not to enumerate the various mechanical aspects of the various models, but to present a unifying, model-independent set of definitions for security and reliability for interactive computation. Though defining properties of interactive computations has proven subtle and elusive in the past, a concise and easily-understood property we call *resilience* captures a long list of desired security properties and provides a sturdy framework for modular protocol design and verification.

**Previous work.** Research into multiparty protocols has provided a variety of robust algorithms, satisfying one major goal of cryptography while simultaneously failing another: to provide confidence that the techniques are in fact reliable. The distinction between using methods based on unproven complexity-theoretic assumptions and using methods that are simply unproven is vast.

The primary reason for a lack of proofs is the lack of good definitions. Good definitions, like cryptographic research, should be:

a.    easy to understand;
b.    easy to use (providing simple, modular proofs);
c.    unified and sufficiently robust to cover many situations.

Ill-chosen or ill-coordinated definitions make the proofs of even easily-understood ideas like secret sharing into complicated, ugly affairs. Worse, researchers are led to believe that all proofs must be complicated, eliminating the motivation to uphold the basic precept of cryptographic research: to demonstrate provably reliable techniques.

In the case of multiparty protocol security, a host of security properties have arisen in the gradual, *ad hoc* progress of research. The definitions vary with the computational and communication models (*eg.* private channels *vs.* public-key-encrypted messages). Properties like correctness and privacy are intuitively easy to understand but extremely sensitive to subtle issues in their formulation. The definition of an "input" is crucial, and while seemingly simple, it has been fraught with problems. What if a player is given an input, for example, but behaves "properly" as though it were given a different input? "Intuitive proofs" and unwieldy or inflexible approaches are often used to finesse such problems. For example, encryptions of each input may be supplied to all players, thereby fixing the inputs [19], or a player may be required to *commit* to its input, say by secretly sharing it [8, 11]. Techniques that specify the input as a function based on the transcript as a whole [3] may avoid fixing a particular committal technique in the definition of "input," but they are less than elegant.

With *ad hoc* definitions, there is no guarantee that new properties will not arise. After correctness and privacy were considered, researchers began to worry about less apparent properties. For example, faulty players should choose their inputs independently of non-faulty players; otherwise, a 2/3 majority vote might be impossible, or a global random coin could be biased. Satisfactory definitions of input independence can be obtained in an information theoretic sense, but in a resource-bounded model, where one player might choose its input to be the encryption broadcast by another, independence becomes tricky. The separate analysis of properties gives an ill-coordinated and perhaps endless list of definitions.

Even the inspiring idea of *zero-knowledge proof systems* [16], which has produced many new techniques and a greater understanding of how to measure information transfer, avoids the question of "choosing" input $x \in L$ by quantifying over all possible $x$. Despite the wide appeal and strength of ZK and simulation-based ideas in addressing issues of privacy (the preservation of *information*), analyzing privacy alone is insufficient to treat correctness, independence, and other properties related to *influence* wielded by an adversary. As we shall see, however, ZK uses a crucial tool — Yao's notion of indistinguishable ensembles [26] — that provides a solid foundation on which to develop a unified definition of security.

**The new approach.** In considering diverse properties and focusing on ZK simulations, researchers seem to have turned from the primary goal: *achieving what an ideal protocol* *achieves.* Normally we assume no player is above corruption; in fact, any $t$-subset is vulnerable. In the ideal case, however, there is one player, the trusted host, whom the adversary cannot corrupt. The trusted host receives all inputs over private channels, computes $F$, and returns the results.

The *influence* and *information* of the adversary in the ideal setting are precisely delineated. The adversary may learn inputs for corrupted players, but it has no information regarding nonfaulty inputs except for the function value. It may substitute inputs for corrupted players, but it has no other influence over the nonfaulty outputs.

In order to state, however, that a protocol is secure by virtue of achieving what an ideal protocol achieves, one must define what it means to achieve the same results. A fixed comparison of a protocol to an ideal is one approach, but it is inflexible and inconvenient for constructing proofs.

**Relative resilience: a security reduction.** We present a reduction among protocols that allows one to compare *any* two protocols and to show that one implements the other with the same or better degree of security and reliability (including privacy, correctness, independence, fairness, *etc.*). Our thesis is as follows: *if any adversary attacking $\alpha$ cannot gain more information or wield more influence than when it attacks $\beta$, then $\alpha$ is at least as secure and reliable — i.e. as* resilient *— as $\beta$.* Defining such an intuitive thesis formally is the crux of our work.

An adversary attacking $\alpha$ may not be compatible with attacking $\beta$; we introduce an interface that translates the adversary's attacks on $\alpha$ to attacks on $\beta$. The interface should not itself give extra advantage to the adversary (*e.g.* through resource-unbounded computations). By considering ensembles describing *all* outputs in protocol executions (not just adversary views) and employing Yao's notion of indistinguishability [26] we give a formal means to compare attacks on $\alpha$ with interface-assisted attacks on $\beta$. Our use of indistinguishability is far broader than that in the analysis of ZK or of pseudorandom number generators.

Given a formal definition for *relative resilience*, an absolute measure of resilience becomes simply a comparison to some standard: a *$t$-resilient* protocol for $F$ is one that is as resilient as the ideal protocol $\mathrm{ID}(F)$ for $F$.

**Modular proof techniques.** The ability to compare arbitrary pairs of protocols provides simple proofs, broader applications of the definitions, and a conceptually easier approach. Rather than using a single yardstick, we design rulers, tape measures, and micrometers, and gain a thorough understanding of the fundamental relations among the objects we measure.

The most important property of our definitions is that they provide an extremely simple and modular way to treat security. Relative resilience is transitive, supporting step-by-step modular proofs (see [4, 2]) in an arena where many protocols lack proofs because of the lack of definitions or the vast complexity of such proofs. Relative resilience makes it easy to analyze the security of concatenating secure protocols, an affair that fixed-comparisons to an ideal fail to support (*cf.* the discussion of alternative approaches in §3, notably *fault-oracles* [13, 3, 21] and *legal-versions* [5, 14]). Proofs of "folk theorems" (transitivity, concatenability, and the share-compute-reveal paradigm) using our definitions reveal insecurities under certain circumstances, clarifying an intuitive understanding of security and contributing to a key purpose of cryptography: giving accurate security ratings. Our definitions have elucidated the important distinction between static and dynamic attacks in the "cryptographic" (computationally-bounded) setting, giving conditions under which protocols provably secure against *dynamic* adversaries can be designed [6] (previously, no proof of security against a dynamic adversary in the cryptographic setting has appeared in the literature).

The modularity in proof and protocol design has inspired vastly simplified, more efficient, and provably secure protocols for cryptographic multiparty protocols [6]. Moreover, formal proofs are short and clear.

Relative resilience unifies the idea of security and reliability for a host of interactive computations: Zero Knowledge, Byzantine Agreement, Oblivious Transfer, Instance-Hiding Schemes, *etc.*. Relative resilience explains the quite disparate collection of alternative and previous formal approaches to multiparty protocol security as particular aspects of a single principle, like electricity and magnetism, without recourse to an intricate and lengthy theory.

Thus, relative resilience satisfies the three important properties of good definitions: it is easily understood, it is easily used to give clear and formal proofs, and it captures at a single blow all desirable security properties — not just for multiparty protocols, but for virtually any kind of interactive computation.

**History of ideas.** In 1988, Beaver [3] developed and generalized the notion of fault-oracles introduced by Galil, Haber, and Yung [12]. Micali and Rogaway [21] independently pursued the same approach. In 1989, after a brief collaboration and exchange of ideas about fault-oracles, Beaver, Micali, and Rogaway employed the fault-oracle approach to security in a joint paper [7].

Beaver found the fault-oracle approach unsatisfactory (for reasons presented within) and went on to develop the ideas presented here. Micali and Rogaway developed the fault-oracle approach further [21] (see also these Proceedings). The reader is strongly encouraged to compare approaches[2] and to decide which is the more natural, the more concise, and the more powerful.

**Contents.** Relative resilience is defined in §2.2 and resilience in §2.3. In §3 we show how resilience captures zero-knowledge and other interactive computations concisely, and we compare it to other approaches to defining security. In §4 we give theorems supporting a modular approach to protocol design and proof, describing the transitivity of security and the security of protocol concatenation.

---

[2]including those presented in [5, 14]

# 2 Defining Security

## 2.1 Ensembles Induced by Protocol Execution

**Preliminaries.** Let $\Sigma = \{0,1\}$ with extra symbols $(\#, \mathbb{C}, \langle, \rangle)$ encoded naturally. Let $[n] = \{1, \ldots, n\}$ and let $\vec{x} = (x_1, \ldots, x_n)$. Let $\text{dist}(X)$ be the set of distributions on some set $X$ (usually finite). Let PFF be the set of functions mapping $(\Sigma^m)^n \to \text{dist}((\Sigma^m)^n)$ described by probabilistic circuit families $\{C_F(n,m)\}$.

The difference between distributions $P, Q \in \text{dist}(X)$ is $|P - Q| = \sum_X |\text{Pr}_P[x] - \text{Pr}_Q[x]|$. A **probabilistic function** is a function whose range contains distributions, namely $f : X \to \text{dist}(Y)$. The **composition** of probabilistic functions $g$ and $f$ is given by $\text{Pr}_{g \circ f(x)}[z] = \sum_y \text{Pr}_{f(x)}[y] \text{Pr}_{g(y)}[z]$. An **ensemble** is a probabilistic function $P : \Sigma^* \times \mathbb{N} \to \text{dist}(\Sigma^*)$ such that $\text{Pr}_{P(z,k)}[x] = 0$ for $|x| > k^c$ and some fixed $c$. Two ensembles $P$ and $Q$ are $O(\delta(k))$-**indistinguishable** ($P \approx^{\delta(k)} Q$) if $(\exists k_0)(\forall k \geq k_0)(\forall z)|P(z,k) - Q(z,k)| < \delta(k)$. Definitions of **perfect** $(O(0))$, **exponential** $(O(d^{-k})$ for some $d)$, **statistical** $(O(k^{-d})$ for all $d > 0)$, and **computational** (for all PPT-tests $T$ and all $d > 0$, $T(P)$ is $O(k^{-d})$-indistinguishable from $T(Q)$) are standard.

**Networks and Protocols.** A **player** is an interactive PPTM having a random tape, input tape, output tape, and work tape. The I/O tapes may encode several $(n)$ different tapes for communication with several machines. The **superstate** $q_i$ of machine $P_i$ is a string describing its finite control, current state, and contents of all tape squares read or written so far. With messages $m_1 \cdots m_j$ written on its input tape, $P_i$ induces a transition $(Q_i, (C_1, M_1) \cdots (C_J, M_J)) \leftarrow \delta(q_i, m_1 \cdots m_j)$, where $(C, M)$ requests that message $M$ be sent on channel $C$.

A **channel** is a probabilistic function $C : \Sigma^* \to \text{dist}(2^{\mathbb{N} \times \mathbb{N} \times \Sigma^*})$. For example, a **private channel** from $i$ to $j$ satisfies $\text{Pr}_{C(m)}[\{(i,j,m)\}] = 1$, while a **broadcast channel** from $i$ is $\text{Pr}_{C(m)}[\{(i,1,m), \ldots, (i,n,m)\}] = 1$. An **oblivious transfer channel** from $i$ to $j$ gives $\text{Pr}_{C(m)}[\{(i,j,(0,0))\}] = \frac{1}{2}$ and $\text{Pr}_{C(m)}[\{(i,j,(1,m))\}] = \frac{1}{2}$. A **network** is a set of channel functions.

**Ensembles describing protocol execution.** A **protocol** is a collection of sets of players $\alpha = \{(P_1, \ldots, P_n)\}_{n \in \mathbb{N}}$. For each $n$ (number of players), $m$ (size of inputs), $k$ (security parameter), $\vec{x} \in (\Sigma^m)^n$ (inputs), and $\vec{a} \in (\Sigma^*)^n$ (auxiliary inputs), a protocol $\alpha$ induces a distribution $\alpha(\vec{x} \cdot \vec{a}, k)$ on outputs and final views;[3] as $z$ ranges over possible $\vec{x} \cdot \vec{a}$ values, this gives an ensemble $[\alpha]$. The messages sent from players in set $A$ to those in $B$ during round $r$ are denoted $\mu(A, B, r)$. Let $R(n, m, k)$ bound the number of rounds until all nonfaulty players halt. Let $\vec{\mu} = \langle \mu([n], 1, r), \ldots, \mu([n], n, r) \rangle$ denote a set of incoming messages, and denote by $\vec{q} \cdot \vec{\mu}$ a global state of the system. Let $Y_i : \Sigma^* \to \Sigma^*$ be an **output function**; the output of $P_i$ is $y_i = Y_i(q_i^{R(n,m,k)})$. The **view** $v_i^r$ of a player at round $r \leq R(n, m, k)$ is the list of states and messages it has seen; in the **memoryless model**, an intermediate view contains only the current state, tape contents, and incoming and outgoing messages. Let $\text{Reformat}(\vec{q} \cdot \vec{\mu}) = \vec{y} \cdot \vec{v}$. A round and an execution of a synchronous

---

[3]If $\vec{x}$ or $\vec{a}$ does not have $n$ components or if some $x_i$ does not have $m$ bits, the distribution gives probability 1 to the empty string.

---

```
Synchronous Protocol Execution
1       For i = 1..n do μⁱⁿ(i,i,0) ← n#m#k#xᵢ#aᵢ      /* (function Init) */
2       For r = 1..R(n,m,k) do
.           For i = 1..n do in parallel
2.1             /* Compute locally (function Local): */
.                   (qᵢʳ, μᵒᵘᵗ(i,[n],r)) ← δ(qᵢʳ⁻¹, μⁱⁿ([n],i,r-1))
2.2             /* Apply channel functions (function Channel): */
.                   μᵈᵉˡ([n],[n],r) ← C(μᵒᵘᵗ([n],[n],r))
2.3             /* Deliver messages output from channels (function Deliver): */
.                   μⁱⁿ([n],[n],r+1) ← μᵈᵉˡ([n],[n],r)
```

Figure 1: Algorithmic description of synchronous, distributed protocol execution.

---

protocol can be expressed as probabilistic functions:

$$\mathbf{Round}(\vec{q}\cdot\vec{\mu}) = \mathbf{Deliver}(\mathbf{Channel}(\mathbf{Local}(\vec{q}\cdot\vec{\mu})))$$
$$\mathbf{Exec}(\vec{x}\cdot\vec{a}) = \mathbf{Reformat}(\mathbf{Round}^{R(n,m,k)}(\mathbf{Init}(\vec{x}\cdot\vec{a}))).$$

Figure 1 describes protocol execution algorithmically.

**Adversaries.** An adversary $\mathcal{A}$ is an interactive TM with one communication line, on which it makes *corruption requests*. A Byzantine adversary requests either the view of a player $i$ or requests to replace outgoing messages from corrupted players. Note that an adversary may change input and random tapes before the protocol starts (*i.e.* before any messages are generated). A passive adversary cannot change messages. If the adversary superstate is $q_A$, let $T = T(q_A)$ denote the set of players it has corrupted. A $t$-**adversary** satisfies $|T(q_A)| \leq t$; an ideal $t$-adversary also satisfies $T(q_A) \subseteq [n]$. A **static** adversary satisfies $T(q_A) = T_0$ for some fixed $T_0$. A rushing, dynamic adversary sees $\mu^{del}(T,T,r)$ (step 2.2) before choosing whom to corrupt and how to corrupt them.

The function **Fault** provides $\mathcal{A}$ with requested information and allows it to compute a new request. The function **Replace** allows $\mathcal{A}$ to change outgoing messages $\mu^{out}(T,[n],r)$, which are then passed through channels, changing some of the messages in $\mu^{del}(T,[n],r)$ in step 2.2. Let $a_A$ be an auxiliary input for $\mathcal{A}$, let $y_A$ denote its output $Y_A(q_A)$, and let $\mathbf{Reformat}(\vec{q}\cdot\vec{\mu}\cdot q_A) = \vec{y}\cdot\vec{v}\cdot y_A$. An execution of a protocol with adversary is:

$$\mathbf{RoundA}(\vec{q}\cdot\vec{\mu}\cdot q_A) = \mathbf{Deliver}(\mathbf{Replace}(\mathbf{Fault}^n(\mathbf{Channel}(\mathbf{Local}(\vec{q}\cdot\vec{\mu}\cdot q_A)))))$$
$$\mathbf{ExecA}(\vec{x}\cdot\vec{a}\cdot a_A) = \mathbf{Reformat}(\mathbf{RoundA}^{R(n,m,k)}(\mathbf{Init}(\vec{x}\cdot\vec{a}\cdot a_A))).$$

An execution thus maps $\vec{x}\cdot\vec{a}\cdot a_A$ to $\vec{y}\cdot\vec{v}\cdot y_A$. The ensemble of outputs induced by a simple adversary attack is the following:

$$[\alpha, \mathcal{A}]' = \vec{y}\cdot y_A = (Y_1(q_1),\ldots,Y_n(q_n),Y_A(q_A))$$

## 2.2 Relative Resilience

**Interfaces.** The principle behind ZK [16] states that the information revealed during a proof is bounded by the fact "$x \in L$" because a simulator can produce an accurate verifier (adversary) view based only on "$x \in L$." This brilliant use of the notion of ensemble indistinguishability [26] covers only half the picture of interaction, though. In addition to *information*, there is the *influence* an adversary has on the outputs of nonfaulty players. ZK-simulation ignores this side because a faulty verifier doesn't "influence" the final output of the prover, which is irrelevant in ZK proof systems — only the verifier's decision is considered. In an interactive protocol, the influence of the adversary is reflected in the distributions on final outputs of nonfaulty players. By examining the ensemble of all outputs, we unify the long list of desired properties (correctness, independence, *etc.*).

To say that $\alpha$ is as secure — *ie.* resilient — as $\beta$ is to say that attacks on $\alpha$ do no better than attacks on $\beta$. An adversary $\mathcal{A}$ attacking $\alpha$ gains *information* and wields *influence* on $\alpha$; its information and influence should be the same as with $\beta$. But $\mathcal{A}$ may be incompatible with $\beta$ for many reasons: the network may differ from protocol $\alpha$, the communication format may differ, *etc.* To allow $\mathcal{A}$ to attack $\beta$, we give it an *interface* $\mathcal{I}$. Interface $\mathcal{I}$ accepts corruption requests from $\mathcal{A}$, performs direct attacks on $\beta$, obtains views $v_i^\beta$ of $\beta$, and returns *pseudo-views* $\dot{v}_i^\alpha$ (apparently of $\alpha$) to $\mathcal{A}$ in response to $\mathcal{A}$'s requests.

The interface should not give $\mathcal{A}$ extra power, though; the combined machine $\mathcal{I}(\mathcal{A})$ acting as an adversary against $\beta$ should not exceed the power allowed to adversaries attacking $\beta$. In cases where adversaries are polynomial-time bounded, this means that the interface itself must be polynomial-time.

**Definition 1** *An* **interface** *is an interactive TM $\mathcal{I}$ with two tapes. On its "environment simulation" tape, $\mathcal{I}$ receives and responds to messages from an adversary; on its "adversarial" tape, $\mathcal{I}$ sends and receives messages as an adversary in its own right. An* **interface from $\alpha$ to $\beta$** *satisfies $\mathcal{I}(\mathcal{A}) \in \text{ADV}_\beta$ for all $\mathcal{A} \in \text{ADV}_\alpha$, where $\text{ADV}_\alpha, \text{ADV}_\beta$ are the respective classes of allowed adversaries for $\alpha, \beta$.*

A preliminary definition illustrates the use of an interface to demonstrate that the information (adversary output) and influence (player outputs) are the same in attacks against $\alpha$ as in $\beta$:

**Definition 2 (Weak Relative Resilience)** *Protocol $\alpha$ is* **weakly as resilient as** *protocol $\beta$ if there exists an interface $\mathcal{I}$ from $\alpha$ to $\beta$ such that for all $\mathcal{A} \in \text{ADV}_\alpha$,*

$$[\alpha, \mathcal{A}]' \approx [\beta, \mathcal{I}(\mathcal{A})]'.$$

**Post Protocol Corruption.** To support protocol concatenation and other issues in modularity, we strengthen this preliminary definition somewhat. In particular, an interface $\mathcal{I}$ from $\alpha$ to $\beta$ should be able to do a good job not only during the execution of $\beta$ but later on, when it may be called upon (as a result of subsequent protocol executions) to respond to requests for new corruptions. Its eternal job is to return outputs and pseudo-views seemingly from $\alpha$. Definition (2), however, says nothing about its ability to do so after protocol $\beta$ is complete.

A **post-protocol corrupting** adversary may, after it sees the end of $\alpha$, generate a request "PPC" to enter a *post-protocol corruption* stage, at which point it receives *all* outputs $\vec{y}$ (but not the views) and then continues to make requests for corruptions in $\alpha$. The interface sees neither the PPC request nor the response $\vec{y}$, but it must continue to answer corruption requests $i$ from $\mathcal{A}$ with (final) pseudo-views $v_i^\alpha$. $\mathcal{I}$ can itself obtain $y_i$ and view $v_i^\beta$ from $\beta$, but the pseudo-$\alpha$-view $\hat{v}_i^\alpha$ that it generates must be accurate enough that, *even knowing all the outputs*,[4] the adversary cannot detect a difference between information from $\mathcal{I}$ and information from corrupting "the real thing," protocol $\alpha$. The interface must satisfy, as usual, $(\forall \mathcal{A} \in \text{ADV}_\alpha)\mathcal{I}(\mathcal{A}) \in \text{ADV}_\beta$.

An execution of a protocol with a post-protocol corrupting adversary induces an ensemble on player and adversary outputs.[5] We denote this ensemble, and the ensemble restricted to adversary output alone or to player outputs alone, as:

$$
\begin{aligned}
{[\alpha, \mathcal{A}]} &= \vec{y} \cdot y_A &= (Y_1(q_1), \ldots, Y_n(q_n), Y_A(q_A)) \\
{[\alpha, \mathcal{A}]}^{Y_A} &= y_A &= Y_A(q_A) \\
{[\alpha, \mathcal{A}]}^{Y_{[n]}} &= \vec{y} &= (Y_1(q_1), \ldots, Y_n(q_n)).
\end{aligned}
$$

When an interface is involved, we write the induced ensembles respectively as $[\beta, \mathcal{I}(\mathcal{A})]$, $[\beta, \mathcal{I}(\mathcal{A})]^{Y_A}$, and $[\beta, \mathcal{I}(\mathcal{A})]^{Y_{[n]}}$.

**Relative Resilience.** With interfaces, post-protocol corruption, and the induced ensembles in hand, the notion of relative resilience can be stated concisely:

**Definition 3 (Relative Resilience)** *Protocol $\alpha$ is as resilient as $\beta$, written $\alpha \succeq \beta$, if there exists an interface $\mathcal{I}$ from $\alpha$ to $\beta$ such that for all $\mathcal{A} \in \text{ADV}_\alpha$,*

$$[\alpha, \mathcal{A}] \approx [\beta, \mathcal{I}(\mathcal{A})].$$

The use of the $\succeq$ symbol is intended. Using Theorem 3 below, it is not hard to show that $\succeq$ defines a partial order. Complexity-theoretic reductions among problems employ a polynomial-time transducer to map one problem to another, thereby comparing their difficulty. Relative resilience is a reduction among protocols, employing an interface to map one protocol to another, thereby comparing their security and reliability.

**Privacy and correctness.** Relative resilience captures *a priori* the notions of privacy and correctness: $\alpha$ is as private as $\beta$ if $[\alpha, \mathcal{A}]^{Y_A} \approx [\beta, \mathcal{I}(\mathcal{A})]^{Y_A}$ and it is as **correct as** $\beta$ if $[\alpha, \mathcal{A}]^{Y_{[n]}} \approx [\beta, \mathcal{I}(\mathcal{A})]^{Y_{[n]}}$. We write these as $\alpha \succeq^{\text{priv}} \beta$ and $\alpha \succeq^{\text{correct}} \beta$, respectively.

**Computational and other issues.** Statistical and computational versions of these definitions are easy modifications using statistical and computational indistinguishability. Some qualifications are necessary in moving from the information-theoretic to the polynomially-bounded scenario. Statements of theorems presented here include polynomial bounds (*eg.* on the number of protocols to concatenate) so that they may apply for each degree of resilience; stronger statements are often possible.

---

[4] Why should $\mathcal{A}$ have *all* outputs? To allow protocol concatenation, we must consider the case that some (naturally ridiculous) later protocol *legitimately* reveals *all protocol-computed* information, which includes all $y$'s — but not all views. $\mathcal{I}$'s efforts must be accurate even in this worst-case situation.

[5] Note that the *player* outputs are the same whether the adversary does post-protocol corruption or not.

## 2.3 Resilience

A real protocol permits an adversary class for which no player is above corruption. An ideal protocol contains one or more *trusted hosts* (players $(n+1), (n+2), \ldots$) who cannot be corrupted. Given a probabilistic finite function $F \in \text{PFF}$, the **ideal protocol for** $F$, $\text{ID}(F)$, has two rounds: (1) each player $i$ sends $x_i$ to host $(n+1)$; (2) host $(n+1)$ computes (or samples) $F(x_1, \ldots, x_n)$ and returns the values (one per player).

**Definition 4 (Resilience)** $\alpha$ *is a t-resilient protocol for* $F$ *if* $\alpha \succeq \text{ID}(F)$, *against t-adversaries.*

# 3  Unifying All Interactive Computations

To demonstrate the conciseness, clarity, and unity of our approach, we redefine a few well-known problems using relative resilience.

**Zero-knowledge.** In the **ideal zero-knowledge proof system**, denoted $\text{ID}(L)$, player $P$ sends $x$ to trusted host $TH$, who calculates whether $x \in L$ and sends "$x \in L$" to $V$ if so. The host otherwise sends "?" to indicate a failed proof. The classical notion of ZKPS [16] is defined in one sentence: A two-party protocol $\alpha = \langle P, V \rangle$ is a **zero-knowledge proof system** for $L$ iff it is as resilient as $\text{ID}(L)$, against static 1-adversaries.

For clarity, let us examine the relation between the two approaches to defining ZK. If the 1 adversary corrupts neither $P$ nor $V$, then resilience ensures that $V$ accepts the correct statement "$x \in L$" from $P$ and checked by the trusted host; *completeness* is satisfied. If the 1-adversary corrupts $P$, resilience ensures that a nonfaulty $V$ never accepts a false statement "$x \in L$"; *soundness* is satisfied. If the 1-adversary corrupts $V$, resilience ensures that the adversary gains no more information than $\mathcal{I}$ corrupting $V$ in the ideal case, where the host ensures that only the statement "$x \in L$" is transmitted.

Notice that a corrupt $P$ does have *influence* over the output of $V$: it can cause $V$ not to believe a proof or it can convince $V$ of a true statement, but its influence is bounded by that permitted in the ideal case. Relative resilience maps the adversary's limitations in the ideal case to the limitations it *should* have in the real case, without having to enumerate all desired properties.

**Secret sharing.** The **ideal vacuous protocol**, $\text{ID}(0)$, returns no result. A *t*-**threshold scheme** is a pair of protocols $(\text{SHA}, \text{REC})$ computing probabilistic functions $(\mathbf{sha}, \mathbf{rec})$ such that

   1.    rec is $t$-robust (*i.e.*, insensitive to $\leq t$ changes in inputs);
   2.    sha is $t$-private (*i.e.*, $\text{ID}(\mathbf{sha}) \succeq \text{ID}(0)$);
   3.    $\text{rec} \circ \mathbf{sha}(x) = x$.

**Other examples.** Byzantine Agreement, Oblivious Transfer, Coin Flipping, Instance-Hiding Schemes, and a host of interactive computations have simple descriptions using relative resilience. These are left to the reader.

**Other recent definitions: their disadvantages; a unified theory.** Several authors [13, 3, 21] have considered the idea of a fault-oracle that performs a single function computation and leaks a subset of the inputs. Extending the ZK-approach, they require a simulator with access to a fault-oracle to generate an adversarial view based on seeing and changing a subset of inputs and receiving a single computation of $F$. Rephrased in the language of relative resilience, a fault-oracle represents a trusted host, and a simulator provides a fixed comparison to the "ideal" protocol. Oracles lack the flexibility of allowing comparisons among various protocols (and exclude those not designed to "compute a function") and do not support an obvious modular framework. For example, it is not clear how the concatenation of two secure protocols may be proven secure without altering the definitions, since the security of each is proven with respect to a separate oracle call, while the simulator for the concatenated protocol may make only one oracle call. The notion of transitivity of security is not expressible in terms of fault-oracles.

The legal-version approach says that a protocol is "legal-robust" if every execution with an adversary corresponds to an execution in which all players behave, except that the inputs of some subset may be different [5, 14]. This approach is again a fixed comparison to an essentially ideal situation, lacking flexibility and modularity. In the language of relative resilience: define the **ideal version** $\text{ID}(\alpha)$ of a protocol $\alpha$ to be the ideal protocol in which the trusted host (1) receives inputs and random tapes from each player and (2) *internally* runs $\alpha$ (without corruption), returning the outputs (not the internal views) to the players. Then, a protocol $\alpha$ is **legal-robust** if the *fixed* comparison $\alpha \succeq \text{ID}(\alpha)$ holds.

# 4    Folk Theorems and Modular Proof Techniques

Many intuitively justified approaches become provable using relative resilience. Resilience brings to light several pitfalls overlooked by imprecisely stated folk theorems. The contribution of this section is a formal statement of provable theorems and the necessary conditions under which they hold. We sketch the proofs; full versions require a little more space than here permitted.

The composition of $f(z, k)$ ensembles is $P^f(z, k) = P_{f(z,k)} \circ \cdots \circ P_1(z, k)$. Protocol concatenation is defined naturally. The concatenation of $f(n, m, k)$ protocols is $\alpha^f(\vec{x} \cdot \vec{a}, k) = \alpha_{f(n,m,k)} \circ \cdots \circ \alpha_1(\vec{x} \cdot \vec{a}, k)$.

The mathematical distinction between uniform and pointwise convergence of functions has a probabilistic counterpart: two families $\{P_i\}$ and $\{Q_i\}$ of ensembles are **uniformly** $O(\delta_i(z, k))$**-indistinguishable** if $(\exists k_0)(\forall i)(\forall k \geq k_0)(\forall z)|P_i(z, k) - Q_i(z, k)| < \delta_i(z, k)$. The term *uniform* does *not* refer to Turing machine computability. We say that protocol family $\{\alpha_i\}$ is **uniformly as $t$-resilient as** family $\{\beta_i\}$ if the ensemble families $\{[\alpha_i, \mathcal{A}]\}$ and $\{[\beta_i, \mathcal{I}(\mathcal{A})]\}$ are uniformly indistinguishable.

*Uniform* convergence is necessary to the following theorems; counterexamples are otherwise easy to find (see below and [2]), showing that folk theorems cannot be applied without care. Luckily for many presumably secure applications, any two *finite* families of ensembles are uniformly indistinguishable if each pair of corresponding ensembles are indistinguishable.

**Lemma 1 (Composing poly-many ensembles)** *If $\{P_i\}$ is uniformly indistinguishable from $\{Q_i\}$ and if $f(z,k)$ is polynomially bounded, then $P^f \approx Q^f$.*

**Proof.** We sketch a proof for perfect and statistical indistinguishability appearing in [2, 4]; the proof for computational indistinguishability is direct and follows the same lines. Unlike probability-walk proofs in other settings, we must explicitly consider the convergence rates — serendipity does not allow us to omit them. Assume by way of contradiction that $\{P_i\}$ is uniformly $\delta_i(z,k)$-indistinguishable from $\{Q_i\}$ and $f$ is poly-bounded, but that $P^f$ is not $\delta(z,k)$-indistinguishable from $Q^f$, where $\delta(z,k) = \sum_{i=1}^{f(z,k)} \delta_i(z,k)$. Let $k_0$ be the uniform convergence parameter. Define $R_l = P_{f(z,k)} \circ \cdots \circ P_l \circ Q_{l-1} \circ \cdots \circ Q_1$. Then for some $k \geq k_0$ and for some $z$,

$$
\begin{aligned}
\sum_{i=1}^{f(z,k)} \delta_i(z,k) &< \sum_z |P_{f(z,k)} \circ \cdots \circ P_1(z,k) - Q_{f(z,k)} \circ \cdots \circ Q_1(z,k)| \\
&\leq \sum_z |R_0 - R_1 + R_1 - R_2 + \cdots + R_{f(z,k)-1} - R_{f(z,k)}| \\
&\leq \sum_z \sum_{i=1}^{f(z,k)} |R_{i-1}(z,k) - R_i(z,k)|.
\end{aligned}
$$

Reversing the order of summation, it follows that for some $i$, $\delta_i(z,k) < \sum_z |R_{i-1}(z,k) - R_i(z,k)|$. From here it is straightforward to show that this demonstrates $P_i$ is not $\delta_i(z,k)$-indistinguishable from $Q_i$ for this $k \geq k_0$, a contradiction. $\square$

A counterexample is easy to describe for *nonuniform* convergence [2]; for example, define:

$$
\begin{aligned}
\Pr_{P_i(z,k)}[0] &= 1 \quad \text{if } k < 2i \\
\Pr_{P_i(z,k)}[1] &= 1 \quad \text{if } k \geq 2i \\
\Pr_{Q_i(z,k)}[1] &= 1 \quad \text{always.}
\end{aligned}
$$

Clearly, for all $i$, $P_i \approx^{O(2^{-k})} Q_i$ since $(\forall i, z)(\forall k \geq 2i)P_i(z,k) = Q_i(z,k)$. Letting $f(z,k) = k$, we see $(\forall z,k)\Pr_{P^f(z,k)}[0] = 1$, because $P^f(z,k) = P_k(P_{k-1}(\cdots),k)$ and $k < 2k$. On the other hand, $(\forall z,k)\Pr_{Q^f(z,k)}[0] = 0$. Hence $(\forall z,k)|P^f(z,k) - Q^f(z,k)| = 2 \neq O(k2^{-k})$, a contradiction. Uniformity of convergence is also necessary when comparing polynomially-many protocols:

**Theorem 2 (Concatenating poly-many protocols)** *If $\{\alpha_i\}$ is uniformly as $t$-resilient as $\{\beta_i\}$ and if $f(n,m,k)$ is polynomially bounded, then $\alpha^f \succeq \beta^f$.*

**Proof.** We sketch a few salient points, following our proof for statistical resilience in [2]. The main idea is to construct an interface $\mathcal{I}$ from $\alpha^f$ to $\beta^f$, using interfaces $\mathcal{I}_i$ between each pair $\alpha_i$ and $\beta_i$. Each interface is taken without loss of generality[6] to be *canonical*, ie.

---

[6]A simple argument demonstrates that no generality is lost for information-theoretic settings; a qualification must be made when defining computational resilience.

the set of corruption requests by $\mathcal{I}_i$ against $\beta_i$ is always a subset of those requested by $\mathcal{A}_i$. Using Lemma 1, the two ensembles $[\alpha^f, \mathcal{I}(\mathcal{A})]$ and $[\beta^f, \mathcal{I}(\mathcal{A})]$ are shown indistinguishable. $\square$

**Theorem 3 (Transitivity of $\succeq$)** $\alpha \succeq \beta$ *and* $\beta \succeq \gamma$ *implies* $\alpha \succeq \gamma$. *Polynomially many applications work as well: If* $\{\alpha_{i+1}\}$ *is* uniformly *as t-resilient as* $\{\alpha_i\}$,[7] *and if* $f(n, m, k)$ *is polynomially bounded, then* $\alpha^f \succeq \alpha_0$.

**Proof.** See [2, 4]; the interface $\mathcal{I}$ from $\alpha^f$ to $\alpha_0$ internally runs $f(n, m, k)$ nested subinterfaces $\mathcal{I}_{f,f-1} \circ \cdots \circ \mathcal{I}_{2,1} \circ \mathcal{I}_{1,0}$. We consider canonical interfaces as in the proof of Theorem 2. $\square$

## 4.1 The Share-Compute-Reveal Paradigm

Define $\text{hide}(H) = \text{sha} \circ H \circ \text{rec}$, the probabilistic function that reconstructs a secretly-shared value, computes $H$, and shares it again. The share-compute-reveal paradigm [18, 19, 8, 11] for multiparty protocols is to express $F$ as $F^f = \circ_1^f F_i$ and compute $\text{rec} \circ [\circ_1^f \text{hide}(F_i)] \circ \text{sha}$. That is, inputs are secretly shared; intermediate values are secretly computed but not revealed; then the final output is reconstructed. The formal and fully provable statement of this methodology is as follows:

**Theorem 4 ("Completeness" paradigm)** *Let* $(\text{SHA}, \text{REC})$ *be a t-threshold scheme, and let* $F = F^f = \circ_1^f F_i$ *for some polynomially bounded* $f(n, m, k)$. *If* $\{\alpha_i\}$ *is* uniformly *as t-resilient as* $\{\text{ID}(\text{hide}(F_i))\}$, *then*

$$\text{REC} \circ [\circ_1^f \alpha_i] \circ \text{SHA} \succeq \text{ID}(F).$$

**Proof.** *Uniformity* is essential. The proof uses Theorems 2 and 3 and the robustness and privacy of $(\text{rec}, \text{sha})$ but is omitted (*cf.* [2, 4], however). $\square$

# 5 Summary

A correct, concise, and useful formulation of security and fault-tolerance is necessary to a proper foundation of the theory and practice of cryptography. We are happy to provide proofs of our theorems upon request and are even happier to discuss them openly and to develop our methodology further.

We have emphasized the important point that protocol security must be treated in a unified manner: security and reliability (privacy and correctness) are two sides of the same coin. Treating a variety of properties separately leads to confusion.

---

[7]Roughly speaking, $(\forall i)\alpha_{i+1} \succeq \alpha_i$ — with uniform convergence.

To say that a protocol is secure is to say it achieves the results of an ideal protocol. Our formal definition of relative resilience states precisely what it means for one protocol to achieve the results of another, avoiding the inflexibility inherent in fault-oracle approaches. Relative resilience provides a natural *reduction* among protocols that supports concise and modular proofs, inspiring newfound confidence in theoretical cryptography and resulting in clearer and more efficient design of provably secure protocols.

# References

[1] M. Abadi, J. Feigenbaum, J. Kilian. "On Hiding Information from an Oracle." J. Comput. System Sci. 39 (1989), 21-50.

[2] D. Beaver. "Secure Multiparty Protocols and Zero Knowledge Proof Systems Tolerating a Faulty Minority." To appear, *J. Cryptology*. An earlier version appeared as "Secure Multiparty Protocols Tolerating Half Faulty Processors." *Proceedings of Crypto 1989*, ACM, 1989.

[3] D. Beaver. "Formal Definitions for Secure Distributed Protocols." *Proceedings of the DIMACS Workshop on Distributed Computing and Cryptography*, Princeton, NJ, October, 1989, J. Feigenbaum, M. Merritt (eds.).

[4] D. Beaver. *Security, Fault Tolerance, and Communication Complexity in Distributed Systems*. PhD Thesis, Harvard University, Cambridge, 1990.

[5] D. Beaver, S. Goldwasser. "Multiparty Computation with Faulty Majority." *Proceedings of the $30^{th}$ FOCS*, IEEE, 1989, 468-473.

[6] D. Beaver, S. Haber. "Cryptographic Protocols Provably Secure Against Dynamic Adversaries." Submitted to FOCS 91.

[7] D. Beaver, S. Micali, P. Rogaway. "The Round Complexity of Secure Protocols." *Proceedings of the $22^{st}$ STOC*, ACM, 1990, 503-513.

[8] M. Ben-Or, S. Goldwasser, A. Wigderson. "Completeness Theorems for Non-Cryptographic Fault-Tolerant Distributed Computation." *Proceedings of the $20^{th}$ STOC*, ACM, 1988, 1-10.

[9] R. Blakley. "Security Proofs for Information Protection Systems." *Proceedings of the 1980 Symposium on Security and Privacy*, IEEE Computer Society Press, New York, 1981, 79-88.

[10] G. Brassard, D. Chaum, C. Crépeau. "Minimum Disclosure Proofs of Knowledge." J. Comput. System Sci. 37 (1988), 156-189.

[11] D. Chaum, C. Crépeau, I. Damgård. "Multiparty Unconditionally Secure Protocols." *Proceedings of the $20^{th}$ STOC*, ACM, 1988, 11-19.

[12] Z. Galil, S. Haber, M. Yung. "Cryptographic Computation: Secure Fault-Tolerant Protocols and the Public-Key Model." *Proceedings of Crypto 1987*, Springer-Verlag, 1988, 135-155.

[13] Z. Galil, S. Haber, and M. Yung. "Minimum-Knowledge Interactive Proofs for Decision Problems." *SIAM J. Comput.* 18:4 (1989), 711–739.

[14] S. Goldwasser, L. Levin. "Fair Computation of General Functions in Presence of Immoral Majority." *Proceedings of Crypto 1990.*

[15] S. Goldwasser, S. Micali. "Probabilistic Encryption." *J. Comput. System Sci.* **28** (1984), 270–299.

[16] S. Goldwasser, S. Micali, C. Rackoff. "The Knowledge Complexity of Interactive Proof Systems." *SIAM J. Comput.* 18:1 (1989), 186–208.

[17] S. Goldwasser, M. Sipser. "Private Coins vs. Public Coins in Interactive Proof Systems." *Proceedings of the 18th STOC,* ACM, 1986, 59–68.

[18] O. Goldreich, S. Micali, A. Wigderson. "Proofs that Yield Nothing but Their Validity and a Methodology of Cryptographic Protocol Design." *Proceedings of the 27th FOCS,* IEEE, 1986, 174–187.

[19] O. Goldreich, S. Micali, A. Wigderson. "How to Play Any Mental Game, or A Completeness Theorem for Protocols with Honest Majority." *Proceedings of the 19th STOC,* ACM, 1987, 218–229.

[20] S. Haber. *Multi-Party Cryptographic Computation: Techniques and Applications,* PhD Thesis, Columbia University, 1988.

[21] S. Micali, P. Rogaway. "The Notion of Secure Computation." Unpublished Manuscript, 1990.

[22] S. Micali, P. Rogaway. "Secure Computation." These Proceedings (*Crypto 1991*), page 9.8.

[23] Y. Oren. "On the Cunning Power of Cheating Verifiers: Some Observations about Zero Knowledge Proofs." *Proceedings of the 19th STOC,* ACM, 1987, 462–471.

[24] T. Rabin, M. Ben-Or. "Verifiable Secret Sharing and Multiparty Protocols with Honest Majority." *Proceedings of the 21st STOC,* ACM, 1989, 73–85.

[25] A. Shamir. "How to Share a Secret." *Communications of the ACM,* **22** (1979), 612–613.

[26] A. Yao, "Theory and Applications of Trapdoor Functions." *Proceedings of the 23rd FOCS,* IEEE, 1982, 80–91.

[27] A. Yao. "How to Generate and Exchange Secrets." *Proceedings of the 27th FOCS,* IEEE, 1986, 162–167.

# Secure Computation

## (Abstract)

Silvio Micali[*]        Phillip Rogaway[†]

### Abstract

We define what it means for a network of communicating players to *securely* compute a function of privately held inputs. Intuitively, we wish to *correctly* compute its value in a manner which protects the *privacy* of each player's contribution, even though a powerful *adversary* may endeavor to disrupt this enterprise.

This highly general and desirable goal has been around a long time, inspiring a large body protocols, definitions, and ideas, starting with Yao [1982, 1986] and Goldreich, Micali and Wigderson [1987]. But all the while, it had resisted a full and satisfactory formulation.

Our definition is built on several new ideas. Among them:

- Closely mimicking an *ideal evaluation*. A *secure* protocol must mimic this abstraction in a *run-by-run* manner, our definition depending as much on individual executions as on global properties of ensembles.

- *Blending* privacy and correctness in a novel way, using a *special type of simulator* designed for the purpose.

- Requiring *adversarial awareness*—capturing the idea that the adversary should know, in a very strong sense, certain information associated to the execution of a protocol.

Among the noteworthy and desirable properties of our definition is the *reducibility* of secure protocols, which we believe to be a cornerstone in a mature theory of secure computation.

## Invocation

The last decade has witnessed the rise of *secure computation* as a new and exciting mathematical subject. This is the study of communication protocols allowing several parties to perform a correct computation on some inputs that are and should be kept private. As a simple example, the parties want to compute the tally of some privately held votes. This new discipline is extremely subtle, involving in novel ways fundamental concepts such as probabilism, information, and complexity theory.

In the making of a new science, finding the *right* definitions can be one of the most difficult tasks: from relatively few examples, one should handle cases that have not yet arisen and reach the highest possible level of generality. It is the purpose of this work both to identify the right notion of secure computation and prove the right fundamental properties about it.

In the last few years, cryptography has been very successful in identifying its basic objectives, properly defining them, and successfully solving them. Secure encryption, secure pseudorandom generation, secure digital signatures, and zero-knowledge proofs—concepts that appeared forever elusive—have all found successful formalizations and solutions. But in contrast to these successes,

---

[*]MIT Laboratory for Computer Science, 545 Technology Square, Cambridge, MA 02139.

[†]IBM, 11400 Burnet Road, Austin, TX 78758. Work performed in part while the author was at the MIT Laboratory for Computer Science, and in part while at Dartmouth College.

J. Feigenbaum (Ed.): Advances in Cryptology - CRYPTO '91, LNCS 576, pp. 392-404, 1992.
© Springer-Verlag Berlin Heidelberg 1992

and despite many beautiful and fundamental ideas that preceded us, not even a satisfactory *definition* of a secure protocol has been proposed so far. This is not surprising, since protocols are extremely complex objects: after all, by defining security for encryption, signatures, and pseudorandom generation, one is defining properties of algorithms; but to properly define protocol security, one needs instead to define properties of the *interaction* of several algorithms, some of which may be deliberately designed to *disrupt* the joint computation in clever ways. The intricacy of this scenario has often encouraged researchers to work either with definitions of security tailored to the problem at hand; or to consider broad definitions, but restricted to specific computational tasks; or to work with only intuitive notions in mind.

Lack of universally accepted definitions can only create confusion and mistakes, and it is only by reaching an *exact* understanding of what we can expect from a secure protocol that can we safely rely on them and further develop them. Powerful computer networks are already in place and the possibility of using them for new and wonderful tasks will largely depend on how successful this development will be.

## In These Proceedings

A full description of our notion of secure computation is beyond the scope of a proceedings' abstract. For this article, we have revised the introduction to [MR91], incorporating a *very* high-level description of the definition and a brief comparison with other notions which have been offered in the literature.

## Secure-Computation Problems

What is secure computation about? Informally, it consists of finding a communication *protocol* that allows a group of *players* to accomplish a special type of *task*, despite the fact that some of them may try to sabotage this enterprise. This said, we now explain terms. Let's start with the easy ones.

*Players* (also called *processors* or *parties* for variation of discourse) can be thought as people, each possessing a personal computer, and capable of exchanging messages. A *protocol* is a set of instructions for the players to follow for sending these messages. The rules of the game are as follows: (1) in executing a protocol, some of the participants may be *bad*, thereby disregarding their instructions and cooperating to disrupt the joint effort; (2) no trusted device or external entity is available; (3) every good party can perform private computation (i.e., computation unmonitored by the bad players).

What is a secure protocol supposed to accomplish? We start by looking at a few archetypal examples. Since our aim is to exemplify various issues and key desiderata that may inspire us to properly define secure computation, in the following list we credit the one who first *posed* the problem.

1. THE MILLIONAIRES PROBLEM (Yao, [Ya82a]). Two millionaires wish to find out who is richer, though neither is willing to reveal the extent of his fortune. Can they carry out a conversation which identifies the richer millionaire, but doesn't divulge additional information about either's wealth?

2. THE DIGITAL VOTING PROBLEM (Chaum, [Ch81]). Is it possible for a group of computer users to hold a secret-ballot election on a computer network?

3. THE INDEPENDENT ANNOUNCEMENT PROBLEM (Chor, Goldwasser, Micali, and Awerbuch [CGMA85]). A group of players want to exchange messages so as to announce their secret

values independently. That is, what the bad players announce cannot be chosen based on the values of the good players.

4. THE COIN FLIPPING PROBLEM (Blum, [Bl82]). How can Alice and Bob, speaking to one another over the telephone, agree on a random, unbiased coin flip—even if one of them cheats to try to produce a coin flip of a certain outcome?

5. THE OBLIVIOUS TRANSFER PROBLEM (Rabin, [Ra81]). Is it possible for Alice to send to Bob a message $m$ in such a way that (i) half the time, Bob gets $m$; (ii) the other half of the time, Bob gets nothing; and (iii) Alice never knows which of the two events has occurred?

6. THE MENTAL POKER PROBLEM (Shamir, Rivest and Adleman, [SRA81]). Can a group of players properly shuffle and deal a deck of cards over the phone?

## Privacy and Correctness

Even the above short list illustrates the enormous variety of types of goals for secure protocols. There may be two parties or many. The output of a protocol may be a single value known to all players (as in digital voting), or to only one of them (as in an oblivious transfer), or it may be a private value for each player (as in mental poker). The output may depend on the players' initial state deterministically (as in the first three problems), or probabilistically (as in the last three problems).

What do such heterogeneous problems have in common, then? Essentially, that the joint computation should both be *private* and *correct*: while preserving the privacy of individually held data, the joint computation manages to correctly perform some computational task based on this data. Correctness and privacy may seem to be conflicting requirements, and capturing in the most general sense what simultaneously meeting them means (within our rules of the game) is quite difficult. As we explain in the full paper, to obtain a satisfactory notion of security privacy and correctness should not be handled independently (like in all prior work), but need to be *blended* in the proper way.

## Prior and Related Definitions

Y-EVALUATION. Distilling a common thread in many prior examples of secure computation, Yao proposed the following general problem [Ya82a]. Assume we have $n$ parties, $1, \ldots, n$. Each party $i$ has a *private* input, $x_i$, known only to him. The parties want to compute a given function $f$ on their own inputs while maintaining the privacy of these inputs. In other words, they want to compute $y = f(x_1, \ldots, x_n)$ without revealing to any player more about the private inputs than the output itself implicitly reveals. If the function is vector-valued, $\vec{y} = f(x_1, \ldots, x_n)$, where $\vec{y}$ has $n$ components, it is desired that every party $i$ privately learn the $i$-th component of $\vec{y}$.

Yao also proposed a notion for what it means for a protocol to solve the above problem. Roughly said, his formalization attempts to capture the idea that the worst the bad players can do to disrupt a computation is to choose alternative inputs for themselves, or quit in the middle of the computation. We will refer to this notion of security as *Y-evaluation*. Subsequently [Ya86], Yao strengthened his notion of a Y-evaluation so as to incorporate some *fairness* constraint. A fair protocol is one in which there is very little advantage to be gained by quitting in the middle. That is, the protocol takes care that, at each point during the execution, the "informational gap" among the players is small. The study of fair protocols was started earlier by Luby, Micali and Rackoff [LMR83], and progressed with the contributions of [Ya86, BG89, GL90].

GMW-GAMES. A more general notion for security has been introduced by Goldreich, Micali and Wigderson [GMW87]. They consider secure protocols as implementations of abstract, but computable, games of partial information. Informally, ingredients of such an $n$-player game are an arbitrary set of *states*, a set of *moves* (functions from states to states), a set of *knowledge functions* (defined on the states), and a vector-valued *outcome function* (defined on the states) whose range values have as many components as there are players. The players wish to start the game by probabilistically selecting an initial global state, unknown to everyone. Then the players take turns making moves. When it is the turn of player $i$, a portion $K(S)$ of the current global state $S$ must be privately revealed to him; here $K$ denotes the proper knowledge function for this stage of the game. Based on this private information, player $i$ secretly selects a move $\mu$, thereby the new, secret, state must become $\mu(S)$. At the end of the game, each player privately learns his own component of the outcome function evaluated at the final state.

[GMW87] envisioned a notion of security which would mimic the abstract game in a "virtual" manner: states are virtually selected, moves act on virtual states, and so on. We will refer to their notion as *GMW-games*. Again putting aside how this can be achieved, let us point out an additional aspect of their notion: namely, in a GMW-game, bad players cannot disrupt the computation *at all* by quitting early. (This condition can indeed be enforced, in a certain communication model, whenever the majority of the players are honest )

OTHER PRIOR WORK. Several noteworthy variants of Y-evaluation and GMW-games have been proposed, with varying degrees of explicitness and care. These definitional ideas include, most notably, the work of Galil, Haber and Yung [GHY87], Chaum, Damgård and van de Graff [CDG87], Ben-Or, Goldwasser and Wigderson [BGW88], Chaum, Crépeau and Damgård [CCD88], Kilian [Ki89], and Crépeau [Cr90].

CONCURRENT WORK. Early in our effort we told our initial ideas (like merging privacy and correctness) to Beaver, who later pursued his own ones in [Be91a, Be91b].

Later, we collaborated with Kilian in developing definitions for secure function evaluation. This collaboration was enjoyable and profitable, and its fruits are described in [KMR90].

Concurrently with the effort of [KMR90], Goldwasser and Levin [GL90] independently proposed an interesting approach to defining secure function evaluation.

## Critique of These Definitions

Definitions cannot, of course, be "wrong" in an absolute sense; but we feel that all previous ones were either vague, or not sufficiently general, or considered "secure" protocols that should have not been called such at a closer analysis. We thus cheerfully decided to clarify the intuitive notion of secure computation. Little we knew that we had taken up a two-year commitment!

Let us very briefly critique some of the mentioned work.

Y-EVALUATION. Though Yao should be credited for presenting his notion with great detail[1], in our opinion his ideas do not fully capture the fundamental intuition of secure computation, leading to several difficulties.

*Blind input correlation.* One of these difficulties we call "blind input correlation." Namely, a two-party Y-evaluation, while preventing a bad player from directly learning the good player's input, might allow him to choose his own input so to be correlated with the good player's. For example, it

---

[1]This precision, however, was made heavier from lacking more modern constructs for discussing these issues, like the notion of a simulator developed by Goldwasser, Micali and Rackoff [GMR89].

is not ruled out that, whenever the good player starts with secret input $x$, the bad player, without finding out what $x$ was, can force the output to be, say, $y = f(x, x)$ (or $y = f(x, -x)$, or ...). In some context, this correlation may result in (what would be considered by most people) a loss of security.[2]

*Privacy/correctness separation.* Y-evaluation considers privacy and correctness as separate constraints and, though with a different terminology, considers secure a protocol that is *both* private and correct. Indeed, privacy and correctness are the fundamental aspects of secure computation, but, as we describe in the full paper, the logical connective "and" *does not* combine them adequately together. In particular, there exists functions $f$ and protocols $P$ such that, under most reasonable-sounding definitions (including Yao's), $P$ correctly computes $f$; and $P$ is private leaking only $f$; and yet $P$ is definitely not a good protocol to securely compute $f$. Basically, the problem is that there can be *tradeoffs* between privacy and correctness, and simply demanding their conjunct does not respect this possible interplay.

GMW-GAMES. GMW-games are most general and powerful, and they are endowed with very strong intuitive appeal. However, the author's main goal was to propose the first general solution to the problem of securely evaluating a function, and so they were less concerned with arriving at a fully general, "protocol-independent" notion of security. In particular, the authors notion of security was tailored for protocols that begin with a "commit" stage, and then perform computation on these committed inputs. While their algorithmic structure has proved to be very successful (indeed, all subsequent protocols designed for the task share it), it should not be embedded in the general definition of our goal. Finally, the authors did not provide full help in their proceedings paper for turning the intuition described into a successful formalization, and several wrong choices could still be made from the level their definition was left at.

CONCURRENT WORK. Concurrent work does not suffer from this drawback, but has other shortcomings. Beaver [Be91a] does not blend the various goals for a secure protocol, but treats them as separate requirements, as Yao first did and incurring in the same type of difficulties. In [Be91b], the author avoids this problem, but offers a notion of security weaker than ours (once cast in the same framework), and one which calls "secure" some protocols which we feel should not be considered as such. Security in the sense of Goldwasser and Levin, in turn, seems to be weaker than the simulation-based notion of [Be91b]. Both, then, admit pitfalls including the following:

*Privacy/correctness unification.* If Yao goes to one extreme in separating privacy and correctness, [GL90, Be91b] go to the other, completely merging them. We do not have space to adequately describe their definitions, but the net result is that if privacy is to be achieved in a computational sense (which, for example is necessarily the case when everyone communicates on a broadcast channel, using encryption to hide private inputs), then correctness also is achieved in a computational sense. While it is OK to say that the adversary cannot understand someone's input because she does not have the resources to make sense of it, it is less acceptable to output wrong results and just be saved by the fact that they "look right" with respect to time-bounded computation. Consider, for instance, the computation that consists of outputting a random quadratic reside modulo

---

[2] Let's see what its effects might be on some of the discussed secure-computation problems. Consider solving the digital voting problem by Y-evaluating the tally function. Then the bad players —though ignoring the electoral intentions of a given good player— might succeed in voting as a block for the opposite candidate. Should we consider this a secure election? We believe not. Similarly, trying to solve the independent announcement problem by Y-evaluating the "concatenation" function (i.e., the function that, on inputs $x_1, \ldots, x_n$, returns the single value $x_1\#\ldots\#x_n$), a bad player might always succeed in announcing the same value as a given good player. Indeed, a poor case of independence!

a composite number whose factorization is unknown by the players. Then a secure protocol in the sense of [GL90] or [Be91b] may well consist of outputting a random quadratic nonresidue of Jacobi symbol +1. Under the proper complexity assumption, no one can notice the difference—yet it seems (to us) that this protocol is not a correct one for performing the specified task.

*Input absence.* Sometimes we define a function part of the purpose of which is to check that its inputs fall in some relation to one another: for simplicity, consider $f(\bar{x}) = 1$ if $x \in OK$, $f(\bar{x}) = 0$ otherwise. A secure computation of $f$ should, when it evaluates to 1, convince the participants that they collectively hold an $\bar{x} \in OK$. However, protocols secure in the sense of [GL90] or [Be91b] allow the good players to each output a 1 even though the bad guys have never chosen their contribution $\bar{x}'_T$—and, in fact, even when there is no such contribution which would result in the function evaluating to 1!

*Reducibility?* In light of the difficulty of designing secure protocols, it is essential that the definition of security supports a "reducibility property" which ensures the possibility of constructing complex secure protocols by properly combining simpler secure protocols in a black-box manner. (This will be further described shortly.) Unfortunately, we do not see any way of proving the reducibility property we are after from their alternative definitions.

## Our Definitions

Our notion of *secure computation* solves the above difficulties, and other ones as well. We plan to build up our definition in two stages. First, as our alternative to Y-evaluation, we define *secure function evaluation*, to which this paper is devoted. Our notion is quite powerful and expressive; for instance, the first three secure-computation problems described earlier are straightforwardly solvable by securely evaluating the proper function. After developing secure function evaluation, we hint how this notion can be successfully extended to that of a *secure game*, our way of fully specifying GMW-games. (The full paper is already quite long, and a different one should be devoted to a detailed treatment of this extension. Also, the present treatment restricts its definitions to there being three or more players.) Secure games capture, in our opinion, the very notion of secure computation. Quite reassuringly, all six problems specified earlier are straightforwardly solved by "playing" a secure game.

The basic intuition behind secure function evaluation is the same one put forward, in quite a different language, by [GMW87]. In essence, two scenarios are considered: an *ideal* one in which there is a trusted party helping in the function evaluation, and a *realistic* one in which the trusted party is simulated by running a protocol. Security is a property of a realistic evaluation, and consists of achieving "indistinguishability" from the corresponding ideal evaluation. While remaining quite informal, let us at least be less succinct.

IDEAL FUNCTION EVALUATION. In an ideal function evaluation of a vector-valued function $f$ there is an external *trusted party* to whom the participants privately give their respective secret inputs. The trusted entity will not divulge the received inputs; rather, it will correctly evaluate function $f$ on them, and will privately hand component $i$ of the result to party $i$. An *adversary* can interfere with this evaluation as follows. At the very beginning, before any party has given his own input to the trusted party, she can corrupt a first player and learn his private input. After this, and possibly based on what she has just learned, the adversary may corrupt a second player and learn this input, too. This continues until the adversary is satisfied. At this point, the adversary chooses alternative, *fake* inputs for the corrupted players, and all parties give the their inputs to the trusted authority—the uncorrupted players giving their initial inputs, and the corrupted players giving their new, fake inputs. When the proper, individual outputs have been returned by the trusted party, the adversary learns the value of the output of every corrupted player. The adversary can still corrupt, one by one, additional players, learning both their inputs and outputs when she does so.

It should be noticed that in such an ideal evaluation the adversary not only learns the inputs of the players she corrupts, but by choosing properly their substitutes, she may learn from the function's output value quite a bit about the other inputs as well.

IDEAL VS. SECURE FUNCTION EVALUATION. While the notion of an ideal function evaluation has been essentially defined above, formalizing the notion of a secure function evaluation is much more complex; we will do it in the next few sections. Here let us just give its basic intuition. To begin with, there no longer is any trusted party; the players will instead try to simulate one by means of a protocol. The adversary can still corrupt players, but this time a corruption will be much more "rewarding." For not only will she learn the private inputs of corrupted players, but also their current computational state in the protocol (and a bit of additional information as well). She will receive all future message addressed to them and she will get control of what messages they are responsible for sending out.

Given the greater power of the adversary in this new setting, it is intuitively clear that a protocol for function evaluation cannot perform "better" than an ideal function evaluation; but it can do much worse! Roughly said, a secure function evaluation consists of simulating *every important aspect* of an ideal function evaluation, to the *maximum extent possible*, so that a secure protocol does *not* perform "significantly worse" than the corresponding ideal protocol.

Setting the stage of security in terms of the above indistinguishability is an important insight of the [GMW87] work. The main difference with their work, though, and the real difficulty of ours, is not so much in the spirit of the solution as in properly realizing what "maximum possible" should mean, and identifying what are the important features, implicit (and perhaps hidden) in an ideal function evaluation that should (and can!) be mimicked in a secure function evaluation.

We point out that none of the alternative definitions proposed for secure function evaluation is motivated by attempting to mimic the ideal evaluation of a function in so direct and strong a manner. Rather, they intend that a protocol should be called "secure" if and only if it is, intuitively, a secure computation. We, instead, are willing to call "secure" only those protocols which mimic the ideal evaluation extremely closely—even if this means excluding "intuitively correct" protocols from being called "secure."

## Key Features of Our Definitions

Let us now highlight the key features of our definitions. These we distinguish as *choices* and *properties*. The former are key technical ideas of our notion of security. The latter are key desiderata: each one is a *condition-sine-qua-non* for calling a protocol secure. Notice, though, that we do not force these necessary conditions into our definitions in an artificial manner; rather, we derive them naturally as consequences (hence the name "properties") of our notion of security, and thus of our technical choices.

### Key Choices

BLENDING PRIVACY AND CORRECTNESS. Secure protocols are more than just correct and private. Simply requiring simultaneous meeting of these two requirements leads to several "embarrassing" situations. In a secure protocol, correctness and privacy are *blended* a deeper manner. In particular, privacy —a meaningful notion all by itself— is taken to mean that the protocol admits a certain type of *simulator*, and correctness is a concept which we define *through the same simulator* proving the protocol private. This merging of privacy and correctness avoids calling secure protocols those which clearly are not, and is a main contribution of this paper, as well as one of our first achievements in the course of this research. We are pleased to see that our idea has been adopted by other researchers in the area.

ADVERSARIAL AWARENESS. In the ideal evaluation of $f$, not only is there a notion of what inputs the adversary has substituted for the original ones of the corrupted players, but also that she is *aware* of what these substituted inputs are! Similarly, she is *aware* of the outputs handed by the trusted party to the corrupted players. We realize that this is a crucial aspect of ideal evaluation, and thus one that should be preserved as closely as possible by secure evaluation. Indeed, *adversarial awareness* is an essential ingredient in obtaining the crucial *reducibility* property discussed below.

TIGHT MIMICRY. Our definition of a secure protocol mimics the ideal evaluation of a function $f$ in a very "tight" manner. (For those familiar with the earlier definition of zero knowledge, the definition of security relies less on "global" properties of ensembles of executions and more on *individual* executions.) In each particular run of a secure protocol for evaluating $f$, one may "put a finger on" *what inputs* the adversary has effectively substituted for the original ones of the corrupted players; *when* in the computation this has happened; *what* the adversary and the players get back from the joint computation, and *when* this happens; and these values are guaranteed (almost certainly) to be exactly what they should be — based on $f$, the inputs the adversary has effectively substituted, and the inputs the good players originally had.

## Key Properties

MODEL INDEPENDENCE. As we said a secure protocol is one that "properly" replaces the trusted external party of ideal evaluation with exchanging messages. There are, however, several possibilities for exchanging messages. For instance, each pair of participants may be linked by a secure communication channel (i.e., the adversary cannot hear messages exchanged by uncorrupted people); alternatively, each pair of players may have a dedicated, but insecure, communication channel; else, the only possible communication may consist of broadcasting messages, and so on. Though for ease of presentation we develop our notion of security with respect to a *particular*, underlying communication model, our notion of security is essentially *independent* of the underlying communication model. Indeed, we prove that the existence of secure protocol in one model of communication entails their existence in all other "reasonable" models. This proof is highly constructive: we show that, for any two rich-enough communication models, there exists a "compiler" that, given a protocol secure in the first model, generates a protocol for the same task which is secure in the second. (Interestingly, the proof, though often considered folklore, turned out to be quite difficult!)

SYNTACTIC INDEPENDENCE. Our definition of security is independent of the "syntax" in which a protocol is written. Designing a secure protocol is easier if one adopts a syntactic structure à la [GMW87]; that is, having the parties first execute a "committal phase" in which they pin down their inputs while keeping them still secret[3] and then they compute on these committed inputs. A different type of syntactic help consists of assuming that a primitive for securely computing some simple function is given, and then reducing to it the secure computation of more complex functions. This also simplifies the design of secure computation protocols (and actually presupposes that secure protocols enjoy the reducibility property we discuss below.) While it is alright to use a right syntax to lessen the difficulty of designing secure protocols, we insist that our definition of

---

[3]This secret commitment is called verifiable secret sharing, a notion introduced by [CGMA85]. For a precise definition and worked out example see [FM90]

security be independent of any specific syntactic restriction for a protocol to be called secure. (Of course, though we insist at remaining at an intuitive level here, being secure is itself an enormous restriction for a protocol, but of a different nature.)

INPUT INDEPENDENCE. There is yet a third, and crucial, type of independence property. In the ideal evaluation of a function $f$, the fake values the adversary chooses are completely *independent* of the values held by *uncorrupted* players. Of course, a secure protocol should have this property too, as closely as is possible. (It is a rather subtle matter how to state this goal satisfactorily.) After the proper definitions are in place, we show that our definition of security captures independence in an *extremely strong sense*—not by "adding it in" as a desired goal, but, rather, by it being a *provable property* of any secure protocol.

REDUCIBILITY. Let us describe this goal. Suppose you have designed a secure protocol for some complicated task—computing some function $f$, say. In an effort to make more manageable your job as protocol designer, you assumed in designing the protocol that you had some *primitive*, $g$, in hand. You proved that your protocol $P^g$ for computing $f$ was secure in a "special" model of computation — one in which an "ideal" evaluation of the primitive $g$ was provided "for free." One would want that you obtain a secure protocol for $f$ by inserting the code of a secure protocol for $g$ wherever it is necessary in $P^g$ that $g$ be computed. This key goal for any "good" definition of security is surprisingly difficult to obtain, *particularly* if one adopts the most natural and innocent-looking notion of adversarial awareness (namely, the result of applying a fixed algorithm to the adversary's entire computational state). Reducibility has always been a key desideratum for us, and, to our knowledge, this is the first definition which provably achieves it.

## The Definition, in a Nutshell

Here we describe, at the highest possible level, our definition of secure function evaluation.

Our notion owes much to the idea of a simulator, originally devised by Goldwasser, Micali and Rackoff [GMR89] in the context of interactive proofs. Recall that, in that context, a simulator which establishes zero-knowledge is a probabilistic algorithm which, knowing only "what it is entitled to" (whether or not $x \in L$) manages to produce a "fake" adversary view drawn from a distribution which closely resembles the distribution on "real" adversary views. To call a protocol secure, we, too, will demand the existence of a simulator—but our simulators are of a different sort. In fact, there are two major differences, which we now describe.

The first difference concerns specifying what information should be provided to the simulator: it is entitled to exactly the information available in the ideal evaluation. This is straightforwardly accomplished by equipping the simulator with a special type of oracle. Specifically, this oracle responds to two types of queries: first, *component queries*, which ask for the values of particular private inputs; and also a (single) *output query*, which asks the value of the function at a (partially) specified input, $\vec{x}_T$.

The second major difference is that instead of being an algorithm which produces a certain distribution on views, our simulator plays the role of the uncorrupted players. In fact, the adversary interacts with a simulator just as though she were interacting with the network. The "good" simulators (those which show that a protocol is secure) manage to interact with *any* adversary in a way which makes it indistinguishable to her whether it is the simulator or the network with whom she speaks. (This type of simulator, which we call an "on-line simulator," is not the same restriction as "black-box" simulation.)

Demanding the existence of such a simulator defines a strong notion of privacy. To capture security as a whole we employ the same simulator demanded for a privacy, as we now describe.

When the simulator asks the output query of its oracle, it computes this query—somehow. We add in a simple restriction: that the adversary *herself* could compute this query as a function $\mathcal{AI}$ of information which she undeniably has assess to (the "message traffic" between herself and the simulator, say). This function $\mathcal{AI}$—the *adversary input function*—captures something important in the ideal evaluation of a function $f$: that at some point in time the adversary inserts a value $x'_T$ into the collaborative computation, and she is necessarily aware of what this value is and when she provides it.

Correctness is defined by looking at individual executions of the network in the presence of the adversary. We demand that in a correct evaluation of $f$, what the good players compute is (almost always) the function $f$ evaluated at what the adversary input function indicates the adversary regards herself as having used for substituted values on this particular execution on behalf of the corrupted players, taken together with the good players' private inputs.

Actually, there is more to correctness than that. As mentioned, in the ideal evaluation of a function, not only is the adversary aware of what she contributes on behalf of corrupted players and when, but she gets an output back from these corrupted players, too! A secure protocol must mimic this. Thus the adversary must be able to compute, on behalf of the bad players, what is their share of the correctly computed function value. This is formalized by demanding the existence of an *adversary output function* $\mathcal{AO}$—again, something easily computed by the adversary—and, thinking of the output from a protocol execution being what the good players do output together with what the adversary "could" output by evaluating $\mathcal{AO}$, the notion of correctness is as before.

(We comment that extra care must be exercised in ensuring that the adversary input and output are properly co-ordinated with one another—roughly, that not only does the adversary regard herself as having inserted a certain value into the collaborative computation, and gotten a certain value back from it, but that these values are, in fact, the values the protocol has acted on.)

## Other Scenarios

One last comment concerning the generality of our notions: that, though the full paper singles out just a few models of computation, one particular adversary, and one particular ideal scenario to mimic, it is the *thesis* underlying this work that the definition given here lifts to many other reasonable scenarios as well, a great many being easy to describe and potentially interesting. Essentially, the thesis is as follows: you specify the communications model, the ideal evaluation you are trying to imitate, and the adversary's capabilities, and we provide, making the right "syntactic modifications," a definition of what it means for a communications protocol to imitate the corresponding abstraction.

## Acknowledgments

In distilling our notion of secure computation we have benefitted highly from the beautiful insights of those who preceded us.

This work may not have come about without the earlier notions of secure function computation set forth by Yao [Ya82a, Ya86], and by Goldreich, Wigderson, and the first author [GMW87].

A more recent, fundamental source of inspiration was provided by the work of Kilian [Ki89] and the joint work of Kilian and the authors [KMR90]. Some of the knots solved here were first identified and/or untangled there.

An equally crucial role was played by the work of Claude Crépeau and the first author [Cr90], which also provided us with a wonderful source of examples that proved crucial for refining our ideas.

We have also gained plenty of key insights from Goldwasser's, Rackoff's, and the first author's work on the earlier, related notion of a zero-knowledge proof [GMR89].

Next, our thanks for recent discussions with Michael Fischer, Leonid Levin, and Adi Shamir.

Last but not least, we would like to thank the many friends with which we exchanged ideas about secure protocols for so many years.

I (the first author) was fortunate to have had Manuel Blum, Shafi Goldwasser, Oded Goldreich, Charles Rackoff, and Michael Fischer as traveling companions in very heroic times, when secure protocols were a totally unexplored and hostile territory. A bit more recently, my very special thanks go to my (cryptography) students Paul Feldman, Claude Crépeau, Phil Rogaway, Mihir Bellare, and Rafail Ostrovsky, from which I continue learning an enormous amount.

I (the second author) happily thank Mihir Bellare and Joe Kilian for many nice discussions on protocols and cryptography.

# References

[Be91a] D. BEAVER, "Formal Definitions for Secure Distributed Protocols," in *Distributed Computing and Cryptography — Proceedings of a DIMACS Workshop*, October 1989. (Paper not presented at workshop but invited to appear in proceedings.)

[Be91b] D. BEAVER, "Foundations of Secure Interactive Computing," these proceedings.

[BG89] D. BEAVER AND S. GOLDWASSER, "Multiparty Computations with Faulty Majority," *Proc. of the 30th FOCS* (1989), 468–473.

[BMR90] D. BEAVER, S. MICALI AND P. ROGAWAY, "The Round Complexity of Secure Protocols," *Proc. of the 22nd FOCS* (1990), 503-513.

[BF85] J. BENALOH (COHEN) AND M. FISCHER, "A Robust and Verifiable Cryptographically Secure Election Scheme," *Proc. of the 26th FOCS* (1985), 372–381.

[BGW88] M. BEN-OR, S. GOLDWASSER AND A. WIGDERSON, "Completeness Theorems for Non-Cryptographic Fault-Tolerant Distributed Computation," *Proc. of the 20th STOC* (1988), 1–10.

[Bl82] M. BLUM, *Coin Flipping by Telephone*, *IEEE COMPCON*, (1982) 133–137.

[BM82] M. BLUM AND S. MICALI, "How to Generate Cryptographically Strong Sequences of Pseudo-Random Bits," *SIAM J. of Computing*, Vol. 13, No. 4, 1984, 850-864. Earlier version in *Proc. of the 23rd FOCS* (1982).

[Ch81] D. CHAUM. "Untraceable Electronic Mail, Return Addresses, and Digital Pseudonyms," *Comm. of the ACM* 24 (2) February 1981, 84–88.

[BCC88] G. BRASSARD, D. CHAUM AND C. CRÉPEAU, "Minimum disclosure proofs of knowledge," *Journal of Computer and System Sciences*, Vol. 37, No. 2, October 1988, 156–189.

[CCD88] D. CHAUM, C. CRÉPEAU AND I. DAMGÅRD, "Multiparty Unconditionally Secure Protocols," *Proc. of the 20th STOC* (1988), 11–19.

[CDG87] D. CHAUM, I. DAMGÅRD AND J. VAN DE GRAFF, "Multiparty Computations Ensuring the Privacy of Each Party's Input and Correctness of the Result," *CRYPTO-87 Proceedings*, 87-119.

[CG89] B. CHOR AND E. KUSHILEVITZ, "A Zero-One Law for Boolean Privacy," *Proc. of the 21st STOC* (1989), 62–72.

[CGK90] B. CHOR, M. GERÉB-GRAUS AND E. KUSHILEVITZ, "Private Computations over the Integers," *Proc. of the 31st FOCS* (1990), 325–344. Earlier version by Chor and Kushilevitz, "Sharing over Infinite Domains," *CRYPTO-89 Proceedings*, Springer-Verlag, 299–306.

[CGMA85] B. CHOR, O. GOLDWASSER, S. MICALI AND B. AWERBUCH, "Verifiable Secret Sharing and Achieving Simultaneity in the Presence of Faults," *Proc. of the 26th FOCS* (1985), 383-95.

[Cr90] C. CRÉPEAU, "Correct and Private Reductions Among Oblivious Transfers," MIT Ph.D. Thesis, February 1990.

[DLM]     R. DeMillo, N. Lynch, and M. Meritt, "Cryptographic Protocols," *Proc. of the 14th STOC* (1982) 383–400.

[DH76]    W. Diffie and M. Hellman, "New Directions in Cryptography," *IEEE Transactions on Information Theory*, 22(6) (November 1976). 644-654.

[Ed65]    J. Edmonds, "Paths, Trees, and Flowers," *Canadian J. of Mathematics*, 17:449–467, 1965.

[FFS87]   U. Feige, A. Fiat, and A. Shamir, "Zero Knowledge Proofs of Identity," *Proc. of the 19th STOC* (1987), 210–217.

[FS90]    U. Feige and A. Shamir, "Witness indistinguishability and witness hiding protocols," *Proc. of the 22nd STOC* (1990), 416–426.

[FS91]    U. Feige and A. Shamir, "On Expected Polynomial Time Simulation of Zero Knowledge Protocols," in *Distributed Computing and Cryptography — Proceedings of a DIMACS Workshop*, October 1989.

[Fe88]    P. Feldman, "One Can Always Assume Private Channels," unpublished manuscript (1988).

[FM90]    P. Feldman and S. Micali, "An Optimal Algorithms for Synchronous Byzantine Agreement," MIT/LCS Technical Report TM-425 (June 1990). Previous version in *Proc. of the 20th STOC* (1988), 148–161.

[GHY87]   Z. Galil, S. Haber and M. Yung, "Cryptographic Computation: Secure Fault-Tolerant Protocols and the Public-Key Model," CRYPTO-87 Proceedings, 135–155.

[Go89]    O. Goldreich, "Foundations of Cryptography – Class Notes," Spring 1989, Technion University, Haifa, Israel.

[GL90]    S. Goldwasser and L. Levin, "Fair Computation of General Functions in Presence of Immoral Majority," CRYPTO-90 Proceedings, 75–84.

[GM84]    S. Goldwasser and S. Micali, "Probabilistic Encryption," *Journal of Computer and System Sciences*, Vol. 28, No. 2 (1984), 270–299. Earlier version in *Proc. of the 14th STOC* (1982).

[GMR89]   O. Goldwasser, S. Micali, and C. Rackoff, "The Knowledge Complexity of Interactive Proof Systems," *SIAM J. of Comp.*, Vol. 18, No. 1, 186–208 (February 1989). Earlier version in *Proc. of the 17th STOC* (1985), 291–305.

[GMR88]   S. Goldwasser, S. Micali, and R. Rivest, "A Digital Signature Scheme Secure Against Adaptive Chosen-Message Attacks," *SIAM Journal on Computing*, 17(2):281–308, April 1988.

[GMW87]   O. Goldreich, S. Micali and A. Wigderson, "How to Play Any Mental Game," *Proc. of the 19th STOC* (1987), 218–229.

[GV87]    O. Goldreich and R. Vainish, "How to Solve any Protocol Problem—An Efficiency Improvement," CRYPTO-87 Proceedings, 76–86.

[Ha88]    S. Haber, "Multi-Party Cryptographic Computation: Techniques and Applications," Columbia University Ph.D. Thesis (1988).

[HU79]    J. Hopcroft and J. Ullman, *Introduction to Automata Theory, Languages, and Computation*, Addison-Wesley, 1979.

[Ki89]    J. Kilian, "Uses of Randomness in Algorithms and Protocols," MIT Ph.D. Thesis, April 1989.

[KMR90]   J. Kilian, S. Micali, and P. Rogaway, "The Notion of Secure Computation," manuscript, 1990.

[Le85]    L. Levin, "One-Way Functions and Pseudorandom Generators," *Combinatorica*, Vol. 17, 1988, 357–363. Earlier version in *Proc. of the 17th STOC* (1985).

[LMR83]   M. Luby, S. Micali and C. Rackoff, "How to Simultaneously Exchange a Secret Bit by Flipping a Symmetrically Biased Coin," *Proc of the 24th FOCS* (1983).

404

[Me83]    M. MERITT, "Cryptographic Protocols." Georgia Institute of Technology Ph.D. Thesis, Feb. 1983.

[MRS88]   S. MICALI, C. RACKOFF AND B. SLOAN, "The Notion of Security for Probabilistic Cryptosystems," *SIAM J. of Computing*, 17(2):412–26, April 1988.

[MR91]    S. MICALI AND P. ROGAWAY, "Secure Computation," manuscript, August 1991.

[Or87]    Y. OREN, "On the Cunning Power of Cheating Verifiers: Some Observations about Zero Knowledge Proofs," *Proc. of the 28th FOCS* (1987), 462–471.

[PSL80]   M. PEASE, R. SHOSTAK AND L. LAMPORT, "Reaching Agreement in the Presence of Faults," *J. of the ACM* Vol. 27, No. 2, 1980.

[Ra81]    M. RABIN, "How to Exchange Secrets by Oblivious Transfer," Technical Memo TR-81, Aiken Computation Laboratory, Harvard University, 1981.

[RB89]    T. RABIN AND M. BEN-OR, "Verifiable Secret Sharing and Multiparty Protocols with Honest Majority," *Proc. of the 21st STOC* (1989), 73–85.

[SRA81]   A. SHAMIR, R. RIVEST, AND L. ADLEMAN, "Mental Poker," in *Mathematical Gardener*, D. D. Klarner, editor, Wadsworth International (1981) pp 37–43,

[TW87]    M. TOMPA AND H. WOLL, "Random Self-Reducibility and Zero Knowledge Interactive Proofs of Possession of Information," *Proc. of the 28th FOCS* (1987), 472–482.

[Ya82a]   A. YAO, "Protocols for Secure Computation," *Proc. of the 23 FOCS* (1982), 160–164.

[Ya82b]   A. YAO, "Theory and Applications of Trapdoor Functions," *Proc. of the 23 FOCS* (1982) 80–91.

[Ya86]    A. YAO, "How to Generate and Exchange Secrets," *Proc. of the 27 FOCS* (1986).

# A Cryptographic Scheme for Computerized General Elections

Kenneth R. Iversen

Department of Electrical Engineering and Computer Science
Norwegian Institute of Technology
7034 Trondheim, Norway
kenneth.iversen@idt.unit.no

### Abstract

This paper presents a novel cryptographic scheme which fully conforms to the requirements of holding large scale general elections. The participants of the scheme are the voters, the candidates and the government. The scheme ensures independence between the voters in that they do not have to be present at the same time or go through several phases together; no global computation is needed. The scheme preserves the privacy of the votes against any subset of dishonest voters, and against any proper subset of dishonest candidates, including the government. Robustness is ensured in that no subset of voters can corrupt or disrupt the election. This also means that no voter is able to vote more than once without being detected. The verifiability of the scheme ensures that the government and the candidates cannot present a false tally without being caught. "Voting by telephone" is possible by employing the proposed scheme.

# 1 Introduction

This paper presents a cryptographic scheme for secret ballot elections. It is a scheme which fully conforms to the requirements of holding large scale general elections. The scheme involves the eligible voters, the government, and the candidates the voters can vote on. The basic assumptions of the scheme are that each voter can communicate all the candidates (from now on, this includes the government) simultaneously, and that at least one candidate do not collaborate with the others. Under these assumptions, the scheme is robust in that no subset of dishonest voters and no proper subset of dishonest candidates can disrupt or corrupt the election, and the privacy of the votes and voters is preserved.

The verifiability of the scheme is restricted to the candidates. (It is possible to include other, possibly more trustworthy parties.) Assuming that every voter trusts one of these parties, this yields public verifiability. The verifiability ensures, with overwhelming probability, that the government cannot present a false tally without being caught.

The scheme is well suited for implementing a "voting by telephone" scheme.

J. Feigenbaum (Ed.): Advances in Cryptology - CRYPTO '91, LNCS 576, pp. 405-419, 1992.
© Springer-Verlag Berlin Heidelberg 1992

## 1.1 Relation to Previous Work

There have been several publications on the problem of holding elections by employing computers and cryptographic protocols, and several cryptographic schemes have been proposed where the voters openly send encrypted messages back and forth until they all are confident of the outcome of the election (boardroom voting) [DLM82, Yao82, Mer83].

The problems with these schemes are that one has to know in advance who wish to vote, and if any voter stops following the protocol during the election, the election cannot be completed. Such schemes are clearly not suitable for real-world elections.

Chaum has given an election scheme that makes use of one or several trusted "mixes" to scramble pairs of votes and digital pseudonyms [Cha81].

Whereas Chaum's scheme hides the identity of the voters, the scheme of (Cohen) Benaloh *et al.* hides the actual value of the vote [CF85, BY86, Ben87]. They take a quite different approach, by employing the hardness of deciding higher residues and interactive protocols.

My work has been much inspired by that of Benaloh *et al.*, and it has adopted many of their ideas. The scheme of this paper does to some extent conform to their election paradigm. The major problem that their scheme succumbs to is that it requires the participants to go through several phases together, where one phase cannot start before all the participants have finished the previous. This problem is solved in my scheme; all voters register and vote totally independent.

The scheme presented is a very practical and flexible election scheme. It can be used to implement almost any election setting; from the conventional setting where each voter show up (independently!) at the voting place, register, vote, and goes back home; to some kind of "voting by telephone" setting.

Chaum has given another method of holding verifiable secret ballot elections that removes the need for a mix [Cha88]. The work is similar to that of a boardroom election in that a failure of a single voter can disrupt the election. However, Chaum's method ensures that such failures can be traced. This allows an election to be restarted without the faulty voter, but this approach is not practical for large-scale elections.

Boyd has proposed a voting scheme based on the use of "multiple key ciphers" [Boy88, Boy90]. It ensures that votes cannot be forged, and privacy is preserved, provided the voters can deliver their votes anonymously. The major problem of this scheme is that the government can see the votes delivered and even worse, produce a false tally by adding votes of its own choice; there is no verifiability.

# 2 The Election Privacy Homomorphism

I here present the privacy homomorphism that is used to construct the ballots of the election scheme. The privacy homomorphism is additive and probabilistic, i.e., the cleartext domain operation is (modular) addition and there are several different and uncorrelated encryptions of the same number. For full details, see Ref. [Ive91a].

## 2.1 Election Triples

**Definition 2.1** Let $k$ be a security parameter, $e$ be a fixed small prime, $p$ be a $k/2$-bit prime such that $e|(p-1)$, and $q$ be a $k/2$-bit prime such that $e \nmid (q-1)$. Further, let $n = pq$. Finally, let $g$ be an element in $\mathbf{Z}_n^*$ such that $e$ divides the order of $g$. For such $e$, $g$, and $n$, I define an *election triple* to be $(e, g, n)$.

I will throughout let $G$ be the set of powers of $g$ modulo $n$; $G = \{g^j \pmod{n} | j \geq 1\}$.

## 2.2 Index Classes

**Definition 2.2** Let $(e, g, n)$ be an election triple. Let $w \equiv g^v \pmod{n} \in G$, for some integer $v$. The *index class* of $w$, denoted $[\![w]\!]_{(e,g,n)}$ (or simply $[\![w]\!]$ when $(e, g, n)$ is given), is $v \pmod{e}$. If $w \notin G$, I say that $[\![w]\!]$ is undefined.

**Definition 2.3** An election triple $(e, g, n)$ is said to be *valid* when $e$ divides the order of $g$. The election triple is said to be *good* if $g$ in addition is a generator modulo $p$.

In Ref. [Ive91b] it is devised an efficient perfect zero-knowledge protocol that enables the publisher of an election triple to convince anyone who wants to be assured that the triple is valid, without giving away any information about the secrets involved.

I am now ready to describe how to use the privacy homomorphism. Given a good election triple $(e, g, n)$, the values to be encrypted must be in the set $\mathbf{Z}_e$.

## How to Encrypt

Suppose a party $A$ wants to encrypt a number $v \in \mathbf{Z}_e$. Then,

A chooses $r \in_R \mathbf{Z}_n$, and computes $x = v + re$,

A computes $E(v) \equiv g^x \pmod{n}$.

In general, $\lfloor \log_2 e \rfloor$ bits of cleartext is expanded into $k$ bits of ciphertext. Since there are several different encryptions of the same value, test for equality is not possible.

## 2.3 The Election Privacy Homomorphism Assumption

In this section, I formally state the intractability assumption for the problem of deciding index classes in the election privacy homomorphism. Clearly, the problem cannot be harder than factoring or computing discrete logarithms modulo a composite integer (see open problems 5 and 22 in Ref. [AM87]). No efficient algorithm for solving the problem without knowing the factorization of the modulus is known.

In order to state the intractability assumption, I introduce the predicate $IND_{(e,g,n)}$. For all $w \in G$,

$$IND_{(e,g,n)}(v, w) = \begin{cases} 1 & \text{if } [\![w]\!] = v \\ 0 & \text{if } [\![w]\!] \neq v \end{cases}.$$

**Assumption 2.1 (EPH Assumption (EPHA))** *Let $v \in \mathbf{Z}_e$. Then for all polynomial size families of circuits $C = \{C_k\}_{k \geq 1}$, with $(3k + |e|)$-bit input gates, for any good election triples $(e, g, n)$ such that $|n| = k$, and for all $w \in G$,*

$$\Pr(C_k(v, w, g, n) = \text{IND}_{(e,g,n)}(v, w)) < \frac{e-1}{e} + \nu(k),$$

*where the probability is taken over the random inputs of $C_k$. The fraction $\frac{e-1}{e}$ is the probability of guessing correctly if $C_k$ always outputs 0. $\nu(k)$ is a function that vanishes faster than the inverse of any polynomial in $k$.*

In Ref. [Ive91a], I show, in a manner similar to that of Goldwasser and Micali [GM84], that the privacy homomorphism is a probabilistic public key encryption function based on the above assumption. I further show that the problem of computing index classes is "everywhere hard".

# 3   EPH Based Votes

I will now describe what the ballots and votes used in the election scheme will look like.

Before the election starts, I assume that every candidate has published a (preferably good, but possibly valid) election triple. Let $(e, g_i, n_i)$ be the election triple of candidate $i$, $1 \leq i \leq \sigma$. $e$ must be larger than the number of eligible voters.

**Definition 3.1** Let $(e, g_i, n_i)$ be the election triple of candidate $i$, $1 \leq i \leq \sigma$. A *vote* $w$ is a $\sigma$-tuple $w = (g_1^{v_1} \pmod{n_1}, \ldots, g_\sigma^{v_\sigma} \pmod{n_\sigma})$.

**Definition 3.2** A *ballot* $W$ is a $\sigma$-tuple $W = (w_1, \ldots, w_\sigma)$ of votes.

**Definition 3.3** *The* index class tuple *(or just index tuple) of a vote* $w = (g_1^{v_1}, \ldots, g_\sigma^{v_\sigma})$ *is the tuple* $(v_1 \pmod{e}, \ldots, v_\sigma \pmod{e})$. *I denote it* $(\!(w)\!)$.

Further, for a vote $w = (g_1^{v_1}, \ldots, g_\sigma^{v_\sigma})$, meaning $v = \sum_{i=1}^{\sigma} v_i \pmod{e}$, I will write $v = \sum (\!(w)\!)$.

**Definition 3.4** A vote $w = (g_1^{v_1}, \ldots, g_\sigma^{v_\sigma})$ is *valid* if $v = \sum (\!(w)\!) = 0$ or $1$. A vote where $v = 0$ is called a *no-vote* and a vote where $v = 1$ is called a *yes-vote*.

**Definition 3.5** A ballot $W = (w_1, \ldots, w_\sigma)$ is *valid* if every vote $w_1, \ldots, w_\sigma$ are valid and $\sum_{j=1}^{\sigma} v_j = \sum_{j=1}^{\sigma} \sum (\!(w_j)\!) = 1 \pmod{e}$.

I will refer to the $v_j = \sum (\!(w_j)\!)$ as the *actual vote* for candidate $j$.

Now, instead of the candidates having to store each ballot from all the voters, the homomorphism property comes into use. Let $W_1$ and $W_2$ be two valid ballots. It should not be hard to see that to store the sum of the actual votes one can store the componentwise product of the votes in $W_1$ and $W_2$.

Let the final net ballot be $\widehat{W} = (\widehat{w}_1, \ldots, \widehat{w}_\sigma)$. Then the final number of yes-votes for candidate $j$ is $\sum (\!(\widehat{w}_j)\!)$.

# 4  Unreusable Eligibility Tokens

The basic assumptions of the election scheme will be applied here also; the voter communicates with all the candidates simultaneously, and at least one candidate is honest. Let the number of candidates be $\sigma$.

The scheme for providing unreusable eligibility tokens is a modification to the scheme for providing unreusable electronic cash presented in Ref. [CFN90].

## 4.1  Initialization

The computations and actions described below can be done at any time before the process of token issuing starts, but only in the order indicated by the numbering.

1. The candidates agree on and publish two (even) security parameters $k$ and $s$, a public one-way collision-free hash function $h$, and a secure public digital signature scheme ([GMR88]) to be used by the voters. Each candidate $j$ then publishes its public RSA key $(e_j, n_j)$ (the corresponding secret key is $d_j$), such that $|n_j| = s$.

2. For $i = 1, \ldots, k$, the voter chooses integers $a_i, b_i, t_i, r_i$, and $z_i \in_R Z_n^*$, where $n = \max_{j=1,\ldots,\sigma}(n_j)$, and computes the inverse of $r_i$ modulo each of the candidates' RSA modulus. The voter then prepares a digital signature on $h(z_1)\|h(z_2)\| \ldots \|h(z_k)$. Let $S_V$ denote this signature.

## 4.2  Token Issuing

Some time before the election day, the voter presents and identifies him- or herself to the candidates (in an election office handling eligibility), and gives his or her public signature key to the candidates. The candidates create a string $ID_V$ which contains the voter's name, ID number, or any other information that the candidates want to establish. The voter and the candidates then perform the protocol below.

1. For $i = 1, \ldots, k$, the voter computes the blinded values

$$v_i = \{r_i^{e_j} \cdot h(h(a_i\|b_i)\|h(a_i \oplus (ID_V\|z_i)\|t_i)) \pmod{n_j}\}_{j=1,\ldots,\sigma}.$$

The voter sends $\{v_i\}_{i=1,\ldots,k}$ to the candidates. In addition, the voter supplies the candidates with the digital signature on $h(z_1)\|h(z_2)\| \ldots \|h(z_k)$; $S_V$.

2. The candidates perform a sub-protocol and send to the voter a random subset of $k/2$ distinct indices $I = \{i_j\}_{j=1,\ldots,k/2}$, where for all $j, 1 \le i_j \le k$.

3. For all $i \in I$, the voter reveals $a_i$, $b_i$, $t_i$, $r_i$, and $z_i$ to the candidates.

4. For all $i \in I$, the candidates check that the voter computed the $v_i$ correctly in Step 1. In addition, the candidates check that $h(z_i)$ is among hash values signed by the voter. If any of the candidates discover any fallacies they terminate the protocol.

5. For simplicity, let the remaining indices not in $I$ be $1,\ldots,k/2$. Each of the candidates computes and sends the RSA signature, $S_{C_j}$, of the $k/2$ unopened values to the voter.

$$\{S_{C_j} = \prod_{i=1}^{k/2} r_i \cdot h(h(a_i\|b_i)\|h(a_i \oplus (ID_V\|z_i)\|t_i))^{d_j} \pmod{n_j}\}_{j=1,\ldots,\sigma}.$$

6. The voter now removes the blinding and extracts the unreusable eligibility token

$$ET = \{\prod_{i=1}^{k/2} h(h(a_i\|b_i)\|h(a_i \oplus (ID_V\|z_i)\|t_i))^{d_j} \pmod{n_j}\}_{j=1,\ldots,\sigma}.$$

After executing the initialization protocol, the candidates store $ID_V$, $S_V$, and $\{z_i\}_{i \in I}$. During the initialization protocol, the candidates have verified that each of the $k/2$ $v_i$'s they examined generates an appropriate $ID_V\|z_i$. I will now assume that the candidates have legal proof that the voter has voted more than once if they can present the preimage of at least $(k/2) + 1$ of the hash values $h(z_i)$ in $S_V$.

## 4.3 Using the Token

On the election day, when the voter is using the token in the voting process, the protocol below is performed by the voter and the candidates.

1. The voter sends $ET$ to the candidates.

2. The candidates perform a sub-protocol to obtain the challenge string $c$, and send it to the voter. $c = \{c_i \in_R \{0,1\}\}_{i=1,\ldots,k/2}$.

3. For $i = 1,\ldots,k/2$, the voter sends the values $y_i$ to the candidates.

$$y_i = \begin{cases} a_i, b_i, h(a_i \oplus (ID_V\|z_i)\|t_i) & \text{if } c_i = 0 \\ h(a_i\|b_i), a_i \oplus (ID_V\|z_i), t_i & \text{if } c_i = 1 \end{cases}$$

4. The candidates check that the $y_i$'s fit $ET$.

   If any of the checks fails, the candidates halt and reject, otherwise they halt and accept.

When the protocol is finished with the candidates accepting, the candidates check whether the token has been used before, by searching in a database where all the previously received tokens are stored. If it is not used before, the candidates store $ET$, the challenge string $\{c_i \in_R \{0,1\}\}_{i=1,\ldots,k/2}$, and the values $a_i$, if $c_i = 0$, and $a_i \oplus (ID_V \| z_i)$, if $c_i = 1$. If the candidates discover that the token has been used before, then with overwhelming probability, any candidate is able to extract the identity $ID_V$ of the voter, and provide a legal proof of the fact that the voter has voted twice.

## 4.4  ET Security

The security of the unreusable electronic cash scheme was left as an open challenge in Ref. [CFN90], and no attempts to solve the problem have been made here. Ref. [Ive91b] gives a proof of unreusability.

# 5  The Election Scheme

The participants of the scheme are the eligible voters and the candidates. Let the number of eligible voters and candidates be $\rho$ and $\sigma$, respectively, such that $\sigma < \rho$. Note that the registration and voting phases can be performed independently by each voter.

## 5.1  Election Initialization

The candidates do what is described in Step 1 in Section 4.1. They then execute the following *election initialization protocol*:

**Agreeing on $e$:** The candidates agree on a prime $e$ which is larger than the number of eligible voters ($e > \rho > \sigma$).

**Generating election triples:** For $i = 1$ to $\sigma$, candidate $i$ secretly produces two random $s/2$-bit primes $p_i$ and $q_i$, such that $e|(p_i-1)$ and $e \nmid (q_i-1)$. Let $n_i = p_i q_i$. Candidate $i$ also chooses an element $g_i \in \mathbf{Z}_{n_i}^*$ which is a generator modulo $p$. $p_i$ and $q_i$ are kept secret, while $(e, g_i, n_i)$ is published as candidate $i$'s election triple.

Each candidate in turn must then give a zero-knowledge proof to show that the election triple is valid to any candidate who wants to be assured.

In the sequel of this chapter, all computations are done modulo the $n_i$'s. Which applies where should be clear from the subscript of the $g_i$ involved.

Finally the candidates compute an initial "net ballot" $\widehat{W}_0 = (\widehat{w}_{0,1}, \ldots, \widehat{w}_{0,\sigma})$, such that for all $j$, $\sum (\![\widehat{w}_{0,j}]\!) = 0$. Each of the candidates then signs a copy of the hash value $h(\widehat{W}_0\|0)$ using the secure digital signature scheme, and then publishes it. $h$ is employed for efficiency reasons only. The zero that is concatenated with the ballot is the (initial) sequence number. This signing is to avoid that, when the election is finished, any proper subset of dishonest candidates can construct their own final ballot and claim it to be the real one.

## 5.2 Voter Registration

An eligible voter first performs the eligibility token initialization described in Step 2 in Section 4.1. After this, she appears and identifies herself at a registration office to obtain an unreusable eligibility token, $ET$, produced by the protocol given in Section 4.2 with security parameter $2k$.

## 5.3 Voter Initialization

At some time before the actual voting is to take place, the voter decides which candidate she wants to give a vote to. A vote on candidate 1 (the government) might yield a blank vote. I will for simplicity assume that the voter votes blank.

The voter then performs the initializing computations shown below. Note that these computations can be done off-line.

1. The voter prepares the ballot $W$ according to the following program:

```
FOR j = 1 TO σ DO
    FOR i = 1 TO σ − 1 DO vᵢ,ⱼ := a random element in Zₙᵢ
    vσ,ⱼ := an element in Zₙσ s.t. ∑ᶦ₌₁ σ vᵢ,ⱼ = IF j = 1 THEN 1 ELSE 0
    wⱼ := (g₁^{v₁,ⱼ}, ..., gσ^{vσ,ⱼ})
END DO
```

$$W := ((w_1, \ldots, w_\sigma), ET)$$

2. The voter prepares the tuple $V = (v_1, \ldots, v_\sigma)$, where $v_i = \sum_{j=1}^{\sigma} v_{i,j}$.

3. For each vote $w_j$ in the ballot the voter prepares $k$ "test-pairs" according to the following program: (for simplicity, I drop the subscript $j$)

```
FOR i = 1 TO k DO
    bit_i := a random element in {0,1}
    FOR j = 1 TO σ − 1 DO
        α_{i,j} := a random element in Z_{n_i}
        β_{i,j} := a random element in Z_{n_i}
    END DO
    α_{i,σ} := an element in Z_{n_σ} s.t. ∑_{i=1}^{σ} α_{i,j} = 0
    β_{i,σ} := an element in Z_{n_σ} s.t. ∑_{i=1}^{σ} β_{i,j} = 1
    a_i := (g_1^{α_{i,1}}, …, g_σ^{α_{i,σ}})
    b_i := (g_1^{β_{i,1}}, …, g_σ^{β_{i,σ}})
    pair_i := IF bit_i = 0 THEN (a_i, b_i) ELSE (b_i, a_i)
END DO
PAIR := {(pair_{1,j}, …, pair_{k,j})}_{j=1,…,σ}
```

## 5.4 Voting

When voting, the voter performs the protocol below with the candidates.

Repeat Steps 1—4 $k$ times ($i = 1, \ldots, k$) (for each vote $w_j$ in parallel). (For simplicity, I drop the subscript $j$.)

1. If $i = 1$, the voter sends the vote $w$ to the candidates. The voter sends $pair_i$ to the candidates.

2. The candidates perform a sub-protocol to obtain a random challenge bit $c_i$, and send it to the voter.

3. The voter answers with $d_i$.

   If $c_i = 0$ then $d_i = ((\alpha_{1,i}, \ldots, \alpha_{\sigma,i}), (\beta_{1,i}, \ldots, \beta_{\sigma,i}))$. If $c_i = 1$ then $d_i = (v_1 + \alpha_{1,i}, \ldots, v_\sigma + \alpha_{\sigma,i})$ if $\sum \langle\!\langle w \rangle\!\rangle = 1$ and $d_i = (v_1 + \beta_{1,i}, \ldots, v_\sigma + \beta_{\sigma,i})$ if $\sum \langle\!\langle w \rangle\!\rangle = 0$.

4. If $c_i = 0$, the candidates check that $pair_i[1] = (g_1^{d_i[1,1]}, \ldots, g_\sigma^{d_i[1,\sigma]})$ and $pair_i[2] = (g_1^{d_i[2,1]}, \ldots, g_\sigma^{d_i[2,\sigma]})$, or possibly vice versa. If $c_i = 1$, the candidates check that $\sum_{j=1}^{\sigma} d_i[j] = 1$ and that $(g_1^{d_i[1]} \ldots, g_\sigma^{d_i[\sigma]}) = w \cdot pair[1]$ or $w \cdot pair[2]$. If any candidate discovers any errors, the candidates halt and the voter is excluded from the election.

5. Finally, when steps 1—4 have been repeated $k$ times, the voter sends $V$ to the candidates.

6. The candidates check that $\sum_{i=1}^{\sigma} v_i = 1$ and that, for each $i$, $g^{v_i} = \prod_{j=1}^{\sigma} w_j[i]$.


Besides the voting protocol the voter and the candidates perform the token usage protocol described in Section 4.3. This can easily be embedded in the voting protocol.

If none of the candidates have discovered any fallacies in the voting protocol or the token usage protocol, they accept the ballot, and indicates this to the voter by sending him or her signed "receipts" (of some sort). The candidates then compute the net ballot $\widehat{W}_m = (\widehat{w}_{m-1,1} \cdot w_{m,1}, \ldots, \widehat{w}_{m-1,\sigma} \cdot w_{m,\sigma})$, where $w_{m,j}$ is vote $j$ of voter $m$. Again, each candidate signs a copy of $h(\widehat{W}_m \| m)$, as described in the election initialization protocol.


## 5.5 Tally Computing

When the election is finished the final net ballot is $\widehat{W}_{\rho'} = (\widehat{w}_{\rho',1}, \ldots, \widehat{w}_{\rho',\sigma})$, where $\rho'$ is the number of voters that actually voted during the election. Now, the total number of yes-votes cast for candidate $j$ is $\sum (\![\widehat{w}_{\rho',j}]\!)$. To be able to compute this tally, the candidates have to publish their "sub-tallies", i.e., candidate $i$ publishes the tuple $([\![\widehat{w}_{\rho',1}[i]]\!], \ldots, [\![\widehat{w}_{\rho',\sigma}[i]]\!])$, and so forth. They must in addition give a (perfect) zero-knowledge proof of the validity of the published "sub-tallies". See full paper for reference.


# 6 Security

The first thing to notice is that the voting protocol is $\sigma$ versions of a computational zero-knowledge protocol, given in Ref. [Ive91b]. Note also that the protocol for each vote in the ballot is run sequentially, so the protocol is still zero-knowledge.


**Theorem 6.1 (Completeness)** *The ballot of an honest voter is accepted by honest candidates with probability one.*

**Proof:** The fact that each valid vote is accepted with probability one follows directly from the completeness part of the proof of zero-knowledgeness of the voting protocol (see Ref. [Ive91b]). In addition, for the whole valid ballot, the check performed by the candidates in Step 6 in the voting protocol will always be accepted. ∎

**Theorem 6.2 (Soundness)** *If at least one candidate is honest, then, with overwhelming probability, a dishonest voter will not succeed in delivering an invalid ballot.*

**Proof:** That this holds for each of the votes in the ballot follows directly from the soundness part of the proof of zero-knowledgeness of the voting protocol (see Ref. [Ive91b]). In addition, the fact that $\sigma < e$ implies that if more than one of the votes are yes-votes, then $\sum_{i=1}^{\sigma} v_i > 1$, and the honest candidates will not accept. ∎

**Theorem 6.3 (Privacy)** *Under the EPHA, if at least one candidate is honest, the privacy of the votes is preserved.*

**Proof:** The voting protocol is proven to be computational zero-knowledge (see Ref. [Ive91b]), and this implies that no information about the value of the votes can be extracted only from executing the protocol. Let $\Gamma$ denote any subset of dishonest candidates such that $|\Gamma| < \sigma$. Let, for simplicity, the candidates in $\Gamma$ be $C_1, C_2, \ldots, C_{\sigma-1}$, and thus $|\Gamma| = \sigma - 1$. First, the candidates in $\Gamma$ cannot extract any information from the index class of the elements they are able to decrypt, i.e., from $[w[i]], i < \sigma$ in any votes. The other element $w[\sigma]$, will to the candidates in $\Gamma$, be a random element in $G_\sigma$.[1]

From the above it follows that a polynomial advantage in determining the actual vote for some candidate in some ballot (delivered by an honest candidate) yields a polynomial advantage in determining the actual vote for any candidate in any ballot.

Assume now that the candidates in $\Gamma$ have gained such a polynomial advantage (somehow). But, then this is a polynomial advantage in determining the index class of at least one element $w[\sigma]$, in any vote in any ballot. This clearly contradicts the EPHA, and our assumption must be wrong. ∎

**Theorem 6.4 (Unreusability)** *With overwhelming probability, no voter is able to vote more than once without being detected by an honest candidate.*

---

[1] Recall that $G_i = \{g_i^j \pmod{n_i} | j \geq 1\}$, where $(e, g_i, n_i)$ is the election triple published by candidate $i$.

**Proof:** This follows from the proof of unreusability of the eligibility tokens. See Ref. [Ive91b]. ∎

**Theorem 6.5 (Tally correctness)** *Under the assumptions that the employed signature scheme is secure and that at least one candidate is honest, then, with overwhelming probability, the published tally is equal to the actual result of the election.*

**Proof:** To be able to claim the validity of a published tally, the (claimed) final ballot must be shown together with signed copies from all the candidates. If this is the case, the properties of the privacy homomorphism ensures that at most one tally can be produced from this final ballot (see Ref. [Ive91a]). By the proof of soundness, every ballot "in" the published net ballot is valid with overwhelming probability, and thus *exactly* one tally can be produced from it.

No proper subset of dishonest candidates can produce a valid final ballot with an equal or larger sequence number without breaking the signature scheme. ∎

**Theorem 6.6 (Eligibility)** *Under the assumption that the RSA blind signature scheme is secure, and if at least one candidate is honest, then with overwhelming probability, only eligible voters are able to deliver a ballot successfully.*

**Proof (sketch):** It is not known under what assumptions the theorem holds. See Section 4.4. ∎

The above election scheme enables voters to deliver their votes independent of each other. No subset of voters can disrupt the election, and the same applies to any subset of less than $\sigma$ candidates.

# 7    Discussion

The scheme is very efficient in that nearly all time-consuming computations can be done offline. In the most time-critical protocol – the voting protocol, the voter need not do any time-consuming computations.

The election scheme presented here has one important drawback; the possibility for a voter to be paid to vote for a dishonest candidate, and afterwards be able to prove to this candidate that he or she actually did so.[2] It remains an open problem to fix this problem.

# References

[AM87]  L. Adleman and K. McCurley. Open Problems in Number Theoretic Complexity. In *Discrete Algorithms and Complexity*, pages 237–262. Academic Press, Inc., 1987.

[Ben87]  J. Benaloh. *Verifiable Secret-Ballot Elections*. PhD thesis, Yale University, USA, September 1987. YALEU/DCS/TR-561.

[Boy88]  C. Boyd. Some Applications of Multiple Key Ciphers. In C. G. Günther, editor, *Advances in Cryptology - EUROCRYPT '88 Proceedings*, volume 330 of *Lecture Notes in Computer Science*, pages 455–467. Springer-Verlag, 1988.

[Boy90]  C. Boyd. A New Multiple Key Cipher and an Improved Voting Scheme. In J.-J. Quisquater, editor, *Advances in Cryptology - EUROCRYPT '89 Proceedings*, volume 434 of *Lecture Notes in Computer Science*, pages 617–625. Springer-Verlag, 1990.

[BY86]  J. Benaloh and M. Yung. Distributing the Power of a Government to Enhance the Privacy of Voters. In *Proceedings of the 5th ACM Symposium on the Principles in Distributed Computing*, pages 52–62, 1986.

[CF85]  J. Cohen and M. Fisher. A Robust and Verifiable Cryptographically Secure Election Scheme. In *Proceedings of the 26th Annual IEEE Symposium on the Foundations of Computer Science*, pages 372–382, 1985.

[CFN90]  D. Chaum, A. Fiat, and M. Naor. Untraceable Electronic Cash. In S. Goldwasser, editor, *Advances in Cryptology - CRYPTO '88 Proceedings*, volume 403 of *Lecture Notes in Computer Science*, pages 319–327. Springer-Verlag, 1990.

[Cha81]  D. Chaum. Untraceable Electronic Mail, Return Addresses, and Digital Pseudonyms. *Communications of the ACM*, 24(2):84–88, 1981.

[Cha88]  D. Chaum. Elections with Unconditionally-Secret Ballots and Disruption Equivalent to Breaking RSA. In C. G. Günther, editor, *Advances in Cryptology - EUROCRYPT '88 Proceedings*, volume 330 of *Lecture Notes in Computer Science*, pages 177–182. Springer-Verlag, 1988.

[2] Thanks to Amir Herzberg for pointing this out.

[DLM82] R. DeMillo, N. Lynch, and M. Merritt. Cryptographic Protocols. In *Proceedings of the 14th Annual ACM Symposium on the Theory of Computing*, pages 383–400, 1982.

[GM84] S. Goldwasser and S. Micali. Probabilistic Encryption. *Journal of Computer and Systems Sciences*, 28(2):270–299, April 1984.

[GMR88] S. Goldwasser, S. Micali, and R. Rivest. A Digital Signature Scheme Secure Against Adaptive Chosen-Message Attacks. *SIAM Journal on Computing*, 17(2):281–308, April 1988.

[Ive91a] K. Iversen. A Novel Probabilistic Additive Privacy Homomorphism. In *Proceedings of the International Conference on Finite Fields, Coding Theory, and Advances in Communications and Computing*, Lecture Notes in Pure and Applied Mathematics. Marcel Dekker, August 1991. To appear.

[Ive91b] K. Iversen. *The Application of Cryptographic Zero-Knowledge Techniques in Computerized Secret Ballot Election Schemes*. Doktor ingeniør-avhandling 1991:15, Norwegian Institute of Technology, February 1991. IDT-report 1991:3.

[Mer83] M. Merritt. *Cryptographic Protocols*. PhD thesis, Georgia Institute of Technology, USA, February 1983. GIT-ICS-83/6.

[Yao82] A. Yao. Protocols for Secure Computations. In *Proceedings of the 23rd Annual IEEE Symposium on the Foundations of Computer Science*, pages 160–164, 1982.

# Efficient Multiparty Protocols
# Using Circuit Randomization

Donald Beaver *
AT&T Bell Laboratories

## Abstract.

The difference between theory and practice often rests on one major factor: efficiency. In distributed systems, communication is usually expensive, and protocols designed for practical use must require as few rounds of communication and as small messages as possible.

A secure multiparty protocol to compute function $F$ is a protocol that, when each player $i$ of $n$ players starts with private input $x_i$, provides each participant $i$ with $F(x_1, \ldots, x_n)$ without revealing more information than what can be derived from learning the function value. Some number $t$ of players may be corrupted by an adversary who may then change the messages they send. Recent solutions to this problem have suffered in practical terms: while theoretically using only polynomially-many rounds, in practice the constants and exponents of such polynomials are too great. Normally, such protocols express $F$ as a circuit $C_F$, call on each player to secretly share $x_i$, and proceed to perform "secret addition and multiplication" on secretly shared values. The cost is proportional to the depth of $C_F$ times the cost of secret multiplication; and multiplication requires several rounds of interaction.

We present a protocol that simplifies the body of such a protocol and significantly reduces the number of rounds of interaction. The steps of our protocol take advantage of a new and counterintuitive technique for evaluating a circuit: set every input to every gate in the circuit completely at random, and then make corrections. Our protocol replaces each secret multiplication — multiplication that requires further sharing, addition, zero-knowledge proofs, and secret reconstruction — that is used during the body of a standard protocol by a simple reconstruction of secretly shared values, thereby reducing rounds by an order of magnitude. Furthermore, these reconstructions require only broadcast messages (but do *not* require Byzantine Agreement). The simplicity of broadcast and reconstruction provides efficiency and ease of implementation. Our transformation is simple and compatible with other techniques for reducing rounds.

*Research supported by AT&T Bell Laboratories, Murray Hill, NJ. Contact: Donald Beaver 313 Whitmore, Penn State Univ., State College, PA 16802; (814) 863-0147; beaver@cs.psu.edu.

J. Feigenbaum (Ed.): Advances in Cryptology - CRYPTO '91, LNCS 576, pp. 420-432, 1992.
© Springer-Verlag Berlin Heidelberg 1992

# 1    Introduction

À quoi bon l'enfant qui vient de naitre?

Benjamin Franklin[1] (1783)

The biggest drawback to current theoretical research in cryptography is its general impracticality: while polynomially-bounded resources are mathematically satisfying, they are often effectively out of reach. In distributed computing, where communication speeds lag behind processor speeds, the number of rounds of communication and the message sizes are significant issues to consider. A factor of ten can mean the difference between utility and impracticality.

Many solutions to secure multiparty function evaluation have been proposed [10, 11, 9, 7, 8, 4, 14, 2, 12, 6, 5] but none seem easily implementable, despite a reasonable clarity in their description and a theoretically small requirement for resources. These methods normally rely on the share-compute-reveal paradigm, in which processors secretly share their inputs, run subprotocols to evaluate gates of a bounded fanin[2] arithmetic circuit $C_F$ that expresses the function $F$ to compute, and reveal the final secret representing the output. Each subprotocol is an addition or multiplication of secrets, and uses a constant number of rounds and a small polynomial number of messages. But an $n^2$ factor or even a constant factor of twenty in a network of a hundred processors is debilitating.

In Shamir's method for secret sharing, each processor $i$ shares secret $s$ by selecting a polynomial $f(u) = a_t u^t + \cdots + a_1 u + s$ with coefficients $a_k$ chosen uniformly at random over a finite field $E$, setting $\text{PIECE}_j(s) = f(\alpha_j)$ (where $\alpha_j \neq 0$ is an identifier for player $j$), and sending $\text{PIECE}_j(s)$ to player $j$ for each $j$. Ben-Or, Goldwasser, and Wigderson point out that when the $\alpha_j$ are selected carefully, the pieces of $s$ turn out to be elements in a BCH code, and a unique secret is reconstructible despite up to $t$ changes, when $t \leq \lfloor n/3 \rfloor$.

A natural advantage of using polynomials is that combining two secrets $r$ and $s$ to form a new secret $q$ whose value is their sum is easy, and requires no interaction: each $j$ sets $\text{PIECE}_i(q) \leftarrow \text{PIECE}_i(r) + \text{PIECE}_i(s)$. If $f(u)$ represents $f(0) = r$ and $g(u)$ represents $g(0) = s$, then $h(u) = f(u) + g(u)$ represents $h(0) = r + s$. Multiplication by a publicly known constant is also easy: $\text{PIECE}_i(cs) = c \cdot \text{PIECE}_i(s)$. Thus a new secret may be computed without having to reveal $r$ and $s$.

When secrets are multiplied, however, problems arise: the degree of the polynomial $h(u) = f(u)g(u)$ determined by the products of the individual pieces is $2t$, which soon grows out of hand. To deal with this problem, an interactive subprotocol for "degree reduction" is employed [7, 8]. We shall not present the solution here, but we shall give a brief outline in order to consider its resource requirements. Essentially, each processor is required to reshare $\text{PIECE}_i(r)$ and $\text{PIECE}_i(s)$ along with a third secret $c_i$, and must then prove interactively that $c_i = \text{PIECE}_i(r)\text{PIECE}_i(s)$. The players also jointly create several uniformly random secrets. Each player's piece of the new secret $q = rs$ then becomes

---

[1] "What good is a newborn child?" —Upon being asked at the launching of one of the first hot-air balloons, what good it would serve.

[2] Multiplicative gates have fanin 2; additive gates have unbounded fanin.

a particular linear combination of the confirmed $c_i$ values along with uniformly random secret values to preserve the uniformity of higher-order coefficients; there is a different linear combination to compute for each player. Thus, a multiplication involves sharing, creating random secrets, proving products are valid, and reconstruction.

A standard protocol to compute $F$ evaluates $C_F$ level by level, creating new secrets at each stage using linear combinations and multiplications. Let $S$ be the number of rounds used to share a secret and let $M$ be that to multiply. If the depth of $C_F$ is $D_F$, then the standard solution requires some $S + D_F M + 1$ rounds. Some improvements can be made for functions $F \in NC$; Bar-Ilan and Beaver [1] slice a $\log n$ factor from the depth of the circuit. But multiplications involving sharing and proofs and reconstructions are still involved at each step.

**Our solution.** We present a protocol that does evaluate the circuit $C_F$ level by level, but *each level is simply a reconstruction of secrets*, rather than a full-blown multiplication. In other words, each level uses *only* one *round of interaction* requiring neither private channels nor broadcast (in the sense of Byzantine Agreement).

Whereas previous protocols employ a great deal of processing to protect against Byzantine (malicious, message-changing) adversaries throughout the execution of the protocols, our protocol requires no elaborate on-line protection during the body of the protocol. Malicious or random errors are easily detected by checking whether $n$ points interpolate to a $t^{th}$-degree polynomial. Byzantine failures are corrected directly using BCH decoding as in normal secret-reconstruction — interaction, proofs, private communication, Byzantine Agreement, and other special procedures are not necessary. In fact, it suffices that all nonfaulty players broadcast a message (broadcasts from faulty players can be incomplete or inconsistent; the players need not agree on the set of messages apparently broadcast).

In addition to reducing network requirements — Byzantine Agreement and private channels can be costly to implement — the body of our protocol (send public messages, do BCH error correction) is easy to implement using established software. The reduction in programming complexity lends a greater degree of confidence in the security of an implementation.

**The cost and the savings.** We achieve these improvements by preprocessing: but the preprocessing stage costs only one phase of multiplication. The total number of rounds drops from $S + D_F M + 1$ rounds to $S + M + D_F$, a significant improvement of a factor of $M$ over standard techniques. The total number of multiplications in our protocol remains *exactly* the same as in [7, 8], namely exactly the number of multiplicative gates in $C_F$, but our multiplications are performed all in parallel. The number of additions is increased slightly in order to generate (just) $N$ uniformly random secrets, where $N$ is the size of $C_F$. The increase in additions is a tiny fraction compared to the number of additions and multiplications required by a standard ([7, 8]) protocol.

**The idea.** Our solution arises from an idea that has no obvious value at first glance: *completely randomize every input and output to each gate in* $C_F$. That is, select random inputs to each gate and compute the results of each gate all at once. Surprisingly, such a mangled circuit turns out to be useful. Through a very simple error-correction procedure, the accurate (and secret) values at each level can be computed without recourse to multiplication.

This error-correcting procedure is based on a technique introduced in [2] for proving that the product of two secrets is a third. Namely: if a dealer wishes to show that $c = ab$, where he has shared $a$, $b$, and $c$, then he chooses random numbers $\Delta_a$ and $\Delta_b$ and shares $d = (a + \Delta_a)(b + \Delta_b)$. A "verifier" (the system) checks the dealer randomly by flipping a coin: the dealer must either (1) reveal $\Delta_a$ and $\Delta_b$, in which case the system checks that the linear combination $d - (a\Delta_b + b\Delta_a + \Delta_a\Delta_b) - c = 0$, or (2) reveal $d$ and linear combinations $(a + \Delta_a)$ and $(b + \Delta_b)$, in which case the system checks $d = (a + \Delta_a)(b + \Delta_b)$. Appropriate repetitions prevent cheating; the dealer must cheat at many random points in order that his secrets be consistent. In the current work, $\Delta_a$ and $\Delta_b$ become corrections to a gate whose inputs $(a + \Delta_a)$ and $(b + \Delta_b)$ have been chosen uniformly at random, and whose output $d = (a + \Delta_a)(b + \Delta_b)$ has been precomputed.[3] Multiplication of two real inputs $a$ and $b$ reduces to computing a correction to $d$ that, in turn, reduces to a linear combination of $a$, $b$, $d$, and the publicly revealed (but uniformly random) corrections $\Delta_a$ and $\Delta_b$.

One-time tables. We coin the term "one-time table" to describe a set of precomputed values that support direct secure computation without broadcast or private channels. This is analogous to a one-time pad, which is a random sequence of bits permitting two parties to send arbitrary messages with perfect privacy over public channels. Our "circuit randomization" constructs a list of independent, secret products of independent, secret random numbers. This list depends on $F$ only insofar as it must contain as many entries as there are multiplicative gates in a circuit for $F$ — in the same way a one-time pad must contain enough bits to mask a given message. The cost of using an entry is one round of open communication and requires neither broadcast nor private channels. Thus, we propose the precomputation of a one-time table, using a few short and initial rounds of costly (broadcast or private) channels, as a general paradigm for secure protocol design.

Contents. We describe the protocol in §2, giving our main theorem in §2.2 and a proof sketch in §2.3. We discuss efficiency and practical issues in §3.

# 2  An Efficient Protocol for Circuit Evaluation

Fix $n$, the number of players; $t(n) < n/2$, a bound on the number of players who can be corrupted in a dynamic and malicious (Byzantine) way; $E$, a finite field such that $|E| > n + 1$; $F$, a function from $E^n$ to $E$ described by a polynomial-size circuit $C_F$ (without loss of generality, this covers finite functions from polynomial bits to polynomial bits [with poly-size circuits] as well as the case where each player learns a private output); and $\alpha_1, \ldots, \alpha_n$, primitive $n^{th}$ roots of unity over $E$. For the sake of exposition, we assume private and broadcast channels are available and that $t(n) < n/3$, but we note that our

---

[3]In [2], the symbols $\Delta_a$ and $\Delta_b$ appear as $r$ and $s$, not to be confused with the use of $r$ and $s$ in this work.

techniques apply to any protocol based on the share-compute-reveal paradigm.

We employ the secret sharing (SHARE ), reconstruction (REC ), linear combination (LINEAR-COMBINE ), and multiplication (MULTIPLY ) protocols of [7] for $t < n/3$; for $n/3 \leq t < n/2$, methods of [14, 2] can be used. We refer the reader to [7, 8, 14, 2] for detailed descriptions. Before describing the protocol, we note that Figure 1 gives a simple and well-known subprotocol UNIFSECRET to generate uniformly random secrets by adding uniformly random secrets shared by each party.

---

UNIFSECRET $(r)$
1    $(1 \leq i \leq n)$          Player $i$ sets $r_i \leftarrow uniform(E)$
2    $(1 \leq i \leq n)$          Player $i$ shares $r_i$.
3                              Run LINEAR-COMBINE : $r \leftarrow \sum_{i=1}^{n} r_i$.

Figure 1: Protocol to produce a uniformly random secret field element $r$.

---

Now, assume that circuit $C_F$ has $N$ wires $x_1, \ldots, x_N$, where $x_1, \ldots, x_n$ carry the inputs. Assume also that there are gates $g_k \in \{+, \times\}$ of fan-in 2, and write $x_k = g_k(x_{i_k}, x_{j_k})$ to mean that gate $g_k$ has inputs $x_{i_k}$ and $x_{j_k}$ and output $x_{k_k}$ with $i_k, j_k < l$. With each gate a depth level$(g_k)$ is associated in a standard way. To evaluate $C_F$, one assigns the input wires the values of $x_1, \ldots, x_n$, then for each level $L$ from 1 to $D_F$, one evaluates all the gates $g_k$ at depth $L$, finally evaluating $g_N$ to produce the circuit output $x_N$.

The share-compute-reveal paradigm follows exactly this pattern, using subprotocols to evaluate gates at each level and thereby produce new secrets $x_k$, until the final secret $x_N$ is calculated. The result $x_N$ can then be reconstructed using REC . We shall take an analogous but somewhat different route.

Let us ignore secret sharing for the moment and focus on the values used in the calculation of $x_N = F(x_1, \ldots, x_n)$.

In particular, let us create N *uniformly random* values $r_1, \ldots, r_N$, one for every $x_i$. For every gate $g_k$, compute $s_k = g_k(r_{i_k}, r_{j_k})$. These values have no apparent connection to the correct $x_k$ values, nor to the final output.

But consider now the *corrections* $\Delta_i = r_i - x_i$ to each wire. We begin the evaluation of $C_F$ by computing the corrections to the inputs: $\Delta_1 = r_1 - x_1, \ldots, \Delta_n = r_n - x_n$. Given an additive gate $g_k = (+)$ with random inputs $r_{i_k}, r_{j_k}$, random output $r_k$, and input wire corrections $\Delta_{i_k}, \Delta_{j_k}$, we can compute the correction $\Delta_k$ for the output wire as $\Delta_k = r_k - s_k - \Delta_{i_k} - \Delta_{j_k}$, because:

$$
\begin{aligned}
\Delta_k &= r_k - (x_{i_k} + x_{j_k}) \\
&= r_k - (r_{i_k} + \Delta_{i_k}) - (r_{j_k} + \Delta_{j_k}) \\
&= r_k - (r_{i_k} + r_{j_k}) - \Delta_{i_k} - \Delta_{j_k} \\
&= r_k - s_k - \Delta_{i_k} - \Delta_{j_k}.
\end{aligned}
$$

We may thus regard $\Delta_k$ as a *linear combination* of previously calculated, "known" constants $\Delta_{i_k}$ and $\Delta_{j_k}$ with the values $r_k$ and $s_k$.

But more interesting, and crucial to our solution, is the observation that for multiplicative gates $g_k = (\times)$, $\Delta_k = r_k - s_k - r_{i_k}\Delta_{j_k} - \Delta_{i_k}r_{j_k} - \Delta_{i_k}\Delta_{j_k}$, because:

$$
\begin{aligned}
\Delta_k &= r_k - (x_{i_k}x_{j_k}) \\
&= r_k - (r_{i_k} + \Delta_{i_k})(r_{j_k} + \Delta_{j_k}) \\
&= r_k - r_{i_k}r_{j_k} - r_{i_k}\Delta_{j_k} - \Delta_{i_k}r_{j_k} - \Delta_{i_k}\Delta_{j_k} \\
&= r_k - s_k - r_{i_k}\Delta_{j_k} - \Delta_{i_k}r_{j_k} - \Delta_{i_k}\Delta_{j_k}.
\end{aligned}
$$

In other words, if $\Delta_{i_k}$ and $\Delta_{j_k}$ are already calculated and "known," then $\Delta_k$ is a *linear combination* of these "known" constants and the values $r_k, s_k, r_{i_k}, r_{j_k}$.

Now, let's return to our worries about security. Say that all values $r_k$ are uniformly random and secretly shared, that all values $q_k = g_k(r_{i_k}, r_{j_k})$ have been secretly computed and are secrets, and that the lowest level of corrections $\Delta_1 = r_1 - x_1, \ldots, \Delta_n = r_n - x_n$ have been computed *and reconstructed*. Then the computation of a new correction at each level is a *linear combination* of publicly known values $(\Delta_{i_k}, \Delta_{j_k})$ and secret values $(r_k, s_k, r_{i_k}, r_{j_k})$, requiring no interaction. In fact, each player computes his piece of new $\Delta_k$ as a linear combination of pieces; with $g_k = \times$, for example, player $i$ computes:

$$
\mathrm{PIECE}_i(\Delta_k) \leftarrow \mathrm{PIECE}_i(r_k) - \mathrm{PIECE}_i(s_k) - \mathrm{PIECE}_i(r_{i_k})\Delta_{j_k} - \Delta_{i_k}\mathrm{PIECE}_i(r_{j_k}) - \Delta_{i_k}\Delta_{j_k}.
$$

The interaction for each level arises from *reconstructing* $\Delta_k$ from these pieces of $\Delta_k$, which involves a single broadcast of each piece by each player. (Byzantine faults — inconsistencies in pieces supplied by faulty players — are covered by BCH error-correction without the need for Byzantine Agreement or other interaction.)

Now, note that because every $r_k$ is uniformly random, every $\Delta_k$ value is also uniformly random, regardless of the inputs. Thus, no information whatsoever is revealed by reconstructing the $\Delta_k$ values. The only reconstruction that contains nonrandom information is the reconstruction of the final output secret $x_N = F(x_1, \ldots, x_n)$.

With this explanation in hand, the reader should be prepared to read Figure 2, which describes the protocol. Note that the final level is computed differently because the secret $x_N$ does not need to be fed into a new, randomized gate.

## 2.1 An Optimization

With a simple optimization, additive layers in the circuit can be ignored, in the sense that they need not lead to interaction. We "compress" additive gates by computing the corrections to their outputs at the same time as the corrections to their input wires. In fact, no "randomization" of additive gates (secret generation of $R_1$, $R_2$, and computation of $S = R_1 + R_2$ during preprocessing) is needed.

Let us illustrate the technique with an example. Let gate $g_5(x_1, x_2) = x_1x_2$, $g_6(x_3, x_4) = x_3x_4$, and $g_7(x_5, x_6) = x_5 + x_6$. That is, the output of $g_7$ is $(x_1x_2 + x_3x_4)$. Rather than go through two stages (multiply, add), we need only one (multiply). Define $\delta_k = s_k - x_k$ for $1 \leq k \leq N$. Although the $\delta_k$ values are not uniformly distributed (and

---

RANDCIRCUIT $(C_F)$

| | | |
|---|---|---|
| **1.1** | $(1 \le i \le n)$ | Player $i$: run SHARE$(x_i)$, dealing secret $x_i$ |
| **1.2** | $(1 \le k \le N)$ | Run UNIFSECRET$(r_k)$ |
| **2.1** | $(1 \le k \le n)$ | Run LINEAR-COMBINE: $\Delta_k \leftarrow r_k - x_k$ |
| **2.2** | $(1 \le k \le n)$ | Run REC$(\Delta_k)$ to reveal $\Delta_k$ |

**2.2** $(N+1 \le k \le N)$ if $g_k = (+)$ then run LINEAR-COMBINE: $s_k \leftarrow r_{i_k} + r_{j_k}$
else run MULTIPLY: $s_k \leftarrow r_{i_k} r_{j_k}$

**3** For $L = 1..(D_F - 1)$ do
($\forall k$ such that **level**$(g_k) = L$):

**3.1** If $g_k = (+)$ then run LINEAR-COMBINE:
$$\Delta_k \leftarrow r_k - s_k - \Delta_{i_k} - \Delta_{j_k}$$
else run MULTIPLY:
$$\Delta_k \leftarrow r_k - s_k - r_{i_k}\Delta_{j_k} - \Delta_{i_k}r_{j_k} - \Delta_{i_k}\Delta_{j_k}$$

**3.2** Run REC$(\Delta_k)$

**4.1** If $g_N = (+)$ then run LINEAR-COMBINE:
$$x_N \leftarrow s_N + \Delta_{i_N} + \Delta_{j_N}$$
else run MULTIPLY:
$$x_N \leftarrow s_N + r_{i_N}\Delta_{j_N} + \Delta_{i_N}r_{j_N} + \Delta_{i_N}\Delta_{j_N}$$

**4.1** Run REC$(x_N)$ to reveal $F(x_1, \ldots, x_n) = x_N$.

Figure 2: Protocol to evaluate function $F$ represented by arithmetic circuit $C_F$ of size $N$ and depth $D_F$ over field $E$. SHARE, REC, LINEAR-COMBINE, MULTIPLY, and UNIFSECRET are described in the text. "$(1 \le i \le n)$" means run in parallel; **for** loops are executed in sequence.

---

hence should not be revealed), they satisfy a set of equations similar to those for the $\Delta_k$ values; thus,

$$
\begin{aligned}
\delta_5 &= -r_1\Delta_2 - \Delta_1 r_2 - \Delta_1\Delta_2, \\
\delta_6 &= -r_3\Delta_4 - \Delta_3 r_4 - \Delta_3\Delta_4.
\end{aligned}
$$

This gives

$$
\begin{aligned}
\Delta_7 &= r_7 - (x_5 + x_6) \\
&= r_7 - (s_5 + \delta_5) - (s_6 + \delta_6) \\
&= r_7 - s_5 - s_6 + r_1\Delta_2 + \Delta_1 r_2 + \Delta_1\Delta_2 + r_3\Delta_4 + \Delta_3 r_4 + \Delta_3\Delta_4,
\end{aligned}
$$

which expresses $\Delta_7$ as a linear combination of secret inputs to $g_5$ and $g_6$, not of inputs to $g_7$. Random secrets $r_5$ and $r_6$ are avoided altogether. Thus, not only need gate $g_7$ not be "randomized," the computation of the correction $\Delta_7$ to its output need not wait for the computation and reconstruction of values $\Delta_5$ and $\Delta_6$.

A simple way to think of this is to set $r_{i_k} = s_{i_k}$ and $r_{j_k} = s_{j_k}$ for every additive gate $s_k = g_k(r_{i_k}, r_{j_k})$; then $s_k = r_{i_k} + r_{j_k} = s_{i_k} + s_{j_k}$, and the formula for $\Delta_k$ depends only on the $\Delta$ values for the inputs to $g_{i_k}$ and $g_{j_k}$. The example given above generalizes in a natural way to give a general technique that "ignores" additive gates.

## 2.2  Main Results

The definitions of *resilience* — a combination of security and fault-tolerance — and of *perfect* and *exponential* are given in §2.3.

**Theorem 1** *Let $t(n) < n/3$. Let $S$ be the number of rounds to share a secret, and let $M$ be the number of rounds to multiply. Let $F$ be any function from $E^n$ to $E$ described by a poly-size circuit $C_F$. Then* RANDCIRCUIT *is a perfectly $t$-resilient protocol for $F$ against Byzantine adversaries and requires only $S + M + D_F$ rounds of interaction, a savings of $\Omega(D_F)$ rounds over previous protocols.*

**Proof.** Referring to Figure 2, step 1 requires $S$ rounds, step 2 requires $M$ rounds, step 3 uses $(D_F - 1)$ secret reconstructions, and step 4 uses one secret reconstruction. Earlier protocols used $S + MD_F + 1$; the improvement is $(D_F - 1)(M - 1) = \Omega(D_F)$ rounds. See §2.3 for a proof of resilience (security). $\square$

Let RANDCIRCUIT′ denote the protocol obtained from RANDCIRCUIT by using secret-sharing, addition, and multiplication protocols designed to withstand $t < n/2$ rather than $t < n/3$ faults, and let $S', M'$ be the number of rounds required by the corresponding subprotocols.

**Theorem 2** *For $t(n) < n/2$,* RANDCIRCUIT′ *is an exponentially $t$-resilient protocol for $F$ against Byzantine adversaries and requires only $S' + M' + D_F$ rounds of interaction, a savings of $\Omega(nD_F)$ rounds over previous protocols.*

**Proof.** As in Theorem 1, the number of rounds used is $S' + M' + D_F$; existing methods for multiplication require $\Omega(t)$ rounds when $t$ faults are possible, so the difference of $(D_F - 1)(M' - 1)$ gives the savings reported. Because of the exponentially small chance of error in the secret addition and multiplication protocols, the resilience of our protocol is only exponential; but better resilience is shown impossible in [7]. $\square$

Using the optimization described in §2.1, we observe that the round complexity depends only on the multiplicative depth of a circuit $C_F$ for $F$. Let RANDCIRCUIT* denote the protocol obtained from RANDCIRCUIT by computing corrections to additive gates at the same time as the corrections to the multiplicative gates that feed them, as described in §2.1; "randomization" is not performed for additive gates. Let $\text{depth}_{\times}(C)$ give the multiplicative depth of circuit $C$, and let $\text{depth}_{\times}(F)$ be the minimum over all polynomial-size bounded-fanin arithmetic circuits $C_F$ computing function $F$.

**Theorem 3** *For $t(n) < n/3$, protocol* RANDCIRCUIT* *is a perfectly $t$-resilient protocol for $F$ against Byzantine adversaries and requires only $S + M + \mathbf{depth}_\times(F)$ rounds of interaction. An analogous result with exponential resilience holds for a protocol* RANDCIRCUIT*' *designed for $t(n) < n/2$.*

We remark that avoiding the randomization for additive gates reduces the message complexity as well; the UNIFSECRET protocol is called only for multiplicative gates, not for all $N$ gates in $C_F$.

**Proof.** The proof follows the lines of the proof of Theorem 1. The improvement in round complexity arises from "compressing" additive gates as described in §2.1. □

## 2.3 Proof Sketch

We adopt the security definitions of [2, 3]. A brief sketch is included here for completeness. An ensemble $P$ is a collection of distributions $P(z, k)$ for $z \in \Sigma^*$ and $k \in \mathbf{N}$. The difference between distributions $\mathcal{P}$ and $\mathcal{Q}$ on finite domain $X$ is $\sum_X |\Pr_{\mathcal{P}}[x] - \Pr_{\mathcal{Q}}[x]|$. Ensembles $P$ and $Q$ are $O(\delta(k))$-**indistinguishable** ($P \approx^{\delta(k)} Q$) if $(\exists k_0)(\forall k \geq k_0)(\forall z)|P(z, k) - Q(z, k)| < \delta(k)$. **Perfect** ($O(0)$), **exponential** ($O(c^{-k})$), **statistical** ($(\forall c)O(k^{-c})$), and **computational** indistinguishability are straightforwardly defined.

A protocol $\alpha$ with $n$ players having $m$-bit inputs $\vec{x} = (x_1, \ldots, x_n)$ and auxiliary inputs $\vec{a} = (a_1, \ldots, a_n)$ induces a distribution $[\alpha](\vec{x} \cdot \vec{a}, k)$ on outputs $\vec{y} = (y_1, \ldots, y_n)$; $k$ is a security parameter given to each player. When an adversary $\mathcal{A}$ with auxiliary input $a_A$ is allowed to attack $\alpha$, the resulting distribution on *all* outputs $\vec{y} \cdot y_A$ is denoted $[\alpha, \mathcal{A}](\vec{x} \cdot \vec{a} \cdot a_A)$. An **interface** is an interactive machine with two tapes; it communicates with an adversary $\mathcal{A}$ on one, and acts as an adversary on the other. The distribution induced by running protocol $\beta$ with adversary $\mathcal{I}(\mathcal{A})$ (*i.e.* $\mathcal{A}$ with interface $\mathcal{I}$ translating its corruptions) is denoted $[\beta, \mathcal{I}(\mathcal{A})](\vec{x} \cdot \vec{a} \cdot a_A)$. Ranging over all $z = \vec{x} \cdot \vec{a} \cdot a_A$ and $k$, we consider ensembles $[\alpha, \mathcal{A}]$ and $[\beta, \mathcal{I}(\mathcal{A})]$.

Protocol $\alpha$ is as resilient (*i.e.* secure and reliable) as $\beta$ if an adversary $\mathcal{A}$, when it attacks $\alpha$, gains the same information and has the same effect on nonfaulty outputs as when $\mathcal{A}$ attacks $\beta$ through $\mathcal{I}$:

**Definition 1 (Relative Resilience)** *Let* ADV$_\alpha$ *and* ADV$_\beta$ *denote the set of allowed adversaries for $\alpha$ and $\beta$. Protocol $\alpha$ is as resilient as $\beta$, written $\alpha \succeq \beta$, if there exists an interface $\mathcal{I}$ from $\alpha$ to $\beta$ such that for all $\mathcal{A} \in$ ADV$_\alpha$, we have $\mathcal{I}(\mathcal{A}) \in$ ADV$_\beta$ and*

$$[\alpha, \mathcal{A}] \approx [\beta, \mathcal{I}(\mathcal{A})].$$

The ideal protocol for $F$, ID($F$), contains an incorruptible host that collects inputs $x_i$ in the first round and returns $F(x_1, \ldots, x_n)$ in the second.

**Definition 2 (Resilience)** *$\alpha$ is a $t$-resilient protocol for $F$ if $\alpha \succeq$ ID($F$), against $t$-adversaries.*

**Proof of Theorem 1.** We must find an interface $\mathcal{I}$ that translates attacks on RANDCIRCUIT to attacks on the ideal, trusted-host protocol $\mathrm{ID}(F)$ for $F$. Because initial messages (preprocessing steps 1 and 2) between nonfaulty players are not seen by an adversary, and because most messages created by nonfaulty players (whether sent to corrupted players or seen when later corrupted) are generated uniformly at random, subject to simple linear algebraic conditions and the input values and output value $F(x_1,\ldots,x_n)$, an interface is neither hard to design nor to prove correct. The following lemmas describe the responses that $\mathcal{I}$ must make in order to supply $\mathcal{A}$ with a proper set of responses to corruption requests while at the same time inducing the same outputs in $\mathrm{ID}(F)$ that $\mathcal{A}$ induces in RANDCIRCUIT.

**Lemma 4** *(Messages from nonfaulty to faulty before final round.) Let $t(n) < n/3$. For any corrupted subset $T \subset \{1,..,n\}$ and any round $r$ except the last, the set of messages from players not in $T$ to players in $T$ consists of uniformly random field elements subject to interpolating to a uniformly random polynomial of degree $t$.*

**Proof.** Simple linear algebra. In the case of messages regarding $\Delta$ reconstructions, the "uniformly random polynomials" have uniformly random $\Delta$ values as their free terms. In the case of messages regarding secretly-shared inputs or random secrets, a set of $t$ messages to players in $T$ is a uniformly random $t$-vector, whether it be generated from a uniformly random polynomial of degree $t$ having free term $x_i$ or from a uniformly random polynomial of degree $t$. $\square$

**Lemma 5** *(Newly corrupt player $i$ before final round; how to generate past view.) Let $t(n) < n/3$. For any corrupted subset $T \subset \{1,..,n\}$, any round $r$ except the last, and any $i \notin T$, the distribution on secret values generated by $i$ through round $r$ is uniform, the distribution on messages through round $r$ from players not in $T$ to player $i$ is uniform subject to interpolating to already revealed $\Delta_k$ values, and the distribution on messages from player $i$ to players not in $T$ is uniform from among the set of solutions consistent with the secret values player $i$ randomly generated, the $\Delta_k$ values revealed through round $r$, and its input $x_i$.*

**Proof.** Simple linear algebra. $\square$

**Lemma 6** *(Messages from nonfaulty at final round.) Let $t(n) < n/3$. For any corrupted subset $T \subset \{1,..,n\}$, at the final round the distribution on messages from players not in $T$ to players in $T$ is uniform subject to interpolating to $F(x_1,\ldots,x_n)$ [with $x_i$ replaced by default value 0 for any player who failed to share an input].*

**Proof.** Simple linear algebra. $\square$

**Lemma 7** *(Newly corrupt player $i$ at final round; how to generate past view.) Let $t(n) < n/3$. For any corrupted subset $T \subset \{1,..,n\}$, any round $r$ except the last, and any $i \notin T$,* the distribution on secret values generated by $i$ through round $r$ is uniform, the distribution on messages through round $r$ from players not in $T$ to player $i$ is uniform subject to interpolating to already revealed $\Delta_k$ values, and the distribution on messages from player $i$ to players not in $T$ is uniform from among the set of solutions consistent with the secret values player $i$ randomly generated, the $\Delta_k$ values revealed through round $r$, its input $x_i$, and $F(x'_1, \ldots, x'_n)$ [where $x'_j$ is $x_j$ for nonfaulty $j$ but is default value 0 for any player $j$ who failed to share an input].

**Proof.** Simple linear algebra. □

The interface collects pieces of $x_i$ distributed by players $i$ corrupted at the start, and sets $x'_i$ accordingly. For every player $i$ corrupted by $\mathcal{A}$, $\mathcal{I}$ requests the corruption of $i$ in $\text{ID}(F)$, obtaining $x_i$, which it then returns to $\mathcal{A}$ along with a view of RANDCIRCUIT constructed according to the lemmas (this involves solutions to simple linear algebraic equations). For messages sent from nonfaulty players to faulty players, $\mathcal{I}$ chooses random elements according to the lemmas and sends them to $\mathcal{A}$. Interface $\mathcal{I}$ records all outgoing messages from $\mathcal{A}$ intended to replace messages from corrupted players, and uses them to construct deterministic responses from nonfaulty, virtual players (in preprocessing steps 1 and 2, nonfaulty players may detect cheating and use default value 0 for cheating players; in later steps, fewer than $t$ modifications to the $n$-vector used in reconstruction does not affect the $\Delta$ value computed by nonfaulty players). For space reasons, we shall not describe the interface in greater detail.

The resilience of RANDCIRCUIT follows directly from the fact that the messages sent to $\mathcal{A}$ from $\mathcal{I}$ are *identical* to responses to corruption requests when $\mathcal{A}$ attacks RANDCIRCUIT, and the inputs $x'_i$ that $\mathcal{I}$ passes on to $\text{ID}(F)$ are exactly what $\mathcal{A}$ chooses and shares (whether or not by default). □

# 3   Theory and Practice

We have reduced the number of rounds of interaction by an order of magnitude, removing yet another obstacle to the use of theoretical results in practice. Our methods apply to any protocol based on circuit evaluation, including cryptographic multiparty protocols, two-party oblivious circuit evaluation, *etc.*. The advantage of circuit randomization over direct evaluation is proportional to the cost of multiplication *vs.* the cost of addition.

Theoretically, the number of rounds can be reduced further by an $O(\log n)$ factor using the results of [1]. In practice, the choice whether to follow this route as well depends on just how large the $O(\log n)$ reduction is. The methods of [1] require multiplying three $3 \times 3$ matrices, which normally costs two multiplications, but which now costs 2 rounds (each matrix multiplication costs a round to correct the ×-gates). Since the submission of this abstract, we have discovered an alternative to [1] that permits unbounded fan-in multiplication but suffers neither from *expected* round complexity (a complication that makes implementation difficult) nor from having to convert circuit layers to matrix products.

The RANDCIRCUIT protocol is, in many senses, simpler than direct circuit evaluation.

The initial processing is perhaps less than immediately intuitive, but it contains the same set of computations that must be done during direct circuit evaluation, parallelized and applied to random secrets. The only added complexity arises from creating random secrets at the start, but this subprotocol is easy relative to the one for multiplication.

In fact, implementation is far easier than for direct circuit evaluation, since the body of the protocol consists of reconstructions, which require simply a weak broadcast (all non-faulty players broadcast their value, without Byzantine Agreement) from each player. A weak broadcast is far simpler to implement than a complicated multiplication subprotocol that itself contains private communications and Byzantine Agreement protocols. In asynchronous settings, using weak broadcast rather than interaction becomes a tremendous advantage, not just for efficiency but for correctness in implementation.

Interestingly, because the steps of the protocol are reconstructions, error correction in the sense of zero-knowledge proofs of behavior is not needed. Error detection and correction is performed locally without interaction. Detection is simple: check whether received pieces interpolate to a degree-$t$ polynomial. Correction uses a local BCH-error-code correction, without interaction. Thus, the overhead of repeated proofs, cut-and-choose methods, or other interactive error detection techniques is not necessary after the first multiplication.

It is interesting to note that the randomization techniques used here apply to circuit evaluation in both the cryptographic and the noncryptographic settings. The techniques we present were inspired by a proof system for multilinear polynomials [2] that has a similarity to recent interactive proof systems for functions expressible as low-degree polynomials, perhaps suggesting deeper connections and a wider applicability than simply to cryptographic protocol optimization. In any case, the practical advantages are evident.

### Acknowledgements

The author would like to thank Donald W. Beaver for his perserverance in keeping the author awake and contemplating new ideas during late-night-early-morning discussions over warm milk.

# References

[1] J. Bar-Ilan, D. Beaver. "Non-Cryptographic Fault-Tolerant Computing in a Constant Expected Number of Rounds of Interaction." *Proceedings of PODC*, ACM, 1989, 201–209.

[2] D. Beaver. "Secure Multiparty Protocols and Zero Knowledge Proof Systems Tolerating a Faulty Minority." To appear, *J. Cryptology.* An earlier version appeared as "Secure Multiparty Protocols Tolerating Half Faulty Processors." *Proceedings of Crypto 1989*, ACM, 1989.

[3] D. Beaver. *Security, Fault Tolerance, and Communication Complexity in Distributed Systems.* PhD Thesis, Harvard University, Cambridge, 1990.

[4] D. Beaver, S. Goldwasser. "Multiparty Computation with Faulty Majority." *Proceedings of the 30th FOCS*, IEEE, 1989, 468–473.

[5] D. Beaver, S. Haber. "Cryptographic Protocols Provably Secure Against Dynamic Adversaries." Submitted to FOCS 91.

[6] D. Beaver, S. Micali, P. Rogaway. "The Round Complexity of Secure Protocols." *Proceedings of the 22st STOC*, ACM, 1990, 503–513.

[7] M. Ben-Or, S. Goldwasser, A. Wigderson. "Completeness Theorems for Non-Cryptographic Fault-Tolerant Distributed Computation." *Proceedings of the 20th STOC*, ACM, 1988, 1–10.

[8] D. Chaum, C. Crépeau, I. Damgård. "Multiparty Unconditionally Secure Protocols." *Proceedings of the 20th STOC*, ACM, 1988, 11–19.

[9] Z. Galil, S. Haber, M. Yung. "Cryptographic Computation: Secure Fault-Tolerant Protocols and the Public-Key Model." *Proceedings of Crypto 1987*, Springer–Verlag, 1988, 135–155.

[10] O. Goldreich, S. Micali, A. Wigderson. "Proofs that Yield Nothing but Their Validity and a Methodology of Cryptographic Protocol Design." *Proceedings of the 27th FOCS*, IEEE, 1986, 174–187.

[11] O. Goldreich, S. Micali, A. Wigderson. "How to Play Any Mental Game, or A Completeness Theorem for Protocols with Honest Majority." *Proceedings of the 19th STOC*, ACM, 1987, 218–229.

[12] S. Goldwasser, L. Levin. "Fair Computation of General Functions in Presence of Immoral Majority." *Proceedings of Crypto 1990*.

[13] S. Haber. *Multi-Party Cryptographic Computation: Techniques and Applications*, PhD Thesis, Columbia University, 1988.

[14] T. Rabin, M. Ben-Or. "Verifiable Secret Sharing and Multiparty Protocols with Honest Majority." *Proceedings of the 21st STOC*, ACM, 1989, 73–85.

[15] A. Shamir. "How to Share a Secret." *Communications of the ACM*, 22 (1979), 612–613.

# Non-Interactive Zero-Knowledge Proof of Knowledge and Chosen Ciphertext Attack

Charles Rackoff
Daniel R. Simon
Dept. of Computer Science
University of Toronto
Toronto, Ontario M5S 1A4
Canada
rackoff@theory.toronto.edu
me@theory.toronto.edu

## Abstract

The zero-knowledge proof of knowledge, first defined by Fiat, Fiege and Shamir, was used by Galil, Haber and Yung as a means of constructing (out of a trapdoor function) an interactive public-key cryptosystem provably secure against chosen ciphertext attack. We introduce a revised setting which permits the definition of a non-interactive analogue, the non-interactive zero-knowledge proof of knowledge, and show how it may be constructed in that setting from a non-interactive zero-knowledge proof system for $NP$ (of the type introduced by Blum, Feldman and Micali). We give a formalization of chosen ciphertext attack in our model which is stronger than the "lunchtime attack" considered by Naor and Yung, and prove a non-interactive public-key cryptosystem based on non-interactive zero-knowledge proof of knowledge to be secure against it.

# 1  Introduction

A fundamental goal of modern cryptography is to formalize and solve the problem of how a group of parties may communicate securely with each other in an environment which does not necessarily prevent adversaries from eavesdropping on, or tampering with, message transmissions. One very strong (but not necessarily sufficient) criterion for prospective solutions has been security of each party's received messages against "chosen ciphertext attack", described informally as an attack on a particular message during which the attacker may obtain decryptions of other messages chosen at will.

Galil, Haber and Yung ([GHY]) showed formally how zero-knowledge interactive proofs of knowledge could be used to make public-key cryptosystems secure against chosen ciphertext attack. The formal argument follows the intuition of Blum, Feldman and Micali ([BFM]); a legal encryption is defined as including an interactive proof that the sender knows its decryption. Thus a machine which can carry out a successful chosen ciphertext attack can be "interrogated" so as to answer its own requests for decryption. It

J. Feigenbaum (Ed.): Advances in Cryptology - CRYPTO '91, LNCS 576, pp. 433-444, 1992.
© Springer-Verlag Berlin Heidelberg 1992

can therefore be used by a "blind" attacker (one without the ability to obtain decryptions of chosen ciphertexts) to break the underlying cryptosystem.

Unfortunately, attempts to remove the interaction from the above system face two closely related problems. Firstly, it is not intuitively clear how one could conceivably prove knowledge non-interactively; such a proof would necessarily not be feasibly produceable by parties not possessing the knowledge in question. However, merely receiving a non-interactive proof of knowledge from someone may well allow one to "produce" the same proof of knowledge to someone else. Secondly, the attacker in a chosen ciphertext attack is in general entitled to exploit this difficulty in proving knowledge by including the attacked ciphertext among the chosen ciphertexts to be decrypted, in a so-called "playback" attack.

Naor and Yung ([NY]) solved the latter problem by using a more restricted form of chosen ciphertext attack, known informally as the "lunchtime" or "midnight" attack. In this form of attack, the attacker is provided with decryptions of any messages it can generate, but only *before* receiving the message it is to attempt to decrypt itself. Thus the playback attack problem disappears. In their solution, each message is encrypted using two independent cryptosystems, and both encryptions are sent along with a non-interactive zero-knowledge proof that the two encryptions encrypt the same message. It turns out that an attacker capable of decrypting messages thus encrypted (when permitted a lunchtime chosen-ciphertext attack) can be used to decrypt messages in an unknown cryptosystem.

However, the "lunchtime" chosen ciphertext attack, being weaker than the unrestricted form, is a less satisfying model of the dangers inherent in real-life applications of cryptosystems, in that there is no reason to assume that an attacker will be bound by the artificial constraint of only being able to obtain information about various ciphertexts *before* discovering the real target message. Rather, the motivation behind the criterion of security against chosen ciphertext attack is the realistic assumption that attackers may be able to obtain information about chosen ciphertexts through ostensibly honest behaviour, which obviously may occur before or after the sending of a particular target message. On the other hand, some restriction on the definition of the attack is necessary in a non-interactive environment, to rule out playback attacks.

As a less restrictive, reasonably realistic alternative, we propose a model in which each sender possesses a "secret" associated with a publicly-known identifying key. For example, the secret could be the private key associated with the public key by which the sender itself receives messages. In this model, a natural definition of chosen ciphertext attack would allow any party to send chosen ciphertext messages to the receiver; a message's "putative" sender, whose identity is determined by the receiver on the basis of some information in the message, is then provided with its decryption. (In more practical terms, the message's decryption can be assumed to be encrypted using the sender's public key, then broadcast.) Thus the playback attack is not eliminated, but an attacker can still be prevented from getting any useful information from it, except by somehow using it to generate a message of which the attacker itself is the "putative" sender.

The problem of securing messages against chosen ciphertext attack (as defined above) in this model can be solved in a manner similar to that used by Naor and Yung. The solution involves the sender encrypting a message using its own public key and the receiver's, and providing a non-interactive zero-knowledge proof that the two encryptions encrypt the same plaintext. The proof of security of this scheme parallels the proof for the scheme of Naor and Yung.

More generally, we now can define non-interactive zero-knowledge proof of knowledge of a string with some property (say, a witness of membership of another string in some $NP$ language) in this model as a non-interactive zero-knowledge proof of existence of such a string from which the prover can recover the string itself (note that such a proof is with respect to a *specific* prover). For example, an encryption using the prover's public key of a string with the desired property, together with a non-interactive zero-knowledge proof that the encrypted string has that property, would in this model be a non-interactive zero-knowledge proof of knowledge of a string with the property in question. This definition is analogous to (and considerably simpler than) the interactive definition given by Fiat, Feige and Shamir ([FFS]), which required that a string with the property in question be recoverable given "complete access" to the prover TM. It also allows us to restate the above solution to the chosen ciphertext attack problem as a non-interactive version of the interactive protocol of Galil, Haber and Yung. That is, if senders are required to include with each message a non-interactive zero-knowledge proof of the sender's knowledge of its decryption, then the resulting (non-interactive) cryptosystem is secure against chosen ciphertext attack.

A still stronger form of chosen ciphertext attack would allow any message other than the one being attacked to be the chosen ciphertext; its (cleartext) decryption would be returned to the *actual* sender/attacker. Adding the requirement of a digital signature of all complete message-proof pairs guarantees security even in this case, since the sender must prove that anyone holding the information enabling it to sign the messages it generates must also know their decryption. Dolev, Dwork and Naor ([DDN]) have independently presented a considerably more complicated cryptosystem which is also secure against this type of chosen ciphertext attack, and does not make use of senders' possession of a "secret". Any further strengthening of this attack to permit playback attacks would necessarily require some kind of "timeliness" constraint on messages, to prevent their re-use.

# 2 The Setting and the Problem

We define here a model for a real-life public-key cryptographic setting similar to that first proposed in [DH], in which every party $u$ is provided by a trusted centre with a secret-key public-key pair, $(s^u, p^u)$, such that messages (which we may without loss of generality assume to be single bits) may be encrypted (using a cryptosystem, as described below) with the receiver's public key such that the receiver's private key is needed to decrypt them.

It is assumed that parties are capable of recognizing "valid" public keys (that is, those actually assigned to someone by the trusted centre). It can be imagined that each party possesses a listing of all assigned public keys; alternatively, the centre can provide parties with its own "digital signature" (described later) for its keys (which no party can then forge in attempting to produce a new valid key). A consequence of this state of affairs is that we can now associate with each message a specific "putative" sender (identified by a public key) as well as a receiver. Moreover, the decryption (indeed, the validity or invalidity) of an encrypted message can then be defined so as to depend on the message's putative sender.

In this setting, a chosen ciphertext attack is one in which an attacker, upon observing an encrypted message from another sender to a receiver, is permitted to generate any feasible number of messages, associated with any assigned public key it chooses, and receive their correct decryptions, according to the receiver. If it can with any significant probability greater than $\frac{1}{2}$ decrypt the intercepted message after this process, it has succeeded in its attack.

We can define the attack in one of two ways, depending on how we view the power of parties to the system to learn from other parties' actions and reactions. We can assume that parties are generally only privy to the consequences of the messages that clearly come from themselves; we would in that case correspondingly provide the chosen ciphertext attacker with only the decryptions of messages for wnich the putative sender is the attacker. Alternatively, we can assume that parties are able to detect the reactions of other parties to any messages sent, and to influence (or attempt to simulate) messages from others. The corresponding chosen ciphertext attack would then allow the attacker to receive the correct decryption of any message the attacker generates, regardless of the putative sender (and, in particular, of whether or not the attacker possesses the secret key of the putative sender). We must in this case of course make an exception in the case of the exact message originally being "attacked", but no other exception is necessary.

**Note.** All polynomial-time TM's defined in this paper are assumed to receive, in addition to their stated inputs, a security parameter $1^n$.

**Definition 2.1** *A* cryptosystem *is a triple* $(M_C, M_E, M_D)$ *of polynomial time-bounded TM's* ($M_C$ *and* $M_E$ *probabilistic), such that on input* $u$ *(the "identity" of user* $u$*)* $M_C$ *outputs a secret-key public-key pair* $(s^u, p^u)$ *with the following property: On input* $(s^u, p^u, p^v, b)$, $b \in \{0, 1\}$, $M_E$ *outputs a string* $e$ *such that on input* $(s^v, p^v, p^u, e)$ $M_D$ *outputs* $b$. *This holds for any two pairs* $(s^u, p^u)$ *and* $(s^v, p^v)$.

Note that $u$ and $v$ might not be distinct; parties may wish to send encryptions to themselves (in fact, this feature will be used later). Note also that "Conventional" public key cryptography (e.g., as defined in [GM]) ignores the identity of the sender altogether; the encryption $M_E(s, p, p', b)$ can be computed by any party without knowledge of any $s$.

We now define a very general type of chosen ciphertext attack, which in no way restricts the attacker's choice of ciphertexts; such an attack is impossible to defend against, because it permits "playback" attacks. The subsequent definitions define the two ways of restricting the attacker's choice of ciphertext appropriate to our model, as described above.

**Definition 2.2** *A* general chosen ciphertext attack *on a cryptosystem* $(M_C, M_E, M_D)$ *is an interactive pair* $(A, U)$, *where* $A$ *is a probabilistic polynomial-time "attacker", and* $U$ *represents the "universe" which responds to* $A$'s *challenges.* $(A, U)$ *behaves as follows: initially,* $M_C$ *creates pairs* $(s^S, p^S)$, $(s^R, p^R)$ *and* $(s^A, p^A)$ *for the sender, receiver and attacker respectively.* $M_C$ *also generates a polynomial number of additional pairs* $(s^1, p^1), \ldots, (s^{q(n)}, p^{q(n)})$ *(representing possible confederates for* $A$*). The plaintext* $b_S$ *is then randomly chosen from* $\{0, 1\}$, *and* $M_E$ *is run on input* $(s^S, p^S, p^R, b_S)$ *to obtain the encryption* $e$. $A$ *is given as input* $(e, K)$, $K = \{p^S, p^R, s^A, p^A, s^1, p^1, \ldots, s^{q(n)}, p^{q(n)}\}$. $A$ *then repeatedly generates triples* $(p^i, p^j, m)$, $p^i, p^j \in K$; *for each such triple,* $U$ *returns* $M_D(s^j, p^j, p^i, m) \in \{0, 1, \text{"?"}\}$. *At the end of this interaction,* $A$ *outputs* $b \in \{0, 1\}$. *We say that* $(A, U)$ succeeds *if for some polynomial* $h(n)$, $b = b_S$ *with probability at least* $\frac{1}{2} + \frac{1}{h(n)}$, *for infinitely many* $n$.

**Definition 2.3** *An* attacker-specific chosen ciphertext attack *is identical to a general chosen ciphertext attack (as defined above), except that on receiving a triple* $(p^i, p^j, m)$, $U$ *always returns "?" when* $i \neq A$.

**Definition 2.4** *A* message-restricted chosen ciphertext attack *is identical to a general chosen ciphertext attack (as defined above), except that on receiving a triple* $(p^i, p^j, m)$, $U$ *always returns "?" when* $i = S$, $j = R$ *and* $m = e$.

# 3 Tools

## 3.1 Public-Key Cryptography

We review here the definition of security for public-key cryptosystems introduced in [GM]; A proposed implementation, based on the assumption of the existence of a trapdoor function, is described there.

**Definition 3.1** *(based on* [GM]*) A* (single-encryption) attack *against a cryptosystem* $(M_C, M_E, M_D)$ *is a probabilistic polynomial-time machine* $A$ *which, on receiving as input* $(p^u, p^v, e)$ *(where* $(s^u, p^u)$ *and* $(s^v, p^v)$ *are generated by* $M_C$, *and* $e$ *is generated by* $M_E$ *on input* $(s^u, p^u, p^v, b)$, *with* $b$ *chosen randomly) outputs a single-bit "guess"* $g$. *We say that* $A$ *succeeds if for some polynomial* $h(n)$, $b = g$ *with probability at least* $\frac{1}{2} + \frac{1}{h(n)}$ *for infinitely many* $n$; *if no such* $A$ *succeeds, then the cryptosystem is* secure *(against single-encryption attack).*

Note again that $u$ and $v$ need not be distinct; $M_E(s^u, p^u, p^u, b)$ should still be difficult to decrypt for pairs $(s^u, p^u)$ generated by $M_C$.

## 3.2 Non-interactive proof systems and zero-knowledge

Non-interactive (zero-knowledge) proof systems were introduced by Blum, Feldman and Micali ([BFM]); the definitions were refined by Bellare and Goldwasser ([BG]) and Naor and Yung ([NY]). We briefly and informally discuss the definitions here, and refer the reader to [NY] for a rigorous treatment of them. An implementation method for any language in $NP$ based on the assumption of the existence of trapdoor functions can be found described in [FLS]. Another implementation appears in [DY].

A *non-interactive proof system* for an $NP$ language $L$ is a pair $(P, V)$ of probabilistic Turing machines, such that given a random bit string $r$ of polynomial length, $P$ can with overwhelmingly high probability construct a "proof" string $\pi$ for any "theorem" $l \in L$ which causes $V$ to accept $(r, l, \pi)$, and with only negligible probability will there be an $\bar{l} \notin L$ such that for some "false proof" $\pi$, $V$ accepts $(r, \bar{l}, \pi)$. Moreover, $V$ runs in polynomial time, and $P$ runs in polynomial time given a witness $w$ that $l \in L$.

Such a non-interactive proof system is *zero-knowledge* if, for every probabilistic polynomial-time "theorem generator" $T$ which observes a random bit string $r$ and interactively generates members $l_i$ of $L$ and observes their proofs, there exists a "simulator" $M$ which, having chosen the fixed "random" bit string $r'$ according to some distribution, interacts with $T$ to generate strings $\pi_i$ such that the distribution on strings $r', l_1, \pi_1, \ldots$ generated by $T$ and $M$ is indistinguishable (to non-uniform polynomial-time distinguishers) from the distribution on strings $r, l_1, \pi_1, \ldots$ generated by $T$ and $P$ after receiving a truly random bit string $r$.

Note that a non-interactive zero-knowledge proof system, as described above, allows repeated use of a single set of public random bits. Hence, the zero knowledge property must take into account the possibility that the theorems which are being proved are chosen *after* the public bits have been revealed, and other theorems have already been proven. The simulator must therefore also allow an adversarial "theorem generator" $T$ to decide what proofs must be simulated based on the simulated pseudorandom public bits and previous simulated proofs.

We can also define a non-interactive zero-knowledge proof of knowledge, analogous to the interactive zero-knowledge proof of knowledge introduced in [FFS]. The definition of the non-interactive version turns out to be much simpler than that for the interactive version, although it assumes a more sophisticated setting. Intuitively, the non-interactive zero-knowledge proof of knowledge is a non-interactive zero-knowledge proof of language membership from which, given certain information, a witness of language membership can be recovered. That information will, in our application, be a secret key associated with a sender's public key (as generated by, say, a trusted centre $M_C$) in a secure public-key cryptosystem.

**Definition 3.2** *Let* $L \in NP$, *and let* $W$ *be a polynomial-time "witness-recognizing" machine which accepts some polynomial-sized input of the form* $(w, l)$ *if and only if* $l \in L$. *Let* $\{D_n\}$ *be a family of distributions on polynomial-length strings of the form* $(s, p)$. *A non-interactive proof-of-knowledge system for witnesses of membership in* $L$, *relative to* $\{D_n\}$ *is a non-interactive proof system* $(P, V)$ *for* $L$ *in which* $P$ *receives as its random bit input the string* $(s, p)$ *chosen according to* $D_n$, *while* $V$ *just receives* $p$ *as its random* *bit input. Moreover, there must exist a polynomial-time "witness-finder" $F$ with the following property: with "overwhelming probability" (that is, with probability $1 - \frac{1}{g(n)}$, where $-\log g(n) \in \omega(\log n)$), $(s,p)$ will be such that for every $l$, and for every string $\pi$, if $V$ accepts $(p, l, \pi)$ then $F((s,p), l, \pi)$ is a witness of membership of $l$ in $L$. The definition of zero-knowledge for proof-of-knowledge systems is essentially the same as for proof systems, except that the theorem generator $T$ receives $p$ as its random bit string inputs, and the simulator $M$ is permitted to generate the $p$ given to $T$.*

## 3.3 Digital signature

Informally, a digital signature is a string $\sigma$ which identifies another string $D$ (the *document*) as originating from the possessor of a particular secret-key public-key pair $(\hat{s}^u, \hat{p}^u)$. A signature scheme is defined by a *key generation algorithm* which produces the secret-key public-key pairs, a *signing algorithm* which given $(\hat{s}^u, \hat{p}^u)$ can generate a signature for any document, and a *checking algorithm*, which uses $\hat{p}^u$ to distinguish valid signatures from invalid ones.

The standard security criterion for a digital signature scheme is security against what is known as *adaptive chosen message attack*. In this attack, the attacker, given $\hat{p}^u$, is permitted to choose any feasible number of documents, and obtain valid signatures for them (interactively, ie. receiving one before choosing the next), before attempting to generate a signature for any document of its choice (distinct from the set of documents whose signatures were obtained). The scheme is secure against this attack if any such attacker succeeds in generating a valid signature for this last document with negligible probabillity.

A rigorous definition for signature schemes and chosen message attack can be found in [GMRi], together with an implementation based a complexity-theoretic assumption. Necessary and sufficient conditions for signature schemes can be found in [R].

# 4 Non-Interactive Zero-Knowledge Proofs of Knowledge and A Cryptosystem Secure against Chosen Ciphertext Attack

We now show how a secure cryptosystem (in the sense of Definition 3.1 above) and a non-interactive zero-knowledge proof system for $NP$ can be used to build a new cryptosystem secure against chosen ciphertext attack. Encryptions in the new cryptosystem consist of encryptions in the old cryptosystem accompanied by non-interactive zero-knowledge proofs of the sender's knowledge of the decryption (as well as a digital signature, in the case of the stronger message-restricted attack). The proof of knowledge simply consists of encryptions, using the sender's public key, of the random bits used in the original encryption, together with a non-interactive zero-knowledge proof that they are in fact just that. The random bits necessary for the non-interactive proof can be assumed provided by the trusted centre that generates public keys (for example, such bits might be appended to each user's public key). These ideas resemble those used by Naor and Yung in [NY] in their setting.

**Theorem 4.1** *Assume that there exist trapdoor functions, as needed for the construction of non-interactive zero-knowledge proofs in [FLS] and of secure cryptosystems (in the sense of definition 3.1) in [GM]; let $\kappa = (M_C, M_E, M_D)$ be such a secure cryptosystem. Then for every $NP$ language $L$ (with witness recognizer $W$) there exists a non-interactive zero-knowledge proof of knowledge for witnesses of membership in $L$ relative to the distribution on strings $(s, (p, r))$ generated by running $M_C$, producing $(s, p)$, and appending a random bit string $r$ to $p$.*

**Proof (sketch):** The prover uses $M_C$ to generate a new secret-key public key pair $(s', p')$, encrypts the witness by running $M_E$ on input $(s', p', p, w_i)$ (for each bit $w_i$ of witness $w$) to produce $e$, and gives a non-interactive zero-knowledge proof that $e$ can be so constructed. (Actually, for technical reasons, the prover should prove that either $e$ can be so constructed, or a particular otherwised unused portion of $r$ is in fact producible by a particular pseudorandom number generator $G$ (as in [FLS]). The simulator $M'$ of the proof-of-knowledge system generates the extra pseudorandom bits using $G$, along with an encryption of an arbitrary string, and produces a legitimate non-interactive zero-knowledge proof of the above (true) theorem, using as a witness the seed input into $G$. Thus the theorems whose proofs are sought from $M$ are always true, and the simulation is therefore indistinguishable from authentic ones.) Full details will be provided in the final paper. ∎

**Theorem 4.2** *If there exist trapdoor functions, as needed for the construction of non-interactive zero-knowledge proofs in [FLS] and of secure cryptosystems (in the sense of definition 3.1) in [GM], then there exists a cryptosystem secure against attacker-specific chosen ciphertext attack.*

**Proof (sketch):** Given the secure cryptosystem $\kappa = (M_C, M_E, M_D)$, consider the new cryptosystem $(N_C, N_E, N_D)$ defined as follows:

**1.** $N_C$ is identical to $M_C$, except that it appends a random bit string $r^u$, of appropriate size for zero-knowledge proofs, to the end of each public key $p^u$;

**2.** $N_E$, given input $(s^u, (p^u, r^u), (p^v, r^v), b)$, runs $M_E$ on input $(s^u, p^u, p^v, b)$ to produce $e$, and appends to it a "proof" $\pi$ generated by $P$ in $(P, V)$, a non-interactive zero-knowledge proof of knowledge (with $(s^u, (p^u, r^u))$ as input to $P$) of a witness that $e$ was so encrypted. $N_E$ outputs $(e, \pi)$.

**3.** On input $(s^v, p^v, p^u, (e, \pi))$, $N_D$ runs $M_D$, obtaining $b$, and outputs $b$ if $V$ of the proof system above (given $(p^u, r^u)$ as random bit input) accepts input $\pi$, and "?" otherwise.

Then no attacker-specific chosen ciphertext attack succeeds against $(N_C, N_E, N_D)$. From any successful such attack, a "breaking" algorithm $B$ can be constructed, using methods similar to those used in [NY], which proves the insecurity of $(M_C, M_E, M_D)$, as follows: given cryptosystem $\kappa$, and $(p^S, p^R, e)$ (the sender's public key, receiver's public key, and the encryption being attacked), $B$ generates $(s^A, p^A)$ (the "attacker's" keys), as well as "confederates' keys" $(s^1, p^1)$, and so on, and produces $\pi$, a simulated non-interactive zero-knowedge proof of knowledge, relative to the distribution on $(s^S, p^S)$, of a witness that $e$ is a valid encryption under $\kappa$ (ie., is output by $M_E$). The algorithm $B$ then simulates *both* $A$ and $U$ ("attacker" and "universe")in the chosen ciphertext attack, taking advantage of the fact that challenges from $A$ containing valid zero-knowledge proofs of knowledge can easily be decrypted by $B$ using $s^A$ and witness-finder $F$ (note also that if $B$ could somehow manage to produce valid-looking encryptions with putative sender $A$, containing convincing but invalid zero-knowledge proofs of knowledge—a feat which would certainly be impossible, except with negligible probability, if $\pi$ were not simulated—then there would exist a means of distinguishing simulated proofs-of-knowledge from real ones). Full details of the proof will appear in the final paper. ∎

**Theorem 4.3** *If there exist trapdoor functions, as needed for the construction of non-interactive zero-knowledge proofs in [FLS] and of secure cryptosystems (in the sense of definition 3.1) in [GM], then there exists a cryptosystem secure against message-restricted chosen ciphertext attack.*

**Proof (sketch):** Consider a cryptosystem $(N_C, N_E, N_D)$ defined as in Theorem 4.2 with the following modifications:

**1.** $N_C$ runs $M_C$ and the key generation algorithm for a secure signature scheme on input $u$ to produce a secret-key public-key pair $((s^u, \hat{s}^u), (p^u, \hat{p}^u, r^u))$.

**2.** On input $((s^u, \hat{s}^u), (p^u, \hat{p}^u, r^u), (p^v, \hat{p}^v, r^v), b)$, $N_E$ appends to its output $(e, \pi)$ (generated using $M_E$, as described in theorem 4.2) a digital signature for it using the private signature key $\hat{s}^u$.

**3.** On input $((s^v, \hat{s}^v), (p^v, \hat{p}^v, r^v), (p^u, \hat{p}^u, r^v), (e, \pi, s))$, $N_D$ obtains $b$ using $M_D$ as described in theorem 4.2, and outputs $b$ if $V$ (as described in Theorem 4.1) accepts input $\pi$ and the checking algorithm of the digital signature scheme accepts the appended digital signature, and "?" otherwise.

Then no message-specific chosen ciphertext attack succeeds against $(N_C, N_E, N_D)$. The proof is similar to that of theorem 4.2, except that the security of signature schemes against chosen message attack is used to show that the attacker has negligible probability of generating a valid message which is not just as easily decryptable by the simulated $U$ as those permissible under an attacker-specific attack. Full details will be presented in the final paper. ∎

Note that the cryptosystems described in theorems 4.2 and 4.3 can both easily be proven, in a similar manner, to be secure against chosen plaintext attack, as well. The proof is necessary, however, because the sender's keys are involved in the encryption process in our revised model (in more "conventional" public-key cryptography, in contrast, chosen-plaintext security follows automatically from the security property described in definition 3.1). The new model therefore raises the issue, for a time somewhat obscured by the prominence of public-key cryptography, of just what kinds of attack a cryptosystem should resist; if the chosen-plaintext and chosen-ciphertext attacks are in some sense incomparable, and must be dealt with separately, then there may be other natural attacks, as well, security against which is guaranteed by neither chosen-plaintext nor chosen-ciphertext security.

# 5   Conclusions

The choice of an appropriate definition and solution to the problem of chosen ciphertext attack can be considered as a first step toward formalizing and solving the much broader problem of securing public-key cryptographic communication in a multiparty setting. Many other issues need to be resolved, including the development of a rigorous definition of security, consideration of the problem of traffic analysis, and examination of the apparently necessary task of implementing timeliness constraints on messages.

# References

[BFM] M. Blum, P. Feldman, and S. Micali, *Non-Interactive Zero Knowledge and its Applications*, Proc. 20th ACM Symposium on Theory of Computing (1988), pp. 103–112.

[BG] M. Bellare and S. Goldwasser, *New Paradigms for Digital signatures and Message Authentication based on Non-Interactive Zero-Knowledge Proofs*, Proc. CRYPTO '89.

[DDN] D. Dolev, C. Dwork and M. Naor, *Non-Malleable Cryptography*, Proc. 23rd ACM Symposium on Theory of Computing (1991), pp. 542–552.

[DH] W. Diffie and M. Hellman, *New directions in Cryptography*, IEEE Trans. on Information Theory 22(6), 1976, pp. 644–654.

[DY] A. De Santis and M. Yung, *Cryptographic Applications of the Non-Interactive Metaproof and Many-Prover Systems*, Proc. CRYPTO '90.

[FFS] U. Feige, A. Fiat, and A. Shamir, *Zero Knowledge Proofs of Identity*, Proc. 19th ACM Symp. on Theory of Computing (1987), pp. 210–217.

[FLS] U. Feige, D. Lapidot and A. Shamir, *Multiple Non-Interactive Zero-Knowledge Proofs Based on a Single Random String*, Proc. 31st IEEE Symp. on Foundations of Computer Science (1990), pp. 308–317.

[GHY] Z. Galil, S. Haber and M. Yung, *Symmetric Public-Key Cryptosystems*, submitted to J. of Cryptology.

[GM] S. Goldwasser and S. Micali, *Probabilistic Encryption*, JCSS Vol. 28, No. 2 (April 1984), pp. 270–299.

[GMRa] S. Goldwasser, S. Micali and C. Rackoff, *The Knowledge Complexity of Interactive Proof Systems*, Proc. 17th ACM Symp. on Theory of Computing (1985), pp. 291–304.

[GMRi] S. Goldwasser, S. Micali and R. Rivest, *A Secure Digital Signature Scheme*, SIAM J. on Computing, Vol. 17, 2 (1988), pp. 281–308.

[NY] M. Naor and M. Yung, *Public-Key Cryptosystems Provably Secure Against Chosen Ciphertext Attacks*, Proc. 22nd ACM Symp on Theory of Computing (1990), pp. 427–437.

[R] J. Rompel, *One-Way Functions Are Necessary and Sufficient for Secure Signatures*, Proc. 31st IEEE Symp. on Foundations of Computer Science (1990), pp. 387–394.

# Towards Practical Public Key Systems Secure Against Chosen Ciphertext attacks

Ivan Damgård

University of Aarhus
Matematisk Institut, Ny Munkegade
DK 8000 Århus C, Denmark
ivan@daimi.aau.dk

## Abstract

We present two efficient constructions aimed at making public key systems secure against chosen ciphertext attacks. The first one applies to any deterministic public key system and modifies it into a system that is provably as hard to break under a passive attack as the original one, but has the potential of making a chosen ciphertext attack useless to an enemy. The second construction applies to the El Gamal/Diffie-Hellman public key system. Again, the modified system is provably as hard to break under a passive attack as the original one, and under an additional cryptographic assumption, a chosen ciphertext attack is provably useless to an enemy. We also point out a connection between such public-key systems and efficient identification schemes.

# 1 Introduction

The question of whether public key encryption schemes can be secure against chosen ciphertext attacks has received at lot of attention in the last 12 years. The problem first came up when Rabin presented his variant of RSA in 1978 based on modular squaring [Ra]. He proved that decrypting a random ciphertext in this system is reducable to factoring. The good news here is that consequently Rabins system has maximal security against passive attacks: the problem of decryption can never be harder than that of finding the private key from the public one. The bad news is that this also implies that the system breaks down completely under a chosen ciphertext attack. This fact mislead many researchers into thinking that no public key system could be secure against a chosen ciphertext attack if the problem of decrypting was reducable to the problem of finding the private key from the public one. A similar "paradox" for public key signature schemes was also discussed in the folklore.

The folkore "proofs" of these "theorems", however, implicitly relied on the assumption that only one trapdoor is used in the system. Goldwasser, Micali and Rivest were the first to observe that the problem could be solved if two independently chosen trapdoors were used. This lead to construction of the first signature scheme secure against an

J. Feigenbaum (Ed.): Advances in Cryptology - CRYPTO '91, LNCS 576, pp. 445-456, 1992.
© Springer-Verlag Berlin Heidelberg 1992

adaptive chosen message attack [GMR]. Later, Naor and Yung [NY] combined the use of two trapdoors with non-interactive zero-knowledge proof systems to build the first public key encryption scheme provably as hard to break under a chosen ciphertext attack as under a passive attack, where the enemy simply observes ciphertexts and tries to decrypt them.

Thus, as far as theoretical results are concerned, the matter is closed. For *practical* schemes, however, we are still very far from a satisfactory solution. The scheme of [NY] relies heavily on non-interactive zero-knowledge, which is a very nice theoretical tool, but in general leads to schemes that no one would try to implement because of the enormous expansion that takes place when going from plaintext to ciphertext.

This paper makes a first step in the direction of finding truely practical public key encryption schemes with optimal security. This will be done by showing how to make modifications of any deterministic public key system (which includes RSA and Rabin), and of the El Gamal/Diffie-Hellman public key system. All the modifications preserve the security of the original system under a passive attack, while extra assumptions are needed to ensure that a chosen ciphertext attack will not help an enemy. The modifications typically require 1 extra encryption/decryption operation of the system in question, and communication of 1 extra multiprecision number.

The model of a chosen ciphertext attack that we will consider here follows that of [NY]: the enemy may specify any (polynomial) number of ciphertexts and receives the corresponding plaintexts. Then he gets a ciphertext as input and must try to decrypt it by himself. Other researchers have suggested different models [RS], where the enemy knows in advance the ciphertext he must attack, but where his choice of ciphertexts to ask for decryptions of is limited in various ways. This model requires that also senders of messages possess secret/public key pairs.

# 2 Deterministic Public Key Systems

A public key encryption scheme is said to be deterministic, when the ciphertext is uniquely determined from the cleartext and the public encryption key. Thus the basic form of the RSA and Rabin systems are deterministic.

For simplicity, we think of deterministic public key systems as trapdoor one-way permutations of bit strings of a given length, although systems like RSA actually are injections into such a set (using injections would complicate the notation, but not change any of the results).

Saying something meaningful about the security of a deterministic system requires that one specifies a distribution of the cleartexts. Throughout this paper, we will assume that the encryption operates on $k$-bit blocks, and that the cleartexts are uniformly distributed $k$-bit strings. This is a natural assumption if no particular application is considered, and is the only reasonable in several cases, e.g. when the system is being used for exchange of keys to a conventional cryptosystem.

## Definition 1

A *family of one-way trapdoor permutations* is a countably infinite family of finite sets $F = \{I_k\}_{k=0}^{\infty}$. An element of $I_k$ is a permutation on the set of $k$-bit strings and is called an instance of size $k$. $F$ must satisfy the following:

1. There exists a probablistic poynomial time algorithm $Gen_F$ called a *generator for F*, which on input $k$ outputs a pair $(f, f^{-1})$. $f$ is a polynomial time algorithm for computing a permutation randomly chosen from $I_k$, while $f^{-1}$ is a polynomial time algorithm for computing the inverse of that permutation.

2. For any probabilistic polynomial time algorithm $A$, let $p_A(k)$ be the probability that $A$ on input $f \in I_k$ chosen randomly by $Gen_F$ and a uniformly chosen $k$-bit $x$ manages to compute $f^{-1}(x)$. Then $p_A(k)$ is superpolynomially small as a function of $k$.

It should be clear that this is just a formalization of the properties that we hope for example RSA has: the permutations would be exponentiations modulo $k$-bit RSA-moduli, and the generator would output randomly chosen $k$-bit moduli, together with the public, resp. secret exponent.

In a chosen ciphertext attack against a system like this, an enemy effectively gets an oracle for $f^{-1}$, for example he may have been able to get temporary access to the deciphering equipment, without being able to get to the secret key itself. By choosing cleverly the ciphertexts to decrypt, he may be able to figure out the entire description of $f^{-1}$. That is precisely what happens with the Rabin system.

A standard practitioner's way of protecting against this would be to require that all cleartexts satisfy a certain redundancy rule, and program the deciphering algorithm such that it refuses to answer, if the cleartext produced does not satisfy this rule. The idea would be that an enemy now cannot produce ciphertexts that he can get decrypted unless he starts by choosing the cleartext, in which case the attack becomes useless: the enemy already knows the cleartexts he gets.

However, such a redundancy rule will be of no use, unless it ensures that a uniformly chosen bit string satisfies the rule with only negligible probability. The problem now is that even if our permutation family satisfies the above Definition 1, the permutations might still become easy to invert, if we restrict the input to the negligibly small subset of messages satisfying the redundancy rule! For example, using this idea on the Rabin system would mean that we would loose the proof of the equivalence of decryption to factoring. Hence we would like to have a solution that makes a chosen ciphertext attack difficult to exploit, *without* having to change the cleartext distribution.

Consider therefore the following public key encryption scheme, which is constructed from two (not necessarily distinct) families $F$ and $G$ as above:

To generate keys, run the generators $Gen_F$ and $Gen_G$ on input $k$ to get outputs $(f, f^{-1}), (g, g^{-1})$, respectively. Let $h$ be an arbitrary but fixed easy-to-invert permutation on $k$-bit strings (we assume for simplicity that $h$ is a generic description of a permutation algorithm that works for any $k$). Let $f, g, h$ be the public key and store $f^{-1}$ as the secret key ($g^{-1}$ may be discarded). The enciphering function $E$ operates on $k$-bit strings and is defined by:

$$E(m) = (f(r), g(h(r)) \oplus m),$$

where $r$ is a uniformly chosen $k$-bit string. To decipher, we have the function $D$, defined by:

$$D(c, d) = g(h^{-1}(f^{-1}(c))) \oplus d$$

It is clear that $D(E(m)) = m$. We then have the following definition and result:

## Definition 2

An algorithm $A$ is said to break $(F, G, h)$ under a passive attack, if $A$ finds $m$ with probability more than a polynomial fraction on input a description of $E$ and $E(m)$. The probability is taken over a random choice of $E$ as above, and a uniform choice of $k$-bit string $m$.

## Theorem 1

If the family $F$ satisfies Definition 1, then no probabilistic polynomial time algorithm breaks $(F, G, h)$ under a passive attack.

# Proof

Suppose $A$ breaks $(F, G, h)$, and let $f$ and $x$ be chosen as in condition 2 of Definition 1. Run $Gen_G$ to get an algorithm for a permutation $g$ and its inverse. Choose a uniform $k$-bit string $s$, and give to $A$ the description of $E$ constructed from $f$ and $g$ and the ciphertext $(x, s)$. Let $m$ be the output of $A$. Then as our guess at $f^{-1}(x)$, we output $h^{-1}(g^{-1}(m \oplus s))$. It is clear that the distribution of the public key $f, g, h$ and the ciphertext $(x, s)$ is precisely the one $A$ expects to see. Therefore we get a correct answer $m$ with nonnegligible probability. Finally, it is trivial that if $m$ is correct, then our answer is also correct□

This theorem says that modifying the public key system defined by $F$, by using $G$ and $h$ as above, does not hurt the security against passive attacks. However, we may hope that the security of $(F, G, h)$ is even better than that of $F$ against chosen ciphertext attacks: suppose that there exists an algorithm that will find the secret key $f^{-1}$ if it is given the public $f$ and a black box that evaluates $f^{-1}$, i.e. the $F$-system has maximal security under a passive attack, but is breakable under a chosen ciphertext attack.

To see how the $(F, G, h)$ system behaves in this respect, observe that what the enemy gets in a chosen ciphertext attack against $(F, G, h)$ is the ability to specify any $x$ to a black box and get back $g(h(f^{-1}(x)))$. Since $g$ is one-way, it is not at all clear that the enemy can find $f^{-1}(x)$ from this information, and therefore $(F, G, h)$ may be secure against a chosen ciphertext attack, even though it provably has maximal security against a passive attack.

It is tempting to conjecture that as long as $f$ and $g$ are independently chosen, seeing $g(h(f^{-1}(x)))$ does not give the enemy any useful extra knowledge, and might in fact as well be a random value, as far as a polynomial time enemy is concerned. This is too optimistic however: suppose we wanted to improve the Rabin system in a simplistic way by letting both $F$ and $G$ be modular squaring and $h$ be the identity. Then an enemy could from a chosen ciphertext attack obtain residues of the same value $r^2$ modulo two different moduli, where $r$ is the square root he is looking for. But from this, the integer $r^2$ (and hence $r$) can easily be found by the Chinese Remainder theorem, and we are no better off than for the original Rabin system!

Thus the functions must be chosen with more care: for example we can define $h$ to be some efficient easy-to-invert bit-scrambling function. One nice way to construct such a function would use a pseudo-random bit generator $\phi$ taking bit strings of length $l < k$

as seed. Then we can define

$$h(r) = r_{k-l} \oplus \phi(r_k) || r_k,$$

where $r_{k-l}$, resp. $r_k$ are the most significant $k - l$, resp. the least significant $k$ bits of $r$, and $||$ denotes concatenation. For concreteness, one can think of $l = 56$ and $\phi = $ DES in output feedback mode, but many ideas are possible here. Another idea is to simply encrypt $r$ under a random, but fixed key using your favorite conventional cipher.

With such a construction, it seems quite resonable to conjecture that $r$ and $h(r)$ will appear to be unrelated as far as modular arithmetic is concerned, and that therefore the above problem will go away. Alternatively, one could let $h = id$, but define $G$ to be RSA with random (large) public exponent.

This leads to the following concrete suggestion for an encryption function $E$:

$$E(m) = (r^2 \ mod \ n_1, \ m \oplus (h(r)^2 \ mod \ n_2)),$$

where $h$ is constructed as above, $n_1, n_2$ are Blum-integers and $r$ is a random square modulo $n_1$ (this ensures that the receiver can reconstruct $r$ from $r^2 \ mod \ n_1$). Decryption is left to the reader. For this construction, the extra security potential comes at a price of very little extra computation - evaluation of $h$ and a modular squaring for both sender and receiver. The bandwidth required is twice that of ordinary Rabin encryption. For applications such as exchange of conventional keys this will often be perfectly acceptable.

Of course, proving chosen ciphertext security for such concrete constructions is probably difficult. Even defining precisely what properties we should demand for $F$ and $G$ is non-trivial. We suggest the construction of $F$, $G$ and $h$ such that security against chosen ciphertext attacks of $(F, G, h)$ can be proved as an interesting open problem.

# 3   The El Gamal/Diffie-Hellman System

This public key encryption scheme was suggested by El Gamal [ElGa] as a variant of the Diffie-Hellman key exchange. The system requires an infinite family of cyclic groups $\{G_k\}$ such that discrete logarithms are hard to compute in $G_k$. One can use the multiplicative groups modulo large primes here, but also other groups might be used, e.g. the groups on some elliptic curves, or the multiplicative groups of extension fields.

To run the system, we are given a generator $g$ of $G_k$ of order $d$, where $d$ is in $O(2^k)$, such that group elements may be represented as $k$-bit strings. The secret key in the system is a number $x$, chosen uniformly in $[0..d-1]$. The public key is $y = g^x$. Let $E$ denote the enciphering operation, $D$ the deciphering. Then

$$E(m) = (g^r, y^r \oplus m),$$

where $r$ is uniform in $[0..d-1]$.

$$D(c_1, c_2) = c_2 \oplus c_1^x.$$

In this description, the $\oplus$-operation may be replaced by any easy to invert group operation on $k$-bit strings. It is clear that this system is not deterministic, but probabilistic: the encryption involves a random choice. For such systems, one may sometimes be able to prove that the system is secure against passive attacks, *independently* of the plaintext distribution. See for example the system of Blum and Goldwasser [BlGo]. However, such a result is not known for the El Gamal system. Moreover, although its security against chosen ciphertext attacks is unknown in general, Bert den Boer [Bo] has shown that for some primes, the Diffie-Hellman problem modulo these primes is equivalent to discrete log, and hence that in these cases the system is breakable under a chosen ciphertext attack.

Hence also for this system, it is of interest to improve its security against chosen ciphertext attacks, without having to change the plaintext distribution. To this end, we propose the following modified version of El Gamal:

The private key consists of $x$ and $z$, chosen uniformly in $[0..d-1]$. The public key is $y = g^x$ and $w = g^z$. Let $E'$ and $D'$ denote the encryption and decryption operations, resp. Then

$$E(m) = (w^r, g^r, m \oplus y^r),$$

where $r$ is uniform in $[0..d-1]$.

$$D(c_1, c_2, c_3) = c_3 \oplus c_2^x, \ if \ c_1 = c_2^z, \ NULL \ otherwise.$$

Here, $NULL$ is a special symbol which can be distinguished from ordinary plaintext, and can be thought of as meaning "no answer".

Security against passive attacks for El Gamal and Modified El Gamal is defined in the same way as in Definition 2, except that the probabilities are also taken over the random coins used in the enciphering. We first have the following easy lemma:

## Lemma 1

Modified El Gamal is as hard to break as El Gamal under a passive attack.

## Proof

Suppose algorithm $A$ breaks Modified El Gamal. Then given an El Gamal public key $y$ and a ciphertext $(c_1, c_2)$, choose $z$ at random in $[0..d-1]$, and give $y, g^z$ as public key to $A$ and $(c_1^z, c_1, c_2)$ as ciphertext. It is trivial to see that the input we generate for $A$ will have the distribution it expects, and that if $A$ is successful, it decrypts the original El Gamal ciphertext.

Intuitively, the reason why this variant may be more secure against a chosen ciphertext attack, is that given only $w, g$, it seems hard to generate a pair of the form $w^r, g^r$, unless one starts by simply choosing $r$. Hence it will be hard for an enemy to come up with a ciphertext that will produce a non-null output from $D$, unless he already knows the plaintext. Formalizing this, we suggest the following assumption:

## Assumption 1

Let $A$ be a probabilistic polynomial (in $k$) time algorithm which receives as input $w, g \in G_k$ and outputs a pair of group elements $a, b$. Then there exists another probabilistic polynomial time algorithm $A'$, which uses the same input and the same random coins as $A$. Except with superpolynomially small probability taken over the random coins, $A'$ will output $a, b, r$, whenever $A$ on the same input produces $(a, b) = (w^r, g^r)$.

The function that maps $r$ to $(w^r, g^r)$ is an example of what one could call *one-way functions with sparse image*: only a very small fraction of the pairs of numbers are in the image, and an element in the image cannot be found in any other way than by computing the function on some input value. Such functions would be extremely useful in other contexts too, e.g. identification protocols, and it is an interesting open problem to find out whether they can be proved to exist.

## Definition 3

A *chosen ciphertext enemy* is a probabilistic polynomial time algorithm that repeatedly gets to choose a ciphertext and receive the output from the decryption algorithm on this ciphertext. It finally takes a random ciphertext as input and tries to decrypt it. The cryptosystem is said to be *secure against chosen ciphertext attacks*, if any chosen ciphertext enemy succeeds with only superpolynomially small (in $k$) probability.

Assumption 1 is enough to prove this type of security for Modified El Gamal:

## Theorem 2

Assume Assumption 1 and that El Gamal is secure under a passive attack. Then Modified El Gamal is secure under a chosen ciphertext attack.

## Proof

By contradiction, let $A$ be a successful chosen ciphertext enemy. Let $C_1, C_2, ...$ be the sequence of ciphertexts of which $A$ requests the decryption. Let $A_i$ be the algorithm that simulates $A$ until the output of $C_i$ and then stops. We can now show by induction that for all $i$, $A_i$ can be simulated *without* access to a decryption oracle: $A_1$ is clear. To do $A_{i+1}$, observe that by induction, $A_i$ can be simulated without the oracle. Therefore Assumption 1 guarantees us the existence of an algorithm $A_i'$ that outputs a quadrouple $(c_1, c_2, c_3, r)$, such that $C_i = (c_1, c_2, c_3)$, and that with large probability, $(c_1, c_2) = (w^r, g^r)$ whenever $C_i$ produces a non-null output from the decryption. Knowledge of $r$ suffices to decrypt $C_i$, and therefore we can simulate also the last steps of $A_{i+1}$. From $A$ we can therefore build an algorithm that breaks the system under a passive attack, and we are done by Lemma 1.

Note that, contrary to Theorem 1, this result works for any plaintext distribution. Note also that we are talking about the ability of an enemy to decrypt entire messages, not whether he can get partial information about the cleartext. However, if we had a result about security of single bits in El Gamal encryption similar to the one for RSA and Rabin bits, it would be easy to reformulate and prove Theorem 2 in terms of probabilistic public key systems, following [NY].

A final remark concerns the model for chosen ciphertext attacks: at first sight, it may seem like a strange condition that the enemy does not get to see the ciphertext he is to decrypt until after his usage of the decryption oracle is over. However, if he knows initally that he eventually wants to decrypt ciphertext $C$, then he might as well give $C$ to the oracle in stead of trying to figure it out himself!

In [RS], it is argued that one could solve this problem in a natural way by allowing the enemy to know $C$ initially, but introduce a restriction on his choice of ciphertexts for decryption in the first phase. One concrete possibility is to demand that he asks the oracle for anything but $C$. It is not clear, however, that this makes the model more natural or realistic: the enemy may well be the only player who knows which ciphertext he is attacking, and in this case, how could the rest of the system possibly impose on him the restriction required by the model?

It is quite possible that we have not yet found the best model to describe this type of problem, and that a final solution would have to include some conditions on the timeliness of messages.

# 4    Connection to Identification Protocols

In this section we point out an interesting duality between the conditions of Definition 3 and the properties of a secure identification system as defined Feige, Fiat and Shamir in [FFS].

Concretely, from any public key encryption scheme that satisfies Definition 3, it is easy to build an efficient identification system: each individual knows a secret key for which the corresponding public key is known by everybody. A prover can identify himself by demonstrating his ability to decrypt messages that were encrypted under the corresponding public key, i.e. the verifier encrypts a random message $m$, sends the encryption to the prover, who decrypts and returns $m$.

By Definition 3, even a cheating verifier who interacts with the honest prover $P$ a polynomial number of times will not afterwards be able to impersonate $P$ with non-negligible probability of success.

Such systems are very efficient in terms of the number of rounds used: only two messages have to be sent. This adds to the interest of solving the open problems listed below: their solution would also lead to construction of very efficient identification schemes.

Note that if Assumption 1 holds, then the protocol in which a verifier receives a public key for the Modified El Gamal system, chooses a ciphertext and receives the decryption, would in fact be zero-knowledge. Despite the small number of messages sent, this does not contradict the result of Goldreich and Krawzyk [GK] because the simulation we get from Assumption 1 is not black-box: it depends on the verifier that participates.

# 5 Conclusion and Open Problems

We have seen that truely practical public key systems can be constructed, for which chosen ciphertext attacks seem totally useless for an enemy, and for which security against passive attacks is provably equivalent to that of well known systems like RSA, Rabin and El Gamal/Diffie-Hellman.

Open problems: prove or disprove Assumption 1. Construct other functions that satisfy an assumption similar to Assumption 1. Find permutation families $F$ and $G$ for which the $(F, G, h)$ system of Section 2 is provably secure against chosen ciphertext attacks.

# References

[BlGo] M.Blum and S.Goldwasser: *An Efficient Probabilistic Public-Key Encryption Scheme which Hides all Partial Information*, Proc. of Crypto 84, Springer Verlag.

[Bo] B. den Boer: *Diffie-Hellman is as Strong as Discrete Log for Certain Primes*, Proc. of Crypto 84, Springer Verlag.

[ElGa] T. El Gamal: *A Public-Key Cryptosystem and a Signature Scheme Based on Discrete Logarithms*, IEEE Trans. on Inf. Theory, vol.IT-31, 1985.

[FFS] U.Feige, A.Fiat and A.Shamir: *Zero-Knowledge Proofs of Identity*, J.Crypt, vol. 1, 1988, Springer Verlag.

[GK] O.Goldreich and H. Krawczyk: *On the Composition of Zero-Knowledge Proof Systems*, Proc. of ICALP 90.

[GMR] S.Goldwasser, S.Micali and R.Rivest: *A "Paradoxical" Solution to the Signature Problem*, proc. of FOCS 84.

[NY] M. Naor and M. Yung: *Public-Key Cryptosystems Provably Secure against Chosen Ciphertext Attacks*, Proc. of FOCS 90.

[Ra] M.O. Rabin: *Digital Signatures and Public Key Encryption as Intractable as Factorization*, Tech. report, MIT/LCS/TR-212. M.I.T., 1978.

[RS] C. Rackoff and D. Simon: *Non-Interactive Zero-Knowledge Proofs of Knowledge and Chosen Ciphertext Attacks*, these proceedings.

# Shared generation of authenticators and signatures[*]

(Extended Abstract)

Yvo Desmedt
EE & CS Department
University of Wisconsin-Milwaukee
Milwaukee, WI 53201
desmedt@cs.uwm.edu

Yair Frankel
EE & CS Department
University of Wisconsin-Milwaukee
Milwaukee, WI 53201
yair@cs.uwm.edu

## Abstract

Often it is desired that the power to sign or authenticate messages is shared. This paper presents methods to collectively generate RSA signatures, provably secure authenticators and unconditionally secure authenticators. In the new schemes, $l$ individuals are given shares such that $k \leq l$ are needed to generate a signature (authenticator) but less than $k$ can not. When the $k$ people have finished signing (authenticating), nobody can perform an impersonation or substitution attack. These schemes are called threshold signature (authentication) schemes. Clearly these schemes are better than each of the $k$ individuals sending a separate authenticator for each message or if each of the $k$ individuals each send their share to a *"trusted"* person who will sign for them.

In all of the schemes we assume that the shareholders (senders) and receiver have secure workstations but the network and servers are not necessarily secure.

# 1 Introduction

The idea of combining cryptosystems with secret sharing (threshold) schemes [Bl, Sh] has been introduced in several papers recently [CH, DQV, DF90]. Shared generation of authenticators using Diffie-Hellman [DH] was presented in [CH], but it is completely insecure against substitution. Threshold decryption of private messages was introduced in [DF90]. Shared verification of authenticators was introduced in [DQV], but the available message space is small. *An important problem not discussed in these papers is the shared generation of secure signatures.* Issuing checks for a corporation is a vivid example of this well-known problem. For security reasons, it may be a company's policy that checks be signed by $k$ individuals rather than one person. An organization may choose $l$ individuals and allow any subset consisting of $k \leq l$ people to sign its checks. This is similar to the concept of threshold schemes [Bl, Sh]. This paper presents *threshold* (a) *RSA* signatures, (b) *provably secure* authenticators and (c) *unconditionally secure* authenticators. Using mental games [GMW], this can be achieved conditionally but the scheme is highly interactive and very impractical.

---

[*]Research is being supported by NSF Grant NCR-9106327

J. Feigenbaum (Ed.): Advances in Cryptology - CRYPTO '91, LNCS 576, pp. 457-469, 1992.
© Springer-Verlag Berlin Heidelberg 1992

Our paper presents techniques where $k$ out of $l$ individuals are required to generate a signature (or authenticator) for a message. This is clearly better than having each of the $k$ individuals create $k$ signatures (authenticators) which would cause an increase in bandwidth overhead. The receiver would also be required to perform more calculations and store a larger key directory. *No interaction between shareholders* is necessary for the generation of signature (authenticator) and the secret key is not revealed to any individual even after signatures (or authenticators) have been created with our schemes. We assume that the shareholders (senders) and receiver have secure workstations but the network and servers are not necessarily secure. A byproduct of this research is a homomorphic group based threshold scheme (see Section 4.2).

Our threshold RSA signature scheme is based on interpolation polynomials over the integers (see Section 3). Even though there exists no threshold scheme over any infinite ring [BS] (see also [CK]), our scheme is secure. A threshold signature scheme based on algebraic integers is also discussed.

RSA signatures [RSA] are weak and not proven secure [Da, Den, dJC, Mo]. Therefore, we present a proven secure solution for threshold authenticators (see Section 4) based on a new *homomorphic threshold scheme over a finite Abelian group* in which inverses can be calculated in polynomial time. These Abelian groups must have an exponent[†] with large prime factors[‡]; the exponent needs to only be known to the distribution center that makes the shares[‡].

A threshold unconditionally secure authentication scheme is presented (see Section 5). It is based on finite geometry.

# 2   The model and notation

Let $(S, R)$ be a signature or an (interactive or non-interactive) authentication scheme, where $S$ is the sender and $R$ is the receiver. Instead of $S$, we have a set $\mathcal{A}$ ($|\mathcal{A}| = l$) such that any subset $\mathcal{B}$, where $|\mathcal{B}| = k$, can replace $S$ as the signature (authenticator) generator. Each time $S$ would send a bit string in $(S, R)$ then all individuals in $\mathcal{B}$, in our $(\mathcal{A}, R)$ signature scheme, will send a *partial result* to some (not necessarily trusted) Combiner $C$. Then $C$ combines the partial results and sends a bit string similar as $S$ would. Observe that no interaction is required between the shareholders and $C$ to create the bit string (see Figure 1). It must be impossible for $C$ to impersonate when $C$ is

---

[†] For a group $G$, the exponent is the smallest integer $e$ such that $\forall x \in G, x^e = 1$.

[‡] Our homomorphic threshold scheme over a finite Abelian group can be adapted to any exponent and there is no need for the key distributor to know the exponent [DF91].

Sending Organization

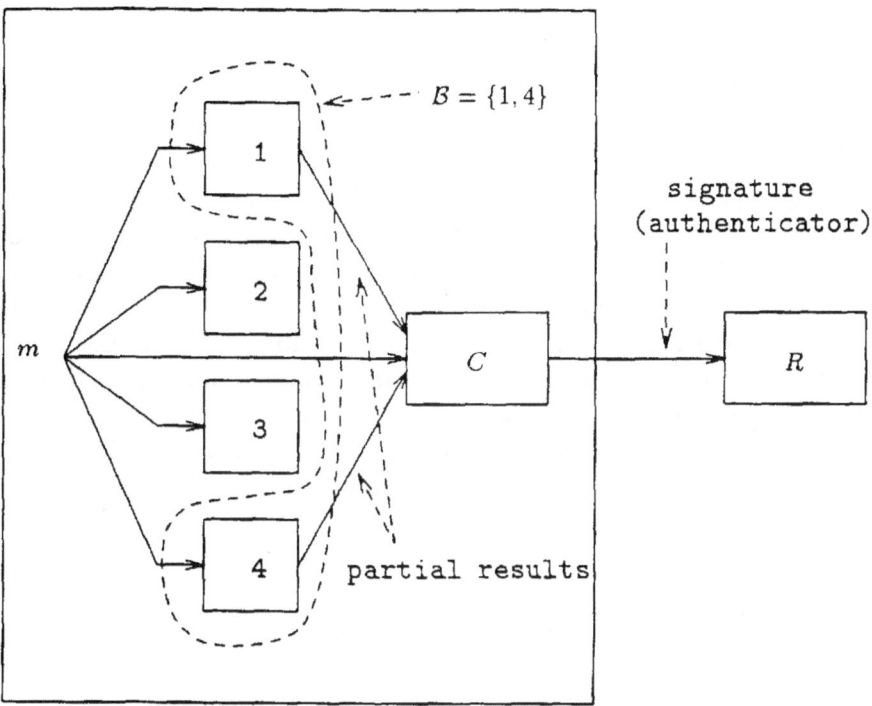

Figure 1: An example of a two out of four threshold signature (authentication) scheme.

collaborating with any $k - 1$ shareholders and for $C$ to substitute a message when $C$ receives additionally $k$ partial results (for the same message). We assume that neither $C$ nor the shareholders will jam the signature generation.

# 3 Threshold RSA signatures

Let $n = pq$ where $p, q$ are safe primes. One condition for $p$ to be a safe prime is that $p = 2p' + 1$ where $p'$ is a prime [BB78, BB79], similarly $q = 2q' + 1$. Normally RSA is defined with the $\phi$ function, however it could just as well have been defined with the $\lambda$ function[§]. Due to the method we chose $n$ note that $\lambda(n) = 2p'q'$. The secret key is $d$ which was chosen at random such that $\gcd(d, \lambda(n)) = 1$. So $d$ is odd. An RSA signature of a message $m$ is $S_m \equiv m^d \bmod n$. In our method, each individual $i \in \mathcal{B}$ will generate a modified share $a_{i,\mathcal{B}}$ such that $\sum_{i \in \mathcal{B}} a_{i,\mathcal{B}} \equiv d - 1 \bmod \lambda(n)$. Each $i \in \mathcal{B}$ will calculate

---

[§] $\lambda$ is the Carmichael function, i.e., the exponent of $Z_n^*(\cdot)$.

the partial result $s_{m,i,\mathcal{B}} \equiv m^{a_{i,\mathcal{B}}} \bmod n$ and send it to $C$. To create the signature, $C$ calculates $S_m \equiv m \cdot \prod_{i \in \mathcal{B}} s_{m,i,\mathcal{B}} \bmod n$.

## 3.1  Polynomial approach

As in the Lagrange interpolation scheme of [Sh], let $f(x)$ be a polynomial of degree $k-1$ such that $f(0)$ is the secret. However, parts of our calculations will be performed over the integers rather than over a field and $f(0) \equiv d-1 \bmod \lambda(n)$. We now discuss a method to calculate $a_{i,\mathcal{B}}$ which circumvents the problem of calculating inverses [DF90] even when $\lambda(n)$ must remain secret to the shareholders. To simplify our discussion[¶], we assume that $\lambda(n) = 2p'q'$, where $p'$ and $q'$ are large primes. This implies that not all $x_i - x_j$ have inverses modulo $2p'q'$ (e.g., when $x_i - x_j$ is even, it has no inverse). Let all the $x_i$ be odd and all $f(x_i)$ be even and let $f(0) = d-1$ ($d$ is odd in RSA). Thus, a share distribution center will choose $p, q$ and $d$, and will send to each $i$ the share

$$K_i' = \frac{f(x_i)/2}{\left( \prod_{\substack{j \in \mathcal{A} \\ j \neq i}} (x_i - x_j) \right) /2} \quad (\bmod\ p'q').$$

Observe now that *no inverses have to be calculated by the shareholder* because

$$f(x) = \sum_{i \in \mathcal{B}} K_i' \prod_{\substack{j \notin \mathcal{B} \\ j \in \mathcal{A}}} (x_i - x_j) \prod_{\substack{j \in \mathcal{B} \\ j \neq i}} (x - x_j) \quad (\bmod\ 2p'q').$$

The correctness of the previous two equations is proven in Theorem 3.1. Let $q_{i,\mathcal{B}} = \prod_{\substack{j \notin \mathcal{B} \\ j \in \mathcal{A}}} (x_i - x_j) \prod_{\substack{j \in \mathcal{B} \\ j \neq i}} (0 - x_j)$, then the modified share, $a_{i,\mathcal{B}}$, is an integer where

$$a_{i,\mathcal{B}} = K_i' \cdot q_{i,\mathcal{B}}.$$

Due to exponentiation, the threshold scheme is actually performed in $Z_{\lambda(n)}$, thus this is not conflicting with [BS]. The above scheme seems to be secure. Some modifications are needed to prove that the scheme is as secure as RSA (see final paper).

**Theorem 3.1** *When $n = pq$ for $p, q$ safe primes and $|\mathcal{A}| \geq 2$, the above scheme creates an RSA signature.*

**Proof:**  (Sketch) Even though $\lambda(n)$ is not known by the shareholders, the exponentiation operation is performed modulo $\lambda(n)$. Using the Chinese remainder theorem the

---

[¶]In general, it is sufficient to assume that $\lambda(n)/2$ is the product of large primes.

above computation is correct modulo 2 (since it is always even) and modulo $p'q'$ (since the inverses exist). Thus the scheme generates the correct signature. ∎

## 3.2 The use of extensions of rings

Since in the above method $q_{i,B}$ becomes a very large integer when $l$ is large, we discuss a different method using algebraic extensions (see [Ja85]) over $Z_{\lambda(n)}$. Let $u$ be a root to the irreducible polynomial $p(x) = x^h + a_{h-1}x^{h-1} + \cdots + a_1 x + a_0$ over $Z_{\lambda(n)}$. We remind the reader that an algebra $A$ over a commutative ring $R$ is a pair of $A$, a ring and an $R$-module $A$ where the additive group for the ring and the $R$-module are the same and $\alpha(ab) = (\alpha a)b = a(\alpha b)$ for $a, b \in A$ and $\alpha \in R$ (see [Ja89, p. 43]). We can now view $Z_{\lambda(n)}[u]$ as an algebra over $Z_{\lambda(n)}$. The regular representation of an algebra $A$ is the map $x \to x_L$ for each $x \in A$ where $x_L$ is the map $a \to xa$ in $A$. This is a homomorphism from $A$ to $\text{End}_R A^{\|}$. A matrix representation $\rho(x)$ for $x_L$ can be made for each $x \in A$. When the inverse of $x$ exits, we define $\bar{x} = x^{-1} \cdot N(x)$ where $N(x) = \det(\rho(x))$ is the norm of $x$ (see also [Ja85, pp. 422-425]). Note that $\rho(x)$ is invertible iff $x$ is invertible. This framework provides us with an alternative method to the polynomial approach.

Now $f(x)$ is a polynomial over $Z_{\lambda(n)}[u]$ with $f(0) = d - 1$. Let the $x_i$'s be chosen such that $\forall i, j \in A : x_i, x_j \in Z_{\lambda(n)}[u]$ and $N(x_i - x_j) < C_p(l)$ where $C_p(l)$ is a small integer independent of $x_i$ and $\gcd(N(x_i - x_j), \lambda(n)) = 1$. We now let

$$q'_{i,B} = \prod_{\substack{j \in A \\ j \notin B}} N(x_i - x_j) \prod_{\substack{j \in B \\ j \neq i}} (\overline{x_i - x_j}) \prod_{\substack{j \in B \\ j \neq i}} (0 - x_j)$$

and $K''_i = f(x_i)/\prod_{\substack{j \neq i \\ j \in A}} N(x_i - x_j)$. Note that $a_{i,B} = K''_i \cdot q'_{i,B}$. We define functions $F_i : R[u] \to R$ such that $F_i(b_0 + \cdots + b_h u^h) = b_i$. Since $d - 1 \in Z_{\lambda(n)}$, we see that $\sum_{i \in B} F_0(a_{i,B}) = \sum_{i \in B} a_{i,B} \equiv d - 1 \bmod Z_{\lambda(n)}$. So each $i \in B$ will calculate $s_{m,i,B} \equiv m^{F_0(a_{i,B})} \bmod n$ and send $s_{m,i,B}$ to the Combiner as mentioned earlier in Section 3.

Modification of the extension ring method can enhance our threshold scheme over some Abelian groups (see Section 4.2) as done in [DF91].

We now analyze the order of the number of multiplications needed in the modified RSA by one shareholder. For that purpose we analyze the largest coefficient in absolute value of $q'_{i,B}$. Let $|a|$ denote the absolute value of the integer $a$ and let $p(x) = x^h + a_{h-1}x^{h-1} + \cdots + a_0$ be an irreducible polynomial mod $\lambda(n)$ with $u$ a root and $a_i < \lambda(n)$. Let, $c(u) = b(u) \cdot b'(u) = (b_{h-1} \cdot u^{h-1} + \cdots + b_0) \cdot (b'_{h-1} u^{h-1} + \cdots + b'_0) = \sum_{j=0}^{2h-2} c_j u^j$ then

---

$^{\|}\text{End}_R A$ is the ring of homomorphisms going from the $R$-module $A$ into itself.

$c_j = \sum_{i=0}^{j} b_i \cdot b'_{j-i}$. We see that when $|b_i| \leq B$ and $|b'_i| \leq B'$, then $|c_j| \leq hBB'$. Now let $c'(u) \equiv c(u) \pmod{\lambda(n), p(u)}$. Since $\lambda(n)$ is unknown to $k-1$ shareholders, each of them cannot do the above reduction. So we define $c''(u) \equiv c(u) \bmod p(u)$ without reducing it modulo $\lambda(n)$ and we use the relation $u^h = -a_{h-1}u^{h-1} - \cdots - a_0$ for $c_j$ with $j > (h-1)$. Thus by calculating the absolute value of the largest coefficient in $c''(u)$, we find that it is less than $hBB'\lambda(n)^{(h-1)}$. When the largest coefficient of $y_i(u)$ are in absolute value less than $A$, then by induction the absolute value of the largest coefficient in $y_1(u) \cdot y_2(u) \cdots y_T(u)$ is at most $h^{T-1}A^T\lambda(n)^{(T-1)(h-1)}$. We now will use this formula to calculate the largest coefficient in absolute value of $\prod_{j \in B, j \neq i} x_j$ and of $\prod_{j \in B, j \neq i}(x_i - x_j)$.

It is easy to see that the largest coefficient in absolute value of $\prod_{j \in B, j \neq i} x_j$ is less than: $h^{k-2}\lambda(n)^{(k-2)h+1}$. The calculation of $\overline{(x_i - x_j)}$ cannot be made in a straight forward manner since $\lambda(n)$ is not known to the shareholders. It is clear that using the extended Euclidean algorithm over the rationals, that $\overline{(x_i - x_j)}$ and $N(x_i - x_j)$ can be computed**. We note that the absolute value of the quotients computed in the Euclidean algorithm are bounded [Kn] by $\alpha = \lambda(n)^{2h-1}(h+1)^h$. We also note that the extended Euclidean algorithm terminates in $\log(h)$ steps. So using the *extended* Euclidean algorithm the largest coefficient in absolute value of $\overline{(x_i - x_j)}$ is less than $\beta = \log(h)h^{\log(h)-1}\alpha^{\log(h)}$. So the largest coefficient in absolute value of $\prod_{j \in B, j \neq i}\overline{(x_i - x_j)}$ is less than: $h^{k-2}\beta^{k-1}\lambda(n)^{(k-2)(h-1)}$.

Now $N(x_i - x_j) \leq C_p(l)$, so $|\prod_{j \in A, j \notin B} N(x_i - x_j)| \leq C_p(l)^{l-k}$. Let $L_{i,B}$ be the largest coefficient in $q'_{i,B}$. Then $\log(L'_{i,B}) \in O(kh \log(h) \log(\lambda(n)) + (l-k) \log C_p(l))$, because $h$ must be much smaller than $\lambda(n)$. We now recall from the first method that $q_{i,B} = (\prod_{j \notin B, j \in A}(x_i - x_j))(-1^{T-1})\prod_{j \in B, j \neq i} x_i$. Observe that the $x_i$ in $q_{i,B}$ are integers. Let $D_{i,B}$ be the absolute value of $q_{i,B}$. In fact $x_i < 2i$, so $D_{i,B} < (2l)^{l-k} \cdot (k-1)!2^{k-1}$. So using Stirling's approximation $\log(D_{i,B}) \in O((l-k)\log(l) + (k-1)\log(k-1))$. So depending from $l$, $k$, $h$, $C_p(l)$, and $\log(\lambda(n))$ one should choose one of the methods. Evidently we can see that the extension ring method can be improved when one optimizes the norms $(C_p(l))$ and $h$. It seems as though this optimization problem is difficult.

A third method to obtain threshold RSA signatures, which can be used, is based on matrices where the determinant is small. This is similar to the method used in [DF90]. Each of the methods of the threshold RSA signatures performs differently depending on $k$, $l$, $h$, $C_p(l)$, and $\log(\lambda(n))$.

---

**In some cases this method does not find the actual conjugate and the actual norm. As long as all shareholders and the key distributor use the same method it does not matter in our context.

# 4 A provably secure threshold authentication scheme

## 4.1 Attempt at a group based homomorphic threshold scheme

We first want to develop a homomorphic threshold scheme [Be] for an Abelian group $G$ whose exponent has only large prime factors. Let $e'_G$ be a multiple of the exponent of $G$ such that $e'_G$ is of similar form as $e_G$. Let $\{g_1, g_2, \cdots, g_m\}$ generate $G$ and $e'_G$ and $g_j$ be known to the key distribution center. Define secret $s = g_1^{\gamma_1} g_2^{\gamma_2} \cdots g_m^{\gamma_m}$. For $0 < j \le m$, let $f_j(x)$ be independently chosen polynomials of degree $k-1$ such that $f_j(0) = \gamma_j$. Similar to the method of Section 3.1, the key distribution center calculates

$$K'_{j,i} = \frac{f_j(x_i)}{\left( \prod_{\substack{t \ne i \\ t \in \mathcal{A}}} (x_i - x_t) \right)} \in Z_{e'_G}, \ \forall i \in \mathcal{A} \text{ and } \forall j \in \{1, \cdots, m\}.$$

In this scheme, however, the share for $i$ is $A_i = g_1^{K'_{1,i}} g_2^{K'_{2,i}} \cdots g_m^{K'_{m,i}} \in G$ and the modified share for $i$ in $\mathcal{B}$ is $a_{i,\mathcal{B}} = (A_i)^{q_{i,\mathcal{B}}}$ where $q_{i,\mathcal{B}}$ is defined as in Section 3.1. Thus $s = \prod_{i \in \mathcal{B}} a_{i,\mathcal{B}}$. This scheme is not practical since the key distribution center must solve the discrete log problem and additionally know the generators and $e'_G$. A similar remark in the context of multiplicative sharing schemes was made in [Be]. For many groups, the discrete logarithm is considered hard [Od, MVO].

## 4.2 Homomorphic threshold scheme over an Abelian group

Since the first attempt is not practical for most purposes, we propose a variation which *requires only that $e'_G$ is known to the key distributor and has only large prime factors*. Let $\{A_1, A_2, \cdots, A_{k-1}\}$ be independently randomly chosen elements in $G$. Then by letting $\mathcal{X}_j = \{1, 2, \cdots, k-1, j\}$ with $j \ge k$, the key distribution center can calculate

$$A_j = (s \cdot \prod_{\substack{i \ne j \\ i \in \mathcal{X}_j}} A_i^{-q_{i, \mathcal{X}_j}})^{q_{j, \mathcal{X}_j}^{-1}}.$$

The use of $A_j$ is as in Section 4.1. Observe that any combination of $k-1$ shareholders do not learn anything new about $e_G$, the exponent of $G$, when given the fact that $e_G$ has only large prime factors. The following concept goes further. The concept of a sharing scheme not revealing anything about the secret *or anything else* is called a zero-knowledge sharing scheme [DF91]. We remind the reader that knowing the exponent of $Z_n^*$ allows one to factor $n$. Using extensions, similar to Section 3.2, we have proposed a zero-knowledge homomorphic threshold scheme for *any* $l$ and $k$ no matter what the exponent $e_G$ is [DF91].

## 4.3 The provable scheme

A provable secure *authentication* scheme based on a zero-knowledge version of [GMR] was presented in [Des]. Its advantage is that no authentication tree is needed.

Let $R \in D_n$ where $D_n = \{x \in Z_n \mid (x \mid n) = 1 \text{ and } 0 < x < n/2\} = G$ and $n = p \cdot q$ where $p$ and $q$ safe primes such that: $p \equiv 3 \bmod 8$ and $q \equiv 7 \bmod 8$. The tuple $(R, n)$ is our public key. First observe that $D_n(*)$ is an Abelian group in which the operation is defined as:

$$x * y = \begin{cases} xy \, (\bmod n) & \text{if } xy \, (\bmod n) < n/2, \\ -xy \, (\bmod n) & \text{if } xy \, (\bmod n) \geq n/2, \end{cases}$$

where $x, y \in D_n$. In $D_n$ we will use this multiplication from now on. The function $f_0(x) = x * x$ in $D_n$ and $f_1(x) = 4 * x * x$ in $D_n$. When $\langle M \rangle$ is the prefix-free encoding [Ga] of $M$ then $\langle M \rangle$ is never a prefix of $\langle M' \rangle$ ($M \neq M'$). Now, $f_{\langle M \rangle}$ is defined as $f_{\langle M \rangle}(x) = f_{i_d}(f_{i_{d-1}}(\cdots f_{i_1}(f_{i_0}(x)) \cdots))$, where $\langle M \rangle = i_d i_{d-1} \ldots i_1 i_0$ in binary. One has to read $f_{\langle M \rangle}^{-1}$ as $(f_{\langle M \rangle})^{-1}$ so that $f_{\langle M \rangle}^{-1}(f_{\langle M \rangle}(x)) = x$. We define $|\langle M \rangle| = d + 1$. When a limit on the length of the prefix free encoding of the message, called $\alpha$, is known beforehand, [Des] works when one knows $\sqrt[2^\alpha]{R}$ and $\sqrt[2^\alpha]{4}$ (see also [Go]). We recall that if $n$ is as in Section 3.1, then the exponent of $D_n$ is $p'q'$, satisfying our conditions. In our scheme the key distributor gives shares of $\sqrt[2^\alpha]{R}$ and $\sqrt[2^\alpha]{4}$ using our group based threshold scheme. In a homomorphic threshold scheme when $A_j$ is a share for $s$ and $A_j'$ is a share for $s'$, $A_j \cdot A_j'$ is a share for $s \cdot s'$. When $|\langle M \rangle| \leq \alpha$, each shareholder can calculate, using his shares, his part of $f_M^{-1}(R_j)$, which we call $S_{i,M}$.

To authenticate a message the following protocol is executed. First $C$ sends the message $M$ to the receiver, called the verifier $V$. Then repeat $|n|$ times:

**Step 1** The shareholder $i \in B$ randomly chooses a $t_i \in D_n$ and squares it $|\langle M \rangle|$ times to obtain $X_i = t_i^{(2^{|\langle M \rangle|})} \pmod{n}$ and sends $X_i$ to $C$. Then $C$ calculates $X = \prod_i X_i \pmod{n}$ and sends $X$ to $V$.

**Step 2** $V$ sends a random bit $E$ to $C$, who broadcasts it.

**Step 3** Each shareholder calculates $Y_i = t_i \cdot (S_{i,M})^E \pmod{n}$ and sends it to $C$. Then $C$ calculates $Y = \prod_i Y_i \pmod{n}$ and sends it to $V$.

**Step 4** $V$ verifies $Y$ by using multiplications, and the organization's public key.

Our method does not leak the factors of $n$ to a collusion of $k-1$ shareholders. It is not difficult to prove that if $k$ is polynomial in $|n|$ that the view that $C$ has is easy to simulate, so that it not necessary to trust $C$. So the shareholders could have secure workstations using an insecure local network to communicate with $C$ (who communicates with the verifier).

Observe that the distributor in the above does not need to be one trusted individual. Mental games [GMW] allow for this.

# 5 An unconditionally secure version

We now develop a method for the threshold unconditionally secure authenticators using a geometric scheme. The method will be performed in $Z_p^{k+1}$, a $(k+1)$-dimensional vector space over a large prime $p$. We denote one of the axis in $Z_p^{k+1}$ as $\mathcal{M}$ and points as $p = (x_1, x_2, \cdots, x_k, n) \in Z_p^{k+1}$ where $n$ is the $\mathcal{M}$ coordinate. Let $P_m$, called the message plane for $m$, contain all points satisfying the equation $n = m$. A secret line $l_s$ known to the receiver, $R$, and not parallel to $P_0$ is generated by the key distribution center $D$ (see Figure 2); $D$ may be $R$. The secret shares generated by $D$ are $k$-dimensional

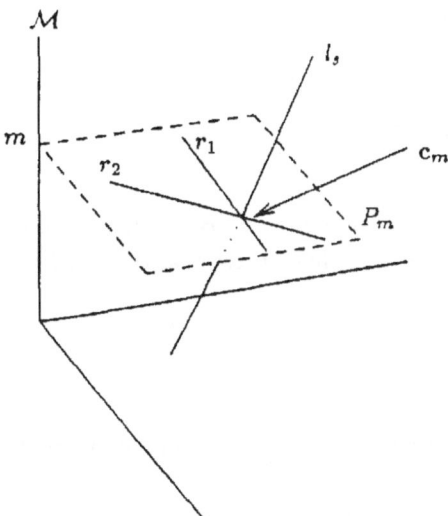

Figure 2: The geometric scheme for a 2 out of $l$ authenticator generator. $C$ calculates the codeword given two planes $R_{i,m}$, which intersect $P_m$ at $r_i$.

planes $A_i$ such that the intersection of any $k$ planes, $A_i$, is $l_s$. The receiver accepts as an authenticated $m$, a point $c_m = (x_1, x_2, \cdots, x_k, m) \in l_s$, called the codeword.

To generate the codeword, each individual $i \in B$ will send to $C$ a $k$-dimensional random plane $R_{i,m}$ which contains the intersection of $A_i$ and $P_m$. $C$ can now generate the codeword $c_m$ given the $k$ planes $R_{i,m}$ and the plane $P_m$. Since the planes are random, $C$ will gain no information about $l_s$ other than the point $p_m \in l_s$ and therefore $C$ cannot perform a substitution attack even if $k-1$ individuals would help additionally. A projective geometry method is easily derived from the above method. In [DF], a method based on polynomials to achieve the above is given.

# 6 Conclusion

Often it is desired that the power to sign or authenticate messages is shared. Key sharing schemes on their own are not suited for this because once used the key is revealed. Our heuristic (RSA), proven secure and unconditionally secure schemes solve this problem. In our scheme the shareholders do not have to interact with one another, while in mental games they do heavily. In all of our schemes we assume that the shareholders (senders) and receiver have secure workstations but the network and servers are not necessarily secure. It is an open problem to determine which systems in general can be executed in a non-interactive distributive way.

# 7 Acknowledgements

The authors would like to thank Josh Benaloh, Bob Blakley, Burt Kaliski and Gus Simmons for discussions and expressing their interest in this work.

# References

[BB78] B. Blakley and G. R. Blakley. Security of number theoretic public key cryptosystems against random attack. *Cryptologia*, 1978. In three parts: Part I: 2(4), pp. 305–321, October 1978; Part II: 3(1), pp. 29–42, January 1979; Part III: 3(2), pp. 105–118, April 1979.

[BB79] G. R. Blakley and I. Borosh. Rivest-Shamir-Adleman public key cryptosystems do not always conceal messages. *Computers & Mathematics with Apllications*, 5(3):169–178, 1979.

[Be] J. C. Benaloh. Secret sharing homomorphisms: Keeping shares of a secret secret. In A. Odlyzko, editor, *Advances in Cryptology, Proc. of Crypto'86 (Lecture Notes in Computer Science 263)*, pages 251–260. Springer–Verlag, 1987. Santa Barbara, California, U.S.A., August 11–15.

[Bl] G. R. Blakley. Safeguarding cryptographic keys. In *Proc. Nat. Computer Conf. AFIPS Conf. Proc.*, pages 313–317, 1979. vol.48.

[BS] G. R. Blakley and L. Swanson. Infinite structures in information theory. In D. Chaum, R.L. Rivest, and A. T. Sherman, editors, *Advances in Cryptology. Proc. of Crypto'82*, pages 39–50. Plenum Press N. Y., 1983. Crypto '82, Santa Barbara, CA, August 1982.

[CH] R. A. Croft and S. P. Harris. Public-key cryptography and re-usable shared secrets. In H. Beker and F. Piper, editors, *Cryptography and coding*, pages 189–201. Clarendon Press, 1989. Royal Agricultural College, Cirencester, December 15–17, 1986.

[CK] B. Chor and E. Kushilevitz. Secret sharing over infinite domains. In G. Brassard, editor, *Advances in Cryptology — Crypto '89, Proceedings (Lecture Notes in Computer Science 435)*, pages 299–306. Springer-Verlag, 1990. Santa Barbara, California, U.S.A., August 20–24.

[Da] G. I. Davida. Chosen signature cryptanalysis of the RSA (MIT) public key cryptosystem. Tech. Report TR-CS-82-2, University of Wisconsin-Milwaukee, October 1982.

[Den] D. E. R. Denning. Digital signatures with RSA and other public-key cryptosystems. *Comm. ACM 27*, pages 388–392, 1984.

[Des] Y. Desmedt. Abuse-free cryptosystems: Particularly subliminal-free authentication and signature. Submitted to the Journal of Cryptology, under revision, April 1989.

[DF] Y. Desmedt and Y. Frankel. Unconditionally secure threshold authentication. In preparation (Available from authors when completed).

[DF90] Y. Desmedt and Y. Frankel. Threshold cryptosystems. Santa Barbara, California, U.S.A., August 20–24, 1990.

[DF91] Y. Desmedt and Y. Frankel. Perfect zero-knowledge sharing schemes over any finite Abelian group. Presented at Sequences '91, June 17–22, 1991, Positano, Italy, to appear in: the Proceedings Springer-Verlag, 1991.

[DH] W. Diffie and M. E. Hellman. New directions in cryptography. *IEEE Trans. Inform. Theory*, IT–22(6):644–654, November 1976.

[dJC] W. de Jonge and D. Chaum. Attacks on some RSA signatures. In *Advances in Cryptology: Crypto '85, Proceedings (Lecture Notes in Computer Science 218)*, pages 18–27. Springer-Verlag, New York, 1986. Santa Barbara, California, U.S.A., August 18–22, 1985.

[DQV] M. De Soete, J.-J. Quisquater, and K. Vedder. A signature with shared verification scheme. In G. Brassard, editor, *Advances in Cryptology — Crypto '89, Proceedings (Lecture Notes in Computer Science 435)*, pages 253–262. Springer-Verlag, 1990. Santa Barbara, California, U.S.A., August 20–24.

[Ga] R. G. Gallager. *Information theory and reliable communication*. John Wiley and Sons, New York, 1968.

[GMR] S. Goldwasser, S. Micali, and R. Rivest. A digital signature scheme secure against adaptive chosen-message attacks. *Siam J. Comput.*, 17(2):281–308, April 1988.

[GMW] O. Goldreich, S. Micali, and A. Wigderson. How to play any mental game. In *Proceedings of the Nineteenth ACM Symp. Theory of Computing, STOC*, pages 218 – 229, May 25–27, 1987.

[Go] O. Goldreich. Two remarks concerning the Goldwasser-Micali-Rivest signature scheme. In A. Odlyzko, editor, *Advances in Cryptology, Proc. of Crypto '86 (Lecture Notes in Computer Science 263)*, pages 104–110. Springer-Verlag, 1987. Santa Barbara, California, U.S.A., August 11–15, 1986.

[Ja85] N. Jacobson. *Basic Algebra I*, volume 1. W. H. Freeman and Company, 2nd edition, 1985.

[Ja89] N. Jacobson. *Basic Algebra II*, volume 2. W. H. Freeman and Company, 2nd edition, 1989.

[Kn] D. E. Knuth. *The Art of Computer Programming, Vol. 2, Seminumerical Algorithms*. Addison-Wesley, Reading, MA, 1981.

[Mo] J. H. Moore. Protocol failures in cryptosystems. *Proc. IEEE*, 76(5):594–602, May 1988.

[MVO]  A. Menezes, S. Vanstone, and T. Okamoto. Reducing elliptic curve logarithms to logarithms in a finite field. In *Proceedings of the Twenty third annual ACM Symp. Theory of Computing, STOC*, pages 80–89, 1991.

[Od]   A. M. Odlyzko. Discrete logs in a finite field and their cryptographic significance. In N. Cot T. Beth and I. Ingemarsson, editors, *Advances in Cryptology, Proc. of Eurocrypt'84 (Lecture Notes in Computer Science 209)*, pages 224–314. Springer-Verlag, 1984. Paris, France April 1984.

[RSA]  R. L. Rivest, A. Shamir, and L. Adleman. A method for obtaining digital signatures and public key cryptosystems. *Commun. ACM*, 21:294–299, April 1978.

[Sh]   A. Shamir. How to share a secret. *Commun. ACM*, 22:612 – 613, November 1979.

# Cryptographically Strong Undeniable Signatures, Unconditionally Secure for the Signer

## (Extended Abstract)

David Chaum[1], Eugène van Heijst[1], Birgit Pfitzmann[2]

## Abstract

We present the first undeniable signature schemes where signers are unconditionally secure. In the efficient variants, the security for the recipients relies on a discrete logarithm assumption or on factoring; and in a theoretical version, on claw-free permutation pairs.

Besides, on the one hand, the efficient variants are the first practical cryptographically strong undeniable signature schemes at all. On the other hand, in many cases they are more efficient than previous signature schemes unconditionally secure for the signer.

Interesting new subprotocols are efficient collision-free hash functions based on a discrete logarithm assumption, efficient perfectly hiding commitments for elements of $\mathbb{Z}_p$ ($p$ prime), and fairly practical perfect zero-knowledge proofs for arithmetic formulas in $\mathbb{Z}_p$ or $\mathbb{Z}_{2^\sigma}$.

## 1    Introduction

The signature schemes presented here combine, for the first time, two independent features that have recently been suggested as desirable for signatures in certain situations: unconditional security for the signer and "invisibility", the characteristic property of "undeniable signatures".

Each of these features will be described separately in §1.1 and §1.2, resp., together with reasons why one might want it and previous schemes realizing it.

In §1.3, we sketch the properties of our new schemes. In particular, for cases where just one of the features is of interest, we mention how the new schemes compare with the previous schemes realizing just this one feature. §1.4 lists interesting new subprotocols, §1.5 gives an overview over the rest of the paper.

### 1.1    Unconditional security for signers

In conventional digital signature schemes, i.e., those according to the idea in [DH], signers can be cheated with forged signatures if a cryptographic assumption, such as the hardness of factoring, turns out to be wrong. This holds even for provably secure signature schemes such as GMR [GMR]. (Recipients, however, are unconditionally secure.)

In contrast, symmetric authentication systems with unconditional, i.e., information-theoretical security for senders of messages (and for recipients, too) have existed for quite a while, e.g., [GMS, WC]. An exponentially small error probability is tolerated. (And this seems unavoidable: An attacker can always guess the complete secret information of the real sender.) Thus unconditional security in this context means that an adversary has no advantage over mere

---

[1]  Centre for Mathematics and Computer Science (CWI), Kruislaan 413, NL-1098 SJ Amsterdam, The Netherlands

[2]  Institut für Informatik, Universität Hildesheim, Samelsonplatz 1, W-3200 Hildesheim, FRG; Fax +49-5121-860475; Phone +49-5121-883-739; e-mail pfitzb@infhil.uucp (via unido.informatik.uni-dortmund.de)

J. Feigenbaum (Ed.): Advances in Cryptology - CRYPTO '91, LNCS 576, pp. 470-484, 1992.
© Springer-Verlag Berlin Heidelberg 1992

guessing and cannot check locally whether a guess is correct. However, with symmetric authentication, disputes between a sender and a recipient cannot be solved.

Recently, unconditional security for signers has been considered with "non-undeniable" signature schemes.

This feature is interesting in practice, even if it is only combined with cryptographic security for recipients [PW2]. In particular, if two parties exchange signed messages, both were only computationally secure before. Now, if one party uses signatures unconditionally secure for the signer, and the other party conventional ones, the former party is unconditionally secure. This is particularly suitable if there is an asymmetry between the parties anyway: One would make the weaker party unconditionally secure.

For instance, one can make individuals unconditionally secure when they exchange signatures with a large organization, e.g., a bank in a payment system. The asymmetry is that the organization usually chooses the signature schemes and the security parameters. Thus it can provide for its own security, whereas many individuals may not even know what a security parameter is. The organization has no disadvantage due to the new scheme, since it had to trust a cryptographic assumption anyway; the individuals certainly have an advantage.

But even the organization may see advantages: If clients appreciate security, there may be a marketing advantage. Also, it may be easier to obtain a guarantee of legal significance for such a system, since the organization bears the whole risk. In particular, in the (hopefully) more likely case that the cryptographic assumption is not broken, the risk that courts believe dishonest clients who falsely claim that their signatures were forged should be much smaller, since such a forgery is (mathematically) impossible. Also, if any forgery ever occurs, the organization itself is sure about this and can stop the scheme or increase the security parameters, in contrast to the case where a client's signature is forged in a conventional scheme.

**Previous schemes:** In [WP, BPW, PW2], fail-stop signatures were introduced. They are cryptographically secure against forgeries in the sense of [GMR]. In addition, if a forgery occurs nevertheless, the signer can prove this (more precisely: the fact that the cryptograpic assumption has been broken) unconditionally (in the sense described above) to everyone, e.g., by showing the factors of a number that she was assumed not to be able to factor. In particular, if signatures become invalid once a proof of forgery has been shown, signers are unconditionally secure, and recipients cryptographically.

In [CR], a signature-like scheme where all parties are unconditionally secure was introduced.

However, so far, none of these schemes is efficient in all cases: Fail-stop signatures are efficient for one-bit messages, but their length grows linearly with the length of the message (up to a certain point, since messages can be hashed). (But note that for some important situations, protocols with one-bit messages exist [PW2].) Unconditional signatures have a complicated precomputation phase and grow linearly with the number of possible recipients.

## 1.2 Undeniable signatures: Invisibility

Undeniable (or perhaps rather "invisible") signatures were introduced in [CA] and further developed, e.g., in [C2, BCDP]. These are digital signatures providing more privacy: A recipient of a signature cannot show it to others without the help of the signer. If, however, the signer is forced to either deny or acknowledge a valid signature, e.g., in court, she cannot deny it.

**Previous schemes:** In the previous schemes, similar to conventional digital signatures, the signers' security relies on a cryptographic assumption. (Don't be confused by the fact that the verification protocols of some schemes are "perfect zero-knowledge": A forger who breaks the cryptographic assumption can compute the secret key from the public key directly.)

All the efficient schemes are based on a discrete logarithm assumption, and they are not cryptographically strong, i.e., proved to be as secure as the discrete logarithm. In particular, no security against active attacks has been shown (cf. [GMR]). There is, however, a cryptographically strong theoretical construction from any one-way function in [BCDP].

## 1.3    The new schemes

We present the first three undeniable signature schemes were signers are unconditionally secure. The security of the recipients is cryptographically strong. In the two efficient variants, this means provably as secure as factoring or a discrete logarithm assumption, resp. In a theoretical variant, the security of the recipients relies on arbitrary claw-free permutation pairs.

If one cares about invisibility only, but not about which of the parties is unconditionally secure: Our schemes are not quite as efficient as the most efficient previous ones. However, if one wants the remaining party's security to be at least cryptographically strong, one must use ours.

If one cares about unconditional security for signers only, but not about invisibility: In many cases, the new schemes are much more efficient than fail-stop and unconditionally secure signatures are so far. However, if one relaxes the requirements on fail-stop signatures like they are in the schemes presented here, i.e., omits the fail-stop property and allows interaction between signer and recipient, one can construct variants of those which are even more efficient [PW2, Pf].

## 1.4    Interesting new subprotocols

Several subprotocols may be interesting in their own right:

We present cryptographically collision-free hash functions based on a discrete logarithm assumption, which need about one multiplication per message bit only. So far, this was only possible on the factoring assumption, whereas in the discrete logarithm case, about one exponentiation per bit was needed [D1].

We also construct efficient perfectly hiding commitments for elements of $\mathbb{Z}_p$, where the unchangeability relies on a discrete logarithm assumption. The commitment is only as long as the message. So far, perfectly hiding commitments where normally made bitwise, which induces a large message expansion. The only efficient version for larger messages was based on factoring [BPW].

The commitments can be added and subtracted locally, like those of [BPW]. We present efficient inequality proofs and procedures to multiply them. This makes fairly practical perfect zero-knowledge proofs (computationally convincing) for arithmetic formulas in $\mathbb{Z}_p$ or $\mathbb{Z}_{2^\sigma}$ possible.

## 1.5    Overview

We first present the basic idea in an informal way (§2). We then desribe the basic parts and security proofs of the discrete logarithm scheme (§3) and the theoretical version (§4) and sketch the factoring scheme (§5). Finally, we sketch the remaining parts, which are quite similar in the three schemes (§6).

## 2 Basic Idea

Our scheme combines ideas of previous undeniable signatures and of fail-stop signatures.

The basic idea to achieve the invisibility characterizing undeniable signatures is that a signature can only be verified by an interactive protocol between the signer and the recipient, preferably in zero-knowledge.

The basic idea of fail-stop signatures is that, given a public key and perhaps previous signatures, each new message has many acceptable signatures $s$. On a cryptographic assumption, however, the signer can compute just one of them, say $s^*$. If the cryptographic assumption is broken and someone forges a signature, still with high probability they will not use $s^*$, since all acceptable signatures look equally likely to them in the information-theoretical sense. Thus the signer now knows two different signatures for one message. This counts as a proof of forgery.

In combination with invisibility, the latter idea is changed a bit: When the real signer receives the forged signature, say $sf$, she cannot prove that $s^*$ and $sf$ are two different signatures for the same message, since she cannot carry out the verification protocol for $sf$. Instead, she will only prove (in zero-knowledge) that her real signature is not $sf$. (However, this is not a proof that the cryptographic assumption has been broken, since it can be done for any value $sf$. Thus this scheme has no fail-stop property.)

## 3 The Discrete Logarithm Scheme

Most things described in §§3.1-3.3 and 3.5-3.6 can be found in more detail in [CHP].

### 3.1 Assumption and notation

The cryptographic assumption, needed for the security of the recipients, is that we have an infinite sequence of groups $G_p$ of known prime orders $p$, where one can perform the group operations and choose random elements efficiently, but the discrete logarithm is hard. (The security of both signers and recipients depends on the primality of $p$.) This is the same assumption as in [CA, C2].

An efficient proposal from [CA] is $G_p = \mathbb{Z}_q^*/\{\pm 1\}$ where $q = 2p+1$ and both $p$ and $q$ are prime. $G_p$ can be represented by $\{1, ..., p\}$. Note that if the discrete logarithm in a group is hard, it is also hard in a large subgroup (i.e., of logarithmic index). Hence this is just the normal discrete logarithm assumption for $\mathbb{Z}_q^*$, restricted to primes $q$ of the form $2p+1$. These are usually considered as particularly hard cases.

Groups $G_p = GF(2^n)^*$ for Mersenne-primes $p = 2^n-1$ or large subgroups on elliptic curves are also possible.

For $g = (g_1, ..., g_n) \in G_p^n$ and $x = (x_1, ..., x_n) \in \mathbb{Z}_p^n$, let
$$g^x := g_1^{x_1} \cdot ... \cdot g_n^{x_n}.$$
(Since the order of $G_p$ is $p$, exponents only need to be defined modulo $p$.)

For $x = (x_1, ..., x_n), y = (y_1, ..., y_n) \in \mathbb{Z}_p^n$, denote the inner product by $x * y := x_1 y_1 + ... + x_n y_n$.

For a message $m \in \mathbb{Z}_p$, let $\underline{m}$ denote its extension to a vector $\underline{m} := (1, 1, m)$.

We will call the signer Sibyl and the recipient Rick.

## 3.2 System structure for one message of fixed length

To give a better idea of the new features of the scheme, we first assume that just one message of fixed length for a given recipient is to be signed. Efficient extensions to many messages of arbitrary length and more recipients, plus extended security definitions, are quite canonical and sketched in §6.

**Key exchange:**

0. All the participants agree on a group $G_p$ of prime order $p$ and a parameter $L$. ($L$ determines that the probability of successful cheating in the following zero-knowledge proofs should be at most $2^{-L}$.)

1. The recipient Rick chooses a triple
$$g = (g_1, g_2, g_3)$$
of generators of $G_p$, i.e., any elements of $G_p{}^*$, with $g_1 \neq g_2$, randomly and publishes it.

The public values $p$, $L$, and $g$ are parameters of the following algorithms, but will be omitted for simplicity.

2. The signer Sibyl checks that $g_1 \neq 1$ and $g_1 \neq g_2$. Then she chooses a secret key
$$SK = (x_1, x_2, x_3) \in \mathbb{Z}_p{}^3$$
randomly and computes and publishes the public key
$$PK = pub(SK) := g^{SK} = g_1{}^{x_1} \cdot g_2{}^{x_2} \cdot g_3{}^{x_3}.$$

**Signing:** To sign a message $m \in \mathbb{Z}_p$, Sibyl forms the signature
$$sign(SK, m) := SK * \underline{m} = x_1 + x_2 + m \cdot x_3.$$

**Verification:** To accept a value $s \in \mathbb{Z}_p$ as a signature on $m$, Rick requires Sibyl to give a perfect zero-knowledge proof of knowledge for the relation corresponding to the following statement (where $PK$, $m$, and $s$ are common inputs):
$$\text{I know } SK: PK = pub(SK) \ \wedge \ sign(SK, m) = s. \tag{1}$$

**Disavowal:** To disavow a value $sf \in \mathbb{Z}_p$ as a signature on $m$, the signer gives a perfect zero-knowledge proof of knowledge of the statement (again, $PK$, $m$, and $sf$ are common inputs):
$$\text{I know } SK: PK = pub(SK) \ \wedge \ sign(SK, m) \neq sf. \tag{2}$$

The description of efficient zero-knowledge proofs for these two purposes is postponed to §3.6 and §3.7.

## 3.3 Security of the signer

We must prove that however a forger Felix (using all the information that he could obtain from Sibyl) forges a signature, the probability that Sibyl can disavow it is exponentially close to 1. We first show this without the information obtained from verifications and disavowals:

**Lemma 1:** $\forall PK$, $m \neq m^*$, in the probability space defined by the random choice of the secret key $SK$: If a forger Felix knows $PK = pub(SK)$ and $s = sign(SK, m)$, then for any forged signature $sf$ for $m^*$, the probability that Sibyl can disavow $sf$ is $1 - p^{-1}$.

**Proof:** Because of the completeness of the disavowal protocol, any signature on $m^*$ other than $sign(SK, m^*)$ can be disavowed with probability 1. Thus it suffices to prove for all $sf$:

$$\Pr(sf \neq sign(SK, m^*) \mid PK = pub(SK) \wedge s = sign(SK, m)) = 1 - p^{-1}. \tag{3}$$

Assume $g_2 = g_1^\alpha$, $g_3 = g_1^\beta$, and $PK = g_1^\gamma$. (This representation is possible, since $g_1$ is a generator.)

Then
$$PK = pub(SK) \iff g_1^\gamma = g_1^{x_1 + \alpha x_2 + \beta x_3} \iff \gamma = x_1 + \alpha x_2 + \beta x_3 \text{ in } \mathbb{Z}_p,$$
$$s = sign(SK, m) \iff s = x_1 + x_2 + m \cdot x_3,$$

and
$$sf = sign(SK, m^*) \iff sf = x_1 + x_2 + m^* \cdot x_3.$$

The matrix of these three equations can be transformed by row operations into

$$\begin{pmatrix} 1 & \alpha & \beta \\ 0 & 1-\alpha & m-\beta \\ 0 & 0 & m^*-m \end{pmatrix}$$

We have $m \neq m^*$, and we explicitly required $g_1 \neq g_2$, i.e., $\alpha \neq 1$. Thus the rank of this matrix is 3. (Since $p$ is prime, a rank is defined.) Hence exactly $p$ secret keys fulfil the condition of the probability in (3), and $sf = sign(SK, m^*)$ holds for just one of them. This proves (3). □

Note that Sibyl's security just depends on $g_1 \neq g_2$, not on the randomness of the generators. Thus it does not harm her if Rick chooses them incorrectly. Also, we have considered an adaptive chosen message attack for this simple case, since "$\forall\, m, m^*$" means that Felix can choose $m$ and $m^*$ in any order.

Of course, Felix does not just see $PK$ and $s$, but he may ask Sibyl to verify $s$ and to disavow other signatures. Here we need one restriction: There are only $p$ possible signatures for $m^*$, thus we cannot allow Felix to try them all. For example, we restrict him to $\sqrt{p}$ attempts. This does not contradict unconditional security, since it is a restriction not on Felix's computing abilities, but on the number of disavowals Sibyl or a court are willing to perform. In practice, for a realistic size of $p$, $\sqrt{p}$ disavowals are impossible anyway.

---

**Theorem 1 (Sibyl's security):** $\forall\, PK, m$: Assume a forger Felix knows $PK = pub(SK)$ and $s = sign(SK, m)$ and can ask Sibyl to verify $s$ arbitrarily often and disavow up to $\sqrt{p}$ adaptively chosen other signatures, i.e., pairs $(m^*, sf) \neq (m, s)$. Then the probability that Sibyl can disavow them all is at least $1 - \sqrt{p}^{-1}$.

---

**Proof (Sketch):** Verification and disavowal are perfect zero-knowledge. Hence a verification gives Felix no information about $SK$ at all, and a disavowal tells him at most $sign(SK, m^*) \neq sf$ for one pair $(m^*, sf)$. By the proof of Lemma 1, this excludes exactly one secret key. Thus no strategy gives him a better chance than $\sqrt{p}$ guesses for $SK$. The probability that he guesses right at least once is at most $\sqrt{p}\,/\,p = \sqrt{p}^{-1}$. □

## 3.4 Invisibility

Invisibility of signatures, i.e., that they cannot be recognized without the help of the signer, was not defined formally in the first publications about undeniable signatures. A definition of computational invisibility (developed independently of the abstract-version of this paper, and probably earlier) ought to appear before this in the final version of [BCDP], a newer one is contained in [CBDP]. Here, however, we need perfect invisibility, corresponding to the unconditional security of the signer.

(Note that the zero-knowledge property in [C2] concerns just verification and disavowal, not the act of issuing the signature. Issuing the signature cannot be zero-knowledge, since it enables the recipient to do something that he could not have done before, i.e., show a signature that Sibyl cannot disavow. More formally: Perfect zero-knowledge (pZKP) implies that the distribution of the prover's output is independent of her secret knowledge. This is not the case with the signatures.) However, with respect to everybody except Sibyl, perfect zero-knowledge seems just what we need. The information that these outsiders have about Sibyl's secret knowledge is modelled by a probability distribution. Thus, as a basic weaker version of perfect zero-knowledge, we define (in the notation of [TW]):

Definition: Let $R$ be a relation, and for each $x$ with $R_x := \{y \mid (x, y) \in R\} \neq \varnothing$, let $p_x(y)$ denote a probability distribution on $R_x$. An interactive TM $P$ is perfect zero-knowledge against outsiders (pZKO) on $(R, (p_x)_x)$ iff for all probabilistic polynomial interactive TMs $V^*$, there is a simulator $M_{V^*}$ so that $M_{V^*}(x, s)$ is polynomial in $|x|$, and for all $x$ with $R_x \neq \varnothing$ and all $s$, $z$:

$$\sum_y (p_x(y) \cdot \Pr((P(y), V^*(s))(x) = z)) = \Pr(M_{V^*}(x, s) = z).$$

(A computational analogue of this definition can be identified in the final version of [BCDP] if one omits the active attacks by the distinguisher and notices that the probabilities there must also be taken over the key choice.)

For the most basic part of invisibility, i.e., defining that the protocol of just issuing one signature is invisible, we can directly apply this definition: $P$ is the TM that, on input $m$, issues $z := sign(SK, m)$ once, $R$ is $\{(PK, SK) \mid PK = pub(SK)\}$, and the distributions $p_{PK}(SK)$ are naturally defined by Sibyl's choice of $SK$.

For the particular system of §3.2, we can easily see that this definition is fulfilled, since one can simulate the signer by choosing $z$ randomly.

If $P$ additionally carries out perfect zero-knowledge verifications, one can show that it is still pZKO by proving that the concatenation of a pZKO and pZKPs is always pZKO. (Although intuitively clear, this is not trivial formally, but there should be no other difficulties than in similar proofs for ZKPs [O, TW].)

For adding disavowals, one may generally relax the requirement to statistical zero-knowledge against outsiders (since before each disavowal, the public information $x$ is slightly increased by revealing $sign(SK, m_i) \neq sf_i$).

Also, for the case where the person to whom the recipient wants to show the signature has information $I$ about $y$ secret from the recipient, one can extend the notion to partial outsiders by computing the expected value of the probability of the outputs $z$ based on the corresponding probability distribution $p_{(x, I)}(y)$. In the simple case considered in this §3, $I$ can only be the little information from disavowals.

This definition, like its computational counterpart, does not consider cooperating verifiers who try to get a signature verified simultaneously, as described in [C2, DY]. (That is, practical cases covered by this model are that a cheating recipient tries to show a signature on private information to third parties who are fairly honest, but might not look away when being shown a conventional signature, or tries to sell a received signature afterwards.) Measures against cooperating verifiers exist [C2, CBDP]: Firstly, the verification protocol should not only be zero-knowledge, but start with verifier-commitments. This is the case in all previous undeniable signature schemes and excludes the practical attack described in [DY], where the verifiers just use a coin-flipping protocol to choose their challenges. Secondly, against more complicated uses of multi-party computations, one can take measures involving timing. However, they are difficult to formalize.

## 3.5 Security of the recipient

We first show that *pub* is cryptographically collision-free, i.e., Sibyl cannot find two secret keys fitting the same public key. A bit more generally, we prove the following lemma:

**Lemma 2 (Collision-freeness of *n*-tuple exponentiation):** On the discrete logarithm assumption of §3.1, and for fixed $n$: For any probabilistic polynomial-time algorithm $\mathcal{A}_n$, any polynomial $Q$, and sufficiently large $p$: The probability that $\mathcal{A}_n$, on input a random $n$-tuple $G_n = (g_1, ..., g_n)$ of generators of $G_p$, finds a $G_n$-collision, i.e.,

$$X_n \neq X_n{}' \in \mathbb{Z}_p{}^n \text{ with } G_n{}^{X_n} = G_n{}^{X_n'},$$

is smaller than $1/Q(\log(p))$.

**Proof (Sketch):** The proof is by induction on $n$. The case $n = 2$ is quite easy. For $n > 2$, we assume that an algorithm $\mathcal{A}_n$ contradicts the lemma and show that the following algorithm would then contradict the lemma for $n-1$:

$\mathcal{A}_{n-1}$: On input $G_{n-1} = (g_1, ..., g_{n-1})$:
1. Choose $e_1, ..., e_{n-1}$ from $\mathbb{Z}_p{}^*$ and $r_1, ..., r_{n-1}$ from $\mathbb{Z}_p$ randomly, and let
$$E := (e_1, ..., e_{n-1}) \text{ and } R := (r_1, ..., r_{n-1}).$$
2. Define an $n$-tuple
$$G_n := (g_1{}^{e_1}, ..., g_{n-1}{}^{e_{n-1}}, g_1{}^{r_1} \cdot ... \cdot g_{n-1}{}^{r_{n-1}}).$$
(If the last component of $G_n$ is not a generator, repeat the choice of $r_{n-1}$ until it is.)
3. Run $\mathcal{A}_n$ on $G_n$ and call the result $C_n$. If $C_n$ is a collision $(X_n, X_n{}')$, output
$$C_{n-1} := ((e_1 x_1 + r_1 x_n, ..., e_{n-1} x_{n-1} + r_{n-1} x_n), (e_1 x'_1 + r_1 x'_n, ..., e_{n-1} x'_{n-1} + r_{n-1} x'_n)).$$

One easily sees that if $C_n$ is a collision and the two components $X_{n-1}$, $X_{n-1}{}'$ of $C_{n-1}$ are different, then $C_{n-1}$ is a collision, too. Next one shows that for fixed $G_{n-1}$, $G_n$, and $C_n$, the equation $X_{n-1} = X_{n-1}{}'$ can be true for just one of the many possible underlying choices of $R$. Finally, one formalizes the following idea: When $\mathcal{A}_n$ is called, it has no information about $R$ except $G_n$. Thus no matter how $\mathcal{A}_n$ chooses $C_n$, with high probability $R$ is not the one for which $X_{n-1} = X_{n-1}{}'$ for the given $G_{n-1}$. ☐

**Theorem 2 (Rick's security):** On the discrete logarithm assumption of §3.1, it is infeasible for Sibyl to prove an $s$ to be a valid signature for a message $m$ and to disavow it later.

**Proof:** The soundness of the interactive proofs implies that if Sibyl can prove $s$ to be a valid signature for $m$ and later disavow it, she can compute secret keys $SK$ and $SK^*$ with

$$PK = pub(SK) \wedge sign(SK, m) = s \wedge PK = pub(SK^*) \wedge sign(SK^*, m) \neq s.$$

Since *sign* is deterministic, this implies $SK \neq SK^*$, i.e., Sibyl has found a collision of the function *pub*. This contradicts Lemma 2. ☐

## 3.6 Efficient verification

A signature is verified by use of the following protocol:

Sibyl (Prover)                                                                Rick (Verifier)

Repeat $L$ times:

Choose $R = (r_1, r_2, r_3) \in \mathbb{Z}_p^3$ randomly.
Compute $SK' = SK + R$, $PK' = pub(SK)$,
$PK' = pub(SK')$, and $s' = sign(SK', m)$  $\underline{\quad PK',\, s' \quad}>$   Choose $b \in \{0,1\}$ randomly.

$<\underline{\quad b \quad}$

(If $b=0$, open the blinding $R$.          $\underline{\quad R \text{ or } SK' \quad}>$
If $b=1$, prove the knowledge          if $b = 0$ or 1, resp.               Check:
for the blinded problem instance.)                              If $b=0$: $PK' = PK \cdot g^R \wedge s' = s + R \cdot m$?
                                                                If $b=1$: $PK' = pub(SK) \wedge s' = sign(SK, m)$ ?

**Protocol 1**     Verification of a signature $s$

**Lemma 3 (Verification):** Protocol 1 is a perfect zero-knowledge interactive proof of knowledge for the relation defined by Formula (1).

**Proof (Sketch):** One can easily show that this is a special case of the proof system for random self-reducible relations of [TW, Th. 4]; the self-reduction is just the addition of a random $R$ to $SK$. (More systematically, one can see that for $\phi_{p,m}(SK) = (pub_p(SK), sign_p(\cdot, m))$ is a homomorphism for all $p, m$, and construct a similar protocol to prove the knowledge of a preimage under any efficient homomorphism.)                                                                      □

One can add verifier-commitments on the challenges $b$ like in the protocol in [Br] (also sketched in [BCLL]), in order to achieve the same robustness against cooperating verifiers as other undeniable signatures have (see §3.4), and probably also to parallelize the rounds. (One would base the commitments on $g_1$, and a simulator could use a cheating verifier to compute $\alpha$, $\beta$, and $\gamma$ from Lemma 1 in order to cheat, too.)

## 3.7 Efficient disavowal

The basic structure of our disavowal is similar to that in [C1]:

In an ideal version, there would be a number $L'$ of rounds, with Rick allowed to choose one of three challenges in each round. We now consider one round: First Sibyl chooses $R$ randomly and computes blinded values $SK' = SK + R$, $PK' = pub(SK')$, $s' = sign(SK', m)$, and $sf' = sf + R \cdot m$. She prepares commitments on $PK'$, $s'$, and $sf'$ (cf. Fig. 1). Rick can choose among the following three challenges:

C1    Sibyl must open the two left commitments and reveal $R$.
C2    Sibyl must open the two right commitments and reveal $SK'$.
C3    Sibyl must prove inequality of the values in the lower two commitments, without opening the commitments. (If they were both opened, Rick could compute the correct signature $s$.)

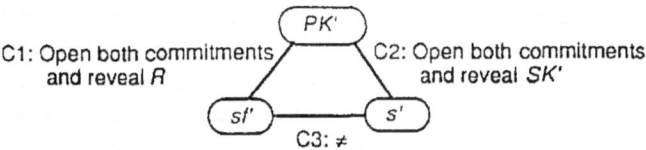

**Fig. 1** Idea of the disavowal protocol; enclosures represent commitments

This idea can be implemented with bit commitments, similar to [C1]. However, bit commitments make the protocol far less efficient than verification. Thus we present a new variant, almost as efficient as the verification, using commitments on complete numbers instead of bits. The main problem will be the inequality proof.

We present the protocol in a generalized version, so that it can also be used in the factoring case. (A different and slightly simpler protocol, with a complete proof, can be found in [CHP], but it is slightly less efficient and could not be generalized to the factoring case.)

**Definition (Sketch):** A homomorphic perfectly hiding commitment scheme for a family of abelian groups consists of an algorithm to choose a key $K$, a test that is passed by all correctly chosen keys, sequences $(G_K)$, $(H_K)$, and $(D_K)$ of abelian groups where all standard operations are efficiently computable, efficient homomorphisms $h_K: G_K \to H_K$ and $\pi_K: G_K \to D_K$, and an efficient algorithm to choose elements of $\pi_K^{-1}(a)$ randomly.

If $h_K(\alpha) = A$ and $\pi_K(\alpha) = a$, we call $A$ a commitment to $a$, and say $A$ is opened by showing $\alpha$.

The two security requirements are: If $K$ passes the test, then for each commitment, all contents are equally probable. If $K$ is chosen correctly, then $h$ is cryptographically collision-free. ♦

For the concrete system, we keep the commitment scheme from [CHP], which has independently been proposed in [Pe], too (but without the inequality proof):

**Lemma 4 (Commitments):** The following parameters define a homomorphic perfectly hiding commitment scheme for a family of abelian groups:

- $K$ consists of a group $G_p$ and two generators $g_1$ and $g_2$ of $G_p$, with $g_1 \neq g_2$.
- $G_K = \mathbb{Z}_p^2$, $H_K = G_p$, $D_K = \mathbb{Z}_p$.
- If $\alpha = (\alpha_1, \alpha_2)$, then $h_K(\alpha) = g_1^{\alpha_1} \cdot g_2^{\alpha_2}$ and $\pi_K(\alpha) = \alpha_1$.
- Given $a$, choose $\alpha := (a, \alpha_2)$ with random $\alpha_2 \in \mathbb{Z}_p$.

**Proof:** Obviously, $h_K$ and $\pi_K$ are homomorphisms. The content is unconditionally hidden since for each $A \in G_p$, $a \in \mathbb{Z}_p$, there is exactly one $\alpha_2$ with $h(a, \alpha_2) = A$. Lemma 2 implies that $h$ is collision-free. □

The inequality proof is based on the following ideas:

1. Since contents of commitments can be subtracted, it suffices to show that the value $a$ in a commitment $A$ is not zero.

2. Our groups $D_K$ are actually rings $\mathbb{Z}_p$ or $\mathbb{Z}_{2^\sigma}$. In $\mathbb{Z}_p$, we can prove $a \neq 0$ in zero-knowledge by proving that it has an inverse $b$, and in $\mathbb{Z}_{2^\sigma}$, by proving that there exists $b$ such that $a \cdot b = 2^{\sigma-1}$. We unify this by saying that $D_K$ has an element $c \neq 0$ such that $\forall a \neq 0 \, \exists b: a \cdot b = c$, and this $b$ can be computed efficiently.

3. Thus we finally need a protocol to prove that the product of the contents $a$ and $b$ of two commitments is $c$. We adapt an idea for shared secrets from [Be]: The factors are blinded as $a'$

$= a + y$, $b' = b + z$, and either a multiplication $a' \cdot b' = d$ is opened, or the correct connection between the original and the blinded multiplication must be shown. The idea is that, once the blinding factors $y$ and $z$ are opened, $a' \cdot b' = a \cdot b + a \cdot z + y \cdot b + y \cdot z$ is a linear equation connecting $c$ and $d$ and can therefore be tested on the unopened commitments. We only need to be able to multiply commitments and the values used to open them by contents. Again, we present a unification of the factoring case and the discrete logarithm case:

**Definition: A semi-homomorphic perfectly hiding commitment scheme for a family of commutative rings** is a homomorphic perfectly hiding commitment scheme for a family of abelian groups if additionally

1. the $D_K$'s are commutative rings with an efficient multiplication algorithm, and
2. there are efficient "multiplications" of elements of $G_K$ and $H_K$ by those of $D_K$, which commute with the homomorphisms (i.e., $h_K(d \cdot \alpha) = d \cdot h_K(\alpha)$ and $\pi_K(d \cdot \alpha) = d \cdot \pi_K(\alpha)$). ◆

Whenever $D_K$ is a ring $\mathbb{Z}_x$, like in our cases, we can obtain suitable multiplications as follows: If $d \in \mathbb{Z}_x$ is represented by $z \in \{0, \ldots, x-1\}$, let $d \cdot g := g + g + \ldots + g$, $z$ times.

In order to manage with just $L$ rounds overall, the protocol from Figure 1 and the multiplication protocol are joined more closely.

About *pub* and *sign*, we only need that they are group homomorphisms, e.g., *pub*: $G^* \to G'$, *sign*$(\cdot, m)$: $G^* \to G''$, and that the results are imbedded into the domain of the commitment scheme, e.g., by injective functions $\iota^*: G' \to D_K$, $\iota: G'' \to D_K$. In our discrete logarithm case, $G'' = \mathbb{Z}_p$, hence the same group $G_p$ can be used here as for the signature scheme itself. For $G' = G_p$, we need an efficient embedding $\iota^*: G_p \to \mathbb{Z}_{p'}$ for a possibly larger prime $p'$. However, e.g., for the first choice of $G_p$ in §3.1, we can use $p' = p$ and $\iota$ only needs to change $p$ into 0.

We obtain the following Protocol 2:

Repeat $L$ times:

Sibyl prepares commitments: (Remember: $c$ is a fixed nonzero value with $\forall a \neq 0 \exists b: a \cdot b = c$.)

Choose $R$, $y$, $z$ randomly.

Let $SK' = SK + R$, $PK' = pub(SK')$, $s' = sign(SK', m)$, $sf' = sf + sign(R, m)$,
$a = \iota(sf') - \iota(s)$, $b$ such that $a \cdot b = c$, $a' = a + y$, $b' = b + z$, and $d = a' \cdot b'$.

Choose commitments $P$ on $\iota'(PK')$, $SF'$ on $sf'$, $S'$ on $s'$, $B$ on $b$, $Y$ on $y$, $Z$ on $z$, $D$ on $d$.

She sends the commitments to Rick, and they both compute locally:

$A = SF' - S'$, $A' = A + Y$, $B' = B + Z$

Rick can choose among 2 possibilities:

| Sibyl: | Rick tests if the commitments are opened correctly and if: |
|---|---|
| C1 Opens $P$, $S'$, $A'$, $B'$, $D$, shows $PK'$ and $s'$, and reveals $SK'$. | $PK' = pub(SK')$, $s' = sign(SK', m)$ $a' \cdot b' = d$. |
| C2 Opens $P'$, $SF'$, $Y$, $Z$ and shows $PK'$ and $sf'$, reveals $R$, and opens $D - z \cdot A - y \cdot B$ by showing $\chi := \delta - z \cdot \alpha - y \cdot \beta$. | $PK' = PK \cdot pub(R)$ $sf' = sf + sign(R, m)$ $\pi(\chi) = c + y \cdot z$. |

**Protocol 2**    Efficient disavowal

**Lemma 5:** Protocol 2 is a perfect zero-knowledge interactive proof of knowledge that Sibyl either knows a satisfying assignment for the disavowal formula or can break the commitment scheme (cf. [BP]).

**Proof:** Omitted in this extended abstract. □

It is easy to see that the proof of Theorem 2 is not much changed by the occurrence of the commitment scheme in Lemma 5.

**Remark:** The multiplication protocol can easily be adapted to the case where $c$ is hidden in a commitment, too (actually, this is closer to the protocol from [Be]). Thus we can compute arbitrary arithmetic terms of commitments, i.e., we can build perfect ZKPs of atomic formulas in $\mathbb{Z}_p$ or $\mathbb{Z}_{2^\sigma}$. Since logical operations can be substituted by arithmetic ones, we can generalize this to all arithmetic formulas in these rings.

# 4 A Theoretical Construction from Claw-free Permutation Pairs

For theoretical purposes, we sketch a construction based on an arbitrary family of claw-free permutation pairs (not necessarily with a trap-door) [GMR, D1]. This seems a sensible assumption, since it is the same one on which collision-free hash functions can be constructed, and we require a similar property from our function *pub*.

**Key exchange:**

0. All participants agree on a family of claw-free permutation pairs and parameters $k$ for cryptographic security, $\sigma$ for information-theoretical security, and $L$ for the ZKPs.

1. Rick chooses a claw-free pair $(d, f_0, f_1)$ and publishes it (cf. [GMR]). ($f_0, f_1$ are the permutations; $d$ is an algorithm to choose a random element from their common domain $D$.) He proves Sibyl in (computational) zero-knowledge that his choice is correct.
   From the claw-free pair, a hiding function $h: \{0, 1\}^\sigma \times D \to D$ is defined as
   $$h((b_1,\dots,b_\sigma), x) = f_{b_1}( \dots(f_{b_\sigma}(x))\dots). \tag{4}$$

2. Now Sibyl uses $d$ to choose a secret key
   $$SK = (sk_1, sk_2) = ((a, x), (b, y)) \in (\{0, 1\}^\sigma \times D)^2$$
   randomly and computes and publishes the public key $PK = pub(SK) = (h(sk_1), h(sk_2)) \in D^2$.

**Signing:** Now we assume that $\{0, 1\}^\sigma$ is interpreted as $GF(2^\sigma)$. The message space is $GF(2^\sigma)$, and
$$sign(SK, m) = a + b \cdot m \text{ in } GF(2^\sigma).$$

**Verification and disavowal** are perfect zero-knowledge proofs of knowledge for the relations defined by Formulas (1) and (2).

The three required ZKPs exist on our assumption (e.g., [GMW, BCC, D1]).

**Security (Sketch):** We use that $h$ is cryptographically collision-free and hides its first argument unconditionally [BPW, PW1], and that for each $PK$, the family $(sign(SK, \bullet))_{SK \in pub^{-1}(PK)}$ is strongly universal$_2$ [WC].

# 5 A Practical Scheme Based on Factoring

An inefficient scheme based on factoring can be obtained as a special case of §4 by using the special claw-free permutation pairs from [GMR]. However, to make the scheme efficient, we need special zero-knowledge proofs. We only sketch this scheme in this extended abstract.

The proof of Lemma 3 implies that one can use an analogue of Protocol 1 for efficient verification if $sign(\cdot, m)$ is a homomorphism on the same group as $pub$. Thus we must change $sign$ from §4 to
$$sign(SK, m) = a + b \cdot m \text{ in } \mathbb{Z}_{2\sigma}.$$

To prove an analogue of Lemma 1 with a probability of $1 - 2^{-\tau}$ (and thus Sibyl's security), we now restrict the message space to $\{0, \ldots, 2^{\sigma-\tau}-1\}$.

To be able to use the efficient disavowal of Protocol 2 and Lemma 5, we use the following commitments (where $h_K$ is the same function as $h$ in §4):

**Lemma 6 (Commitments):** The following parameters define a homomorphic perfectly hiding commitment scheme for a family of abelian groups:
- $K$ should be a Blum-integer $n$. (This defines a GMR claw-free pair.) The test checks $n \equiv 5$ mod 8 and $n = p^s \cdot q^t$ with $p \equiv 3$ mod 4 for odd $s, t$, using the efficient proof-system from [GP].
- $D_n = \mathbb{Z}_{2\sigma}, H_n = \pm \mathrm{QR}_n/\{\pm 1\}, G_n = \mathbb{Z}_{2\sigma} \times H_n$ with an operation $\cdot$ defined by
  $$(a, x) \cdot (b, y) := ((a + b) \bmod 2^\sigma, \lfloor x \cdot y \cdot 4^{(a+b) \operatorname{div} 2^\sigma} \rfloor).$$
- If $\alpha = (a, x)$, then $h_K(\alpha) = \pm (4^a \cdot x^{2\sigma})$ and $\pi_K(\alpha) = a$.
- Given $a$, choose $\alpha := (a, x)$ with random $x \in H_n$.

**Proof:** The main parts follow from [BPW]. It only remains to show that the GMR claw-free pairs are still permutations when $n$ is not a Blum-integer, but of the form that Sibyl checks. This is quite easy. □

# 6 Efficient Extension to Many Long Messages

Everything in this section is only sketched in this extended abstract.

**Definitions:** First, of course, the definition of the security of the signer (in Theorem 1) must be extended to more than one message. This means introducing the possibility for $sign$ to need memory, and a real adaptive chosen message attack, i.e., an additional "$\forall m_1, m_2 \ldots$: assume Sibyl signed $m_1, m_2 \ldots$ in this order ...". (Thus an active attack by an unrestricted attacker is easier to formalize than a normal one, see [GMR].)

The security of the recipient can still be defined as in Theorem 2.

In the definition of invisibility, one must include that both the recipient and the (partial) outsider to whom the signature is shown can have received more signatures. (For the computational variant, one can see this in detail in the future versions of [BCDP]. An additional complication is that our schemes are not memory-less; however, like in all "perfect" definitions, we need not model the outsider explicitly as a distinguisher, but only in the "$\forall$" over the public and private information $(x, I)$ that he can obtain.)

**Prekeys:** If there are many participants, of course each recipient Rick publishes just one triple $g$, which can then be used by all signers when signing a message for Rick. The participants can also jointly choose one triple $g$ whose randomness they all trust. In the discrete logarithm case, they just need a coin-flipping protocol; this is feasible. (In this case, one might even let a center make the choice alone, since no way of choosing a trap-door is known yet.) If participants disrupt, the computation is repeated without them. Although a bias results, security can still be proved for $g$'s chosen this way. In the following, we consider the case of one $g$ only.

**Tree-authentication:** As usual, one can extend the scheme to many signatures, without augmenting the public key, by two versions of tree-authentication. First, the previous public keys can be used as leaves of a hash tree [M1]. The new public key is just the root. (However, for invisibility, the signer must tell the recipient the leaves of the tree, and must use the leaves in random order.) A collision for the hash function *hash* used counts as disavowal, and for the recipient's security, *hash* must be cryptographically collision-free. There are such functions based on claw-free permutation pairs, and an efficient one based on factoring [D1]. For an efficient *hash* based on the discrete logarithm, we can use Lemma 2 directly, since we only need to hash messages of fixed length.

Generating the complete secret key in advance is the most efficient possibility; however, if one wants the scheme to go on "polynomially forever", one can use some signatures to sign new "public" keys in a tree-like fashion [M2, NY].

**Message hashing:** Similarly, long messages can be hashed before signing. For this, we can use the general construction of computationally collision-free hash functions *hash\** for messages of arbitrary length from hash functions *hash* for messages of fixed length from [D2], starting with *hash* from the previous paragraph.

Hence, public keys and signatures are as short as in conventional signature schemes, such as GMR. The information exchanged during verification or disavowal is about $L$ times the length of a signature.

# Acknowledgements

We are happy to thank *Manfred Böttger* for initializing this cooperation and for saving us a lot of time by quickly spotting a principle problem in an early version of this scheme, *Matthijs Coster* for his hospitality, *Ivan Damgård, Eiji Okamoto, Torben Pedersen*, and *Andreas Pfitzmann* for helpful discussions, and *Michael Waidner* for helpful discussions and tedious proof-reading.

# References

(All references can, if nowhere else, be obtained from the third author.)
[BCC] Gilles Brassard, David Chaum, Claude Crépeau: Minimum Disclosure Proofs of Knowledge; Journal of Computer and System Sciences 37 (1988) 156-189.
[BCDP] Joan Boyar, David Chaum, Ivan Damgård, Torben Pedersen: Convertible Undeniable Signatures; Crypto '90, Abstracts, 195-208.
[BCLL] Gilles Brassard, Claude Crépeau, Sophie Laplante, Christian Léger: Computationally Convincing Proofs of Knowledge; STACS '91, LNCS 480, Springer-Verlag, Berlin 1991, 251-262.
[Be] Donald Beaver: Multiparty Protocols Tolerating Half Faulty Processors; Crypto '89, LNCS 435, Springer-Verlag, Berlin 1990, 560-572.
[BP] Joan Boyar, René Peralta: On the concrete complexity of zero-knowledge proofs; Crypto '89, LNCS 435, Springer-Verlag, Heidelberg 1990, 507-525.
[BPW] Gerrit Bleumer, Birgit Pfitzmann, Michael Waidner: A Remark on a Signature Scheme where Forgery can be Proved; Eurocrypt '90, LNCS 473, Springer-Verlag, Berlin 1991, 441-445.

[Br] Gilles Brassard: Efficient constant-round perfect zero-knowledge; Département d'informatique et de R.O., Université de Montréal, C.P. 6128, Succ. "A", Montréal, Québec Canada H3C 3J7, Dec. 1990. (Manuscript available from the author.)

[C1] David Chaum: Zero-Knowledge Undeniable Signatures; Eurocrypt '90, Abstracts, Århus 1990, 419-426.

[C2] David Chaum: Zero-Knowledge Undeniable Signatures; Eurocrypt '90, LNCS 473, Springer-Verlag, Berlin 1991, 458-464.

[CA] David Chaum, Hans van Antwerpen: Undeniable signatures; Crypto '89, LNCS 435, Springer-Verlag, Heidelberg 1990, 212-216.

[CBDP] David Chaum, Joan Boyar, Ivan Damgård, Torben Pedersen: Undeniable Signatures: Applications and Theory; July 1, 1991. (Manuscript available from Ivan Damgård.)

[CHP] David Chaum, Eugène van Heijst, Birgit Pfitzmann: Cryptographically Strong Undeniable Signatures, Unconditionally Secure for the Signer; Fakultät f. Informatik, Univ. Karlsruhe, Internal Report 1/91, February 1991.

[CR] David Chaum, Sandra Roijakkers: Unconditionally secure digital signatures; Crypto '90 Abstracts, 209-217.

[D1] Ivan Damgård: Collision free hash functions and public key signature schemes; Eurocrypt '87, LNCS 304, Springer-Verlag, Berlin 1988, 203-216.

[D2] Ivan Damgård: A design principle for hash functions; Crypto '89, LNCS 435, Springer-Verlag, Heidelberg 1990, 416-427.

[DH] Whitfield Diffie, Martin Hellman: New Directions in Cryptography; IEEE Transactions on Information Theory 22/6 (1976) 644-654.

[DY] Yvo Desmedt, Moti Yung: Weaknesses of Undeniable Signature Schemes; Eurocrypt '91, Brighton, 8-11 April 1991, Abstracts, 111-116.

[GMR] Shafi Goldwasser, Silvio Micali, Ronald L. Rivest: A Digital Signature Scheme Secure Against Adaptive Chosen-Message Attacks; SIAM J. Comput. 17/2 (1988) 281-308.

[GMS] E. N. Gilbert, F. J. Mac Williams, N. J. A. Sloane: Codes which detect deception; The Bell System Technical Journal 53/3 (1974) 405-424.

[GMW] Oded Goldreich, Silvio Micali, Avi Wigderson: Proofs that Yield Nothing But their Validity and a Methodology of Cryptographic Protocol Design; 27th FOCS, IEEE Computer Society, 1986, 174-187.

[GP] Jeroen van de Graaf, René Peralta: A simple and secure way to show the validity of your public key; Crypto '87, LNCS 293, Springer-Verlag, Berlin 1988, 128-134.

[M1] Ralph Merkle: Protocols for Public Key Cryptosystems; Proceedings of the 1980 Symposium on Security and Privacy, April 14-16, 1980 Oakland, California, 122-134.

[M2] Ralph Merkle: A digital signature based on a conventional encryption function; Crypto '87, LNCS 293, Springer-Verlag, Berlin 1988, 369-378.

[NY] Moni Naor, Moti Yung: Universal One-way Hash Functions and their Cryptographic Applications; 21st STOC, ACM, New York 1989, 33-43.

[O] Yair Oren: On the cunning power of cheating verifiers: some observations about zero-knowledge proofs; 28th FOCS, IEEE Computer Society, 1987, 462-471.

[Pe] Torben Pedersen: Non-Interactive and Information-Theoretic Secure Verifiable Secret Sharing; Crypto '91, Santa Barbara, CA, 11.-15. August 1991, Abstracts 3.12-3.17.

[Pf] Birgit Pfitzmann: Fail-stop Signatures: Making Signers Unconditionally Secure; invited for Compsec, London 30.10.-1.11.1991, Proc. to be published by Elsevier.

[PW1] Birgit Pfitzmann, Michael Waidner: Formal Aspects of Fail-stop Signatures; Fakultät f. Informatik, Univ. Karlsruhe, Internal Report 22/90, 1990.

[PW2] Birgit Pfitzmann, Michael Waidner: Fail-stop Signatures and their Application; Securicom 91, Paris 1991, 145-160.

[TW] Martin Tompa, Heather Woll: Random self-reducibility and zero knowledge proofs of possession of information; 28th FOCS, IEEE Computer Society, 1987, 472-482.

[WC] Mark Wegman, Lawrence Carter: New Hash Functions and Their Use in Authentication and Set Equality"; Journal of Computer and System Sciences 22 (1981) 265-279.

[WP] Michael Waidner, Birgit Pfitzmann: Unconditional Sender and Recipient Untraceability in spite of Active Attacks – Some Remarks; Fakultät f. Informatik, Univ. Karlsruhe, Interner Bericht 5/89, 1989.

# Author Index